SIR JOSEPH GOLD MEMORIAL SERIES
International Financial & Economic Law
Vol. 4

FINANCIAL CRISES IN THE 1990s: A GLOBAL PERSPECTIVE

Dedman School of Law, Southern Methodist University
International Financial Law Unit, Centre for Commercial Law Studies
London Centre for Financial Studies and the Rule of Law

FINANCIAL CRISES IN THE 1990s:
A Global Perspective

Editors

Douglas Arner
Mamiko Yokoi-Arai
Zhongfei Zhou

In cooperation with
Centre for Commercial Law Studies, University of London (IFL Unit);
Dedman School of Law, Southern Methodist University;
The British Institute of International and Comparative Law;
The London Centre for Financial Studies and the Rule of Law;
The Asian Institute of International Financial Law (HKU);
London Institute of International Banking,
Finance, & Development Law Ltd.

BIICL
British Institute of
International and
Comparative Law
www.biicl.org

Published and Distributed by
The British Institute of International and Comparative Law
Charles Clore House, 17 Russell Square, London WC1B 5JP

British Library Cataloguing in Publication Data
A Catalogue record of this book is available from the British Library

ISBN 0–903067–52–8

Typeset by Cambrian Typesetters
Frimley, Surrey
Printed in Great Britain by Biddles Ltd.,
Guildford and King's Lynn

Preface

The 1990s was a decade marked by significant and ongoing financial crises on a global basis, involving and affecting a broad range of developed, developing, emerging, and transitioning economies. The roots of such crises stem back into the 1970s with the breakdown of the Bretton Woods-based international monetary system and the resulting international monetary and financial instability and uncertainties that resulted, and became reinforced and fueled by a variety of disparate international, regional and domestic events through the 1980s. Today, one speaks of an incipient 'new international financial architecture', which supposedly is to eliminate or at least reduce and to mitigate future financial crises— hopefully.

However, for this new 'architecture' to attain a good level of practical success in terms of implementation and enforcement, it will need to be based in large part upon the lessons learned (or which should have been learned) from the series of domestic financial crises in the 1990s. This most impressive volume provides the historical perspectives and context for scholars and policymakers to assist in this end, analysing financial crises in over sixteen divergent jurisdictions.

The editors and contributors to this volume are largely drawn from scholars who have been studying financial crises over the past decade in conjunction with the efforts of the Centre for Commercial Law Studies (International Financial Law Unit) at Queen Mary College, London, the SMU Institute of International Banking and Finance (based at the Dedman School of Law, SMU, Dallas, Texas) and (more recently) also at the Asian Institute of International Financial Law at the University of Hong Kong and at the Stockholm Centre for Commercial Law Studies. While there are a number of senior scholars who have contributed to this volume, what is even more significant is this major research effort and the bulk of this volume have been spearheaded and contributed to by a most outstanding group of young international financial law scholars. In particular special recognition should be given to Associate Professor Zhongfei Zhou of the Law Faculty of Shanghai University of Finance and Economics, Assistant Professor Douglas Arner of the HKU Law Faculty, and Queen Mary, London Lecturer Ms. Mamiko Yokoi-Arai—all of whom began this major research project at the CCLS-London.

While this major research project was underway, this CCLS-based research team (in conjunction with the London Institute of International Banking, Finance and Development Law and its SMU counterpart) conducted over six major international research seminars and produced three volumes and a series of scholarly articles on various aspects of the law-based dimensions of the new international financial architecture. In addition, this team learned from practical experiences by being involved in legal technical assistance projects in Thailand, Korea, Indonesia, the CEE, Latin America and Southern Africa.

For myself, I have been incredibly blessed and fortunate to have been able, in part, to provide a supportive academic environment for such important research and practical efforts. In doing so, I and my other colleagues at the University of London, SMU and HKU have learned very much and have benefited greatly. I simply do not have the words to express my gratitude to and pride in this wonderful group of young scholars dedicated to improving economic conditions in the developing world through a search for global, regional and domestic financial stability. Thank you so much Zhongfei, Douglas, and Mamiko for heading up this most impressive and much needed historical and comparative study of financial crises in the 1990s. I also wish to especially recognise the significant support efforts of Ms Eun Yee Chung from SMU. Hopefully, we all can learn many important lessons from your collective efforts.

London
1 October 2001

Joseph J. Norton, SJD, DPhil, LLD(hc)

Table of Contents

Sponsoring Organisations

CENTRE FOR COMMERCIAL LAW STUDIES AND ITS INTERNATIONAL FINANCIAL LAW UNIT (a 5*, highest-rated UK academic postgraduate research and teaching institution)

The Centre was established in 1980 as a distinct department within the Faculty of Laws of Queen Mary College, University of London. The primary objectives of the Centre are to promote the systematic study and research of national and international commercial law and its social and economic implications and to develop a body of knowledge, information and skills that can be placed at the service of government, public bodies, overseas institutions, the legal profession, industry and commerce.

The IFLU engages in integrated and cross-disciplinary activities in banking and finance law, from both developed and emerging market standpoints. The establishment of the Sir John Lubbock Chair of Banking Law and the creation of various Visiting Professorial and Senior Fellowships involving leading UK, European and international banking and finance law experts within the IFLU have resulted in making the IFLU the leading banking law Centre in Europe.

DEDMAN SCHOOL OF LAW, SMU

The Dedman School of Law at Southern Methodist University, Dallas, Texas, is one of the leading U.S. law schools with over 50 years of international programmes for both LL.M and J.D. students. It has an internationally oriented faculty that enjoys an outstanding reputation as a community of dedicated teachers and scholars. The Dedman School of Law is involved in an impressive range of international law publications, including the editing of *The International Lawyer* and a co-sponsorship arrangement with the Kluwer Law International Group of a leading international book publication series. The School of Law is the home of the SMU Institute of International Banking and Finance.

THE BRITISH INSTITUTE FOR INTERNATIONAL AND COMPARATIVE LAW (BIICL)

This is an academic institution established in 1895 specialising in all aspects of international law. One of its distinctive features is its genuinely international membership and approach. Membership is worldwide and open to all without restrictions on nationality. The Institute is best suited to bring together judges and practitioners, academic lawyers and civil servants and to provide both authoritative legal analysis and practical experience.

London Institute of International Banking, Finance and Development Law, Ltd

The London Institute is a privately incorporated, educational institution based at the British Institute of International and Comparative Law (BIICL). Among other functions, the Institute assists the International Financial Law Unit at the Centre for Commercial Law Studies at Queen Mary College, University of London and BIICL in directing research seminars, professional conferences, executive training sessions, law reform and consulting projects, and major journals and book series. This legal think-tank is also responsible for conducting research and publishing articles and essays on an array of important legal issues concerning banking, finance and development, including a series of *Studies in International Financial and Economic Law* and of *Yearbooks of International Financial and Economic Law*.

The Centre of International Financial Studies and the Rule of Law

This is a recently formed academic joint venture between the London Institute and BIICL (in which the CCLS/IFLU) is a sponsoring and participating institution) to bring together interdisciplinary talents within the academic research community of the University of London and the British academic community at-large. The Centre is dedicated to developing legal scholarship in the area of international economic, financial and banking law as they relate to questions of the Rule of Law. The Centre has the following basic functions: to coordinate the significant legal, financial and economic talents and expertise available within the London and British academic and professional communities for the purpose of assembling working groups or teams for significant rule-of-law/financial sector reform research and consultancy projects for governmental and intergovernmental purposes; to identify significant areas for ongoing research projects; actively to pursue possibilities of ongoing joint research projects with external 'partners'; to build up significant expertise in assisting IFIs and RFIs independently evaluate their financial sector law reform projects; to sponsor or co-sponsor, on a regular basis, distinguished lectures and high-level research seminars and conferences; and to oversee the Sir John Gold Memorial Book Series on International Financial Economic Law.

List of Contributors

EDITORS

Douglas Arner, Assistant Professor and Deputy Director, Asian Institute of International Financial Law, Faculty of Law, University of Hong Kong; Visiting Fellow and former Sir John Lubbock Research Fellow in International Financial Law, Centre for Commercial Law Studies, Queen Mary, University of London.

Dr Mamiko Yokoi-Arai, Sir John Lubbock Research Fellow in International Financial Regulation, Centre for Commercial Law Studies, Queen Mary, University of London.

Dr Zhongfei Zhou, Associate Professor of Law Faculty of Shanghai University of Finance and Economics, PRC; Visiting Fellow and former Sir John Lubbock Research Fellow in Chinese Financial Law, Centre for Commercial Law Studies.

ASSISTANT EDITOR

Eun Ye Chung, J D Fellow, SMU Institute of International Banking and Finance and Member of State Bar of Texas.

CONTRIBUTORS

Douglas Arner, see above.

Kai Chen, Research Fellow, SMU Institute of International Banking and Finance, Dedman School of Law, Southern Methodist University.

Chunghsing Chou, Taipei Economic and Cultural Office, Philippines; Research Fellow, Centre Commercial Law Studies, University of London.

Jorge Guira, Lecturer in Law, Warwick University; Fellow in Latin American Financial Law, London Institute of International Banking, Finance and Development Law; Senior Visiting Fellow, Law Institute of the Americas, Dedman School of Law, Southern Methodist University.

Yoshihisa Haykawa, Associate Professor of Law, Rikkyo University, Tokyo.

Dr Berry Hsu, Associate Professor in Law, Department of Real Estate and Construction, University of Hong Kong.

Byung-Tae Kim, Research Fellow, SMU Institute of International Banking and Finance, Dedman School of Law, Southern Methodist University.

Dr Ruth de Krivoy, President, Síntesis Financiera, Caracas, Venezuela.

Christine Lang, Visiting Scholar, Central Economic Mathematical Institute, Russian Academy of Sciences, Moscow, Russia; Assistant Professor, University of Geneva, Switzerland.

Dr Chuanjie Li, former General Manager, Bank of China, New York.

Dr Joseph J. Norton, James L. Walsh Distinguished Faculty Fellow and Professor of Financial Institution Law, Dedman School of Law, Southern Methodist University; Sir John Lubbock Professor of Banking Law, Centre for Commercial Law Studies, University of London.

Dr Gerald N. Olson, Visiting Senior Fellow, Centre for Commercial Law Studies, University of London; Associate Director, London Institute of International Banking, Finance and Development Law.

Maria Laura Patiño L., Central Bank of Ecuador, Quito, Ecuador.

Sungchul Shin, H.D. Vest International Fellow, SMU Institute of International Banking and Finance, Dedman School of Law, Southern Methodist University.

Thomas Slover, Jackson Walker LLP, Dallas, Texas; Visiting Fellow, Law, Law Institute of the Americas, Dedman School of Law (SMU).

Georgi Spasov, Senior Assistant Professor of Commercial Law, Kliment Ohridski University, Sofia, Bulgaria; Managing Partner, Spasov & Bratanov Lawyers' Partnership.

Marcelo Rafael Tavarone, Estudio Bunge, Smith & Luchía Puig—Abogados, Buenos Aires; former Research Fellow in Latin American Financial Law, Centre for Commercial Law Studies, University of London.

Dr Manuela Tortora, former Executive Secretary of SELA, and Latin America Trade expert of WTO, Geneva.

Dr Tull Traisorat, Ministry of Foreign Affairs, Bangkok, Thailand; former Research Fellow, London Institute of International Banking, Finance and Development Law and former Visiting Scholar, Dedman School of Law (SMU).

Dr Shlomo Weber, Dedman Trustee Professor of Economics, Department of Economics, Southern Methodist University.

Dr Mamiko Yokoi-Arai, see above.

Dr Zhongfei Zhou, see above.

Foreword

Yes, It Can Happen Anywhere: the Swedish Financial Crises of the 1990s

I am most pleased to have been asked to provide this Foreword to what certainly must be viewed as one of the best historical, legal perspectives on financial crises occurring during the past decade. I, my colleagues at the Stockholm University Law Faculty, and now also our new Stockholm Centre for Commercial Law Studies enjoy very close academic relations with the Centre for Commercial Law Studies, Queen Mary College, University of London, the 'breeding ground' (along with the Dedman School of Law, SMU) of this most impressive global study. Over the past decade, we have participated in a number of significant academic ventures with the London CCLS, several of which focussed upon issued relating to global financial crises. What always impressed me from these collaborative efforts were the similarities, yet the uniqueness as to the characteristics and nature of these various financial crisis. The additional perspective I wish to add to this volume via this Foreword is that financial crisis is not simply a problem for emerging and transitioning economies, but is an ongoing area of concern for *all* economies.

Yes, financial crisis can happen anywhere, even in a country such as my Sweden; and wherever and whenever it may happen, possible contagion implications are always present. For example, the most recent Turkish crises raised very significant problems in countries as far away and as supposedly disconnected as Argentina—a strange but real phenomenon of our unfolding global financial system. But, back to the Swedish saga.

One could clearly say that Sweden is a country without dramatic incidents; it is a state that has not been in war for nearly 200 years and where earthquakes, state coups and revolutions do not exist. Therefore, as Sweden entered into the 1990s, few foresaw that the then so glamorous 1980s would make way for a decade where the financial sector would offer such drama as not seen since the famous business man Ivar Krüger shot himself in Paris in 1932. The 1990s also offered a re-distribution of wealth and a change in the political views as few could have expected.

Since Sweden was blessed from the horrors of the Second World War, it started the post war era with a relatively strong financial position that came to distinguish the character of the nation through to the late 1970s. It was, however, a country characterised by trade political isolation, where the so-called EFTA project had no effect on the citizens' private economies. In reality, the post war era meant a self-assumed isolation, where the regulations from the war era were still applied. The legislation was hardly governed by market economical views. Both corporations and individuals were under complete supervision. The banks' lending operations as well as its monetary transactions were only carried out subject to actual government approval. Not even the new liberal trends that Thatcher and Reagan represented, with heavy tax reductions, had any effect in Sweden. Instead, the Swedish economy during the 1980s represented high taxes and significant inflation.

A biased locking of the Swedish currency to a set exchange rate did surprisingly not give rise to any reactions outside the boarders of the nation. During the 1980s, the Swedes became—as the Argentinians ten years later—consumers that drew benefit from the country's wealth abroad. A sudden cost crisis in the end of this period pushed the social democrats to an unexpected declaration to apply for membership in the European Union. The political decline in the East made the government less willing to maintain the economical and political isolation. Thus, several reforms were implemented during the late 1980s and the early 1990s. The extreme marginal income taxes—that in practice made it impossible to increase one's wealth by working— were replaced by much lower marginal income taxes.

Even if the government had declared that it intended to take measures to increase the inflation driven speculation in real property, this type of investment was for a long time the only type of wealth increase that seemed to take place.

When the banking business was reformed in the 1980s, extensive lending resulted in large funds poured into the real property market. Even if signs in the form of a banking conflict and worries on the international political scene were shown during the spring and summer of 1990, few understood what was going on. In September 1990, a financial company with large lending activities related to the current speculation economy suspended its payments. This was only the starting signal of a financial crisis that characterised the whole last decade of the 20th century.

The tax reform and an expressed will to tighten the inflationary economy together with an economic recession resulted in prices dropping substantially on real estate during 1991. Unsurprisingly, several real estate and insurance corporations, who during a few years had made big profits on credit insurance, were affected by urgent economical problems. However, only a few seem to have suspected that these highly speculative financial institutions were depending on credits from more reputable commercial banks.

What started as a crisis related to real estate and investment corporations, grew to full storm during the summer and fall of 1992. Suddenly, the international monetary market started to distrust the foundations of the Swedish economic welfare. In connection with a crisis in the European monetary collaboration, the Swedish krona was exposed to a great pressure. Despite big efforts from the Riksbank (the Swedish Central Bank), who during certain phases raised the interest rate up to 500 per cent and with a supportive purpose purchased the Swedish krona, it did not manage to maintain the value of the Swedish krona. The Riksbank then decided to let go of it, which led to a decline of almost 30 per cent. This started additional crises on the real estate and the financial markets, since many actors had believed in the financial declarations made by politicians; that the value of the Swedish krona would be held intact.

The Swedish banks' organisations were now in an urgent financial crisis. Credit losses in the real estate and financial markets led to a large number of Swedish banks suffering heavy losses. Suddenly, the risk of bankruptcy of banks and insurance companies was a reality. The lack of similar experiences brought about an absence of legislation protecting investors and consumers. However, many politicians judged bankruptcy of Swedish banks as a political impossibility.

After two insurance companies with extensive commitment on the credit insurance market, as well as another big insurance company, were close to being dragged into the collapse, the saving banks organisation and a smaller commercial bank were facing bankruptcy. At this time, even some of the biggest commercial banks in the country could not present satisfactory results. Perhaps, the insecurity regarding the account of the real estate values on the real estate market, which practically were standing still, saved these banks' position. The government grasped the crises as a tangible threat towards the Swedish State's credit rating. Therefore, it decided to give unlimited warrants to secure the Swedish banks' capacity of repayment. The Swedish Ministry of Finance even issued letters of comfort to the creditors of the Swedish banks. Even though the Swedish government lacked constitutional possibilities to issue such warrants, the political unity in the parliament was apprehended as a political—although not a legal—binding warranty. Thus, the Swedish taxpayers had to pay large sums to redeem the commitments that had been made by real estate operators in the 1980s.

The period with high inflation was superseded by a period of high interest rates and low inflation. However, not until the Swedish people in the middle of the 1990s after a dramatic plebiscite decided to join the European Union, the financial crises slowly ebbed away.

As a reflection of the strong American economy and a substantial growth of the IT-sector, the dramatic financial crises gradually released its grip on the Swedish economy.

After the crisis Sweden had however lost a big part of its self-esteem, which had characterised the country during the post-war period. The political discrepancy increased as the states tax subsidising welfare programme was reduced. To handle the large public finances, a political unity was forced to make extensive savings programmes to cut down the public expenses. Reflecting upon the fact that regulations regarding restriction of the state's expenses were established at this time, it should be kept in mind that balanced budgets had not even been discussed before. Further, an end of reforms was carried through. The requirements that the Swedish economy to a larger extent should adjust to the other states in the European Union meant that a fifty-year-old financial political isolation was brought to an end. The politicians had deprived themselves of the possibilities to protect the Swedish economy from competition. Today, only a strong political aversion to accede to the European Central Bank and to replace the Swedish krona with the Euro remains.

However, it seem like the heavily decline of the Swedish krona in relation to the stock exchange fall in 2000–2001, opens up to an accede to the Euro. If this takes place, a weapon which has been used for over thirty years will be deprived by the politicians; the possibility to reduce the effects of significant increase in salary without real economic basis through devaluation.

As in other financial crises, the Swedish financial crisis was associated with macroeconomic circumstances, banks' credit booms in the real property market and enhanced competitive pressures from inside and outside. When deregulation occurred in financial systems, out-of-date regulations with a characteristic of strict controls were not accordingly adjusted to this transition. Delayed and inadequate policy responses deteriorated the crisis and distorted economic incentives to take prudent risk taking. The lesson learned from the Swedish crisis is that the prevention and correction of a financial crisis need all-round efforts at macro and micro levels.

Stockholm, 17 September 2001

JAN KLEINEMAN
Professor in Private Law
Stockholm University

Chapter 1

Introduction
Financial Crises: Early Warning Systems and Institutional Mechanisms from a Comparative Perspective

Mamiko Yokoi-Arai

I. INTRODUCTION

There is an ongoing international debate on how best to prevent and manage financial crises with no seeming conclusion available. However, the consensus is that the social consequences of a financial crisis make prevention essential.

To detect a financial crisis at the earliest possible stage, regulators need to be able to identify traits of a crisis and take timely action. Hence, it is necessary to analyse characteristics that a financial crisis exhibits before its outbreak and what regulatory schemes are appropriate to prevent, detect, manage, and protect. Thus, this paper analyses early warning systems of financial crises and, legal and institutional mechanisms available to prevent and manage against them.

In this chapter, characteristics of a financial crisis are discussed taking into considering unique features of banks. Section II reviews early warning systems of financial distress. Section III analyses legal and institutional mechanisms to contain a financial crisis. The UK, US, and Japanese are analysed in a comparative context.

A. Notion of a Financial Crisis

'Financial crises' have been the subject of numerous analytical studies over the past century[1] suggesting the causes to be evolving and dynamic. The

[1] Such studies date back to AD 33. G. Caprio, Jr. and D. Klingebiel, 'Bank Insolvencies: Bad Luck, Bad Policy, or Bad Banking?' *in* M. Bruno and B. Pleskovic (eds), *Annual World Bank Conference on Development Economics 1996* (1997), p. 80 (World Bank).

advance in information technology has made contagion from crises more pronounced and threatening.

A clear definition of a financial crisis is difficult because not two crises are the same. Kindleberger, who is renown for his studies of financial crises, defines 'the financial crisis [. . .] is the culmination of a period of [business cycle] expansion and leads to a downturn.'[2]

Financial crises can be defined as having the following four stages of economic and financial characteristics enabling analysis of regulations in the respective stages:

- Build up of high demand in the financial market;
- A rush to exit market by market participants;
- Difficulty to finance which was not present before; and
- Market failure to efficiently distribute funds.

The underlying cause of a crisis is often deficiencies in the financial system, enabling market participants to fulfil the above conditions. Causes to a financial crisis are intertwined economic, institutional, political and social elements without exception.

Timing is essential because the earlier the detection, the more effectively and efficiently it is prevented. Contagion and self-fulfilling crisis make it difficult to avoid a crisis just by abiding the rules of preventive management. Investors' sentiment will also play a role because they are likely to rush to exit in a financially distressed situation. Regulatory agencies will find it necessary to issue assurances to the financial market that the government intends to stand by financial institutions in difficult situations since preservation of public confidence is the key to prevent the proliferation of a crisis.

B. Uniqueness of the Banking Sector

While the failure of an individual bank is not in itself considerably distinct from corporate failure, the possibility of systemic failure justifies special treatment. The difference in quality of financial service is opaque or indistinguishable from users. Banks with a higher risk profile will free ride on the reputation and trust of conservatively operating banks, leading to a failure of one bank to cause bank runs because depositors cannot determine the safety of a bank and would prefer to hold assets in liquid currency.[3]

Despite the widespread economic assumption that depositors would shift their deposits to other banks for safety, in practice, this is costly and time consuming. The credibility that depositors earn from long-term dealing

[2] C. P. Kindleberger, *Manias, Panics and Crashes* (1978), p. 1 (1996, 3rd edn., Macmillan).
[3] C. A. E. Goodhart, *The Evolution of Central Banks* (1988), p. 61 (MIT Press).

with one bank is sacrificed if they shift their account, disadvantaging them when taking out a loan.

Banks are considered susceptible to contagion for three reasons: (1) low capital-to-assets ratio (high leverage with little capital), (2) low cash-to-assets ratio (fractional reserve banking requiring sales of assets to meet deposit obligations), and (3) liquid liabilities and illiquid debt (maturity mismatch of assets and liabilities).[4] Further, contagion in the banking industry is considered to occur faster, spread wider, more failures, and larger losses to creditors.[5]

II. EARLY WARNING SYSTEMS OF A FINANCIAL CRISIS

Early warning systems (EWSs) are economic variables, financial ratios and accounting measures that predict a bank panic or financial crisis. They are devised to deal with financial distress in a timely fashion and for regulators to be proactive against financial distress.

A. *Bank specific early warning systems*

A bank specific EWS is a microeconomic evaluation of the financial system. Bank supervisors examine the books of banks, financial performance, and information in the market for individual bank's EWS.

1. ON-SITE EXAMINATIONS

On-site examination requires bank regulators to enter the premise of banks and directly examine the books and operations of the financial institution to evaluate the soundness of business and management. An assessment of the financial institution is made after an overall examination which is either reported to the examined bank undisclosed, or disclosed to the public.

The frequency of examination varies depending on the regulatory tradition and available resources. For example, while the US and Japan have annual on-site examinations,[6] the UK traditionally stressed the use of management interviews instead.[7] It is difficult for developing countries to conduct frequent inspections because of lack of staff and expertise.

[4] G. G. Kaufman, 'Bank Failures, Systemic Risk, and Bank Regulation' (1996) 16(1) *Cato J.*

[5] Ibid.

[6] The US conducts annual examinations by coordinating with other federal agencies to lift the regulatory burden on the regulator and regulatee.

[7] The UK had a tradition of self-regulation with a 'clubby' approach, where BOE exerted authority through 'nods and winks', and moral suasion was emphasised, as opposed to the US confrontational approach. *See* V. P. Polizatto, 'Prudential Regulation and Banking Supervision'

On-site examinations are usually conducted on a surprise basis and at random.[8] The rationale behind this is to inspect the financial institution under circumstances of its daily operations.

On-site examination requires a large number of experienced bank examiners whose training is costly and time consuming.[9] Therefore, a long-term human resource strategy is indispensable to acquire good bank examiners. When a country liberalises its economy, sufficient time needs to be taken not only for financial institutions to adjust, but also for the regulatory agency to build up its supervisory ability.

2. CAMEL/CAMELOT/CAMELS

The CAMEL system is the most well-known on-site EWS. CAMEL was developed to objectively rate the financial performance of banks in the US. It is considered an international guideline for bank supervision and bank regulators are expected to supervise on the five components of CAMEL. In the US, the CAMEL rating is the prime concern to regulators while for developing countries covering all components it a more immediate task.

CAMEL makes a rule based assessment of: Capital adequacy, Asset quality, Management, Earnings, and Liquidity. Each item is assigned a rating of 1–5 which together aggregate into a composite rate.[10] More recently, the Federal Reserve System has adopted CAMELS, adding Sensitivity to market risk. This reflects the impact of market risk affecting the soundness of business.[11]

There is also CAMELOT adding the quality of Operations and Treasury management,[12] or Operating environment and Transparency.[13] Operation quality has been a common theme for examiners since major institutions

in Dimitri Vittas (ed.), *Financial Regulation: Changing the Rules of the Game* (1992), at p. 298 (World Bank). A revision of this approach was made following Lord Justice Bingham's report on the Bank of Credit and Commerce International (BCCI) scandal.

[8] A. Sheng, 'Bank Supervision Principles and Practice' (1990) *World Bank Institute*, Working Papers, at p. 18.

[9] It is said to take four to five years just to learn the skills necessary to examine small, well-managed institutions. *See* n. 7, at p. 310.

[10] A rate of 1 is strong performance, while 5 is considered having an unsatisfactory performance that is critically deficient and in need of immediate remedial action. R.A. Cole *et al.*, 'FIMS: A New Monitoring System for Banking Institutions' (1995) 81 *Fed. Reserve Bull.* (January), p. 2.

[11] 'Uniform Financial Institutions Rating System' (1996) *Board of Governors* (27 Dec.), SR Letter 96–38 (SUP)(Washington, D.C.), and 'Interagency Guidance on Common Questions About the Application of the Revised CAMELS Rating System' (1997) *Board of Governors* (5 Mar.), SR Letter 97–4 (SUP) (Washington, D.C.),

[12] CAMELOT was developed by the Canadian Office of Superintendent of Financial Institutions. A. Sheng, 'Resolution and Reform: Supervisory Remedies for Problem Banks' *in* A. Sheng (ed.), *Bank Restructuring: Lessons from the 1980s* (1996), p. 51 (World Bank).

[13] World Bank, *East Asia: The Road to Recovery* (1998), p. v.

collapsed as a result of operational flaws.[14] Transparency is an important element because robust financial institutions usually do not hesitate to disclose. Encouraging transparency of operations will give an incentive for banks to conduct safe business.

a. Capital adequacy

Capital adequacy is a standard method of defining the strength of a financial institution because capital acts as a cushion to absorb losses. Losses should be first borne by shareholders rather than depositors, which is why a minimum capital requirement and capital adequacy are set.[15]

A proposal has been made by the Basle Committee on Banking Supervision (Basle Committee) to amend the risk weights on assets in the Capital Accord of June 1999.[16] The proposal reflects the dilemma of industrial countries, where their financial structure is too complex to regulate by a singular formula.[17] The US is following a two-track system of standardised and customised approach.[18] Japan encourages banks to self-assess their loss loans reflecting a customised approach too. The repeal of the Glass-Steagall Act in the US and Big Bang in Japan both have the effect of dismantling the Chinese wall between securities and banking business which is bound to complicate the measurement of capital adequacy.

The European Union (EU) has a universal banking approach to regulation. The books of a bank are separated into a 'trading book' and a 'banking book'.[19] The EU approach is functional rather than institutional regulation providing other countries implications to an evolving financial structure.

[14] Such as Barings and Daiwa Bank closure of US operations. R. M. Lastra, *Central Banking and Banking Regulation* (1996), p. 115 (LSE).

[15] Capital is paid in capital of shareholders used to finance the banking operation. D. Ware, 'Basic Principles of Banking Supervision' (1996), *Bank of England*, Handbooks in Central Banking No. 7, p. 10.

[16] The amendments include minimum capital requirements, supervisory review process, and effective use of market discipline. Basle Committee on Banking Supervision, *A New Capital Adequacy Framework* (1999) Consultative paper (June), Publication No. 50.

[17] Banks and credit rating agencies have criticised the use of external credit assessment by rating agencies' for sovereign and bank claim. IMF has expressed concern from disincentives they have to downgrading, lack of information sources, insufficient political consideration, poor probabilistic approach, too narrow scope of country risk analysis and possible human resources deficit. IMF, *World Economic Outlook* (1999), pp.110–52 (Sept.).

[18] Alan Greenspan, 'The Evolution of Bank Supervision' (1999) *Remarks Before the American Bankers Associations* (11 Oct.) and R. Spillenkothen, 'Bank Supervision and Regulation in the Next Millennium' (1999) *Remarks At the New York State Banking Department* (25 Oct.).

[19] Banking book calculates CAR of deposit taking business and trading book that for securities trading. Art. 1 of 1989 O.J. (L386) 14 (Council Directive 89/647/EEC) and Art. 2 of 1993 O.J. (L141) 1 (Council Directive 93/6/EEC).

Although, capital absorbs temporary and unexpected losses for a short period, it is not sufficient to cover a loss caused from a structural reason or accumulating losses.[20] For one, capital is usually recorded at its historical value which is the value at the time of acquisition. So the value of shares held for a long period can be significantly higher than its market value depending on the market situation,[21] especially when the economy downturns causing capital to be insufficient to assist the bank.[22] Through a periodic and systemic review of capital values, CAR can reflect the true financial condition and strength of the bank.

Regulatory agencies take advantage of the non-definite feature of financial institution insolvency. The CAR criteria for prompt corrective action do not necessarily reflect a bank's economic insolvency but when the rescue of a financial institution is initiated. It is an ex ante criterion, not always reality motivated which the market is also affected by.

In reality, capital cushions losses only when earnings are used up.[23] So, as long as a financial institution has sufficient earnings to cover losses, low CAR does not necessarily mean an unsafe financial institution.

b. Asset quality

Asset quality determines the ability and willingness of borrowers to service and repay loans. If the quality of loans is declining and losses increasing, pressure will be put on the capital. Bank examiners check whether banks are following their documented lending policies in supervision in terms of:[24] adequacy of documentation, collateral, and payment records of most large loans and a sample of small loans to predict the risk exposure of the bank. Accordingly, loans are classified into good, substandard, doubtful and loss categories. Following is a list of recommended loan classifications:

[20] J. H. Noonan and S. K. Fetner, 'Capital and Capital Standards' (1983), *Econ. Rev.* (Nov.), p. 51 (Federal Reserve Bank of Atlanta).

[21] Japanese banks have traditionally cross-held shares in corporate group. This led to long-term share holding and long term business planning. However, as the number of foreign investors increased in the market, significance of individual shareholders is growing since shares are more likely to be sold for short-term gains.

[22] A. Demirgüç-Kunt, 'Deposit-Institution Failures: A Review of Empirical Literature' (1989) 25 *Econ. Rev.* (Fourth quarter), p. 4 (Federal Reserve Bank of Cleveland).

[23] B. H. Putnam, 'Early Warning Systems and Financial Analysis in Bank Monitoring: Concepts of Financial Monitoring' (1983), *Econ. Rev.* (November), p. 12 (Federal Reserve Bank of Atlanta).

[24] The lending policies of banks consists of standard of borrowers, credit assessment and loan authorisation procedure, monitoring of each loan, and periodic review by staff independent of lending officers. Ware, above n. 15.

Standard Loan Classifications (US model)

	Characteristics	Considerations
Pass or Normal	– Reasonable credit risk. – Payments of interest are current. – No evidence adverse tends affecting borrower's present or prospective ability to repay.	– Adequately protected by the net worth and expected debt-service capacity of borrower. – Minimum provisioning requirement varies between 1 and 2%.
Special mention	– Potential deficiency or potential problem identified. – Adverse trends or characteristics. – Credit risk is relatively minor, yet higher than normally acceptable.	– Deserves management's special attention. – If not corrected, may result in deterioration of repayment prospects. – A declining trend in borrower's operations or an unbalanced position in the balance sheet, but not at point that repayment is jeopardized.
Classified or Nonperforming Loans		
Sub-standard	– Clearly defined credit weaknesses. – Bank may suffer some loss deficiencies are not pomptly corrected.	– Credit is inadequately protected by current net worth and cash-flow of borrower. – Can jeopardize the liquidation of debt by reduction in borrower's income, demand for borrower product, devaluation risk, high leverage, low profitability of borrower. – Minimum specific provision of between 20 and 25% required.
Doubtful	– Collection in full is highly questionable. – Possibility of significant loss (though not readily defined) is extremely high.	– Have all the weaknesses inherent in substandard classification, with added characteristic that payment in full is highly questionable and unlikely. – Possibility of loss is extremely high, but because of certain important and reasonably specific pending factors that may strengthen the credit, its classification as estimated loss is defered.
Loss	– Uncollectable.	– Little value to continue classifying them as assests. – Banks should provision 100% of the loan. – Losses should be taken in the period in which they surface as uncollectable.

Source: D. Ware, 'Basic Principles of Banking Supervision' (1996), *Bank of England*, Handbooks in Central Banking No 7, p.10 and Board of Governors of the Federal Reserve System, 'Commercial Bank Examination Manual' (March 1994), Section 2040.1.

Loan classifications should not be too abstract since banks become discouraged from collecting loans past substandard, and small improvements in the possibility of repayment will then not be officially recognised.

Depending on the maturity of financial market, regulators may recommend the use of self-regulation. Self-regulation of asset classification and loan-loss provisions are effective for mature financial markets where strong market discipline is imposed.

c. CAMEL ratings and regulatory action

The judgment of economic insolvency compounds two concepts: equitable insolvency (failure to pay obligations as they fall due) and balance sheet insolvency (the condition in which liabilities exceed assets).[25] Further, there is a difference between economic insolvency and regulatory failure of a bank. While the former indicates a situation in which an institution can no longer meet its contractual obligations out of its own resources, the latter is a decision by a regulatory agency to close a financial institution.

There will be a time lag between bank failure and economic insolvency because regulators base their judgment on the book value of the balance sheet which is the acquisition value.[26] If the market value becomes higher, the book value will be lower than the current.

However, the reality is that financial institutions are more likely to come under pressure in a declining market, and thus the book value of capital becomes closer to the market value. Also, the capital and asset levels are volatile and difficult to measure. As a result, regulatory failure becomes delayed beyond economic insolvency.

d. Nonperforming loans (NPL)

NPL are a fruition of credit risk, and the source of future losses. Many writers have proposed using the ratio of nonperforming loans to total loans to evaluate the financial fragility of banks and use it as a trigger for regulatory action. Sheng has modelled a 15 per cent threshold of nonperforming loans to total assets for a bank to be totally decapitalised at a CAR of 8 per cent.[27] This threshold could be used as a warning point for regulators to

[25] H. N. Schiffman, 'Legal Measures to Manage Bank Insolvency in Economies in Transition' *in* R. M. Lastra and H. N. Schiffman (eds.), *Bank Failures and Bank Insolvency Law in Economies in Transition* (1999), p. 96 (Kluwer Law).

[26] E. J. Kane, 'Comment on 'Understanding Financial Crises: A Developing Countries Perspective,' by Fredric S. Mishkin', *in* M. Bruno and B. Pleskovic (eds.), *Annual World Bank Conference on Development Economics 1996* (1997), p. 70 (World Bank).

[27] This is modelled on the assumption that loan portfolio has an average maturity of seven years and yields 10 per cent a year and a capital-asset ratio of 8 per cent. A. Sheng, 'Banking Fragility in the 1980s: An Overview' *in* A. Sheng (ed.), *Bank Restructuring: Lessons from the 1980s* (1996), p. 10 (World Bank).

pay special attention to the effect of non-performing loans on bank performance.

Current early warning systems use information available *ex post* the failure. However, *ex post* information does not reflect the condition in which the bank fell into distress. Hence, Gonzalez-Hermosillo has proposed the use of a composite indicator adding the ratio of capital equity to total assets and loan reserves to total assets, and subtracting NPL to total assets (coverage ratio) to indicate bank fragility.[28] An increase of nonperforming loans and deteriorating capital ratio are leading indicators of financial distress *ex ante*.

However, the diversity of nonperforming loan definitions make the use of NPL ratio problematic. Banks, especially in developing countries, have opportunities to window-dress NPLs if accounting standards are inadequate.[29] The lack of accuracy of statistics used in conjunction with bank-reported data is also a problem.

3. Off-site supervisory systems

While on-site examinations are usually conducted at random, off-site supervision is carried out to complement the period in between. Banks are required to submit their statutorily required reports (call reports) on a predetermined basis[30] which is often quarterly, but some regulators demand more frequent reporting.[31]

Based on the call report, regulators evaluate the changes in the condition of a financial institution. Supervisors have an advantage over private parties in judging the health of financial institutions through their access not only to confidential, micro information but also to prior supervisory ratings.[32]

a. Reporting requirements

The contents of call reports vary depending on the financial structure, stage of development, and size of institution. Possible contents are financial condition (balance sheet on a consolidated basis), income and dividends, profit/loss statement, deposit/loan growths, international operations, foreign exchange exposures, past due loans, NPL, ownership, capital adequacy, and off-balance sheet activities.[33]

[28] B. Gonzalez-Hermosillo, 'Developing Indicators to Provide Early Warnings of Banking Crises' (1999) 36 *Fin. and Dev.* (June).

[29] C.-J. Lindgren *et al.*, *Bank Soundness and Macroeconomic Policy* (1996), p.11.

[30] Frequency and format of mandatory report should be unified to lighten regulatory burden. Above n. 17, p.111.

[31] Federal Home Loan Bank Board (FHLBB) requires a monthly report. *See* Putnam, above n. 23, p. 8.

[32] *See* Lindgren *et al.*, above n. 29, p.12.

[33] *See* Lastra, above n. 17, p. 111 and A. Sheng, above n. 8, p. 14.

The frequency of reporting is crucial since it affects the regulatory burden on financial institutions. A cost and benefit analysis should be made on both the contents and frequency of reports, weighing the supervisory need and cost especially on smaller financial institutions.[34]

b. Market activity monitoring

The mobility of banks has given rise to the need for on-going monitoring and ability to evaluate them in a short time span. Most central banks conduct off-site monitoring through daily contact and exchange information in the money market. The objective of money market monitoring is to obtain information on the liquidity position of financial institutions and sound market rumours.

Central banks have access to this information through their open market operations. Maintaining daily contacts with financial institutions is costly, but places them in an advantageous position compared to other bank regulators. It also supplements their role to oversee the stability of the financial system. However, market monitoring is a subjective assessment and is difficult to incorporate the findings into regulatory action.

B. Financial system early warning systems

Bank supervision does not directly contribute to comprehend the health of the financial system. Due to the contagion effect of banking problems, more emphasis is being placed on systemic fragility.

A financial system EWS enables understanding of the multiple factors affecting a financial crisis. Regulators need to have at hand a broad spectrum of analytical tools, where conventional supervisory methods are essential but not sufficient.

The three main financial system EWS are considered: 'macroeconomic' approach, 'bottom up' approach, and 'aggregate' model. IMF surveillance is also examined as a valuable systemic EWS.

1. Macroeconomic approach

The 'macroeconomic' approach looks at macroeconomic variables that reflect the health of banks because it in turn reflects the robustness of their clients. If the real economy is experiencing difficulties, it affects banks as well.

[34] *See* A. Sheng, above p. 112.

2. Bottom-up approach

A 'bottom-up approach' predicts the probability of banking system fragility by consolidating the financial condition of each bank in the financial system. The performance of each bank is analysed by deriving financial ratios from figures in its balance sheet. The financial ratios of each bank are consolidated into financial system-wide ratios.

When a system-wide ratio is flashing a warning signal and a significant proportion of bank assets are held with banks with a high probability of insolvency—derived from the financial ratios of individual banks—then systemic bank failure becomes of concern. The sum of asset-weighted probabilities[35] would provide an objective account of the financial system fragility.[36]

The drawback of CAMEL to initiate a regulatory action is the degree of subjectiveness—regulatory action is a discretionary decision of the regulator. The bottom-up approach rectifies this problem since it is a statistical analysis.

The disadvantage of the bottom-up approach is the lack of bank data in most countries. An analysis based on partial information is unlikely to provide the full picture on the condition of the financial system since those that are unwilling to disclose are likely to be those with a worsening condition. Also, it ignores sectoral or geographical functions of banks. Financial distress in one sector of the economy will not be detected in this approach.[37]

3. Aggregate approach

The 'aggregate approach' analyses the aggregated financial data of all banks to determine the systemic fragility of the financial system. The advantage of this method is the availability of aggregate financial data, usually in the form of statistics published from the central bank or national statistics bureau. Based on these statistics, financial ratios similar to those used in the bottom-up approach are calculated.

To make available financial data more widely, the International Monetary Fund (IMF) has established a data dissemination system. Members are required to publish data on the website of IMF so the general public can easily obtain statistics.

The drawback of the aggregate approach is that the trouble of one financial institution is distributed and hidden in the statistics. If a category of

[35] It would be 0 when all assets are in banks with no probability of insolvency and 100 when all nation's assets are with banks insolvent.

[36] *See* Lindgren *et al.*, above n. 29, pp. 14–16.

[37] Ibid., p.16.

banks is developing problematic factors and their size of assets are smaller than other categories, the systemic danger will not emerge in the aggregate approach. If all banks have similar investment portfolio and asset sizes, the aggregate approach would present a sufficient picture. However, the banking sector is more likely to have diverse institutions in size and sectors.

4. IMF SURVEILLANCE

Through Article IV surveillance,[38] IMF is able to obtain substantial information on the economic and financial condition of each member economy. IMF itself is founded on the principle that an 'internationally agreed arrangement is [. . .] basically *self-enforcing*'.[39] The IMF has the ability to enhance this mechanism through its surveillance.

Surveillance is held annually with each member.[40] The IMF mission holds discussions with officials from the finance ministry, central bank, and other government ministries on fiscal and monetary policy,[41] providing an opportunity to submit policy advice to them.[42] After the mission, a staff report is submitted to the Executive Board and if the member country agrees, it is published as a Press/Public Information Notice (PIN).

IMF itself uses the surveillance results for lending,[43] and the information is beneficial to private parties to measure sovereign risk. As a response to the increasing demands from private parties to disclose surveillance reports,[44] IMF has established the Special Data Dissemination Standard (SDDS).[45] Member countries that seek to tap the international financial and capital market will subscribe to this standard, enhancing transparency of its financial system. It also mitigates information asymmetry.

C. *Issues in early warning systems*

All authors agree on the need to look at a wide range of variables and financial ratios, and detect unusually high or low movements of ratios. By monitoring multiple fronts, there is a higher possibility of detecting financial troubles.

[38] Section 3, Article IV of Articles of Agreement of the IMF.

[39] M. Guitian, 'The Unique Nature of the Responsibilities of the International Monetary Fund' (1992) *IMF*, (June) Pamphlet Series No. 46, p. 8.

[40] IMF, *IMF Surveillance—Factsheet* (5 Sept. 1999).

[41] IMF, *External Evaluation of IMF Surveillance: report by a group of independent experts* (1999), p. 25.

[42] Ibid., p. 17.

[43] Ibid., p. 20.

[44] Institute of International Finance, *Report of the Working Group on Financial Crises in Emerging Markets* (Jan. 1999), p. 27.

[45] SDDS is a standard on data access, integrity, and quality.

It is essential that internationally approved accounting standards are applied and enforced for any EWS. Strict application will not always be appropriate given the different market maturity and regulatory cost. Nevertheless, the core concepts of loan classification, disclosure items, frequency, and timing of reporting should be adhered to.

III. INSTITUTIONAL MECHANISMS TO CONTAIN FINANCIAL CRISES

This analysis looks at existing institutional mechanisms that trigger regulatory actions, and contemplates who and how these mechanisms should operate for future prevention and protection in the context of Japan, UK, and US. Their markets have distinct legal cultures but are all obliged to cope with progressing financial innovations. The following mechanisms are examined: lender of last resort, changes in supervisory ratings, sanctions, recapitalisation and restructuring, and revocation of banking license.

A. *Lender of Last Resort*

The lender of last resort (LOLR) is a facility under which the central bank extends credit to a solvent but temporarily illiquid bank. It is made available in an emergency situation when a bank is subject to a bank run, either retail or interbank, or when failure of an institution might trigger systemic contagion.[46] The objective of LOLR is to restore confidence and re-establish the credibility of banks. Thus, it is more likely that the central bank will consider use when a general loss of confidence is imminent with systemic implications.[47]

The conventional wisdom of LOLR developed by Thornton[48] and refined by Bagehot[49] was: (i) to provide liquidity freely, (ii) at a penal interest rate relative to the pre-crisis period, (iii) to any bank with good collateral, and (iv) to banks that are illiquid but not insolvent.[50]

There are increasing occasions when strict application of these principles are no longer realistic. Central banks often lend to insolvent institutions

[46] *See* R. M. Lastra, 'Lender of Last Resort, An International Perspective' (1999) 48 *Int'l and Comp. L.Q.* (Apr.), p. 342.

[47] *See* X. Freixas *et al.*, 'Lender of Last Resort: a review of the literature' (1999) *Financial Stability Review* (Nov.), pp. 157–8 (BOE).

[48] H. Thornton, *An Enquiry Into the Nature and Effects of the Paper Credits of Great Britain* (1802)(1962, F. A. v. Hayek edn).

[49] W. Bagehot, *Lombard Street: A Description of the Money Market* (1873, repr. 1962).

[50] *Refer to* T. M. Humphrey, 'Lender of Last Resort: The Concept in History' (1989) *Econ. Rev.* (Mar./Apr.), pp. 8–16 (Federal Reserve Bank of Richmond).

because there are no other sources of lending, and immediacy of the need for assistance makes it difficult to assess insolvency.[51]

Whether illiquidity or insolvency is first depends on the degree of confidence in the bank and its transparency. Financial institutions can conceal losses by attracting new deposits or other liabilities. When problems become severe enough, the net flow of funds turn negative and illiquidity becomes evident although insolvency was already present. On the other hand, an illiquid bank can become insolvent as a result of a fire sale of its assets.

1. The UK

The UK is discreet in the provision of LOLR since the Bank of England (BOE) is neither statutorily required to provide emergency credit nor to oversee the stability of the financial system. Financial stability and LOLR are clearly roles which the Bank of England is responsible for,[52] although not statutorily defined when BOE became independent in 1998.

The role of ensuring financial stability was laid out in the Chancellor's statement[53] and subsequently agreed between BOE, the Treasury, and the Financial Services Authority (FSA) on October 1997. A Memorandum of Understanding (MOU) was exchanged to clarify the framework for financial stability.[54]

The Financial Stability Standing Committee was established as a result of the MOU to meet monthly 'to discuss individual cases of significance and other developments relevant to financial stability'.[55] When an 'exceptional circumstances' arises, a support operation will be needed but only when 'a genuine threat to the stability of the financial system to avoid a serious disturbance in the UK economy'.[56]

BOE's LOLR function has evolved over the past decades reflecting the global trend of moral hazard concern. Previously, troubled institutions were encouraged to seek refinancing from shareholders. Although BOE limited its financial exposure and extended emergency credit only when other parties were not willing to assist,[57] it was reluctant to leave a troubled bank unattended, whether it was illiquid or insolvent.

[51] *See* Lastra, above n. 46, p. 346.

[52] *Refer to* BOE, *Fact Sheet: Bank of England* (Aug. 1998).

[53] *See* P. Rodgers, 'Changes at the Bank of England' (1997) *Bank of England Q. Bull.* (Aug.), at p. 246.

[54] *See* ibid., 'The Bank of England Act' (1998) *Bank of England Q. Bull.* (May), at pp. 97–9.

[55] Ibid., paragraph 10 and 11 at p. 98.

[56] Ibid., paragraph 11.

[57] Christos Hadjiemmanuil, *Banking Regulation and the Bank of England* (1996), p. 267 (LLP).

Following the enactment of the BOE Act, LOLR execution will be conducted even more carefully since it involves consultation with two other parties. In addition, accountability will necessitate clear reasoning and criteria when any such operation is carried out.[58]

2. The US

The US approach is contrary to the UK where Regulation A states the conditions in which Federal Reserve Banks (FRBs) can extend credit, not limited to depository institutions.[59]

LOLR is usually extended through discount window lending. The debate of whether LOLR should be extended to insolvent banks has been a legislative issue of emergency credit assistance. Provision of LOLR is explicit when the institution is solvent, but lending to insolvent institution gives rise to moral hazard concerns. 'Constructive ambiguity' was seen to limit moral hazard of LOLR.

Federal Deposit Insurance Corporation Improvement Act of 1991 (FDICIA) clarified this by limiting discount window lending to undercapitalised banks.[60] It reflects the intention to prevent delays in regulatory intervention and create clear guidelines to when and how the regulator acts. The discount window is, in principle, provided to a financial institution that is solvent, but with the discretion of the bank regulator it can be provided to insolvent bank in exceptional cases of systemic concern. One criterion for a depository institution to receive credit advancement is when there is no alternative source of funding.

Those who can access extended credit are limited: those appraised as 'undercapitalised' or 'critically undercapitalised', or insured depository institutions. The criteria of a critically undercapitalised depository institution were set out in FDICIA.[61]

3. Japan

Under the former Bank of Japan (BOJ) Law,[62] LOLR was affected either by a collateralised credit facility[63] or credit for 'preservation of the credit system'.[64] LOLR was a convenient method of providing temporary funds to troubled institutions.[65] LOLR provided to securities companies were

[58] S. 15 of the Bank of England Act 1998, ch.11 (Eng.) requires any decision involving intervention in the financial market to be published.

[59] 12 CFR 201. In unusual and exigent circumstances, FRB can extend credit to individuals, partnerships, and corporations.

[60] Federal Reserve Act sections 10(a) and 10(b) amended by FDICIA.

[61] 12 CFR 201.2(b) in Regulation A required from 12 USC 1831o(b)(1)(E).

[62] Kyuu Nihon Ginkouhou [former Bank of Japan Law], Law No. 67 of 1942.

[63] Ibid., Art. 20-2.

[64] Ibid., Art. 25.

[65] LOLR was extended to securities companies facing bankruptcy during the 1965–9 securities recession, and insolvent banks until 1995 as stopgap measures.

transferred through private banks inhibiting the healthy operation of LOLR since transfer obscures the true justification of LOLR.

The new BOJ Law enacted in 1998,[66] stated that LOLR was for 'temporary loans to financial institutions'[67] and 'business contributing to the maintenance of an orderly financial system'.[68]

The four principles of LOLR are: 1) threat of systemic risk is imminent, 2) provision is absolutely necessary, 3) responsibility of related parties will be clarified to prevent moral hazard, and 4) due consideration to the fiscal soundness of BOJ.[69]

However, BOJ's power to provide LOLR to prevent systemic risks has become somewhat limited in the new BOJ Law. While BOJ has the responsibility to conduct LOLR for temporary illiquidity caused by computer failures, LOLR for the preservation of the financial system is carried out by the instruction of the Minister of Finance (MOF).[70] Whereas the former BOJ Law gave BOJ the initiative to activate a LOLR, the new BOJ Law reverses this process.[71] The restrictive nature of LOLR to BOJ may inhibit timely provision of funds which defeats the objective of the new BOJ Law.

B. Deterioration in Supervisory Rating

CAMEL rating is the international best practice in supervisory rating, but probably less often they are accumulated and more so published. The more common measurement of prudence is the capital adequacy ratio (CAR). Bank regulators typically require financial institutions to maintain a certain CAR depending on their geographical or functional characteristics. If a financial institution fails to meet this threshold, it will be subject to scrutiny and required to review its operations.

1. The UK

Financial institutions in the UK are required by the Banking Act 1987 to conduct their business in a prudent manner, which is the foundation of FSA's capital adequacy test.[72] Financial institutions are required to 'maintain own

[66] Bank of Japan Law, Law No. 89 of 1997.

[67] Ibid., Art. 37.

[68] Ibid., Art. 38.

[69] Bank of Japan, *Heiseil Onendo Gyoukyougaikyoushyo[Operational Report for the Fiscal Year of 1998]* (1999).

[70] H. Shiono *et al.*, 'Kouhoutekikanntennkaramita Nihon Ginkounogyoumunohoutekiseikakutouneinoarikata [The Legal Characteristic and Operations of the Bank of Japan from a Public Law Point of View]' (1999), *Kin'yu Kenkyu [Monetary and Economic Studies]* (Dec.) BOJ, p. 100.

[71] H. Kanda, 'Nihon Ginkouhounokaisei [the Amendment of the Bank of Japan Law]' (1997) 1119 *Juristo* (15 Sept.), p. 20.

[72] *See* paragraph 4, Sch. 3 of Banking Act 1987.

funds which, together with other financial resources available to the institution of such nature and amount are considered appropriate . . .'[73]

A trigger ratio, the minimum CAR, is required above 8 per cent in accordance with the Council Directive on a Solvency Ratio for Credit Institutions,[74] although banks are expected to maintain a higher ratio.[75] Financial institutions also have a target ratio (a 'warning light' ratio), which breaches are reported although consequences of a breach are unclear.

The possible interpretation is that a breach of a trigger ratio indicates that 'a bank has insufficient capital safely to support the risks in its business and is therefore unable to satisfy one of the Schedule 3 criteria',[76] thus it is a violation of the Banking Act. There are no clauses as to sanctions for violating the Banking Act, but could lead to takeovers or mergers.

The target and trigger ratios are determined upon consultation with the financial institution according to their nature and size.[77] The minimum being 8 per cent, from most regulatory ratio requirements, it can be deduced that a 1–2 per cent difference will exist between the target and trigger ratios. Thus, it can be assumed that when the 8–10 percent CAR is not maintained, the financial institution is subject to close surveillance and review of its management.

2. THE US

Supervisory ratings are the core of the regulatory framework in the US. It allows regulators to conduct explicit, rule-based regulation. FDICIA[78] laid the foundation of quantitative evaluations of financial institutions' safety and soundness. FDICIA was a result of the many bank failures that occurred in the 1980s[79] resulting from late regulatory intervention as well as political forbearance.

Each bank regulator is required to set a standard of safety and soundness.[80] Based on these standards, regulators take action appropriate to the level of deterioration in the rating. This is the concept of 'structural early intervention and resolution (SEIR)' advocated by Benston and Kaufman[81] subsequent to the S&L debacle. For example, a cease-and-desist order is

[73] Ibid.

[74] Art. 10 of 1989 O.J. (L 386) 14 (Council Directive 89/647/EEC).

[75] *See* Financial Supervisory Authority, *A Guide to Banking Supervisory Policy* (Sept. 1998), 4.1.1.3.

[76] Ibid., 4.2.4.14.

[77] *See* above n. 75.

[78] Public Law 102–242.

[79] Between 1980 and 1994, more than 1,600 banks insured by FDIC were closed or received financial assistance. Federal Deposit Insurance Corporation, *History of the Eighties: Lessons from the Future* (1997), p. 3.

[80] 12 USCA 1818 p-1.

[81] G. J. Benston and G. G. Kaufman, 'Risk and solvency regulation of depository institutions: Past policies and current options' (1988), *New York University*, Monograph Series in Finance and Economics, No. 1988–1.

issued when a financial institution displays unsatisfactory asset quality, management, earnings, or liquidity in an unsafe or unsound manner.[82] These components are in fact those of the CAMEL rating.

3. JAPAN

The Banking Law states that the Financial Revitalisation Commission (FRC) and MOF can establish a standard that measures the safety and soundness of financial institutions.[83] Accordingly, FRC has issued a CAR guideline.

For internationally operating banks, a well-capitalised bank must maintain an 8 per cent CAR; an undercapitalised bank 4–8 per cent; a significantly undercapitalised bank 2–4 per cent; and a critically under-capitalised bank 0–2 per cent.[84]

For a financial institution to receive a capital injection, it has to be significantly or critically undercapitalised (CAR below 4 per cent)[85] and measures need to be taken to remedy the financial condition.

Considering the lag of CAR measurement, the 4 per cent threshold is a lax criteria for intervention since they are likely to be more undercapitalised by the time the CAR is disclosed.

C. Sanctions

Sanctions are applied when non-compliance with regulatory requirements or criminal activities occur.[86] They aim to provide banks an incentive to operate soundly by punishing those who have failed to comply. The prerequisite for this incentive to work is enforcement.

The degree of penalty differs depending on the wrongdoing of the bank. Sanctions include dismissal of management, termination of deposit insurance, monetary fine, cease-and-desist order, and closure.

While the objective of sanctions is to provide the incentive to operate safely and soundly, their implementation may in fact result in the worsening of situation. If the penalty is too severe, it will lead to eventual failure of the already financially distressed institution. It could also trigger a loss of confidence in the institution resulting in a self-fulfilling bank run. On the other hand, if the sanction is not penalising, compliance becomes lax. The balance of a carrot-and-stick is essential for effective functioning.

[82] 12 USCA 1818(b)(8).

[83] *See* art. 14–2 of Ginkouho [Banking law], Law, No. 59 of 1981.

[84] Art. 2 and 3 of Kin'yunosoukikenzenkanotamenokinkyuhsochinikansuruhouritsusekoukisoku [Rules for Implementation of Financial Function Early Strengthen Law], Rule No. 3 of Financial Revitalisation Commission.

[85] Kin'yukinounosaiseinotamenosoukikenzenkanikansuruhouritsu [Financial Function Early Strengthen Law], Law No. 143 of 1998 (hereinafter Early Strengthen Law), art. 6–4.

[86] *See* Lastra, above n. 17, p. 122.

1. THE UK

Prior to the Banking Act in 1979, the UK did not have a statutory requirement that a bank or depository institution had to fulfil. The statutory authorisation process was established after a number of events during the 1970s.[87]

The UK does not have a set framework for the handling of troubled institutions but rather an informal approach to resolve difficulties.[88] Sanctions are likely to be imposed when there is a threat to depositors' claim, or a looming crisis.

2. THE US

There is a gradation of sanctions imposed depending on the bank's CAMEL rating. This links the supervisory intensity with rating. A comprehensive revision of sanctions was made by FDICIA aiming to limit morally hazardous behaviour and restrict the cost of bank rescues. There were four developments to restructure the regulatory framework:[89] (1) the supervisory system was revised to ensure 'prompt corrective action (PCA)', (2) federal banking regulators were required to conduct annual safety and soundness examinations of all insured institutions and set safety and soundness standards, (3) deposit insurance premium was changed to risk-based, and (4) FDIC was required to use the 'least-cost resolution'.

PCA is based on the CAR of a financial institution. The critical capital level range is specified as tangible equity in an amount not less than 2 per cent of total assets, and not more than 65 per cent of the required minimum level of capital under the leverage limit.[90] This implicates that equity stock cannot be lower than 2 per cent of total assets.

The action taken against each category is specified by each banking regulator.[91] A depository institution is subject to PCA if it does not satisfy the undercapitalised level. Thus the capital category of undercapitalise is the warning level of banking troubles.[92]

[87] 'Lifeboat' rescues happened in the early 1970s when some fringe banks fell into liquidity difficulty after consecutive interest rate rises. Then the UK joined EEC in 1973, and subsequently the First Banking Co-ordination Directive was introduced in 1977 requiring an authorisation process for credit institutions. V. Robbs, 'The Genesis of Regulation' (1997) 3 *Financial Stability Rev.* (Autumn), pp. 29–31 (BOE).

[88] Hadjiemmanuil, above n. 57, p. 267.

[89] *Referring to* Federal Deposit Insurance Corporation, above n. 79, p.103.

[90] 12 USCA 1831o(c)(1)(B).

[91] 12 USCA 1831o(c)(2).

[92] A bank is defined as undercapitalised if: (i) it has a total risk-based capital ratio that is less than 8 per cent; or (ii) it has a Tier 1 risk-based capital ratio that is less than 4 per cent; or (iii) has a leverage ratio that is less than 4 per cent, or has a leverage ratio that is less than 3.0 per cent if the bank is rated composite 1 under the CAMEL rating system in the most recent examination of the bank and is not experiencing or anticipating significant growth. 12 CFR 208.33(a)(3).

Summary of PCA provisions of the FDICIA

Zone	Mandatory provisions	Discretionary provisions	Capital ratio (%)		
			Risk based		Leverage
			Total	Tier 1	Tier 1
1 Well capitalised			>10	>6	>5
2 Adequately capitalised	– No brokered deposits allowed without approval of FDIC.		>8	>4	>4
3 Under capitalised	– Suspend dividends and management. – Require capital restoration plan. – Restrict asset growth. – Approval required for acquisitions, branching and new activities. – No brokered deposits.	– Order recapitalisation. – Restrict interaffiliate transactions. – Restrict deposit interest rates. – Restrict certain other activities. – Any other action that would better carry out.	<8	<4	<4
4 Significantly under-capitalised	– Same as for zone 3. – Order recapitalisation*. – Restrict interafiliate transactions*. – Restrict deposit interest rates*. – Pay of officers restricted.	– Any zone 3 discretionary actions. – Conservatorship or receivership if fails to submit or implement plan or recapitalise pursuant to order. – Any other zone 5 provision, if such action is necessary to carry out prompt corrective action.	<6	<3	<3
5 Critically under-capitalised	– Same as for zone 4. – Receiver/conservator. within ninety days*. – Receiver if still in zone 5 four quarters after becoming critically under-capitalised. – Suspend payments on subordinated debt*. – Restrict certain other activities.				<2

* Not required if primary supervisor determines action would not serve purpose of PCA or if certain other conditions are met.

Source: Charles Goodhart *et al.*, *Financial Regulation: Why, how and where now?* 56 (Routledge, 1998).

For each capitalisation category, the regulatory action is explicit, although each banking regulator sets the specific terms. PCA and sanctions are summarised below. Besides the material sanctions listed, there are also reputational sanctions at the point where managerial intervention is made.

In the US, all national banks and all members of the Federal Reserve are required to be insured by the Federal Deposit Insurance Corporation (FDIC).[93] Hence, the termination of insurance will equate to the inability of a depository institution to continue business. Thus, FDIC and banking regulators both have the power to cease the operations of a depository institution.

The safety and soundness standards established by bank regulators cover:[94] (1) operational and managerial standards, (2) compensation standards, and (3) standards relating to asset quality, earnings, and stock valuations. FDIC,[95] OCC Treasury,[96] and Federal Reserve[97] have established similar standards.

The term 'unsafe and unsound' relates to the overall operations of a financial institution, thus it is difficult to define a rigid and all-inclusive definition,[98] especially when the US financial system is complex and will be more so as a result of the Financial Services Modernisation Act. The very least condition of unsafe and unsound banking would be a insolvent bank operating, and a conduct that poses a threat to the financial system or is an imprudent conduct in relation to the general standards set by the banking regulators. Allowing a financial institution that has violated the law or regulation to continue operation is also an unsafe and unsound conduct.

The US General Accounting Office (GAO) has questioned the enforcement of safety and soundness standards and whether it has resulted in increased early regulatory action.[99] The abstract nature of these standards allows subjective judgment contradicting the objective of FDICIA. Some have questioned the effectiveness of PCA on the basis that regulatory forbearance occurred from infrequency of supervisory examination rather than lack of early intervention.[100] Also, the level of capital required in each category could be inadequate for early intervention to be useful.[101]

[93] 12 USCA 1814(b).
[94] 12 USCA 1831p-1.
[95] 12 CFR 364.101.
[96] 12 CFR 30.6.
[97] 12 CFR 208.60.
[98] E. L. Symons, Jr. and J. J. White, *Banking Law: Teaching Materials* (1984), at p. 574 (2nd edn).
[99] *See* 'Bank and Thrift Regulation: Implementation of FDICIA's Prompt Regulatory Action Provisions' (1998), *General Accounting Office* (Nov.) GAO/GGD–97–18, p. 49.
[100] J. Peek and E. S. Rosengren, 'Will Legislative Early Intervention Prevent the Next Banking Crisis?' (1997) *Southern Econ. J.* (July), p. 268.
[101] *See* Kaufman, above n. 4, p. 10; J. Peek and E. S. Rosengren, 'How Well Capitalised are Well-Capitalised Banks?' (1997) *New England Econ. Rev.* (September/October), p. 42 (Federal Reserve Bank of Boston); and G. J. Benston and G. G. Kaufman, 'Deposit insurance reform in the FDIC Improvement Act: The experience to date' (1998) *Econ. Perspectives* (second quarter), p. 7 (Federal Reserve Bank of Chicago).

3. JAPAN

The concept of PCA was first brought into Japanese regulation with the enactment of the Financial System Reform Laws of 1997. Article 26–1 of the Banking Law states that financial institutions are required to take necessary measures to ensure the safety and soundness of their operations. If necessary, FRC can require the submission of a restructuring plan by the financial institution. When not satisfied with the restructuring plan or implementation of restructuring, FRC can issue a cease and desist order.[102]

The Banking Law states that FRC and MOF can establish a standard that measures the safety and soundness of financial institutions.[103] Accordingly, Financial Supervisory Agency (FSA-J) issued the CAR guideline so as to assist regulatees understand the method of how PCA will be implemented.[104] Financial institutions will ultimately use a self-developed asset classification, although they tend to be more lax than that of FSA-J. Criticism has been expressed towards the regulatory method of the Japanese authorities on loss loan classifications and provisions encouraging delayed response by financial institutions to write off their bad loans.[105]

A financial institution is to be significantly or critically undercapitalised to receive capital injection.[106] For other capital levels to receive capital assistance, the actions required are shown in the table on page 23.

D. *Recapitalisation and Restructuring*

Capital assistance to troubled banks is provided when a financial institution is solvent but needs recapitalisation to continue business on a sound basis. If the capital level is low, there is a threat that it will conduct morally hazardous and risky business. So, when financial institutions become undercapitalised, governments often conduct a capital boost and purchase NPL to revitalise the financial intermediation function.

Capital assistance can also be made to banks taking over or merging troubled banks. A bridge bank could take over a troubled institution until it is ready for resale.

102 *See* Banking Law, above n. 83, art. 26–1.

103 *See* ibid., art. 14–2.

104 *See* Yokin tou ukeirekin'yu kikan ni kakawaru kensa manyuaru ni tsuite [Supervisory Manual with regard to Deposit Taking Institutions], Guidance of the Financial Supervisory Agency No. 177, 1 July, 1998 (hereinafter FSA-J supervisory manual).

105 *See* T. Hoshi and A. Kashyap, 'The Japanese Banking Crisis: Where did it come from and How Will It End?' (1999), *National Bureau of Economic Research* (July) Working Paper No.7250, at p. 26–31.

106 *See* Financial Function Early Strengthen Law, above n. 85, art. 6–4.

Criteria for financial institutions to receive capital assistance

Zone	**Mandatory provisions**	**Basle capital adequacy ratio**[107]	
		Internationally operating banks	**Other banks**
1 Well capitalised	– Merger or acquisition of an undercapitalised bank or a sudden tight credit condition.[108] – Enhance management efficiency of management/staff and cost cutting.[109] – Prevention of profit loss.	>8	>4
2 Sub-standard capitalised	– Same as zone 1.[110] – Reduction of dividends and restore management strategy. – Pay of officers restricted.	>4	>2
3 Significantly under-capitalised	– Suspend dividends and management.[111] – Efficacy of staff number, branching, and international operations revised.	<2	<1
4 Critically under-capitalised	– Same as for zone 3.[112] – The continuation of the operation is essential for the local economy.	<0	<0

1. The UK

The UK does not have a framework for capital assistance to troubled banks besides LOLR. It has traditionally sought the support of shareholders and other banks instead of exposing itself financially. There has not been much need of capital injection because financially troubled banks are often taken over.[113]

Also, the tradition of self-regulation has discouraged the government from financially assisting banks. Regulators have acted more as a coordinator than a main player in takeovers and mergers.

[107] *See* art. 2 and 3, Kin'yu no souki kenzenka no tameno kinkyuh sochi ni kansuru houritsu sekou kisoku [Rules for Implementation of Financial Function Early Strengthen Law], Rule No. 3 of Financial Revitalisation Commission.

[108] *See* Financial Function Early Strengthen Law, above n. 85, art. 7–1–5–1 and 2.

[109] Ibid., art. 7–2–11.

[110] Ibid., art. 7–2–2.

[111] Ibid., art. 7–2–3.

[112] Ibid., art. 7–1–4.

[113] The most recent example is Barings taken over by ING.

2. The US

Restructuring takes place as recapitalisation, or merger and acquisition with another bank. The variety and complexity of restructuring measures make it difficult to form a clear-cut distinction between closure and restructuring in some cases. When an institution is merged, the unsound institution will cease to exist while its operations will be taken over by a healthy institution.

FDIC provides monetary assistance to troubled banks:[114] (i) to prevent default of insured institution,[115] (ii) to restore an insured bank that has defaulted its normal operations,[116] and (iii) severe financial conditions exist that threaten the stability of a significant number of insured depository institutions.[117] The Board of Directors of FDIC has the discretion to determine whether the three conditions exist.[118] The condition that is of highest concern is the systemic risk to other insured depository institutions because FDIC has an obligation to take the least cost resolution.[119]

3. Japan

The Financial Function Early Strengthen Law[120] legislated for the first time the requirements for injection of public funds. The principle condition for a capital injection is the threat to the financial intermediary function of Japan.[121]

Resolution and Collection Corporation (RCC) carried out the capital injection by underwriting stock of the financial institution. For stock with a voting right to be underwritten by the RCC: (i) it is indispensable to obtain public confidence, (ii) to remedy the mismanagement, (iii) liabilities cannot be repaid with the capital, (iv) the financial institution is either critically undercapitalised or undercapitalised, and (v) the operation of the financial institution is indispensable for the local economy.[122]

Deposit Insurance Corporation (DIC) can purchase the assets of financial institutions to safeguard the soundness and safety of the financial system, protect depositors,[123] and provide financial assistance to take over troubled banks. The condition for financial assistance for merger is: (i) is

[114] 12 USCA 1823(c).
[115] 12 USCA 1823(c)(1)(A) and 1823(c)(2)(B)(i).
[116] 12 USCA 1823(c)(1)(B) and 1823(c)(2)(B)(ii).
[117] 12 USCA 1823(c)(1)(C) and 1823(c)(2)(B)(iii).
[118] 12 USCA 1823(c)(1).
[119] 12 USCA 1823(c)(4).
[120] *See* Financial Function Early Strengthen Law, above n. 85.
[121] Ibid., art. 3–1.
[122] Ibid., art. 6.
[123] Kin'yukinounosaiseinotamenokinkyuhsochinikansuruhouritsu [Law Concerning Emergency Measures for the Revitalisation of the Functions of the Financial System], Law No. 132 of 1998 (hereinafter Revitalisation Law), art. 53 and 1.

beneficial for protection of depositors, (ii) without it, the merger is not possible, (iii) without merger, great inconveniences in financing will be experienced by the local community and sector which the default financial institution is conducting business with, and (iv) the merged financial institution is insolvent and must be closed.[124]

The Japanese also use damage to public confidence as a condition of financial assistance. Taking into account that the loss of public confidence is the greatest danger to a financial institution, the maintenance of confidence is significant although difficult to detect the deterioration.

E. *Revocation of License or Closure of a Bank*

When a bank is facing financial difficulty and it culminates in closure, unless it is outright fraud of mismanagement, it is likely that other banks might be facing similar difficulties.

1. The UK

The authorisation and revocation of financial institutions were transferred from BOE to FSA in 1998. The revocation condition stated in the Banking Act 1987 as amended by BOE Act is 'the interests of depositors or potential depositors of the institution are in any other way threatened . . .'[125] or when the financial institution is insolvent. The meaning of 'insolvency' is stated as 'the institution (i) is unable to repay deposits which are due and payable; and (ii) has no current prospect of being able to do so'.[126] Revocation is also conducted when the financial institution has entered a winding up or insolvency proceeding.[127]

2. The US

The closure of a bank can only be implemented by OCC for national banks[128] and by state bank regulators for state banks. The offences that result in a closure and receivership are wide ranging. The foremost cause is insufficient assets to cover obligations,[129] substantial dissipation of assets or earnings,[130] unsafe and unsound condition,[131] and a cease and desist order.[132] A failure to recover from an undercapitalised situation can also

[124] Art. 61–3 of Yokin hokenho [Deposit Insurance Law], Law No. 34 of 1971.
[125] Sec. 11(1)(e) of Banking Act 1987, ch. 22 (Eng.).
[126] Sec 59(1)(a) of Banking Act 1987.
[127] Sec 11(6), (7), (8) and (9) of Banking Act 1987.
[128] 12 USC 1821(b).
[129] 12 USC 1821(c)(5)(A).
[130] 12 USC 1821(c)(5)(B).
[131] 12 USC 1821(c)(5)(C).
[132] 12 USC 1821(c)(5)(D).

lead to closure.[133] Money laundering practices found guilty of criminal offences will lead to immediate closure.[134]

The payoff of deposit insurance is conducted when closure of the depository institution takes place.[135] In practice, payoffs of deposits have been rare due to the cost burden on FDIC and inconvenience to depositors.

The view that market discipline is an effective bank regulator opposes this argument.[136] Potential loss of deposits will encourage depositors to monitor the safety and soundness of banking operations. The risk incorporated in deposit insurance does provide a valuable inhibition of excessively risky business.

Considering the inconveniences to depositors and the effort depositors might take to avoid these inconveniences, while not dismissing its applicability, limiting deposit payoff to when it is the least cost option will maintain the benefit of deposit insurance. Depending purely on depositors' action will cause collective action problems with the vast number of depositors.

3. Japan

There are two routes that a financial institution's license is revoked in Japan: the Banking Law of 1981 stated termination of operations and subsequent revocation of license, and a cease and desist order due to the threat posed to the financial and local community.

The termination of operations will be carried out if: (i) finances of institution are insufficient for safe and sound operation,[137] and (ii) capital is inadequate for operation.[138] License is revoked if (i) there is a violation of the law, articles of association, or order from FRC,[139] (ii) the financial institution's conduct is against the public interest,[140] or (iii) the revocation of license is necessary out of systemic concern.[141]

The termination of operation of a financial institution must constitute a threat to repay deposits—or a bank run—and a systemic risk to the domestic and international community. The conditions are narrower because the threat will have to pose a threat to a greater community than just the financial system to amount to a termination.

A bank shall be insolvent but illiquidity is also a condition of termination.[142] For revocation of license, there is a further requirement of violation

[133] 12 USC 1821(c)(5)(K).

[134] 12 USC 1821(c)(5)(M).

[135] 12 USC 1821(f).

[136] J. R. Macey and G. P. Miller, 'Bank Failures, Risk Monitoring, and the Market for Bank Control' (1988) 88 *Colum. L. Rev.* (Oct.), p. 1192.

[137] *See* Banking Law, above n. 83, art. 26–1.

[138] Ibid., art. 26–2.

[139] Ibid., art. 27–1.

[140] Ibid.

[141] Ibid., art. 28.

[142] Ibid., art. 26.

of law and regulations, and acting against the interest of public. Japanese authorities consider financial institutions to be quasi-public institutions, acting in the interest of public, different from other commercial entities.

The Financial Revitalisation Law stated the termination of operation and receivership, merger, or nationalisation to be carried out if: (i) the financial institution cannot repay its liabilities with its assets,[143] (ii) possible termination of repayment of deposits or it has been terminated,[144] (iii) continuation of operation is critically inappropriate,[145] (iv) unless taken over, the operation of the financial institution is a great inconvenience to the community or sector,[146] (v) a systemic threat to the financial system of Japan,[147] (vi) financial institution's lending constitutes a high proportion of lending to local community or sector,[148] and (vii) unless taken over, the operation of the financial institution has a serious effect on the international financial market.[149]

IV. CONCLUDING REMARKS

A financial crisis occurs when there is an unanticipated shock to the economy, and this shock triggers an alteration in investment behaviour. Prior to this event, there are underlying micro or macroeconomic weaknesses which have been latent due to the preceding positive outlook. The shock activates a revision by investors of the true financial condition according to the new information available. This correction causes a mass and sudden withdrawal of investments resulting in a financial crisis.

Early warning systems (EWSs) have been developed to mechanically predict a financial crisis. Capital adequacy has been the main emphasis of supervision because it is considered the main measurement of bank soundness. CAR is often used as a threshold to initiate PCA.

Through the analysis of the institutional mechanisms to contain a financial crisis, there are two perspectives: individual financial institution problems, and systemic risk concerns. The attitude and regulatory method of each country is considerably distinct. Nevertheless, the analysis delineates a picture of a possible financial crisis to be more or less uniform in the three financial centers. This is a threat to financial stability with an illiquid situation indicating a possible bank run. Termination of deposit repayment by an insolvent institution is another situation. A threat to the

143 *See* Revitalisation Law, above n. 123, art. 8–1, stating the principle for receivership to be imposed. Also a principle condition of the nationalisation of a financial institution, art. 36–1 of Revitalisation Law.

144 Ibid.

145 Ibid., art. 8–2–1.

146 Ibid.

147 Ibid., art. 36–1–1–1.

148 Ibid., art. 36–1–1–2.

149 Ibid., art. 37–1–1.

financial intermediary function and loss of public confidence is also a financial crisis situation. Finally, a CAR that is less than 6 per cent indicates a bank's problem with a financial crisis potential.

There is no one universal financial system that will prevent a financial crisis. The diversity of causes and innovation of finance has made prediction of a crisis even more difficult. To contain such an evolutionary economic phenomenon effectively while limiting the regulatory burden on financial institutions, objective monitoring is a prerequisite. Where political interference is inherent, regulators might choose to delegate this to an external observer. Second, accumulation of experience and expertise of supervision is necessary. Highly qualified individuals with high morale should carry out technical analyses of economic conditions and share information with other regulators. Third, there should be a mechanism that such analyses can be recommended to the government and made public to prevent politicisation of the suggestions. Fourth, flexibility of regulations should be guaranteed by preserving financial regulations to independent bodies consulted by the government.

There is no one system that would fit all financial systems. It is necessary to consider various economic, legal, and social factors together with historical elements to implement the appropriate regulatory framework to prevent a financial crisis.

PART I

Prelude: 1990–1995

Chapter 2

Lessons from the American Debt Crisis

Gerald N. Olson[1]

I. INTRODUCTION

In the twenty-two years following the abandonment of the Bretton Woods Accord by the United States, fuelled by rapid technological development and increasingly interdependent world trade, a global financial economy has been unleashed. The global financial economy is approximately fifty times larger than the so-called global 'real economy'.[2]

According to Joel Kurtzman, Executive Editor of the Harvard Business Review,

> the ascendancy of trading means that finance has shifted its orientation from 'investing' to one of 'transacting', a consequence of the ability of computers and telecommunications network to manipulate vast quantities of information effortlessly and send it around the world.
>
> The information age has moved finance from its age-old static-even passive-framework of buying assets or making investments and holding them, into something new, making money by harvesting minute shifts in value across various exchanges.[3]

The growing dominance of the global financial economy, combined with the floating rate currency exchange system which followed the collapse of Bretton Woods, and accompanied by the accelerated velocity of high-tech trading, has resulted in increasingly volatile financial markets; highs are higher; lows are lower; and cycles are closer together as a result of 'hot money' and electronic 'portfolio investment'. All of these developments have put tremendous pressure on the international monetary system.

Unless the increasingly destabilising and volatile effects of the global financial economy on the financial arrangements integral to domestic real

[1] The author is most grateful to his former colleagues at Winstead, Sechrest & Minick P.C., who participated in the preparation of prior unpublished versions of certain materials contained in this chapter. This chapter primarily speaks as to the historical period of 1970 to the mid-1990s.

[2] Joel Kurtzman, *The Death of Money: How the Electronic Economy has Destabilised the World's Markets and Created Financial Chaos*, at 12 (1993).

[3] Ibid., at p. 25.

economies are mitigated through international currency stabilisation and trading regulation, the pernicious problems presented in resolving insolvencies, liquidations, reorganisations and effecting debt restructures will increase.

The United States has benefited, and expects to continue to benefit, from the abandonment of the Bretton Woods fixed exchange rate system through the devaluation of its international financial obligations. Because the dollar has continued to serve as the world's reserve currency, currency stabilisation through the adoption of a fixed or semi-fixed exchange rate system is viewed as highly unlikely. Similarly, no nation or group of nations has been willing to take the lead in regulating trading in the global financial economy. Consequently, as pressures from the growing global financial economy increase, the world may expect an increasing incidence of company and bank insolvencies and increasing size and complexity of those insolvencies. Emerging economies are facing the brunt of this pressure. As an example, following the collapse of the Mexican peso in late December 1994, nonperforming loans in Mexican banks rose from a 1994 rate of 9 per cent of all bank loans to a 1995 rate of approximately 17 per cent. Under US accounting standards, however, the 17 per cent rate would equate to about 27 per cent.[4] A bank bailout programme is ongoing, with the non-performing loan largely in the hands of banks. By the year ending March 1995, fourteen Venezuelan banks had collapsed. The government has not yet developed a plan to sell off banking assets that have fallen under state control as a result of interventions.[5] According to the International Monetary Fund, 'Crises in the banking systems of Argentina, Mexico and Venezuela and costly bank bailouts in Brazil, have raised concerns that weak financial systems may be one of the most important Achilles heel of the region's economic reforms.'[6]

This chapter examines the practical and legal issues addressed in the American banking crisis of the late 1980s and early 1990s, at the point where the author's experience intersected with an awareness of the extraordinary systemic nature of the collapse of asset values, and thus debtor and bank capital, in America in the mid-1980s.

According to Congressional testimony by Bernard Weinstein, Director of the Center for Economics Development and Research, 'Mexico's current financial emergency mirrors Texas' and then the America's S & L crisis of a decade ago. An inadequate capital base, rising loan losses, inexperienced

[4] US GAO Report on Mexico's Financial Crisis, 23 Feb. 1996, at p. 21.

[5] Ibid., *see also*, R. Karoglan and M. Lubrano, *Mexico's Banks After the December 1994 Devaluation: A Chronology of the Governments Response*, 16 NWJ OF Int'l. L. and Bus. 24 (1995).

[6] Stephen Fidler, *IMF to do more in Monitoring Banking*, Fin. Times, 26 Mar. 1996, at p. 4.

management and a sky-high cost-of-funds all sound familiar.'[7] Despite cultural and legal differences among the Latin American countries, including Mexico and the United States, the causes of these financial crises are in many ways the same (albeit in many ways different). The issues presented in their resolution at the bank asset level through loan restructures also are essentially the same. Indeed, 'the deflation visible in Mexico is part of a larger, global asset and revenue collapse that is apparent in Japan, China, Europe and in many emerging markets'.[8]

In the United States, the deflating erosion of asset values was reflected first in debtors' capital. As loan defaults proliferated, both debtors and creditors sought to protect their balance sheets by shifting apparent losses to others through broad-based, multiparty negotiations of consensual workouts, foreclosures, litigation and bankruptcy, followed by widespread bank failures, rescues and bailouts. This process is distinguished from the legal and economic effects of prior boom and bust cycles, following the Great Depression in the late 1920s and 1930s and in the mid-1970s in America and worldwide. It has been said that the earlier cycles resulted in a winnowing of the weaker and less capable debtors and creditors, whose misfortune was often predicated by mismanagement, and in some cases, fraud. The recent systemic crisis of capital adequacy, however, struck both the strong and the weak, and was thus devastating in its effect.

The more astute participants changed tactics in these new circumstances. These changes were reflected by both debtor and creditor desires to resolve widespread defaults in credit transactions on a 'global', 'planned', or 'integrated' basis, as opposed to narrow enforcement of contractual and legal rights and remedies. There was, in effect, a tacit acceptance by the more sophisticated players that the broad based economic crisis was well beyond the consequences of occasional mismanagement or fraud. Less astute participants in this growing drama, most particularly politicians and bank regulators, however, continued to view the growing number of loan defaults as a moral crisis, founded in widespread fraud and criminal activities. Tragically, the American legal and bank regulatory system has been largely limited to this perspective.[9]

[7] Testimony of B. Weinstein, Director, Center for Economic Development and Research, Professor of Applied Economics, University of North Texas, before the Senate Committee on Banking, Housing and Urban Affairs, US Congress, 24 May 1995.

[8] Testimony of C. Whalen, Chief Financial Officer, Legal Research International, Inc., before the Senate Committee on Banking, Housing and Urban Affairs, US Congress, 24 May 1995.

[9] *But see*, C. Whalen, who observes that 'the criminal economy . . . [is] by far the largest of the three sectors of the Mexican economy, which is built around narcotics trafficking, arms smuggling, kidnapping and other forms of illegal activity. The criminal economy has mushroomed in size over the past decade and now clearly dominates the entire political economy of Mexico. By way of comparison, consider that the $25 to $30 billion in profits from the $100

This chapter explores the dichotomy, first by examining the immediate context of the American crisis of capital inadequacy during the period 1985 to 1995, then the distinctive characteristics of the loss recognition and allocation processes between debtors and creditors which brought the systemic nature of the American crisis to light, and which is, in the most basic sense, the battle ground for debtor and creditor solvency.

In the late 1980s and early 1990s, debtors and creditors in the United States were in the grip of a systemic cycle of capital deterioration of unprecedented proportion. Superficial public and governmental opinion suggested that the current problem of capital deterioration was driven by collapsing real estate values, first in the Southwest, and then in New England, the Mid-Atlantic States and the Southeast, but that the problem did not extend to other parts of the country. The problem of collapsing real estate values, however, was pervasive throughout the United States. The effects of collapsing real estate values, when combined with other problems with national implications (including increasing rates of default on LBO's, junk bonds and other highly leveraged transactions) and regional economic problems, such as the oil and gas problems in the Southwest and sagging performance by the so-called 'high tech' industry in the Northeast, precipitated broadbased credit constriction and an alarming rate of business failures, resulting in the erosion of the nation's financial institutions' capital footings. This process has often been described as the 'deleveraging' of American business in the 1990s.

Experience revealed recurring patterns of reaction to this crisis by both debtors and creditors. These reactions were marked by early and persistent denial of the problem. Experience has also showed that, when regulatory examiners of federally regulated financial institutions forced recognition of the problem, both debtor and creditor management were thrown into an intractable reactionary mode. Debtors faced abrupt and precipitous termination of longstanding, historical credit relationships. Creditors were often unable to withstand against the pressure of constantly increasing and restrictive regulatory action, including the effect of regulators' actions on their operations, the constant turmoil of resulting crisis management, the distortion on the institution's balance sheet caused by a dramatic shift from earning to nonearning assets, increased levels of other real estate owned ('OREO') and other repossessed collateral and the wave of litigation and

billion per year narcotics trade is twice the total revenues of Mexican oil sector . . . It is impossible to have sound solvent banks in an economic environment that is as hostile and difficult is the one that I have just described.' Ibid., citing an FBI report by James Moody, head of that agency's narcotics section, Whalen notes that 'companies in the process of privatisation in Mexico under President Salinas were purchased by narcotics trafficking organisations in Mexico and Columbia.' Ibid.

bankruptcies which the repossession and foreclosure process invited, as the debtor's ticket to survival.[10]

The cycle of industry-wide in-substance and actual foreclosure or repossession, of collateral marking to market of collateral value mandated by accounting and regulatory policy, increasing costs to carry and manage assets and to administer problems which the creditors were inadequately prepared to manage and resolve, and the dramatic effect of negative leverage on both debtors and creditors, resulted in recurring unavoidable capital losses, unless a proactive approach was taken by debtor and creditor management early in the cycle. The mission of management was to minimise capital loss, stabilise the downward spiral of negative leverage and deflect as much loss as possible to hapless, unprepared competitors. Failure to act quickly, decisively, and proactively, pursuant to a clear plan and established priorities, resulted in the dissipation of both the debtor's and the creditor's liquidity and capital and in the elimination of their remaining flexibility. This process of loan workout and restructure was distinct from the usual loan-by-loan enforcement tactics generally employed in previous cycles.[11]

This chapter examines the context for the American national crisis of capital adequacy, describes in more detail the indicia of the problem and prescribes a proactive general programme to minimise the effect of this crisis on a given debtor or creditor by early problem recognition; prompt, detailed and anticipatory response, accurate asset valuation, early loss allocation and consensual balance sheet restructuring. The goal of both the

[10] See Whalen's observations with respect to the developing situation in Mexico and Latin America. Ibid. See also, *Credit Crunch, the Banking Disaster in Mexico Whipsaws an Ailing Economy*, WSJ, 25 Jan. 1996, at p. A-1. Moreover, Mexican banks have been reluctant to recognise the extent of their losses . . .' Banks prefer to wait for the economy', with the hope that growth will lift the prices of these properties again, says Pedro Azcue, managing partner at La Salle [La Salle partners]. Mexican business culture contributes, too, to the unwillingness of bank to acknowledge their mistakes and make changes. Short of a government takeover, few Mexican banks have made a major management change, though many executive teams left their banks vulnerable. Mexican boards tend not to hold managers as accountable as US companies do, especially because many Mexican companies are still dominated by families.'

[11] See M. Tangman, 'The Once, and Future, Banking Crisis?', Institutional Investors, at p. 19, Nov. 1995. 'Mexicans' debt bind, with its potential for sparking social unrest, so worries the government that in late August Zedillo and Ortiz presented an emergency four-point plan to restructure bank loans. It was clearly aimed at stemming a growing tide of borrower sentiment for a payments moratorium, an idea first championed by rural debtors' organisation El Barzon on 1993. The borrowers' movement has gone urban and consumerist since interest rates soared to more than 140 per cent on credit card accounts during the first quarter this year. The number of debtors' associations nationwide is now estimated at 100. Threatened with a debt moratorium, bankers and government officials were adamant that loan restructuring on a case-by-case basis was the only acceptable alternative. Says Elizabeth Barrera, banking analyst with Interacciones Casa de Bolsa: 'If you get borrowers to agree to that, you weaken the promoratorium movement. But if you can't, you could get to a very dangerous situation.'

debtor and the creditor should be to recognise this problem early, deal with it in at least as favourable a manner as the debtor's creditors and the bankruptcy courts ultimately would require, and take painful but acceptable losses necessary to ensure the financial survival of both debtor and creditor.[12] As we will discover, there are many more restraints on the debtors' and creditors' ability to act in their mutual best interest than initially meets the eye.

[12] Although loan restructures are an important component of resolution of the current Mexican banking crisis, there remain many difficulties in the process. See, C. Torres, 'Out of the loop, Mexican Restructuring of Firms' Debt Often Hurts Foreign Holders' WSJ, 13 May 1996 at p. A-1. 'Because Mexico's creaky legal system is ill-equipped to handle complex bankruptcy cases, many decisions are made by a clubby group of Mexican bankers and businessmen. Left out-of-the-loop and in some cases, out-of-the-money are the foreign bondholders who bought more than $20 billion of high-yield Mexican corporate debt in the early 1990s. 'There was a lot of greed and blind trust in a system that was fundamentally different' from that in the US,' says Mitchell Sahn, a partner at Latin Tactical Trading Group Ltd., a New York investment firm. 'Investors have clearly had a wake-up call.' A Different Debt Crisis Mexico's current debt crisis, stemming from its 1994 peso devaluation and subsequent recession, contrasts sharply with the one in the early 1980s. Then, most foreign debt owned by the Mexican government and corporations was in the form of loans from a manageable number of international banks. By presenting a united front, they extracted favourable restructuring terms. But now, most Mexican borrowings are in-bonds, and the foreign holders are a diverse and fractious lot, ranging from pension plans and mutual funds to wealthy individuals scattered around the world. Nearly all were caught flat-footed by the recession, and few are sufficiently organised to form bondholder groups and negotiate with the Mexican companies. The Mexican government itself has managed to stay current on its roughly $90 billion bailout arranged early last year by the US government and the International Monetary Fund. Corporate Problems Corporations are another story. Mexico's slow recovery from the recession has left many of them strapped for cash, and international markets are in most cases loath to refinance their maturing debts. Investment bankers estimate at least a dozen companies with some $3 billion in foreign bonds outstanding have already started restructuring their debts or will do so later this year. Corporate blowups, though painful, are typically viewed by bondholders as a cost of doing business with high-risk, high-yield issuers. But what happens in the aftermath here is causing serious concern. Debt negotiations are always a rough business in which secured creditors-those with the strongest guarantees-win the choice cuts of a company's value; unsecured creditors get the scraps. But in the US bankruptcy procedures are well defined, and even out-of-court settlements follow an orderly process. No so in Mexico. 'An out-of-court restructuring in the US usually incorporates the concerns of all creditors,' says Agustin Berdeja, managing partner of Berdeja and Associados, a law firm hiere. 'The lack of a specific legal framework for out-of-court restructures in Mexico sometimes results in some creditors being treated more advantageously than others.' As a substitute for law, the Mexican government has approved an unusual new office in Mexico City to negotiate out-of-court debt settlements. In charge is Eduardo Robinson Bours, a young poultry baron who helped negotiate some of the North American Free Trade Agreement's agricultural accords for Mexico. He has become, in essence, Mexico's one-man bankruptcy system. He says he was chosen because his government, banking and business contracts allow him to 'knock on all three doors' with ease. Mr Bours says he has no governmental authority. But sitting near his desk is a big red phone, a hot line linking him with government ministers and President Ernest Zedillo. Mr Bours's office is just a few steps away from the National Banking Commission, the bank regulatory agency. His expenses are paid by the government's bank-bailout fund. Shaky Banks Some investors suspect that Mr Bours's real job is to keep Mexico's banking system afloat. The banks were so badly damaged by the Dec. 1994 devaluation that last year they had to ask their

II. IMMEDIATE LEGAL AND ECONOMIC CONTEXT.

The apparent roots of the United States' capital adequacy crisis were found in the late 1970's. This period was characterised by the following factors:

1. high inflation in all goods and services;
2. an abrupt increase in interest rates, with prime exceeding 20 per cent;
3. an oil crisis that made marginal production profitable;
4. resultant heavy investment in real estate and energy as inflation hedges; and
5. severe problems experienced by financial institutions, particularly thrifts, arising from:
   a. Significant undercapitalisation and overleverage. While the early 1970's had been a period of growth, the US Federal Home Loan Bank Board ('FHLBB'), during these relatively 'good times', consistently reduced capital requirements, rather than holding the line in requiring a relatively high ratio of capital to liabilities. This retreat was made during a time when the thrifts had sufficient earnings to develop an adequate capital base;
   b. Limitations imposed by law with respect to the rates banks and thrifts could pay for small deposits. Unregulated financial institutions were not so limited. Disintermediation was the logical result, as small depositors sought to minimise the ravages of high inflation by taking advantage of the rates offered by money market funds and cash management accounts;
   c. Banks and thrifts being forced to replace the small depositors with large certificates of deposit at competitive rates. This had a particularly devastating effect on thrifts whose assets consisted primarily of lower fixed-rate residential mortgages. The resulting negative spread caused thrifts to lose capital at an alarming rate.

These factors led to a series of reactionary events in the early 1980s, which resulted in a 'finance/tax push' on real estate values. First, Congress passed the Depositary Institutions Deregulation & Monetary Control Act of 1980 ('DIDIMCA'),[13] under which three major actions were taken. First,

shareholders for more than $1 billion in new cash. Now, the weakened banks can't afford to have their clients, the debt-swamped corporations, fall.' See also, D. Darrow, *et al.*, 'Restructuring Strategies for Mexican Eurobond Debt,' 16 NWJ. Int'l. L. and Bus. 117 (1995).

[13] Pub. L. No. 96-221, 94 Stat. 132 (1980). §202 indicates that DIDIMCA was promulgated as an attempt at an orderly phase-out and, ultimately, an elimination of limitations on the maximum rates of interest and dividends which could be paid on deposits and accounts by depository institutions. Congress determined that all depositors were entitled to receive a market rate of return on their savings as soon as it was economically feasible for depository institutions to pay such a rate. 12 USC §3501 (1996).

Federal Deposit Insurance Corporation ('FDIC') and Federal Savings and Loan Insurance Corporation ('FSLIC') deposit insurance was increased to $100,000 from $40,000.[14] Next, the liability side of the balance sheet for banks and savings and loans was deregulated. Banks and savings associations could now pay competitive rates for deposits without restriction.[15] Finally, federal laws were adopted, pursuant to which state usury laws were preempted, to provide for unlimited interest rates on first lien loans on residential property (houses, condominiums, apartments, townhouses)[16] and interest rates (on business and agricultural loans of $25,000 or more) that could equal 5 per cent above the discount rate at the Fed window.[17] (At this time, rates were still at an historical high and the Fed discount rate exceeded 14 to 15 per cent.) These provisions allowed deposits to be brokered in fully insured $100,000 increments,[18] with rates on deposits at whatever level was needed to attract the deposit[19] and investment of deposits at rates exceeding state usury laws.[20] DIDIMCA superficially may have alleviated the disintermediation problem, but it did not stop the huge losses of the thrifts which were still carrying lower fixedrate assets.

Meanwhile, inflation in real estate prices continued, even as the general inflation rate abated. Real property inflation was fuelled by the tax shelter business, which received a large push from the Economic Recovery Tax Act of 1981 ('ERTA').[21] ERTA improved tax shelter opportunities in real estate principally by reducing the depreciable life of improvements to 15 years from 35 years.[22] In addition to this new incentive, investors already could deduct

[14] DIDIMCA §308(a)(1)(A).

[15] Ibid. at §204. Authority to control the rates paid on deposits by depository institutions under Pub. L. No. 89-597, 80 Stat. 823 (1966) was provided for a term of six years from the date of enactment of the legislation in order to give thrift institutions time to incorporate the new powers granted to them so that they might increase their earnings and be in a position to attract deposits by paying market interest rates. The Federal Reserve Board, the FDIC and the FHLBB, however, were permitted to regulate depository institutions' advertising of interest rates. 12 USC §1735f-7a (1996).

[16] DIDIMCA §501. States were permitted to override the federal preemption of state usury limits on home mortgage loans within the period after 1 Apr. 1980, and prior to 1 Apr. 1983. The override could consist of the adoption of a law or a vote by voters in favour of any provision, constitutional or otherwise, which stated explicitly that the state did not want the federal preemption to apply to loans made in that state.

[17] DIDIMCA §511.

[18] Ibid. at §308(a)(1)(A).

[19] Ibid. at §204.

[20] Ibid. at §§501, 511.

[21] Pub L. No. 97-34, 95 Stat. 172 (1981). §212 of ERTA amended §§46 and 48 of the IRC and increased the investment tax credit for rehabilitation expenditures to 15 per cent for non-residential 30-year-old buildings, 20 per cent for non-residential 40-year-old buildings; 25 per cent credit for residential and nonresidential certified historic structures; and repealed the accelerated cost recovery and demolition disincentives for certified historic structures.

[22] ERTA §201; IRC §168 (the recovery period was subsequently extended to 18 years by the Deficit Reduction Act of 1984 and then to 19 years in 1985). The taxpayer was given the option to elect to use the straight-line depreciation method over 15 years, 35 years, or 45 years for 15 year public utility property.

investment interest paid or accrued, and could take advantage of non-recourse mortgage financing for purposes of deducting losses.[23] If the property were held for longer than one year, it was entitled to the 60 per cent long-term capital gains exclusion,[24] thus insuring a maximum tax of 20 per cent on disposition (in 1984, the holding period was shortened to six months).[25] Before long, limited partnerships or syndications became an attractive way to invest in real estate because they generated tax savings and profits that passed through to investors. Broader participation in the apparently highly profitable real estate business was seen as a panacea for the thrifts.

Congress passed the Garn-St Germain Depository Institutions Act of 1982 ('Garn-St Germain').[26] Garn-St Germain allowed thrifts to expand their lending powers by allowing commercial and non-residential real estate lending[27] (so-called acquisition, development and construction loans, as well as commercial loans[28]), make direct investments in real estate[29] (state chartered institutions in some jurisdictions already enjoyed broad investment authority), participate in ownership of real estate through joint ventures, partnerships and similar vehicles,[30] eliminate loan-to-value ratios for residential mortgages[31] and, in some instances, utilise loan-to-value ratios up to 100 per cent.[32] The result was that a savings and loan charter was more flexible than a bank charter.

Entrepreneurs were encouraged to acquire savings and loans and operate them as giant real estate companies. State laws were amended, giving state savings and loans expanded powers. California, Florida and Texas were examples. California allowed 100 per cent of an in-state thrift's assets to be contributed to a subsidiary service corporation for investment activities. Texas allowed leverage of 20-to-1 on capital in service corporations.[33] Capital requirements of savings associations were dropped to 3 per cent of liabilities on a long-term averaging basis, as opposed to 5 per cent.[34] Banks' capital requirements remained at 5½ per cent primary and 6 per cent secondary. Leverage in the savings and loan industry was thirty-three times capital raised, and in the banking industry, fifteen times capital raised.

Regulatory and examination forces of state and federal regulatory bodies were not expanded to handle effectively the regulation of the broadened

23 IRC §163.
24 IRC §1202(a).
25 Tax Reform Act of 1984, Pub. L. No. 98-369, 98 Stat. 494 (1984), §1001(a)(1).
26 Pub. L. No. 97–320, 96 Stat. 1469 (1982). Federal savings associations were granted expanded lending and investment authority by this Act, as an attempt to provide them with the flexibility necessary to maintain their role of providing credit for housing.
27 12 USC §1464(c)(1)(B).
28 12 USC §1464(c)(1)(R).
29 12 USC §1464(c)(1)(B).
30 12 USC §1464(c)(1)(N).
31 12 USC §1464(c)(1)(B).
32 Ibid.
33 Tex. Rev. Civ. Stat. Ann., art. 342–606 (Vernon 1973). This act was repealed by 69th Leg. R.S. Ch. 639 §21 1985 Tex. Gen. Laws 237.
34 Texas Savings and Loan Department, 10 Tex. Reg. 3429 (1985) (codified at 7 Tex. Admin. Code 64.7(b)).

powers arising from DIDIMCA and Garn-St Germain. In addition to new powers, there was a quantifiable risk increase as the amount of deposit insurance rose two and a half times from $40,000 per account to $100,000. Incredibly, the FDIC system had ten times more personnel than the FSLIC system. In the midst of all this change, the Federal Home Loan Bank ('FHLB') of Little Rock, Arkansas, was moved to Dallas, Texas, causing significant loss of experienced personnel. Then several events occurred:

- oil and gas prices dropped;
- Empire Savings of Texas failed;
- Continental Illinois Bank failed;
- Penn Square Bank of Oklahoma failed;
- certain instances of fraud, deceit and abuse appeared; and
- active reregulation commenced.

These events precipitated the crisis which emerged first in the thrift industry and in Texas banking and spread throughout the capital base of the nation's businesses and financial institutions. Reregulation of the financial institutions and elimination of tax incentives for real estate removed the finance/tax push on real estate values and caused values to shrink and capital to 'evaporate' from our financial system. The crisis began slowly, but quickly gathered momentum.

Beginning in 1984 and 1985, reregulation of the thrifts commenced in earnest. Personnel in the FHLB of Dallas were shaken up, with tough regulators appointed to key positions. New appraisal standards were adopted,[35] resulting in lower values and lower comparables, and often were applied on a retroactive basis. New capital regulations were adopted requiring more capital,[36] when the aim should have been to preserve existing capital. New growth restriction regulations were adopted,[37] and classification of asset regulations were also adopted.[38]

[35] These standards are currently located at CFR §563.17-1a(c)(1). The Code sets forth three appraisal standards that, at a minimum, must be included in the appraisal policies of every insured institution and service corporation. First, the appraisal must be based upon the definition of market value as set forth in the regulation. This definition contemplates the consummation of a sale as of a specified date and the passing of title from buyer to seller under open and competitive market conditions requisite to a fair sale. Secondly, the appraisal must be presented in a narrative format. The appraisal report must be sufficiently descriptive to enable a reviewer to readily ascertain the estimated value reported and the rationale for that estimate. The analysis is required to be as detailed and in depth as the complexity of the real estate requires. Third, an appraisal must contain a sales history of the real estate appraised. Generally, sales within the three previous years must be disclosed.

[36] 50 Fed. Reg. 6891 (1985) (codified at 12 CFR §563.13 (1985)).

[37] 12 CFR §563.98 (1990). This section established new restrictions for equity risk investments by savings associations. The limits for investments were based on tangible capital in relation to total liabilities. In addition, permissible investments were described and diversification was required.

[38] Fed. Home Loan Bank Board Memo. No. R41C; Fed. Banking L. Rep. (CCH) §40.185.176.

All of these measures treated the emerging thrift crisis as one that could be cured simply by tightening the rules. However, these measures failed to take into account their effect on the dynamics of the real estate industry and its interrelation with the value of assets held by thrifts and banks. The upshot of the sudden change in the rules was that property values depreciated quickly and insidiously in a downward spiral. The FHLBB's overreaction led to:

1. a precipitous decline in available financing by thrifts;
2. revised appraisal standards and nervous appraisers causing lower appraised values that, by way of comparables, caused still further lowering of values;
3. existing capital evaporating from this loss of real property value;
4. incipient negative leverage;[39] and
5. the loan portfolios of many of the financial institutions began to consist primarily of term loans which were due to be paid in full at maturity.[40]

New tax legislation then took tax incentives out of property ownership, causing further loss of real property value and hence financial institution capital.

The Tax Reform Act of 1986 ('TRA-86')[41] virtually eliminated tax as a consideration in the purchase of real estate. The easy write-offs that once made otherwise marginal real estate development profitable were gone.

Nineteen eighty-six was the last year that developers could take advantage of the faster depreciation allowed under the old law. Under TRA-86, the depreciable life for real estate improvements went from 19 years to 31 years.[42] The 'at risk' rules changed, limiting tax write-offs to the amount actually invested.[43] The deductibility of interest used to finance investment property was limited to the amount of net investment income.[44]

39 For each dollar of capital loss, thrifts were required to shrink assets $33 ⅓, and banks $15. Shrinkage was difficult, however, since the depreciating values meant that there were no buyers or new financing available. When shrinkage did occur, it usually was from the sale of earning assets, and the loss of income from those earning assets' further reduced capital, requiring still more asset shrinkage. The consequence of this downward spiral is obvious.

40 Needless to say, the majority of these loans were not paid at maturity. As a result, the institutions were deprived of a major source of asset shrinkage.

41 Pub. L. No. 99–514, 100 Stat. 2085 (1986) (hereinafter 'TRA'). The 60 per cent deduction for long-term capital gains were repealed; residential real estate was to be depreciated over 27½ years under the straight-line method, nonresidential real estate was to be depreciated over 31½ years under the straight-line method; the investment tax credit was repealed; the Rehabilitation tax credit was substantially reduced; 'at risk' rules now applied to real estate; and losses from 'passive activities' could be offset income from other passive activities.

42 TRA 1986 §201. This section amended IRC §168.

43 TRA 1986 §503. This section repealed IRC §465(c)(3)(D), which excluded the holding of real property from the application of the 'at risk' rules.

44 TRA 1986 §511. This section amended IRC §163(d), such that after the Act was passed, investment interest expense was only to be deducted against net investment income.

Moreover, new 'passive loss' rules required that losses from an activity in which an individual did not materially participate could be deducted only from income derived from a passive activity.[45] Prior to these rules, an investor could deduct these losses from any income, including salary.[46]

The capital gains tax exclusion was repealed,[47] resulting in a maximum tax rate of 28 per cent instead of 20 per cent.[48] Finally, the investment tax credit was eliminated[49] and the rehabilitation credit substantially reduced.[50]

As a result of the initial finance/tax push in real estate values and the subsequent removal of that finance/tax push, a spiralling depression in values occurred with losses in value as high at 50 per cent, rivalling the October 1987 stock market debacle. There was not a shift of wealth; there was a loss of wealth. Operating losses become monumental. For banks and thrifts, these were caused by:

1. loss of operating income:
   a. no new loans being made since no growth is allowed (i.e., there is no capital to support any growth; to the contrary, shrinkage is required);
   b. borrowers not paying interest, much less principal; and
   c. income not being realised from collateral by reason of legal issues and lender liability considerations;
2. increase in operating expenses:
   a. increase in cost of funds, despite FDIC insurance (the so-called Texas premium);
   b. legal fees running up to $500,000 per month at many thrifts;
   c. consultant fees equal to that same amount being incurred per month;
   d. property operating and management costs increasing with respect to OREO in non-performing assets; and
   e. hidden costs arising from constant regulator involvement, required independent reappraisals and additional accounting and personnel expense;
3. delays in dealing with non-performing loans caused by:
   a. borrowers' lender liability lawsuits (sometimes successful), often

[45] IRC §469.
[46] IRC §165.
[47] TRA 1986 §301. This section amended IRC §1202.
[48] Ibid. at §302(a)(1).
[49] Ibid. at §211.
[50] Ibid. at §251. The rehabilitation tax credit for certified historic structures was reduced from 25 per cent to 20 per cent, a credit of 10 per cent was provided for substantial rehabilitation of buildings placed in service before 1936, there was to be no credit for any buildings placed in-service after 1935, that was not certified historic, and the credit was subject to the limitations on passive losses and credits.

brought to buy time to deal with the adverse tax consequences of foreclosure;
b. injunctions and restraining orders limiting enforcement of creditors' rights against security;
c. regulatory delays-most thrifts and many banks were under some type of regulatory control or scrutiny; and
d. inter-creditor disagreements on participated loans.

The rush to real estate investment, inspired by previously favourable tax legislation and fuelled by the massive availability of capital for real estate investment provided by banks and thrifts, created an enormous constituency of owners who, in the face of the loss of tax benefits due to changes in the tax laws, were confronted with significant adverse tax consequences on asset disposition. The problem of adverse tax consequences was exacerbated by collapsing values and the resulting lack of resources from asset sale proceeds to pay the tax bill. Owners generally could not sell for a price which would pay the tax bill for the phantom gains from the disposition of property upon which the outstanding debt is in excess of the owner's adjusted basis in the property, as reduced by depreciation deductions, much less provide for recovery of equity or the making of a profit. Just as importantly, the debtors who owned the real estate could not permit foreclosure on the collateral by the creditors since that would trigger the same tax problems for the debtor as a sale to a third party. Financial institutions, which were under pressure to shrink, sought to enforce foreclosure against the collateral, but generally paid no attention to the underlying systemic tax and value problems which faced the debtor. This often resulted in costly and time consuming litigation and bankruptcies initiated as protective action by debtors and designed, in most cases, to delay and afford to the debtor some opportunity to shift the unrecognised losses already in the system, including both tax losses and real losses of equity, to others.

In the late 1980s, in continuation of the quest for higher returns and fee income and, based in part on the commercial acceptability of borrowing on the basis of expected cash flow and anticipated asset dispositions as well as the introduction and market acceptance of non-investment grade corporate high yield debt, as an alternative to real estate financing and equity investments, investors began to concentrate heavily in these highly leveraged transactions ('HLTs'), such as leveraged buyouts. These HLTs afforded significant tax incentives by allowing interest on corporate debt to be deducted, as distinguished from non-deductible dividends on equity. The rise in HLTs corresponded to the general tendency of American businesses to leverage themselves to unprecedented levels. Debt service required ever larger portions of debtor companies' cash flow. The decline of business revenues due to regional economic woes and increases in interest rates eroded the liquidity margin between success and default. Debtor companies with substantial amounts of floating rate debt, zero coupon debt or short or medium-term debt that must be refinanced, found that there was no practical alternative to a reorganisation when faced with the reduced flexibility of federally insured financial institutions which could no longer freely refinance these HLTs and when faced with a contracting market where the debtor could not readily spinoff assets at acceptable prices. The real question in any reorganisation became how the cost of that deleveraging and loss recognition would be shared and how it would be effected.[51]

While the scenario described above was suffered primarily by thrifts and banks in Texas, New England and the Mid-Atlantic states, it inevitably spread in varying degrees to financial institutions in other regions. On 19 December 1989, the Office of the Comptroller of the Currency ('OCC') issued a Fact Sheet,[52] in which it clearly set out its intention to identify those banks which may be vulnerable to softening real estate markets and to review those banks with potential problems. Those banks most likely to be subject to an OCC target exam were those that had a large real estate loan portfolio, or were in a market that the OCC macroeconomic model indicated as approaching an overbuilt condition. The Fact Sheet stated that 'if banks are not recognising problem real estate loans, examiners will ensure that they do so in the future'.[53]

The intermediate term effect on these institutions was unpleasant, at best. Federal banking regulations required that OREO be marked to market no less frequently than annually.[54] Actual practice of the OCC in a pervasively declining regional market was been to require that banks anticipate future value declines by establishing 'OREO valuation reserves', also a direct charge to capital, unlike the 'loan loss reserve'. As the real estate market in a region dried up, comparable sales become so infrequent that they were deemed meaningless by bank regulators. The Texas and New England experience showed that the value of a bank's OREO portfolio was

[51] See Cieri, *An Introduction to Legal and Practical Considerations in the Restructuring of Troubled Leveraged Buyouts*, 45 Bus. Law 333 (Nov. 1989) with respect to restructuring of HLTs.

[52] Under the heading 'Current and Future Actions,' the Fact Sheet states that the OCC is using its experts in real estate lending problems to assist in reviewing targeted banks. The Fact Sheet states that the purpose of this review is to help assess banks' vulnerability to softening real estate markets and review real estate loan portfolios in banks with potential problems. The Real Estate Valuation Model was to be used to identify those banks with potential problems or weaknesses in targeted markets. The OCC stated that this model would be refined to fit the characteristics of individual markets.

[53] The Fact Sheet also stated that the OCC would require the targeted banks to take whatever corrective action was necessary with respect to real estate lending practices and loan portfolios.

[54] 12 CFR §7.3025 (1990).

then determined by the judgment of regulators, using discounted cash flow computer models and the regulators' assumptions, even when those regulators were based in other parts of the nation and likely had no personal knowledge of the regional market. This discounted cash technique was also used to value land, an appraisal method not sanctioned by any professional appraisal body. The effect of OREO write-downs and valuation reserves on banks' earnings and capital was devastating. These same write-down and valuation practices were applied to other assets, including HLTs. The impact of these events on the marketplace included general credit tightening and restrictive requirements for additional collateral and equity support for businesses generally.

All of these developments received high profile attention as they affected US financial institutions. The deterioration of capital and the intransigence of US financial institutions in their battle for survival placed a premium on the peaceful and nondestructive allocation of loss and the preservation of the base of businesses in the most efficient manner possible. The goal of a debtor's non-judicial workout is to provide for such an efficient and equitable loss allocation with respect to that debtor, short of bankruptcy, and to preserve its business as a valuable going concern.

III. IMPACT ON DEBTORS.

In a collapsing economy, debtor companies tend to recognise and attack problem assets or financing on an individual basis. This tendency is exacerbated when one or more of the debtor's creditors, caught in the downward spiral of the systemic capital adequacy crisis, behaves in a reactionary mode and focuses only on its own problems with the debtor, disregarding the debtor's other credit relationships and problems. At some point, the debtor may come to realise that it is unable to maintain many separate negotiations for the resolution of its problems simultaneously on a coherent basis. The debtor will recognise that many of its problems are interrelated and that some of its lenders or investors are more aggressive in seeking collection and pursuing default remedies than others. The debtor will have been prone to resolve its problems with its most troublesome creditors on a preferential basis and to defer the resolution of problems or potential problems with its more patient creditors, to their mutual detriment.

Each creditor considers its loan transaction and prospects for collection from a narrowed perspective. As the debtor's financial condition deteriorates, each creditor seeks to spread its grip over the debtor's resources to maximise its prospects for collection. When the debtor seeks to respond to each creditor on an individual basis, and where each creditor adopts its hegemony over the debtor's financial resources through cross-collateralisation, requirements of completion deposits, establishment of performance hurdles or deadlines which limit flexibility and distort decision making, the debtor may find that, in the process, its financial resources are insufficient to meet the demands of all its creditors.

The formulation of an overall workout plan for a debtor in the environment of a systemic capital adequacy crisis and the responses generated by its financial institution creditors, requires a change of focus or frame of reference by the debtor, as well as its creditors. Unless the debtor's efforts are coordinated properly and the work handled efficiently, the debtor's efforts will become paralysed and the expense undertaken in the preparation of a consensual workout plan will be wasted. No overall workout plan can be accomplished without successful individual workouts, through renegotiation of the affected loan or credit transactions. Conversely, the only way in which the debtor can achieve a successful workout is by placing these individual successful workout renegotiations in the context of an overall plan, which is designed to maximise return to all of the creditors on a fair and equitable basis and to motivate the debtor to follow through with the plan and ultimately avoid judicial reorganisation or liquidation. The plan must accommodate the financial and legal positions inherent in each individual workout negotiation situation, and each individual negotiation situation must be placed in the context of the overall workout plan.

In its initial stages, the plan is a reflection of a coherent communication of the debtor's legal and financial condition. The effect of this broad-based communication to the creditors of the debtor will have the effect of repositioning many of the debtor/creditor relationships from their status prior to presentation of the plan. This process of repositioning generally will go through several stages in which the overall nature of the plan may shift based upon shifting individual workout negotiations and individual negotiations will vary in light of the economic implication of the plan upon the specific transaction and based upon the legal implications of the relationship and of the plan itself. The objective of a consensual reorganisation is to obtain the essential benefits of protection afforded under the federal bankruptcy laws without the attendant costs, stigma, and potential loss of control. The basic equitable principles underlying a successful consensual reorganisation are the same basic equitable principles that underlie the completion of a successful reorganisation under Chapter 11 of the US Bankruptcy Code.[55] A consensual reorganisation, however, is not the legal equivalent of a proceeding under the Bankruptcy Code. Any discussion of reorganisation under the Bankruptcy Code is beyond the scope of this chapter.

[55] See 11 USC §§1101–74 (1988).

IV. CONSENSUAL WORKOUTS

A. Advantages of Consensual Workouts for Both Debtors and Creditors

Consensual workouts fix the rights of the parties and avoid the uncertainties of litigation in bankruptcy. Other advantages afforded by consensual workouts, as opposed to bankruptcy, include the following:

1. Consensual workouts are more flexible; workouts permit legitimate agreements to accomplish the consensual intent of the parties, limited primarily by depth and breadth of imagination;
2. Consensual workouts preserve higher asset values; debtors are given incentives to maximise recoveries to limit deficiency liability;
3. Consensual workouts are generally less expensive, both from an administrative perspective and from a legal perspective. Workouts limit costs and avoid burdens of litigation and bankruptcy;
4. Consensual workouts often afford more benefits to creditors and debtors, both tangible and intangible:
   a. management retains control of business;
   b. debtor avoids 'stigma' of bankruptcy;
   c. debtor's principals may avoid or defer liability on personal guaranties;
   d. creditor might obtain acknowledgment of outstanding indebtedness and of validity of liens and encumbrances;
   e. creditor might obtain waiver of defences, setoffs and counterclaims;
   f. creditor might obtain additional collateral and guaranties; and
   g. creditor might correct deficiencies in loan or security documents.

B. Disadvantages of Consensual Workouts from the Debtor's Standpoint

Since a workout is a consensual arrangement, neither debtor nor cooperating creditors can bind nonassenting creditors nor halt litigation or foreclosure proceedings by uncooperative creditors. Substantial unanimity is required of all creditors. This unanimity is often difficult to obtain.

Claims by governmental entities are frequently more difficult to deal with in workouts because governmental or government-controlled creditors tend to be less flexible; their respective regulatory guidelines frequently do not permit flexibility.

Additional problems include:

1. The debtor is unable to reject burdensome leases or other executory contracts;
2. The debtor is unable to recover property in possession of foreclosing creditors or to defeat prior attachment, garnishment or levy;

3. The debtor is unable to recover preferential, fraudulent or voidable transfers that otherwise might be avoidable in bankruptcy; and
4. The debtor has no convenient forum (such as an experienced bankruptcy court) for expeditious resolution of disputes, enforcement of sales free and clear of liens and encumbrances, determination of priority of liens and the like.

C. *Disadvantages of Consensual Workouts from the Creditor's Standpoint*

Unlike bankruptcy, consensual workouts do not subject actions of the debtor and its principals to judicial scrutiny and control. Participation in a consensual workout might perpetuate ineffectual or dishonest management. It may also permit continued erosion of collateral or other asset values if control of timing and price of liquidation remains with the debtor. Participation in a consensual workout does not prevent a subsequent bankruptcy filing if the workout fails.

D. *Conditions for a Successful Consensual Workout*

Participation in a consensual workout makes no sense if the crucial components of a successful workout are not present. Those elements depend upon the attributes of the particular workout. For example, inability to survive in the long term is inconsequential if the workout contemplates an orderly liquidation of assets, as opposed to continuing business operations. Many consensual workouts initially envision long-term survival, but as negotiations progress, they evolve into more or less of an orderly liquidation. In evaluating a proposed consensual workout, some of the most important factors relating to its potential success include:

1. adequate liquidity (cash) available to fund the workout;
2. readjusted and realistic expectations by all parties;
3. adequate disclosure of information; a consensual workout is, in a sense, a private bankruptcy proceeding, where the scope of information provided by debtor should be substantially equivalent to that disclosed in a formal bankruptcy filing;
4. flexibility of the legal rights and practical leverage of each of the participants;
5. appreciation of the legal rights and practical leverage of each of the participants;
6. absence of significant avoidable transfers which prefer one creditor over others in the same class, as well as equal treatment of classes of creditors;

7. perceived fairness in the treatment of differing creditor and equity classes;
8. continuing cooperation of critical creditors, employees and management personnel;
9. confidence in management;
10. confidence in the debtor's business plan; and
11. ability to operate profitably within the applicable regulatory climate.

E. *Pitfalls which Creditors Should Seek to Avoid in a Consensual Workout*

Assuming that the key elements for a successful consensual workout are present, creditors should guard against:

1. inducing others to extend credit to the debtor;
2. paying debtor's employees without making adequate provisions for trust fund taxes or funding the payroll with knowledge that debtor's management will not surrender or withhold appropriate taxes;
3. failing to comply with bulk transfer provisions;
4. failing to take immediate possession of surrendered collateral;
5. becoming enmeshed in unintended admissions, waivers or releases during negotiations; and
6. exercising control over the debtor.

V. EVOLUTION OF INSOLVENCY LAW AS A CONTEXT FOR CONSENSUAL WORKOUTS

Awareness of the evolution of insolvency law brings context to current national, as well as international, problems of insolvency. Historically, the United States has addressed the problem of insolvency through its bankruptcy laws. The Bankruptcy Act of 1800 was the first bankruptcy law adopted by the United States Congress.[56] The Bankruptcy Act of 1800 closely followed the English Statute of Bankrupts.[57] In turn, the origins of the English Statute of Bankrupts may be traced back to the laws of other European countries, the Italian city-states of the fourteenth Century, and even further to the Roman Empire.[58]

[56] Robert L. Jordan and William D. Warren, *Bankruptcy*, 20 (1985) (Univ. Casebook Series 1985).

[57] Ibid.

[58] Ibid. at 17. On ancient Roman collection practices, 'If the debtor be insolvent to serve creditors, let his body be cut in pieces on the third market day. It may be cut into more or fewer pieces with impunity, or, if his creditors consent to it, let him be sold to foreigners beyond the Tiber.' Twelve Tables, Table III, 6 (*c.*450 BC).

The various practices employed in dealing with the problem of a debtor who either refused, or was unable, to pay its debts date back as far as the extension of credit itself. In the primitive and ancient cultures, public opinion provided two sanctions by which a debtor could be compelled to perform his part of a contract. Each of these sanctions was extremely powerful. One sanction was religious, while the other was more primitive and severe: Execution.[59]

In thirteenth-century England, the common law provided for imprisonment of the debtor until he 'made agreement (with his creditors) or his friends for him'.[60] Imprisonment was intended to compel payment of the debt and not to punish the debtor for his failure to pay.[61]

The most important early English bankruptcy law was the Statute of Bankrupts.[62] The Statute of Bankrupts was directed toward punishment of fraudulent debtors[63] and only applied to debtors who were merchants, providing that a debtor who committed 'an act of bankruptcy'[64] was to be reputed, deemed and taken for a bankrupt. Upon complaint, the Lord

[59] Levinthal, *The Early History of Bankruptcy Law*, 66 U. Pa. L. Rev. 223, 229 (1918). For instance, in India of old, and currently in Nepal, creditors engaged in the practice of 'sitting d'harna' and, in ancient Ireland, creditors engaged in 'fasting on' debtors. These practices involved the creditor placing himself before the debtor's doorway and remaining until the debt was paid. This practice was extremely effective, in light of the fact that debtor would have been instantly and severely punished by public opinion if he were to permit his creditor to suffer from exhaustion or die of starvation at his door. Ibid. at 229, citing Tarde, 'Evolution of Procedure,' in Primitive and Ancient Legal Institutions 700 (A. Kocourek and J. Wigmore (eds.), 1915). The Hindus employed a system of self help. In this system, the creditor could take his debtor and force him to perform labor for him or he could resort to violence and kill or maim the debtor, confine his wife, his sons or his cattle. Lang, 'Origin of Exogamy and Totemism', in Primitive and Ancient Legal Institutions 230 (A. Kocourek and J. Wigmore (eds), 1915), citing Manu. XIII, 48 ff. The Egyptians, however, only provided for the attachment of the debtor's property, not his person. The rationale for this was that the state might at any time require the debtor's service, in peace as an official or labourer, and in war as a soldier. Ibid., at 230–1, on the authority of Diodorous, I, 79; Reveillout, Cours de Droit Egyptien, at 42. In time, legal process against insolvents evolved to the point where execution was had against the property of the debtor, rather than against the debtor himself. Undoubtedly, this was the result of a change in objective from retaliation to compensation. Tarde, at 232. In ancient systems of law, whether the debtor was actually honest or dishonest, insolvency was seen as something that was irregular and fraudulent. However, in time the unfortunate insolvent was distinguished from the fraudulent bankrupt. See, e.g., Code of Hammurabi, §§116, 117, where protection from creditors was provided to the debtor who was made insolvent by misfortune.

[60] J. Cohen, *The History of Imprisonment for Debt and Its Relation to the Development of Discharge in Bankruptcy*, 29 U. Chi. L. Sch. Rec. 5, 6 (Fall 1983), citing 13 Edw. 1, §14 (1285).

[61] Ibid. While some may argue that imprisoning the debtor was punitive in nature, the debtor could always terminate his imprisonment by paying the debt.

[62] 13 Elizabeth, c.7 (1571).

[63] Jordan, above. note 56, at 18.

[64] 'Acts of bankruptcy' include[d] the debtor's departure from the realm, his taking refuge in his home, his taking sanctuary and various other acts if his purpose was to avoid process with the intent of defrauding or hindering his creditors.

Chancellor could appoint a commission of 'wise, honest and discrete' persons who were authorised to seize the property of the bankrupt and sell it for the payment, pro rata, of the debts of the bankrupt. The bankrupt, however, remained liable to the extent that his creditors were not paid in full. The commissioners had the power to imprison the bankrupt and, by virtue of a later statute, could be subject to pillory and the loss of an ear as well.[65] The design of early English bankruptcy law was to protect creditors and to punish debtors who were trying to avoid payment of just debt.[66]

In the early eighteenth century, the harshness with which bankrupts were treated was greatly reduced by statutes which provided for the granting of a discharge to the bankrupt of the debts owing at the time of bankruptcy.[67] This development was attributed to the notion that bankrupts were not always fraudulent, and sometimes failed because of circumstances beyond their control; such bankrupts were entitled to relief.[68] Society recognised that unlimited incarceration of the debtor did not usually lead to reimbursing his creditors.[69] In addition, creditors came to believe that a law which was 'all penalty and no reward' was self-defeating; forcing bankrupts to relinquish all of their property to satisfy some creditors and then exposing them to unlimited imprisonment by others encouraged evasion, even by merchants who otherwise would have been willing to cooperate.[70] Finally, creditors acknowledged that mercantile credit was given in the interest of the creditor, as well as of the debtor, and that the giving of credit necessarily involved some risk and, therefore, it followed that the business of the merchant should insure against this risk by adding on a per centage for the credit which he advanced and that all a debtor ought to pledge to this credit was his estate, and not his future earnings or personal liberty.[71] Not until well into the nineteenth century did the notion of allowing a debtor to declare bankruptcy voluntarily become a part of English bankruptcy law as a means of finding relief from creditors.

Insolvent debtors historically have received different treatment, dependent upon whether they were merchants. A merchant was entitled to bankruptcy in which, upon surrender of his available assets, he was discharged from liability to his creditors. Insolvency also applied to nonmerchants, who however, after released, remained obligated to pay the remainder of their debt. Blackstone probably best expressed the rationale for restricting bankruptcy to the merchants when he stated:

[65] See Levinthal, *The Early History of English Bankruptcy*, 67 U. Pa. L. Rev. 1, 16–18 (1919).

[66] D. G. Boshkoff, Limited, *Conditional and Suspended Discharges in Anglo-American Bankruptcy Proceedings*, 131 U. Pa. L. Rev. 69, 105–6 (1982).

[67] 4 Anne c. 17 (1705); 10 Anne c. 15 (1711). These statutes applied only to merchants, however.

[68] Jordan, above, note 56, at 18.

[69] Boshkoff, above, note 66, at 69.

[70] Levinthal, above, note 65, at 18–19.

[71] Cohen, above, note 60, at 5–6.

But [the laws] are cautious of encouraging prodigality and extravagance by this indulgence to debtors; and therefore they allow the benefit of laws of bankruptcy to none but actual traders; since that set of men are, generally speaking, the only persons liable for accidental losses, and to an inability of paying their debts without any fault of their own. If persons in other situations of life run in debt without the power of payment, they must take the consequences of their own indiscretion, even though they meet with sudden accidents that may reduce their fortunes: the law holds it to be an unjustifiable practice, for any person but a trader to encumber himself with debts of any considerable value. If a gentlemen, or one in a liberal profession, at the time of contracting his debts, has a sufficient fund to pay them, delay of payment is a species of dishonesty, and a temporary injustice to his creditor; and if, at such time, he has an insufficient fund, the dishonesty and injustice is the greater. He cannot, therefore, murmur, if he suffers the punishment which he has drawn upon himself. But in mercantile transactions, the case is far otherwise. Trade cannot be carried on without mutual credit on both sides: the contracting of debts is therefore here not only justifiable, but necessary. And if by accidental calamities, as by loss of a ship in a tempest, the failure of brother traders, or by the nonpayment of persons out of trade, a merchant or trader becomes incapable of discharging his own debts, it is his misfortune and not his fault.[72]

In the United States, Congress was given the authority, under the Constitution, to enact laws concerning bankruptcy. Every bankruptcy law in the United States has been the product of some financial crisis or business depression.[73] The bankruptcy legislation in the United States is a reflection of changes in economic conditions and viewpoints in this country. Bankruptcy law in the United States has evolved through periods of pro-debtor tendencies, pro-creditor tendencies and compromises between each.[74] The United States generally has accepted the principle that bankruptcy is required in the public interest of the nation, apart from the effect of the law upon particular individuals upon whom the law was to operate. The interest of the nation lies in the continuation of business and the conservation of property for the benefit of creditors and the debtor, and not in the sale and distribution of the assets among the creditors, or even in the debtor's own immediate discharge from debt. The forced sale of property and the stoppage of business in times of financial crisis constitutes a loss to the nation at large, as well as to the individual debtors and creditors.[75] Thus, bankruptcy law has developed into a system which attempts to achieve three objectives:

[72] W. Blackstone, 2 Commentaries on the Laws of England, 417, 473–4 (photo reprint 1979)(1765–1769)

[73] Charles Warren, *Bankruptcy in United States History*, Harvard Press 9 (1935).

[74] Ibid.

[75] Ibid.

1. protect creditors from each other;
2. protect creditors from dishonest debtors; and
3. protect the honest debtor from his creditors by means of discharge.[76]

Those laws that seek to protect creditors from one another attempt to prevent any one creditor from obtaining more than its proportionate share of the debtor's assets. Such a law provides for the collective execution of process directed against all of the property of the debtor for the benefit of, and at the common expense of, all the creditors. When the debtor is unable to pay all of its debts in full, the principle of contribution is invoked, and any loss due to insolvency is thereby spread among all of the creditors. The bases for this execution process are both social and economic. In order to achieve these objectives, a method of managing the debtor's estate during the pendency of the process is required. Some entity must be given control over all of the property of the debtor to collect, manage and distribute all the assets. When this process is handled through bankruptcy law, the expense of the process and depletion of the debtor's estate to the detriment of the creditors is significant.[77] The objective in a consensual workout is, through a voluntary and forthright action by the debtor, to inspire in the creditors a high level of trust and confidence in the debtor's adherence to the fundamental principles of bankruptcy law and the likelihood of achievement of their mutual objectives by voluntary and consensual management, and thereby to avoid the polarisation and expense of a judicial achievement of those objectives and to thereby maximise repayment.

VI. CONSENSUAL WORKOUT THEORY

Consensual workouts are based upon the fundamental assumption that the debtor has been honest and forthright in its operations and that current economic difficulties leading to workout or reorganisation are due to honest mistakes of business judgment or market conditions not susceptible of anticipation or accommodation by the debtor. The systemic problem of deteriorating capital adequacy is precisely such a circumstance. Resolution of the resulting financial problems between a debtor and creditor then need not necessarily be a violently adversary process. A calm and dispassionate evaluation of the factors leading to the defined economic problem, however, should lead to a fairly clearly defined set of options under existing legal and

[76] Levinthal, above, note 70, at 25. It should be noted that not all systems of bankruptcy law seek to achieve this third goal.

[77] Warren, above, note 73, at 112, citing Am. L. Rev. VII (July 1873), '[F]rom the beginning to the end, there is one continuous, increasing plucking at the estate. Merchants have come to believe it best to settle with their debtors out of the bankrupt court. In its details, the law is perplexing, cumbersome, annoying, and expensive.'

financial structures for problem resolution. The mission of both the debtor and the creditor in a consensual workout is to go past artificial adversary posturing and to seek to understand the underlying root of the economic problem and allocate the loss occasioned by that problem in accordance with the legal and economic facts. If both the debtor and the creditor see the facts clearly, their interests should be aligned in resolving the allocation of loss in accordance with those facts and the law in the most expeditious and efficient manner possible. These parties are in the position to suffer the most pain in the absence of such a consensual agreement and are in the position to gain the greatest economic benefits from its success. A successful consensual workout requires, and is the product of, this alignment and agreement.

The organisation of the legal and economic facts into a workout plan, however, involves a complex interrelated set of decisions which, in each case, must be measured against the available alternatives. The test in each case for each of the constituent decision makers, both the debtor and the creditor, and the constituents within the debtor organisation, including partners, investors and employees, is to measure and prioritise the consequences of each decision under various alternatives. A consensual workout should produce an alignment of the constituents' best legal, economic and personal interests. A correct alignment among the constituents in the face of the legal and economic facts will produce a will to action and to execution of the workout.

Performance incentives or inducements can be built in with respect to any or all of these constituents to further their will. Examples of such incentives or inducements include preferential treatment for risk-taking by creditors, incentive fees or participation in residuals and limitation or elimination of personal liability for debtors under certain circumstances. If will, action and performance by the debtor, combined with time and space afforded by a consensual workout plan, will not produce a greater repayment to creditors than a liquidation, the creditors will not permit any economic incentive or inducement to such will, action and performance. The objective of the consensual workout and the definition of its success is the effectuation of the lowest cost and most efficient allocation of loss on the most equitable basis, considering the facts and the law, which produces the maximum repayment to creditors. Every decision and the consideration of every alternative must be considered against this test of success.

Debtors should be cognisant that, in many cases, lenders do not act rationally. The motivation of loan officers and lender management is often inconsistent with their role in the workout process. Many decision-making motivations for these individuals are personal and relate to internal politics in or external pressures on their employer organisations or to regulatory pressures. Often, the responsible officers are not given any incentive to understand and do not understand their factual and legal position. The debtor must be mindful of the problems presented by these anomalous situations and of the effect of the state of mind of the various decision makers on their approach to the workout process.

Although it is the objective of a consensual reorganisation to avoid adversary positioning, it may be necessary for the debtor or for the creditors to utilise adversary tools, such as bankruptcy proceedings, litigation and other aggressive and adversary actions, from time to time, to level the field of negotiations and protect consensual participants from creditors who seek to obtain an advantage without providing a corresponding benefit to the consensual workout process or to force reluctant or misguided participants to the bargaining table. This process is often required in one of two situations:

1. where responsibility for negotiations on behalf of a creditor must be moved out of the hands of a defensive loan officer, who may desire to avoid the issues and protect his personal position in the organisation; or
2. where responsibility for negotiations on behalf of a debtor rests with an individual whose ego and self image dominate strategy.

In each of these situations responsibility and control must be delegated and moved into the hands of a professional problem solver. Creditors will often take a very tough position from both a legal and a business point of view to flush out the level of commitment and will of a debtor who proposes a consensual workout or plan. The debtor must remain calm, stick with the workout plan and utilise appropriate adversary proceedings sparingly, but with sufficient definition and purpose, to protect its position and move the workout process forward, stopping short of polarising positioning.

The plan formulation process must recognise creditor preferences for reaching separate individual workout agreements, rather than global agreements. Creditors consistently demonstrate a strong desire to avoid master creditor agreements which extend over a long period of time. Each plan, therefore, should seek to accommodate the individual creditor relationships to the maximum possible degree through consistent treatment and, if possible, to accomplish satisfaction of undersecured or unsecured claims through available assets which can be segregated on a fair and equitable basis. Only where unsecured and undersecured claims cannot be satisfied in this way should a collateral pooling mechanism be utilised. Creditors will often prefer to waive their unsecured claims or undersecured claims to avoid the complication of participation in a complex collateral pool or they will be willing to advance new funds outside of the collateral pool context, but subject to a requirement for additional collateralisation or specific cross-collateralisation not related to the other unsecured or undersecured claims, in effect, creating individual creditor-by-creditor collateral pools. An important component of the plan will be to clearly communicate to the creditors that undersecured or unsecured claims can be waived, or collateralised, if new consideration is given. In addition, if there is enough collateral to go around, and if it can be divided equitably and if there is an incentive to the debtor to go through with this process, a master, or global collateral pool may not be required.

The purpose of a collateral pool is to effect a mechanism to capture equity for repayment of unsecured or undersecured creditors, subject to any reasonable residual incentives reserved to the debtor. Collateral pools are an important plan component in consensual reorganisations, but are not absolutely necessary if claims can otherwise be satisfied on a fair and equitable basis.

A consensual workout plan is no panacea. There is no magic to the process; just the hard work of uncovering, organising and recording the economic and legal facts, developing a detailed knowledge of the circumstances and communicating these clearly and persistently to the constituents of the plan. The legal and economic facts will define the plan, and internal and external relationships will be changed, based upon the development of these factual and legal positions. Development of a consensual workout plan is difficult and requires the alignment of a large number of disparate parties, each of whom undoubtedly will recognise some change in their legal and economic position from the position they thought they had before the process began. Those changes must be accepted and alternative decisions based on the commonly understood legal and economic facts must be measured, in each case, against the legal and economic alternatives, the anticipated effectiveness of the workout plan and its cost measured against the cost of alternatives. Where there are reasonable prospects for the development and execution of a consensual workout plan, both the creditors and the debtor have the duty to pursue it and to honestly and vigorously seek its implementation.

VII. IMPACT ON CREDITORS.

Lessons learned by federal regulators in the Texas experience and in New England were applied with swiftness to banks in other regions of the country. Regulators relied heavily on the doctrine of bank safety and soundness in order to halt practices to which it objected. Prior to the Texas experience, the application of the standard of safety and soundness was unclear when applied to real estate loan portfolios and OREO and by extension to LBO portfolios. Although no clear consensus has yet developed in the courts, the application of the standard now has much more focus.

The statutory underpinning of safety and soundness is found in 12 USC §1818, which authorises federal banking agencies to take enforcement action necessary to halt unsafe and unsound banking practices. Such enforcement actions range from informal administrative action, such as letters of commitment or board resolutions, through memoranda of understanding to cease and desist orders. These documents require the bank's board to direct specific positive action by management and proscribe continued unsafe and unsound practices and violations of law. The consequences of engaging in practices found to be unsafe and unsound or in violation of law can include restitution for losses by and/or civil monetary penalties against and/or temporary or permanent disbarment from the banking industry of members of management and the board of directors.[78] Enforcement actions often contain allegations of violations of law, fraud and breach of fiduciary obligations by directors and officers. The Financial Institutions Reform Recovery and Enforcement Act (FIRREA)[79] and the Crime Control Act of 1990 (CCA)[80] greatly expanded the enforcement authority of regulators and increases civil penalties for violations.

Regulators applied the standards of safety and soundness subjectively based on a retrospective factual analysis. Consequently, bank management and its board of directors were required to be proactive and anticipatory in demonstrating to regulators their awareness of and serious concern for safe and sound practices. This awareness and concern must be carefully documented. For example, documentation should show that the board and management are aware of the effect which explosive growth in non-performing assets can have on the financial condition of the bank. It should show that management has examined and evaluated alternative courses of action. It should demonstrate that a specific course of action has been adopted and put into effect. Most importantly, documentation should demonstrate that the board and management have exercised reasonable business judgement in dealing with the problem. Reasonable business judgement is generally regarded as the ultimate standard to which management may be held accountable. However, some recent public sentiment indicates a call for a higher and more rigorous standard of care by management in dealing with other people's money. Unless or until the requirement of a higher standard of care actually develops, the reasonable business judgement should be the test of managing the bank safely and soundly.

[78] See J. Crawford, 'Scandal Gives Parties a Chance to Fire Away at Each Other', 48 Cong. 2204, 2205 (1990). See also Competitive Equality Banking Act (CEBA) PL-100–86 101 Stat. 552 (codified in various sections of 2, 12, 15 and 31 USC) (1987). and the Federal Deposit Insurance Corporation Improvement Act of 1991 (FDICIA) PL-102–242, 105 Stat. 2236 (codified in various sections of 12 and 15 USC) (1991).

[79] PL-101–73, 103 Stat. 183 (codified in various sections of 12 and 15 USC) (1989).

[80] PL-101–647, 104 Stat. 4789 (codifies in various sections of 11, 12, 18 and 28 USC) (1990).

The early 1980s, late 1980s, and early 1990s in the Southwest, New England, and the Middle Atlantic states, clearly demonstrated that the excesses in real estate, LBO's and ill-conceived mergers had created an absolute loss in value in many assets which were collateral for banks' loans. This loss was systemic and unavoidable. It could not have been escaped by 'better underwriting'. Indeed, underwriting to a large degree had become irrelevant.

Thus, the task of bank asset management is to shift this unavoidable loss to others and away from the bank to the greatest extent possible.

The shift of loss may be to the debtor or it may be to his other creditors who are not as aware nor as proactive as bank.

VIII. BASIC PRINCIPLES OF LOAN RESTRUCTURES

A. Balancing Collection Efforts with Effect on Bank Results

1. The dilemma: Ultimate loss protection vs. Non-Performing Asset Minimisation

Banks are guarded by rating agencies and bank stock analysts on current and projected levels of nonperforming assets('NPAs') compared to total assets, loss reserve and capital.

- High ratios cause higher cost of funds.
- Thus, management is deeply concerned about NPAs and reserves.
- The real loss is the ultimate loss on an asset. The rest is interim accounting.
- So which is more important? How do you balance these concerns?
- Establish a clear rule.

2. Regulator Confidence

- Importance
- Benefit of doubt in close calls.
- Higher cut-off.
- Examiners examine from centralised, organised files. Examiners give no credit for what's in your head or your desk file.
- Knowledge of credit and pursuit of a proactive plan action must be demonstrated by road map memos.
- Examiners are the most experienced reviewers of appraisals today.

3. Rating Agency Expectations

- Identify potential credit watch banks with regional statistics on

vacancy, rent rates, absorption, general business conditions and job creation.
- Are particularly interested in bank's tracking systems and early proactive address of problems.
- Can have as much effect on bank earnings and capital as the examiners.

B. Important Accounting Issues and Their Effect on Workout Action

Although Mexico and many Latin American countries do not follow US Generally Accepted Accounting Principles (GAAP), on 11 March 1996, officials at the Mexican National Banking and Securities Commission announced that by 1 January 1997, Mexican banks would be following accounting standards much closer to GAAP standards. When implemented, '[a]ccording to Jose Garcia-Cantrera, Latin American bank analyst at Solomon Brothers, the new accounting rules could mean that past due loans increase by as much as 100 per cent, which would cut in half the amount of reserves has against loans in default.' (Reuters, 11 March 1996, Mexico City). Suddenly, GAAP accounting issues are of immediate importance to Mexican bankers and borrowers.

1. Capitalisation of interest

Capitalised interest on loans is defined as uncollected interest which is added to the unpaid principal balance in accordance with a contractual loan agreement.[81]

It is common in construction lending for the loan agreement to contain a line item loan allocation for the costs of construction. One of the line items is often an 'interest reserve' out of which advances are made periodically to pay interest charges on the outstanding balance of the construction loan. When construction is complete and all line item allocations including the interest reserve are fully advanced, the loan is repaid through permanent financing or sale of the project in the normal course of business. The result, of course, is that the loan including the interest allocation is paid.

Capitalised interest concerns arise when the project loan is not paid at maturity through permanent financing or sale as was expected. In these cases, the 'interest reserve' has been fully advanced, the loan has matured, but the source of repayment is delayed. If the loan is renewed pending receipt of the source of repayment, the interest reserve by definition has been capitalised into the loan.

Another situation causing interest capitalisation concerns arises from

[81] OCC Examining Circular 229.

opening a new loan or increasing the original loan to create a new interest reserve to carry the renewed loan pending its repayment. Depending on the source of repayment of the new loan, it too may be deemed capitalised interest on the original loan.

Capitalisation of interest for reporting purposes is appropriate only when the borrower has the ability to repay the debt in the normal course of business.[82] The preceding sentence does not mean that any construction loan which is not repaid at maturity must automatically be placed on non-accrual. It is not unusual in the real estate development business for permanent financings and sales to be temporarily delayed and for additional well structured loans to be extended to pay interest on the original loan during the delay. The purpose of this section is to give workout officers guidance on the circumstances under which continued accrual is appropriate.

Capitalisation of interest on short term real estate loans should be based upon the borrower's ability to discharge the indebtedness in the normal course of business considering the surrounding circumstances and based upon prudent credit judgement including source of repayment and value of collateral.

The appropriateness of interest capitalisation for accounting purposes is based primarily on the creditworthiness of the borrower and guarantors. In addition to the general criteria for creditworthiness, the following questions should be considered in determining whether capitalisation of interest is appropriable:

(a) Was interest capitalisation anticipated upon approval of the initial loan?
(b) Is the loan well secured (i) by collateral that has a realisable value sufficient to discharge the debt (including capitalised interest) in full, or (ii) by the guaranty of a financially responsible and capable party?
(c) Is repayment of the loan based upon a reasonably ascertainable event in the future?
(d) Can the borrower obtain funds from sources other than the bank on similar terms and rates?
(e) Is there little or no doubt as to the ultimate collection of all principal and interest?

If the answer to these questions is predominantly affirmative, then capitalisation of interest may be acceptable. The primary test remains the overall credit quality of the loan. Credits of sound quality may merit interest capitalisation even if some of these questions are answered negatively. However, only in very unusual circumstances will a loan classified substandard merit interest capitalisation.

[82] OCC Examining Circular 229.

2. INSUBSTANCE FORECLOSURE (ISF)

Loans should generally be considered insubstance foreclosures where they meet all of the following criteria:[83]

(a) The debtor has little or no equity in the collateral, considering the current fair value of the collateral; and
(b) Proceeds for repayment of the loan can be expected to come only from the operation or sale of the collateral; and
(c) The debtor has either:
   i. formally or effectively abandoned control of the collateral to the creditor, or
   ii. retained control of the collateral but, because of the current financial condition of the debtor, or the economic prospects for the debtor and/or the collateral in the foreseeable future, it is doubtful that the debtor will be able to rebuild equity in the collateral or otherwise repay the loan in the foreseeable future.

The first two criteria are used to identify situations where most of the risks and rewards of ownership of the collateral have passed from the borrower to the bank. Even if the value of the collateral securing the loan has dropped so that there is little or no equity in that particular investment, the borrower or guarantor may currently have demonstrable sufficient strength or outside sources of cash to service and eventually retire the debt. In such case, the second criteria is not met and there is no insubstance foreclosure. Thus, value of collateral for a secured loan may drop to zero without a finding of ISF if the borrower or guarantor has the demonstrable current wherewithal to repay the loan from other sources. Likewise, if all loans to a borrower are cross collateralised and total debt is reasonably exceeded by the value of all cross pledged collateral, then the first criteria is not met and there is no finding of ISF.

The third criteria leaves room for subjective evaluation of the borrower's ability to rebuild equity in the collateral or otherwise repay the loan in the foreseeable future. This subjective evaluation should be prudently exercised by the workout officer and management. For example, when using forecasts to assess the borrower's ability to repay the loan or to assess the prospects for improvement in the value of the collateral, the workout officer making the determination should be mindful that the longer the time projected, the less reliable the projected results. Projections should be reasonably near term and be based on independently derived supportable assumptions.

[83] US Securities and Exchange Commission FRR §401.09(c)(FRR 28)(6AAP Release 17,9189), *see also*, Statement of Financial Accounting Standards No. 15, at para. 28 and 29.

Workout officers should be cognisant that determination of ISF affects only the bank's accounting for a loan as substantially repossessed. Legal title to the asset remains in the borrower until it is passed to the bank either consensually or through foreclosure. The loan is not in default solely by being found to be an ISF. It may be in the bank's best interest to obtain control over the price and timing of the sale of the collateral to eliminate an asset acquired for debt previously contracted as soon as possible, but action must be taken in a way to protect the bank from lender liability allegations. Therefore, it is extremely important for lending and supervised workout officers to maintain a course of dealing that minimises the bank's exposure to such allegations.

Even though an ISF real estate loan must be accounted for as OREO, compliance with 12 USC §7.3025 is limited to the initial appraisal and annual reappraisal of the value of the underlying real estate. It is not necessary to obtain prior regulatory approval to fund a borrower's draw request,[84] although the bank may opt to refuse such funding under its loan agreement if the loan is in default.

3. Troubled debt restructures

A troubled debt restructure (TDR) is one 'in which the bank, for economic or legal reasons related to the borrower's financial difficulties, grants a concession to the borrower that it would not otherwise consider.'[85]

Basic knowledge of TDR accounting is important to workout officers in (a) preventing nonaccrual status for certain loans and, (b) restoring existing non accruals to performing status. A finding that a restructure is a TDR requires the restructure to be carried on the bank's financial statement as a nonperforming asset even if the loan is current as to interest. TDR's are governed by FAS 15[86] which is extremely complex. This section undertakes only to outline the basic rules of TDR's and make certain suggestions rather than attempt a comprehensive review of FAS 15.

The point is to make workout officers aware that a restructure that makes perfect business sense may nonetheless be deemed a TDR by the bank's independent accountants with the result that the goal of reducing non-accrual assets is not achieved. However, the workout officer should not negotiate a less favourable business deal in an attempt to achieve more favourable accounting treatment.

Because of the complexity of FAS 15, the advice and counsel of the bank's internal accounting staff should be sought as soon as a plan begins to take shape and before commitments are made to the borrower.

[84] Conference with legal staff OCC Southwestern District Office.
[85] Banking Circular 195, 1 May 1985, emphasis added.
[86] Statement of Financial Accounting Standards No. 15.

Note from the underscoring in the definition of TDR that the touchstone is granting concessions because of the borrower's difficulty. For example, extending a loan at an interest rate equal to that generally charged for loans with similar risk would not be a TDR even if the rate were lower than the rate on the original loan.

If the new terms of the troubled debt restructuring provide for a reduction of either interest or principal (referred to as a modification of terms), FAS 15 requires that the recorded amount of the loan on the bank's books (principal plus accrued interest) be compared to the total future contractual cash payments (including both principal and interest) expected to be collected. A loss is recognised only if the total of such future combined payments is less than the recorded amount of the loan. Otherwise, no loss is recognised and the only additional accounting requirement is to determine the new effective interest rate for income recognition purposes. However, the restructured loan will be carried as a non-performing asset.

Often, the new effective interest rate is equal to the stated loan rate included in the restructured loan document. However, adjustments may be required if (a) the loan principal is reduced, (b) the new contractual rates are on a graduated basis (e.g. 8 per cent first year, 10 per cent second year, etc.), (c) due and unpaid interest is not added to principal or otherwise included in the contractual interest rate amount, or (d) the repayment terms have other unusual provisions. If an effective interest rate computation is required, it should be based upon future contractual payment terms excluding all payments which are contingently payable. This rate is calculated so as to yield a constant rate of interest over the remaining life of the loan. It is expected the rate will generally be less than the original loan rate and may be as low as zero without any requirement to recognise a loss.

Subject to the rules on capitalisation of interest discussed in Section VII B(1), infra the bank may extend additional credit to a borrower at interest rates below the current market rate. Since this is a new loan to the same borrower, no special accounting rules apply. Accordingly, discounting or loss recognition is not necessary. However, if the new loan is granted in connection with the restructuring of an existing loan, it will be considered part of the restructuring and accounted for as previously described.

In all troubled debt restructuring the collectibility of future payments may be questionable. Therefore, a credit analysis should be performed to determine if any additional amounts should be charged to the allowance for loan losses. The analysis should include the borrower's ability to meet the new terms of the loan based upon projected cash flows, profitability and other credit factors.

C. *How to Force Hidden Problems to the Surface*

1. STRICT ENFORCEMENT OF LOAN AGREEMENT.

- Require full compliance with all conditions to new advances (advising borrower, if necessary, that any prior waiver of certain conditions will no longer be granted).
- Make sure that financial statements and borrowing base/construction progress reports are provided on time and accompanied by any required certificate of compliance.
- Obtain detailed computation of any financial covenants required by loan agreements, such as current ratio, leverage ratio, tangible net worth, etc.
- Obtain on a regular basis agings of all payables and receivables and an analysis of concentrations.
- Inspect borrower's book and records and properties as permitted by loan agreement.

2. NO REALLOCATION.

In order to keep a loan on accrual, the lending officer is sometimes tempted to reallocate from, say, the tenant finish line items to the interest reserve after the initial interest reserve has been depleted. The debtor will offer convincing arguments that tenant finish requirements are lower or will be paid by the tenant. This type of action hides problems because the tenant finish is always higher than originally projected, not lower.

3. BORROWER'S DEPOSITS

Borrower deposit requirements are included in loan agreements to capture the borrower's cash into a project as soon as a line item cost overrun is known. Failure to exercise this right allows the borrower to divert his cash to other uses thus exposing the bank to additional cost and probable loss to complete the end of the job.

4. BORROWING BASE OVERADVANCES

A clear sign of problems in an accounts receivable and inventory financing is when the borrowing base report, either directly or indirectly through an analysis of specific items contained therein, discloses that the principal balance of the loan exceeds the stipulated borrowing base. In nearly all situations, the borrower will argue that the overadvance is temporary in nature and will correct itself over time so that a waiver should be granted. In the overwhelming majority of cases, the overadvance will not cure itself over time, and the bank is well advised not to grant the waiver unless the borrower makes specific concessions designed to protect the bank's interests (e.g. lock box, additional collateral and/or personal guaranties).

5. Breaches of Financial Covenants

A primary purpose of financial covenants in a loan agreement is to provide an early warning signal of a borrower's potentially serious financial difficulties. Clearly, the financial covenants will fail to serve such purpose if their breach is treated by the bank as a mere 'technical' default and readily waived. The breach of any financial covenant should be carefully analysed to determine if it represents an isolated occurrence based on special circumstances or is indeed a harbinger of future distress for the customer (and bank). If such breach raises concerns, consideration should be given to obtaining specific concessions from the borrower in exchange for granting a waiver. In any event, the waiver should always be given in writing and make clear that it applies only to the specific date or period involved.

D. Understanding Economic and Market Forces

1. Market for the Product

In troubled real estate markets, the debtor often depletes his resources in covering overhead or feeding projects with perceived positive potential. He has little left to support the bank's projects.

In these cases, the banks primary source of interest carry and principal payment is the collateral itself. Thus, it is critical for the workout officer to know how to evaluate the project. This is discussed in detail in Section VIII, below.

2. Current Feasibility

Appraisals are important in evaluating collateral, but appraisals do not produce the cash to repay a loan. They only give an indication of what the collateral is worth on the day of the appraisal. Consider that appraisals are for accounting purposes. The workout officer needs to know current feasibility of the project. This is also expanded in section VII.A.3, below.

3. Lease Rules

- Importance of bank approval rights.
- Effect on value and salability.

- Free rent rules.
- Lease profitability rules.

4. Sales of subsidiaries

In many highly leveraged transactions, it is common for the lender to require the parent company borrower to grant liens in the stock or assets of subsidiary companies. While the cash flow of the consolidated group may be sufficient to pay interest on the loan, the sale of one or more subsidiaries may be needed to make principal payments. The sale of subsidiaries may not have been contemplated at the time the leveraged buyout originally occurred. In any case, the workout officer must carefully analyse the potential value of various subsidiaries and their prospects for sale, taking into account that the overhead charges allocated by the parent company to such subsidiaries may skew their apparent operating results. Such analysis will require a review of consolidating financial statements as well as the possible retention of an industry consultant.

E. Bank's Rights to Collateral

1. Negative Pledges

The bank may have required a 'negative pledge' which, although not acquiring a lien against the assets, limits the debtor's right to dispose of or encumber certain assets. The theory of a 'negative pledge' is that the debtor agrees with the bank that it will not sell, lease, convey, or otherwise dispose of specified assets of the debtor or permit to exist any encumbrances with respect to such assets. The negative pledge may be coupled with the debtor's agreement to provide collateral to the bank (i.e. that the debtor will execute documents necessary to grant the bank a lien against certain property) upon the happening of certain events which typically may be tied to circumstances evidencing a deteriorating financial condition of the debtor. This type of arrangement may provide little comfort to the bank if the loan becomes troubled. To the extent that the debtor may be in default for failure to make any required payments to the bank or is otherwise in default to the bank, the debtor may have little motivation to deliver the requisite lien documents at that point, as its failure to do so will simply be another event of default. The bank may be in no better position than it would be if the loan were 'unsecured,' although the bank could perhaps argue that the debtor's agreement and obligation to provide collateral is specifically enforceable or that the collateral is held in a constructive trust for the benefit of the bank. Significant litigation expense would likely be incurred in such cases.

2. ASSIGNMENT OF PARTNERSHIP INTERESTS

In a restructure or in connection with the original loan, the bank may attempt to obtain or may have obtained a collateral assignment of a partnership interest held by the borrower. The assignment of the partnership interest should in most cases be a collateral assignment (security interest or lien on the partnership interest) and not an absolute assignment (bank owns partnership interest) in order to avoid obligating the bank for any partnership duties or liabilities. Prior to obtaining an assignment of a partnership interest, the partnership agreement should be reviewed with the bank's counsel in order to determine any issues relating to partner's consents to a transfer, securities law restriction and future capital contribution obligations of the partner. The collateral assignment of the partnership interest typically will provide the bank with a more valuable assetthe entire equity interestthan simply an assignment of proceeds from the partnership interest.

3. ASSIGNMENT OF PROCEEDS

In connection with a restructure, a bank may attempt to obtain an assignment of proceeds from certain collateral, typically a partnership interest or some types of contracts (e.g. lot sale contracts, income generating service contracts). The assignment of proceeds will typically only provide the bank with remedies or recourse in the event proceeds are received by the borrower from a partnership interest or from contracts and such proceeds are not delivered to the bank. The bank will not have obtained a security interest in or lien on the actual interest which produces the proceeds, so the true balance sheet value of such an assignment may be nominal. In certain cases (e.g. service contracts) the bank may very well not want to obtain an assignment of a contract so as not to impose liability on the bank. One other consideration is that if bankruptcy is likely the proceeds received by the bank within the preference period prior to bankruptcy may be required to be disgorged.

4. LIENS, SENIOR AND SUBORDINATE

Typically, the bank will obtain a first or senior lien on the primary collateral for its loan. In many instances, either in obtaining additional collateral for the original loan or in shoring up a troubled loan, the bank may have acquired a subordinate lien on an additional piece of collateral. The subordinate lien would be subject to one or more prior liens in favour of other creditors. An analysis of the actual value of the subordinate lien must include consideration of the total value of the collateral, the amount of debt secured by senior or prior liens against the collateral and the actual willingness of the bank to advance funds to protect its interest in the collateral in the event the borrower is in default in payments to a senior lienholder or in the event the senior lienholder exercises remedies against the collateral. Another consideration in the use of a subordinate lien is to 'tie up' the collateral so that no consensual sale or conveyance of the collateral by the borrower can occur without the bank having the opportunity to require payment of the proceeds from the sale of the property to the bank prior to the release of its lien.

5. Related personal property

Often loans secured by real property will be additionally secured by personal property and fixtures used in connection with the real property. The bank should have valid security interests that have been perfected by financing statements currently filed and effective with the property filing offices. Liens on personal property are extremely important in relation to multifamily properties and hotel properties.

6. Remedies under UCC Article 9

Upon default in a loan secured by personal property which is subject to a valid and enforceable security interest under Article 9 of the Uniform Commercial Code, Article 9 affords the secured creditor the following non-judicial (i.e. self-help) remedies:

(a) right to notify account debtors to make payment directly to the secured creditor;
(b) right to repossess tangible collateral without causing a breach of the peace;
(c) right to require the debtor to assemble the collateral and make it available at a reasonably convenient location designated by the secured creditor;
(d) right to retain the collateral in satisfaction of the loan; and
(e) right to sell, lease or otherwise dispose of the collateral by public or private proceedings.

The most significant remedy available under Article 9 is the secured creditor's right, after giving prior notice to the debtor and certain other interested parties, to conduct a private or public sale of all or a portion of the collateral without any judicial involvement.[87] While the power of sale under Article 9 represents an efficient method of liquidating collateral,

[87] UCC §9–504.

there is imposed on the secured creditor the responsibility of assuring that every aspect of the sale if conducted in a 'commercially reasonable' manner.[88] Article 9 does not expressly define what constitutes 'commercially reasonable' conduct, and litigation has frequently resulted seeking to determine whether a secured creditor's conduct was commercially reasonable in the specific circumstances presented. The importance of conducting the Article 9 sale in a commercially reasonable manner is that the secured creditor who fails to meet this standard may be denied the right to pursue any deficiency claim against the debtor or any guarantor and may be restrained from or ordered to conduct the sale in a specified manner or be liable for damages.[89]

7. Bank's remedies–local law determination

The determination of the specific legal remedies available to the bank in the event of a loan default is made under the local law of the governing jurisdiction and is an inherent part of that state's economic and political structure. The workout officer must consult with the bank's legal department and local legal counsel to ascertain the legal advantages and disadvantages of specific workout structures and enforcement strategies.

F. Overview of Borrower's Problems

1. Federal income tax liability

A properly counselled debtor will first be concerned with his liability for income tax arising from involuntary or voluntary conveyance of title to collateral or from forgiveness of debt. Income tax planning is a very significant element of virtually every real estate workout. In fact, in many workouts, the tax considerations become the single most important factor in developing a strategy and ultimate consummation of the workout. Although certain taxes incurred more than three years before the filing of a bankruptcy petition may be dischargeable in bankruptcy, more recent federal income taxes, including taxes generated pursuant to the transactions involved in the workout, are not dischargeable. Consequently, it may be advisable for the debtor to pursue virtually any course that would minimise federal tax liabilities, including incurring additional personal liability which may be subsequently discharged in bankruptcy.

88 UCC §9–504(3), *see also* UCC §9–507(2).
89 UCC §9–507.

a. *Information To Be Gathered*

In order to apply the foregoing legal principles and to further develop the strategies described below, the following information must be examined:

(i) A detailed description of each asset owned by the debtor, including its fair market value, adjusted tax basis, and usage by the debtor (i.e. investment, personal, trade or business, inventory, etc.).
(ii) A detailed description of all fixed and contingent liabilities of the debtor, including whether they are recourse or nonrecourse, guaranteed, sellerfinancing, etc.
(iii) All agreements relating to the assets and liabilities of the debtor, including notes, loan agreements, guarantees and partnership agreements.

b. *Analysis and Strategies*

In a comprehensive real estate workout, the following steps of tax planning and analysis must be taken:

(i) Evaluate the market value, indebtedness and adjusted basis of each property and determine the taxable gain or loss that would be recognised upon the voluntary or involuntary conveyance of each such property.
(ii) Determine the taxable income of the debtor for the current taxable year to date and project the taxable income for the remainder of the year, other than income or loss that may be generated upon the disposition of the real properties.
(iii) Determine the solvency or insolvency of the debtor.
(iv) Determine the practical likelihood of bankruptcy and the willingness of the debtor to consider bankruptcy.
(v) Consider and plan for the amount of gain or loss and timing of disposition of each and every property of the debtor.

2. Reputation, future earning power and family

A debtor will be concerned with his reputation in the community since it will greatly affect his ability to earn money in the future. These concerns are driven by his perceived need to preserve a reasonable life style for himself and his family. These are powerful psychological motivations and should not be treated lightly by the workout officer.

3. Alternatives

Absent fraud or other malfeasance, a borrower can accomplish his objectives by filing for bankruptcy, an action which is expensive and time consuming for the bank, invariably leads to greatly reduced value of collateral if the stays are finally lifted or may expose the bank to a cram down plan of reorganisation resulting in write downs and permanently non-performing assets. Thus, heavy handed action by a workout officer without consideration of the factors described above can adversely affect the bank. Conversely, if the bank is an undersecured or unsecured creditor, it may prefer the debtor to be in bankruptcy in which case a different approach is appropriate. As noted in section VIIIA., *infra* the facts generated in connection with the initial analysis of the existing status of the credit will dictate the workout plan.

G. *Basic Workout Strategy*

Time is always critical. First, it is important to the bank's well being that nonperforming and classified assets be reduced quickly. Secondly, if the workout plan requires foreclosure and resale, ultimate actual loss is minimised by doing so as quickly as possible especially in a deteriorating market. Finally, the bank is greatly benefited by achieving its workout before other creditors are mobilised.

It is imperative to understand the bank's plan and focus on alternatives for achievement of the plan. The workout officer should prioritise actions to achieve the plan and move quickly and effectively with these actions. Remain calm and cool; avoid recriminations in meetings and exchanges where the borrower or guarantor face the same facts you have uncovered. Do your best to avoid exchanges of legalism which polarises the objectives. Seek to align the borrower's and guarantor's plan with that of the bank. The officer should remember to stick to the loan documents and the bank's legal position within the context of the bank's plan. All parties should focus on a resolution and not waste money and time arguing about 'who shot John'.

1. Objective: Prevent Non-Performing Asset Classification

The first goal of every workout plan is to prevent the subject loans from being placed on non-accrual or to restore the subject loans to accrual status, if possible. If accrual is not possible, then the plan goal is to minimise interim charge-offs and ultimate actual loss.

2. Downside Protection

It is axiomatic that the lender who (i) addresses problems with the debtor first, (ii) acts consistently and in good faith, (iii) addresses debtor concerns, and (iv) is knowledgeable, reasonable and creative will achieve a better solution to a troubled credit whether that solution is loan restructure or amicable acquisition of title to collateral. Debtors, however, are not always cooperative. Thus, the workout officer must put the bank in the strongest position if restructure efforts fail and the relationship becomes acrimonious. Always first position the bank for maximum recovery if the events critical to the workout's success do not occur.

The following actions should be part of, or at least given consideration in formulating, every workout plan:

(a) Find the best available collateral and get it pledged to support future value declines, accrued unpaid interest or possible working capital loans. The best collateral is that which produces income in addition to value.
(b) Get all unsecured debt secured by anything of real value immediately.
(c) Control the cash flow of the bank's collateral by entering into a cash collateral agreement with the debtor under which he pays over monthly to the bank all net operating income without deduction for capital improvements, taxes or insurance. The expense component of monthly NOI should be tightly negotiated and the debtor should agree to strict accounting subject to audit by the bank. Refusal of the debtor to comply with these requirements is a clear indication of bad faith necessarily requiring the workout officer to control cash flow through the bank's legal remedies.
(d) Get all loans to the debtor cross collateralised and cross defaulted as an early objective. If cross collateralisation cannot be obtained at the asset level because of ownership by partnerships without common partners, at least obtain cross collateralisation of all the common partnership interests. The workout officer can expect a sophisticated debtor to use granting of cross collateralisation as a bargaining chip, for example, for a working capital loan or release of liability. Any other deficiencies discovered in the analysis of the documentation should be corrected in any restructure modification agreement relating to a troubled credit.
(e) Get the bank's deal done before other creditors wake up. Start the preference period running.

3. Press remedies in the documents

Correctly drafted loan documents will provide for non-monetary covenants, undertakings and representations and warranties by the borrower. Non-compliance with these provisions usually constitutes a default after appropriate notices to the borrower and his failure to cure within the time limits provided. Often it is necessary to get the attention of an uncooperative borrower by methodical enforcement of the bank's rights and remedies under the loan documents. Such enforcement should stay strictly within the bounds of the documents (e.g. written notice, grace period, etc.) in order to avoid allegations of lender liability. By demonstrating its seriousness through methodical enforcement of rights and remedies, the bank encourages the borrower to be willing to negotiate restructure.

Even after restructure negotiations begin, the bank should continue to give all notices and other actions required of it by the documents. The bank can always suspend legal enforcement if negotiations are proceeding satisfactorily, but not lose time (and money) through a 'start-stop-start' approach to enforcement if negotiations break down.

To avoid surprising the borrower (which often leads to emotional allegations of bad faith by him), the bank should inform the borrower at the outset of negotiations that it intends to follow this dual track course of action (legal enforcement while simultaneously negotiating).

4. Encourage borrower's proposals

The borrower should be encouraged to propose solutions to the problem. By encouraging borrower's proposals the workout officer keeps the borrower involved and obtains insight into the borrower's management ability.

5. Be responsive, but firm and sceptical

Be sceptical of the debtor's optimistic projections of lease up, rent rates, low tenant finish requirements, sales volume, sales prices and operating income. The market is always worse than the developer perceives. Feasibility analysis previously ordered will give the workout officer his own independent realistic view of the market. The restructure should be based on the realistic view.

Set performance benchmarks in the restructure which the debtor must meet to earn the right to continue the workout. Make them reasonably achievable, but not easy. Often the debtor will propose a 'cash flow' mortgage to the bank. In all but the rarest circumstances, the workout officer should reject such a proposal. Cash flow mortgages leave the debtor in control of timing and pricing of sale, give him the opportunity to manipulate net operating income to the disadvantage of the bank (even if he has executed a cash collateral agreement) and leave the bank with all of the risk of value decline either from market deterioration or from debtor mismanagement. If a cash flow mortgage is accepted, it must be made 'defaultable' by requiring a minimum monthly payment regardless of cash flow and prompt payment by the debtor of taxes and insurance.

Some debtors with many lenders will propose a consensual reorganisation of their business in an attempt to reach a global resolution of all their debt, see Sections V and VI, above. Even though these plans usually involve cash flow mortgages (called 'pass-throughs'), they should not be rejected out of hand. Features of such plans also include a 'collateral pool' into which the debtor places all of his business assets for the benefit of all of his creditors and usually involve partial or complete release from liability. The plan requires equal treatment of all creditors and full disclosure. They are similar in many respects to bankruptcy but without judicial supervision. If the bank is under secured even after cross-collateralisation, it may be beneficial to consider consensual reorganisation to gain access to the collateral pool. The plans are extremely complex and should be discussed thoroughly with the workout officer's manager.

6. One broken promise for another

Do not trade one broken promise to pay for a new promise to pay. Always obtain something tangible for any concession, however small.

7. Borrower's affidavits

When problems begin to arise with respect to a lending relationship, a bank finds it increasingly difficult to get current financial information from the borrower. Its borrower may well be encountering difficulties with other creditors and will want to reveal as little information as possible about its current affairs while it considers possible courses of action to protect its interests as against all creditors. The bank's ability to evaluate the status of the loan and the prospects for repayment are made more difficult by its inability to determine the overall financial condition of the borrower. It is essential that the bank obtain a full and complete disclosure of the financial condition of the borrower as a part of and as a condition precedent to any workout arrangement. The borrower should provide a detailed sworn financial statement which described and identifies all assets and liabilities and prior transfers of assets. The affidavit of financial condition, when examined against prior financial information received from the borrower, may assist the bank in identifying any fraudulent transfers which may have been made by the borrower and also should provide the bank with either support for the borrower's oral representations regarding its financial condition or reveal that the borrower has been untruthful or fraudulent during workout discussions. The borrower should be able to show that his financial affairs are such that a restructure of a problem loan can be successful in order for a bank to consider that alternative. Likewise, to the extent that a borrower who claims to have few assets from which the creditor may recover seeks to be released from liability in consideration of his cooperating with the bank in the bank's realisation on any collateral for the loan, the borrower should be able to evidence such financial condition to the bank.

H. Techniques to Maintain Loan Performance

1. UNSECURED LOANS, ADDITIONAL COLLATERAL, CROSS COLLATERALISATION

A primary objective in any workout is to improve the bank's prospects for repayment by obtaining any new collateral which is available to be pledged to it. In the case of an unsecured loan, obtaining collateral, even if it provides considerably less than full coverage for the loan, will be the only means of acquiring a specific source of repayment and prevents the bank from being treated in the same manner as the borrower's trade creditors who, in a bankruptcy context, will receive only pennies on the dollar.

Even if the bank's loan is currently secured, there may be additional collateral which is available to be pledged to improve the bank's secured status. Obviously, assets which are currently unencumbered are the best form of collateral. However, it may be extremely advantageous for the bank to obtain a lien against assets which have previously been encumbered since the current or future value of such assets may exceed the amount of the first lien. In evaluating the borrower's assets which may be available to serve as collateral, do not hesitate to be creative. For example, a borrower's intangible assets, such as patents, copyrights, trademarks, servicemarks and franchise rights, could be very valuable but may not have been taken as collateral by other lenders who only loan against 'hard' assets.

An extremely important objective in any workout is for the bank to obtain cross collateralisation of all of its loans. Cross collateralisation means that particular assets serve as collateral for more than one loan or indebtedness. For example, if a bank's relationship with its borrower consists of a revolving line of credit secured by accounts receivable and inventory, a term loan secured by equipment and real estate an letters of credit secured by the proceeds of specific contracts, the workout officer's objective would be to revise the existing documents to make sure that all the assets which have been pledged by such borrower secure all three types of financing provided. The reason that cross collateralisation is so important is that it will enable the bank to apply 'excess' value attributable to collateral for one loan against the outstanding balance of another loan. Using the example discussed above, it is quite conceivable that if the borrower were to file for bankruptcy, its accounts receivable and inventory which secure the revolving line of credit would be insufficient to pay off such line of credit. On the other hand, liquidation of the borrower's equipment and real estate may result in proceeds in excess of the term loan.

Unless the revolving line of credit and term loan were cross collateralised, the bank would not be entitled to apply the excess proceeds of equipment and real estate to the outstanding balance of the revolving line of credit, thereby resulting in a loss on the revolving line of credit which would otherwise be avoided.

2. Cash collateral agreements

Often the bank will be faced, in a workout situation, with the opportunity to enter into an agreement with a borrower whereby the borrower will turn the revenues from the property over to the bank and the bank will be allowed to deal with the property by taking control of the property and managing it prior to the time that the bank actually acquires the property pursuant to a foreclosure action. Generally, the bank is presented this opportunity in relation to income producing real estate, and it may appear to be an ideal way to obtain possession of the revenue from the property and protect the collateral pending foreclosure. When the bank and a borrower agree to this type of arrangement, they usually enter into a cash collateral agreement to govern the collection and application of the rents from the property. The borrower generally attempts to obtain a full release and an indemnification from the bank in relation to the activities of the bank during the period that the bank is in possession of the property prior to the bank's acquisition of the property through foreclosure. Notwithstanding that a cash collateral agreement may seem to be the ideal arrangement in cases where the foreclosure process is lengthy, there are numerous pitfalls which the bank should consider.

Once the bank takes possession of the property it becomes a 'mortgagee in possession'. This term has slightly different meanings in various jurisdictions; however, the principles and warnings set forth below are generally applicable. A mortgagee in possession is one who takes possession of property pursuant to a contract (e.g. a cash collateral agreement) and is entitled to remain in possession until the bank's debt is paid in full.

Generally the standard of care of a mortgagee in possession is that of a constructive trustee and the mortgagee is under a duty to manage the property in a reasonably prudent and careful manner in order to keep the property in a good state of preservation and to make it productive. When a mortgagee comes into possession of the property in other than a lawful manner, then the mortgagee generally is responsible for the reasonable rental value of the property, if any, during the time the mortgagee is in possession. If the mortgagee's possession is lawful, then the mortgagee must account for the rents and profits received or which might have been received by the use of reasonable diligence and care. The mortgagee in possession may be liable as the landlord under the leased that cover the property and will be liable for negligent acts occurring on the property. Indemnities from borrowers are generally of little or no help in protecting the bank; however, insurance can cover some of the risk assumed by a mortgagee in possession.

Because of the bank's control over the borrower and the property resulting from its being a mortgagee in possession, there are number of lender liability concerns which should be considered. If a borrower subsequently seeks the protection of the bankruptcy courts and the bank is found to be in control of the borrower's business, the bankruptcy court has the power to 'equitably subordinate' the bank's lien to the liens of other creditors. If the bank is found to be in control of the borrower's business, it can be held liable under federal and state environmental statutes for the cost of cleanup of various hazardous wastes. Certain liability for federal withholding taxes also can be successfully asserted by the Internal Revenue Service if the bank controls the borrower's business. In addition, notwithstanding the fact that the bank may act properly, a borrower seeking to prevent foreclosure may raise allegations of improprieties related to the bank's possession of the property which the borrower may allege prevented the borrower from making payments on the debt.

There are circumstances when the bank will clearly desire to become a mortgagee in possession (e.g. where the borrower has abandoned the property). However, in most cases careful consideration should be given to the facts surrounding a proposed cash collateral agreement and the circumstances relating to the collateral, especially in light of the numerous liabilities which inure to a mortgagee in possession. If the risks are such that a cash collateral agreement is deemed to be appropriate and possession of the property is desirable, the provisions of the agreement with the borrower should be carefully drafted to protect the bank. The bank should attempt to structure a cash collateral agreement under which the borrower retains control of the property by leaving the borrower responsible for the management and operation of the property while obtaining the net revenues from the property.

3. Loan splitting

A $10,000,000 loan on an office building which is producing $600,00 in NOI from credit tenants. No outside support available from the debtor/guarantor. No concessions on rate or terms other than extension of maturity are made. Can the loan be internally restructured on the bank's books as a $5,000,000 performing loan ($600,000/$5,000,000 = market rate) and a $5,000,000 non-accrual loan? Generally no. If there is no outside debtor/guarantor support and the building produces $600,000 in NOI, it will be difficult to show a value in excess of the $10,000,000 loan amount. These factors would combine to produce an insubstance foreclosure (see section VII B(2), above). If an independent, accurate appraisal of the building showed value in excess of $10,000,000, then the workout officer should discuss the possibility of this internal 'restructure' with the bank's internal accountants.

One exception to the general rule is a change in circumstance after the loan has been placed on non-accrual and been charged down. For example, a new credit-worthy tenant could be obtained producing new cash flow which would carry and begin amortising the loan as charged down. In such case, the loan may be returned to accrual.

4. Trading borrowers

Original borrower arranges to sell project for amount equal to current debt to unrelated buyers. Bank agrees to finance 100 per cent of purchase price for new buyers at below market rate but no other concessions such as limited liability to new buyers. The new loan is not technically a TDR under FAS 15 because it is not to the original borrower. However, the new loan may still be a non-performing asset if there was a finding that the original loan was an insubstance foreclosure because the downpayment requirement of 12 USC §7.3025 and FAS 66 was not met. Even if there was no finding of insubstance foreclosure, the principal balance of the new loan may be required to be marked to market to reflect a belowmarket interest rate. These are only two of many complex considerations. Advice of the bank's internal accountants should be sought early on.

Warning. Workout officers are often tempted to negotiate with inhouse and independent accounts to comply with the literal accounting rules and to twist the deal to meet accounting requirements. The new borrower immediately picks up on the bank's problems and extracts substantive concessions for his cooperation in helping the bank with its accounting issues. This often weakens the restructure and can led to greater ultimate loss. Build hammers, not watches.

5. Additional compensation for added risk

Obviously, if the bank structures a workout with the borrower that reduces the bank's current return, causes it current loss or exposes it to future loss, the bank should be and is entitled to a higher reward. The bank contracted for interest risk and interest reward. if the bank's risk is converted to equity risk, it should participate to some degree in equity reward if such occurs because of a rising market.

However, the bank must beware of lender liability issues inherent in increasing its reward. The bank must maintain its position as a secured lender and not a partner of the debtor.

6. MARKETING AGREEMENTS WITH BORROWER

As an alternative to forced liquidation of assets and litigation, a bank may consider affording the borrower a reasonable period of time in which to market the property prior to the bank's ultimate enforcement of its remedies pursuant to the loan documents. The bank may assist the borrower in its marketing efforts by obtaining from the borrower a nonexclusive right to market the property. The bank must exercise care in this area to avoid the exercise of control over the borrower which could subject the bank to potential claims.

I. Borrower Conferences

1. PURPOSE

When arranging a conference with the debtor, the workout officer should specify the purpose of the meeting. The debtor should then be informed that the initial meeting will commence with execution of the pre-workout agreement which should be provided to the debtor in advance. He should be advised to come prepared to bring the bank up to date on his financial condition, cash flow, property status, other debt and other pertinent topics, and to present his own workout alternatives.

Debtors may approach this meeting with a 'wait and see' attitude to get an understanding of what types of alternatives the bank will consider before they make a proposal. The meeting will be more productive if the workout officer encourages the debtor to make a proposal at the meeting.

2. HOW TO PREPARE

In order to conduct a meaningful and fruitful working meeting, the workout officer must be prepared to enter into an open-minded discussion of the facts as presented by the debtor so he can fully understand the circumstances and review alternatives, some of which may be suggested by the debtor. By beginning the working conference in this manner, the workout officer can establish the 'ground rules' for future discussions, the results of which will be more fruitful under these circumstances.

Because of the debtor's potential fears or anger, the conference may become antagonistic and unproductive. For this reason, the workout officer must have the discipline and professional attitude to maintain the purpose of the meeting and maintain the 'ground rules' for meaningful resolution.

3. Use of Attorneys

Many conferences relating to workout resolution can be handled directly between the workout officer and the debtor. Depending upon the nature of the workout, the size of the loan and the potential for non-accrual or loss, certain discussions should include an additional workout officer, preferably the group manager. If a debtor indicates he will arrive at a meeting with his attorney, the workout officer must review the situation with his manager to determine if it is appropriate for the bank to engage legal counsel at this juncture. By all means, when an attorney for the debtor is present, the workout officer should include in the conference his manager or legal counsel so two people are representing the bank.

Examples of instances when the meeting should include the bank's legal counsel follow:

- Debtor has made claims of lender liability.
- Litigation between the bank and the debtor is pending or being actively considered.
- Debtor has revealed plans to file bankruptcy.
- The workout officer considers there are issues for which a claim may arise in the future against the bank.
- Debtor's relationship is already antagonistic, in which case the bank may be best served by utilising legal counsel as the primary contact with the workout officer support.
- A discussion of legal issues is expected.

Prior to the meeting, either the workout officer, his manager, or another workout employee should be designated as the person to take notes and prepare a follow-up memorandum summarising the meeting.

4. Topics for Discussion

Topics for discussion include:

- Status of debtor's loans with other creditors.
- Status of debtor's other real and personal property investments (leasing, cash flow).
- Status of pending transactions or litigation which may positively or negatively impact the debtor's financial condition.
- Possibility of raising additional equity, refinancing, sales.
- Future plans.
- Operating standards for the collateral property during the period of negotiations (What happens to the cash? Is the property secure?)

At the initial debtor conference, the workout officer should explain the bank's requirements regarding turnover of property NOI and present the debtor with the proposed cash collateral agreement discussed above. One objective is to make clear to the debtor that the bank intends to enforce its remedies thoroughly.

5. Memorialising Meeting and Next Steps

Immediately after the meeting, the person designated to summarise the meeting in report form generates a report memo. The original of the memo should be sent to the Credit file with a copy sent to each participant. The memo should be factual, objective, and not draw any subjective conclusions as to the outcome of negotiations.

As a result of conferences with the debtor and his analysis of information provided, the workout officer will have obtained new information which must be investigated and verified in order to fully understand the debtor's financial condition and the potential for repayment from liquidation or refinancing of the collateral. As the workout officer assesses certain key factors, and defines more clearly the particular problems, resolutions can then be developed.

Essentially, there are four options which can apply in a workout:

- Reinstatement of the loan.
- Restructure.
- Foreclosure.
- Negotiation of a deedinlieu of foreclosure.

As stated above, the workout officer must remain mindful of the bank's objectives and the debtor's concerns discussed above in developing his proposed resolution.

J. Settlement Agreements and Releases

If a bank and a borrower determine that the loan will be restructured, it is important that the parties focus on the lending relationship going forward and that any disputes which have arisen during the term of the loan be laid to rest. As a part of a bank's agreement to restructure a loan, the bank should require the borrower to release the bank from, and indemnify the bank against, all claims and causes of action which the borrower may have against the bank in relation to the loan arising prior to the time of the restructure.

To the extent that resolution of a problem loan involves the bank's foreclosure of its lien against property or a conveyance to the bank by deed in lieu of foreclosure, the borrower and any guarantors may have negotiated a release from all or a portion of personal liability in connection with the loan. To ensure that the borrower any guarantors do not interfere with the bank's exercise of its foreclosure rights, it may be appropriate to condition their releases on their not taking any such actions. Because the borrower's overall financial condition may be in jeopardy and there is the possibility of a bankruptcy filing by the borrower, it may also be appropriate to provide that the releases of the borrowers and any guarantors will not be effective in the event of a bankruptcy filing for a one-year or longer period following foreclosure to the extent that the foreclosure is set aside by a court of competent jurisdiction.

K. Multi-Creditor Loans and Relationships

There are several distinct types of multiple creditor loans. In the lending community the word 'participation' is often used generically to describe a multiple creditor loan. However, it is helpful to categorise the types of arrangements between creditors. Loan participations are those loans where the 'lead lender' sells a participation to one or more other creditors in the loan made by the lead lender to a borrower. A participation is evidenced by a participation agreement and a participation certificate executed by the participant and the lead lender. There is only one note and only one set of security documents. The participant's rights are contained in the participation agreement with the lead lender. A loan syndication, on the other hand, is an arrangement where each creditor has a direct-creditor relationship with the borrower. There are several types of syndications including agented credits, non-agented credits governed by an intercreditor agreement, and arrangements where each creditor has a separate agreement with the borrower. The problems encountered by the bank in the workout of a multiple creditor loan vary depending upon whether the bank is the lead lender, a participant or part of a bank group governed by an intercreditor agreement.

1. Considerations of lead lender or agent

Set forth below are some of the issues that should be considered by the lead lender or agent.

a. Documentation

The bank should carefully review the documentation which relates to the participation or the syndication. The participation agreement, agent's agreement or intercreditor agreement will spell out the duties and obligations of the lead lender in relation to the other creditors that are participants in the loan. A thorough understanding of the position of the lead lender or agent and its duties and obligations is necessary for the bank to proceed through the workout process. Under no circumstances should the bank take an action which is not authorised by the loan documents or the documents governing the multi-creditor relationship. The bank's failure to honour the contractual obligations in the agreements can subject the lead lender or agent to liability to the other creditors and the borrower.

b. Is the Participation Interest a Security?

If the participation interest is characterised as a security, the lead lender may have other responsibilities to the participants in relation to the loan. The note or the participation agreement may be a security under the Securities Act of 1933 or the Securities Exchange Act of 1934. If the participation interest is a security, the offer and sale of the security would be subject to the anti-fraud provisions of the applicable securities acts. Whether the participation interest in any given situation is a security depends upon many factors. Even if an exemption is relied upon, the bank must be sure to make full disclosure to the participants at all times during the administration and workout of the loan.

c. Conflicts of Interest

Generally, participations and syndications involve large lending relationships where the lead lender or agent has other loans to the borrower, guarantors, or affiliates of the borrower. Full disclosure of the lead lender's relationships is essential when the loan is sold or syndicated. If during the workout process it is discovered that there is or were conflicts or potential conflicts, they should be dealt with openly and fully disclosed. It is important to remember that when the loan becomes troubled the participants will likely not share a common view as to what the proper course of action may be to resolve the problems with the borrower. The various participants will have different financial resources, different guidelines for loan workouts, different regulatory pressures and different concerns relating to earnings and liquidity.

d. Regulatory Guidelines

There are certain regulatory guidelines with which the workout specialist should be familiar in this area. The Comptroller of the Currency, Banking Circular No. 181 (Revised 2 August 1981 and 1984) sets forth certain informational guidelines in relation to which the lead lender should supply information to the participant including (i) accrual status, (ii) status of principal and interest payments'. (iii) financial statements, collateral values and lien status, and (iv) factual information in relation to the borrower's credit standing. If these guidelines have been followed by the lead lender, it will be a better position when the loan becomes troubled.

If a loan was classified during the last examination, is in a nonaccrual status, is in default as to principal or interest or has been renegotiated or compromised due to the weakening financial condition of the borrower, the loan is a 'low quality' loan, and the purchase or sale of the loan may be considered to be unsafe and unsound. Care should be taken not to participate or syndicate a loan that has any of these characteristics without full disclosure.

Loan repurchase arrangements will require the lead lender to include the amount for which the lead lender is obligated to repurchase as a part of the lead lender's portion of the loan for loan limit purposes. Any obligation to repurchase (whether written or oral) will be treated as an extension of credit to the lead lender by the participant, and must be documented in writing and so reflected on the books and records of both creditors. Arrangements which provide that the participant's interest will be funded and paid back on a last-in-first out basis require the participant's interest to be added to the lead lender's portion of the loan for loan limit purposes.

The documentation between the creditors will not cover all of the issues that will face the lead lender or agent in the context of a workout of a troubled multi-creditor loan. Many of the issues which arise will require the creditors to resolve the practical business problems and make decisions that are beyond the scope or even the contemplation of the documents governing the rights and duties of the parties. The lead lender or agent must ensure that the decision-making process goes forward and that decisions are made by the requisite number of creditors (as provided in the documentation) in a timely manner. Often this will require great patience and negotiating ability.

2. Bank as a participant

There are a number of concerns that the bank must be aware of when it is a participant in a troubled loan. The first thing that the bank must determine is the legal relationship between the bank and the creditor that sold the bank its interest. Depending upon the documentation, the relationship between the lead lender and the participant may be: (a) tenants in common, (b) trustee-beneficiary, (c) partners, (d) credit-borrower, or (e) principal-agent. Generally, if the bank (as a participant) has purchased a partial or fractional interest in the loan, the bank will own the right to the bank's proportionate share of future payments of principal and interest. The insolvency of the lead lender should not affect the bank to the lead lender which is unsecured (most participations that are not sales are unsecured or, at least, the security interest is unperfected), the effect of the insolvency of the lead lender may be fatal to the bank's recovery.

With respect to a syndicated multi-creditor loan, if the bank holds its own note and is a party to each security agreement it should be well protected in the case of the lead lender's insolvency as the insolvent lead lender should have no legal interest in the bank's portion of the loan. The agent agreement or the intercreditor agreement should deal with the administration of the loan in the event of the agent's insolvency or the insolvency of one of the creditors.

If the bank is a party to a participant agreement, the provisions of which indicate that the arrangement is a sale, the position of the bank should be fairly safe. There are certain risks of which the bank should be aware, however, and which it should attempt to protect against, (a) including commingling the funds, (b) the note should either indicate the interest of the bank on its face or a third party should hold the note to avoid the risk of the lead lender transferring the note to a holder in due course, and (c) the participation agreement should be amended, if necessary, to allow continued administration of the loan in the event of the insolvency of the lead lender. If the bank is a party to a participation agreement that characterises the arrangement as a loan by the bank to the lead lender, then the bank should seek to accomplish one of the following, if at all possible: (a) an amendment of the participation agreement to recharacterise the loan as a sale, or (b) assurance that the participation agreement contains an enforceable security agreement and perfection of the security interest, if possible, under applicable law. If these steps cannot be accomplished, careful negotiation with the lead lender that leads to a reworking of the interecreditor relationship will be necessary.

IX. REMEDIAL ACTION BY BANKS

A. *Overview*

It is common for a troubled credit relationship to be transferred to the workout officer in a state of disarray. The workout officer is often faced with disorganised files, a fearful borrower/guarantor and no clear direction. The first step, then, in rehabilitating the relationship is to determine what the bank has in terms of collateral and outside sources of repayment and what the problems are. Clear understanding of the facts is an absolute necessity, for a clear and comprehensive understanding of the facts will dictate the plan of action. The workout officer should make no assumptions about the credit nor should he rely completely upon his predecessor's version of the facts. He must make his own complete investigation of the situation. Otherwise, he may develop a workout plan that blows up because it was predicated on unreliable information and incorrect assumptions.

The correct procedure for investigation revolves around creation of proper files which accurately reflect the credit relationship. In order to create proper files, the workout officer must necessarily

- gather all information from all sources in the bank and outside the bank including all existing credit files, working files, desk files and so forth,
- order or otherwise obtain unbiased information about the collateral and the feasibility of its providing all or part of debt service and ultimate repayment,
- organise this disparate information chronologically within subject matter (i.e. collateral, outside ability to pay),
- eliminate duplicates and organise notes on, scraps of paper,
- analyse the facts the file reflects as it is organised, and
- synthesise the facts into a plan.

Information and analysis obtained or performed by the workout officer which is subject to attorney–client privilege should be segregated.[90] If the

[90] The attorney–client privilege generally refers to the client's privilege to refuse to disclose and to prevent other parties from disclosing confidential communications which are made to facilitate the rendition of professional legal services. Communications between the client or the client's representative and the lawyer or the lawyer's representative which are confidential are protected. See *United States v Kovel*, 296 F.2d 918 (2d Cir. 1961) (if is necessary that the communication be confidential). Confidentiality requires an intention that the communication not be communicated to third parties. See *Dorothy K. Winston & Co. v. Town Heights Development, Inc.*, 376 F. Supp. 1214 (D.C. Dist. 1974) (the communication must be intended to be confidential). In some states the attorney–client privilege is given a strict construction because of its tendency to suppress the truth, see, e.g., *San Francisco v Superior Court of San Francisco*, 37 Cal. 2d 227, rehearing denied, 231 P.2d 26 (1951) (because of its tendency to suppress the truth, attorney–client privilege receives a strict construction), while in other states a more liberal construction is adopted on the theory that a client should be free to discuss all circumstances of a matter with his attorney without fear that his statements will later be used against him. See, e.g., *People v Shapiro*, 308 NY 453, 126 NE 2d 559 (1955) (court favored a liberal construction on the theory that one consulting a lawyer should be encouraged to communicate all the facts without fear that his statements may possibly be used against him in the future). The privilege belongs to the client, see *Radiant Burners, Inc. v American Gas Ass'n.*, 320 F.2d 314 (7th Cir. 1963), cert. denied, 375 US 929 (1963), and only the client may waive its right to the privilege, see *Baird v Koerner*, 279 F.2d 623 (9th Cir. 1960) (attorney cannot divulge information that was communicated to him in confidence until the protection afforded by the privilege has been properly waived by the client). In order to insure protection of the confidentiality of the relationship between the attorney and client, policies should be adopted which limit the scope of the parties, to whom information is disseminated and who are in attendance at meetings. The attorney work product protects, from the discovery process, the work produced and developed by an attorney, for his client, in anticipation of litigation. The 'work product' of an attorney in preparing for litigation includes the mental impressions, conclusions, opinions, and legal theories of the attorney or other representative of a party to the litigation, see Fed. R. Civ. P. 26(b)(3), and is reflected in such things as memoranda, statements, correspondence, interviews and briefs. See *Hickman v Taylor*, 329 US 495 (1947). The

workout officer has any doubts or concerns with respect to the nature of the information in the file, its sensitivity in the event of litigation or the applicability of the attorney–client privilege, the bank's counsel should be consulted for advice.

File gathering, organisation, culling and written analysis has the important side benefit of demonstrating to internal and external reviewers that workout officer has complete understanding of the credit relationship and a plan to rehabilitate or collect the loan or to realise on the collateral.

B. Credit File

Analysis of a troubled credit relationship is divided into two parts:

(a) the borrower's or guarantors capacity to service and amortise his debt from sources outside the asset(s) financed including the availability of additional collateral or financial support, and
(b) the assets' susceptibility to providing repayment of debt through sale or refinancing.

A properly constructed credit file will contain the information and analysis necessary to determine borrower/guarantor capacity to pay.

The credit file must first be organised by subdividing it into appropriate sections, eliminating duplicate information, identifying and finding missing information and filing each section in chronological order.

As various components of the file are built, the workout officer should study and make reading notes from analytical memos, correspondence, borrower/guarantor financial statements and cash flow with focus on the borrower/guarantors:

- sources of cash,
- required and optional uses of cash,
- unpledged liquid assets such as tradable securities,
- debt to other lenders and their collateral,
- unpledged liquidable assets such as seasoned income producing property, and
- unpledged cash flowing assets such as seasoned notes receivable, available second liens on cash flowing property or, much less desirable, interests in cash flowing partnerships.

work product doctrine encourages effective preparation for litigation consistent with the adversarial system, based on the theory that each side should prepare its case independently without unnecessary interference. Ibid., Particular litigation need not have actually been commenced in order for the doctrine to apply, but there must be some probability that particular litigation will occur. See *Diversified Industries, Inc. v Meredith*, 572 F.2d 596 (8th Cir. 1977) *en banc* (1978). The degree to which specific litigation must be contemplated, and the question of whether the work product doctrine protects documents which were generated other than in the case in which discovery is sought, varies from state to state.

Outdated or extraneous information should be noted and properly filed, but no time should be spent on in depth analysis.

Careful study and complete reading notes will facilitate analysis of the borrower/guarantor capacity to service the existing loan or any form of restructured loan.

C. *Project Files*

The second part of analysis of a troubled credit relationship comes from gaining thorough understanding and knowledge of the assets pledged. This is accomplished through collection, organisation, and analysis of material necessary to build a project file for each collateral asset.

The workout officer should gather from every source in the bank all information relating to each collateral asset including:

- the original loan underwriting memo,
- draw requests and certifications,
- appraisals and feasibility studies, if any, made in connection with initial underwriting,
- all subsequent appraisals and feasibility studies,
- inspection reports,
- all contracts and closing statements in connection with prior partial releases of for sale properties such as buildings, lots or homes,
- rent rolls on income producing collateral,
- all leases and lease summaries on income producing collateral,
- year to date and current month operating statements on income producing collateral,
- copies of service contracts such as janitoring, equipment, etc.,
- copies of all other third-party contracts, if any,
- all environmental studies and assessments, if any,
- all borrowing base reports and aging reports of accounts receivable,
- letters of credits,
- all correspondence to and from the borrower/guarantor(s) relating to the property, and
- all internally generated memoranda describing the property.

The workout officer should request and receive the desk files of his bank predecessor which files often contain items not found in official files. Any information listed above which is not in the bank's possession should be requested of the borrower in writing.

Concurrently, the workout officer should order: (i) a title report to identify any mechanic's or materialman's liens or other claims filed of record on the property; (ii) an ad valorem tax certificate from all applicable taxing authorities; and (iii) a certificate of insurance from the borrower if not already taxing authorities; and (iv) a UCC search in all applicable jurisdictions with respect to any personal property collateral. Environmental issues should be addressed at this point. The project file of each collateral asset should then be organised in the format outlined in Procedures. Extraneous and duplicate information should be discarded unless it contains an original signature.

Finally, the workout officer should order from a competent appraiser an updated appraisal of the collateral based on current market conditions and the current status of the collateral. The appraisal should be supplemented by a feasibility study which considers current market conditions. The appraisal gives guidance in determining correct accounting treatment of the loan. The feasibility study gives guidance in development of a plan of restructure.

As the project file is being constructed, the workout officer should analyse appropriate documents to give him knowledge of:

- status of completion,
- current market for the product offered,
- waste or mismanagement by the borrower,
- recent sales volume (for sale properties),
- recent leasing activity and current operating costs (income properties),
- current and near term identifiable cash flow produced by the property,
- claims of others on the property, and
- the value and salability of the property.

Again, careful study and complete reading notes will facilitate analysis of the situation.

D. Legal Files

The legal documentation of the loan should be in reasonably good order if closed by the bank's own legal staff or outside counsel. Any missing documentation such as recorded deeds of trust, mortgages, UCC financial statements, paid tax receipts or insurance certificates should be obtained by collateral cage personnel under the workout officer's oversight.

The legal documentation of loans not closed by the bank's attorneys may be incomplete. In such case, collateral cage personnel with the assistance of a paralegal (if necessary) should gather all missing documents, cure filing defects and organise the file.

The workout officer should carefully review the note, guaranties and loan agreement for business points to determine, for example, whether the guaranties are of payment and performance or only of collection, whether the guaranties are limited in any way, whether the construction loan agreement contains a provision requiring a borrower's deposit in certain circumstances and whether all loans are cross collateralised or cross defaulted. These and other points will become important leverage either to the bank or to the borrower in negotiations. The workout officer must know whether he is dealing from strength or weakness. Typical business deficiencies in loan documents include:

- No cross default or cross collateralisation;
- No right to approve leases;
- No borrower deposit requirement;
- No time limit on right to cure defaults;
- No penalty interest provision;
- Limitations on exercise of certain remedies;
- Inadequate insurance provisions;
- Inadequate restrictions on sale of personal property; and
- No lock box provisions relating to receivables.

Legal sufficiency of the loan documents should be reviewed by the bank's counsel. After review, counsel should report any significant deficiencies to the workout officer along with required remedial action and a cost estimate therefor.

Loan participations purchased present additional complexity. Often, the lead lender has virtually unlimited decision making powers in a workout effectively foreclosing the banks' legal right to participate meaningfully in negotiations with the debtor. The participation agreement may contain a buy-sell provision under which the bank could take out the lead lender or force being taken out itself, invariably at a loss. However, being taken out at a loss may be less costly than being an unwilling participant in oafish negotiations by an unskilled, or worse, financially weak lead lender. Also, the lead lender may be constrained in debtor negotiations by its obligations to the other participant(s).

Legal leverage and significant documentation deficiencies should be identified and analysed with the assistance of the bank's counsel.

E. Physical Inspection

Collateral assets should be personally inspected by the workout officer promptly upon his receipt of the case. The extent and nature of the physical inspection should be made only in accordance with the rights of the bank under the loan documents and applicable law. During inspection, particular attention should be paid to design, quality, maintenance, location, access, traffic, neighbourhood ambiance, evidence of competition such as 'for lease' and 'for sale' signs on surrounding properties and so forth. The workout officer should approach the collateral asset with the view of a tenant or buyer as the case may be. What about the property would encourage or discourage its lease or sale?

During inspection, the workout officer should be alert for signs of obvious construction defects, deferred maintenance or environmental hazards. If he suspects any, professional engineers should be engaged to make a thorough investigation and written report immediately.

F. Environmental Issues

Case law under the federal Comprehensive Environmental Response, Compensation and Liability Act ('CERCLA')[91] and comparable state statutes is developing toward the perceived deep pockets of lenders. For example, in *US v. Fleet Factors Corp.*,[92] the 11th Circuit Court of Appeals found that a secured lender may incur liability under CERCLA merely by participating in the financial management of a facility to a degree which would indicate that it had the capacity to influence the borrower's treatment and disposal of hazardous waste.

Thus, it is incumbent on the workout officer to become thoroughly knowledgeable of environmental procedures and pitfalls and to be aware of circumstances which could expose the bank to unlimited claims under environmental laws.

G. Special Issues in Construction Loans

It is often in the bank's best interest to retain the debtor's interest and cooperation at least through completion of construction since, if he is honest he can usually complete the project faster and cheaper. If the bank has lost confidence or the debtor has given up, the following issues must be addressed if the bank intends to complete the project.

- Contractor and subcontractor status.
- Legal access to plans and specifications in absence of debtor.
- Subcontractor liens and lien waivers.
- Defenses to mechanics liens.
- New permits in name of bank.
- Cost of construction delays.
- Feasibility of restriction of project scope.
- Preservation of payment and performance bonds.

[91] 42 USC §§9601-75 (1988 Supp. IV 1992).
[92] 901 F.2d 1550 (11th Cir. 1990), cert. denied, 498 US 1046 (1991).

X. CONCLUDING OBSERVATIONS

This chapter has explored the circumstances facing debtors and creditors in America in the grip of a national crisis of capital inadequacy. Although America had faced a relatively recent banking crisis in the mid 1970s, it paled in comparison to the recent distress. Loan underwriting became irrelevant. The absolute loss in value of many assets which served as collateral for bank loans was systemic and unavoidable by the debtors and creditors. This systemic loss is distinguished from the 'systemic' banking crises alluded to by many commentators as the risk of one bank's failure to the solvency of other banks in the banking system. Although the systemic crisis of capital adequacy in America did, in fact, pose bank-to-bank system risks, the issues presented were far more fundamental to overall American financial stability and bank solvency.

The American systemic crisis of capital adequacy was manifest where capital reposes, in assets; assets which collateralise loans, and which comprise the asset side of a banks' balance sheet, and which are the source of a bank's solvency and liquidity. Although the American crisis has been characterised as the consequence of regulatory and supervisory failure and management abuse, while true in part, such a characterisation obscures and begs the more fundamental questions regarding the source of the systemic problem and encourages a localised 'micro' response from government regulators, supervisors, examiners and bank managers.

This chapter has focused on the 'micro' manifestations to the problem, and outlines a small part of the context of the problem in America. Debtors and creditors as well as regulators in other jurisdictions such as Mexico, Latin America, Central and Eastern Europe and even Japan, who continue to categorise their banking and credit 'problem' as local and explainable by focusing blame and recrimination on obvious participants in an echo of the early foundations of insolvency law, must accept that the problems are not limited to America.

The world-wide systemic problem of capital adequacy and bank insolvency is not, fundamentally, a problem of bank mismanagement, fraud or crime, but represents a broad-based world-wide systemic problem of capital adequacy, whose roots predate the recent American crisis, and which has spread throughout both so-called 'developed economies' as well as emerging and transitional economies. As international pressure for 'transparency' in financial information disclosures as well as consistency and clarity in accounting rules and laws relating to banking, credit and security creation and enforcement increase, borrowers, bankers, accountants and lawyers in emerging economies will find the principles and strategies presented in this chapter to be of increasing relevance and importance.

Attention to the principles, practical issues and strategies presented in this chapter should be of benefit to debtors and creditors in other jurisdictions who now face the consequences of the global crisis of capital inadequacy.

Chapter 3

The Mexican Currency Crisis of 1995

Douglas Arner and Thomas Slover

I. INTRODUCTION

Capital provides the engine for growth in any economy, whether developing or developed, and is by its nature a scarce and costly resource, especially for developing countries where resources are short and financial systems evolving and fragile. For these reasons, developing countries such as Mexico acted to open their financial systems and seek out sources of foreign capital in the first half of the 1990s, in many cases as the result of policies directed by international financial institutions such as the International Monetary Fund (IMF) and the International Bank for Reconstruction and Development (World Bank), as well as by developed countries such as the United States, and regional processes such as the European Union and the North American Free Trade Agreement (NAFTA).

This quest for capital, however, may not be without its drawbacks, as has been demonstrated by Mexico's financial problems beginning in December 1994 and arguably continuing to the present. Mexico, considered a leader among the LDC (lesser developed country) world, had vigorously pursued just these sorts of policies and had in fact succeeded in encouraging large amounts of foreign capital to flow into its financial system. Due to external factors such as rising US interest rates, internal factors such as perceived political instability, and due to the growing mobility of international capital flows, Mexico's economy has been severely impacted by a significant liquidity crisis, subsequently termed the Mexican Peso Crisis of 1994–5.

In December 1994 Mexico's devaluation of the peso triggered a severe crisis in the country's financial system. The crisis created serious liquidity and solvency problems for the entire banking system, exposing its weak capital base and widespread portfolio problems. International financial markets reacted with panic, and investor confidence all but disappeared. The large inflows of capital that followed Mexico's economic liberalisation and accession to the NAFTA abruptly shifted outwards, prompting a massive rescue effort from the US, the IMF, and Mexican authorities.

Although the peso devaluation proved to be the catalyst that triggered the crisis, it was widespread instability in the banking sector that created the environment necessary for a crisis to occur and that, arguably, transformed what should have been an economic adjustment into a near financial collapse. The Mexican Peso Crisis caused havoc in the Mexican economy and also negatively impacted the domestic capital markets of many other emerging economies, especially in Latin America, but also throughout the entire world (popularly dubbed 'the Tequila Effect'). Due to perceptions of Mexico's leadership position among LDCs and due to US policy pressures, a massive international rescue practice was assembled in 1995 to help Mexico weather its liquidity crisis, to prevent contagion to other LDCs, and to stave off a potential debt crisis.

This chapter is divided into six main parts. Following this introduction, Part Two provides a legal and economic overview of the Mexican financial system. The first two sections of Part Two focus on the historical development of Mexico's banking system and the government's financial liberalisation under President Salinas's administration. The third and fourth sections present an overview of Mexico's financial system prior to the crisis and the impact of the NAFTA provisions on financial services.

Part Three describes the crisis of 1994–5. The first section under Part Three presents the background to the crisis. The second and third sections discuss several factors that analysts now view as the underlying causes of the banking crisis, paying particular attention to the macroeconomic policy decisions and political events in Mexico during 1994 leading up to the peso devaluation. The third, fourth, and fifth sections describe the immediate economic effects of the crisis on the banking system, internationally and the international rescue effort.

Part Four provides a detailed analysis of the Mexican government's reform initiatives in response to the crisis and the extent to which these initiatives have fostered financial soundness and stability in Mexico. The first section under Part Four discusses some of the most significant short-term government initiatives, such as fiscal austerity measures, liquidity assistance, the temporary capitalisation programme, and debtor-relief programmes. The second section describes several significant long-term structural reforms, such as the relaxation of foreign investment limitations under NAFTA, the facilitation of bank mergers and sales, and the establishment of peso futures markets. The third section explains some of the vast and far-reaching supervisory and regulatory reforms implemented, such as stricter lending standards, increased reporting and disclosure requirements, and proposed measures to amend the structure of the Mexican financial regulatory system.

Part Five consists of an assessment of Mexico's legal and economic reforms. The first two sections provide an analysis of some of the key successes of the new reforms and gives examples of recent positive developments. The third section discusses some of the deficiencies which remain in Mexico's financial system. Finally, Part Six concludes the chapter with a few comments regarding the future of Mexico's financial system.

II. HISTORIAL OVERVIEW OF MEXICO'S BANKING SYSTEM

The recent history of Mexico's banking system is one of turbulence. Mexico has experienced several financial crises since the mid-1970s, and on a number of occasions has been forced to seek financial assistance from the US and the IMF to help it manage such crises.

Following the nationalisation of the banking system in 1982 and the efforts of Mexico to reform its economy in the late 1980s and early 1990s, Mexico substantially reformed its domestic financial system. In 1990, constitutional amendments and new banking legislation[1] set the stage for the return of the commercial banking system to private hands, and between June 1991 and July 1992, all of the commercial banks were privatised, most of which became subsidiaries of newly established financial holding companies.[2] At the same time as the new privatised banking regime was set in place, deposit lending rates, reserve requirements, requirements to lend to specific sectors, and other limitations on bank lending activities were significantly deregulated.[3]

A. *The 1982 Crisis and Nationalisation*

The last major financial crisis prior to 1994 began in 1982 when Mexico announced that its foreign exchange reserves had run out and that, without financial assistance, it would be forced to default on US$80 billion in

[1] The Credit Institutions Law (*Ley de Instituciones de Crédito*) was introduced in July 1990 and has been amended on a number of occasions. It replaced an earlier law that was drafted to govern the activities of the banks nationalised in 1982. Together with the Financial Groups Law (*Ley para Regular las Agrupaciones Financieras*), it established the basis for the conglomerate banking model in effect in Mexico today. The Credit Institutions Law was intended to provide an appropriate legal framework for the capital structure, activities and supervision of the reprivatised banking system as well as for the activities of state-owned development banks. Roy A. Karaoglan and Mike Lubrano, 'Mexico's Banks After the December 1994 Devaluation—A Chronology of the Government's Response', 16 *NW. J. Int'l L. and Bus.* 24 (1995), at 25.

[2] Ibid.

[3] In July 1993 amendments to the Credit Institutions Law and Financial Groups Law were approved which weakened the restrictions on the types of services which could be provided by banks and other financial entities. New regulations were also issued governing the treatment of newly introduced financial instruments, securities activities of banks, and the establishment of independent credit bureaux. Ibid. at 28.

mainly dollar-denominated foreign debt obligations to US and other foreign banks.[4] The US and IMF arranged a US$4.55 billion rescue package which entailed a substantial rescheduling of Mexico's debt obligations.[5]

Soon after the crisis began, President Lopez Portillo nationalised all but two of Mexico's sixty private commercial banks, imposed exchange controls, and initiated a series of consolidations which continued until only eighteen commercial banks remained.[6] In addition, the Mexican congress amended its constitution to provide that all banking and financial services activities were to be the exclusive domain of the government.[7]

During this period of state ownership of the commercial banks, Mexico was severely 'underbanked'.[8] The government's control of the banking system resulted in crowding out credit to the private sector as banks' investment portfolios shifted toward government securities and loans were made to state-controlled enterprises rather than to private sector entities.[9]

State ownership had several other adverse effects on Mexico's banking system. An immediate problem was that the commercial banks lost many experienced officers who strongly disapproved of the nationalisation and subsequently resigned their posts rather than accept the government as their employer.[10] Those bank officers who remained, or who were acquired to fill the vacancies created by the departing officers, did not receive proper training in the credit business since only a small fraction of loanable funds were channelled to the private sector.

Additionally, since the principal borrower was the government, a sovereign entity, the risk evaluation function was practically ignored during this period.[11] Excluded from the capital markets, the Mexican banking system stagnated, and credit growth reached its lowest rate in years. Further,

[4] *See* Nora Lustig, 'Mexico in Crisis, the US to the Rescue: The Financial Assistance Packages of 1982 and 1995', 2 UCLA J. Int'l L. and Foreign Aff. 25, 31 (1997); *see also* United States General Accounting Office, *GAO Report: Mexico's Financial Crisis: Origins, Assistance, and Initial Efforts to Recover* (GAO/GGD-96–56, 23 Feb. 1996) (hereinafter '*Mexico's Financial Crisis*').

[5] The debt obligations were repeatedly rescheduled throughout the 1980s until eventually the remaining debt was converted into bonds under the Brady Initiative. *See* Rory Macmillan, 'The Next Sovereign Debt Crisis', 31 Stan. J. Int'l L. 305 (1995).

[6] *See* Sri-Ram Ayer, *Anatomy of Mexico's Banking System Following the Peso Crisis*, World Bank Sector Report (1996); *see also* Carlos M. Nalda, 'NAFTA, Foreign Investment and the Mexican Banking System', 26 Geo. Wash. J. Int'l L. and Econ. 379, 386 (1992).

[7] *See* Nalda, above note 6, at 386.

[8] *See* Roy A. Karaoglan and Mike Lubrano, 'Mexico's Banks After the December 1994 Devaluation—A Chronology of the Government's Response', 16 N.W. J. Int'l L. and Bus. 24, 25 (1995).

[9] Eventually, nearly 100 per cent of bank credit was directly or indirectly allocated by the government.

[10] *See* Miguel Mancera, *Problems of Bank Soundness: Mexico's Recent Experience, in* BANKING SOUNDNESS AND MONETARY POLICY, International Monetary Fund (Jan. 1997).

[11] Ibid. at 229.

Mexico's insulation from foreign bank competition created an environment of lax complacency. Internal controls received little attention and bankers failed to develop disclosure and informational systems in pace with their counterparts from other world banking systems. In such an environment, there was little incentive for either the public servants administering the commercial banks or the supervisory authorities to worry much about loan portfolio risk.

B. *Privatisation and Liberalisation Under the Salinas Administration*

Since 1988, the Mexican financial system has undergone deep structural changes. During the first days of 1989, President Carlos Salinas de Gotari initiated comprehensive reforms in an effort to promote sustained economic growth while controlling excessive inflation, which stood at an annual rate of 160 per cent.[12]

A central aspect of the government's plan was the privatisation of the state-owned Mexican banks and the encouragement of limited foreign investment in the banking system. The government hoped that foreign investment in the banks would encourage the transfer of technology and the modernisation of the banking system and thus allow the banking system to reverse the decline in productivity experienced during the 1980s.

Bank privatisation and financial liberalisation began in earnest in 1990. Among the legal reforms made were the liberalisation of deposit and lending rates, elimination of the mandatory requirement for commercial banks to hold long-term government paper to maturity, and the elimination of reserve requirements.[13] By the end of 1992, all of Mexico's eighteen state-owned banks had been reprivatised.[14] Twelve of the eighteen banks were purchased by holding companies, which were dominated by brokerage houses and which generally have a higher risk tolerance than banks.[15] Moreover, many of the new bank purchasers were far from seasoned bankers and they generally paid higher than average prices in order to acquire the banks.

[12] *See* John H. Chun, 'Post-Modern Sovereign Debt Crisis: Did Mexico Need an International Bankruptcy Forum?', 64 Fordham L. Rev. 2647, 2654 (1996).

[13] *See* Ayer, above note 6.

[14] The privatisation of the banking system was far more successful than originally anticipated. The first eight banks, representing 56 per cent of Mexico's nationalised bank assets, sold for a total of US$7.68 billion at an average of 3.12 times their book value. Several reasons explain the high prices paid for the banks, including industrial growth, profit potential, and the desire to secure a place in the growing Mexican market. By the time the privatisation process was completed in 1992, Mexico had garnered a total of US$12.4 billion. *See* Ayer, above note 18; *see also* Nalda, above note 6, at note 106.

[15] *See* Stephen L. Fluckiger, 'The Mexican Banking Crisis: Remedies and Opportunities', 50 Consumer Fin. L.Q. Rep. 76 (1996).

In addition to the privatisation of the state-owned banks, Mexico instituted numerous changes in the legal framework governing the financial sector. These structural changes were designed to encourage increased competition in financial services from foreign institutions, but at a gradual rate so that domestically controlled financial institutions could have time to adjust by adopting new technologies, internal infrastructure, and services.

In 1990, Congress enacted the Law for the Regulation of Financial Groups.[16] This statute allowed conglomerate banking whereby a single holding company could carry out separate commercial banking, brokerage, and other financial services activities.[17] Unfortunately, the legislation lacked important prudential requirements.[18]

Congress simultaneously enacted the Law of Credit Institutions[19] which allowed majority private sector ownership of commercial banks. The statute created a legal framework for the capital structure and operations of the banking system, under which investors could acquire one or more of three different types of stock in Mexican banks dependent upon the investor's status.[20] The statute also dictated the maximum levels of foreign investment allowed for Mexico's domestically controlled financial institutions.[21]

C. *Mexico's Financial Regulatory System*

The Mexican financial regulatory system is a purely national system. Accordingly, all of the authorities which are involved in the supervision and regulation of banking activities are part of the federal government. Authority for regulating the activities of banks in Mexico is shared among the Banco de Mexico,[22] the Ministry of Finance and Public Credit, and the National Banking and Securities Commission ('CNBV').[23] The Ministry of

[16] Ley Para Regular las Agrupaciones Financieras, D.O. 18 July, 1990.

[17] *See* Miguel Angel Garza, 'The Mexican Financial System: Toward a German Universal Banking Model? A Comparative Analysis', NAFTA L. Rev., Autumn 1997, at 46.

[18] Such prudential requirements might include: producing consolidated financial statements, following credit exposure rules, and other practices designed to limit a holding company's exposure to the insolvency of one of its entities.

[19] Ley de Instituciones de Credito, D.O. 22 July, 1994.

[20] *See* Nalda, above note 6.

[21] The law limited foreign ownership of a single bank's capital stock to 5 per cent, but allowed up to 10 per cent ownership with government approval and under certain conditions. These limitations were later amended to comply with the provisions under Chapter 14 of the NAFTA Treaty. *See* Ayer, above note 6.

[22] In June 1993 the Mexican Constitution was amended to grant the Banco de Mexico greater autonomy and more clearly define its functions as those relating to conduct of monetary policy and supervision of the payments system and foreign exchanges markets. *See* Karaoglan and Lubrano, above note 8, at 28.

[23] The CNBV was created in May 1995 through a merger of the National Banking Commission (CNB) and the National Securities Commission (CNV).

Finance is considered the head of the financial sector and is the only authority with legal powers to interpret financial laws.[24] Other principal functions of the Ministry of Finance include: determining the composition of capital in all banking corporations and providing the legal basis to calculate the specific amounts of money available for loans and to diversify the risks in all active operations of credit institutions.[25]

The CNBV's mandate is to perform the supervisory, remedial, and regulatory functions concerning the operation of all financial entities.[26] Under its supervisory authority, the CNBV conducts liquidity and solvency examinations to evaluate the possible risks to which banks may be subject. The CNBV also conducts periodic bank inspections and establishes operative programmes to reduce existing irregularities that may affect the liquidity and solvency in banking corporations.[27]

The CNBV may impose monetary penalties against banking corporations and, in cases of serious or repeated violations, may issue a decree for the suspension of the financial entity's charter.[28] Additionally, the CNBV may recommend that bank managers and directors be removed from office and may operate as administrative receiver of the institution.

Since April 1994, the Banco de Mexico has been an autonomous entity responsible for the country's monetary and price stability policies.[29] The Banco de Mexico also serves as the depository, lending institution, and clearing house regulator for credit institutions.[30] The Banco de Mexico is further authorised to impose sanctions against financial intermediaries, including civil monetary penalties and suspension of operations in foreign currencies, gold, and silver.[31]

Beyond the primary supervisory authorities, the Law of Credit Institutions established the Banking Fund for Savings Support (*Fondo Bancario para Proteccion de Ahorro*, or 'FOBAPROA') and defined the legal basis for its provision of 'preventative support' to troubled banks.[32]

FOBAPROA's role went beyond simple deposit insurance. FOBAPROA had broad powers to extend preventative support to banks to permit them to meet their obligations, securing such support through a pledge of shares of the commercial bank recipient or its financial holding company. Under amendments approved in February 1995, FOBAPROA was further

24 *See* Garza, above note 17, at 50.

25 *See* Jose D. Guerra-Sanchez, *Overview of the Regulation of Banks in Mexico* (1996) <http://www.natlaw.com/pubs/spmxbk2.htm>.

26 Ibid. 27 Ibid. 28 Ibid.

29 Ley del Banco de Mexico, D.O. 23 Dec., 1993, arts. 1–2.

30 Ley de Instituciones de Credito, D.O. 22 July, 1994, art. 122.

31 Ley del Banco de Mexico, arts. 24, 29, 32.

32 *See* Karaoglan and Lubrano, above note 8, at 30. Pursuant to legislation passed in December of 1998, FOBAPROA was dismantled and replaced by a more formal deposit protection fund, 'IPAB'.

empowered to exercise the voting rights of shares that have been pledged to it, take majority control of the bank or financial group, replace management, write down the bank's capital in accordance with the results of a full audit, and sell the bank if amounts extended as preventative support were not repaid or if serious undercapitalisation or irregularities were discovered.[33]

Although steps to improve banking supervision were taken at the time of the privatisation of the commercial banks, efforts to fully equip the CNBV to supervise the new system began only in 1994.[34] As such, one of the principal goals of the new system was to facilitate the effective supervision of financial groups on a consolidated basis by placing the supervisors of Mexico's brokerage houses under the same roof as the supervisors of their banking affiliates. While a basic framework for implementing new policies and procedures for bank inspections had been put in place by the CNBV, there was not sufficient time before the onset of the Peso Crisis to prepare an adequate number of trained and experienced inspectors to be fully effective.[35]

Not surprisingly, once privatised, banks competed fiercely to gain market share in the provision of loans, both by increasing the volumes of their existing lines of business and by entering the markets for relatively new financial services, such as home mortgages and credit cards.[36] Unable to attract conventional deposits fast enough to support new lending,[37] many banks increased their reliance on interbank funding, the bulk of which consisted of lines of credit from foreign banks.[38] A rapid expansion of lending to private enterprises usually takes place at the cost of a drop-off in portfolio quality, and the development of the Mexican banking system was

[33] The flexibility accorded FOBAPROA under the Law of Credit Institutions permitted it to function as the instrument for a number of the Mexican government's responses to the effects of the peso crisis on the banking sector. *See* Douglas W. Arner, 'The Mexican Peso Crisis: Implications for the Regulation of Financial Markets', NAFTA L. Rev., Autumn 1996, at 2.

[34] Ibid.

[35] Ibid. at 29–30.

[36] Between 1991 and 1994, aggregate assets of the commercial banks increased by 111.3 per cent in nominal terms (64.6 per cent in real terms), equivalent to a real annual growth of 18.1 per cent. In 1994, assets of the commercial banking system averaged new pesos (N$) 735bn, equivalent to 58.8 per cent of GDP, compared to 42.5 per cent in 1991. Ibid. at 25–26.

[37] Although deposit mobilisation improved significantly after privatisation, with the ratio of average deposits to GDP increasing from 21.4 per cent in 1991 to 31.3 per cent in 1994, the rate of growth of loan portfolios outstripped that of deposits. The ratio of loans to deposits increased steadily from 94.1 per cent at the end of 1991 to 113.8 per cent in 1993, and to 124.0 per cent in 1994. Ibid. at 26.

[38] Interbank credit lines increased from the equivalent of N$34bn at the end of 1991 (of which N$23bn were denominated in foreign currency) to N$124bn at the end of 1994 (of which the equivalent of N$92bn (US$17.3bn) were denominated in foreign currency). Ibid. at 26.

not an exception.[39] Notwithstanding the shortfall in banks provisions,[40] the banks' capital adequacy ratios improved during the period 1991–4, as the financial authorities instituted a phased increase in the minimum required ratio of net capital to risk-weighted assets, from 6 per cent at the end of 1991 to 7 per cent by the end of 1992, and then to 8 per cent by the end of 1993.[41]

D. *NAFTA Provisions on Financial Services*

Mexico's pre-crisis financial reforms culminated in 1994 with the enactment of the North American Free Trade Agreement (NAFTA)[42] between Mexico, the United States, and Canada. Under the agreement, Mexico agreed to allow US and Canadian financial institutions to provide financial services through the establishment of subsidiaries or affiliates in Mexico.[43] Mexico further agreed to provide both 'national treatment'[44] and 'most-favored-nation treatment'[45] to cross border financial service providers and investors from other NAFTA countries.

Financial services are governed principally by Chapter 14 of NAFTA.[46]

[39] Aggregate past due loans of commercial banks (excluding Banco Union and Banco Cremi, both of which were already subject to intervention at this time) accounted for 4.09 per cent of gross loans at the end of 1991, increased to 7.25 per cent by the end of 1993. During the first half of 1994, the ratio increased to 8.30 per cent, before decreasing to 7.33 per cent by year end, largely due to a 27 per cent increase in gross loans during the second half of 1994. Ibid. at 26–7. Note that in analysing the Mexican banking system, it is important to keep in mind that until 1997, Mexican banks prepared their financial statements under Mexican Generally Accepted Accounting Principles (Mexican GAAP) and that these differred in a number of important respects from US GAAP, including the definition and treatment of non-performing loans, of provisions, and of the accrual of interest on loans. Ibid. at n. 4.

[40] Aggregate loan-loss provisions more than doubled from nearly N\$5.0bn at the end of 1991 to more than N\$13.0bn by the end of 1993; however, the ratio of provisions to past due loans actually decreased from 50.8 per cent to 42.7 per cent during the two-year interval, before rebounding somewhat to 47.9 per cent by the end of 1994. Ibid. at 27.

[41] The average ratio actually increased from 7.73. per cent at the end of 1991 to 9.94 per cent in 1993, to 10.27 per cent at the end of Sept. 1994, before decreasing to 9.60 per cent by the end of 1994. Ibid. at 27–28, citing CNBV data.

[42] North American Free Trade Agreement, 17 Dec. 1993, US-Can.-Mex., ***available in*** WESTLAW, NAFTA file (hereinafter 'NAFTA').

[43] In order to facilitate the control of monetary policy by the Banco de Mexico, the Mexican government chose not to allow foreign banks to establish branches. *See* Garza, above note 17, at 53–54.

[44] National treatment requires each NAFTA party to treat another party's financial institutions and investors no less favorably than domestic financial institutions and investors. *See* PAUL, HASTINGS, JANOFSKY AND WALKER, NORTH AMERICAN FREE TRADE AGREEMENT 68 (1993).

[45] Most-favoured-nation treatment requires each NAFTA party to treat another party's financial services providers and investors no less favorably than financial services providers and investors from any other country. Ibid.

[46] For an excellent analysis of the financial services provisions under NAFTA, *see* NAFTA AND BEYOND: A NEW FRAMEWORK FOR DOING BUSINESS IN THE AMERICAS (Joseph Norton and Thomas Bloodworth, eds. 1995).

Chapter 14 requires each party to permit individuals and companies from the other NAFTA countries to establish financial institutions in its territory and to expand the operations of such institutions throughout its territory.[47] To be eligible for the benefits under Chapter 14, the foreign institution or investor must already be engaged in the business of providing financial services.[48]

The agreement, however, also provided Mexico with several significant reservations. Section B of Annex VII (Schedule of Mexico) imposed capital limits during the six-year transition period following the effective date of the agreement.[49] There are two types of capital limits: individual limits for each foreign-owned institution and aggregate limits for all foreign-owned institutions of the same type.[50] The capital limits apply only during the transition period, with some exceptions.[51] The original capital limit for individual institutions began at 1.5 per cent.[52] The aggregate industry capital limit began originally at 8 per cent.[53] Both of these limits were to increase yearly throughout the transition period until the year 2000, at which point all limits would expire.[54]

The agreement further opened Mexico to foreign investment and bolstered foreign investor confidence because investors perceived that with the signing of the NAFTA, Mexico's long-term prospects for stable economic development were likely to improve.[55]

III. THE MEXICAN PESO CRISIS OF 1994–95

The evidence suggests that the causes of the Peso Crisis can be found in the interplay of a number of complex financial, economic, and political factors that developed in the period prior to December 1994.[56] According to an

47 NAFTA art. 1403.

48 NAFTA art. 1403(5).

49 NAFTA Annex VII(B)(1)-(7)-Mex. The six-year transition period ended on 1 Jan. 2000.

50 NAFTA Annex VII(B)(2), (5) and (6)-Mex.

51 NAFTA Annex VII(B)(1), (9) and (C)(Definitions)-Mex.

52 NAFTA Annex VII(B)(2)-Mex.

53 NAFTA Annex VII(B)(5)-Mex.

54 The agreement included a further safeguard provision permiting Mexico, under certain conditions, to freeze for three years the aggregate capital limits.

55 For further analysis of the NAFTA provisions and implications, *see generally* Judith H. Bello, Alan F. Holmer, and Joseph J. Norton (eds.), *The North American Free Trade Agreement: A New Frontier in International Trade and Investment in the Americas* (1994).

56 *See generally* William A. Lovett, 'Lessons from the Recent Peso Crisis in Mexico', 4 *Tul. J. Int'l and Comp. L.* 143 (1996); Edwin M. Truman, 'The Mexican Peso Crisis: Implications for International Finance', 82 *Fed. Res. Bull.* 199 (Mar. 1996); Magda Kornis, 'The Peso Crisis Revisited', 5:4 *Mex. Trade and L. Rep.* 14 (Apr. 1, 1995); ibid., 'Financial Crisis in Mexico', 5:2 *Mex. Trade and L. Rep.* 5 (Feb. 1, 1995). *See also* GAO, 'Mexico's Financial Crisis', below note 57.

analysis by the US General Accounting Office (GAO),[57] Mexico's financial crisis originated in the growing inconsistency in 1994 between Mexico's monetary and fiscal policies and its exchange rate system. Due in part to an upcoming presidential election, Mexican authorities were reluctant to take actions in the spring and summer of 1994, such as raising interest rates or devaluing the peso, that could have reduced these inconsistencies. These fundamental policy inconsistencies were exacerbated by the Mexican government's response to several economic and political events that created investor concerns about the likelihood of a currency devaluation and generally reduced investor confidence in the political and economic stability of Mexico. In response to these investor concerns, the Mexican government issued large amounts of short-term, dollar-indexed notes (*tesobonos*), so that by the end of November 1994,[58] Mexico had become particularly vulnerable to a financial market crisis because its foreign exchange reserves had fallen to US$12.9 billion,[59] while it had *tesobono* obligations of US$28.7 billion maturing in 1995.[60]

A. *The Origins of the Mexican Peso Crisis*

In a broad sense, policy decisions that Mexican financial authorities took in 1994 need to be considered in the context of Mexico's recent financial and economic history. From the mid-1970s through the late 1980s, Mexico was caught in a destructive cycle of inflation and currency devaluations that seriously set back the country's economic development and eventually culminated in the nationalisation of the Mexican banking system in 1982. Further, prior to the 1994 Peso Crisis, Mexico had experienced several financial crises since 1976 and on a number of occasions had received US financial assistance to assist it in dealing with such crises as well as with other difficulties. Prior to 1994, Mexico's last major financial crisis

[57] As a result of the US commitments resulting from the Peso Crisis, the US General Accounting Office (GAO) prepared a comprehensive report on Mexico's 1994–5 financial crisis at the request of the Chairman of the House Committee on Banking and Financial Services, James A. Leach. *See* United States General Accounting Office, GAO Report: 'Mexico's Financial Crisis: Origins, Assistance, and Initial Efforts to Recover' (GAO/GGD-96–56, 23 Feb. 1996) [hereinafter 'Mexico's Financial Crisis']. In preparing the report, the GAO interviewed all major particpants from all entities involved, as well as significant private participants, and reviewed substantially every available piece of information regarding its mandate.

[58] During October and November, high-level US officials cautioned Mexican officials that the peso seemed overvalued and indicated that it was risky to continue the existing exchange rate policy. US officials, however, were undecided about the extent to which the peso was overvalued and if and when financial markets might force Mexico to take action. Moreover, Federal Reserve and Treasury officials apparently did not foresee the magnitude of the crisis that eventually unfolded. *See* 'Mexico's Financial Crisis', above note 57, at 77–109.

[59] 'Evolution of the Mexican Peso Crisis', above note 56, at 56.

[60] Ibid. at 61, Table I.3.

occurred in 1982, when Mexico was unable to meet its obligations to service US$80 billion in mainly dollar-denominated debt obligations to US and foreign banks.[61]

By the late 1980s, however, Mexico had largely resolved its debt crisis and was able to resume economic growth, although it continued to rely to a great extent on foreign investment to finance such growth. Since 1988, Mexico has instituted comprehensive reforms in an effort to make its economy more open, efficient, and competitive, and has sought to address both domestic and international restrictions that limited its economic growth. Most importantly, to attract foreign capital, the Mexican government undertook major structural reforms in the early 1990s designed to make its economy more open to foreign investment. These reforms included privatising many state-owned enterprises, removing trade barriers, removing restrictions on foreign investment, and reducing inflation and government spending. Finally, in 1994, Mexico became the twenty-fifth member of the Organisation for Economic Cooperation and Development (OECD), thereby apparently signalling its full membership in the world economy and its position as a leader in the LDC world.[62]

The flow of capital to and from Mexico between 1983 and 1994 serves to illustrate the effect of its various actions on the perceptions of investors, both foreign and domestic.[63] Between 1983 and 1989, Mexico experienced net capital outflows of US$15 billion, reflecting the impact of the 1982 Debt Crisis, but this reversed to net inflows of US$102 billion between 1990 and 1994, signalling the perceived effectiveness of its domestic and international actions. The importance of Mexico in terms of its position as a leader among LDCs can be seen from its significance in world capital flows: in 1993, Mexico received US$31 billion of capital inflows—accounting for 20 per cent of net capital flows to all LDCs.

As this evidence suggests, at the beginning of 1994, Mexico was experiencing a boom in foreign investment, related in part to investors' perceptions that Mexico's economy was fundamentally strong, and further bolstered by the approval of NAFTA.[64] A substantial part of the financial

[61] *See* 'Mexico's Financial Crisis', above note 57, at 29–31. *See generally* Stephany Griffith-Jones and Osvaldo Sunkel, *Debt and Development Crises in Latin America: The End of an Illusion* (1986), and sources cited, above note 5.

[62] Mexico was formally invited to become a member of the OECD on 14 Apr. 1994. *See* Christian Schricke, 'Mexico, 25th Member of the OECD', 188 *OECD Observer* 4 (June 1994) (analysing the accession process).

[63] Domestic flows take the form of flight capital, which flows out of and back into an economy such as Mexico with remarkable speed. For an interesting analysis of the magnitude of flight capital in Latin America and other emerging economies, *See generally* Rudy Naylor, *Hot Money and the Politics of Debt* (1994).

[64] For an analysis of capital flows to Mexico in the period preceding Dec. 1994, *see* José Angel Gurría, 'Capital Flows: The Mexican Case', in Ricardo Ffrench-Davis and Stephany Griffith-Jones, *Coping with Capital Surges: The Return of Finance to Latin America* (1995).

inflow, however, was in the form of equity and debt portfolio investments that could be withdrawn quickly, especially as the result of declines in investor confidence.

B. Banking Fragility and Unsustainable Economic Expansion

The NAFTA agreement, and the financial liberalisation which preceded it, sparked significant foreign investment in the banking sector. With a rapidly expanding population of almost 90 million people, most of whom were under-banked and under-leveraged, Mexico's consumer market presented an attractive opportunity for the highly developed retail banking industries of the Untied States and Canada.[65] The period immediately following the agreement's effective date on January 1, 1994 saw exceptionally high growth.[66]

Not surprisingly, once privatised, Mexican banks competed fiercely to gain market share in the provision of loans, both by increasing the volumes of their existing lines of business and by venturing into relatively new financial services, such as home mortgages and credit cards.[67] The consolidation of public finances shifted banks' lending behaviour away from financing the government and toward riskier lending to the private sector. As banks were privatised, their risk evaluation staffs, either brand new or inherited from the period when the government owned the banks, were ill-prepared to operate in this new environment.[68] As a result of both macroeconomic stabilisation and financial liberalisation, a financial deepening occurred in which the availability of domestic loanable funds increased significantly for Mexican banks.

Naturally, the newly available funds found many eager takers in the private sector. Between 1988 and 1994, the ratio of bank credit to the private sector increased from 13.4 per cent of GDP at year-end 1988 to 50.7 per cent in 1994.[69] Private sector demand for bank credit was strong for several reasons, including:

[65] *See* Nalda, above note 6, at 397.

[66] By 17 Oct. 1994, the Finance Ministry had approved fifty-four applications from foreign financial services firms to operate in Mexico. *See* Fluckiger, above note 15, at 77.

[67] As a consequence, between 1991 and 1994, aggregate assets of the commercial banks increased by 111.3 per cent in nominal terms, or by 64.6 per cent in real terms, equivalent to a real annual growth rate of 18.1 per cent. In 1994, assets of the commercial banking system averaged N$735 billion, equivalent to 58.8 per cent of GDP, compared to 42.5 per cent for 1991. The bank's loan portfolios grew at an even higher rate than their assets. From year-end 1991 to year-end 1994, aggregate gross loans (excluding discounted loans) increased by 142.9 per cent in nominal terms, or by 89.2 per cent in real terms, equivalent to an annual real growth rate of 23.7 per cent (more than eight times the rate of GDP growth during the period). *See* Karaoglan and Lubrano, above note 8, at 25.

[68] *See* Banco de Mexico, *The Mexican Economy 1996*, IV(2)(a) (1996) <http://www.banixco.org.mx/public_html/doyai/mexecon96/mexecon.html> (hereinafter '*The Mexican Economy 1996*').

[69] *See* Mancera, above note 10, at 229.

1. Favourable expectations of Mexican economic performance;
2. The need to modernise and expand Mexico's industrial plant in light of increased competition resulting from a more open economy;
3. The appalling housing shortage;
4. Higher perceived permanent income;
5. Consumers wishing to replace obsolete stocks of durable goods; and
6. The need to finance the acquisition of public enterprises being privatised.[70]

To a certain extent, the greater availability of credit and the increased private sector consumption of that credit were viewed favourably; they were the intended results of Mexico's financial liberalisation policies. However, improved expectations about the future course of the economy caused inexperienced bank credit officials and bank managers to confuse good and bad credit risks.[71] In such an environment, too many borrowers seemed to have profitable projects and reasonably good prospects for servicing their debts. Moreover, borrowers who had forgotten how to use credit prudently, or who had never had any prior experience in paying debts, often failed to practice caution.

Several developments accompanied the expansion of credit to the private sector. First, the structure of credits shifted conspicuously toward financing consumer and mortgage credit. Mortgage and consumer credit is riskier than a business loan because legal proceedings to recover the collateral in the case of default are particularly cumbersome, often rendering the collateral of little use. Additionally, credits denominated in dollars—which are subject to exchange rate risk—grew rapidly until 1992 when the central bank imposed restrictions on the increase of foreign currency liabilities of commercial banks.[72] Overall, the imprudent expansion of lending to the private sector led to a significant drop-off in portfolio quality.[73]

The 'crawling peg' exchange rate system[74], although effective in controlling Mexico's high inflation, contributed to the current account deficit by overvaluing the peso and thereby artificially increasing the price of Mexican exports and reducing the price of imports.[75] Mexican imports exploded

[70] *See* Mancera, above note 10, at 230.

[71] *See The Mexican Economy 1996*, above note 68, at IV(2)(a).

[72] *See* Mancera, above note 10, at 230.

[73] Aggregate past due loans of commercial banks grew from 4.09 per cent of gross loans at the end of 1991 to 7.25 per cent of gross loans at the end of 1993. *See* Karaoglan and Lubrano, above note 8, at 26.

[74] Under a 'crawling peg' exchange rate system, the domestic currency is pegged to a foreign currency, such as the US dollar, at a fixed rate, but the rate is allowed to fluctuate within a narrow band. This band can be adjusted periodically to accommodate upward or downward trends in the exchange rate. It is through these periodic adjustments that the peg 'crawls'.

[75] *See* Chun, above note 12, at 2656.

from 1987 to 1994 while exports grew more slowly during this period.[76] Real GDP growth in Mexico was modest, averaging only 2.7 per cent a year in the early 1990s.[77]

These trends in Mexico were perceived as manageable since the system had sufficient flexibility in interest rates and the exchange rate band to manage macroeconomic imbalances. To subsidise its current account deficit, Mexico relied on portfolio investors to purchase short-term, peso-denominated treasury notes, called '*cetes*'. Cognisant of the volatility created by the short-term nature of the *cetes*, the government nevertheless hoped that Mexico's continued attractiveness to foreign investors would prevent capital flight. The government fully anticipated that exports would expand as Mexico's competitiveness and productivity improved, and that this would lead to a reduction in the current account deficit and a decrease in the dependence on foreign capital.

Moreover, the Salinas administration needed to present an image of stability to international investors and to the US Congress during the NAFTA negotiations. The US Congress had not yet embraced the prospect of entering into a trade agreement with Mexico and there was already mounting opposition to the agreement from the Senate and House Democrats. Any attempt to correct the current account deficit and shrinking foreign exchange reserves with a substantial peso devaluation before completing the NAFTA negotiations (or prior to the vote in Congress) would likely have resulted in an economic recession and could have easily derailed the negotiations and jeopardised the progress achieved during the previous five years. Those were risks that the government was unwilling to take.

The Mexican banking system was still in its infancy just a few years after privatisation. Accordingly, banks were relatively fragile and were beginning to show signs of weakness toward the end of 1993. The supply of capital was becoming increasingly insufficient due to the relatively high level of past due loans that had not been adequately provisioned. Moreover, some commercial banks were operating with serious problems, which were not readily noticeable from the information disclosed to financial authorities.[78] In such a fragile state, the banking system was ill-prepared for the macroeconomic and political events which unfolded in 1994.

[76] The Mexican trade balance deteriorated from an export surplus of US$8.4 billion in 1987, to a deficit of US$0.7 billion in 1989, and reached US$–20 billion in 1992 and US$–18.5 billion deficit in 1994. At the same time, Mexico's current account balance declined from a US$4.0 billion surplus in 1987 to a US$–4.0 billion deficit in 1989, getting much worse with a US$–22.8 billion deficit in 1992, and a US$28.8 billion deficit in 1994. As a share of Mexican GDP, the current account deficit was 1 per cent of GDP in 1987, 0.9 per cent of GDP in 1989, –4.1 per cent in 1992, and –5.2 per cent in 1994. *See* William A. Lovett, 'Lessons From the Recent Peso Crisis in Mexico', 4 Tul. J. Int'l and Comp. L. 143, 152 (1996).

[77] *See* Ayer, above note 6, at 5.

[78] *See* Mancera, above note 10, at 231.

C. *The Events of 1994*

Sadly, Mexico suffered a series of unfortunate political and economic shocks in 1994 that forced investors to reconsider their investments and also endangered the sustainability of Mexico's spending policies.

The first significant drop in investor confidence in Mexico in 1994 and the related drop in Mexican foreign currency reserves occurred following an armed uprising of Indian rebels that broke out on 1 January 1994 in the Chiapas region. The uprising was timed to coincide with the effective date of the NAFTA treaty and was a significant blow to Mexico's image as a stable and mostly conflict-free modernising country seeking to join the developed world.[79] Then on 23 March 1994, Mexico's image was again tarnished by the assassination of presidential candidate Louis Donaldo Colosio. On the day after the assassination, the Mexican Stock Exchange fell by 22 points. Additionally, Mexico experienced large losses in foreign exchange reserves due to investors' increasing fears of political turmoil in Mexico.[80] In response, the government allowed the peso to depreciate approximately 1 per cent against the dollar, combining with a 7 per cent devaluation that had taken place in the month preceding the assassination.[81] As well, Banco de México (Mexico's central bank) increased domestic interest rates on short-term (91-day), peso-denominated Mexican government notes (*cetes*) in an attempt to stem the outflow of capital.

In spite of higher interest rates, investor demand for *cetes* continued to lag, and investors were demanding higher interest rates on new issues because of their perception that the peso would eventually be subject to a relatively large devaluation. Options available to the Mexican government at this time included: (i) offering even higher interest rates on *cetes*; (ii) reducing government expenditures to reduce domestic demand, decrease imports, and relieve pressure on the peso; or (iii) devaluing the peso.[82] From the perspective of the Mexican authorities, the first two options were unattractive in a presidential election year because they could have led to a significant downturn in economic activity and could have further weakened Mexico's banking system. The third option, devaluation, was also unattractive since Mexico's success in attracting foreign investment depended significantly on its commitment to maintaining a stable exchange rate, both from the standpoint of perceptions of international investors and in order to continue to reduce the rate of inflation, especially since a stable exchange rate had been an essential ingredient of long-standing agreements between

[79] *See*, *Mexico's Financial Crisis*, above note 57, at 49.

[80] By 22 Apr. barely a month after the assassination, foreign reserves had declined by US$10.8 billion. Ibid. at 52.

[81] *See* 'Mexico's Financial Crisis', above note 57, at 51–60.

[82] Ibid., at 60–6.

labour, government, and business, with the perception being that these agreements were necessary to ensure continuing domestic stability.

Rather than adopt any of these options, the government chose, in the spring of 1994, to increase its issuance of *tesobonos*. Since *tesobonos* were dollar-indexed, the government reasoned that *tesobonos* would be more attractive to foreign investors because foreign exchange risk would effectively transferred from investors to the Mexican government.[83]

As *tesobono* sales rose, however, Mexico's vulnerability to a financial market crisis increased because many *tesobono* purchasers were portfolio investors who were very sensitive to changes in interest rates and risks. Further, *tesobonos* had short maturities, increasing the threat of changes in perceptions because investors might not roll them over if investors perceived either an increased risk of a Mexican government default or higher returns elsewhere. While this was not necessarily the best choice in hindsight, Mexico's foreign exchange reserves did in fact stabilise at a level of about US$17.7 billion for a period of about four months.[84]

By the middle of 1994, Mexico was entering into another expansionary stage and there was an evident need for measures to reduce the current account deficit. However, with Zedillo trailing in the polls only three months before the presidential election, the government ruled out a substantial devaluation in the peso as too disruptive.[85] Indeed, the government exacerbated the problem by pumping credit into the economy through government development bank lending. Finally, the government ruled out any significant increases in interest rates because it was fearful that higher interest rates could severely impact a banking system that had already been weakened by the growing volume of past-due loans.

The government's failure to respond adequately to the current account deficit was based in part on the assumption that, once the August presidential elections had concluded successfully, the stabilisation of the political situation would calm the markets, causing capital inflows to resume and allowing the government a greater opportunity to engineer a smoother adjustment.

Following the election, however, foreign investment flows did not recover to the extent expected by Mexican authorities, in part because peso interest rates were allowed to decline in August and were maintained at that level until December.[86] During the autumn of 1994, it became increasingly

[83] Between January and November 1994, *tesobonos* rose from 6.4 per cent to 70.2 per cent of total foreign investment in Mexican government securities. *See* Ibid., at 60–6, esp. Table 2.12 (citing data from Banco de México).

[84] Ibid.; *see also* 'Evolution of the Mexican Peso Crisis', above note 56, at 54–6.

[85] The peso had already depreciated 10 per cent since March. *See* Lovett, above note 74, at 154.

[86] 'Mexico's Financial Crisis', above note 57, at 66–73.

clear to some officials in Mexico, the US, and the IMF, that Mexico's mix of monetary, fiscal and exchange policies needed to be adjusted; however, no action was taken.[87] The current account deficit worsened during the year, partly as a result of the strengthening of the economy related to a moderate loosening of fiscal policy, in turn motivating a step up in domestic lending.[88] Further, imports had surged as the peso became increasingly overvalued, and Mexico had become heavily exposed to a run on its foreign exchange reserves as a result of substantial *tesobono* financing.[89] Moreover, US interest rates became increasingly attractive during this period, thereby diverting capital flows away from Mexico.[90]

In November of 1994, Mexican authorities had to draw down foreign currency reserves in order to meet demands for dollars, at least partially in response to further increases in US interest rates.[91] In late November and early December, renewed fighting in Chiapas and an unfolding scandal surrounding the September 1994 assassination of PRI Secretary General Francisco Ruiz Massieu renewed apprehensions among investors regarding Mexico's political stability, which were compounded further with the release of government figures in December projecting a higher current account deficit, but without an announcement of any alteration of exchange rate policy.[92] These factors led to a further loss of confidence among investors, increased redemptions of Mexican securities, and resulted in a significant drop in foreign exchange reserves, to approximately US$10 billion.[93] At the same time, Mexican government officials continued to assure investors that the peso would not be devalued even though Mexico's outstanding *tesobono* obligations had reached US$30 billion.[94]

On 20 December, Mexican authorities sought to relieve pressure on the exchange rate by announcing a widening of the peso/dollar exchange rate band, effectively devaluing the peso by approximately 15 per cent. The government, however, did not announce any new fiscal or monetary measures to accompany the devaluation.[95] This combination resulted in an

[87] *See generally* ibid. at 76–109. Overall, the GAO's analysis suggests that the US knew of Mexico's problems, but did not think the outcome would be so severe, while IMF simply did not have sufficient information to gauge the extent of the problem or its possible impact. Ibid.

[88] *See* 'Mexico's Financial Crisis', above note 57, at 66–73.

[89] Outstanding *tesobono* obligations increased from US$3.1bn at the end of Mar. to US$29.2bn in Dec. 'Evolution of the Mexican Peso Crisis', above note 56, at 60–2.

[90] Between Jan. 1994 and Nov. 1994, US 3-month Treasury bill yields rose from 3.04 per cent to 5.45 per cent. 'Mexico's Financial Crisis', above note 57, at 56.

[91] On 15 Nov., the Fed raised the federal funds rate by ¾ of a per centage point. Ibid.

[92] 'Mexico's Financial Crisis', above note 57, at 66–73.

[93] 'Evolution of the Mexican Peso Crisis', above note 56, at 57, Table I.8. Interestingly, most of the pressure during this period came from the funds of Mexican nationals leaving the country.

[94] 'Mexico's Financial Crisis', above note 57, at 66–73.

[95] An example would have been an increase in interest rates.

additional loss of US$4 billion in foreign reserves on 20–21 December, forcing the Mexican government to freely float its currency on 22 December. The discrepancy between the stated exchange rate policy of the Mexican government throughout most of 1994 and its devaluation of the peso on 20 December, along with its failure to announce any appropriate economic policy measures, significantly reduced investor confidence in the newly elected government and increased fears that default was imminent.

Events after the devaluation did not lead international investors to conclude that Mexico was stable, either. To the contrary, investors' scepticism regarding Mexico's financial future grew in light of the Mexican government's apparent unwillingness raise interest rates to market levels. Perception became reality as investors, concerned that Mexico would not be able to finance its short-term debt, refused to roll over their maturing *tesabonos*.[96] Because its reserves had fallen to such a low level, the government was no longer able to meet the redemption demands of all the bondholders. These events pushed an already weak banking system toward insolvency. Consequently, downward pressure on the peso continued, and by early January 1995, investors realised that *tesobono* redemptions could soon exhaust Mexico's reserves and, in the absence of external assistance, that Mexico might default on its dollar-indexed and dollar-denominated debt. This pressure was exacerbated by the fact that information beginning to emerge on Mexico indicated that its reserves were lower than had generally been believed.[97] The Mexican Peso Crisis of 1994–95 was now full-blown, and at this point, Mexico was forced to turn to international sources for assistance.

D. The Effects of the Peso Devaluation on the Banking System

According to Banco de México officials, the fragile state of Mexican commercial banks during 1994 presented a serious challenge to financial authorities' ability to use monetary policy to decrease the current account deficit that eventually necessitated the devaluation and the international rescue package.[98] Beyond its impact on attempts to prevent the crisis, the Mexican financial system was severely impacted by the crisis. According to the IMF, overall net capital outflows totalled more than US$11.5 billion in the first quarter of 1995. As an example, the Bolsa index declined sharply

[96] Sixteen billion dollars worth of *tesabonos* were due to mature in early 1995 and payment obligations on *tesabonos* for the entire year exceeded reserves by US$23 billion. *See* Chun, above note 12, at 2659.

[97] Ibid. Mexico had not announced its declines in reserves in November until after the devaluation of the peso in Dec. 'Evolution of the Mexican Peso Crisis', above note 56, at 56.

[98] 'Mexico's Financial Crisis', above note 16, at 40–9.

in the wake of the devaluation, falling 39 per cent in nominal peso terms from the end of 1994 to February 27, 1995.[99]

After the devaluation, Mexican banks came under pressure in a number of ways.[100] First, many banks faced an immediate dollar liquidity problem in January because pesos continued to be converted to dollars, and foreign lenders were reluctant to roll over their dollar claims on Mexican banks in significant volume.[101] Secondly, the banks' capitalisation levels were negatively impacted by their dollar-based obligations as the peso continued to decline against the dollar.[102] Third, banks' asset quality suffered as the per centage of non-performing loans continued to rise[103] and portfolio values continued to fall[104] in the face of dramatically rising Mexican interest rates.

[99] During this period, the peso declined 32 per cent against the dollar, reaching a low of 7.45 to the dollar—53 per cent below its devaluation level. Ibid. at 63.

[100] *See* 'Mexico's Financial Crisis', above note 57, at 143–6.

[101] At the end of 1994, aggregate deposits with the commercial banks (excluding Union and Cremi) totalled N$413.9bn, of which 18.3 per cent was denominated in foreign currency and 73.6 per cent consisted of time deposits. As a result of the Peso Crisis, the banks came under significant liquidity pressure as they found it extremely difficult to roll over maturing CDs, and during the first three months of 1995, aggregate foreign currency-denominated deposits with the commercial banks (including Union and Cremi) decreased by 23 per cent, or by more than US$3.5bn, to stand at the end of Mar. 1995 at US$11.8bn, equivalent to 15.8 per cent of total deposits. Although the liquidity assistance provided by FOBAPROA to the commercial banks, amounting to US$3.3bn during the first quarter of 1995, significantly improved the banks' liquidity position, the liquidity crunch still had significant adverse effects on the banks' average cost of funds, and hence, on their profitability during the first half of 1995. Karaoglan and Lubrano, above note 8, at 32.

[102] Although under prevailing regulatory guidelines, banks are required to limit their foreign currency liabilities to no more than 20 per cent of total liabilities, and their open short or long foreign currency positions to no more than 15 per cent of net capital, for the system as a whole, fourth quarter foreign exchange losses totalled about N$4.6bn, equivalent to more than 10 per cent of equity. Ibid. at 31.

[103] As previously described, the high rate of growth of Mexico's banking system in the period after privatisation was accompanied by an increase in the level of non-performing loans. As a result of loan-loss provisions due to this increase, combined with the foreign exchange losses, the impairment in the values of securities portfolios, and the unrealised losses from the banks' subsidiaries, the banking system (excluding Union and Cremi) recorded an aggregate loss before tax of N$3.5bn during the fourth quarter of 1994, equivalent to 43 per cent of profits (before tax) during the first three quarters of the year, and to 7.9 per cent of the equity at year end. Ibid. at 33.

These effects were further accentuated by the increase of interest rates on consumer debt, mortgages and commercial credit to above 80 per cent during the months immediately following the devaluation, before falling to 30–40 per cent by late spring. Ibid.

[104] The banks' aggregate investment portfolio increased by about 84 per cent in 1994 to reach a level of N$85.9bn at the end of the year. The bulk of these investments consisted of fixed income securities (N$55.8bn), whose value was impaired by the sharp hike in interest rates. In the aftermath of the devaluation, the CNBV issued in January 1995 a new regulation requiring banks to value their securities at market prices and to disclose their unrealised gains or losses on their financial assets and liabilities in their off-balance sheet accounts as of the end of 1994. Including Banamex (Mexico's largest bank and the only bank to show realised losses on its securities portfolio), the losses (both realised and unrealised) amounted to N$660mn, equivalent to 1.5 per cent of the system's equity at year end. Ibid. at 31–32.

The overall result of these effects was a significant drop in bank capitalisation, with the average ratio of net capital to risk-weighted assets of the nineteen major Mexican commercial banks decreasing from 9.40 per cent to 7.75 per cent.[105]

In the first quarter of 1995, interest rates on home mortgages, consumer credit, and commercial credit rose to over 80 per cent per annum.[106] Furthermore, the December devaluation of the peso and the further depreciations in subsequent months, along with the higher interest and inflation rates[107], the over-indebtedness of households and companies, and economic recession, made it much more difficult for debtors to make their debt service payments.[108] This brought about further increases in banks' past-due portfolios and significant declines in their capitalisation ratios.

E. The Tequila Effect

By the end of the first week of January, it became clear to the Mexican Secretary of Finance that the situation was much more grave than first anticipated. News that some of the Mexican banks were unable to renew their certificates of deposit held by foreigners triggered another wave of flight from the peso. The peso continued to slide. Investors panicked, not only those in the Mexican stock market and debt instruments, but also investors in similar instruments issued by borrowers from countries in the same part of the world or perceived to be in similar circumstances. Thus began the so-called 'tequila effect'. The tequila effect was induced by two types of factors. First, as perceived risks rose and expected returns fell, individual investors were persuaded to divest. Secondly, institutional holders, such as mutual funds faced with actual or threatened redemptions, were led to liquefy their holdings not only of Mexican paper but also of the paper of other countries, especially if they could do so while limiting their capital losses.[109]

Stock market indexes for emerging markets compiled by the International Finance Corporation (IFC) showed that markets in Argentina and Brazil in particular suffered heavy trading losses immediately after the

[105] In fact, at the end of Feb. 1995, nine of the nineteen banks had ratios below 8 per cent as compared to only 3 per cent at the end of 1994. Ibid. at 34, citing CNBV data. The figures exclude Cremi, Union, Banpaís, and Oriente, all of which were then intervened or controlled by FOBAPROA.

[106] However, in the second quarter after the devaluation, interest rate growth subsided and nominal rates declined to approximately 35 per cent. Ibid.

[107] The inflation rate between Dec. 1994 and Dec. 1995 was 51.97 per cent. *See The Mexican Economy 1996*, above note 68, at Part I.

[108] Ibid.

[109] *See* Edwin M. Truman, *The Risks and Implications of External Financial Shocks: Lessons from Mexico* 10 (Board of Governors of the Federal Reserve System No. 535, 1996).

Peso Crisis.[110] Once the international assistance package was announced[111] and the initial reaction subsided, investors began to discriminate significantly against countries such as Argentina and Brazil which were viewed as having the same general characteristics that afflicted Mexico; namely: (i) low savings rates, (ii) large current account deficits, (iii) weak banking systems, and (iv) significant volumes of short-term debt. While the overall international efforts were significant in reducing the ultimate contagion effect, the resulting lessons taught by international investors are instructive for LDC policies.

F. The US/IMF Rescue

A few days after the devaluation, the governments of Mexico and the US realised that the source of the instability was the Mexican debt profile. Mexico took action by seeking a financial assistance package from the US to help stave off the liquidity crisis.[112] Although Mexico had sufficient incoming oil revenue to honour the random repayment demands of its bondholders, it did not have sufficient resources at hand to redeem all of the maturing bonds from the panicking multitude of bondholders.[113] This prompted the arrangement of an US$18 billion rescue package, announced on 2 January 1995.

Authorities presumed at the time that such a large assistance package would calm the market since it covered the outstanding *tesabonos* held by foreign investors coming due in 1995.[114] However, the rescue package was too small to cover the bank certificates of deposit and other short-term obligations coming due in 1995. Through simple arithmetic calculations, investors estimated that, assuming no investors were willing to roll-over their investments, the US$50 billion in public and private short-term debt obligations coming due in 1995 was far greater than the resources available.[115]

In an attempt to bridge the immediate crisis and prevent a total economic collapse of the Mexican economy, Clinton announced on 12 January 1995

[110] 'Mexico's Financial Crisis', above note 57, at 112–13, Tables 4.1–4.2. *See* 'Evolution of the Mexican Peso Crisis', above note 56, at 64–9.

[111] *See* above, section II.C.

[112] *See* Lustig, above note 4, at 53.

[113] *See* Chun, above note 12, at 2659.

[114] Mexican authorities assumed (or rather hoped) that a large portion of the certificates of deposit would be rolled over. This assumption, however, was not shared by investors. *See* Lustig, above note 4, at 54.

[115] International reserves in the Bank of Mexico were approximately US$6 billion and the rescue package was US$18 billion. Thus, the rescue package plus the international reserves would have barely covered half of Mexico's US$50 billion in financial obligations for 1995. Ibid.

a proposal to extend a new and larger rescue package of US$40 billion to Mexico in loan guarantees.[116] The package was slated for quick congressional approval, with endorsements from congressional leaders from both parties, the Federal Reserve, and Wall Street.[117] However, the bailout quickly drew controversy. Opposition grew rapidly as populist Democrats, alarmed at the prospect of further US job losses and shrinking US exports after the peso devaluation, and isolationist Republicans, unsympathetic to NAFTA and Mexico, attached numerous conditions to the approval of the bailout.[118] Others questioned details and demanded a more complete accounting for the bailout and stronger guarantees for repayment.[119] Approval of a bill that would be acceptable to both the US Congress and the Mexican government became increasingly unlikely. Investors reacted to this development with another wave of capital flight.

Still determined to prevent the collapse of the Mexican economy, Clinton announced on 1 February 1995 that he would use executive authority to provide Mexico with a new emergency bailout package totaling more than US$50 billion. Under the package, the US pledged up to US$20 billion in US Treasury emergency stabilisation funds ('ESF').[120] As part of the amount, the Fed agreed to provide up to US$6 billion in short-term swaps from its pre-existing swap line, and the Treasury agreed to provide backing for the Fed swaps as part of the ESF programme by assuring repayment of

116 *See* Lustig, above note 4, at 56.

117 *See* Lovett, above note 56, at 155.

118 *See* Lustig, above note 4, at 56.

119 Tim Carrington and Jackie Calmes, *US Rescue Plan for Mexico Prompts Conditions from Both Liberals, Conservatives in Congress*, Wall St. J., 19 Jan. 1995.

120 US–Mexico Framework Agreement for Mexican Economic Stabilisation, 21 Feb. 1995, Art. III [hereinafter Framework Agreement]. *See* 'Mexico's Financial Crisis', above note 57, at 118–23 and Appendix I, 148–52 (discussing the use of the ESF and Federal Reserve resources). Congress established the ESF in 1934 pursuant to section 10 of the Gold Reserve Act of 1934 'for the purpose of stabilising the exchange value of the dollar'. 31 USC s. 5302. Since its passage, the statute has been amended to broaden its purpose from the stabilisation of the dollar to include the promotion of orderly exchange arrangements and a stable system of exchange rates. *See* House Rep. No. 94–1284, 94th Cong. 2d Sess., 13–14 (1976).

Although Congressional approval is not required for US Treasury emergency stabilisation funds, the legality of the use of the ESF for this purpose was questioned by many. *See, e.g.*, Russell D. Covey, 'Note: Adventures in the Zone of Twilight: Separation of Powers and National Economic Security in the Mexican Bailout', 105 *Yale L. J.* 1311 (1996); James D. Humphrey II, 'Student Note: Foreign Affairs Powers and 'The First Crisis of the 21st Century': Congressional vs. Executive Authority and the Stabilisation Plan for Mexico', 17 *Mich. J. Int'l L.* 181 (1995). The Treasury and the Department of Justice, however, provided legal opinions stating that the requisite legal authority was in fact present. *See* letter from Edward S. Knight, General Counsel of the Department of the Treasury, to Robert E. Rubin, Secretary of the Treasury, 21 Feb. 1995; and memorandum from Walter Dellinger, Assistant Attorney General of the US Department of Justice, to Edward S. Knight, General Counsel of the Department of the Treasury, 2 Mar. 1995 (both on file with the authors). Not surprisingly, the GAO agreed. 'Mexico's Financial Crisis', above note 57, at 114–17.

any short-term drawings that were counted against the US$20 billion limit.[121]

Specifically, US assistance was offered through three mechanisms:[122] (i) short-term currency swaps for up to 90 days, with renewals for a maximum term of 1 year for Treasury swaps and renewals up to three times for Fed swaps; (ii) medium-term currency swaps for up to 5 years; and (iii) securities guarantees under which ESF funds could be used to back up securities issued by the Mexican government for up to 10 years. Under this package, Mexico effectively pays the same interest rates that other countries pay for short-term currency swaps[123] and other longer-term lending.[124] Further, as part of the package, Mexico agreed to abide by certain economic criteria,[125] and the US and Mexico entered into an oil agreement to ensure that in the event of a default by Mexico, the US would be repaid through earnings from Mexico's oil exports.[126]

The second largest component of the assistance package for Mexico came from the IMF. The IMF pledged up to US$17.8 billion[127] in financial

[121] Framework Agreement, above note 120, Art. III. *See* 'Mexico's Financial Crisis', above note 57, at 118–23.

[122] To put the US assistance package into place, the US and Mexico entered into four financial agreements: (i) the Framework Agreement, above note 120; (ii) the Oil Proceeds Facility Agreement, Framework Agreement, above note 120, Annex A [hereinafter Oil Agreement]; (iii) the Medium-Term Exchange Stabilisation Agreement, 21 Feb. 1996; and (iv) the Guarantee Agreement Dated as of February 21, 1995 among The United States Department of the Treasury, and The Government of the United Mexican States, 21 Feb. 1995.

For an analysis of the package, *See* Patricia A. Wertman, 'Peso Crisis: The Mexican Support Package: A Survey and Analysis' [Part I], 5:8 *Mex. Trade and L. Rep.* 19 (Aug. 1, 1995) (analysing the structure of the rescue package and public policy issues related to US involvement); ibid., 'Peso Crisis: The Mexican Support Package: A Survey and Analysis' [Part II], 5:9 *Mex. Trade and L. Rep.* 9 (1 Sept. 1995) (analysing protections for US taxpayers and Mexico's use of the package).

Note that in fact Mexico has made use of this package and that in fact the US has made a profit on its commitments. *See* 'Mexico's Financial Crisis', above note 57, at 136–9.

[123] *See* 'Mexico's Financial Crisis', above note 57, at 123–7. For example, as of the end of October 1995, this rate was 5.25 per cent.

[124] Ibid. For example, Mexico was charged 9.2 per cent in July 1995 for its longer-term borrowings.

[125] Framework Agreement, above note 120, Arts. V, VI. *See also* Framework Agreement, Annex B, Letter to Michel Camdessus, Managing Director, International Monetary Fund from Guillermo Ortiz Martinez, Secretary of Finance and Public Credit of Mexico and Miguel Mancera Aguayo, Governor, Bank of Mexico, and Mexico—Memorandum of Economic Policies; Annex C, Economic Policy Memorandum; and Annex D, Public Availability of Government and Bank of Mexico Statistical Information.

[126] Oil Agreement, above note 122. Under this mechanism, all of Mexico's foreign oil revenues flow through an acount at the Federal Reseve Bank of New York. While these revenues probably would not be sufficient on a daily basis to cover a major default, their existence makes the likelihood of eventual repayment far more likely. *See* 'Mexico's Financial Crisis', above note 57, at 123–7.

[127] IMF, 'Camdessus to Recommend that IMF Commit an Additional $10 billion for Mexico, Raising its Total Commitment to $17.8 billion', *IMF News Brief* No. 95/5, Jan. 31, 1995. The IMF actually approved assistance for Mexico for up to special drawing rights (SDR) 12.07bn. The

assistance in the form of a standby arrangement for Mexico to be disbursed over a period of 18 months.

As part of the terms and conditions of the international rescue package, the government of Mexico released a new economic plan on 9 March 1995, to address the required economic criteria provided in the agreements with the US and the IMF.[128] Overall, the goals of the plan were to restore financial stability, strengthen public finances and the banking sector, regain confidence, and reinforce the groundwork for long-term sustainable growth. In general terms, the plan addresses monetary policy, exchange rate policy, fiscal policy, banking policy,[129] incomes and social policy, and improved transparency[130]—all consistent with IMF conditionality.[131] The announcement of the new rescue package, followed by Mexican government's announcement of its new economic programme, was successful in halting the peso's nose-dive and stabilising the markets.

The new package, however, received its share of criticism as well. At the IMF, many parties were shocked by the size of the IMF contribution.[132] The IMF contribution was nearly seven times larger than Mexico's quota[133] and three and a one-half times more than the IMF had ever lent in its history.[134] Opponents further cautioned that excessive lending would create moral hazard and establish lending precedents that the IMF could not meet in the future.

SDR is the international reserve asset created and used by the IMF to denominate all its accounts. It is comprised of a basket of five currencies, of which the US dollar is the most significant.

[128] *See* 'Mexico's Financial Crisis', above note 57, at 128–31, 133–6; Patricia A. Wertman, 'Economic Recovery: Mexico's 1995 Economic Programme and the IMF', 5:6 *Mex. Trade and L. Rep.* 4 (June 1, 1995); ibid., 'Peso Crisis: Mexico's 1995 Economic Programme and the IMF', 5:3 *Mex. Trade and L. Rep.* 7 (1 Mar. 1995). Mexico actually proposed an initial economic plan in January 1995; however, without the international rescue package in place, it was largely ignored.

[129] The World Bank, the Inter-American Development Bank (IADB), and other sources agreed to provide up to US$3bn to strengthen Mexican banks.

[130] The plan included a promise by Mexico that information on foreign currency reserves and domestic credit conditions should be announced on a weekly basis. Such disclosure was also mandated by the Framework Agreement, above note 120, Annex D, above note 122. Presumably, this will be consistent with new IMF disclosure policies. *See* below, section IV.

[131] Framework Agreement, above note 120, Annex B, above note 122. *See* 'Mexico's Financial Crisis', above note 57, at 133–6.

[132] *See* George Graham *et al.*, *Bitter Legacy of Battle to Bail Out Mexico*, *Financial Times*, 16 Feb. 1995, at 4; *See* also Chun, above note 12, at 2662.

[133] Quotas are the contributions of IMF members to its General Resources Account. In 1995, access rules to the General Resources Account allowed a country to borrow 100 per cent of its quota with cumulative limit of 300 per cent. Mexico's quota was about US$2.6 billion and, thus, the IMF loan was nearly an unprecedented 700 per cent times greater than Mexico's quota. *See* Daniel Bradlow, *The International Monetary Fund: Overview of its Structure and Functions*, *in* INTERNATIONAL BORROWING: NEGOTIATING AND STRUCTURING INTERNATIONAL DEBT TRANSACTIONS 399 (Daniel D. Bradlow ed. 2nd edn 1986).

[134] *See* Banco de Mexico, *The Mexican Economy 1997*, III(1)(b) (1997) <http://www.banixco.org.mx/public_html/doyai/mexecon97/mexecon.html> (hereinafter '*The Mexican Economy 1997*').

The criticism in the US Congress was even louder. Members of Congress were outraged that the Clinton Administration had circumvented congressional approval for such a large financial rescue package. Many representatives questioned the wisdom of bailing out Mexico, a country with a 'long and painful past of undisciplined financial mismanagement'.[135]

The US and international response to the Peso Crisis was one of the largest multilateral economic assistance packages ever extended to any one country. The objectives, then, of the US and IMF assistance packages, following the December devaluation and the subsequent loss of confidence in the peso, were twofold: first, to help Mexico overcome its short-term liquidity crisis, and secondly, to limit the adverse effects of the Mexican crisis spreading to the economies of other emerging market nations and perhaps beyond.[136] Along the same lines, the stated purpose of the US assistance package was 'to assist Mexico in stabilising its exchange and financial markets by providing resources to be used in such manner as to facilitate the redemption, refinancing or restructuring of Mexico's short-term debt obligations [. . .]'.[137] Some observers opposed any US financial assistance to Mexico, arguing that investors should not be shielded from financial losses, and that neither the danger posed by the spread of Mexico's crisis to other nations nor the risk to US trade, employment, and immigration were sufficient to justify the assistance.[138] As can be seen by the US response, US officials disagreed.

IV. THE MEXICAN RESPONSE

Following the peso devaluation, the government of Mexico has taken several measures designed to assist the banking sector deal with the problems associated with Mexico's financial difficulties. Several of these were initiated unilaterally by Mexico, while others were undertaken with the direct support of the international financial community.[139]

A. Domestic Regulatory Measures in Response to the Impact of the Crisis

Since the onset of the crisis, the Mexican government has undertaken a number of important actions designed to assure adequate capitalisation of

[135] *See US and International Response to the Mexican Financial Crisis: Hearings Before the US House Comm. on Banking and Financial Services*, 104th Cong., 1st Sess. 215, 215–17 (1995) (statements by Representatives Bob Barr and Carolyn B. Maloney).
[136] 'Mexico's Financial Crisis', above note 57, at 110–14.
[137] Framework, above note 120.
[138] *See* 'Mexico's Financial Crisis', above note 57, at 117–18.
[139] *See* Ibid.

financial institutions and continued public confidence in the banking system.[140] The goal throughout has been to avoid a banking crisis that would exacerbate the contraction in the real economy and to set the stage for a recovery of the financial system based on sound institutions and efficient financial markets. Similar to the probable situation in future liquidity crises in most developing countries, the rapid devaluation of the peso and its after-effects hit a relatively new banking system which was still undergoing a process of maturation, with both the banks and the supervisory authorities working to improve their institutional capacity in order to be effective in their new environment.

The different schemes to support the banking system and indebted bank clients were developed with the following principles in mind:

1. Prevent systemic risk;
2. Protect the legitimate interests of depositors and other bank creditors;
3. Help debtors strained by the macroeconomic crisis;
4. Resist pressures to bail out the stockholders of financial institutions;
5. Avoid expansion of the central bank's credit;
6. Minimise the fiscal costs of the crisis management;
7. Interfere as little as possible with the normal functioning of the markets;
8. Minimise incentives which can lead to moral hazard problems; and
9. Implement simple and transparent programmes which foster confidence.[141]

The steps taken included amendments to the legal framework for foreign ownership of banks, reinforcement of supervision, programmes for recapitalising troubled banks, the introduction of inflation-indexed lending and the provision of indexed funding to banks, a debtor relief programme, and direct intervention to those banks that proved unable to weather the crisis and its after-effects. Further, Mexican officials received technical assistance from several international organisations, including the World Bank, to help strengthen their supervisory capability, and also received a US$1.7-billion loan to recapitalise the deposit insurance fund of FOBAPROA, thereby allowing it to purchase assets and resolve failing institutions more effectively.

The government responded to the banks' immediate needs for liquidity following the devaluation with the establishment of a special FOBAPROA window to provide dollar liquidity, while the Banco de México provided short-term peso credit in its function as lender of last resort. In an effort to attract additional capital to the Mexican banking system, Mexico substantially

140 Karaoglan and Lubrano, above note 8, at 24.

141 *See The Mexican Economy 1996*, above note 68, at IV(2)(a).

reduced restrictions on foreign investment,[142] and Mexico's financial sector legislation was amended in February 1995 to permit foreign individuals and companies as a group to hold up to 49 per cent of the voting shares of a Mexican-controlled financial holding company, commercial bank, or brokerage house.[143] Further, in order to encourage take-overs or mergers between better capitalised foreign financial institutions and existing Mexican banks, the amendments permitted foreign financial institutions to purchase a controlling interest in any Mexican commercial bank with a market share of less than 6 per cent.[144]

In addition, the Mexican government took several measures to bolster the capitalisation of the Mexican banking system. In an effort to address asset quality problems, Mexico undertook a series of measures throughout 1995 to address the increase in non-performing loans resulting from the peso's devaluation and the subsequent financial turmoil.[145] Recognising the need to deal with the deterioration of asset quality in the banking system at the onset of the financial crisis, Mexican regulators implemented a more stringent system for maintaining adequate loan loss reserves in early 1995. Mexico also created a new programme to help banks restructure portions of their loan portfolios to increase the likelihood that loans will continue to perform in the face of high inflation and interest rates. These measures, in addition to others, are discussed in greater detail in remainder of Part IV.

B. Short-Term Initiatives

1. The Macroeconomic Austerity Programme

Almost immediately after the devaluation, the Mexican government began the implementation of another painful austerity plan. On 3 January 1995, the government announced a new emergency economic agreement designed to restore financial stability, strengthen public finances, assist the banking sector, rebuild confidence, and reinforce the foundations for long-term sustainable growth.[146]

Because the plan failed to prevent foreign investors from continuing to

[142] *See* 'Mexico's Financial Crisis', above note 57, at 143–6.

[143] The previous ceiling for Mexican-controlled commercial banks had been 30 per cent. Ibid. at 36.

[144] For a detailed description of the Feb. 1995 amendments, *see* Lubrano, 'Mexico Amends Financial Sector Legislation to Attract Greater Investment and Reinforce Supervision', 2 *North Amer. Corp. Law.* 90–3 (1995).

[145] *See* 'Mexico's Financial Crisis', above note 57, at 143–6. *See also* Karaoglan and Lubrano, above note 8, at 39–40.

[146] *See Mexico's Financial Crisis*, above note 57, at 133.

withdraw their funds from Mexico,[147] the government was prompted to announce a new economic plan on 9 March 1995 of monetary, fiscal, banking and social measures. The plan contained stringent economic policy adjustments consistent with agreements reached with the US and the IMF. The main objectives of the new plan were to contain inflation and reduce the current account deficit. In contrast to previous plans, the new plan was not accompanied by a *Pacto* between the Mexican government, business and labour.[148]

The plan consisted of several elements dealing with monetary, exchange rate, fiscal and social policies. In order to stabilise the exchange market, the plan entailed a 20 per cent reduction in the domestic money supply in real terms through higher interest rates and increased financial regulation.[149] The floating exchange rate policy, adopted by necessity in December 1994, was maintained. The government ruled out any measures to limit currency convertibility because of the negative effect it would have had on Mexico's attempts to access the capital markets in the future.[150]

Mexico adopted several new fiscal policy measures in accordance with IMF guidelines. These measures included: (1) an increase in the value-added tax; (2) a reduction in budgetary outlays equal to 1.6 per cent of GDP for fiscal year 1995; (3) an immediate tax increase on gasoline and diesel fuel, and an increase in electricity prices; and (4) an increase in the fiscal surplus of 2.1 per cent of GDP.[151]

Finally, Mexico made several changes to its social policies. Minimum wages were increased by 10 per cent in addition to a previously announced increase of 7 per cent.[152] Other measures included an extension in health benefits for unemployed workers from two to six months, and a rural employment programme.[153]

[147] Some of the economic projections incorporated into the initial plan, such as maintaining a current account deficit of US$14 billion and reducing the expected rate of GDP growth from 4 per cent to 1.5 to 2 per cent for 1995, were not viewed as credible by international investors. Ibid. at 133–4.

[148] Although the government wanted to obtain the endorsement of the plan from the members of the old Pacto, its efforts to do so were unsuccessful because the Pacto disagreed with the austerity measures. Ibid. at 134.

[149] According to the Federal Reserve, Mexico's monetary programme was intended to target a particular growth rate of net domestic assets which, given flat net international reserves, would produce a particular growth rate of the nominal monetary base. The extent of real reduction in the monetary base would then depend on inflation. Ibid.

[150] The mere hint that a country might impose exchange controls can preclude it from access to international capital markets because mutual fund managers cannot tolerate the possibility that they might be prevented from quickly dumping their holdings and shifting them elsewhere. *See* Cynthia Lichtenstein, 'The Mexican Crisis, Who Should Be a Country's Lender of Last Resort?', 18 *Fordham Int'l L.J.* 1769, 1775 (1995).

[151] *See Mexico's Financial Crisis*, above note 57, at 135.

[152] However, because the two increases were well below the projected inflation rate of 42 per cent, real wages were projected to decline. Ibid. at 136.

[153] Ibid.

2. LIQUIDITY PROGRAMMES

a. Dollar Liquidity Facility

In the immediate aftermath of the peso devaluation, Mexican banks encountered extreme difficulty in renewing their maturing dollar obligations. Mirroring the government's *tesabono* difficulties, commercial banks discovered that their CD depositors and other lenders were unwilling to roll over their investments. The Banco de Mexico responded in early January by establishing a special dollar liquidity facility whereby FOBAPROA provided short-term, 28-day dollar loans to enable banks to pay all foreign currency liabilities as they came due.[154] The purpose of the dollar liquidity facility was to stop, and eventually reverse, the run on the external liabilities of commercial banks.

In order to encourage commercial banks to substitute the loans with private sector funding at the earliest possible time, FOBAPROA charged interest on the loans of up to 25 per cent and required the loans to be secured by government securities, debt securities of Nacional Financiera, SNC (the state development bank), or equity securities of the recipient bank.[155] To further encourage the prompt repayment of these loans, it was established that early repayment of even a portion of the loans would reduce the interest charged on a portion of the outstanding balance.

b. Peso Liquidity Facility

Mexican banks also found it difficult to maintain their peso funding. Banks' increasing need for pesos to buy dollars to retire maturing dollar-denominated CDs caused interbank peso lending rates to rise substantially. Smaller banks were put under additional pressure as their depositors transferred peso deposits to larger and presumably sounder institutions in a 'flight to quality'.

Acting as lender of last resort, the Banco de Mexico addressed the problem by providing short-term peso credit through special credit auctions. Credit was initially provided on an unsecured basis for banks that were experiencing a shortage of collateral. However, to ensure that liquidity provision did not become a means to delay recognition of insolvency, the

[154] Dollar financing under this programme was extended to seventeen commercial banks. At its peak in Apr. 1995, the outstanding credit granted through the dollar liquidity facility had reached US$3.9 billion. By Sept. 1995, however, all dollar denominated advances had been repaid as banks took advantage of renewed access to international financial markets. *See The Mexican Economy 1996*, above note 68, at IV(2)(c)(iii); *see also* Mancera, above note 10, at 233.

[155] *See* Karaoglan and Lubrano, above note 8, at 35.

Banco de Mexico began requiring banks after 20 March 1995 to post government securities, securities of National Financiera, and loans provided to prime borrowers as collateral.[156] By 31 March 1995, outstanding balances stood at the equivalent of US$3 billion, with most established banks participating in the auctions at some point.[157] After the immediate crisis had subsided, banks were able to obtain peso liquidity from private money markets and no longer required the assistance of the Banco de Mexico for peso liquidity.

3. Temporary Capitalisation Programme (PROCAPTE)

The devaluation of the peso drastically increased the domestic currency value of bank loans denominated in foreign currency, causing the capital-asset ratios of many Mexican banks to fall below the accepted level.[158] To remedy this situation, the government introduced the Temporary Capitalisation Programme (*Programa de Capitalizacion Temporal* or 'PROCAPTE') in February 1995 to assist the banks that had capitalisation levels below the internationally accepted standard of 8 per cent of risk-weighted assets. This programme was administered on a voluntary basis and was intended for use by viable banks that were facing short-term capital needs, rather than by problem banks requiring intervention.[159]

Using resources obtained from the Banco de Mexico, FOBAPROA purchased subordinated convertible debentures from participating banks in amounts sufficient to raise the banks' ratio of net capital-to-risk-weighted assets to 9 per cent. To prevent unwarranted expansion of the Banco de Mexico's net domestic credit, the commercial banks were required to deposit the resources thus obtained in an account at the Banco de Mexico.[160] Interest rates on the deposits were fixed to match the rates on the debentures to avoid negatively affecting the banks' income statements. While the debentures remained outstanding, participating banks were required to maintain a capital ratio of at least 9 per cent and were restricted from paying dividends or issuing new equity or subordinated debt.[161]

Banks operating under PROCAPTE were kept under strict supervision by the CNBV. If a participating bank's capitalisation ratio fell below 8.5 per cent, FOBAPROA had discretion to approve additional subordinated convertible debentures to restore the bank's 9 per cent capitalisation ratio. If a bank failed to repay the debt within five years, FOBAPROA could

156 Ibid.

157 Ibid.

158 *See The Mexican Economy 1996*, above note 68, at IV(2)(c)(ii).

159 Although the programme was stated to be voluntary, a bank which did not recapitalise faced suspension or revocation of its operating charter. *See* Mexico's Financial Crisis, above note 57, at 144.

160 *See* Camdessus, above note 127, at 221.

161 *See* Fluckiger, above note 15, at 80.

convert the debentures into equity capital of the bank, thereby becoming an owner of the bank.[162] In addition to converting shares that were not repaid within five years, the convertibility feature could be invoked earlier if a participating bank's capital deteriorated to below 2 per cent of its risk-weighted assets, or if the bank's capitalisation, excluding the PROCAPTE obligations, varied more than 25 per cent from the trend of average capitalisation of all the banks participating in the programme.[163] If a bank's capitalisation ratio improved to exceed 9 per cent, however, the bank was rewarded by attaining the right to redeem in advance all or part of the subordinated debentures held by FOBAPROA.

The programme allowed banks a relatively long time to obtain fresh capital and pay their debts to FOBAPROA. At the same time, the programme provided incentives to the banks to recapitalise as promptly as possible through the threat of dilution of interest or even total loss of investment presented by the mandatory conversion of the debentures after the five-year period.[164] Indeed, faced with the mere possibility of having to rely on PROCAPTE's resources, some banks made an immediate effort to obtain capital on their own.[165] Moreover, many participating banks were anxious to leave the programme as soon as possible due to the stigma that the market attached to these banks in the form of higher interbank rates for funds.[166]

By the end of March 1995, six banks had entered into the PROCAPTE programme, including Mexico's third largest bank, Serfin.[167] However, by June 1995 all participating banks except one had exited the programme by injecting new capital from shareholders in return for the purchase of non-performing assets by FOBAPROA.[168] The programme had a positive effect on depositor confidence. The effect on future profitability, however, has been less than positive because of the high level of subordinated debt in the composition of the banks' capital.[169]

162 Under no circumstances would the government retain any ownership interest in the banks. In keeping with its commitment to financial liberalisation, the government was eager to demonstrate to the markets that it had no intention of renationalising any banks, however weak. *See* Ayer, above note 6, at 8.

163 *See* Karaoglan and Lubrano, above note 8, at 38.

164 *See The Mexican Economy 1996*, above note 68, at IV(2)(c)(ii).

165 Ibid.

166 *See* Ayer, above note 6, at 8.

167 The other five banks were Inverlat, Bital, Confia, Centro, and Oriente. The average capitalisation ratio of these banks had declined from 8.13 per cent at the end of 1994 to 5.82 per cent by the end of Feb. 1995. Collectively, the six banks issued N$6.5 billion of convertible subordinated debentures to the government which enabled them to raise their average capitalisation ratios to 9.6 per cent. *See* Fluckiger, above note 15, at 80; *see also* Karaoglan and Lubrano, above note 8, at 39.

168 The remaining capital-deficient bank, Probursa, was given additional time to meet the minimum capital requirements in anticipation of an agreement by Banco Bilbao Vizcaya to make a substantial capital infusion and convert Probursa into an affiliate. *See* Karaoglan and Lubrano, above note 8, at 39.

169 Six of the healthy banks had subordinated debt totaling more than $N seven billion, equivalent to 13 per cent of their total capital. *See* Ayer, above note 6, at 9.

4. Debtor Programmes

According to literature published by the Banco de Mexico, all of the programmes in support of debtors were designed with the following objectives in mind:

1. To foster responsible payment practices among debtors;
2. To carry incentives for banks to grant additional credit to certain sectors which the programmes were designed to help and thereby contribute towards economic recovery in those sectors;
3. To limit financial support to small debtors and to limit the extent of support;
4. To structure the cost of the programmes so that they be shared equally between banks and the Federal Government; and
5. To structure the programme to have no monetary impact.[170]

a. Debt Restructuring Programme (UDI)

The rapid devaluation of the peso led to a substantial increase in the inflation rate during 1995.[171] Mexico responded to this problem by introducing an inflation-indexed unit of account for financial transactions called the *Unidad de Inversion* ('UDI') on April 1, 1995. Under the programme, both new transactions and pre-existing loans can be denominated in UDIs.

The UDI is designed to be a constant value unit of account used to denominate credits. The value of the UDI is updated daily by the Banco de Mexico to reflect the behaviour of the consumer price index. The value of credits denominated in UDIs remains constant in real terms with regard to both principal and interest so that the credits are protected against the accelerated amortisation caused when high inflation eats away at the principal.[172] Lenders are thus guaranteed a rate of return in excess of inflation while borrowers are shielded from interest rate volatility.[173]

Under the programme, the banks' loan portfolios are transferred to special

[170] *See The Mexican Economy 1997*, above note 134, at III(2)(a).

[171] During periods of high inflation, the value of a loan's principal remains constant in nominal terms but not real terms. In fact, inflation causes the real value of the principal to continuously deteriorate. Generally, the creditor charges a high rate of interest to compensate for the erosion of real value of the principal. Thus, except when highly negative real interest rates prevail (e.g. when the inflation rate is higher than the interest rate), the real amortisation will be paid by debtors through interest payments. These higher interest payments, in turn, reduce the likelihood that a bank's loan portfolio will continue to perform. *See* Mancera, above note 10, at 234; *see also* Karaoglan and Lubrano, above note 8, at 41.

[172] *See The Mexican Economy 1996*, above note 68, at IV(2)(c)(vi).

[173] The UDI programme further eases debt burdens by extending loan maturities. Participants are granted a variety of grace periods and terms permitting maturities of up to 12 years. *See* Ayer, above note 6, at 12.

purpose off-balance sheet trusts, administered by the banks themselves, that restructure the loans and denominate them in UDIs.[174] To carry out the restructuring, the trusts obtain loans from the government, also denominated in UDIs. In exchange for their loan portfolios, commercial banks receive long-term government bonds that pay interest only at maturity. Through the restructuring, commercial banks' peso-denominated liabilities are matched by assets in the same currency. The banks are required to keep the trusts adequately provisioned and to assume the credit risk of the loans in the UDI portfolio.

The government is left with domestic currency-denominated liabilities (the bonds acquired by banks) and UDI-denominated assets (the loans to the trusts). Consequently, the government bears the risk that the interest rates charged on its UDI loans will be lower than the real interest rates it pays on the aforementioned bonds while the commercial banks bear the credit risk.[175]

Unfortunately, the complexity of the UDI programme led to problems with its implementation. Both bank officials and borrowers had great difficulty understanding the economic effects of the new unit of account.[176] Since banks were initially slow to make full use of the UDI programme, the government was forced to intervene to facilitate the restructuring of a large number of viable loans and encourage their redenomination in UDIs. Although the programme was a disappointment initially, borrowers and banks in non-mortgage lending areas eventually caught on to the programme's benefits. By the end of 1996, approximately $NP 167 billion of the loan portfolio had been restructured in UDIs to the benefit of approximately 375,000 debtors.[177]

b. *Debtor Relief Programme (ADE)*

After the initial shock of the first few months of the crisis had passed and once interest rate volatility began to subside, the government turned its attention toward relieving the debt burden of consumers created by high interest rates and the substantial decrease in economic activity. The government and the banks were equally anxious to encourage enterprises and consumers to reach agreement with lenders and return to servicing non-performing loans.[178]

[174] *See* Mancera, above note 10, at 235.

[175] Ibid.

[176] The response to the programme from mortgage lenders and borrowers, however, was overwhelming. Mortgage borrowers generally had a greater understanding of the UDI programme due to their previous experience with indexed instruments in connection with mortgage loans.

[177] Market volatility during Oct. and Nov. 1995 required authorities to extend the UDI programme in an effort to reduce the negative impact of interest rates on banks' fourth quarter results. The limit on the size of foreign currency loans available for restructuring was raised to US$2 billion and the deadline for the commercial loan UDI restructuring programme was extended. Additionally, authorities increased funding for the UDI mortgage programme by 12,000 UDIs, which represented a 28.6 per cent increase over the original amount. *See* Fluckiger, above note 15, at 81; *see also* Mancera, above note 10, at 235.

[178] *See* Karaoglan and Lubrano, above note 8, at 42.

In August 1995 the Mexican government introduced the Agreement of Immediate Support of Bank Debtors (*Acuerdo de Apoyo Inmediato a Deudores de la Banca* or 'ADE') targeted at consumer, credit card, small business, agricultural, and mortgage loan debtors.[179] ADE was intended to assist debtors in remaining current on their loans, thereby reducing the systemic risk to the banking system stemming from widespread default. Within this framework, the government shared losses with banks, seeking to minimise fiscal costs and distribute them over time, while preventing further distortions in credit markets.[180]

Borrowers wishing to be eligible for the programme were required to sign a letter of intent by 31 October 1995 to renegotiate their debts with creditors. The signing of the letter of intent obligated the lending bank to refrain from instituting legal proceedings against delinquent debtors until 31 January 1996 and to waive all accrued penalty interest.[181] Interest rates payable by the borrower were capped for the year of the programme's duration (1 September 1995 to 1 September 1996) at 38.5 per cent for credit card balances, 34 per cent for consumer loans and 25 per cent for commercial loans.[182] The programme was intended to bridge the gap between what borrowers were willing to pay and what lenders were willing to accept.[183]

Participation in the ADE programme was extensive. The programme enabled 75 per cent of borrowers from Mexican banks to completely refinance their debts.[184] The cost of the interest rate subsidy was split evenly between the banks and the government and was much lower than had been initially anticipated.[185]

[179] The programme was intended to preempt more extreme measures being promoted by certain borrower pressure groups and to foster responsible payment practices by providing viable borrowers with interest relief and a legal truce. Ibid.; *see also The Mexican Economy 1996*, above note 68, at IV(2)(c)(vii).

[180] Importantly, the programme entailed no monetary expansion because the subsidy provided by the ADE programme was financed through the issuance of bonds to the commercial banks rather than through the lending of funds. Furthermore, the ADE programme helped to improve the quality of commercial banks' loan portfolios, and induced payment discipline and reductions in required provisions. *See* Karaoglan and Lubrano, above note 8, at 42; *see also* Mancera, above note 10, at 236.

[181] *See* Fluckiger, above note 15, at 81.

[182] Mortgage loans restructured into UDIs were capped at UDI + 6.5 per cent. *See* Karaoglan and Lubrano, above note 8, at 42.

[183] The government planned to absorb up to 16 per centage points on the difference between the concessional interest rate, which varied depending upon the class of debtor and type of loan, and the market reference rate. If such limit had been surpassed, commercial banks would have borne half of the additional cost. Ibid., *see also* Mancera, above *note* 10, at 237.

[184] *See* Ayer, above note 6, at 13.

[185] The government reimbursed the full amount of the ADE subsidy, in cash rather than bonds, from Nov. 1995 to Jan. 1996 to alleviate liquidity and interest margin pressures stemming from market volatility.

c. Other Debtor Programmes

Although the UDI and ADE programmes helped tremendously by providing liquidity to banks and preventing a wave of defaults by borrowers, further assistance was necessary. To provide extra assistance in certain critical areas, the Mexican government implemented a number of additional support programmes.

Because existing bankruptcy laws and procedures were inadequate to enable a 'work out' between insolvent shareholders and their creditors, the Mexican government established the Coordinating Unit for Bank-Enterprise Agreements (*Unidad Coordinadora para Creditos Corporativos* or 'UCABE') in December 1995 to lay the foundation for the financial restructuring of large corporate debtors.[186] Although the banks' largest debtors (with loans totalling between US$150 to US$500 million) accounted for only 8–10 per cent of total bank lending, the programme nevertheless had a positive impact on reducing the overall debt burden.[187] By year-end 1996, thirty-one loans were restructured by UCABE, for a total of US$2.57 billion, allowing seven large firms to resolve their payment-suspension situations.

The government launched a mortgage subsidy programme (*Programa de Beneficios Adicionales a los Deudores de Creditos para Vivienda*) to ease mortgage borrowers' heavy burden stemming from high interest rates and reduced purchasing power. As a result of the recession, property values fell, in many cases below the remaining balance on the mortgage loans. Under such circumstances, mortgage debtors lost the incentive to remain current on their payments. Defaults occurred even with mortgage loans restructured under the UDI programme.

The programme contained several key components designed to encourage mortgage debtors to avoid default. First, a 30 per cent discount was made available on payments due in 1996, which will gradually decline to 5 per cent in 2005 and applies only to the first 500,000 UDIs of the total loan.[188] Secondly, the amount available to restructure mortgages in UDIs was increased by 43,000 million UDIs, to a total of 100,000 million UDIs (about US$22.3 billion as of mid-January 1997).[189] Thirdly, a scheme of minimum payments equivalent to rent was introduced to help mortgage debtors that, notwithstanding the benefit of the discount, were unable to service their loans.[190]

[186] *See* Ayer, above note 6, at 13.

[187] Ibid.

[188] *See The Mexican Economy 1997*, above note 134, at III(2)(a)(ii).

[189] *See* Mancera, above note 10, at 237.

[190] Under this scheme, the debtor transfers title to the property as full payment of the loan but retains the right to repurchase it for up to six years. The government bears the cost of the discount by paying the banks in either cash or five-year credits bearing an interest rate equal to that on 91-day *cetes* treasury bills. Ibid.

The agricultural sector was particularly affected by the economic crisis. In July 1996, the government introduced the Agricultural, Livestock, and Fisheries Loan Support Programme (*Acuerdo para el Financiamiento del Sector Agropecuario y Pesquero* or 'FINAPE'), a loan restructuring mechanism designed to provide debt relief to Mexican farmers, fishermen, and ranchers.[191] The mechanism provided discounts of up to 40 per cent, depending on the amount of the outstanding loan and the lending banks' willingness to forgive part of the loan.[192] As with other support programmes, the cost of the discounts were shared between the government and banks. However, since the programme also sought to promote flows of new financial capital to the agricultural sector, the cost borne by the government depended on the amount of new resources that banks injected into the sector.

Small and medium-sized firms also encountered difficulty in coping with the economic crisis. In August 1996 the government launched the Support Programme for Small and Medium-Sized Firms (*Acuerdo de Apoyo Financiero y Fomento a la Micro, Pequeña y Mediana Empresa* or 'FOPYME') to help alleviate the heavy financial burden faced by smaller, but viable, firms and to help them finance their current activities. Discounts under the programme ranged from 17 per cent to 30 per cent depending on the amount of the outstanding loan. To be eligible, loans were required to be under $NP 6 million and to have been contracted as of 31 July 1996.[193] Banks promoted economic activity under the programme by providing up to $NP 13 billion in new financing to creditworthy firms. Banks were committed to maintaining these lines of credit in real terms for at least three years.

C. *Long-Term Structural Reforms*

1. Relaxation of Foreign Investment Limitations Under NAFTA

Under the 1993 amendments to the Law of Credit Institutions, foreign-controlled commercial banks were subjected to individual and aggregate market-share limitations. No single foreign-controlled bank could represent more than 1.5 per cent of the capital of the Mexican banking system and all foreign banks taken together were limited to 8 per cent of the market.[194] NAFTA provided for gradual increases in the aggregate market share limitation until its elimination in the year 2000.

In an effort to encourage more capital investment into the financial

191 *See* Mancera, above note 10, at 237. 192 Ibid. at 238.
193 *The Mexican Economy 1997*, above note 134, at III(2)(a)(v).
194 NAFTA, Annex VII(B)(2) and (5)-Mex.

system, the Mexican government amended its financial sector legislation in February 1995 to permit foreign individuals and foreign companies as a group to hold up to 49 per cent of the voting shares of a Mexican-controlled financial holding company, commercial bank or brokerage house.[195] Under prior law, the limit on foreign holdings of shares of Mexican-controlled commercial banks had been 30 per cent.[196]

Just as importantly, the financial sector legislation was amended to allow the Ministry of Finance to waive the limits on market share in NAFTA on a case-by-case basis in certain circumstances.[197] To encourage well-capitalised foreign financial institutions to merge with or take over existing Mexican banks, the amendments allowed foreign financial institutions to buy a controlling stake in existing Mexican commercial banks as long as the resulting foreign-controlled bank had no more than 6 per cent market share.[198] The amendments also raised the aggregate market-share ceiling by restricting foreign-controlled banks to 25 per cent of the aggregate capital in the banking system. The new limits were designed to allow mergers or takeovers of smaller institutions while placing the three largest Mexican banks, Banamex, Bancomer, and Serfin, off limits.[199]

2. Bank Consolidation and Recapitalisation

a. Mergers/Acquisitions

Since the outbreak of the crisis, the Mexican banking system has witnessed significant consolidation through a succession of financial mergers and acquisitions. For example, Spain's Banco Bilbao Vizcaya took over Mercantile Probursa in May 1995, as well as two other banks, Cremi and Banco de Oriente, in 1995 and 1996.[200] Additionally, Canada's Bank of Nova Scotia bought a controlling interest in Mexico's Banco Inverlat in 1995, while the Bank of Montreal bought a 16 per cent stake in Mexico's Bancomer in 1996.[201]

195 Brokerage houses were not subject to market share limitations. *See* Karaoglan and Lubrano, above note 8, at 36.

196 Ibid.

197 Relaxation of the previous 1.5 per cent individual market share limitation was crucial to permitting the recapitalisation of Probursa by Spain's Banco Bilbao Vizcaya. Ibid.

198 *See* Ayer, above note 6, at 12; *see also* Mancera, above note 10, at 235.

199 The 6 per cent limit and the 25 per cent aggregate cap on foreign controlled banks were added to the amending legislation during Congressional consideration on the grounds that permitting foreign control of any of Mexico's three largest banks might compromise the domestic payments system. *See* Mike Lubrano, 'Mexico Amends Financial Sector Legislation to Attract Greater Investment and Reinforce Supervision', 2 *N. Am. Corp. Law* (1995).

200 *See Banking/finance/insurance: Spain's Banco Santander Buys Out Invermexico*, Mexico Business Monthly, 1 Dec. 1996, *available in* 1996 WL 12545247.

201 *See Banking/finance/insurance*, above note 200.

In January 1998, London-based HSBC Holdings PLC agreed to purchase 19.9 per cent of Banca Serfin as part of a recapitalisation programme.[202] In the same month, Banco Industrial signed an initial agreement with Far East National Bank, the US subsidiary of Taiwanese financial group SinoPac, to sell a 51 per cent stake. A few months later, in May 1998, Mexican authorities formally agreed to allow Citibank de Mexico to purchase a majority stake in Confia Bank.[203] As a result of the consolidation of the banking system, the number of national commercial banks dwindled from 18 banks prior to the devaluation to just nine banks by 1998.[204]

b. Loan Sale / Capitalisation Programme

Although measures to provide temporary liquidity and capitalisation to troubled banks helped to avoid bank failures in the short-term, it was evident that long-term measures for bank restructuring and recapitalisation were necessary in order to assure the prolonged soundness of the Mexican banking system. Thus, authorities began focusing their efforts on attracting fresh capital to the banking system.

An agreement between the Mexican government and Banco Bilbao Vizcaya ('BBV') for the recapitalisation of Probursa provided an informal model for an *ad hoc* programme to restructure and recapitalise other vulnerable Mexican banks. BBV agreed to increase its 20 per cent stake in Grupo Financiero Probursa to 70 per cent, with an aggregate investment of US$350 million.[205] In exchange for the new capital, FOBAPROA agreed to purchase approximately US$780 million of Probursa's troubled loans, essentially cleansing the bank's balance sheet.[206] FOBAPROA purchased the Probursa portfolio with ten-year bonds bearing interest at a rate equal to that on the 28-day *cetes* treasury notes.[207] Pursuant to the agreement, Probursa maintained responsibility for administering and collecting the loans on behalf of FOBAPROA.

In July 1995, a variation of the Probursa agreement was reached with Mexico's third-largest bank, Banca Serfin, in which the bank's controlling Mexican shareholder group agreed to inject additional capital.[208] Serfin

202 *See* Rogelio Varela, *Mexico's Banking System: Renewal of Credit Seen*, Dow Jones Int'l News Serv. (29 Jan. 1998), *available in* the Westlaw NORTHNEWS database.

203 *See Citibank Mexico Unit Buys Confia Bank*, Reuters News Servicé (11 May 1998).

204 *See* Rogelio Varela, *Mexico's Banking System Continues Consolidating in 1998*, Dow Jones Int'l News Serv., 29 Jan. 1998, *available in* the Westlaw NORTHNEWS database.

205 *See* Fluckiger, above note 15, at 80.

206 Ibid. As a result of this agreement, Probursa's ratio of net capital to risk-weighted assets increased to 10.1 per cent by the end of July 1995. *See* Karaoglan and Lubrano, above note 8, at 40.

207 *See* Ayer, above note 6, at 9.

208 FOBAPROA purchased loans from Serfin totaling more than NP$4.9 billion on the condition that Serfin's shareholders purchase NP$1.24 billion in shares, NP$930 million in

was permitted to exit the PROCAPTE programme by retiring the mandatory convertible subordinated debentures issued under that programme and was able to increase its ratio of net capital to risk-weighted assets from 10 per cent at the end of March to 11 per cent by the end of July.[209] Several other banks, including Banco Atlantico[210], took advantage of the programme as well.[211]

Although the agreements were tailored to suit the particular needs of each bank, they all shared common characteristics. First, FOBAPROA purchased loans from the banks in return for a contribution of fresh capital by shareholders, generally at a 2:1 ratio. Secondly, loan loss provisions pertaining to the sold portfolio were negotiated between the banks and FOBAPROA. Thirdly, banks continued to maintain responsibility for administering and collecting the loans sold. Fourthly, banks retained between 20–25 per cent of the risk on losses from the sold portfolio. Finally, loans were purchased with ten-year bonds paying the *cetes* rate for the amount of peso denominated loans sold and the LIBOR rate for the amount of dollar denominated loans sold, and all principal recovered from the sold portfolio was used to redeem the bonds.[212]

c. *Creation of the Asset Valuation and Sale Agency (VVA)*

In March 1996, Mexico announced the creation of the Asset Valuation and Sale Agency (*Valuacion y Venta de Activos* or 'VVA'), an agency with functions similar to the US Resolution Trust Corporation.[213] It was charged with the duty of appraising and selling the assets that FOBAPROA acquired from the banks. The main objectives of the VVA were to: (1) maximise revenues from the sale of financial assets, real estate, and other property acquired by FOBAPROA; (2) sell assets through a transparent and open process as quickly as conditions permit; (3) design formulas to help restructure viable companies; and (4) promote the development of secondary

convertible subordinated bonds, and NP$600 million in non-convertible subordinated bonds. In addition to maintaining responsibility for the administration and collection of the loans, Serfin agreed to share 20 per cent of any losses which the portfolio might have generated, thereby preserving its incentive to effectively manage the portfolio. *See* Karaoglan and Lubrano, above note 8, at 40.

209 Ibid.

210 Banco Atlantico agreed to sell NP$2 billion to FOBAPROA in return for new capital injections from shareholders of NP$1 billion. *See* Department of the Treasury, *Monthly Report by the Secretary of the Treasury Pursuant to the Mexican Debt Disclosure Act of 1995* (6 Dec. 1996) <http://www.ustreas.gov/treasury/mexico/archive/mex9611.htm>.

211 By the end of 1997, the banking sector had increased its capital by almost 158 per cent over Dec. 1994 levels. *See The Mexican Economy 1997*, above note 134, at III(2)(b)(ii).

212 *See* Karaoglan and Lubrano, above note 8, at 40.

213 *See Banking finance insurance Banks Seek to Survive in 1996*, Mexico Business Monthly, 1 Apr. 1996, *available in* 1996 WL 8155014.

markets for banks' debt instruments and other financial and non-financial assets.[214] Due to a shift in government strategy, however, the VVA was later dissolved.

3. Establishment of Futures Markets

Derivatives and other financial innovations provide useful vehicles which enable investors to manage the types of risk which are common in emerging markets, namely currency risk and interest rate risk. The Banco de Mexico, realising that futures markets are an efficient mechanism for hegdging risks and for determining prices and exchange rates, began actively facilitating their development. In an effort to provide a more efficient market, Mexico took steps to introduce new financial instruments to modernise Mexican financial markets and serve the needs of investors.

In 1995, the Chicago Mercantile Exchange ('CME') established a new division, called the Growth and Emerging Markets Division, to provide risk management of emerging market currencies, equity, and interest rates, including those of Mexico. In concert with the establishment of the new division, the Bolsa and the CME developed distinct peso and interest futures contracts to create a North American standard for futures trading for pesos and Mexican Treasury interest rates.[215] Today, in addition to currency forwards and options, the division offers products such as interest rate swaps and forward agreements, credit derivatives, and structured notes.[216]

In November 1996, the CNBV inaugurated Mexico's first futures market called the Mexican Derivatives and Futures Market ('Mex-Der').[217] The market offers products such as peso currency forwards and options, interest rate swaps, and IPC index contracts.[218] Since the introduction of the futures markets, Mexico has been gradually introducing other derivative financial instruments, such as warrants on individual Mexican securities and options on individual Mexican stocks.[219] Importantly, the level of volatility in the peso exchange rate has declined, in part due to the addition of the peso futures contract, since international investors can now hedge against exchange-rate risk.

214 *See The Mexican Economy 1997*, above note 134, at III(2)(c)(i).

215 *See* 'Mexico's Financial Crisis', above note 57 at 133–6.

216 *See* Ovidio E. Diaz Espino, *Emerging Markets Derivatives Set to Expand*, 1071 PLI/Corp 669 (1997).

217 However, due to the amount of infrastructure required to set up a futures market, the Mex-Der did not become operational until 1998. *See Mexico Derivatives Market Expected to Begin 1Q 1998*, Dow Jones International News Service, 4 Dec. 1997.

218 Ibid.

219 For a full discussion of devivatives, their uses, and implications, *See* GAO, 'Financial Derivatives: Actions Needed to Protect the Financial System' (GAO/GGD-94-133, 18 May 1995).

4. PENSION SYSTEM PRIVATISATION

Historically, Mexico has lacked strong internal financing and has continuously experienced a significant leakage of domestic savings to foreign investments. Indeed, the economy's overall savings rate in 1994 fell to just 16 per cent of gross domestic product, which contributed to Mexico's reliance on short-term foreign capital and to the subsequent financial crisis.[220]

To rectify this situation, Mexico passed a new Social Security Act (*Ley del Instituto Mexicano del Seguro Social*) in late 1995 and the Retirement Savings Systems Act (*Ley de los Sistemas de Ahorro para el Retiro*) in April 1996 to privatise the nearly bankrupt government social security system.[221] Pension privatisation was heralded as a cornerstone of President Ernesto Zedillo's efforts to deepen Mexico's financial markets, increase the domestic savings rate, and diminish reliance on foreign capital.[222]

The pension acts required all Mexican workers to choose by the year 2001 which private pension fund administrator (called an 'AFORE')[223] they wished to look after their pension contributions. Regulations pursuant to the law also include a provision permitting US and Canadian financial institutions to own equity in AFORES on a basis consistent with NAFTA and thus to participate fully in the management of the pension funds.[224]

The new system gives many Mexicans their first opportunity to participate in financial markets. Instead of having money taken out of their paycheques, employees will actively invest in their own retirement. Under

[220] *See Mexico: January 1998*, Barclays Bank Country Rep. 1, 1 Jan. 1998, *available in* 1998 WL 10591500; *see also Private Pension Funds Out to Lure Mexicans, Financial Times* (London), 4 Feb. 1998.

[221] The government pension system, run by the notoriously inefficient IMSS, was already US$6 billion in debt and expected to be completely bankrupt by 2006. The government pension system was further criticised as unfair because of the poor correlation between benefits and lifetime contributions. *See* Luis Cerda, *The Mexican Pension Reform* (no date) <http://www.shcp.gob.mx/english/docs/pension.html>.

[222] *See Private Pension Funds*, above note 220; *See also* Department of the Treasury, *Dec. Monthly Report to Congress: Summaries of the Treasury Secretary's Monthly Reports, July–Dec., 1996*, (10 Jan. 1997) <http://www.ustreas.gov/treasury/mexico/archive/mex9612.htm>.

[223] AFORES are financial institutions whose purpose is to professionally administer individual pension retirement accounts and to channel these funds into the corresponding subaccounts in accordance with the social security laws, as well as to administer specialised retirement mutual funds, called 'SEIFORES'. *See The Mexican Economy 1997*, above note 134, at III(6)(a).

[224] Department of the Treasury, *Semi-Annual Report to Congress by the Secretary of the Treasury Pursuant to the Mexican Debt Disclosure Act of 1995*, III (5 Aug. 1996) <http://www.ustreas.gov/treasury/mexico/semi626.htm>. Participation by other foreign institutions is limited to 49 per cent of the AFORE capital. Additionally, no individual or corporation may control more than 10 per cent of the AFORE stock unless specifically authorised by the National Retirement Fund System Commission ('CONSAR'), the pension system regulatory agency. *See* Cerda, above note 221.

the new system, workers' future pension benefits will be tied directly to their contributions, time spent working, and to their savings. Thus, at least in theory, a change of perception will be brought about by turning the worker into the sole owner of his contribution and of the capital that it generates. Initially, AFORES were restricted to investing in government and domestic corporate bonds within Mexico, but investment restrictions were expected to be liberalised within a year or two.[225] Until then, the funds would be vulnerable to any major peso devaluations.

While not the first pension system to be privatised in Latin America, Mexico's is by far the largest privatisation and will draw the heaviest participation.[226] Response to the programme has been overwhelming, as more than 8 million workers had already signed up for the programme by mid-September 1997.[227]

D. *Regulatory and Supervisory Reforms*

1. Amended Loan Loss Reserve Requirements

New guidelines were announced in March 1995 requiring Mexican banks to implement more stringent loan loss reserves. Under the guidelines, banks are required to maintain either reserves for non-performing loans of at least 60 per cent of past due loans, or reserves equal to 4 per cent of the total loan portfolio or provisions as required from quarterly loan classifications under earlier rules, whichever is highest.[228] Prior to the new guidelines, banks were required only to make quarterly provisions based on self-assessed risk rating categories.[229] The new guidelines were prompted by the government's concern that the crisis, and its negative effect on the majority of Mexican borrowers, was preventing banks from properly provisioning for loans. As a result of the new guidelines, aggregate loan loss provisions increased substantially from N$24.5 billion at the end of 1994 to N$54.1 billion by the end of July 1995.[230]

[225] *See Mexicans Rush to Switch Funds to Private Pensions Economy: Marketing Blitz and Disenchantment with Social Security Fuel Move*, *Los Angeles Times*, 16 Sept. 1997, *available in* 1997 WL 13980468.

[226] *See Mexicans Rush to Switch Funds*, above note 225.

[227] The enormous response was due in part to an aggressive, US$135 million advertising campaign launched by owners of the *Afores* hoping to acquire the largest share possible of the funds from the contributions equaling 8.5 per cent of employees' gross wages. *See Mexicans Rush to Switch Funds*, above note 225.

[228] *See Mexico's Financial Crisis*, above note 57, at 145. *See also* Karaoglan and Lubrano, above note 8, at 38.

[229] Under the previous system, Mexican banks had discretion in classifying their loan portfolios in five categories. Banks created loan loss reserves based on requirements for each level of classification. *See* Ibid., at 27, note 5. Under this system, in Dec. 1994, provisioning for past due loans across all categories averaged 47.9 per cent.

[230] *See* Karaoglan and Lubrano, above note 8, at 38.

2. Stricter Bank Lending Standards

Connected lending, insider dealing, and fraud were major contributors to the instability of the Mexican banking system before the crisis. To address these problems, the government instituted legislative reforms to prohibit self-lending or '*autoprestamos*', a practice in which a bank officer makes loans to himself or a corporation in which he has an equity interest.[231] In the past, self-lending in Mexico was not considered an unethical practice, as long as bank officers complied with requirements to report all such loans to regulatory authorities. But with hundreds of millions in losses due to insider dealing at banks, savings and loans, and leasing firms, the Mexican government reversed its former policy of giving bankers the benefit of the doubt regarding the legitimacy of their self-lending transactions.[232]

3. Enhanced Supervision

In May 1995, the Law of the National Banking and Securities Commission (*Ley de la Comision Nacional Bancaria y de Valores* or 'CNBV')[233] went into effect. The key feature of the law is centralised supervision. The National Banking Commission and the Securities Commission were combined to form the CNBV and, importantly, the staffing of the new commission was strengthened.[234]

In 1997, the CNBV published an official agenda, entitled the *Programmea Institucional, 1997–2000*, which outlined four principle areas for improvement: (1) prudential regulation; (2) supervision; (3) market self-regulation; and (4) corrective actions.[235] In order to address the new challenges presented by Mexico's transition to a universal banking system, the CNBV developed a consolidated 'MACRO' supervision scheme to manage and coordinate on-site inspections and off-site monitoring of financial institutions and to assist in the evaluation of financial institutions' management of funds, capital adequacy, asset quality, profitability and organisation. [236]

The MACRO scheme significantly changes the method of on-site inspections. Previously, inspectors were permanently stationed within the financial institution. The MACRO scheme abolished that practice in favour of

[231] *See Proposed Banking Reform Would Prohibit 'Insider-Lending' Practice*, US Mex. Free Trade Rep., Mar. 31, 1996, *available in* 1996 WL 10175326.

[232] The reforms may cause significant problems for some Mexican industrial groups which bought into banks during the 1991–1992 privatisation and do much of their lending to associated industrial groups. Ibid.

[233] Ley de la Comision Nacional Bancaria y de Valores, D.O. 1 May, 1995.

[234] *See The Mexican Economy 1996*, above note 68, at IV(2)(c)(i).

[235] *See* Comision Nacional Bancaria y de Valores, *Programa Institucional 1997–2000*, 8 (no date) <http://www.cnbv.gob.mx/aspgral/prestrateg.htm> (hereinafter 'Programa Institucional').

[236] Ibid. at 15.

using teams of inspectors stationed outside the financial institutions to carry out regular on-site inspections. On-site inspectors are now responsible for monitoring the financial institutions' internal control systems for risk-management, paying particular attention to the institutions' operations, procedures, internal controls, management, and compliance with rules and regulations.[237]

Off-site inspection has been strengthened through the development of the Financial Analysis System ('SAF'). The SAF is a computer database that electronically receives the financial information that institutions must provide to the CNBV, eliminating the need for physical delivery. The receipt of consistent and uniform financial information allows off-site inspectors to create individual, comparative, and sectoral analyses concerning the performance of financial institutions and thereby develop early warning mechanisms that make it possible to detect in a timely manner any atypical behaviour, whether individual or systemic, that may pose risks to the financial position of an institution, and to address those risks before they reach critical levels.[238]

Additionally, the CNBV is considering a new system of internal and external audits to complement the supervision of financial institutions. Under the new system, external auditors must register with the CNBV and be evaluated regularly regarding their performance and opinions.[239] External auditors will also be subject to sanctions for poor performance. Internal auditors must report directly to a financial institution's board of directors rather than the intermediate management of the institution. The CNBV will supervise internal auditors by examining the scope and regularity of audits, audit procedures, and the content of internal audit reports.[240]

Lastly, to foster market confidence in Mexico's financial institutions, the Institutional Programme called for the public dissemination of quality financial information, in financial terms, so that markets may make their own evaluations regarding a Mexican institution's exposure to risk.

4. Adoption of GAAP Accounting Standards

In an effort to improve the quality of information provided to markets by banks and to improve overall transparency of the financial system, the CNBV issued regulations in December 1995 requiring banks to implement accounting standards consistent with US generally accepted accounting principles ('GAAP').[241] As of 1 January 1997, all financial statements must be reported under the GAAP standards exclusively.

237 Ibid. at 16.

238 Ibid. at 18.

239 Ibid. at 20.

240 Ibid. at 19–20.

241 In an explanatory bulletin published at the end of 1995, CNBV President Eduardo Fernandez outlined the reasons for the changes. 'Considering the globalisation of the financial

Mexican institutions' financial statements prior to the adoption of GAAP differed considerably from the US and other industrial nations. The areas of divergence included the valuation of fixed assets, the definition of non-performing assets, and the treatment of interest income on loans.[242] These and other differences in the accounting practices between the two countries led to many complaints that the true nature of the Mexican banks' asset quality during the months before the devaluation had been disguised.

Under GAAP accounting requirements, banks must include in their past-due loan portfolios the total balances of delinquent loans, including past-due, due, and current balances.[243] Once a loan has been classified as past-due, banks may not continue to apply interest charges. Another important change under the requirements is that practically all securities portfolios are now valued at mark-to-market.[244] The purpose of the new criterion is to provide a clearer determination of the real value of financial institutions' investments and, consequently, of their equity.

Reporting financial statements using GAAP accounting standards makes it easier to compare banks' accounts internationally and makes the accounts more credible in the eyes of international money markets. Moreover, it is essential to proper credit analysis, the lack of which contributed greatly to the loan defaults which have plagued banks since the crisis began. The use of the new principles should also encourage market discipline to become the basic means for maintaining a healthy financial system.

markets and the complexity which some Mexican banking operations have reached in the last years it's necessary to reset the accounting standards, the valuation of assets and liabilities as well as the presentation and publication of financial information of these institutions.' *See*, *Switch to GAAP Seen To Clarify Banks' Loan Losses*, Special Report, The Business Times (Singapore), Mar. 1996.

[242] Specifically, using previous Mexican standards, only the missed payment of an installment loan is classified as past due (after 30 days), while under US GAAP, the loan itself is classified as past due after 90 days. Additionally, in the US, interest accrued on loans is discontinued when it appears likely that the borrower will not be able to make payments. All unpaid interest accrued is reversed. In Mexico, however, interest is allowed to continue to accrue on loans except in cases where the entire balance of the underlying loan principal is past due. Unpaid interest accrued does not have to be reversed. *See* Ayer, above note 6, at 13; *see also* Fluckiger, above note 15, at 79.

[243] *The Mexican Economy 1997*, above note 134, at III(4). Prior to 1997, past-due loan portfolios included only the unpaid amortisations of each loan. Thus, the transition to GAAP was particularly burdensome for many banks because it had the immediate effect of increasing the ratio of bad loans to total loans in the banks' portfolios by approximately 24 per cent. *See Switch to GAAP*, above note 241.

[244] Under a mark-to-market valuation, assets are valued at their current market price rather than their nominal value. *See The Mexican Economy 1997*, above note 134, at III(4).

5. PARTICIPATION IN SDDS

In March 1996, the Executive Board of the IMF approved an initiative to create the Special Data Dissemination Standard ('SDDS'). This standard seeks to improve the practices for the dissemination of information by countries participating in international capital markets.[245] It was established by the IMF in response to lapses in the publication of economic and financial data prior to the Mexican crisis. Mexico accepted the IMF's invitation to participate in this initiative and collaborate as a pilot country in the implementation of the first stage of the SDDS. In September 1996, Mexico and seventeen other countries inaugurated the Dissemination Standards Bulletin Board ('DSBB').[246]

The SDDS emphasises four aspects: (1) the coverage, periodicity and timeliness of data; (2) public access; (3) integrity of the data; and (4) the quality of data.[247] The rationale behind the SDDS is that informed financial markets are likely to be less volatile and that prompt simultaneous release of government statistics prepared according to adequate and harmonised standards will be an antidote to runs by investors caused by leaks, rumours, and the decision to act on inside information before one's competitor does.[248]

6. REVISED CAPITAL ADEQUACY VALUATIONS

In September of 1996, the Banco de Mexico issued regulations requiring banks to adjust their capital adequacy reports to reflect market risk (changes in share prices, interest rates, exchange rates, and inflation) as well as credit risk.[249] This change was designed to move Mexico closer to international

[245] The *Mexican Economy 1997*, above note 134, at III(8).

[246] The group of subscribing countries included industrialised nations (United States, United Kingdom, Japan, Germany, Italy, France and Holland), countries 'in transition' (Croatia, Lithuania, Hungary, and the Slovak Republic), and 'emerging' economies (Chile, Argentina, Philippines, Singapore, Peru, Thailand, and Mexico). Each subscribing country is required to post the main characteristics of twenty selected variables on the DSBB, including the methodology for computing the data, the procedures for publishing the information, the publishing institution, and the individual responsible for answering any question posed by users. Moreover, the bulletin board must also include a schedule for the release of information indicating the dates on which the data will be published in the four subsequent months. *Id.*

[247] In order to increase the public's trust in the statistics published on the DSBB, equal access is guaranteed to all users, the clarity and objectivity of the information is ensured, and basic statistical information is published in the real, fiscal, financial, and external sectors. Ibid.

[248] Cynthia Lichtenstein, *The New Financial World of Cross Border Capital Movements: The International Monetary Fund Agreement in the Light of the 1994 Mexican Peso Crisis*, WAHRUNG UND WIRTSCHAFT: DAS GELD IM RECHT 197 (Albrecht Weber, ed., 1996).

[249] *See* Department of the Treasury, *Monthly Report by the Secretary of the Treasury Pursuant to the Mexican Debt Disclosure Act of 1995* (17 Oct. 1996) <http://www.ustreas.gov/treasury/tnews102.htm>.

regulatory standards and to increase transparency in the system. In an effort to further boost the quality and quantity of bank capital, the Banco de Mexico issued a package of measures in September of 1999 which included a gradual lowering of the amount of deferred taxes banks can consider basic capital to 20 per cent by the year 2003.[250] Under the measures, banks are also forbidden to consider as basic capital special subordinated obligations or debt instruments.[251]

7. Encouragement of Credit Bureau System

In February 1995, the Mexican government enacted new regulations designed to encourage the creation of credit bureaus covering areas such as credit card obligations, auto financing, and mortgages. Prior to the new regulations, only one credit bureau existed. This credit bureau, owned by a group of the largest Mexican banks, operated only on behalf of its owners, as banks historically have been unwilling to share credit information between each other. The lack of a common credit database made it extremely difficult for Mexican banks to access the information necessary to value new loans or to determine a potential borrower's creditworthiness. The new regulations outline the procedures for collecting and disseminating consumer credit information as well as the procedures for applying to the Finance Ministry for operating licenses.

8. 1998 Financial Reform Legislation

On 26 March 1998, the President of Mexico presented to Congress a reform package calling for significant structural changes to the financial regulatory agencies. The reform package included measures to grant the Banco de Mexico independence on exchange rate decisions[252], eliminate limits on foreign ownership of domestic banks[253], simplify the shareholder structure of financial groups,[254] create a limited deposit insurance system,

[250] Previously there was no specific limit on how much deferred tax could be considered capital. S&P estimated that as of Mar., 1999 37 per cent of the banking system's reported equity was in the form of deferred taxes, compared with 1.55 per cent in Argentina. *See* Richard Jacobsen, *Mexico Moves to Strengthen Ailing Banks*, Reuters News Service, 12 Sept. 1999.

[251] Ibid.

[252] *Decreto* que Reforma la Ley del Banco de Mexico, 26 de Marzo, 1998.

[253] The legislation called for the elimination of the limitation restricting foreign-controlled banks from acquiring a controlling interest in a bank whose net capital exceeds 6 per cent of the aggregate capital in the banking system. The elimination of this restriction would make it possible for foreign institutions to acquire controlling interests in Mexico's three largest banks. *See Government Proposes Restructuring Banking Regulatory Agencies*, Sourcemex Econ. News and Analysis on Mex., 18 Mar. 1998, *available in* 1998 WL 8779038.

[254] The proposal to modify the shareholder structure of the controlling entities of financial groups, banks, and brokerage houses entailed the issuance of a new, single series of 'O' shares

transform the CNBV into a semi-autonomous agency, and convert all of FOBAPROA's holdings into public debt.

Perhaps the most important initiative in the 1998 legislation was the proposal to transform the CNBV into a semi-autonomous entity with increased regulatory and supervisory powers. Under the proposal, the CNBV would become dependent on the Banco de Mexico rather than the Ministry of Finance. Since the Banco de Mexico is an autonomous entity, the CNBV would gain similar autonomy. This reform would dramatically redistribute financial system supervisory powers from the Ministry of Finance to the Banco de Mexico. The Ministry of Finance would continue to exercise limited influence over the CNBV, however, since one of six seats on the proposed Governing Board of the CNBV would be filled by the Secretary of Finance.

Moody's Investor Service, a credit rating agency, voiced its support for the legislation in a special comment which stated that 'the progress made by Mexican authorities during the past three years in terms of the quality of official oversight, if reinforced with energetic and rigorous implementation of the proposed March 1998 reforms, will move the industry toward a stable and more efficient banking system.'[255] The agency added that without the reforms, the Mexican banking system could continue to suffer periodic meltdowns.[256]

The legislation's most controversial measure proved to be the proposal to eliminate FOBAPROA and transfer its functions to the Banco de Mexico and the Ministry of Finance. The measure would entail transferring the assets currently controlled by FOBAPROA into public debt by converting them into bonds.[257] The proposal hit an immediate roadblock in Congress as legislators from opposition parties questioned whether the increase in public debt would hurt economic growth and hamper any efforts to boost the purchasing power of the peso, ease unemployment and underemployment, and reduce poverty.[258] Controversy grew stronger in the wake of US

to be freely subscribed, thus allowing a broader participation in the institutions by foreign corporate entities and individuals. Ibid.

255 *See Moody's Comments on Mexican Bank Credit Strength*, Moody's Investors Service, 4 May 1998.

256 Moody's has long identified the issue of 'moral hazard' that occurs when the government bail outs become conducive to excessive risk exposure. Measures that would burden even large depositors with bank risk would go far in addressing this problem. Moody's described the reform proposals as 'the culmination of an almost four-year-long journey to reduce moral hazard through structural changes'. Ibid.

257 FOBAPROA was unable to dispose of much of the debt acquired from troubled banks and had amassed over US$65 billion in non-performing assets, primarily in real estate and bad loans. Officials estimated that the government could expect to recover no greater than approximately US$24.5 billion from the sale of the bonds. *See Mexico's Werner optimistic on financial reform*, Reuters News Service, 15 May 1998.

258 *See Government Introduces Controversial Bank-Reform Legislation*, Sourcemex Econ. & Analysis on Mex., 15 Apr. 1998, *available in* 1998 WL 8779051.

accusations in the summer of 1998 that officials from twelve of Mexico's top banks were involved in money-laundering schemes.

A tumultuous debate and political stalemate continued in the lower house for several months. During this period, the level of bad bank loans rose from approximately 552 billion pesos (US$55 billion) on 28 February 1998 to over 640 billion pesos (US$64 billion) by late November.[259] Outraged leaders from both the pro-business National Action Party (PAN) and the leftist Democratic Revolutionary Party (PRD) called for the resignation of Banco de Mexico Chairman Guillermo Ortiz for his former role as Minister of Finance in the Fobaproa bank bailout.

Congress eventually approved a compromise plan on 12 December 1998 which called for the creation of a new Bank Savings Protection Institute ('IPAB') to replace Fobaproa.[260] Under the compromise plan, Fobaproa's liabilities will not be immediately assumed as public debt. Instead, the liabilities will be financed each year as a separate category in the federal budget. In addition, the current 100 per cent *de-facto* deposit insurance which banks and depositors enjoyed under the old Fobaproa system will be scaled back gradually beginning in 2003 until it reaches around US$105,000 per depositor in 2005.[261] Finally, the plan called for a team of auditors hired by Congress to perform detailed audits of the liabilities to determine which loans are tainted with fraud or other improprieties.[262] Those loans found to be tainted by fraud were to be returned to the banks that originally issued them.[263]

V. ASSESSMENT OF MEXICO'S REFORMS

A. *Successes*

In many respects, the support programmes and legal reforms adopted by the Mexican Government conform to what are generally considered to be

[259] *See* Caroline Brothers, *Bank Rescue Stalemate Boosts Costs to $64 Bln-Gurria*, Reuters News Service, 26 Nov. 1998. Figures released in Aug. 1999 put the estimate of the total cost of the bailout at NP$988.3 billion, representing 21 per cent of GDP for 1999. *See Bailout Costs Continue to rise for Mexico Banks*, Reuters News Service (31 Aug. 1999) (citing SandP press release).

[260] *See* Brendan M. Case, *Mexican Parties Back Bank Bailout Amid Debtors' Protests*, The Dallas Morning News, 13 Dec. 1998.

[261] *See* Michael Christie, *Mexico's Banks in Race to Beat Clock*, Reuters News Service, 16 July 1999.

[262] Ibid.

[263] A six-month independent audit conducted by Canadian auditor Michael Mackey exposed only 6.0 billion pesos (US$640 million) as clearly illegal. However, the audit did succeed in targeting 45 billion pesos (US$4.5 billion) in Fobaproa liabilities as 'dubious' because they were the result of loans by banks to related parties and another 24 billion pesos (US$2.5 billion) as worth highlighting because they did not comply with Fobaproa's original criteria for taking on bad bank loans. *See* Michael Christie, *Mexico Bank Audit Blasts Privatisation Failings*, Rueters News Service, 20 July 1999.

'best practices' for dealing with bank crises.[264] In particular, Mexican authorities responded quickly in arranging the support and liquidity packages to stem the massive outflow of capital. Furthermore, regulators were able to successfully constrain the growth in the number of impaired institutions without resorting to inflationary financing to resolve banks.

Additionally, Mexico made significant progress in the areas identified by a special Working Party formed by the Group of Ten[265] as 'key indicators' of a robust financial system.[266] For example, Mexico has considerably improved its accounting practices and disclosure techniques. The switch to GAAP was a particularly meaningful achievement as it will now enable markets to see a more realistic picture of the financial condition of Mexican banks. Participation in the SDDS programme is also important because it gives markets the ability to monitor on a daily basis the condition of the Mexican financial system on an aggregate level, as well as monitor the activities of the Mexican financial regulatory authorities. One of the chief criticisms expressed by the markets after the crisis began was that the Banco de Mexico's practice of providing information only on a quarterly basis disguised the true nature of its dwindling foreign reserves between quarterly reports.

Mexico has also made progress in creating a market structure that favours free competition and promotes the efficient use of resources. The relaxation of the limits on foreign ownership of Mexican financial institutions has heightened competition by reducing barriers to market entry. Moreover, foreign bank owners from developed financial systems have promoted the use of advanced and efficient market practices by their Mexican affiliates and this has had a positive effect on the Mexican financial system as a whole.

In addition to promoting disclosure and free competition, Mexico has made improvements in stakeholder oversight and institutional governance

[264] For an in-depth discussion of 'best practices' for dealing with bank crises, *See* Liliana Rojas-Suarez and Steven R. Weisbrod, *The Do's and Don'ts of Banking Crisis Management*, *in* BANKING CRISES IN LATIN AMERICA 121 (Ricardo Hausmann and Liliana Rojas-Suarez, eds., 1996).

[265] The Working Party was made up of representatives from the Group of Ten countries and of emerging market economies, including Mexico. In the course of the work, the working party consulted officials from the Basle Committee, the IMF, IOSCO, the World Bank, and other international organisations with expertise in financial matters.

[266] The key elements of a robust financial system outlined by the G-10 Working Party are: (1) a sound and well-developed legal and juridical framework; (2) comprehensive and well-defined accounting practices and disclosure techniques; (3) improved stakeholder oversight and institutional governance; (4) a market structure which favors free competition and promotes the efficient use of resources and the maximisation of returns; (5) a financial regulatory and supervisory system designed to support and enhance market functioning, rather than displace it, by promoting the integrity of the market infrastructure and fostering the efficient operation of the financial system; and (6) a financial safety net designed to minimise moral hazard. *See* Group of Ten, above note 265, at 74–6.

and has taken measures to strengthen its regulatory and supervisory system by giving it increased independence and authority to impose penalties on wrongdoers.

B. Positive Developments

Several important developments since the first quarter of 1995 provide convincing evidence that Mexico's financial system has emerged from the crisis and is now beginning the process of transformation into a robust financial system. A particularly noteworthy development was that Mexico regained access to international capital markets in the second quarter of 1995, only five months after the December 1994 devaluation. This was in sharp contrast to the aftermath of the 1982 crisis, when Mexico needed almost seven years in order to tap capital markets again.[267]

According to a report by the Ministry of Finance, growth dynamics during 1997 confirmed that the economic recovery had been consolidated.[268] Moreover, real GDP grew 7 per cent in 1997, the strongest performance since 1981.[269] The report gave a very favourable outlook for 1998, predicting GDP growth at 5 per cent in real terms, a current account deficit completely financed by foreign direct investment, and a continued commitment by the government to sound public finances.[270]

Financial and foreign exchange markets have been substantially more stable since 1995. Annual inflation maintained a clear downward trend, from 51.9 per cent in 1995 to 27.7 per cent in 1996, and then to 15.7 per cent in 1997.[271] The reduction in inflationary pressures since March 1995 has induced a downward trend in interest rates, which has been interrupted only by temporary setbacks. Whereas in mid-March 1995 the interbank 28-day interest rate was 110 per cent, a year later it had declined to 46 per cent, and at year-end 1997 it closed at 20.4 per cent.[272] Real interest rates

[267] *See The Mexican Economy 1996*, above note 68, at Part I.

[268] Economic growth was mainly financed through domestic savings, which reached 21.9 per cent of GDP in 1997. *See* Secretaria de Hacienda y Credito Publico, *Mexico Quarterly Report: Fourth Quarter 1997* (no date) <http://www.shcp.gob.mx/english/docs/qr497.html> (hereinafter 'Mexico Quarterly Report').

[269] Furthermore, in contrast to 1981, the economic expansion in 1997 was accompanied by a significant decrease in inflation and higher domestic savings. Significantly, domestic demand (consumption and investment) featured as the main engine of economic activity. *See* Jose Angel Gurria Trevino, *Address at the Economic Club of New York* (11 Mar. 1998) <http://www.shcp.gob.mx/english/docs/pr980312.html>.

[270] *See* Mexico Quarterly Report, above note 239. In fact, Mexico's GDP grew by only 4.8 per cent because of negative pressures from the financial crisis in Asia. *See* Banco de Mexico, *Informe Anual 1998* (Apr. 1999) at 19 <http://www.banxico.org.mx/public_html/inveco/doctos/infanual/anual98/infor98.pdf>

[271] *See The Mexican Economy 1997*, above note 134, at I(1); *See also Mexico: Jan. 1998*, Barclays Bank Country Rep. 1, 1 Jan. 1998, *available in* 1998 WL 10591500.

[272] *See Mexico: Jan. 1998*, Barclays Bank Country Rep. 1, 1 Jan. 1998, *available in* 1998 WL 10591500.

(adjusted for inflation) moved in the same direction. In 1995 the average interbank 28-day rate was 11.6 per cent whereas in 1996 it declined to 9.4 per cent, both in real terms.[273]

The volatility of the peso-dollar exchange rate has been considerably reduced since 1995. In fact, based on a sample taken in 1996 of 12 major currencies under floatation regimes *vis-à-vis* the US dollar, the Mexican peso exchange rate was the second-least volatile.[274] Moreover, Banco de Mexico's international reserves have risen considerably since the peso devaluation, reaching the level of US$30.776 billion as of 3 November 1999, higher than the pre-crisis peak of US$29.2 billion in February 1994.[275]

Mexico demonstrated its creditworthiness by repaying the funds lent to it by the US and the IMF in 1995 ahead of schedule. On 17 January 1997, Mexico prepaid the remaining outstanding balance of US$3.5 billion owed to the US under the Financial Assistance Package granted to Mexico at the onset of the financial crisis.[276] The repayment ahead of schedule also saved the Mexican government a significant amount of money in interest.

Not only has Mexico paid off its external debt, it has made a meaningful reduction in the debt incurred from the various financial support programmes implemented since the crisis began. By year-end 1997, nearly one-fifth of the cost of the financial support programmes (71.3 billion pesos in net present value) had already been covered.[277]

Finally, the international financial community appears to have given the Banco de Mexico its seal of approval.[278] In its reunion of 9 September 1996, the Board of Governors of the Bank for International Settlements ('BIS')[279] invited the Banco de Mexico and eight other central banks to become BIS members. The selection of the new members was based on selective economic and financial criteria, as well as contributions to global economic and financial cooperation. The invitation extended to the Banco de Mexico

[273] *See The Mexican Economy 1997*, above note 134, at I(1). [274] Ibid.

[275] *See Banco de Mexico Net Assets Static, Reserves Slip*, Reuters News Service, 3 Nov. 1999.

[276] *See The Mexican Economy 1997*, above note 134, at III(1)(a).

[277] *See* Secretaria de Hacienda y Credito Publico, *Economic Policy Guidelines for 1998* (Nov. 1997) <http://www.shcp.gob.mx/english/docs/crit98/crit98e.html>, at Appendix D.

[278] In the Fall of 1997, S&P, an international financial credit rating agency, revised its outlook on Mexico from 'stable' to 'positive', reflecting its favourable view of the unprecedented political liberalisation, the sustained economic expansion, the strengthening of balance-of-payment fundamentals, and the recuperation of the banking system. *See S&P Affirms Outlook on Mexico's Currency*, Mexico Business Monthly, 1 Oct. 1997, *available in* WL 13104353.

[279] The BIS is the world's oldest international financial institution. It is the only central banking institution at the international level which is owned and controlled by central banks. The BIS carries out a number of highly specialised services for central banks, provides a forum for international monetary cooperation, and functions as a centre for monetary and economic research. *The Mexican Economy 1997*, above note 134, at III(7). See http://<www.bis.org>.

recognises Mexico's economic and financial significance, the role the Banco de Mexico has played in promoting cooperation among central banks around the world, and the Banco de Mexico's active participation in the BIS.

C. *Remaining Deficiencies and Areas for Improvement*

Although developments since the first quarter of 1995 have been mostly positive, Mexico's financial system still suffers from inadequacy in several areas. Until these inadequacies are addressed, the financial system will remain vulnerable to major economic shocks such as the December 1994 peso devaluation. In fact, some financial advisors continue to urge investors to use caution when considering investments in Mexico.[280]

One conspicuous deficiency in Mexico's financial system is that it provides numerous incentives for moral hazard. The incentives for moral hazard are due, in part, to the way in which the intervention and recapitalisation of troubled banks were carried out. First, the regulatory authorities failed to compel managers and shareholders to share enough of the losses. Moreover, instead of a single bailout, there were multiple bailouts. As a result, bank managers and shareholders may now be more inclined to incur excessive risk on the assumption that the government will consent to similar bailouts in the future.

Other aspects of the response to the crisis could induce moral hazard as well. For instance, the general extension of debtor aid programmes, such as ADE, FINAPE, and FOPYME, could encourage some debtors to defer paying their debt obligations until they receive government assistance, notwithstanding their ability to pay.

Mexico continues to suffer from a weak and inadequate bankruptcy system. An ideal robust financial system possesses a sound and well-developed legal and juridical framework, including a developed bankruptcy system. Well-defined bankruptcy laws are necessary so that the taking possession of collateral, as well as other legal recourse, is possible without undue delay. The bankruptcy laws in effect in 1995 (and still in effect today) are largely unchanged since their enactment in the 1940s. The laws are so cumbersome and inefficient that they afford many debtors virtual immunity from collection efforts.[281] The deficient bankruptcy system also

[280] In May of 1998, Moody's Investors Service cautioned that the Mexican banking system still suffered from extremely weak financial fundamentals. For example, during that period Mexico had the lowest average bank financial strength rating (E+) of any major country in Latin America. Moreover, although it was not reflected on banks' balance sheets, banks remained liable for contingent losses on approximately 25 per cent of loans sold to FOBAPROA, which created a significant exposure to credit risk. *See Moody's*, above note 255.

[281] In 1994, an initial draft of a bankruptcy reform programme was proposed which would have lifted the effective immunity of debtors. Unfortunately, the legislation was never enacted. Ibid.

hampered corporate restructurings and this had a negative effect on the quality of bank portfolios since a significant per centage of the banks' debtors were corporations. President Zedillo sent a bill to Congress in the autumn of 1999 to modernise the bankruptcy system. Unfortunately, political experts immediately predicted that the bill would stall as a result of the July 2000 presidential elections.

Although Mexico has made substantial improvement in the capacity and effectiveness of its regulatory and supervisory system, there still remains room for improvement. Above all, it is important that supervisors break free from the 'rituals' of banking supervision, which for years have allowed formal compliance with regulations without addressing the crucial issues of bank solvency, profitability, and competition. Recent CNBV initiatives to eliminate the practice of permanently stationing on-site inspectors within the financial institutions should help to reduce this problem.

Conflicts of interest have also arisen from the government regulators' dual role as 'watchdog' and supporter of financial institutions. At the same time that regulators helped to orchestrate the bank bailouts, they were also responsible for monitoring the banks and disciplining improper behaviour. The result has been that while regulators focused on performing the role of supporter, organising various bailouts and facilitating sales and mergers of institutions, they somewhat disregarded their role as watchdog of the same financial institutions. The consequences of this failure have been made painfully evident by the discovery that a drug cartel was successful in purchasing a small Mexican bank in 1995[282], and also by the 1998 sting operation conducted by US law enforcement officers that uncovered widespread involvement by Mexican banks in money laundering schemes.[283] These two revelations demonstrate the shortcomings of the previous supervisory practices and the need for the regulatory agencies to shift their focus more towards the role of watchdog.

282 Mexican officials from the CNBV discovered in early 1998 that Mexican drug traffickers from the Juarez Cartel obtained a license from the Ministry of Finance in Apr. 1995 to purchase a small domestic bank. The true owners of the bank were only uncovered after regulators detected fraud at the bank 19 months later. *See* Leslie Crawford, *Mexico Drug Men 'Bought Bank'*, *Financial Times* (London) 17 Mar. 1998.

283 In May 1998, US prosecutors announced that they had broken a vast drug-money laundering scheme involving twelve of Mexico's nineteen largest banks. The three-year sting operation, termed 'Operation Casablanca', was described by Treasury Secretary Robert Rubin as the 'largest and most comprehensive drug-money laundering case in the history of the United States law enforcement.' *See Mexican Banks Indicted in Drug-Cash Laundering*, *Dallas Morning News*, 19 May 1998.

VI. CONCLUSION

It is evident from the developments since 1995 that Mexico has emerged from its immediate financial crisis. Recent economic indicators demonstrate that the economy has revived significantly and is showing signs of progress. However, Mexico's financial system has far to go before it reaches the level of robustness. Accordingly, to fully reap the benefits of the renewed growth in private capital inflows and financial integration with developed markets, the Mexican government must continue to pursue an aggressive programme of structural reforms in the banking sector to increase stability. Unless further improvements to the banking sector are made, the Mexican economy risks being dragged down by the banking sector and will remain vulnerable to external economic shocks.

Chapter 4

The Venezuelan Banking Crisis, 1994–5

Ruth de Krivoy

I. INTRODUCTION

The Venezuelan banking crisis 1994–5 was largely a microeconomic problem, rooted in bad regulation and supervision, and bad banking. However, the process was also related to macroeconomic problems, rooted in a long history of pro-cyclical policies, and directly affected by a poorly sequenced economic reform programme, and negative shocks due to the fall of oil prices and political turbulence. The cost of the crisis further increased as a result of crisis management policies.

The Venezuelan experience holds lessons with respect to macroeconomic policy, banking regulation and supervision, and crisis management, which might be especially useful for supervisors and bankers in transition economies.

II. THE VENEZUELAN ECONOMY

The Venezuelan economy is highly dependent on oil, and very sensitive to international oil prices, as more than 50 per cent of fiscal revenues and 75 per cent of exports are oil based. Oil has a decisive influence on market expectations and also plays a key role in the country's politics.

Ample oil revenues paved the way to a state-centred rentier society that grew accustomed to negative real interest rates, heavy subsidies, and low tax rates. Government expenditures grew over time due to a bloated bureaucracy, numerous entitlements and a wide array of inefficient Government-owned companies and institutions set up over time to redistribute oil revenues.

Oil shocks, both positive and negative, have always been felt at full strength due to the lack of stabilisation policies. Rising oil prices have invariably translated into higher Government expenditures and booms, while the impact of falling oil prices has been dampened as demonstrated by the ensuing fiscal and balance of payments deficits. The country's inability to adjust to oil shocks reflects the lack of political consensus with respect to the need to adjust.

Oil prices fell in real terms since the mid-1970s, and declined especially in 1982–3, 1986–8 and 1992–4. The political establishment traditionally took the decline in oil prices as transitory, expecting prompt recoveries and hoping to muddle through difficult times. Administrative controls were the usual policy response to external shocks, originating cycles of containment and partial adjustment measures, which were abandoned as soon as oil prices began to recover.

Sound long-term strategies translated into sustained growth in the oil sector, while import substitution policies implemented since the early 1960s led to a non-competitive and inefficient non-oil sector. Controls on prices and interest rates, credit allocation rules, widespread subsidies, foreign exchange controls and exchange rate policies resulted in a highly volatile real exchange rate and hindered long term private investment. The non-oil sector has also been largely affected by the country's deficient legal and institutional framework.

This set of policies resulted in poor performance throughout the 1980s. Non-oil real GDP stagnated, investment (both private and public) declined, and unemployment rose, partially masked by the rising levels of informal sector employment. Towards the end of the decade, fiscal and balance of payments deficits led to an untenable situation, and economic reforms could no longer be avoided.

III. THE FINANCIAL SYSTEM

Venezuela's banking system is relatively small, as it has been confined to channelling domestic savings onto private non-oil investment.

Government owned banks were established in the 1930s and 1940s as a means to channel oil rent onto the non-oil sector through loans at subsidised interest rates. By December 1988, they accounted for only 6.2 per cent of total deposits. Public sector financial institutions repeatedly received preferential treatment by the regulators, and were often used to influence market conditions and distort competition.

The banking system is largely private and centres on commercial banks. It developed on the basis of specialised institutions legally restricted to conduct only certain types of business, and prevented from others. Consequently, more than 150 financial institutions were operating in Venezuela by the end of 1993. Despite the large number of institutions, the financial system has been heavily concentrated. The largest six banks accounted for over 50 per cent of total financial system assets prior to the 1994 crisis.

Ownership of banks and financial groups has also been highly concentrated, controlled by small groups of individuals or families. Only fourteen banks are listed in the Caracas Stock Exchange and the proportion of traded shares has usually been very low. Disclosure rules on beneficial ownership have been lax and minority shareholders have been treated with disdain.

Financial institutions were grouped in conglomerates of legally independent financial entities controlled by common shareholders. The set up has been analogous to universal banking but less efficient and transparent. A commercial bank has usually been the core of the group, which also included mortgage banks, investment banks, leasing companies, insurance, securities firms, trusts, money management funds and offshore banking operations. Banks have also been closely linked to industry and commerce through common ownership, often through opaque arrangements.

In the 1970s, Venezuelan banks began to establish offshore operations as affiliates, subsidiaries or firms linked to the banks by common ownership. This came in part as a market reaction to exchange controls, portfolio allocation rules, interest rate regulations and high cash reserve requirements. However, offshore operations were also used as outlets for problem assets, as they were not subject to any kind of supervision. Heavy losses in the offshore operations were unveiled when parent banks ran into problems at the time of the crisis, making problems more complicated in the most strenuous times.

Bank capitalisation declined since the early 1970s oil boom, as capital adequacy rules were progressively loosened. Franchise value of Venezuelan banks rose as a consequence of the 1975 reform of the banking law which closed the Venezuelan market to foreign banks and severely restricted the scope of business for all foreign banks that decided to remain doing business in the country. From there on, only Latin American banks could only be authorised to operate in Venezuela, on the basis of reciprocity. However, they never played an important role.

Politically influenced entry barriers and equivocal exit rules helped shape oligopolistic behaviour. Operating costs grew to the point where they could no longer be covered by deposit spreads, which were frequently contained by interest rate controls or other administrative restrictions. Profits became highly dependent on fee income and extraordinary revenue items generated by asset sales, often conducted with related companies.

The regulatory framework and the closed ownership structure largely explain the corporate governance problems, which led to pervasive insider and connected lending practices. The usual corporate checks and balances turned were largely ineffective, and internal controls were loose.

Furthermore, external auditor reports were not required at all for a long time. They became mandatory in 1985, but turned out to be inconsequential and misleading in many cases.

Large individual bank failures occurred in the 1960s, when political and economic shocks affected the country. Although problems were limited to individual banks, and never reached systemic proportions, these failures were very costly (28 per cent of GDP). There were further cases of individual bank bankruptcies in the 1970s and 1980s, all of them following similar patterns.

These episodes contributed to shape the moral hazard problems that would later on feed into the 1994 crisis. As a rule, the banks collapsed largely due to insider loans and imprudent risk taking. Government action always came too late, intervening in bankrupt banks long after the capital was gone. Although shareholders lost their equity capital, substantial profits had already been made in connected businesses funded by the bankrupt banks. Depositors were bailed out by the government. Most of the banks were liquidated in a drawn out process that, in some cases, lasted up to twenty years. Despite the changes in regulations that came after each large bank failure, supervision and regulation weakened over time.

Venezuela's chief regulator is the Superintendent of Banks, under the authority of the Minister of Finance. The central bank has been the lender of last resort, in charge of monetary policy, international reserves management and, until 1992, numerous development-related responsibilities. The central bank had been the nucleus of all bail-outs prior to the 1994 crisis.

Deposit insurance was established in 1985 by means of a special fund, Fondo de Garantía de Depósitos y Protección Bancaria (FOGADE). The fund was given the assets that the central bank had acquired from previous failures, and later on funded through bank contributions. The fund had been severely undercapitalised throughout its existence, and concentrated on managing its assets.

The banking system's fragility was evident by 1989, as the government initiated economic reforms. The non risk-weighted capital/asset ratio had fallen from 13 per cent in 1970 to 5.5 per cent in 1988, and poor quality assets and low profitability affected many banks.

IV. THE 1989 ECONOMIC REFORM PROGRAMME

Market oriented reforms were implemented in 1989, in line with what was generally happening in Latin America. Exchange controls were abolished, and the differential exchange rate system gave way to a single floating exchange rate, though largely influenced by the central bank's intervention in the foreign exchange market.

Prices of most goods and services were deregulated. Administrative restrictions on direct foreign investment were virtually eliminated, except where mandated by law (banking, insurance and media). Lower tariffs and non-tariff barriers quickly exposed the Venezuelan industry to international competition. Interest rates were deregulated and the central bank moved from direct controls to market based instruments.

Unfortunately, reforms lagged on two fronts that were key to the country's monetary and financial stability: the financial sector and the fiscal sector. Both of them required legislative changes to move ahead, and became the subject of heated and protracted discussions, as vested interests worked effectively against the needed changes. The consequences would soon be felt.

In 1989, the first year of the programme, real GDP fell sharply (–8.6 per cent) and inflation rose to unprecedented highs (81 per cent p.a.). However, the economy rapidly recovered and started to grow again in 1990–1, while inflation declined to the 30 per cent range. The oil-export windfall caused by the Gulf War (1990) quickly weakened the commitment to fiscal adjustment. Soon after, a few highly visible and successful privatisations overshadowed the need for fiscal reforms, and nothing was done to offset the large decline in the government's oil revenues in 1991.

Government expenditures rose while monetary policy was also being eased in 1990–1 in an effort to speed up economic recovery after the political commotion of the early days of the programme. Capital inflows further fed the boom, as overly optimistic expectations influenced the markets. Consequently, the economy began to grow rapidly (perhaps too rapidly) in 1990–1.

Financial deregulation allowed banks to bid freely for deposits. Aggressive competition for market shares led many banks to rapidly expand their balance sheets by paying high interest rates. The decline in the franchise value of banks due to reforms, deregulation, and increased competition added incentives to bad banking. Weak banks engaged in questionable banking practices, risky investments and insider lending, taking advantage of the lax oversight. The common pattern in those banks was aggressive growth, risky lending, and over-investment in the stock market, real estate, and tourism.

Venezuela went through a speculative bubble that lasted for two years. Huge and quick profits were made in real estate and in the capital market, attracting both local and foreign investors. In fact, share prices increased by 440 per cent in real terms in 1990–1, but fell substantially in 1992 once the country entered into political turmoil.

Several banks began to pay exceedingly high interest rates on deposits, thus signalling their difficulties to the markets. Interest rate spreads declined while operative costs were on the rise, leading banks to mask their operational losses with extraordinary revenues originating largely from the sale of assets to related parties. (Off balance sheet operations grew, issuing both bolívar and dollar denominated deposit-like liabilities—mainly to their Venezuelan depositors—and lending on the funds to the parent bank or its affiliated companies).

Meanwhile, economic reforms were taking their toll in the banks loan portfolios. The substantial devaluation in 1989, shifts in relative prices, positive real interest rates and import liberalisation affected borrowers. Large Government-owned companies, which had heavily borrowed in the domestic and international markets in previous years, also ran into difficulties and Venezuelan banks had to bear the cost of major debt restructurings.

No effective steps were taken in the boom years to reinforce banking regulation and supervision and its enforcement. Although legislation was drafted and presented to congress as part of the commitments of the World Bank–IMF sponsored reform programme, the only outcome was the approval of the new Central Bank Law in December 1992, which established the independence of the central bank and improved monetary policy instruments.

V. 1992–3: THE LEAD UP TO THE CRISIS

Banking problems intensified as the country entered into a period of severe political turbulence. The financial bubble burst in February 1992, after the first attempted coup. Real estate and share prices plummeted, and the overly optimistic environment of the early 1990s gave way to two years of riots, strikes, and demonstrations. Market expectations were further hurt as commitment to reforms diminished, oil prices declined, and Venezuela's 36-year old democracy was further shaken by a second coup attempt in November 1992 and the President's impeachment in June 1993.

Additionally, fiscal problems worsened due to declining oil prices. Venezuela was virtually excluded from the international financial markets, reflecting widespread concerns about the country's political and economic outlook. Real interest rates rose both in bolívar and dollar terms.

Demand for money became extremely volatile, and declined sharply after 1992. Capital outflows were recurrently triggered by political disturbances and banks got hurt by the sharp erosion of deposits and lending in real terms, falling real estate and share prices, and the deterioration of loan portfolios. Financial market risks associated with capital flows became extremely high, and the domestic saving rate fell to a low of 16 per cent of GDP in 1993.

Signs of financial distress became evident as the government and PDVSA (the state-owned oil industry) began to borrow heavily in the domestic market, pushing interest rates up. The group of ailing banks continued to deteriorate, and their deposit rates rose far above the market. It is worth noting that most of the banks that faced major problems in the last quarter of 1993 (and collapsed as the crisis unfolded in 1994) had embarked on aggressive expansion strategies since the early 1990s. As they had heavily invested in real estate, tourism and construction, all of which were hurt by the asset price slump in 1992–3, they were especially hurt by the changing business environment.

After the attempted coup in February 1992, approving the financial sector reform became increasingly difficult. Prudential regulations were drafted to bridge the gap until the new banking law would be enacted, but these were not enough to reverse the debilitating trend. Lacking the legal powers to impose them, regulators had to craft these rules through protracted consensus building exercises. Although some improvements were made in 1991–3 to the accounting rules, information requirements, and loan portfolio classification and provisioning rules, systemic risk was rising to dangerous levels.

A new Banking Law was approved in October 1993 by a transition government, which had been given special legislative powers by congress. The new Banking Law established the Basle capital adequacy rules and consolidated supervision, opened the banking system to foreign competition, allowed for a more competitive environment and strengthened sanctions for directors and bank management. This law was to become effective on 1 January 1994.

VI. THE BANKING CRISIS, 1994–5

The banking crisis erupted in January 1994 after 24 months of severe political turbulence and growing economic problems. The triggering event was the collapse of Banco Latino (the second largest) on 13 January 1994.

The bank was placed under government control once it proved to be unable to meet its check clearing obligations. Banco Latino and all its related institutions were closed, affecting 1.2 million accounts, more than 10 per cent of total bank deposits, as well as a sizeable amount of trust funds, pension funds, public sector deposits, and inter-bank funds. Unfortunately this happened when both the government and congress were in their last weeks in office, soon to be replaced by the winners of the December 1993 national elections.

The unclear policy response to Banco Latino's breakdown fuelled a violent contagion effect. Heavy capital flight and runs on bank deposits began a few days later, hurting particularly a group of banks that were related to Banco Latino or thought by the public to have difficulties of their own. Market expectations were also affected by uncertainties regarding the new government's economic policies and widespread fears of exchange controls, devaluation and nationalisation of bank deposits.

The group of ailing banks got virtually excluded from the overnight inter-bank market and had to resort to the unusual practice of guaranteeing short term inter-bank loans with ad hoc trusts, which made their weaknesses even more evident to the market. Runs also affected the money desks and the offshore operations of Venezuelan banks, as the bankruptcy of the Latino Curacao NV revealed the existence of a substantial mass of off-balance sheet deposits with virtually no asset coverage.

The subsequent contagion effect became extremely destructive, largely due to the way the crisis was handled. In the first three weeks almost 40 per cent of the banking system virtually collapsed. Popular anger increased and recurrent waves of runs on deposits affected the banking system as Banco Latino remained closed for 77 days, and its depositors were kept in total uncertainty. The combination of severe fiscal difficulties, concerns with respect to the other ailing banks, and dragging uncertainties with respect to the new Government's banking and macroeconomic policies further eroded depositor confidence and stimulated capital flight.

Economic and financial conditions continued to worsen due to the lack of a comprehensive strategy to cope with the crisis. Several episodes of banking problems ensued throughout an 18-month period, each one evoking a different response from the authorities with respect to depositors and shareholders.

The first was Banco Latino, placed under government control and closed in January 1994. It was reopened in April with special funding by the government, run by government appointees, and has been in operation since then. Certain restrictions applied to the withdrawal of funds by depositors. Emergency financial legislation approved by congress in March 1994 set the rules for Banco Latino's rehabilitation.

The second episode included a group of eight banks, which received special liquidity support from FOGADE, funded by the central bank as a means to prevent the chaotic collapse of those banks and, consequently, that of the payment system. The programme lasted from 25 January to 17 June 1997. Holding measures were imposed and existing management was kept in place until the banks were taken over by the government and closed in June. The previously announced policy of avoiding further bank closures had been abandoned. Several months later the government approved the liquidation of these banks. Until the take over, no restrictions applied to the withdrawal of funds by depositors. After the closure, deposit insurance rules became effective. The intervention in and further closure of these banks in mid-1994 aggravated capital outflows and contributed to the derailing of macroeconomic policy. Foreign exchange and price controls and the suspension of Constitutional rights came shortly after, in early July 1994.

The third episode included three major banks. One of them was nationalised in August, without interrupting its normal operations, and the other two were subject to recapitalisation agreements with their owners. As deposit outflows continued, these agreements could not be fulfilled. Consequently, the authorities nationalised these two banks in September and December 1994, respectively. Upon nationalisation, the banks' management was replaced by government appointees. Meanwhile, a small bank was placed under management control of Banco Industrial, a government-owned bank, and later on nationalised. In this group of banks, the withdrawal of funds by depositors was not restricted.

The fourth episode affected three medium size banks, which were nationalised and closed in early 1995. Their deposits were assumed by the group of previously nationalised banks, at FOGADE's expense.

In 1994 the financial system was also hurt by a tax applied to bank debits. The government's decision to establish this tax was confirmed in the first quarter of 1994, while runs on banks were at full strength, effective in the period May–December 1994. The bank-debit tax stimulated capital flight and fuelled distortions in the payment system, as depositors moved to offshore accounts, shifted funds among banks and increased the use of cash, thus intensifying the trends originated by the banking crisis itself. The proportion of cash in M2 rose sharply, from 7 per cent in March to 11 per cent in December 1994.

The Venezuelan deposit insurance system was unable to stave off the bank panic in the 1994–5 crisis. FOGADE was ill prepared to deal with a systemic crisis. Although explicit deposit insurance was limited, the markets operated under the assumption of implicit deposit insurance, as had been the experience in earlier bank failures. Depositors totally disregarded the decline in the real value of deposit insurance, from US$18,000 (in 1985) to US$2,700 (in 1993).

In response to strong social and political pressures at the time of the crisis, congress quadrupled the deposit insurance coverage and extended the safety net to uninsured deposits and deposit-like liabilities, off-balance-sheet risks, and bolívar-denominated off shore liabilities. Paradoxically, runs on banks continued in spite of these legislative changes, reacting to the lack of crisis management guidelines and policies.

Legal and administrative barriers led to a protracted and cumbersome resolution process. Subsequent legislative reforms expanded the government's powers to seize the banks' shareholders' assets, but did not improve the regulators' ability to deal with the crisis.

Bank failures placed economic policies under great stress, especially monetary policy. In its inevitable sequel, the crisis fuelled heavy capital outflows, sharp drops in asset values, recession, unemployment, and inflation. The crisis eroded market confidence, contributed to derail economic reforms and deepened economic problems. It also obstructed Venezuela's relationship with the international financial community, as the country remained excluded from the financial markets until mid-1996. Stability and growth prospects suffered a severe setback.

The political system was also hurt as democratic institutions came under pressure. The judicial system confronted difficult challenges. All government institutions dealing with financial issues were hurt by the crisis, regardless of their specific role and duties.

VII. THE ROLE OF THE CENTRAL BANK

The role of the Central Bank of Venezuela in this crisis was severely constrained by its legal status. Its first efforts, throughout 1992 and 1993, went to alert the government about growing weaknesses in the banking sector. The central bank also addressed the imminent collapse of Banco Latino, seeking to avoid its closure. A joint private and public sector solution was sought but failed, mainly due to the lack of appropriate and timely information on the situation of the bank. Subsequently, the central bank also promoted Banco Latino's prompt reopening, under government control, but this also failed as it required a major political decision and the active participation of all government agencies involved.

Once the crisis emerged, the central bank acted to prevent the chaotic collapse and closure of banks that would have otherwise occurred in the early weeks of the new Administration. Reserve requirements were reduced as a means to alleviate the liquidity problems of the banking system, while at the same time trying to minimise monetary expansion. A special recycling facility was also established to allow the more liquid banks to channel funds onto the less liquid ones. However, this only lasted for a few days, as the risk that these operations involved for the lenders rose quickly.

Voluntary lending to the ailing banks virtually ceased in the ensuing days. On 25 January 1994 a special liquidity assistance programme was implemented by FOGADE, with central bank funding, in order to prevent the chaotic collapse of banks and protect the payment system. This programme was buying time until competent authorities could resolve the fundamentals of the crisis. Although conceived for a short duration, this programme lasted for almost six months. Throughout this protracted period, the central bank recommended and urged the government to address the banking system's solvency, management and profitability problems, in its advisory capacity.

VIII. THE AFTERMATH

Today Venezuela is moving from damage control to healing the wounds in its financial system. It took almost two years to return to market oriented policies under a new IMF programme. Banking supervision is gradually improving.

After the 1994 crisis, nonperforming and past due loans declined as corporate borrowers pre-paid part of their bolivar denominated debt to banks; the low interest rate environment allowed banks and borrowers to work out problem loans; and banks became more aggressive in their collections, improving collateral and foreclosing on loans. Higher provisioning requirements were also established.

Information on risk-weighted capital ratios for Venezuelan banks is available since September 1996. Reflecting the banks slow lending activity and increased investments in government and central bank bonds (zero risk assets), the ratio rose from 14.2 per cent in September to a record high of 17.9 per cent in December 1996. It has been declining gradually to the 15 per cent range as lending activity has been picking up.

Competition has become fierce, and the banking industry is going through a consolidation process. Foreign banks have aggressively entered the Venezuelan market, both through the privatisation of banks previously taken over by the government at the time of the crisis, or by acquiring control ownership of privately held Venezuelan banks. As of October 1997 foreign owned or controlled banks account for more than 50 per cent of the market.

Banks have also been availing themselves of the option to convert into universal banks, which are allowed to undertake all kinds of operations open to banks and other financial institutions in accordance with the banking law. Universal banks have resulted from the merger of banks and other specialised financial institutions previously organised as conglomerates (specialised institutions linked by common ownership), or from the transformation of banks or other specialised financial intermediaries into universal banks.

IX. RECOMMENDATIONS

The Venezuelan banking crisis holds lessons with respect to macroeconomic policy, banking regulation and supervision, and crisis management. It was essentially a microeconomic problem, rooted in bad regulations and bad banking. Problems worsened due to poorly sequenced economic reforms, macroeconomic shocks and political turbulence.

A. *Macroeconomic Policy Issues*

1. Financial Deregulation

The Venezuelan experience demonstrates the high risk of financial deregulation if pre-conditions are absent. Successful financial deregulation requires stable macroeconomic conditions; banks with positive net worth that can reasonably be expected to remain solvent; competitive financial markets; effective bank supervision and reliable information on the true state of bank balance sheets. These were clearly not in place in Venezuela when deregulation was implemented, thereby leading to its failure.

The Venezuelan experience shows that financial deregulation must be carefully planned, adapting the sequence and pace of the process to the financial system's ability to cope with the risks that may emerge during the process.

2. Sequencing of Economic Reforms

Proper sequencing of the reform process is crucial. Political circumstances normally determine the speed and sequence of the reform process, and governments may find that moving on with reforms is better than waiting for a safe and sound banking system to emerge, as by then, the window of opportunity for reforms may be gone. Therefore, I would stress that the health of the banking sector must be one of the top priorities. As the Venezuelan case demonstrates, reforms can be jeopardised at a very high cost if banking sector reforms are postponed and imprudent risk taking by banks is not prevented.

Economic reforms put pressure on banks and might lead to systemic risk in different ways. Deregulation and more responsible fiscal and monetary policies lead to positive real interest rates, slower growth and more competition. Interest rate spreads tend to shrink, and the traditionally high overhead costs might no longer be manageable. Asset quality may deteriorate due to financial market volatility.

More openness and competition in the domestic financial market will also expose the difference in asset quality between banks, giving rise to potentially destabilising market reactions. The money market becomes an efficient early indicator of distress, when ailing banks either have to pay exorbitant rates or are excluded from the inter-bank money market, and risks of runs on banks will further rise as soon as the markets become aware of it. Volatile international capital flows add another dimension to the problem, as substantial amounts of money can leave the country at very short notice, and directly impact the banking system.

3. THE RISK OF DERAILMENT

If macroeconomic imbalances couple with financial market fragility, the potential impact of a banking crisis can easily derail economic reforms and deepen macroeconomic disequilibria. As the Venezuelan case proves, under those circumstances a banking crisis can easily induce heavy capital flight and declines in asset values. Thin capital markets and limited investment opportunities contribute to this fragility and illustrate the importance of capital market development in order to build up resilience to banking crises.

In the acute phase of a banking crisis, the authorities might find that they have no effective tools to deal with the situation other than exchange controls, as was the case in Venezuela. Once controls become the only option, the need for proper policies is even greater in order to be able to remove them quickly.

B. *Banking Regulation and Supervision*

1. INSTITUTIONS AND PROCESSES

The institutional framework will be conducive to stable money and safe and sound banking only if it fulfills three basic requirements: political independence, coordination between the monetary policy function and banking regulation and supervision, and effectiveness, by enabling the incumbents to anticipate systemic risk and to react to it both timely and efficiently.

a. Strong and Independent Bank Supervisors

The basis for effective bank supervision is to have strong and independent bank supervisors shielded from day to day political pressures by means of a clear mandate, and political support to perform their role. Weak bank supervisors, lacking funds and political support, will be unable to enforce regulations that effectively address the sources of bank weaknesses.

b. Where Should Bank Supervision Be?

There is no simple answer to the question as to whether banking supervision should be placed in the central bank or in a separate body. Countries have chosen a diversity of institutional arrangements in their search for a proper interaction between monetary policy and banking supervision and there is no simple nor universal solution to this, as country-specific issues largely determine what kind of arrangement serves each country best.

My views are obviously influenced by my personal experience, but I strongly believe that the central bank -responsible for monetary and financial stability—must be able to ensure that all critical factors converge on this goal. As the Venezuelan case demonstrates, if bank supervision is weak, a strong case can be made in favour of an independent central bank vested with bank supervisory powers as part of an overall strategy for banking crisis avoidance. If the central bank is unable to prevent a banking crisis (or deal with it if it arises), as was the case in Venezuela, its charter to pursue monetary stability and protect the payment system is almost impossible to accomplish.

If coordination between the central bank and bank supervisors is impaired by historical, cultural or political reasons, a single and accountable authority with an unequivocal mandate for stable money and for sound and safe banking would seem a more appropriate arrangement.

A multiple-agency system will be more effective when the country's institutions are strong and stable, the political leadership is truly committed to monetary and financial stability, and anti-inflationary constituencies are strong enough to keep policies on track. If politicians depend on constituencies with a strong pro-inflation bias, as has been the case in Venezuela, a multi-agency system will tend to be less effective as efforts and resources will dissipate, and conflicting views and responsibilities will ultimately lead to poor results.

A single regulatory agency might also facilitate crisis resolution, as expeditious decision making and a clear voice could cope with contagion effects and restore depositor confidence more effectively.

c. Clear Authority

Banking supervisors must have clear authority to sanction banks and to handle bank insolvencies. Unclear rules will place regulators at great personal risk and will make passivity the less risky course of action. Furthermore, their decisions are always politically sensitive and might involve tax payer money. Personal liability should arise only in case of violations of the law, malfeasance or fraud. If these public servants will be personally liable for the actions taken in their official capacity, laws might breed procrastination instead of prudence and effectiveness.

d. Disclosure and Transparency

Disclosure is a powerful tool to strengthen supervision, improve corporate governance and market surveillance, especially if a country is in the early stages of financial sector reform and trust needs to be built up. Market participants should have access to timely, meaningful and accurate information both on banks and on the regulatory process.

Disclosure ultimately strengthens market surveillance and helps protect supervisors from day-to-day political pressures.

e. The Role of External Auditors

External auditors can perform a useful role as an arm of banking supervision by conducting on-site inspections on behalf of the authorities and ensuring that the information provided by the bank accurately reflects its financial position. External auditors must be accountable to the supervisors. However, the contribution that ought to be expected to this end is limited, especially when bank supervisors are perceived to be weak. In the Venezuelan experience, the information provided by external auditors in many cases turned out to be ineffective and misleading.

f. Private Credit Rating Agencies

Independent rating agencies improve market information and awareness, and complement official information. While enhancing their role, rules should prevent misconduct, promote competition, and avoid conflicts of interest. Let us be reminded that, although useful, bank supervision by the markets—the depositors—does not prevent runs on banks. On the contrary, even a slight drop in the rating of a bank could give rise to serious liquidity problems, especially when the markets are unstable or under the influence of a crisis, as happened in Venezuela.

2. Regulatory Issues

a. Licensing

Authorisation policies and procedures contributed to the fragility of the Venezuelan banking system. The approval process has been opaque, allowing for bureaucratic decisions often influenced by politics. Sound business plans and fitness for banking were not central to the approval process. These authorisation policies later on translated into the banks internal governance problems and the weakness of the supervisors.

In order to build stronger banking systems, bank licensing should foster competition and build incentives for strong internal governance. Rules should also offer some assurance that the new banks will be well capitalised, owned by shareholders who are putting their own capital at risk, and managed by individuals with the ethics, skills, and prudence required to run a healthy bank. If the new bank is owned by corporations, beneficial ownership must be known, as only individuals are ultimately accountable. The same criteria should be applied in case of re-licensing and change of ownership control.

The approval process must be transparent, by publishing and uniformly applying the laws, regulations and requirements for a licence, including the application process, and publishing reasoned decisions on licensing applications and the register of licensed banks. However, disclosure must be carefully crafted. The information to be disclosed in each step must be clearly defined and checks and balances must be established in each step. The law must give the supervisory authorities the right to demand pertinent information, a strong responsibility to maintain confidentiality and strict penalties for violating confidentiality. The law must also punish applicants that provide false information.

b. Ongoing Supervision

The Venezuelan experience proves the damage that can result from a deficient regulatory framework, loaded with perverse incentives. The main sources of bank weaknesses came from the lack of capital, loose rules on high risks, no restrictions on loans to shareholders and related companies, lack of consolidated supervision, and loose accounting rules.

I would suggest focusing on the following regulatory issues:

(i) Capitalisation
Regulators must ensure that banks are properly capitalised, with shareholders having real capital at stake.

(ii) Investment climate
Raising the capital adequacy level in the banking system can only be successfully implemented when the overall investment climate in the economy is favourable. If such a policy is not actively undertaken while investor confidence is high, it becomes an impossible mission once the economy enters into a recession and a crisis emerges, as was the case in Venezuela.

(iii) Capital adequacy ratios
Capital adequacy ratios should reflect the true level of risks that the banking sector faces. It is advisable to set minimum ratios above the minimum Basle reference level of 8 per cent if asset quality and financial market volatility expose the banking system to higher risks.

(iv) Tier 1 and Tier 2 capital
Tier 1 capital should be the priority, as it does not require the issuance of sophisticated financial instruments for which a developing or transition economy might not have proper legislation or markets. Tier 1 capital is also easier to use for the reconstruction of a bank.

Tier 2 capital allows for a variety of market mechanisms to be used to capitalise banks. However, its main virtue—flexibility gains through market mechanisms—is not a real advantage when capital markets are thin and underdeveloped. If Tier 2 capital requires major regulatory changes otherwise not needed, it might be advisable to leave it for a later stage, so as not distract the supervisors.

(v) Insider and connected lending

Insider and connected lending problems should be effectively addressed, especially if banks are closely held and linked to commerce and industry. Until 1994, in Venezuela there were no restrictions on loans to shareholders or to related companies. Direct loans to directors and management were limited to first-home mortgage loans. Connected lending can definitely be a problem because the banks may be used to rescuing related borrowers at the expense of the bank and its depositors. The key is to ensure that all loans are treated equally but this might be an impossible goal if not sustained by the proper regulatory powers. I believe that clear and enforceable rules limiting loans to shareholders and management, and to related companies, are strongly needed, especially if banks are closely held and disclosure of financial data is poor. Consolidated supervision is an effective tool to cope with these risks. Connected lending problems may further be avoided if, whatever the rules are, information regarding beneficial ownership of banks, loans to affiliates, shareholders, management and connected borrowers is properly disclosed to the markets.

(vi) Regulations on high risks

In Venezuela, until 1994 credit exposure to a single borrower was limited to 10 per cent of capital, while maximum credit exposure to related borrowers was set at 20 per cent of capital. However, an extremely loose definition of related borrowers made these rules totally meaningless. In fact, two borrowers of a bank would be classified as 'related' only if a borrower owned more than 50 per cent of another borrower's equity capital and if both parties engaged in the same economic activity within the same State of the country. Additionally, complex arrangements—involving third parties and offshore jurisdictions—were used to circumvent lending restrictions and obscured the nature of the transfers.

In 1994 both the Banking Law enacted by the government prior to the crisis and the Emergency Law approved after the crisis broke out, improved the rules on high risks and established severe sanctions in the event of violations, thereby recognising the importance of the problem.

(vii) Asset quality is the key

Although capital is important, asset quality is even more crucial because poor quality assets will negate the effect of any capital adequacy rule. Supervisors must focus on asset quality, especially if banking supervision has been weak. This task includes assessing the valuation, classification and provisioning rules, and strict enforcement through on site inspections.

Asset valuation criteria should ensure prudent valuations, especially in an unstable environment. Market value accounting generally produces an accurate measure of the bank's tradable assets. However, there are some caveats to it in a volatile environment. Asset values in times of transition are unstable and marking assets to market could increase the risk factor in the bank's balance sheet. In the boom phase, prices rise sharply and marking to market practices by themselves do not prepare the bank to absorb the shock that a downturn might cause at any time.

Specific valuation and accounting problems may also arise in small and underdeveloped financial markets in connection with assets that are 'illiquid', either because of the nature of the individual asset or because of exceptionally difficult market conditions in times of distress or crisis.

Prudent asset valuation could be achieved by applying cost or market value, which ever is lower, and by setting clear rules in order to avoid relying simply on the banker's 'prudency' or the 'feeling' of the bank supervisor.

(viii) Accounting rules

Two recommendations essentially arise from the Venezuelan experience. First of all, accounting rules must be clear, and uniformly applied to all banks. Decisions cannot be left for management to be made.

Secondly, no matter who sets the accounting rules, I strongly recommend that *all* overnment agencies involved in banking matters (the Ministry of Finance, the central bank, the deposit insurance fund and bank supervisors) agree on the accounting principles. This will facilitate the decision making process, strengthen prudential supervision and facilitate early action if a bank runs into problems.

(ix) Consolidated supervision

Consolidated supervision is the key to building and maintaining the safety and soundness of the banking system. Venezuelan regulations did not establish consolidated supervision until 1994. As the crisis emerged, insider lending, off balance sheet liabilities and offshore operations proved to be the source of substantial losses. With home country consolidated supervision, alarms could have been sounded at an earlier stage.

c. Liquidity: An Early Warning

Liquidity rules may serve as an early warning system, as illiquidity is often on the road to insolvency. Liquidity must be closely followed by the supervisors, and enforcement must be supported by specific sanctions. The failure to closely follow the situation of the banks that confronted severe liquidity problems in 1993 largely explains the depth of the Venezuelan banking crisis. Important signs were missed at times when supervisory actions could have avoided the collapse of certain banks, and sanctions in the case of violation of the cash reserve requirements (the only rule in place) were meaningless and ineffective.

Liquidity rules might also help prevent problems that arise from inadequate asset-liability management. Medium and long term funding has not been available in Venezuela for decades. Average maturity of bank deposits fell from the 90-day range to less than 30 days, as the Venezuelan economy became increasingly unstable, while loans were booked as 90 day operations regardless of their true term. Maturity mismatch in some Venezuelan banks reached extreme proportions prior to the crisis, as some banks funded 12- to 14-year projects with 8-day funds. Not surprisingly, they failed.

It might thus be useful to supplement the usual liquidity ratios with relevant information on the bank's assets and liabilities, i.e. the concentration of refinancing dates, and the cash flow needs of the issuers of the securities held by a bank, and those of its main borrowers.

Cash reserve requirements were not useful in Venezuela. They have been extensively used over time, both for monetary policy purposes and as a line of defence for the check clearing system. However, numerous distortions arose from this system. First of all, they were a strong incentive to disintermediation, and contributed to the build up of off-balance sheet risks. Secondly, they affected competitive conditions and could easily be evaded, as cash reserve requirements were not uniformly applied to all types of institutions.

d. Preventative Measures and Insolvency Rules

Until 1993, Venezuela's insolvency rules were extremely loose. The lax and highly discretionary regime reflected the desire to give the regulators and the government ample leeway when dealing with problem banks, and allow them to postpone decisions to the limit.

The banking law required that losses of at least 25 per cent of capital be determined by the Superintendent of Banks in order to trigger any corrective action. If the Superintendent of Banks determined that a bank lost 25 per cent of its capital, it would have to be liquidated unless the shareholders preferred to recapitalise the bank or, alternatively, to reduce the bank's capital to the new level. The only requirement in the latter option would be to comply with the minimum capital requirements established for each type of institution, a nominal parameter whose real value declined over time to meaningless levels. The law did not require recapitalisation if the losses were less than 25 per cent of capital.

A more general rule allowed the Superintendent of Banks to impose special measures and/or appoint advisers, if a bank was perceived to have severe liquidity or solvency problems (though not stipulated in the law) or engaged in grave and recurrent violation of the law. These measures should be previously discussed with the central bank and FOGADE. The bank could subsequently be intervened if it did not comply with the measures imposed or remedy the problem within the set deadlines. In an environment burdened by poor information and lax supervision, this kind of regulation was meaningless.

Intervention had to be approved by the Minister of Finance. An interventor or board of interventors would be appointed by the government with the mandate to present a report within 90 days recommending whether the bank should be reorganised or liquidated. The government would then have 30 days to make a decision.

Bank losses could be subject to deferred amortisation only in the following circumstances: (1) if the losses were caused by government or central bank decisions; (2) if the losses were the result of the sale of assets received in foreclosures; (3) loan losses.

The 1994 Banking Law improved the scope for these supervisory actions. A graduated system of preventive measures was established, so as to force the Superintendent of Banks to look closely into the banks and to make sure that corrective steps were taken at earlier stages.

Unfortunately, the law came too late. It was crafted throughout 1991–3 and designed for normal times, but it was enacted when the crisis was already full blown. Consequently, the rules turned out to be a straight jacket for the supervisors when having to deal with banks that were bankrupt but had not been subject to the prior measures.

This graduated system also presupposed that accurate and timely information would be available to the supervisors, while—as was later found out—information available to the supervisors was inaccurate and outdated in all cases. A transition system was not included in the law.

The system established in the 1994 law in case of bank losses can be summarised as follows:

(1) The Superintendent of Banks has the power to suggest corrective measures to any bank
(2) If these were not accepted and implemented, the bank can be forced to apply corrective actions within a specified deadline
(3) General or specific loss provisions may be directed by the Superintendent of Banks
(4) If problems are deeper, and the bank incurs in losses of 15–25 per cent of capital for two consecutive semesters, special restrictive measures can be applied: no new loans and trust operations, no dividend payments, orders to sell assets, and suspension of management.

(5) If losses are 25–50 per cent of capital, the shareholders will be instructed to recapitalise the bank in cash (without a specific deadline established in the law). The bank could also be prevented from granting new loans, obtaining loans from the central bank, and being forced to deposit any extra cash at the central bank. A special supervisor could also be appointed to look after the bank.

(6) If losses exceed 50 per cent of capital, the law established a 90 day period for recapitalisation. The bank would not be allowed to borrow from the central bank, and the Superintendent of Banks would appoint a supervisor with veto powers over the bank's board decisions.

These measures may be useful if action is taken at an early stage and applied to an individual bank, in normal times. If applied to a large number of already insolvent banks, while they are facing heavy runs, it can help destroy whatever is left of the bank.

These regulations made crisis management more difficult. When confronted with an insolvent bank that needed government intervention, the fact that these newly enacted prior actions had not been taken led to defer decisions or to time consuming rituals.

With the benefit of hindsight, if a country has a weak a supervisory body and poor information, and banks are believed to be weak, it seems advisable to craft a transition system along with the permanent regulatory framework, in order to give the regulators the flexibility they might need to cope with a crisis. Early action, triggered by specific indicators, should be the rule.

Powers to allow for and promote early mergers and acquisitions might also be useful.

e. Deposit Insurance and Bank Resolution

The key question is to assess the credibility of the government's commitment to limit itself to the pre-determined amount of deposit protection

As the Venezuelan case illustrates, the role of deposit insurance in a banking crisis depends on the potential impact of the crisis on the payments system, and on the accountability of bank supervisors. If bank failures pose a severe threat to the operation of the payments system, as was the case in Venezuela, the authorities will face great political difficulties while trying to limit the Government's support to the amount of insured deposits. Under those circumstances, the cost of a major banking crisis could more effectively be contained if the Government issues a full guarantee on deposits upon the eruption of the crisis.

3. Crisis Management

The Venezuelan experience proves that inadequate crisis management can significantly increase the cost of the crisis and compound its effects. Unclear crisis management destroyed depositor confidence throughout a protracted period of heavy runs on banks which translated into massive capital outflows, substantial falls in asset values, pressures in the foreign exchange market, wider macroeconomic imbalances, and thus, a major economic crisis.

a. Early Action

Authorities must move decisively when confronted with a banking crisis. Uncertainties caused by tardy decisions and unclear rules contributed to an overall loss of confidence, both in the banking system and in the currency. The Venezuelan case is a clear example of the damaging consequences of delayed decision making.

b. A Single Authority for Crisis Management

If public institutions are weak, a single and accountable authority with an unequivocal mandate is more appropriate to deal with a major crisis, as expeditious decision making and a clear voice can restore depositor confidence more effectively.

Avoid excessive checks and balances among institutions. It does not ensure coordination and can do a lot of harm.

c. Early Decisions on Burden Sharing

Crisis management can be more efficient if an early decision is made as to how the cost of the crisis will be shared between shareholders, depositors and the taxpayer. Improvisation as the crisis unfolds will most probably lead to the most damaging outcome for the taxpayer as seen in the Venezuelan case.

The Venezuelan experience also shows that in the event of a banking crisis, it should also be made clear from the outset that the banking crisis must be properly accounted for in the fiscal accounts. The notion of quasi-fiscal costs incurred through Central Bank intervention is difficult to convey and this may contribute to delays in fiscal adjustment.

d. Information

Reliable and timely information on the situation of the banking system, and especially of problem banks, is of utmost importance for expeditious decision making as a banking crisis unfolds. Reliable information is also the key to implementing effective and prompt private sector solutions for problem banks, and thereby minimise the cost to the taxpayer. In large part, the failure of the rescue plans for Banco Latino and the trial and error process with respect to many other banks can be traced to the lack of proper information.

e. *Handle Bank Closures With Care*

The closure of a bank can have devastating effects, as proven in the case of Banco Latino, and therefore ought to be avoided. If a bank must inevitably be closed, the fate of the depositors should be promptly defined. Persistent depositor uncertainty while banks are being closed had a highly damaging impact on depositor confidence in Venezuela, increased the contagion effect and fuelled capital flight.

f. *Central Bank Independence Can Only Be Sustained If Banking Supervision Is Effective*

The Venezuelan experience illustrates the threat that weak bank supervision poses to the independence of the Central Bank. If the Central Bank has no supervisory powers and cannot act directly to prevent a banking crisis or deal with it effectively if it arises, as has been the case in Venezuela, its commitment to preserve a functional payments system may endanger monetary stability. In an environment of weak bank supervision, a strong case can be made in favour of an independent Central Bank vested with bank supervisory powers.

4. Bank privatisations

Privatising banks cannot be seen merely as a divestiture by government. It may impact systemic risk. Consequently, a key goal of bank privatisation policies should be to enhance the soundness of the banking system.

Three major Venezuelan banks were privatised in 1990–1, while banking supervision was weak and competition restricted. All banks were purchased by Venezuelan banks that collapsed in the 1994 crisis. Here are the lessons from this questionable experience:

(1) Strict bank supervision should be in place before banks are privatised.
(2) Stringent tests must be applied to the applicants: the new bankers should be fit and proper investors and/or professionals, and have a

clean and competent record in their previous business activities. The origin of the funds that will be used to pay for the transaction should be clear.

(3) The government should be satisfied with the business plans submitted by the new bankers, setting the bank's objectives as a contribution to the economy.

(4) The privatised bank must be adequately capitalised. The government should capitalise the bank before the sale. If new owners take charge of an undercapitalised bank, regardless of the supervisors ability to enforce the buyers commitment to recapitalise it at a later stage, the outcome will be uncertain.

(5) The privatisation process must fulfil the needs of competitive and transparent bidding but must also establish the proper incentives for the buyers. If conducted through a bidding process, the price cannot be the only consideration. A price that is too high will induce the shareholders to undertake riskier business. The price should be related to the net asset value of the bank.

(6) Government must be liable for the accuracy and quality of the information provided to the prospective buyers, and for all the terms of the contract. The rule of law in the country must ensure that buyers will be able to enforce their rights.

5. Special Implementation Issues

Moving towards a stronger banking system poses special transition problems that need to be dealt with. Many of these transition problems were a valid reason for concern in the Venezuelan experience. However, the discussion of these issues often led to postponement of key decisions instead of tackling them up front.

Competitive advantages and disadvantages for the banks might arise during the financial sector reform process, especially if the country is moving out from an over-regulated system. Anti-competitive regulations must be carefully revised in order to allow banks to compete effectively as the domestic market is opened to foreign banks.

Transition towards international banking standards has to be managed. This raises the issue of gradualism, as the challenge is twofold: setting the rules and enforcing them effectively. Gradualism seems attractive, but can also backfire as it may be used to defer the approval and/or enforcement of better supervision and regulation, thus weakening the banking system while people are led to believe that efforts are being made to make it stronger. The Venezuelan experience during the pre-crisis years offers many relevant examples of this problem.

In developing countries and transition economies, education deserves a special effort. The public must be made aware of the limits of banking supervision, clarifying who is and who is not supervised by a meaningful supervisor, and what instruments are and are not covered by deposit insurance. The community must also understand that risks cannot (and should not) be eliminated.

Another important issue in times of transition is that prudent lending cannot be ensured by merely improving the quality and depth of banking supervision. The soundness of a bank is primarily the banker's responsibility. Regulators should thus actively encourage bankers to enhance the banks' risk management systems.

Last but not least, financial sector reform must go hand in hand with the effort to improve the ability of the judicial system to support the banks' ability to get loans serviced and the supervisors' ability to enforce regulations. The latter is of utmost importance in civil law countries, as modern banking regulations are developing on the basis of common law.

Chapter 5

Regulatory Issues of the Banking Crisis in Bulgaria

Georgi Spasov

I. INTRODUCTION

The 1996–7 'black period' of banking business in Bulgaria brought the invention (or maybe the translation) of a joke: 'How could one kill a bank and a fly ?—By a newspaper.'

This piece of black humour was, of course, provoked by the behaviour of the media towards the banks, but considering the reasons for the systematic collapse of the banking market it is just the top of the iceberg. Much more serious reasons than depositors' confidence lie under the ruin of about half of the banks in the country. And the depositors confidence is much more complex phenomenon, because depositors from the countries in economic transition do not trust not just the banks—much more important is that initially they have lost trust in the legal tender and in the state. So trust in banks which by the way are also dependent on (and suffering from the negatives) of macroeconomics, regulatory and political factors, in the end is a secondary phenomenon, which is not caused by the behaviour of the banks only.

The Bulgarian banking system has undergone a systemic collapse which few of the developed economies would survive—roughly up to 40 per cent of the then existing banks were proclaimed insolvent or are under administration.

The predominant opinion (inclusive of the analyses of the International Financial Institutions[1]), also broadcast by the mass media, is that the reasons for the collapse of the banks, are at micro-level, mainly poor management including fraud. Without denying such instances, the present paper will concentrate on some more basic reasons for the poor performance of the Bulgarian banks in the period of transition to market economy, also involving incorrect decision-making, but at a higher level. It might be stated, that substantial contribution to the present status was

[1] Further within the text the abbreviation 'IFIs' will be used for short.

made by the decision-making of the IFIs, the Government[2] and the Bulgarian National Bank[3] as home supervisor. Too much regulatory pressure was put on the recently established Bulgarian banks, and in any of the known channels—formal and informal, direct and indirect. Actually, from more economic point of view, it might well be said that in Bulgaria the burden of the transition of the economy was wholly laid on the banks, which of course, could not deal with it in a way to survive themselves.

It should be also considered, while examining the case study of the banking collapse in Bulgaria that it is not an isolated case and comes within the trend of a world-wide banking crisis, especially with the recent Asian dimension examples of Japan, South Korea, Hong Kong, Indonesia, etc. Considering the globalisation of the banking business an estimation of the depth of the world-wide banking crisis should also be made on the basis of the regulatory aspects of banking, because it seems that the very concept of central banking should be changed radically in order to prevent 'isolated' case from becoming the rule.

II. VULNERABILITY OF BANKS

It is well known that financial markets can be broadly divided into money markets and investment markets and that banks are generally the basic players at the money markets. It is also well known that the pillars of financial markets are: liquidity of investments, return on investments, performance risk and integrity of the market. All these are, of course, much dependant on the overall macroeconomic performance within a certain jurisdiction. The Bulgarian case might illustrate how systemic breaches of all these principles of all these principles within an unstable economic environment could affect a banking system.

An universal bank is expected to take part into three major fields of banking : deposit-taking; extension of credit; and, clearing of payments. The balance between these three interrelated functions is controlled by various means of monitoring the allocation of the risks through capital controls and economic ratios, addressing the solvency and liquidity of the bank. One of the major characteristics is that a bank trades in financial instruments only, and the consideration for most of the transactions is based on the basic legal modifiers—conditions and expiration of time. This trade is completed through actually reselling other persons' funds[4] (the own funds

[2] 'Government' will be used as term indicating the institution only, without particular reference to any of the eight Cabinets Bulgaria has had since 1989.

[3] Further within the text the abbreviation 'BNB' will be used.

[4] J. J. Norton, and S. C. Whitley, in: European Banking Law : The Banker–Customer Relationship. LLP Ltd. 1995, p. 248 : 'Banking institutions primarily derive their funds for

of a bank are very small compared to the funds entrusted by other persons to the bank). In fact, banks are thus functioning as undisclosed agents, redistributing the available funds of their depositors towards the demand of such—to their borrowers.

From purely legal point of view (under the basic continental concepts of agency[5]) a bank is unique exception among the undisclosed agents—it is allowed to keep all the profit from the reselling the funds of the principal (the depositors). Any other intermediary is under strict obligation to account for the profit of the subsequent transaction. The same area is covered by the fiduciary duties of the agent under common law[6]). The banks are exempt from accounting for the results[7] of their disposal of the depositors' moneys, because in modern law the rules for bank deposits are generally governed by the rules for loans[8]. And ever since Roman law the loan of consumable (what money undoubtedly is) effectively transfers the title of property over the consumable lent. Thus the banks lend their own money, but on the other hand owe the same money to the depositors. Which, in short, means that all the profits made are unaccountable for to their depositors, but on the other hand, the eventual negative results of a bank's investments can not be transferred to the depositors, but have to be borne by the bank itself. This mismatch of liabilities and claims allows a bank to benefit more in case of successful and smooth conduct of its business, but the consideration for it makes a bank vulnerable to any instance of disharmony. Besides, the depositors, as a rule, are entitled to accelerate their claims to the bank, and a bank, on the contrary, can accelerate its own claims only under exceptional circumstances, which are of such a nature that usually the acceleration brings little comfort. Provided that a bank can not make profits if it does not convert its liabilities for claims, it has no alternative, especially in a competitive environment, but to assume more risks, attached to its intermediary position. To put it into other words, a bank is primarily liable to its depositors, and it also warranties to the depositors for the performance of the persons to whom credit has been extended—technically—with the money of the depositors (and in order to earn interest for the depositors), as well as for the correctness of its own decision-making on the usage of depositors' money—especially for the

loans and investments by accepting deposits from the public and by borrowing from non-depository institutions and the general public.'

[5] Cf Cranston, R. Principles of Banking Law, Clarendon Press Oxford 1997, p. 149 et seq. e.g. (at p. 149) 'Civil lawyers have sometimes used the concept of mandate to categorise the relationship between customers and their bank.'

[6] The same area is covered by the fiduciary duties of the agent concept in the Common law.

[7] *Joachimson v. Swiss Bank Corp.* [1921] 3 KB 110, 127 per Atkin LJ: 'proceeds so received are not to be held in trust for the customer, but the bank borrows the proceeds and undertakes to repay them.'

[8] e.g. s. 257, para 2 of the Law on Obligations and Contracts (Bulgaria).

availability of liquidity (which in legal terms means—the readiness to perform on short notice or even without any notice). Thus, going back to the differentiation between the two segments of the financial markets, it should be noted that in the purely legal sense of the term, liquidity at money market is much more of a problem than liquidity at investment market. This means that from legal point of view the claims of the investors at the money market (the banks' depositors) are modified (if modified at all) only by expiration of time; while the claims of the investors at the investment market are also and primarily modified by the occurrence of some conditions (e.g. availability of dividends). At the same time, since a universal bank has no choice of doing business but to either participate directly at the investment market, or, to extend credit and thus assume borrowers' default risk, it comes into a position to swap the uncertainty of expectations of higher return for the certainty of its own liability to its depositors. Which, in a normally operating and stable economic environment means to make profits out of banks institutional standing (protected by licensing) of an intermediary, but in an unstable (whether developing, emerging, boosted or otherwise) economic environment may put banks into the position of a losing bumper.

Therefore, in the latter situation much will depend on the regulation of banking business at the different levels of regulation—legislative, administrative, economic, and professional, including the implementation of the internationally established instruments for such regulation. An early warning should be observed at the stage of introducing such regulation : what might be excellent in a perfect environment, might be crucial in an imperfect environment. It seems that this was underestimated at the very beginning of the rebuilding of the banking system in Bulgaria under the free market principles, and it also seems that this underestimation to a great extent resulted from the directions of the international financial institutions.

III. IFIS REQUIREMENTS ON THE MODEL OF BANKING SYSTEM

A. *Methods of Access*

The international financial institutions (IFIs) had and have easy access to each state with emerging or developing economy—they are on one hand lenders (potential and then—actual), and on the other hand—experts. By the time of the pulling down of the 'Iron Curtain' the IFIs were quite proud of the newly established international regulatory standards[9], and they did not hesitate to offer them to the emerging economies immediately.

9 i.e. under the Basle Concordat and the matching EU regulations.

Through the stand-by credit offers and other means of funding of the structural reform in the economies in transition, the IFIs[10] were and are in a position to demand certain behaviour from governments, central banks and law-making bodies[11]. Thus the well-known international standards of prudential banking were introduced in the banking sectors of the economies in transition. Of course, these standards are, perhaps, the best for a bank, operating within a developed market. But a crucial question is to be asked: weren't they too good for a starting bank, fighting its way through an imperfect surrounding?[12] It seems now, that the answer to this question is definitely positive. Just three examples will be given of this—the effect of the compulsory universal banking, the effect of the endowment capital requirements, and the concept of zero risk of the sovereign.

B. Universal Banking Requirement

One of the requirements of the International Monetary Fund[13] and the World Bank was that universal banks only be licensed in Bulgaria[14]. Of course, the point of this is clear—to avoid the systemic risk within a certain branch of the unstable national economy. But the other side of it, also quite important in terms of a banking system in transition from commanded economy to market economy, is the lack of experience. Thus it should be noted that certain fraud in extension of credit and losses for other reasons became possible because of the lack of experience of Bulgarian bankers to be universal bankers. The universal banking meant, in the understanding of the supervisor, that a banker should not deny credit to any commercial initiative. In the short history of contemporary banking Bulgarian banks other than the BNB and the Bulgarian Foreign Trade Bank) started in mid-1980s as branch banks, which was manifested even in their trading names (some of which survived until today—Mineralbank (natural resources and mining), Biochim (chemical industry), Autotechnica (transport), Stroybank (building industry), etc. Each of these was experienced in financing certain

[10] In Bulgaria particularly active is the International Monetary Fund.

[11] For example, the pressure of the IMF to close down Bulgarian banks, nominated as insolvent, was recently admitted by the former Governor of the BNB in an interview for the 'Free Europe' radio (23 Jan. 1998).

[12] Cf. C. Hadjiemmanuil, In: Emerging Financial markets and the Role of International Financial Organisations, J.J. Norton, and M. Andenas, (co-eds), Kluwer Law International, 1996, p. 207 et seq. (Western-style capital based prudential regulation : an appropriate tool for banking reform?)

[13] Further within the text the abbreviation 'IMF' will be used.

[14] Memorandum of the World Bank Mission to Sofia (23 Sept. 1991–4 Oct. 1991) on SAL negotiations, see Information Bulletin of the BNB, No.10/1991, and Annual Report of the BNB (1992), p. 106; also (on negotiations with the IMF) Annual Report of the BNB (1991), p. 68, Information Bulletin of the BNB No. 7/1992, 23/1992, etc.

type of economic activities. The universal banking requirement forced all the banks into supporting projects into activities, of which the bankers had no particular knowledge, especially of cash flows and return. Also, the aspect of taking security for the extended credit also proved to vary on the particular type of credit, so a serious number of fraud or instances of ignorance were revealed at the beginning[15].

C. *Endowment Capital Requirements*

Also, being based mainly on capital ratios and indicators, the modern supervisory standards are very prudent for the banking of any country, which legal tender is convertible under Art. VIII of the IMF. In a country with an unstable currency this caused, at least, much uncertainty in the amount of the endowment capital of the banks, which had to be adjusted with each more significant drop into the exchange rate of the national currency versus the convertible currencies. Thus the endowment capital requirements, in an effort to be kept up to the EU currencies and US dollar equivalents, were always quite high (and therefore—expensive), and some pressure was put to their crawling increase in order to follow the devaluation of the national currency. This requirement caused the BNB to be in formal breach of the law, which had fixed the endowment capital at 10 000 000 BGL[16] in 1991 and by the time of its enactment the BNB already refused to discuss any applicants with less than 50 000 000 BGL. Later, that law was amended so that the endowment capital requirement be fixed by a separate act (the then anticipated Banks and Credit Activities Act) but it in turn delegated the power to fix the endowment capital of banks to BNB which still does this by a regulation. Correspondingly, the endowment capital requirements rose to 200 000 000 BGL, then to 800 000 000 BGL, then to 2 200 000 000 BGL, and currently amount to 10 000 000 000 BGL, (i.e. 1 000 times more than in 1991) while no comprehensive re-evaluation of available assets (other than foreign currency assets) was allowed at all. Thus banking was growing more and more costly in terms of general corporate finance, also for the cases where banks already operated and had to keep up with the capital in order to retained their licences. Although the burden of increasing the capital was laid upon the shareholders, the controls over

[15] There is a notorious example within the Bulgarian banking community of a person (in fact—acting as guarantor for commission), pledging one and the same lot of artificial joints, which were very expensive indeed for accounting purposes, but there was no market demand for so expensive goods of the sort because of the structure of the health care system and of the lack of experience of doctors.

[16] 'BGL' stands for Bulgarian Lev ('Leva' in the plural), which is the official name of the national currency unit (the legal tender) in Bulgaria under s. 24 of the BNB Act (1997). Since the beginning of July 1999 a denomination was performed, so now 1 000 BGL are equal to 1 BGN, but herein the original figures are shown.

them were as strict as within the most stable economies. At a time the business had found a way out from the double trap of increasing requirements towards the own funds and the taxation on banks, which discouraged the payment of dividends—the capital was increased for the account of undistributed profits and through this actual re-evaluation, appreciation of the invested capital was reached as the shareholders received free shares instead of taxable dividend. When this gap was in turn regulated, the cost of the own funds started to become unbearable for the shareholders (especially for the controlling shareholders) and since there was no alternative for legal return on the invested fresh money—it actually started to provoke banking fraud—mainly by extending credit to the group, because banking was itself unattractive business, which should be noted as the other side of overregulation.

D. Solvency Ratio Requirements and Lending to the Government

It is an international standard, that lending to the own Government incurs zero risk weighting on the solvency ratio of the lending bank from supervisory point of view. Besides a demonstration of respect to the own legal tender and institutions, in a country of a convertible currency and of stable economic growth the reasoning is the good standing of that currency. In the other case, a possible reason may be that the institution in charge of issuing currency is subordinated to the Government, which has been resented for temptation of generating inflation. Anyhow, neither of the above two reasons exists in Bulgaria, nor existed at the time of introduction of the new model of banking. Lending to a Government of a state with unstable currency involves a credit risk perhaps of a bit more different nature (indirect enhancement of inflation), but still an actual credit risk. A possible reason for offering of a model by the IFIs stimulating banks to lend to such a Government might be that it is quite convenient—without jeopardising the current state budget (express and standard requirement of the IFIs) the Government can still generate social stability or so by implementation of funds other than external debt, i.e. this is an instrument to swap internal debt for external debt. Finally, the effect of stability is undermined, because actually this technique generates inflation within the system, and besides, makes banks share the costs of it. At a later stage, it seems that this technique was coupled with expert directions to substitute the Government payment obligations for 'guilt-edged' securities[17], which additionally affects the standing of the banks, even those that did not lend to the Government.

[17] The terms 'gilt-edged' and 'gilts' are being used for convenience within the text, although the different classes of securities, issued by the Bulgarian Government are dematerialised only.

E. General Remarks

Of course, the position of the IFIs is more than understandable, especially with a view of the third issue just considered above. Being lenders to the state budget rather than charities, they ought to be primarily concerned with the return of their own extensions of credit. Therefore, a model of a banking system which is dominated (although not legally subjected) by state administration, is much better security for these extensions, than an economically independent banking system; and, if the internal debt be subordinated to the external debt, then return on the external debt is at least a bit better. So the very principles of the model undermine the standing of the banks within the system.

As it was mentioned within the introduction to this Chapter, the global dimensions of the banking crisis conduct the idea, that perhaps the global pattern of the organisation of the finances might be inadequate. Concentration of finances is public issue by its nature, and banks thus cease to be subjects of private law only, even if privately owned. They acquire a kind of social aspect and go beyond the field of application of purely commercial law. This is the basis for introduction of specific regulation by different institutions, but the other side of this complexity is that the proper functioning of private bodies ceases to depend only on their own performance. The public feature, attached to banks, obviously has induced the global model (heavily exploited by the IFIs) of subordination of banks to governments, central banks and other bodies of public powers, but this model contains the 'pyramid' structure within itself and weakens the importance of the performance of banks at macro level, thus actually exposing them to crisis. Even the 'currency board' regime, recently relied upon at as panacea for weaker economies[18], is just a simplified version of the same concept and thus could hardly help resolve the crises, but just postpone the dramatic effects at the price of amplifying the country risks, as it attaches the risk of the country of the nominated currency to the original risk as well. The banking crises in the world seem to be the crisis of the IFIs pattern of central banking model, drifting away from the gold standard and co-mingling politics and extension of credit, which was forecasted in Milton Friedman's speech at the Annual meeting of the IMF in the autumn of 1997 in Hong Kong.

Therefore, the systematic occurrence of crises all over the world seems to indicate the exhauster of the existing central banking model of regulation of the banking business, as the central banks are hardly 'fit and proper' to function both as state budget operators and currency issuing authorities at one

[18] The Currency Board regime was introduced in Bulgaria in July 1997, employing the German Mark as reference currency.

hand, and, of supervisors of the banking system, on the other hand. It seems that they cannot remain impartial and are ready to favour the more public issue—the budget, rather than the less public issue—the banks[19]. Quite the same problems seem to be predictable within the European Union, regarding the issue of the European Central Bank and the 'euro' currency unit.

The approach and the policies of the IFI's (the IMF being the most active among them) in their interference into the restructuring of the banking systems of the former socialist countries were definitely inadequate to the existing situation. Speaking of the IMF, it is hardly arguable that its strongest part are the patterns, designed for and tested in industrially developed countries. Another strong point are the patterns and the experience in stabilising absolutely undeveloped and practically—non-existing economies. The fall of the 'Iron Curtain' seemed to be a surprise also for the IFI's and they did not have patterns applicable to former socialist contries, where economies were actually functioning and the banking system—operating, but under different rules of the game. Considering the then existing banking system in Bulgaria in brief, it was administered by the BNB which was subordinated to the Ministry of Finance; the rate of the concentration of finances was enviable; and, the system of accepting deposits, payment and clearing, and extension of credit was quite simple and clear, though administrative. What happened was, that the IFIs just mechanically applied their available knowledge and experience that were formed in a very different environment. Even the background of the officers, commissioned to East Europe is an exellent evidence of this attitude—practically all of the senior executives came from African and Asian missions to countries of devastated economies, which fairly indicates the position of the IFIs—to negate the existing operative systems in order to clear the way for application of the available patterns and to rebuild all of the systems in 'Western' style[20]. It seems now that this was an enormous mistake with far reaching consequences to be experienced not only within East Europe.

IV. THE PARLIAMENT AND THE ROOTS OF THE BANK CRISIS

A. *Banking Legislation*

The Parliament has interfered into the banking business through promulgating acts on the Bulgarian National Bank (in 1991 and a new one in

[19] Even in the USA the permanent issue of new and new T-bonds seems to create problems in repayment of the interest promised, which seems to force riskier investments outside the USA in expectation of higher return.

[20] Perhaps, much more effective in the case of Bulgaria would be to stick to the experience of the IMF with Italy, where the state participation into the banking system and some other indicators seem to be fairly close to the situation in Bulgaria in 1989 and after.

1997) and on Banks and Credit Activities[21] (1992) also cancelled in 1997 by the new Banks Act (which, by the way, also introduced Currency Board regime)[22]. The Parliament also controls the supreme supervisor of banking—the BNB—through appointment to the offices of Governor and Deputy-Governors of BNB, as well as (nominally) by voting on the Annual Report of the BNB. Indirectly, the Parliament can, of course, also affect the business of banking through passing other acts, some of which will be mentioned later. Since the matter of banking legislation is quite specific, it is no wonder that actually the drafts, prepared by the central bank experts have been adopted without much amendments, both in 1991 and in 1997. These drafts are, of course, induced by the IFIs and thus the branch of banking law came to be the first one fully harmonised with the EU (then—still EC) standards of banking. Another specific feature of these acts is, that a lot of the specific issues regulation is delegated (back!) to the BNB to be covered by regulations at the discretion of BNB. Thus primary normative regulation occurs quite often at the level of these regulations, which could be much more dynamically amended. It should be noted here that these liberties were heavily used by the BNB to help resolve the budget problems to the detriment of the banks.

Thus a very interesting technique of legislative initiative on specific banking acts is being displayed—the Parliament adopts a piece of legislation (drafted by the BNB on the inspiration of the IFIs) in order to place back with the BNB the power to decide on implementation of monetary instruments and controls, which makes the Parliament seem to be more a kind of a tool in the hands of the BNB (which is primarily liable for the payment balance of the state and is an agent of the Government in its relations to the IFIs). On the other hand, the Government enjoys the primary legislative initiative on the legal environment of the banking business, although formally neither the BNB, nor banks are subordinated to it.

B. Other Legislation in Support of the Model

The Parliament also passed legislation, that enabled the Government to make extensive use of gilts to the detriment of the bank system, which will be discussed later in more details. It also let the Government retain full control over the operation of the currency exchange regime, which the latter enjoyed to an extent that the Court had to correct some of the governmental decrees.

[21] Hereinafter referred to as 'BCAA'.

[22] Cf. R. Cranston, op. cit, p. 153. 'Once a bank offers services to the public, the relationship of bank and customer is potentially subject to regulation. The state acts as surrogate for the customer and compels banks to meet standards *purportedly (emphasis added)* in the customer interest.

Quite an important point is that the legal framework of privatisation was structured in such a way, that the banks were ousted as potential holders of shares and stock of privatised enterprises. This was made at a point when banks had extended credits to such enterprises in anticipation to convert these in capital holdings in privatisation. Besides, the liabilities of such enterprises (which were not converted in gilts) were by virtue of law included within the price of the enterprises and through privatisation contracts were assumed by the latter. Thus actual revenues out of privatisation flowed into the state budget only, and the banks had just to substitute one debtor for another.

And finally, without going into details, from tax point of view (taxation may be levied only by acts of Parliament), banks are regarded as concentrated money and are taxed heavily, even on some of the obligatory reserves. The accounting system for convertible currency, through compulsory conversion of the value of assets from and into Bulgarian leva, allowed the so-called in the banking jargon 'hollow profits' to misrepresent the financial status of banks in an inflation environment, which profits, on the other hand, were an excellent chance for tax purposes.

V. THE GOVERNMENT AS CONTROLLER, COMPETITOR, AND REGULATOR OF THE BANKING SYSTEM

A. *The Government as Controller*

The Government, as sovereign[23] of the executive powers of the state, has interfered into the banking business by all the various means of the different powers, enjoyed by it, of course the most effective being the one of rule-making. From private point of view, the state budget also needs finance during times of transition, and thus Government has come out both as debtor to the banking system—for existing internal debt, and for new loans (being prohibited from overborrowing from the BNB by law) and as depositor of some funds available for usually short periods of time. Banks are legal persons which concentrate liquid funds, and the temptation to make use of these is great, even for a Government when it is in need of such. Thus, a Government steps out as a very special client—one, who also can change the rules of the game[24].

There are few major steps that were taken by the Government, although

[23] See, e.g., G. A. Penn, A. M. Shea, A. Arora, 'The Law and Practice of International banking', BANKING LAW, v. 2, (London, Sweet & Maxwell, 1997), 46 et seq. on 'Sovereign risk' in the context of international banking.

[24] P. Honohan, 'Banking System Failures in Developing and Transition Countries : Diagnosis and prediction'. BIS Working papers No. 39—Jan. 1997 (particularly 1.1.3. 'Endemic crisis in a government-permeated banking system')

it should also be noted, that the Government did not have appropriate information database on banking after the liberalisation of the system. One of these was that within the structural reform the former BNB (at the beginning—accountable to the Ministry of Finance although later it was declared independent and accountable directly to the Parliament), was restructured and its former regional branches were given the status of independent small banks. Thus the overcrowding and decapitalisation of the banking system started.

In an effort to retain control over the already open banking system, the Government formed a special purpose vehicle, although under the general provisions of the Commercial Act—the Banking Consolidation Company[25]. This company was created by concentration of the shareholdings of the state owned companies into the banks. Actually these shareholdings were compulsory collected and exchanged for shares into the BCC's capital, but the control over the company itself was retained by the BNB and the Government (through the Board of Directors, as nominees of the BNB and cabinet ministers *ex officio* formed this Board—initially 3 : 2, then the Government took over the control) and currently is shared between the Government and the BNB. Thus BCC is in fact a very special holding company, which used to own proportions of the capital of almost all Bulgarian banks, exercising control through the capital over those, where it owned the majority shares.[26] BCC sold its minority shareholdings into some banks, but concentrated its holdings into other banks (upon the permission granted by the BNB for controlling more than 5 per cent of the voting shares) up to even over 99 per cent.[27] For this reason the banks where majority capital was thus controlled by BCC became popular as 'state banks', considering that BCC became itself controlled jointly by the Government and the BNB. It is obvious that besides the other means of interference, the Government (and BNB) acquired a 'market' mechanism of influencing the banking market, inclusive of influencing it directly by those banks and destroying competition.

Another very important issue in macroeconomic aspect is that slightly the actual burden of the period of transition was shifted to the banks. Certain investment loans were made before the transition began, when credit granting was operated in administrative way. Then, when the new banks were formed, the existing loans made to different commercial structures in administrative manner, were assigned to some of the specialised

[25] Hereinafter referred to as 'BCC'.

[26] Cf. M. Goldstein, and P. Turner, 'Banking Crises in Emerging Economies: Origins and Policy Options' *BIS Economic Papers*, No. 46—Oct. 1996, p. 18 (on the effect of heavy government involvement).

[27] Meanwhile, in 1998 through 2000, most of the controlling shareholdings of the BCC were sold to foreign banks.

banks and the former branches of the BNB, which made them have a fresh start with already troubled balance sheets, sharing the negatives of former managerial mistakes, for which they had no fault. This, in combination with the lack of regulation (besides the pressure of the IFIs to introduce such) and later—the reluctance to apply the scarce provisions of insolvency towards stately owned enterprises (perhaps—in anticipation of successful privatisation, which unfortunately proved to be extremely slow) effectively overthrew the burden of the economic history and the burden of the transition, to the portfolios of the banks. In fact, some losing enterprises were kept going (under the motive of avoiding social distress—which is more political problem), at the cost of being subsidised by the banks.

B. *Trading in Gilts and Competing the Banks*

In an attempt to balance the burden of transition between the different economic structures, in the very end of 1993 was enacted a piece of legislation—Settlement of Unserviced Credits (negotiated before 31 December 1990) Act—under which the Government compulsory exchanged the 'bad loans' which were before attached to the banks, for gilt-edged' bonds with 25-years maturity[28]. The original aim of this move was to give a break to the banks (where the concentration of the financial negatives of the transition started to bring troubles) and, as it was then believed that privatisation is going to start at high speed—to remove by operation of law the banks as creditors to the enterprises which could be privatised. Anyway, the banks had no choice, but to accept these rules. This manoeuvre helped banks to clear their balance sheets, accepting the prime rate debtor—the Government—for low rated debtors, but it did not bring back the money that was systematically poured into the said enterprises. To make them more attractive, these gilts were allowed for trade at the secondary market and acceptable as legal tender for some proportion of the price in the cash-privatisation deals. This was primarily designed as a vehicle to allow banks to collect some cash in exchange for the gilts allocated to them, of course at substantial discount on at par-value because of the maturity, which additionally worsened the balance of the banks, which opted to improve their solvency. A side effect of this Act was, that it covered the 'bad debts' of 'state banks' actually, as the time limit set was such that effectively excluded the credits, extended by 'private' banks to the very same debtors, kept running because of social, political, etc. reasons, although operating at losses. In effect, the Government subsidised these enterprises (in fact, the IFIs continued to demand their closing down or insolvency, but perhaps

[28] Popular as ZUNKs—after the name of the Act in Bulgarian language—'Zakon za Urezdane na Neobsluzhvani Krediti'.

for formal excuse there was no insolvency legislation adopted until mid-1994).

Even worse adverse effects brought the attachment of secondary rights to the above described gilts, which convenience for the state budget was later well exploited through new and new issues of different classes of gilts. Neither of these issues, including the original one, could be introduced without the former consent of the IFIs (and perhaps, even on their initiative). The state budget, which was prohibited by the law to use extensions of credit from the BNB (another express requirement of the IFIs, in order to curb inflation) even before the introduction of the currency board regulation in mid-1997, soon realised the advantages of borrowing directly from the population and the legal entities in search of additional funding. As the demand of gilts for privatisation payments purposes was low, the additional rights attached to them were gradually designed (with the assistance of the BNB of course) to develop the gilts as investment instruments. Then the primary market in the Government bonds attracted a substantial part of the banks own investment business (these received very favourable supervisory treatment) and the secondary market in turn attracted many of the depositors—obviously, to the detriment of the banks. Thus, starting from a point meant originally to help banks clear their balance sheets, the Government ended as the strongest competitor to the banks in the very core of the banking business—collecting deposits from the public. Of course, the Government was then able to allocate these available funds with some banks, which further destroyed the fair competition among them. In most cases these 'favourites' were the 'state' banks, and there were special decrees of some governments prohibiting the placement of public funds with other banks—allegedly, for purposes of safety of these funds. It might be said that these were serious instances of destroying the public confidence into banks and the integrity of the banking market.

C. *Exchange Control Regulation*

Bulgaria is a jurisdiction of strict exchange control,[29] considered to be a major tool for controlling the payment balance of the country, especially *vis-à-vis* the external debt in convertible currencies.[30] Until 2000,[31] the

[29] See R. *Dixon, Banking in Europe: The Single Market* (Routledge, London, 1991), 50: 'As far as provision of cross-border services is concerned, the main direct barrier to this is the existence of exchange controls.'

[30] The external debt of the country is a specific factor to be considered in the examination of the banking system and its regulation. *Inter alia*, the ratio of the debt (external and internal) versus the GNP is (in rough average) 150 per cent, which is about five times more than the standard norm.

[31] Since the beginning of 2000, upon the enactment of the Currency Act, the currency regulation rests with the BNB and the regime has been liberalized, but partly only.

exchange control was exercised jointly by the Ministry of Finance and the BNB. The idea was that through these regulations the outflow of convertible currency and other valuables will be restricted, so that personal wealth will be actually national wealth[32]. Basically, the same regime applies to the banks, and in fact there are two types of banks depending on their licence—one, that are allowed to participate directly at the international interbank market (popular as 'full licence'), and others, that are allowed to operate by themselves only at the national interbank market (popular as 'internal licence'). In any case though, the direct investment of banks abroad, inclusive of forming branches and subsidiaries, is subject to express former permission of the BNB. On the other side, foreign investment in banking business was basically subject to registration, and in some cases—to formal permission. These restrictions, had a side effect, which enhanced the collapse of the national banking system—they did not allow the Bulgarian banks to integrate properly within the international banking community, and the crisis was endemic only, that is—cheap. It wiped out some of the savings, i.e. reduced the inflation, but it did not affect the external debt. Since there were no major foreign interests involved, there was no international rescue or so, as could be recently observed in Asian economies. In fact, the currency controls regime limited the banking crisis only within the country, which is a good point to weight the costs (economic and social) of such a crisis and its possible economic benefits to the overall balance of the country.

D. Benefits Out of a Bank Crisis

Perhaps, although it might look cynical, a collapse of the banking system is a good instrument to transfer some of the costs of the transition to the public at a moment when banks are already exhausted and might need costly rescue operations themselves. Insolvency reduces the outstanding debts to the amount of the available assets only. Therefore, it reduces the overall amount of monetary obligations, which is quite favourable to reduction of inflation. On the other hand, the state budget is traditionally ranking quite ahead among the unsecured creditors, which means that it might benefit from such a situation. The system of deposit insurance, introduced by a special Act of the Parliament (initiated by the Government) only in May 1996, also contributed to this transfer of the costs to the public. It provides for state guarantees for some of the deposits with failed banks, which liabilities are (of course—again) covered by gilts. Being better than nothing, especially as the BNB did not itself complete such a system,

[32] See, e.g., G. A. Penn, A. M. Shea, A. Arora, op cit., p. 75 et seq. on private law effects of exchange controls.

provided for into the BCAA, this seemed a strange step of the Government, designed for purposes of social stability only. In fact, it was also quite successful in economic terms, considering the terms and conditions of repayment under the guarantee, such as : financial institutions, shareholders of more than 1 per cent, directors, etc. were excluded as beneficiaries, legal personalities were entitled to receive their foreign currency deposits in BGL and only half of the balances of their deposits in BGL, etc. It should be particularly noted that the application of this protection is to be triggered upon the discretion of the BNB (15 days after the decision of BNB to demand the insolvency of a particular bank to be proclaimed by the Court). This petition was usually filed only upon the expiration of the maximal one-year period of administration of troubled bank, during which deposits were simply blocked. Thus further difference on interest on these (before the introduction of the currency board the interest went up to 360 per cent per annum at a time) and on currency exchange rates (also very volatile) was easily realised to the detriment of the public. The act on deposit guarantee by the state also subjected the property of the members of the boards of an insolvent bank to unlimited liability, which raised the concept of fraud and crime as independent part of bank management and further destroyed the public confidence and the integrity of the market.

VI. THE BULGARIAN NATIONAL BANK AS REGULATOR AND SUPERVISOR AND THE BANK CRISIS

A. *General*

Banking supervision is art, which is not much different from the art of banking itself. It is perhaps even more ambitious and certainly requires more experience and skills than banking itself. Banking supervision in Bulgaria is exercised by the BNB, roughly following the German supervisory model. Thus the BNB in fact acts in a dual capacity—supervisor and competitor to the supervised banks, and by virtue of law it is exempt from liability for its actions or omissions as supervisor and regulator.[33] It is actually a competitor because, being primarily responsible for the payment balance of the country, it engages in actually the same banking business (especially in currency exchange and trading) as the supervised banks do. Such a position is tempting, even for an institution—to resolve some of the state budget problems it has to meet, through inventing or amending the market rules for the supervised banks. It could be, perhaps, argued, that the BNB could not resist this temptation, and some conclusive evidence based on supervisory policies, will be discussed hereinafter.

[33] See C. Hadjiemmanuil, *Banking Regulation and the Bank of England* (LLP, 1996) 336 et seq.

The BNB facilitated and promoted the development of the market in gilts, thus allowing the partial substitution of external debt for internal debt as it itself is the Governmental agent on foreign debt. Being the single institution to issue legal tender, the BNB did not object to attaching special rights to the gilts, so that these be used as means of payment in privatisation. What is more, in order to support the trade in guilts, the BNB allowed these to be used for meeting supervisory criteria of banks, such as increases in the endowment capital. This radically affected the standing of state-controlled banks (which by definition had exchanged a lot of 'bad debts' for guilts) versus the private banks, which had to find cash to meet the increased requirements. This also allowed some state-controlled banks to gear their endowment capital to the full face value of their gilts, which was much more than the required minimum standards. Automatically, their supervisory standing, including the rights to extend credit, were boosted, which was to the detriment of the competition in the business of banking. Thus from the viewpoint of allocation of funds for supervisory purposes, the private banks were forced into rather incompetitive position. Another effect was, that by employing various legal means, the state control in some banks (through the holdings of the BCC) was substantially increased tens of times over the supervisory minimum, ousting the minority private shareholders who could not compete with pouring in more money to exercise their pre-emptive rights.

The actual lack of investment market and the stability of the gilts attracted a substantial part of the banks' depositors, which was a further blow to the stability of the banking system. Most of the banks had to invest in gilts themselves, which made the return of banks deposits in fact subject to the return on gilts. Finally, the BNB adopted a new formula on calculating the basic interest rate (which is within its prerogatives), openly based on the revenue on gilts, which effectively and wholly subordinated the deposit market to that of gilts.

B. Foreign Currency Politics

Another instrument of the BNB to make use of the supervised banks traditionally (even now, under the Currency Board regime) is the regulatory policy on bank assets, kept in foreign currencies. An easy way to conduct the exchange rate in an inflation environment proved to be the limits on holding such assets and regulations on the nature of the required reserves. Banks tend to hedge their assets against inflation simply by holding foreign ('hard') currencies, and the BNB, primarily responsible for the stability of the national currency, stuck to the international rules that such holdings are exposures, that are undesirable—which was finally recognised untrue by the very fact of introducing Currency Board regulation. At a time, the BNB would play even more elaborate schemes, such as letting these controls off when the Bulgarian lev was especially low, so that banks buy out expensive currencies, and tightening the same controls in order to make the banks sell currency assets quickly when itself had to buy such (pending payments on the external debt or for other currency denominated liabilities of the Government). Sometimes these fluctuations coincide even with minor occasions, such as when larger state-owned companies had to meet currency liabilities (especially for import of fuel and other energy resources). Thus the BNB obviously manipulated the supervisory regime in order to transfer the currency exchange risks to the banks within the system.

C. *Regulatory Non-performance*

Next issue is, that the BNB did not regulate strictly the whole of the banking market. It was strict only to the banks, their shareholders, directors, etc., which in fact did not prevent incidents of fraud and crime, but it did not regulate the business of lending credit properly. Thus, for example, the BNB was under legal duty to organise a system for exchange of information between banks on the creditworthiness of borrowers. Such a system does not exist even until now. This allowed the existence of so-called 'credit millionaires'—people who borrowed and borrowed funds from different banks without an intention to return the money, and as a result, instead of suing the borrowers, the banks litigated between themselves.

Also, the BNB was supposed to organise a sort of security registrar, where securities given to banks were to be duly registered. A most amazing point in this line is, that finally the European Bank of Reconstruction and Development commissioned a draft of Specific Pledges Act, based on its Model Law on Secured Transactions[34]. Finally, in November 1996 the law was ready, and was enacted in April 1997. Ever since it remains inoperative, as there is no institution formed to carry the functions of a Registrar, which was, in fact, duty of the Government. A funny point is that the law proclaimed the unenforceability of any liens, even the already existing ones, that would not comply with its requirements, while, since there is no registrar, not a single lien could be made in compliance with the law[35]. This was particularly inconvenient in a jurisdiction, which is easy to define as 'debtor-protective' in terms of enforcement.[36] The competition among the banks also favoured unhealthy lending policies by itself and 'new bad loans' came into existence, and all the above discussed issues (while the list is by

[34] J. Simpson, and J. M. Rover, in: Emerging Financial Markets . . . op. cit., p. 165 et seq.

[35] See M. Giovanioli, in: R. Cranston (ed.), *European Banking Law* (cit.), p. 220: 'From a very general viewpoint, it might be said that pledging a dematerialised (book entry) security would be quite similar to pledging a claim.'

[36] See P. Wood, *Law and Practice of International Finance : Comparative Financial Law*. (Sweet & Maxwell: London, 1995) 40 et seq. (the 'Litmus test').

no means exhaustive) brought to assuming of too high credit risks by the banks, which definitely contributed to the bank crisis.

The BNB was the only supervisor of the financial markets until the appointment of the Securities and Securities Exchange Commission in 1995. Yet the BNB simply ignored the existence and operation of structures (later nick-named 'pyramids') which actually took deposits from the public without being regulated and supervised, of course, avoiding also the costs of these. Because of unprecise legislation such structures pretended to be 'popular banks' as a sort of co-operative organisations, or—issuers of bonds and other securities in exchange of deposits, etc. These attracted deposits from the public with promises of much higher return, and most of their directors soon changed their residence in foreign countries. These instances seriously damaged the public confidence in banking and related services, and also undermined the position of banks on the deposit market, but the BNB would not take any measures against these structures, waiting for the Public Prosecution Office to react.

D. *Enjoying Discretion*

The BNB was the lender of last resort and still is (with certain limitations) under the Currency Board. Thus it could choose its rescue politics[37] *vis-à-vis* a particular bank. This discretion allowed enhancement of its informal pressure and 'moral suasion' standing, as it could differentiate between, say, 'obedient' and 'disobedient' banks. The statistics read that most of the insolvent banks were privately owned, while for some of the state owned banks specific rescue instruments were tailored, amounting even to special issues of gilts, sold at the necessary discount to the necessary bank, nominations of depositories of large budget funds in order to inject liquidity, or even applying funds from IFIs to support a particular bank.

In the end, it came out that even the judiciary are to be subordinated to the decisions of the BNB and judiciary control over the decisions of the BNB on administration or insolvency of banks is in practice, denied, especially under the 1997 Banks Act. This was the regulatory response to the inability of the BNB to persuade the Court that some banks have to be closed down, although in the litigation the banks were represented by the administrators appointed by the BNB, and not the former directors. The most notorious case is that of First Private Bank, when litigation continued for over one year, the Court unable to find it insolvent, although the BNB closed it down.

[37] S. Bristoll, and R. Goode, in: *The Single Market and the Law of Banking* (cit.), p. 121 : 'Indeed, there is a strong pressure on central banks to ensure that failure is avoided, not least to avoid criticism that their licensing and supervision of the failed bank have been inadequate.'

Considering the competition in terms of lack of integrity of the market of banking services, following the Governmental policies of approaching the European Union, the BNB, as well as the Government itself, ignored the provisions of s. 46, para 2 of the European Agreement for Association between the European Communities and their member-states, and Bulgaria, which allowed (until the beginning of February 2000) the discretion to protect the national market of financial services on the grounds of monetary policy, the integrity and stability of the financial system, etc. Perhaps with an expectation of promoting foreign investment, freely allowed branching of foreign banks in Bulgaria. Generally, these branches are exempt from maintaining capital adequacy standards and operate upon a guarantee by the mother bank, which obviously is cheaper. Besides, as representatives of well-known institutions they have ready correspondent agreements serving transfers of funds abroad and also benefit from the lack of integrity and the lack of public confidence in the Bulgarian banks, which puts them in a further competitive position versus local banks. These factors have led to shifting of substantial part of the banking services to these branches. From macroeconomic point of view this certainly pumps out part of the GNP.

The same tendency of favouring foreign banks could be observed in the bank privatisation to be. Technically it is conducted by the BCC, but, as it was already mentioned, it is controlled by the BNB and the Government. Negotiations, also for the sale of the insolvent banks, are taking place basically with foreign banks, thus substantial delays being caused to the privatisation procedures besides the pressure of the IFIs to speed up.

VII. 'WITCH-HUNTING' FOR THE CAUSES OF THE CRISIS

Considering the social aspects of the bank crisis, some policies of 'witch-hunting' for the exposure of the guilty persons has been started, of course, at micro-level only, perhaps following the explanatory analyses of the IFIs for the crisis. These policies are now mentioned separately, because in fact all the above mentioned regulatory institutions, perhaps in an effort to deny the regulatory responsibilities, are involved to some extent, enjoying powerful support by the media. Some two trends may be observed so far—of personal attacks on bank directors, and on so-called 'credit millionaires'—persons, who have received extensions of credit by the banks, but have not settled these in full.

The personal attacks towards bank management were raised by the Ministry of Internal Affairs and the Chief Prosecutor's Office (which is actually part of the Judiciary System). So far there is no one found guilty and jailed for substantial fraud or crime involved in bank insolvency, but many investigations were made, and some directors were arrested for months. The public opinion thus formed, was that all the reasons for losing of money in the banks were at micro-level, bank directors being always crooks or at least, lacking any common sense. The consequences were that the directors of the banks still operating effectively stopped lending credits, opting for not being investigated some day. The new requirements towards bank directors, recently introduced by a regulation of the BNB, ban from holding such office people who have been directors of an insolvent bank for five years before the insolvency, regardless of their merits. Thus a lot of inexperienced people joined the banking community because of just being eligible under the requirements. A funny point is, that some of the directors of the branches of foreign banks in Bulgaria are not eligible to continue to hold their office.

Also, the Parliament enacted a special piece of legislation,[38] aiming at collecting the information on credit misperformance by banks' clients by the BNB, and obliging it to make it public The target group of clients concerned are from the so-called 'new bad credits' as the initial time limit set back for such investigation is since 1 July 1991. The point is that these lists be made public, so that those guilty for the bank crisis be personally condemned, then, the information to be made available to the Parliament and to the tax and customs' offices, as well as to the Ministry of Internal Affairs in order to commence criminal etc., investigations. The law also obliges the Chief Prosecutor to start investigations on his own and to report to the Parliament of the eventual results. The measures thus prescribed so far had only one partial positive effect—a small part of the indebted persons did clear out their outstanding debts. On the other hand, it came out of the published lists that the worst concentration of 'new bad loans' is again with the biggest state owned enterprises, which continue to operate still forming losses. Otherwise, such retrospective measures at such individual level may perhaps satisfy populist feelings of revenge, but could hardly be considered properly effective at the regulatory level of the institutions. Even if the goals set by this law be genuine, then the social result of the strict application might be disastrous—criminal and related proceedings might well eliminate some on-going businesses, and, chain insolvencies of bank debtors will inevitably result, which at this point, might be even worse than the already experienced bank crisis from macroeconomic viewpoint.

[38] Information On Unserviced Credits Act (Zakon za informatzijata otnosno neobsluzvani krediti), enacted in Oct. 1997.

VIII. TOWARDS A FUTURE MODEL: POST-CRISIS ALTERNATIVE CONCEPTS

Lessons are to be learned from the Bulgarian bank crisis—by the Bulgarian institution, by the IFIs and even by the developed economies. The critical evaluation of the costly experience of bank crises in East Europe has already started,[39] by taking into account that under East European circumstances of transition, classic banking should be modified significantly. The attack of Professor Jeffrey Sachs (also adviser to the Bulgarian president) towards the IMF was a hot piece of news in the early autumn of 1997 and especially his severe attack in mid-December 1997 in *The Financial Times*[40]. Some hints that the necessary modifications mean 'back to basics' of the nineteenth-century banking in order to start building gradually the bank system from the natural beginning instead of boosting it to the most advanced standards, have already been made[41]. Assuming that it is a matter of systemic risk and therefore a macroeconomic approach is required, they suggest that what a banking system is (especially where there is currency board and therefore—no lender of last resort, or the ability of that lender to interfere is quite limited) needs, are: 100 per cent liquid reserves on all the deposits within the banks—in order to stabilise the bank money[42] (wide money) to the same extent, to which the base money (the narrow money) is stabilised, in which case investor confidence and public panics will matter much less; and, separation of the money in the bank from the credit facilities, and the funding of the credit facilities be made for the account of own funds only, or loans by commercial banks only. Actually this is an invention of a *sui generis* lender of last resort in terms of currency board—by means of self-help, i.e. sharing of the risks between the banks only.

If these recommendations be followed automatically, then few major results will have to be considered:

- depositors will be quite sure about the amount of money deposited, but they will have perhaps, to pay for the service of keeping their money by banks, rather than expecting interest to be paid to them; this could further discourage thrift activities of the population, which would have bad macroeconomic results.

[39] See G. N. Olson, in: *Emerging Financial Markets* . . . (op cit.), p. 144 et seq. (suggestions regarding issues of bank capital adequacy in emerging and transitional economies).

[40] Jeffrey Sachs, 'Power Unto Itself'. *The Financial Times*, 11 Dec. 1997.

[41] See, e.g., S. Hanke, and Burnsteen, as cited by '168 hours' (weekly newspaper in Bulgarian language), 29 Aug.– 4 Sept. 1997, p. 23.

[42] Cf. F. A. Mann, *The Legal Aspect of Money* 5th edn (Clarendon Press: Oxford, 1992), 5 et seq.

- there will be no reason to expect easy access to credit facilities, which will also bring down the free economic initiative. Considering the rather narrow funds for credit the banks would perhaps have to credit only their groups or shareholders, etc. which is currently known as 'internal credit'. The restrictions against it should be lifted in the above circumstances, because there is no reason to expect that 'club money' would be lent to the public. Also it would be a good reason that within the group the 'know-your-customer' rule is better defended.

Of course, if there be banks subjected to other supervisory standards, i.e. branches of foreign banks, these will attract all the public or general needs of credit.

What is interesting in the above discussed suggestion, is that provisions (reserves) are to be made on the deposits, and not on, as the current practice in the world is—on the extensions of credit. Actually, for the formerly pointed out legal reasons, a bank is double-exposed—to its depositors, and to its borrowers. To put it flat—a money which is gone to some borrower, is gone[43]. It is a general matter of law to sue the borrower and try to recover the money due. Each diligent creditor, not only a bank, would normally try to hedge the risk of non-payment, but hardly a reasonable creditor would put aside more money not to be used by him, in order to cover eventual losses. On the other hand, a diligent borrower (what a bank ultimately is to its depositors) would try to save some money (make reserves) so that it be easier for him to perform back on the due date. Therefore, it seems that (especially for the eastern European realities) a requirement for provisioning of the deposits—inclusive of those made for purposes of payment transfers only—with a bank seem to be much more relevant as an alternative to a deposit-guarantee scheme, than wasting fresh money to provision money that is gone (plus the costs of the guarantee scheme). Broadly, the same principle is the core of any deposit-guarantee schemes. But a deposit-guarantee scheme of the existing sort is just an instrument to share the risks between the banks and the state budget (in some states). Rather more important for the informed decision of a depositor will be to know that a bank has some individual commitment of funds towards securitisation of the claims for returning the money deposited.

The 'narrow banking' concept perhaps is also worth examining, as it is actually based on building up a kind of 'Chinese wall' within the bank to separate its different functions. Yet a combination of this instrument with provisioning of reserves may, perhaps, defer the lending potential of the bank.

The separation should be considered also necessary within the BNB

[43] See J. Cooper, *The Management and Regulation of Banks* (Macmillan, 1984), 165: 'The first risk confronted by a banker is the credit risk of the borrower . . .'.

itself. From the above discussed examples, it seems to appear that an institution that unites the functions of a central bank and of supervisor of the banking system, is tempted to incur collision of the different interests. The formal separation of the supervisory body under the 1997 BNB Act (as one of the three departments of the BNB) does not seem effective enough so far. Perhaps a model of an independent supervisory body, directly accountable to the Parliament, might be a better solution.

And last but not least—in drafting a new model of the banking system, the particular features and traditions in banking of the country[44] should be considered very carefully, instead of trying to find an universal model, readily applicable anywhere in the world.

IX. PECULIAR FEATURES OF BULGARIAN BANKING TO BE CONSIDERED

A. *Depositors*

In Bulgaria deposits are traditionally made by physical persons. This is typical for the culture of the older generation, which believes that money to be spent are only part of the 'dry money', i.e. from the savings, and they would not readily live on credit to be repaid later. Also, there is a very popular saying 'white money for black days', which once again expresses the readiness to save in anticipation of future problems. Also, the elderly people in Bulgaria, at least formally belonging to the said generation, are about one third of the whole population. Yet exactly this social group, because of the former lack of investment market, is now with reduced ability to generate money and to save money. The younger generation, is more ready to spend the whole lot of earnings, perhaps mostly because the high inflation rates actually prove senseless any savings. The experience of the last few years shows that any savings in BGL prove to be a continuously losing investment, as the rate of inflation is much more than the interest, and the actual value of the deposit together with the accrued interest in the end is much less than the initial value of the money deposited. A recognition of this fact is, for example, that even tax authorities which seem ready to tax everything, will not tax the interest on deposits, acknowledging that such a tax would be mocking.

Thus the actual savings of that part of the population which can afford to save, are made in fully convertible ('hard') currency, typically US dollars, to the extent that the existing exchange controls would allow this.

[44] See (on the gradual development of supervision in the UK, for example): J.J. Norton, *Designing International Bank Supervisory Standards* (Graham and Trotman/Martinus Nijhoff, members of Kluwer Academic Publishing Group: The Netherlands, 1995), 70 et seq.

Furthermore, because of the same exchange controls, and the lack of confidence both in the banking system and in the law-making and administration, people would rather waive the advantages (such as safety and interest-bearing) of depositing their foreign currency personal reserves into banks for the advantages of independence from eventual bank failures or passing normative acts restricting the disposal of the deposited currency in one or another way. The macroeconomic price for these considerations is, that effectively, substantial part of the money saved is out of the banking system, which, by the least, ruins all calculations and plans based on such statistics.

On the other hand, there seem to be no national professional investors. There are hardly any funds available for investment at the money market, other than those kept with the commercial banks with the Bulgarian National Bank for supervisory purposes. Both the commercial companies (privately or stately owned) and the budget operators (centralised or municipal) experience the shortage of funds for performance of their activities. Thus, these are rather borrowers than depositors. There are no health-care funds (and decentralised pension funds are just being established) looking for investing their collections, and the few special funds controlled by the state administration that are not so heavily used, are attached to one or two 'trustworthy' banks by special administrative orders. Alongside, the capital market is practically absent (save for some 'gilts', so it could be hardly expected that funds be raised by professional investors and kept within banks. For reasons of general instability, exchange controls and taxation, there are virtually no deposits in the line of foreign investment. Thus, banks have to rely on classic deposit-raising in a hostile environment, which brings along shortage of funds, competition among them to attract such deposits, increased expenses of maintaining branches and offices, etc. Actually, there are no investment Bulgarian banks in the functional sense of the internationally recognised classification. On the other hand, as the current jargon is, there exist some 'boutique' banks, which have stuck to a club of depositors and live on reselling funds to other banks on the interbank market.

B. *Payment Functions*

The payment function of the banking system is typically underestimated[45] for purposes of evaluation of the inherent to the banking business risk, but the practice, including that in Eastern Europe, has proved that it is crucial

[45] Cf. R. Cranston, op cit., p. 304: 'netting has a relevance for banking well beyond payment systems. . . . It is now a recognised concept in bank regulatory law. In all, it is central to the safety and efficiency of modern banking.'

for the systemic effect to the banking system, as well as for the macroeconomic climate of the country. Of course, the matter is the channelling of payments, or the role of banks into the national clearing. The primary responsibility for this is also laid with the universal banks within the system. Therefore, the non-performance of a single bank endangers the standing of the other banks. Thus, the Bulgarian experience showed that as a rule, there were no 'sudden deaths' of the type of Herstatt Bank. On the contrary, the troubled banks caused significant delays in their performance of payments ordered by customers, some of which were cleared with th assistance of the Bulgarian national Bank (then still lender of last resort). Thus, for reasons of 'maintaining the stability of the financial and credit system' which was (under s. 42 of the 1991 BNB Act) and is (under s. 2 of the 1997 BNB Act) primary responsibility of the BNB, it actually allowed the crisis to deepen, and caused other banks within the system to be affected by the problems of the limited number of initially troubled banks. Thus, in completion of its task as part of the state administration, the BNB waived the timely performance of its duties as supervisor and regulator. The reason for this was that the BNB could not allow the payment system of the Bulgarian banking system to be struck. The cost of this was, that the liquidity and solvency of more banks within the system, were contiguously affected, some—irrecoverably.

X. CONCLUSION

The alternatives discussed in part VII also support the conclusion that something was wrong with the model of regulation introduced. The lessons to be learned from the banking crisis in Bulgaria thus are that some balance has to be struck between the securitisation of the payments on the foreign debt and the maintenance of an operative banking system. Subordination of the system to these payments only might damage irreversibly the economic transition going.

It could be summarised, that all the three major aspects of the banking business of a universal bank (the attracting of deposits, the extension of credit and the channelling of the payments) are endangered by the bank failures. Perhaps the most public aspect of these is the running of the payment system. Thus, when it is run by the bank supervisor (as the case is in Bulgaria) it is tempted to save the payment system first. But the decision of the supervisor is not always that easy. To put it in terms of economics of law, a decision to close down a bank affects all the aspects of banking in a certain manner, and namely:

- Depositors suffer the reduced ability of repayment of their claims—either pro rata in insolvency, or even in case of restarting the banking activities, or under a deposit-protection scheme—at least suffer the delay in these repayments, which, besides the general inconvenience, in an highly inflation environment, means in fact substantial loos in the actual value of money, even paid at par. By operation of law, any liabilities in currencies different from the legal tender, are automatically transformed into liabilities in the legal tender, at the rate current for the day of the decision of the court to proclaim the insolvency of the bank. Thus, in an environment of quick falls into the exchange rates the devaluation or the exchange rate risk is laid with the depositors.

- Debtors to the bank may suffer the inconveniences of calling their loans immediately upon insolvency, losing the chances to restructure or renegotiate the repayment of their loans. These could destroy even sound corporate finances, and in the terms of transitional economy (poor self-financing and tight credit market) actually may end in additional chain- insolvencies.
- Payment services through a bank are stuck, which also affects foreign creditors, trustees, beneficiaries, etc. And under s. 305 of the Commercial Act a payment is made only after the money is disposable with the account of the beneficiary.

The decision to close down a bank might depend on some related interest and being thus in a position of conflict of interest, a regulator and/or a supervisor will not have a proper move to make. To put it in cynically flat economics, the decision to close a bank down will be economically useful, if the credit risk (attached to collection of prematurely called loans) is less than the reduction on the return of deposits and payments. Therefore, if the regulator is concerned with macroeconomics, the closing down of a bank may have attractive effects, such as: reduction the available money into the system and relaxation of the pressure of inflation. From political point of view it might bring to the reduction of the inter-state indebtedness (and if the legal tender is fully convertible—which is not the case in Bulgaria—also the international indebtedness). Condemnation of banks and bankers as the guilty ones for the crisis also has important social and political aspects in a society in transition. On the other hand, the obvious and easy advantages of such a move, motivates the 'shadow economics' and keeping money (both deposits and payment funds) outside the banking system. Therefore, a 'tax amnesty' is being mentioned from time to time, both for money kept within the residing into the country population, and for the money that is believed to be kept (perhaps already laundered) in foreign banks and enterprises.

Hopefully, the above shown examples evidence that the model of the banking system, adopted by the relevant national institutions under the guidance of the IFIs and following the established rules of the banking business of the developed economies has failed under the terms of transitional economy in Bulgaria and to considerable extent the features of the model itself caused the broad dimensions of the collapse of so many banks in Bulgaria. It ought to be repeated that of course there were incidents of fraud and crime, but these were hardly of a scale to be considered being the only or even the main reason for such a collapse.

It ought to be mentioned, that in 1997 a new Bulgarian Bank Act and a new Banks Act were adopted and enacted, in an attempt to fight the crisis. Failing to admit the regulatory mistakes of the near past, the underlying concepts of both the acts rest on enlarging the set of tools available to the BNB to regulate the banks and, taking away any existing until then opportunity for the banks to challenge the decisions of the BNB. Thus the concept of confronting the bank crisis by administration rather than jurisprudence or market tools has merely been polished.

In drafting a new regulatory model, which would obviously be necessary, more attention has to be paid to the peculiarities of the social environment in the particular economy in transition, rather than formally introducing the most advanced supervisory and regulatory models available for the advanced economies. Thus regarding a future model of the banking system in Bulgaria, perhaps, some national peculiarities, interwoven within the economic transition have to be considered separately.

As for the global aspect of the regulatory model, perhaps, the time for a new Bretton Woods has come.

ATTACHMENT 1

Total Banks Operating in Bulgaria [by the end of September 2000]

License Type	Number
Commercial banks with an international banking license	26
Commercial banks with domestic and limited license	1
Branches of foreign banks in Bulgaria	8
TOTAL	35

Commercial Banks Declared Bankrupt

No.	Banks
1	BEP 'Mineralbank', Sofia
2	Kristalbank, Madan

No.	Banks
3	Slaviani Bank, Sofia
4	Balkan Universal Bank, Sofia
5	Balkanbank, Sofia
6	Bank of Agricultural Credit Ltd., Sofia
7	Businessbank, Sofia
8	International Bank of Investments and Development, Sofia
9	CB Dobrudjanska, Dobrich
10	Capital Bank, Sofia
11	Creditbank Ltd., Sofia

Commercial Banks under Liquidation

No.	Banks
1	CB Bobov Dol, Bobov Dol
2	Bulgarian Agricultural and Industrial Bank, Sofia

Banks Removed from Commercial Register

No.	Banks
1	Agrobusinessbank, Plovdiv
2	Economic Bank, Sofia
3	CB Elit, Sofia
4	First Private Bank, Sofia
5	Private Agricultural and Investment Bank Ltd., Sofia
6	Trade and Savings Bank (TSBank), Sofia

ATTACHMENT 2

History of Bank Failures in Bulgaria

Date of BNB decision on insolvency	Name of the Bank
[17 March 1993]	Commercial Bank 'Bobov Dol'[46]
[29 April 1996]	Bulgarian Agricultural and Industrial Bank[47]

[46] By then bank insolvency was unknown to Bulgarian law. In fact, the liquidation is insolvent.

[47] The reason for winding up of this bank is order of court based on misrepresentation in the payment of the endowment capital and therefore, initial invalidity of incorporation.

Date of BNB decision on insolvency	Name of the Bank
	'black period'
31 May 1996	First Private Bank
	BEP Mineralbank
17 June 1996	Agrobusinessbank
	Kristalbank
	Private Agricultural and Investment Bank
31 October 1996	Economic Bank
	Commercial Bank 'Mollov'
	Yambolska Commercial Bank
	Trade and Savings Bank
	Bank 'Slaviani'
	Dobrudzhanska Bank
	Businessbank
	Balkanbank
24 January 1997	Elitbank
	Bank for Agricultural Credit
27 March 1997	Capitalbank
1 September1997	International Bank for Investment and Development
1 February 1999	Credit Bank[48]
29 February 2000	Balkan Universal Bank[49]

[48] The failure of this bank was due to the disruption of the Russian bonds market and possibly, managerial fraud related to the acquisition of these bonds.
[49] This bank failed to meet the increased own funds requirement.

PART II

The East Asian Financial Crisis: 1997–1998

Chapter 6

The Thai Financial and Economic Crisis of 1997–8: An Opportunity to Re-Address the Fundamentals

*Tull Traisorat**

In the past decade, the East Asian 'economic miracle'[1] appeared to be an on-going and sustainable economic reality.[2] Several East Asian countries,

* The author extends appreciation to Christopher Olive, JD, LLM, his colleague at the Centre for Commercial Law Studies, for the useful comments and constructive criticism.

Author's Note In making certain pointed and critical observations on certain aspects of Thai society, this author does *not* wish such observations to be taken out of context as a general political critique of Thai society and government in this article. Clearly, the Monarch has been a most constructive force in the educational and political development of modern Thai society, and in the course of Thai history has been viewed favourably by the Thai people as a benevolent ruler. Further, though Thailand's current state of democratic government tends to be ineffective in many important stances due to the practical realities of 'coalition politics', Thai democracy and the most recent Thai Constitution are to be revered and encouraged. Moreover, there has been much done in a positive vein by the Bank of Thailand and the Ministry of Finance in revamping and developing the Thai economy and financial sectors over the past several decades. In addition, the presence of a large Chinese and selected Thai family influence in Thai business society has helped bring many positive results, including a generally favourable post-Second World War economic environment (at least up until the recent 1997–8 financial crisis).

The focal point of this author's critique is directed to Thailand's stated national commitment to become (i) a more economically developed and more democratically mature society, (ii) a more integrated and influential part of the East Asia Region, and (iii) an economy that comports with international standards of liberalisation, openness, non-corruption and competitiveness—all most worthy shared-national objectives for Thailand as it enters the twenty-first Century. However, to attain these lofty objectives, Thailand (as with any other society similarly disposed) needs to take account of its 'historical and cultural baggage'—sifting through both the positive and negative dimensions.

[1] *See generally* World Bank, *The East Asian Miracle: Economic Growth and Public Policy* (1993): 'East Asia has a remarkable record of high and sustained economic growth. From 1965 to 1990 the . . . economies of East Asia grew faster than all other regions of the world. Most of this achievement is attributable to seemingly miraculous growth in just eight economies: Japan; the Four Tigers'—Hong Kong, the Republic of Korea, Singapore, and Taiwan . . .; and the three newly industrialising economies (NIEs) of Southeast Asia, Indonesia, Malaysia, and Thailand', at 1 and Figure 1. Those eight economies including Japan were termed as High-performing Asian Economies (HPAEs); *See also* Michel Sarel, *Growth in East Asia* (1996); Peter G. Warr, *The Thai Economy in Transition* (1993); Peter G. Warr and Bhanupong Nidhiprabha, *Thailand's Macroeconomic Miracle:Stable Adjustment and Sustained Growth* (1996); Kalpana Kochhar *et al.*, 'Thailand: The Road to Sustained Growth', *IMF Occasional Paper No 146*, Dec. 1996.

[2] During the period from 1992 to 1995, the economic growth rate of the region (including

including Thailand, were recognised as models of economic development for other emerging economies.[3] The economic performances were generally attributed to policies of low inflation and macroeconomic stability,[4] a growing openness of the national economies,[5] and 'high investment rates.'[6] 'Human capital formation'[7] and strong public and private savings were also suggested as reasons for East Asian economic successes.[8] East Asian economic growth not only facilitated prosperity within the region but also to the world as a whole, as the region provided significant and growing markets for the developed nations to indulge in.[9]

The year 1997, however, evidenced drastically adverse changes to the economic fortunes of most East Asian countries, particularly for Thailand. The decade-long period of dramatic economic growth[10] proved to be unsustainable. The East Asian economic crisis of 1997 became plainly visible with the Spring and Summer 1997 speculative attacks against the baht, the official currency of Thailand.

Thailand) was on average around 9 per cent annually, 'significantly above their recent historical averages and probably unparalleled at any time by any group of economies of comparable size'. *See* IMF, *World Economic Outlook: Interim Assessment* (Dec. 1997), at 2.

[3] *See* Shigemitsu Sugisaki, 'Economic Crises in Asia', address at the 1998 Harvard Asia Business Conference, Harvard Business School, 30 Jan. 1998: '[T]hese economies have been the envy of the rest of the world. We have sought to derive policy lessons for high and sustainable growth that could be replicated by other developing countries'; *See also* Joseph Stiglitz, 'Bad Private-Sector Decisions', *Wall Street Journal,* 4 Feb. 1998, at A22.

[4] East Asian countries maintained low fiscal deficits so that their finances 'could be prudently financed without increasing inflationary pressures and responded quickly when fiscal pressures were perceived to building up'. The average inflation rates of the HPAEs were approximately 9 per cent during 1963–93, compared with 18 per cent in 'other low- and middle-income economies' during the same period. *See* World Bank, above note 1, at 12–13.

[5] Most East Asian countries recently liberalised trade in both goods and services. *See* Shigemitsu Sugisaki, above n 3, at 2.

[6] Alan Greenspan, Chairman of the Governing Board of the US Federal Reserve System, Testimony before the Committee on Banking and Financial Services of the US House of Representatives in Washington DC on 13 November 1997, *BIS Review* 105/1997.

[7] East Asian nations have emphasised on the significance of education. The allocation of public expenditure in East Asia nations for basic education has been 'consistently higher . . . than elsewhere'. *See* World Bank, above n 1, at 195–203.

[8] Shigemitsu Sugisaki, above n 3, at 2.

[9] *See* Stanley Fischer, 'The Asian Crisis: A View from the IMF', Address at the Midwinter Conference of the Bankers' Association for Foreign Trade, 22 Jan. 1998: 'Asia's success has also been good for the rest of the world. The developing and emerging market economies of Asia have not just been major exporters; they have been an increasingly important market for other countries' exports. For example, these countries bought about 19 per cent of US. exports in 1996, up from about 15 per cent in 1990'; *see also* Robert Rubin, Address on the Asian Financial Situation to Georgetown University, Washington DC, 21 Jan. 1998: 'Thirty per cent of US exports go to Asia, supporting millions of US jobs, and we export more to Asia than Europe. In states like California, Oregon and Washington, exports to Asia account for more than half of each state's total exports.

[10] Averaged annual GDP growth in ASEAN-5 which includes Indonesia, Malaysia, the Philippines, Singapore and Thailand was nearly 8 per cent over the past decade. *See* Stanley Fischer, below n 42, at 9.

The effects of the speculative attacks in turn triggered, on 2 July 1997, the floatation of the Thai baht which had been pegged to a 'currency basket' significantly tied to the US dollar since November 1984.[11] The resulting *de facto* currency devaluation brought down Thailand's latently weak and financially over-exposed banking and finance sectors. In addition, the *de facto* devaluation of the baht engendered a contagious ricochet of untoward economic and monetary consequences throughout the East Asian countries and arguably throughout the global financial markets.[12]

This chapter considers various aspects of Thailand's recent financial crisis. While recognising the devastating effects the crisis has caused to the country (*e.g.*, bankruptcies and unemployment) and the ensuing social safety net problems, the article primarily concentrates on the need for restructuring the banking and financial sectors and for reconsidering the chronic long-term economic, social, political, and legal problems which have to date undermined or impeded banking and financial sector reform.

This chapter begins by reviewing the contextual implications of historical and cultural 'overlays' which have contributed significantly to the dysfunctional system of prudential supervision of Thai financial institutions. Next, the article addresses the origins of the current financial crisis *vis-à-vis* unsound macroeconomic policymaking and resulting imbalances that underpinned the chronically unsafe and unsound banking and financial sectors. The chapter then considers certain factors internal to Thailand (i.e. economic and exports slowdown and domestic political uncertainties) and other external factors (i.e. the speculative attacks on various recent occasions against the Thai currency) and how such factors culminated in the floatation of the baht, the loss of investor confidence in the Thai financial markets, and ultimately the severe domestic foreign exchange liquidity crisis.

This chapter thereafter considers the policy responses to the ongoing currency and liquidity crisis, from the international and internal domestic perspectives. In particular, the International Monetary Fund (IMF) assistance package and 'conditionality' measures of *inter alia* financial restructuring and ratification of economic and legal measures designed purportedly to reverse the processes of unsound monetary and fiscal policies will be analysed critically. The merits and the short-comings of the IMF package, as well as the difficulties arising from the economic and legal

[11] Financial Markets Operation, Banking Department, Bank of Thailand, *A Review and Assessment of the Bank of Thailand's Foreign Exchange Interventions* (Oct. 1997), at 1.

[12] The crisis spreaded quickly to Malaysia, Indonesia, the Philipines and South Korea, causing *de facto* devaluations in their respective currencies. Further, the East Asian financial crisis engendered significant volatility in the Hong Kong Stock Exchange during the Summer of 1997, and adversely affected stock markets in New York and London, as well as those in European and Latin American countries. *See*, e.g., Chronology of the Asian Currency Crisis and its Global Contagion <http://www.stern.nyu.edu/~nroubini/asia/AsiaChronology1.html>.

'conditionality' measures, will be the focus of this analysis. The chapter concludes with a consideration of whether long-term economic, legal and political benefits (metaphorically, a 'silver lining') may arise from the Thai financial crises.

II. INTRODUCTION: CONTEXTUAL IMPLICATIONS OF THAI HISTORICAL AND CULTURAL 'OVERLAYS'

The history of Thailand has shown that policy actions and the development of administrative and legislative powers have resulted in an inclination towards unduly benefiting influential business or social elites. This inclination is due in large part to an ingrained, feudal-derived system of patronage between politicians and bureaucrats holding political power on the one hand, and the business elites controlled by a select group of families on the other hand.[13] The patronage system is well reflected in the histories of other East Asian nations as well.

Thai history reflects the fundamental need for rooting out political corruption that tends to breed from the patronage system. The current financial crisis manifests the depth of the trauma that an excessive and nontransparent interconnection of government and business elites can have on a national economy in our modern era of globalisation. Unfortunately, the Thai general public has held a long-time perception that politics and economics operate separately and are disconnected matters. In the era of globalisation and increasingly open financial markets, however, economic performance and investor confidence are increasingly influenced by political stability or instability as the case may be. Moreover, capital flows and financial market perceptions and reactions are increasingly contingent upon levels of investor confidence in the respective market. As such, any significant loss of investor confidence may well generate unfavourable capital flow reversals, resulting in a severe foreign exchange liquidity crisis and resulting domestic currency crisis.

There may be fruit borne from the ongoing crisis, however, which produces fundamental but positive reforms. Most importantly, the crisis resulted in the long-awaited and long-overdue passage of a new Thai

[13] This was evidenced in 1979 when the Commercial Banking Act (No 2) BE2522 (AD 1979) was in the process of enactment. The Commercial Banking Act was designed to alleviate the Thailand's peculiar problem of single control on a commercial bank which had resulted in favoured connected lending and frauds. Its successful enactment was traded off with an interim provision which in effect rendered the Act not applicable to the existing commercial banks. *See* Commercial Banking Act (No 2) BE2522 (1979), s 22, *Royal Gazette,* vol 96, part 31, special edition, 7 Mar. 1979. Further, an attempt to establish a deposit insurance institution in 1980 and 1991 was unsuccessful although a draft act to found such an institution was completed.

Constitution aimed at putting an end to Thailand's traditional 'money politics'.[14] In addition, the current crisis may provide Thailand with an opportunity to restructure the chronically unsafe and unsound banking and finance sectors, and to revise the inefficient and largely ineffective framework of prudential supervision. If such reforms are properly effected, implemented, monitored, and enforced, a new era of safe and sound financial institutions could be established in Thailand.

Unfortunately, the aforementioned patronage system and resultant 'crony capitalism' has contributed to inefficient and ineffective prudential supervision in Thailand. The societal concept of providing favours to family and friends have long been engrafted into Thai cultural mentality: the interests of the general public are too often relegated to a second priority.[15] Thai governance is viewed as both an incongruity of Western capitalism and as a 'traditional system of patronage networks, a system built on personal connections to allocate values and resources.'[16]

The patronage relationship between groups possessing economic power and groups possessing administrative power can be traced back five or six hundred years in Thai history to the period of Ayutthaya.[17] At the time, Thai feudalism called the 'Sakdi Na' system was in place and the economic and administrative powers were concentrated in the Monarch, and the Monarch exercised those powers via aristocrats working under his auspices. Commoners called 'prais' were obliged to work for aristocrats for a certain period of time during a year,[18] which attributed to the underdevelopment of the business framework in Thailand.[19]

[14] Money politics in Thailand can be broadly defined as the politics whereby vote-buying is prevalent and politicians successfully obtain office by such means. As a result, they would attempt to recoup the expenses incurred in vote-buying from the office. *See*, e.g., Paitoon Boonyawat, 'Election System which Reduces Vote-Buying and Gives More Possibility For Good People, In Replace of the Current System', 18 *Chulalongkorn Law Journal* (Jan. 1998), at 108, 116.

[15] *See* Thinapan Nakata, *Bureaucratic Corruption in Thailand: Incongruities of Legal Codes and Social Norms* (1977); *See also* Anand Panyarachun, 'An Inward Look May Change Thailand for the Better', the First Asia–Europe Foundation Annual Lecture, *Bangkok Post,* 18 Feb. 1998.

[16] *See* Anand Panyarachun, above n 15, at 3–4; *see also* Thinapan Nakata, above n 15, at 17–18.

[17] Ayutthaya period started from 1350 until 1767. It lasted 417 years and was thus far the longest period in the history of Thailand.

[18] 'Prai's' were required to work for aristocrats six months in a year on a one-month-on-one-month-off basis. *See* Suthy Prasartset, *Evolution of Thai Economic System During the Last 200 Years* (1982), at 28. The obliged period was reduced to four months and three months during the reign of King Rama I and III, respectively. *See* Boonrod (Kaewkanha) 'Chalaluk, "Suai" Collection in the Early Ratanakosin Period', in Chattip Nartsupha and Somphob Manarungsan (eds.), *The Economic History of Thailand Until 1931* (1984), at 89; *See also* Kajorn Sukpanich, *Status of Prai's* (1976), at 43–9.

[19] *See* Suthy Prasartset, above n 18, at 30; *see also* Ian Brown, *The Elite and the Economy in Siam c.1890–1920* (1988), at 173.

The feudal period also witnessed collaboration between the aristocrats and Chinese merchants who did not have an obligation to work under the prevailing 'Sakdi Na' system. The collaboration was purely one of self-interest in the form of economic benefits for the aristocrats[20] and security and business protection for the Chinese merchants.[21] This collaborative system of 'protection buying' continued through the later development of the 'Sakdi Na' system whereby the Chinese merchants became 'tax farmers' or tax collectors under the monopoly system pertaining to the manufacture of certain products,[22] and/or possessed the sole right to collect taxes out of those/certain products.[23] The needs of the general public were largely ignored under this system.[24]

Protection buying and crony capitalism continued to thrive even after the Thai revolution of 1932, which effectively abolished the absolute monarchy system.[25] In particular, when Thailand was subject to military rule from 1958 to 1973, the collaborative protection buying scheme became quite onerous, as those in power collaborated with Chinese merchants in their groups to greatly exploit the benefits of the nation.[26] This system of protection buying and cronyism continued unabated into the period of democracy both within bureaucratic and political circles, in a marginally less transparent manner. No 'check and balance' system could be properly implemented in such an environment, especially as systematic 'vote-buying' became more prevalent. Many commentators have recognised that '[P]oliticians spend enormous sums to win office . . . [; they] often put the need to recoup their expenditures before rational policy-making.'[27] In short, the same parties with their affiliations always managed to retain power, regardless of their past performance in government.

As a result of these historical and cultural 'overlays', the legal teeth for serious reform could not be sharpened. Thai financial laws became much like 'paper tigers'. For example, prudential regulation of financial institutions was more of an illusion than a reality, as regulatory measures could

[20] *See* Siriluk Sakkriengkrai, *Origin of Capitalist Class in Thailand (B.E. 2398–2453 (A.D. 1855–1910))* (1980), at 26–8, 43.

[21] Ian Brown, above n 19, at 172.

[22] *See inter alia* Yada Prapapun, *Tax Farming in Thailand in the Early Bangkok Period* (1976).

[23] *See* Sangsit Piriyarungsan, *Thai Aristocratic Capitalism* (1983), at 31; *see also* Siriluk Sakkriengkrai, above n 20, at 69.

[24] *See* Deja Chayabongse, *Force Labour in Thai Feudal System* (1974), at 1; *see also* Ian Brown, above n 19, at 171.

[25] It was a peaceful revolution, as King Rama VII concurred to abdicate the throne for the interest of the country and the people. The absolute monarchy system began during the Ayutthaya period.

[26] *See* Pannee Bualek, *Analysis on Thai Commercial Bank Capitalists* (1986), at 89–93.

[27] 'Ailing Tiger', *Financial Times*, 6 Aug. 1997.

rarely be properly implemented or enforced.[28] Moreover, banks and finance companies generally operated with inadequate levels of reserve capital, and readily became overexposed to growing risks from the ailing property sector and other speculative activities.[29] Even as fundamental legislative changes were made in the banking laws to improve regulation during the financial crisis in the 1980s,[30] these changes have generally not subsequently materialised in practice due to the excessive power of the vested interests.

In addition, the parties that clearly violated Thai banking and financial laws have generally not been prosecuted. The Bangkok Bank of Commerce scandal in 1996 represents an unfortunate example of how corrupt bank management easily eluded criminal prosecution. In this instance, the bank management in question violated the Thai banking laws by disregarding the Bank of Thailand's order[31] as to recapitalisation and the rectification of other unsafe and unsound operations. The public prosecutors moved for dismissal on procedural grounds, finding that the time according to the law of limitations had elapsed.[32] In response to this incident, a committee was established to conduct an investigation into the matter and to temporarily suspend certain relevant officials of the Bank of Thailand in the interim.[33] The end result of the investigation, however, was the determination that the officials of the Bank of Thailand were not guilty of deliberate or negligent actions which had caused the case against the management of the Bangkok Bank of Commerce Plc. to be dismissed.[34]

Thai financial institutions have also received overly generous and undiscriminating 'bailouts' from the Thai government, creating implicit expectations of government support and therefore serious problems of 'moral hazard'.[35] The Thai government has attempted to justify such actions by

[28] The history in Thailand showed that those violating prudential regulation were hardly prosecuted. Or only those of lower ranks were prosecuted. This was due to the significant influence of those controllers of financial institutions. *See* n 32, below, and related text.

[29] 'Joint Statement by the Ministry of Finance and the Bank of Thailand: Thailand Financial Restructuring Package', *Bank of Thailand News*, No 70/1997, at 1.

[30] Commercial Banking Act (No 2) of 1979, s 5 *bis*.

[31] The statutory penalty for such violations is imprisonment of no more than one year, and/or fine no more than 300,000 bahts. *See* Commercial Banking Act of 1962, s 46 *bis*.

[32] *See* Office of the Supreme Public Prosecutor News Re: Violation of the Order of the Bank of Thailand of Mr. Krirkkiet Jalichan and his accomplice, 12 Feb. 1997. The criminal offence needed to be prosecute within one year from the date the offence was discovered; *see also* Commercial Banking Act of 1962, s 46 *bis*.

[33] *See* 'Establishment of Disciplinary Committee', *Bank of Thailand News*, No 12/1997.

[34] *See* 'Result of the Investigation of Disciplinary Committee', *Bank of Thailand News*, No 20/1997.

[35] In 1997 government bail-outs for distressed finance companies cost Thai taxpayers five hundred billion bahts (approximately twenty billion US dollars, at the time the exchange rate was in the region of 25 bahts per US dollar). *See* 'Thais unveil tough economic reforms', *Financial Times*, 6 Aug. 1997. Since 1985, government bail-outs in Thailand have been implemented through the Financial Institution Development Fund (FIDF), an 'arms-length' institu-

focusing on concept of systemic risk avoidance,[36] due in part to the absence of a national deposit insurance regime.[37]

Finally, the Thai banking sector was largely closed to foreign and domestic competition over the past twenty years. During this period, only fourteen foreign banks had branch operations in Thailand[38] and these institutions competed with fifteen powerful and politically connected domestic banks owned and controlled largely by elite Thai families. The Thai supervisory authorities nonetheless consistently argued that adequate competition existed so as to ensure that the financial system remained robust, healthy and efficient. In addition to a tendency toward inefficient prudential supervision and a noncompetitive environment, favoured connected lending practices plagued the Thai banking sector.[39] In conclusion, these submerged foundations of the modern-day Thai banking and financial systems became incapable of avoiding serious economic and financial crisis in the new and more open globalised environment.

II. THE IMMEDIATE CAUSES OF THE THAI FINANCIAL CRISIS

While the Thai banking and financial systems rested upon these insidious and generally non-transparent 'overlays', the more immediate causes of the Thai crisis were generically twofold: (1) the existence of unsound macroeconomic policies and imbalances, and (2) chronically unsafe and unsound banking and finance sectors. These factors are interconnected, as each factor has influenced and exacerbated the other through cause and effect.

A. *Unsound Macroeconomic Policies and Imbalances*

In the modern era of international finance, advancements in technology and financial innovation have facilitated international capital mobilisation. In

tion controlled by the Bank of Thailand, set up in 1985 amidst a financial crisis to give financial support to distressed financial institutions 'to rehabilitate and develop [Thailand's] financial system to achieve its stability, especially in time of crisis'. *See* Note on the Emergency Decree of 1985 Amending the Bank of Thailand Act BE 2505 (AD 1962), *Royal Gazette,* vol 102, part 177, special edition, 26 Nov. 1985, at 50.

[36] Bank of Thailand and Board of Investment, *Board of Investment Q&A* (Sept. 1997), at 1.

[37] A deposit insurance was unsuccessfully attempted to be established in 1980 and 1991 somehow. *See* Financial Institution Development Fund, *One Decade of Financial Institution Development Fund B.E. 2528–2538 (A.D.1985–1995)* (1995), at 29–31. The reason of that may have been attributed to influences from banking elites whose benefits would be negatively affected by such establishment.

[38] Foreign banks were only permitted to establish branch operations in Thailand. *See* Commercial Banking Act of 1962, s 6.

[39] Favoured connected lending is also a reflection of crony capitalism and insufficient prudential supervision in Thailand.

the global environment of unrestricted capital flows, financial markets play a crucial and influential role in dictating where, when, and in what amount to place or to move funds. The unrestricted capital flows also expose and punish underlying weaknesses in economies 'swiftly and decisively',[40] and can represent a brutal but potentially effective form of market discipline.

Commentators have opined that the East Asian crisis of 1997–8 was not a surprise to the world as there were numerous signs of the respective national crises.[41] For example, in the case of Thailand, there were alleged warnings by the IMF to Thai officials during the 18 months prior to the crisis; however, the Thai government denied this assertion.[42] In any event, Thai government officials remained focused primarily on sustaining the external perceptions that Thailand had encountered continuing economic growth for over a decade as part of the 'East Asian growth miracle'. Thus, no internal governmental pressures existed to prompt the implementation of pre-emptive measures or shifts in economic policies in order to mitigate the unfolding crisis.[43] Moreover, although certain signals appeared to manifest market awareness of macroeconomic pressures and imbalances, such as decreasing domestic property and equity prices and renewed pressure on the currency,[44] substantial capital inflows moved into Thailand and other East Asian nations in general persisted right up until the very onset of the crisis.[45] The inaction of the Thai government to signs of the impending crisis is explained in part by the 'complacency' of both the Thai authorities and investors who provided capital 'somewhat beyond the prudent limit'. The situation was also worsened by the so-called 'reverse herding' whereby investors (notably mutual fund and collective investment agents) failed to react prudently to the signals and simply followed each other in remaining in the Thai markets.[46] The complacency of the 'herd' also resulted in the overreaction once the crisis materialised, as the same mutual fund and collective investment groups rushed to exit the Thai markets and move funds to safer havens for investment such as the United States.[47]

40 Alan Greenspan, Testimony Before the Committee on Banking and Financial Services, US. House of Representatives, 30 Jan. 1998, at 1.

41 Those included a significant and widening current account deficit of 8 per cent of GDP at the end of 1996, declining property sector, and stagnant export growth.

42 *See* Stanley Fischer, 'IMF Deputy Stanley Fischer on the IMF and the East Asian Crisis', the Forum Funds Lecture at UCLA, Los Angeles, 20 Mar. 1998, at 9. The denial may have resulted from complacency from the past economic success or from the political difficulties in implementing politically unpopular measures; *see also* Kevin Muehring, 'Is anyone listening?', *Institutional Investor*, Sept. 1997.

43 Michel Camdessus, Managing Director of the IMF, 'Lessons from Southeast Asia', remarks at a Press Briefing, Singapore, 13 Nov. 1997, IMF 97/16.

44 Ibid.

45 *See* BIS, *The Maturity, Sectoral and Nationality Distribution of International Bank Lending, First Half 1997* (Jan. 1998) at 4 and table 1.

46 Paul Krugman, below n 121, at 7.

47 Michael Mussa, 'The IMF Approach to Macroeconomic Policy', IMF Seminar: Asia and the IMF, 19 Sept. 1997, at 6.

As to unsound macroeconomic policies, there was a severe overreliance by the *private sector* on short-term foreign currency denominated loans, premised largely on the exchange rate structure of the baht. At end of 1996, short-term *private* debt obligations with maturities of one year or less amounted to nearly fifty billion US dollars, from total private sector debts of nearly seventy billion US dollars (accounting for approximately 65 per cent).[48] During 1994–6, short-term capital inflows accounted for 7 to 10 per cent of GDP.[49] There was a significant increase in short-term foreign currency denominated bank loans from abroad during 1995–6.[50] The short-term foreign currency debt composition in Thailand prior to the crisis was different from that of Mexico in 1994–5 in this respect. In the case of Mexico, most of the foreign currency loans were owed by the Mexican government,[51] whereas in the case of Thailand, the Thai government ran consistent fiscal surpluses during 1988–6 and the foreign currency loans were largely owed by the private sector banks and corporations.[52]

The crux of the problem relevant to the overabundance of capital inflows was that the substantial inflows were directed to less productive sectors of the Thai economy, notably the property sector in the form of speculative lending to fund residential and commercial real estate development. Speculative lending caused the supply of property to increase significantly, creating a dangerous 'asset overvaluation bubble' in the property market. Property value inflation began to mitigate from the beginning of 1996 onward as a result of an increasingly stagnating economy and a reduction in credit extensions when commercial banks finally came to realise that they were over-exposed to the property sector.[53] The asset overvaluation bubble finally came under overwhelming pressure, however, and the distressed property market values in turn translated into nonperforming loans for the Thai banking sector. The 'bubble' eventually burst when high interest rates were imposed by the Bank of Thailand in order to support the falling value of the baht in 1997. The Thai economic success story was therefore underscored by the risk of a 'bubble economy'. In the absence of a prudent banking and finance sector, the capital inflows arrived in abundance, and excess flows lacking distinct investment opportunities were applied to speculation and 'pumped up' prices in the property and equity markets to unrealistic levels.[54]

[48] BIS, above n 45, at 4.
[49] IMF, *World Economic Outlook: Interim Assessment* (Dec. 1997), at 4 and table 1.
[50] BIS, *International Banking and Financial Market Developments* (Nov. 1997), at 12.
[51] Ibid.
[52] IMF, above n 49, at 3, statistical appendix, table A1, at 51.
[53] Bank of Thailand and Board of Investment, above n 36, at 6.
[54] *See* Joseph Stiglitz, 'Restoring the Asian Miracle', *Wall Street Journal*, 3 Feb. 1998.

There are various reasons why such massive capital inflows were allocated for investment in Thailand. Thailand became attractive to international investors due to the perceived strength of its economy after a decade of impressive economic performance, augmented by financial liberalisation policies implemented by the authorities since the late 1980s.[55] Importantly, exchange controls had been gradually dismantled in the wake of Thailand's adoption of Article VIII of the IMF Articles of Agreement in May 1990.[56] Moreover, beginning in 1992 the Thai Ministry of Finance and the Bank of Thailand initiated policies designed to promote Thailand as a regional financial centre for the other fast-growing and reconstructing nations of Indochina. The Thai authorities permitted the formation of international banking facilities[57], called 'Bangkok International Banking Facilities' (BIBF).[58] The BIBF was designed to facilitate international borrowings and to encourage capital inflows as a means of financing the current account deficit.[59] The BIBF also offered tax incentives to attract foreign capital inflows.[60]

These developments facilitated significant short-term capital inflows into Thailand.[61] At the beginning of 1996, short-term foreign currency debt

55 Liberalisation policies encompassed among other things the dismantling of interest rate ceilings and foreign exchange control. Government intervention as regards requirement of lending to particular sectors e.g. agriculture was also reduced. *See generally,* Financial Institutions Supervision and Development Department, *Financial Institutions Supervision and Development in Thailand* (Mar. 1995), at 26–38; *see also* Pakorn Vichyanond, *Thailand's Financial System: Structure and Liberalisation* (1994), Thailand Development Research Institute, Research Monograph No 11, ch 10.

56 IMF Articles of Agreement of the International Monetary Fund, Article VIII. *See* Weston B., *et al, Supplement of Basic Documents to International Law and World Order* (1997), at 681; *See generally* Chaiyawat Wibulsawasdi, 'Relaxation of Exchange Control', Seminar for Supreme Court Judges on Thailand's Economic and Monetary Condition, 17 Sept. 1990.

57 The concept of 'International Banking Facilities' actually originated in the USA in December 1981. IBF can be simplistically defined as a conventional Eurocurrency business with an additional scope of business to operate transactions denominated in local currency also. The business is permitted to be operated with only non-residents. *See* Sydney Key, 'International Banking Facilities', 68 *Federal Reserve Bulletin* (Oct. 1982), at 565–77; *see also* Cynthia Lichtenstein, 'US Banks and the Eurocurrency Markets: The Regulatory Structure', 99 *Banking Law Journal* (June/July 1982), at 484–511.

58 The scope of BIBF business can be categorised into three types: (1) offshore lending business whereby capitals in local or foreign currencies are obtained abroad and lent to entities offshore; (2) 'domestic lending' business whereby funds, in foreign currencies only, are obtained from non-residents abroad and lent in domestically; and (3) certain investment banking services, viz, foreign exchange business, issue of letter of credits, debt guarantees. *See* Notification of the Ministry of Finance *Re: The Operation of International Banking Facilities by Commercial Banks*, *Royal Gazette*, vol.109, part 119, 17 Sept. 1992.

59 'Detailed Measures of BIBF to Reduce Risks, An Interview with Mr. Vijit Supinit, the Governor of the Bank of Thailand' (in Thai), *Journal of Finance and Banking (*Mar. 1993), at 212.

60 Special rate of corporate tax, 10 per cent instead of 30 per cent was granted to BIBF businesses.

61 Research Department, Bangkok Bank PCL., *Financial Institution Crisis: from Japan, Korea to Thailand* (1998) <http://www.bbl.co.th/research/jun_pr1.htm>.

obligations of with maturity of one year or less accounted for nearly 90 per centof the total foreign debts originated as BIBF business.[62] The Thai economic and financial liberalisation policies were similarly designed to promote Thailand as a regional funding centre.[63] Other external contributing factors which facilitated significant capital inflows included the stagnant economic growth prospects of Japan and the European Union during the early 1990's, and the 1995 Mexican foreign exchange liquidity crisis fallout which diverted capital flows from emerging markets in Latin America to emerging markets in East Asia.[64]

The following points consider how the massive short-term capitals inflows triggered the explosion of the Thai crisis. Metaphorically, short-term capital flows can be compared to a 'two-edged sword'. On the one hand, short-term capital inflows fuel the burgeoning economic growth and produce economic welfare for the entire nation. On the other hand, serious reliance on short-term capital flows engenders significant latent hazards for funding current account deficits and ill-considered investment projects. The direction and allocation of short-term capital flows hinge upon investor confidence[65] in the health of the domestic economy and financial system, and perhaps more importantly in political stability. Therefore, sustained reliance on short-term capital inflows requires sound macroeconomic policies, a flexible exchange rate regime, stable government, and the establishment of safe and sound banking and financial systems.[66] Absent such underpinnings, any sudden loss of global investor confidence would predictably generate a severe and sudden foreign exchange liquidity crisis, as Thai-denominated assets are liquidated in force by fleeing investors who have collectively lost confidence. The 'double-edged sword' paradigm has clearly manifested in Thailand and other East Asian nations in 1997–8, most notably in Indonesia and South Korea.

Notwithstanding the overreliance on short-term capital inflows, the fixed exchange rate regime also played a significant role in the resulting crisis. The pegged exchange rate regime had been in operation since November 1984. The exchange rate of the baht was fixed to a 'currency basket' consisting of the currencies of Thailand's main trading partners. As

[62] This data actually raised concern among many economists. Interestingly, the Bank of Thailand asserted that there had long been imbalances towards long-term debt obligations and long-term investment, and that such imbalances should not be viewed as problematic. *See* 'Foreign Debts of BIBF Business', *Bank of Thailand News*, No 24/1997.

[63] *See generally* Ministry of Finance, Bank of Thailand, and the Securities Exchange Commission, *Financial System Development Masterplan (1 Mar. 1995–29 Feb. 2000)*, part 2.7.

[64] Shigemitsu Sugisaki, above n 3, at 3.

[65] Joseph Yam, 'Asian Monetary Cooperation', the Per Jacobson Lecture, 21 Sept. 1997, at 6.

[66] IMF, above n 49, at 5.

the US was the most important trading partner of Thailand, the Thai currency basket was heavily weighted in favour of the US dollar. In fact, the currency basket was approximately eighty to ninety per centdenominated by the US dollar.[67] The currency peg was designed to stabilise the currency to promote exports and foreign investment,[68] and it had been the 'hallmark of successful macroeconomic management in Thailand over the past decade or so'.[69]

The fixed exchange rate policy, however, came to contribute to the crisis in four respects.

First, the exchange rate regime guaranteed that the value of the Thai currency would fluctuate proportionately with the US dollar. The value of the baht would therefore mirror the economic conditions of the US, and would not necessarily be representative of the underlying the economic conditions of Thailand. When the US dollar weakened against the Japanese yen during the early 1990s, Thai exports were more globally competitive. Conversely, when the US dollar strengthened during mid-1995, the competitiveness of Thai exports abated, and the Thai current account deficit widened substantially.[70] Thus, the fixed exchange rate regime had become inappropriate, as the value of the baht contradicted with the state of the country's real economy. Under these circumstances, the fixed exchange rate regime became vulnerable to massive 'speculative attack' by institutions both foreign and domestic seeking to exploit or hedge the exchange rate imbalance by selling physical baht and baht-denominated instruments and purchasing dollars and dollar-denominated instruments. The 'speculative attacks' simply accelerated the unveiling of the crises which was basically the result of the macroeconomic and exchange rate imbalances and incompatibility.[71] Second, it became very expensive for the Bank of Thailand to maintain the fixed exchange rate regime. Domestic interest rates needed to be sustained at high levels to maintain interest rate parity with the United States, which adversely affected the profits and growth of domestic businesses. Unfortunately, the Thai government exhausted virtually all of its foreign reserves in the attempts to defend the baht from speculative attacks along traditional central bank operations,[72] and these failed attempts ultimately liquidated the country of dollar reserves

[67] Commission Tasked With Making Recommendations to Improve the Efficiency and Management of Thailand's Financial System, *Report of the Analysis and Evaluation on Facts Behind Thailand's Economic Crisis* (1998), at 11 (hereinafter Nukul Report).

[68] *See* 'Change in Thailand's Exchange Rate System', *Bank of Thailand News*, No 45/1997, at 1.

[69] Financial Markets Operation, Banking Department, Bank of Thailand, *A Review and Assessment of the Bank of Thailand's Foreign Exchange Interventions* (Oct. 1997), at 1.

[70] Shigemitsu Sugisaki, above n 3, at 3.

[71] Paul Krugman, above n. 46, at 6.

[72] From Thailand's experience, Thailand spent more than thirty billion US dollars, both by direct intervention and swaps in futile defenses of her currency. *See Report of the Analysis and Decision*, above n 67, ch 2.

and left it heavily exposed to open forward contracts and other off-balance sheet arrangements in the OTC derivatives markets. Third, the fixed exchange rate regime substantially encouraged artificially large capital inflows into the country, which then became a contributing cause of the problem as the pegged exchange rate provided a perceived guarantee as to the value of the baht. Financial returns in Thailand during the era of economic success were generally higher than those in the United States, Western Europe, or Japan. Thus, undisciplined foreign capital flows moved into Thailand and were targeted for investments with high growth prospects, and such investments were deemed to fail in the short-run as the baht came under heavy selling pressure and devalued enormously relative to the US dollar.[73] Last but not least, the fixed exchange rate regime also created a self-deceptive 'security blanket' for Thai businesses that failed to hedge against exchange rate risk. As the bath-dollar exchange rate began to decline the existence of large unhedged foreign debt obligations panicked businessmen into obtaining foreign currencies to repay their debts, thus creating further negative pressure on the exchange rate.[74]

Interestingly, in response to the fixed exchange rate regime becoming unsustainable, the Bank of Thailand planned to shift the exchange rate regime to a 'managed float regime', but decided to 'adopt a more systematic approach'. But, before doing so, the authorities determined they would 'maintain macroeconomic stability by curtailing inflation'[75] and enhance the safety and soundness of banking and finance sectors in the first place in order to minimise possible risks.[76] Nonetheless, when the remarkable pressures mounted on the baht:dollar exchange rate, the central bank authorities failed to respond promptly by discontinuing the fixed exchange rate regime, but instead fought the 'speculative attacks' with direct intervention[77] in the cash, forward and derivative foreign exchange markets, together with certain measures of exchange controls[78] and dramatic interest rate hikes.[79] The central bank intervention was merely an invitation to domestic and international investors and businesses to test the Bank of Thailand's resolve in its initial decision to defend the fixed exchange rate regime at all costs which nearly exhausted the foreign currency reserves. Thus, the Bank of Thailand's decision to use direct intervention coupled

[73] Alan Greenspan, above n 6, at 1. *See also* Joseph Yam, above n 65, at 6.

[74] Michel Camdessus, above n 43, at 2.

[75] Bank of Thailand and Board of Investment, above n 36, at 11.

[76] Ibid., at 3, 11.

[77] Such intervention was also supported by certain neighbouring countries such as Singapore. *See* 'Joint Action in the Foreign Exchange Market', *Bank of Thailand News*, No 28/1997.

[78] *See Report of the Analysis and Decision,* above n 67, para 182–3.

[79] Overnight inter-bank rate was increased from 9–15 per cent to 30 per cent at the beginning of 1997. *See* Financial Markets Operation, above n 69, at 2–3.

with the abandonment of planned macroeconomic reforms contributed greatly to the depth of the ensuing crisis in 1997–1998. The courses of action taken by the Bank of Thailand were by no means unique, as governments in other East Asian nations, notably South Korea, also followed the Thai initiative in this respect.

The speed and manner of the implementation of liberalisation policies in the Thai domestic financial sector have been widely criticised both before and after the eruption of the crisis as being 'too early' and 'too fast'.[80] It has been suggested that the establishment of a 'safe and sound' financial sector should have been a prerequisite of such liberalisation policies.[81] The question as to whether Thailand had the alternative not to open up the domestic financial sector to foreign competition needs to be taken into account. In the GATS forum,[82] Thailand was not necessarily required to open the domestic financial sector to foreign competition as a result of the Uruguay Round Negotiation.[83] Nonetheless, the US consistently levelled enormous pressure on Thailand to open up the domestic financial sector to foreign competition under the threat of the extraterritorial enforcement of US trade laws.[84]

80 According to Dr Ammar Siamwalla, former president of Thailand Development Research Institute, Thailand's liberalisation towards free capital flows 'in retrospect has been far too rapid'. *See* Paul M. Sherer, 'Distrust of Western Economics Grows in Thailand Amid Crisis', *Wall Street Journal,* 20 Jan. 1998. The initiation of the Bangkok International Banking Facilities (BIBF) was widely viewed as an ambitious step, which resulted in the significant of capital inflow. As a matter of fact, onshore lending was intended and aimed to finance current account deficits.

81 *See* Joseph Stiglitz, above n 54. Thailand admitted the lesson from of the liberalisation that safe and sound financial market is indispensable. *See* Bank of Thailand and Board of Investment, above n 36, at 14.

82 In the Uruguay Round of negotiations, beginning in September 1986, trade in services was successfully included in the scope of the General Agreement of Tariffs and Trade (GATT). The General Agreement on Trade in Services (GATS) 'embracing the traditional GATT concepts (MFN, national treatment, . . . [and transparency])', was agreed. The Agreement functions as a 'framework agreement'. Obligations of member states are 'general obligations and disciplines', and 'specific commitments' committed to be bound by each member state. *See generally* John Jackson, *The World Trading System* (1997), ch 12. The Agreement covers four modes of services supply, i.e. cross-border supply, consumption abroad, commercial presence, and presence of natural persons. *See* General Agreement on Trade in Services, art. 1 (2).

83 Negotiation in the area of financial services was politically sensitive and came to the deadlock at the end of the Uruguay Round. Specific commitment in the Schedule of Commitments mainly were those existing barriers of each member state.

84 Section 301 of the US Trade Act of 1974 was used to 'open up foreign markets' for the US trade. Determining that a country conducts an 'unreasonable or discriminatory practices that burden or restrict' the US trade, the US Trade Representatives (USTR) can among other things revoke any trade benefits for that country, or imports barriers to the goods of the country. *See* Folsom and Gordon, *International Business Transactions* (1995), ch 14.

B. *Unsafe and Unsound Banking and Finance Sectors*

In the modern period of globalisation and liberalised capital flows, it is essential for a market-oriented economy to have a safe and sound financial system to sustain economic growth. Otherwise, the capital inflows could be exploited in a way creating and exacerbating a 'bubble economy'.[85] Notably, the 'bubble economy' concept has manifested in the property and financial asset sectors in nations that claim to have developed prudential supervisory frameworks when there exists considerable amounts of capital inflows, such as the United States in the 1980s and Japan in the 1988–1.[86]

In the case of Thailand, the lack of supervision, regulation, and enforcement in the banking and finance sectors may be considered as the most important fundamental problem that led to the current crisis. The unfortunate reality was that Thailand's banking and finance sectors had been unsafe and unsound for a great period of time. Thai commercial banks were consistently undercapitalised and favoured connected lending practices, lax lending criteria, insider fraud and mismanagement were prevalent. The banking sector was also consistently over-exposed in terms of overlending to the ailing property sector. Further, the banking and finance sectors, as with other business sectors of the Thai economy, substantially depended upon short-term foreign loans to finance investment.[87] Indeed, the banking sector, acting as the primary intermediary of flow of funds, served as a proactive conduit for the considerable capital inflows in this respect. In the face of an apparently robust economic growth, however, such weaknesses in the banking and finance sectors remained submerged or were ignored.[88] The lack of transparency and corrupt practices in the political and financial systems temporarily obscured the true condition of these sectors.[89] In addition, the Thai banking and finance sectors remained unsafe and unsound due to the absence of efficient and serious financial institution prudential supervision and regulatory enforcement by Thai authorities. In short, prudential supervision and regulatory enforcement have been rather inefficient and token as a matter of course in Thailand throughout the 1980s and 1990s.[90]

The deficiencies in prudential supervision and regulatory enforcement largely are logical extensions of the patronage system and attendant crony capitalism prevalent in Thailand. The sustained excessive concentration of

[85] Joseph Yam, above n 65, para 25.

[86] Michel Mussa, above n 47, at 5.

[87] Robert E. Rubin, above n 9, at 2.

[88] Stanley Fischer, above n 9, at 3.

[89] Robert E. Rubin, above n 9, at 2.

[90] *See* n 92, below, *see also* Paul Handley, 'Is the Bank of Thailand part of the problem?', *Institutional Investor*, Dec. 1996; Barry Johnston, 'Distressed Financial Institutions in Thailand: Structural Weaknesses, Support Operations, and Economic Consequences', in V. Sundararajan and Tomas J. T. Balino, *Banking Crises: Cases and Issues* (1991).

power within the business elites and the military leadership systematically rendered proper supervision and enforcement difficult and convoluted or otherwise nonexistent. For instance, the Thai Military Bank was regarded as one of the least sound banks in the country as a result of significant low-quality, favoured connected lending. Military influence shielded the Thai Military Bank from the supervisory and regulatory practices of the Bank of Thailand.[91] The Bangkok Bank of Commerce scandal previously discussed in this article is another blunt example of how crony capitalism generated failures in prudential supervision and inefficient or nonexistent regulatory enforcement.[92]

The unsafe and unsound conditions that permeated the Thai banking and financial systems resulted in various other notable problems. For instance, capitals inflows and savings were mobilised excessively through inefficient financial intermediation into non-productive and/or overcapacitated sectors such as property and equity speculation. Thai banks and finance companies were overexposed to the property sector since the late 1980s, estimated to be approximately a quarter of total credit extension of commercial banks and finance companies.[93] The overexposures were unmistakably linked to serious 'moral hazard' issues in Thailand due to the perception of implied government bailouts held by domestic and international financial institutions alike.[94] This perception facilitated excessive risk-taking by domestic financial institutions, especially Thai finance companies, and generally resulted in overzealous credit extensions to the property sector and fueled a property price bubble that was destined to be unsustainable. The property price bubble, in Thailand as in other nations such as Japan, became a self-fulfilling prophecy. The overpriced property assets served as collateral for bank and finance company lending to the property sector, and when the price bubble burst, the property asset prices suddenly deflated, and the loans secured by such properties became both seriously undercollateralised and distressed. The resulting property asset price deflation engendered significant amounts of non-performing loans

[91] *See* Paul Handley, 'Bangkok's long road to recovery', *Institutional Investor*, Sept. 1997.

[92] The Bank's unsafe and unsound condition resulted from significant favoured connected lending, generally lax lending practices, and various other imprudent activities such as credit extension for purposes of the Bank's own recapitalisation. The Bank of Thailand ordered the Bank to rectify such conditions and to improve operations, but the order was ignored. Nonetheless, at the time there was no legal enforcement from the Bank of Thailand. Rather, the Bank of Thailand extended a financial support to the Bank without the prior write-down of the Bank's capital. The Bank of Thailand's response was widely criticised and discussed in the Parliament, and the ensuing political pressure forced the resignation of the then Governor of the Bank of Thailand.

[93] Economic Research Department, Bank of Thailand, *How the Bubble Economy in Thailand Began* (1998).

[94] Thai supervisory authorities emphasised on the prevention of systemic risk. Financial institutions especially commercial banks were hardly allowed to fail.

extended to property developers.[95] The Thai finance companies began liquidating property collateral to remain solvent, and these actions further depreciated the value of underlying and overpriced property assets.[96] The finance companies engaged in sales of property collateral to protect themselves from nonperforming loans, and these actions in turn exacerbated the property price decline in a vicious cycle.[97] Lending to the property sector all but ceased, and new projects for property development halted. Property values declined to an even greater extent because of the liquidity crunch. The 'vicious cycle' of real property asset inflation and deflation was complete. The property asset value deflation was accompanied by significant decreases in equity prices, as well as previously stated the exchange rate depreciation and interest rate hikes resulting from central bank defence of the currency resulted in a further burden on the unhedged foreign exchange liabilities, which further helped to undermine the loan portfolios of finance companies.[98]

Beginning in 1989, the Bank of Thailand persistently warned Thai commercial banks in relation to the significant lending to property sector by way of 'moral suasion' type of 'credit monitoring'.[99] This informal guidance was clearly disregarded.[100] In March 1997, the Thai Ministry of Finance, in response to the non-performing loan problem, established the Property Loan Management Organisation (PLMO). The purpose of the PLMO was to reduce the burden of non-performing loans to the property sector and to assist property developers to continue their businesses by purchasing and restructuring their debt obligations from Thai banks and finance companies.[101] In June 1997, Thai financial institutions[102] were permitted unilaterally to establish 'Property Management Corporations'.[103] The Thai government measures unfortunately proved to be 'too little-too late'.[104]

[95] Joseph Yam, above n 65, para 25.

[96] Alan Greenspan, above n 6, at 1.

[97] *See* Paul Krugman, *What happened to Asia?* (1998) <http://web.mit.edu/krugman/www/DISINTER.html>. Professor Krugman viewed the asset boom-bust cycle as the main reason for Asia crisis, preceding the currency crisis.

[98] *See* Letter of Development Policy, Proposed Loan for Restructuring Finance Companies, to the World Bank, 16 Dec. 1997, at 1–2.

[99] *See* Bank of Thailand, *Financial Institutions and Market in Thailand* (Dec. 1990), at 35. Bank of Thailand has preferred to use the moral suasion means, although it is empowered according to the banking laws to issue legal restriction in this respect. *See* Commercial Banking Act of 1962, s 13 ter.

[100] *See* Bank of Thailand and Board of Investment, above n 36, at 2.

[101] *See* 'Thai Authorities Take a Major Step to Resolve Property Loan Problems', *Bank of Thailand News* No 13/1997.

[102] Those institutions include commercial banks, finance companies and securities companies.

[103] Bank of Thailand, Circular Letter Re: Procedures in Establishment of Property Management Corporation, 17 June 1997.

[104] In restrospect, the Bank of Thailand should have implemented more serious warning by

III. THE FINANCIAL CRISIS: EXACERBATING FACTORS

A. Economic and Export Growth Slowdown

Given the pegged exchange rate with the US dollar, the Thai baht appreciated as the US dollar appreciated since early 1996. The appreciation of the baht served to undermine the competitiveness of Thai exports. The continued failure of Thai economic policymakers to effectively shift and diversify export concentrations from the labour-intensive manufacturing sectors to capital-intensive industries further aggravated the situation. The Thai labour-intensive manufacturing sector already was facing very strong competition from nations such as China and Vietnam[105] and 'restructuring' Eastern European countries, where the labour costs were less onerous.[106] The decision by China to devalue its currency, the yuan, in 1995 also contributed to the growing lack of competitiveness of Thai exports. Further, the enhanced competitiveness and market access of Latin American countries to US markets as a result of the North American Free Trade Agreement (NAFTA)[107] was another reason underlying the slowing growth of Thai exports. In addition, the declining Thai export competitiveness was influenced by asset price inflation.[108] As a consequence, Thailand's export growth became so sluggish that by 1996 export growth was zero per cent.[109] Notwithstanding these clear signals, Thai authorities nonetheless asserted that the drastic slowdown in export growth could not have been anticipated.[110] The marked decline in Thai exports resulted in increasing current account deficits. The current account imbalances rendered the fixed exchange rate regime inappropriate and vulnerable to speculative attack in a 'cause and effect' ratification by market participants.

B. External Factors and Speculative Attacks

As a result of macro-economic imbalances and the unsustainable pegged exchange rate regime, certain market participants perceived the Thai situation as a great opportunity for profit-taking.[111] Speculative attacks have

ways of regulations rather than moral-suasion-type means. (As a matter of fact, the Bank of Thailand is empowered to issue a prohibition according to s 13 ter. of the Banking Act of 1962 (as amended). Once significant amount of lending had been for long extended to property sector and thus properties had been considerably overvalued, it became too late to cure.

105 Economic Research Department, above n 93, at 1.

106 Joseph Yam, above n 65, at 8.

107 Ibid.

108 Ibid. para 25.

109 *See* Bank of Thailand, Key Economic Indicators, available at <http://www.bot.or.th/research/>.

110 Bank of Thailand and Board of Investment, above n 36, at 3.

111 Mixed policies between pegged exchange rate regimes and the 'free movement of international capital' may render a nation very susceptible to speculative attack, as it permits 'speculators

long been viewed as catalysts for the evolution of currency crises, caused by market participants exploiting inconsistencies between macroeconomic policies and fixed exchange rate regimes by trading in the foreign exchange and interest rate markets.[112] The speculative attacks against the baht started in 1996 and re-occurred in earnest in May 1997. The Bank of Thailand directly confronted market participants by taking positions in the cash, forward and derivative foreign exchange markets in defence of the baht instead of adjusting macroeconomic policies and facilitating a managed floatation of exchange rates[113] as allegedly suggested by the IMF.[114] These direct actions resulted in the Bank of Thailand undertaking enormous positions in the forward foreign exchange market and significant losses of foreign currency (US dollars) reserves[115] (estimated to be thirty billion US dollars) through direct intervention in attempting to stabilise the fixed exchange rate regime.[116]

Apart from the liquidation of foreign currency resources, the Bank of Thailand had to maintain interest rate parity relationships and therefore high interest rates needed to be maintained to support the defence of the baht. The sustained high interest rates effected a slowdown in the domestic business sector expansion and development as the cost of domestic funds increased. Further, during early 1997, there were widespread rumours regarding the *de facto* or *de jure* devaluation of the baht, which substantially undermined investor confidence in the baht and further put pressure on the exchange rate. The Bank of Thailand, in response to the situation, officially denied the rumour in February 1997 and again in May 1997. Nonetheless, the baht was suddenly *de facto* devalued in July 1997, as Thai authorities similarly released the currency from the pegged exchange rate regime and attempted to bring about a managed flotation regime.[117] Under the new managed float exchange rate regime, Thai authorities declared that 'the value of the baht will be determined by market forces to reflect economic fundamentals'.[118] Unfortunately, after the *de facto* devaluation of

to build a position without turning the price against themselves . . . [, but on the other hand, the fixed exchange rate regime] does not allow the . . . authorities . . . to keep supplying foreign reserves at a fixed price'. *See* I. J. Macfarlane Speech to the American Australian Association, in conjunction with the Asia Society, The Downtown Economists Inc., New York Association of Business Economics and the International Economics Club held in New York on 11 Mar. 1998, *BIS Review* 20/1998, at 2.

112 Paul Krugman,, above n 46, at 5.

113 *See* Michel Camdessus, above n 43, at 2.

114 IMF has claimed to have warned Thailand on many occasions *vis-à-vis* the pending crisis. *See Report on Analysis and Decisions*, above n 67, at 101–2.

115 Michel Camdessus, above n 43, at 2.

116 *See Report on Analysis and Decisions*, above n 67, ch 2 and 3.

117 *See* Notification of the Ministry of Finance Re: Change in Exchange Rate Regime, 2 July 1997.

118 *See also* Joint Statement Between the Ministry of Finance and the Bank of Thailand *Re: Change in Thailand's Exchange Rate System*, above n 68, at 1.

the baht, the exchange rate declined 17 per cent the next day,[119] and further decreased to the record low level of approximately 56 bath-dollar by mid-January 1998.[120] The enormous reduction in the exchange rate held devastating effects on the Thai economy.[121] Thai domestic businesses shouldering large amounts of foreign currency debt could not survive through the turbulent exchange rate crisis, as it became considerably more expensive to service and otherwise to repay their debts. The Bank of Thailand now held massive underlying positions in the forward and derivatives markets which obligated it to pay billions of dollars in the near future, but held very little dollar reserves with which to pay them.

Notwithstanding the analysis set forth above, it would not by any means be fair to blame the Bank of Thailand for causing the crisis. The implementation of monetary and exchange rate policies by the Bank of Thailand has always been presumably aimed at achieving macroeconomic and monetary stability, and resulting gains or losses are presumably incidental in part to the achievement of this objective.[122] Further, it is always easier and more straightforward looking at the situation from hindsight.[123] Under the circumstances before the *de facto* devaluation of the baht, the Bank of Thailand was in an extraordinarily difficult position, and the policies it followed must have been exceedingly difficult and politically dangerous to make in an environment of a coalition government.

C. *Political Instability*

Political risk is one of the primary criteria that investors consider in deciding whether or not to allocate funds to investments in a particular country. A country with political instability must presumably offer a more lucrative return (the so-called 'risk premium') for investors to compensate them for the greater political risks incurred, relative to investment risks in other countries or regions.[124]

In the case of Thailand, the post-1932 Revolution political leadership has been generally unstable, alternating between coalition democratic governance and military dictatorship. In times where the government has been a coalition democracy, the government leaders were drawn from within the Thai Parliament from several political parties with different policies and

119 Simon Kuper, 'The Pound Soars on "Loose" Budget', *Financial Times*, 2 July 1997.

120 'SET ends 3 per cent lower as baht sinks to 56.45', *The Nation*, 13 Jan. 1998.

121 *See* Paul Krugman, *Currency Crises* (1998) <http://web.mit.edu/krugman/www/crises.html>, at 3.

122 See 'Denial of Reports on the Bank of Thailand's Exchange Losses', *Bank of Thailand News* No 58/2540.

123 Bank of Thailand and Board of Investment, above n 36, at 11.

124 *See* Richard A. Brealey and Steward C. Myers, *Principles of Corporate Finance* (1996), ch 7.

vested interests. Political stability in Thailand has also been consistently undermined by perceived vulnerabilities to military influence.[125] Nonetheless, investors were attracted to Thailand because of the prospects of explosive growth of an emerging economy. If the prospects for explosive economic growth diminished, the investment incentives abated correspondingly and risks became exaggerated by political instability.

The convoluted 'management of the crisis' by Thai authorities due to political instability further greatly exacerbated the financial crisis in 1997.[126] The ambiguous and cautionary stance of Thai authorities in addressing the crisis facilitated enormous and unnecessary uncertainty and generated sustained losses of investor confidence.[127] In fact, various commentators charged that Thai political instability was not only an exacerbating cause of the crisis but the primary cause thereof.[128] Political influence and responses of vested interests, both foreign and domestic, resulted in indecisiveness and superficial responses by Thai authorities in addressing problematic aspects of macroeconomic policy and the fixed exchange rate regime preceding the crisis. The stagnation of political leadership and corrupt intervention of vested interests directly resulted in ineffective and inefficient prudential supervision and regulation of Thai financial institutions when supervision and regulation were clearly needed most. In short, political instability is a key aspect of crony capitalism, and is undoubtedly at the root of Thailand's dysfunctional economy and banking and financial systems and ensuing financial crisis.

D. Consequences As Accelerating Causes

Few people would have anticipated that the contagion effect of the crisis would spread so rapidly and broadly from Thailand to the remaining East Asian nations. In the wake of Thailand's financial crisis, the Philippines,

[125] In the environment of fragmented government, the military circle is considered as the best organised, disciplined institution in Thai society. Therefore, in times of political distress or deadlock, it normally ended up with the government being overthrown by a military group. Since the revolution that ended the era of absolute monarchy in Thailand in 1932, 'the military as an institution has been the preeminent political force'. *See* David Morell and Chai-anan Samudavanija, *Political Conflict in Thailand: Reform, Reaction, Revolution* (1981), at 55–64.

[126] For instance, oil tax increase as a part of austerity measures to meet a budget surplus required by the IMF was rescinded only after three days. As a result, the then Finance Minister decided to resign. *See* 'The year they sunk the baht', *Bangkok Post Economic Review 1997* <http://www.bangkokpost.net/ecoreview97/review9704.html>, at 7–10; *see also* Wichit Chaitrong and Surachai Chupaka, 'Economic action held up by political turmoil: Coalition stalemate delays moves on urgent issues', *The Nation,* 21 Oct. 1997.

[127] The indecisiveness and ambiguity of the General Chavalit Yongchaiyut government resulted in several successive changes of finance ministers and central bank governors, which in large part undermined investor confidence. General Chavalit was criticised by the press as a 'directionless, ineffective leader'. *See* Paul Handley, above n 91, at 1.

[128] *See* 'Economic Crisis Claims Thai Leader', *International Herald Tribune,* 4 Nov. 1997.

Malaysia, Indonesia, and South Korea all eventually suffered massive *de facto* devaluations of their respective currencies in 1997. The devaluations were caused principally by market participants selling currencies in the form of physicals, forwards, futures, options and other OTC derivative instruments as speculative measures, as a part of hedging strategies, and as arbitraging across asset classes and markets and the inability of the respective central banks to defend their currencies using traditional defence measures. The contagion effect was exacerbated by the lack of investor confidence in the East Asia region as a whole due to the impact of suddenly devalued currencies having reinforcing effects on crises in respective countries.[129] The contagion effect as an expansionary phenomenon can be generally explained in the following manner. Thailand's crisis alerted investors to be beware of underlying crises and/or possible opportunities for profit-taking in other countries with similar fundamental weaknesses (e.g. asset price inflation, unsafe and unsound financial system, 'crony capitalism', over-reliance of public and/or private on short-term foreign debts, and short-term reserve account imbalances and/or deficits).[130] In turn, Thailand's *de facto* devaluation tended to undercut other fragile East Asian economies with similar fundamental weaknesses, especially those with concentrations in the same or similar exports.[131]

These factors tended to facilitate adverse investor reactions, *en masse*, which is sometimes referred to as a 'herd reaction', resulting in massive capital flow reversals.[132] Without investors' confidence in the Thai financial markets and those of its neighbours, the significant short-term public and/or private foreign currency debts became in serious risk of being suspended temporarily and/or not repaid as the respective exchange rates declined to record low levels in early 1998. The countries respectively failed to recognise the need for timely debt restructuring and/or 'rolling over' of foreign debt obligations to avoid the liquidation of forcign currency reserves. The end results were very serious liquidity crises.

129 *See* Callum Henderson, *Asia Falling?: Making Sense of the Asian Currency Crisis and Its Aftermath* (1998), ch 6; *see also* Ranjit Gill, *Asia Under Siege: How the Asian Miracle Went Wrong* (1998), ch 5–8; Dan Biers, *Crash of '97: How the Financial Crisis Is Reshaping Asia* (1998), at 77–93.

130 Michel Camdessus, above n 43, at 2.

131 Paul Krugman, above n 121, at 8.

132 Capital flow reversal and herding are included in the risks as regards financial integration. Besides, the integration increased volatility from the economy's exposure to more sources of shocks in the international economy and from the magnification of domestic shocks. *See* World Bank, *Private Capital Flows to Developing Countries: The Road to Financial Integration* (1997), at 25–32.

IV. RESPONSES TO THE FINANCIAL CRISIS

A. IMF Assistance Package

The Thai authorities were initially reluctant to seek financial assistance from the IMF, despite the IMF's apparent readiness to provide assistance. The Thai government attempted to avoid facing the difficult legal and economic problems underlying the banking and financial systems and the politically unpopular measures required to resolve them under IMF 'conditionality' requirements that accompanied such assistance.[133] Immediately following abandonment of the fixed exchange rate regime and the subsequent currency devaluation, Thailand initially sought bilateral financial assistance from Japan. The Japanese Ministry of Finance, under great pressure from the US, asserted their preference that financial assistance be provided as part of an international response 'organised' by the IMF. After the failed attempt to negotiate bilaterally with Japan, Thailand resorted to seeking a financial assistance package from the IMF.

The IMF financial rescue package for Thailand amounted to a credit facility of US$ 17.2 billion. Of that amount, the IMF provided stand-by credits to Thailand under the Emergency Financing Mechanism (EFM)[134] of up to SDR 2.9 billion, equivalent to approximately US$ 4 billion.[135] The World Bank and the Asian Development Bank provided credit facilities of US$ 1.5 billion and US$ 1.2 billion, respectively. In addition, Japan committed financial support of US$ 4 billion; Australia, China, Hong Kong, Malaysia, and Singapore, committed facilities of US$ 1 billion each; and Indonesia, South Korea and Brunei committed facilities of US$ 0.5 billion each.[136] The IMF assistance package was destined to support the

[133] *See* 'Of crashes and conspirators', *The Economist,* 2 Aug. 1997, at 57; *see also* 'Government turns to IMF for help', *Bangkok Post,* 28 July 1997. As a matter of fact, the government was not certain as regards its ability to meet the IMF austerity measures; Soonruth Bunyamanee, 'Foreign funding package seems inevitable', *Bangkok Post,* 28 July 1997.

[134] Emergency Financing Mechanism (EFM) is a set of procedures to facilitate rapid Executive Board approval of IMF financial support while ensuring the conditionality necessary to warrant such support. It is used only in circumstances representing, or threatening to give rise to, a crisis in a member's external accounts that requires an immediate IMF response. It was introduced in the wake of Mexican Crisis in 1995. *See* IMF, 'Financial Facilities and Policies: IMF Financing Seeks to Cusion Impact of Members' Adjustment Policies', IMF Survey Supplement on the Fund 1996, available at <http://www.imf.org, at 4>.

[135] The stand-by credit is equal to 505 per cent of the quota of Thailand in the IMF which is SDR 573.9 million or around US$ 780 million. The first tranche of SDR 1.2 billion (approximately US$ 1.6 billion), would be ready for withdrawal upon the approval, and second tranche of SDR 600 million (approximately US$ 810 million) would be available after 30 Nov. and on the condition that 'end-Sept. performance targets have been met and the first review of the program[me] has been completed'. *See* 'IMF Approves Stand-by Credit for Thailand', IMF Press Release No 97/37, at 1.

[136] Bank of Thailand, *Bank of Thailand News*, No 56/1997, at 1; *see also* IMF, Fact Sheet, *IMF Bail Outs: Truth and Fiction,* Jan. 1998 <http://www.imf.org/external/np/exr/facts/bailout.htm>, at 4.

balance of payments and maintenance of foreign reserves,[137] and not for bailouts of distressed financial institutions.

The IMF attached various restructuring requirements to the financial assistance package as 'conditionality' measures. Thailand is obliged to meet performance criteria formulated by the IMF during the period of the thirty-four month programme.[138] The financial and restructuring aspects of the IMF package function collaboratively with each other. While the restructuring of economic fundamentals and financial system are in process, the 'temporary' financial assistance is to provide necessary 'breathing room' until investor confidence is restored,[139] and 'industrial and business structure is adjusted (over the next one to two years) to be able to export competitively in the world market'.[140] The financial assistance is also intended to facilitate the 'rolling over' of external debt obligations owed by Thai financial institutions and businesses.[141] In rehabilitation of the banking and financial sectors, money supply will not raised beyond 'an appropriate level needed for solving problems of the financial institutions'.[142]

Nonetheless, Thailand's acceptance of the IMF financial assistance package failed to preclude further downward spirals in asset prices and private capital outflows.[143] Yet, given financial and technical assistance from the IMF, the World Bank, the Asian Development Bank, and various other nations, Thailand would presumably seek to create new and sustainable economic growth opportunities, based on appropriate macroeconomic and structural foundations for such renewed economic expansion. Of course, behind this laudable objective there existed huge political and economic sacrifices ancillary to the implementation of IMF conditionality measures.

B. IMF Conditionality Measures

In exchange for receiving distributions and stand-by facilities under the IMF financial assistance package, Thailand was required to submit a sovereign Letter of Intent drafted with the IMF assistance committing the nation to IMF 'conditionality'. The First Letter of Intent reiterated the government's assurances of the intent to implement plans to rectify monetary and fiscal policies, and to restructure the distressed banking and financial systems. The First Letter of Intent was co-signed by the Minister of Finance

137 Thai Board of Investment, 'Getting the economy back on track with the "IMF formula",' *BOI Investment Review*, vol 6, No 3, 15 Sept. 1997.

138 Ibid.

139 Robert E. Rubin, above n 3, at 4.

140 Board of Investment, *Business Focus: Finance Sector Rehabilitation Program*, Address by Deputy Prime Minister, Dr Virapongsa Ramangkura, on 14 Oct. 1997.

141 Robert Rubin, above n 3, at 4.

142 Board of Investment, *Business Focus*, above n 140, at 2.

143 BIS, *International Banking and Financial Market Developments*, Feb. 1998.

and the Governor of the Bank of Thailand on 14 August 1997, and was approved by the IMF on 21 August 1997. The Letter of Intent stipulated that the government's 1997–2000 policy framework is 'designed to restore confidence and economic stability at an early stage and lay the foundation for sound growth over the medium-term'.[144] This envisioned policy framework included conditions respecting the adjustment of macroeconomic policies by committing the Thai government to maintain economic growth at the rates of 3 to 4 per cent during 1997 and 1998, and of 6 to 7 per cent in the medium-term. Thailand also committed to maintain a cap on inflation at the rate of seven to eight per cent during 1997–8, and to reduce inflation to 4 to 5 per cent in the medium-term. Finally, Thailand committed to reduce its significant current account deficits, which amounted to eight per cent of GDP at the end of 1996,[145] to 5 per cent of GDP in 1997, and 3 to 4 per cent thereafter.[146] The IMF Letter underscored the significance of tight monetary policy in order to support the currency[147] and to preclude high inflation.[148]

All of these conditions have apparently been implemented and satisfied the first review of the IMF in September 1997. Nonetheless, the economic situation, both domestically and regionally, was significantly worsened as a result of the sustained losses of investor confidence. The baht continued to depreciate considerably more than expected, which necessitated that high interest rates be maintained[149] and further aggravated the liquidity crisis.

Hence, the newly installed government of Thailand proposed a Second Letter of Intent to the IMF in order to readjust macroeconomic policies developed in the First Letter of Intent according to the changed economic environment. The Second Letter of Intent stipulated that the Thai government desired to 'lay a foundation for a decisive turnaround in confidence and economic performance, and lead to a resumption of capital flows'.[150] Economic growth projections were readjusted from 2.5 per cent in the First Letter of Intent to 0.6 per cent in 1997, from 3.5 per cent to 0–1 per cent in 1998. Inflation rate limitations were raised to 10 per cent at the end of 1997 instead of 9½ of per cent, and 10 per cent rather than 8 per cent at

144 'IMF Approves Stand-by Credit for Thailand', above n 135, at 2.

145 *See* Summary of the First Letter of Intent, *Bank of Thailand News*, No 56/1997. Note that the First Letter of Intent dated 14 Aug. 1997 has not been made public. However, the Thai government has enhanced their transparency by the official disclosure of the Second Letter of Intent dated 25 Nov. 1997 and the Third Letter of Intent dated 24 Feb. 1998, on the Bank of Thailand website. The Letters of Intent are also available on the IMF website.

146 *See* Summary of the First Letter of Intent, *Bank of Thailand News*, No 56/1997.

147 IMF, *IMF Survey*, vol 2, No 2, 26 Jan. 1998, at 18.

148 Board of Investment, above n 36, at 2.

149 Thailand's Second Letter of Intent (visited 20 Feb. 1998) <http://www.imf.org/external/np/loi/112597html>, at 1.

150 The Second Letter of Intent, para 20.

the end of 1998, respectively.[151] The Thai government also committed to a privatisation programme as one of the key goals in the medium-term. Incorporated state enterprises will be initially privatised. For example, government-owned equity in the Thai Airways International of 93 per cent, and in Bangchak Petroleum Ltd. of 80 per cent, are set to be reduced considerably less than 50 per cent by the middle of 1998.[152]

Notwithstanding the adverse economic environment, the Thai authorities strived to maintain certain of its prior commitments. For instance, although the government ran a 133 billion baht revenue shortfall, equivalent to nearly 2½ per cent of GDP, the Thai government committed to maintain a fiscal surplus of 1 per cent, which 'will ensure an orderly offset to the anticipated costs of the financial sector restructuring'.[153] The Thai government also committed to adhere to the overall original commitment as regards international reserve maintenance of minimum 23 billion US dollars, with an exemption for an 'adjust[ment] on net international reserves for balance of payments support in excess of the program baseline'. This occurred because the balance of payments support would be lower than anticipated.[154] Conversely, the Thai authorities successfully met or exceeded certain performance criteria. The current account deficit was considerably reduced to 3.9 per cent in 1997 instead of 5 per cent as originally programmed. The current account deficit in 1998 was reprogrammed to 1.8 per cent rather than 3 per cent as originally programmed.[155] The substantial positive improvement in current account position was contributed by the increased export competitiveness in both goods and services as a result of the abandonment of the fixed exchange rate regime and substantial declines in imports.[156] Export growth targets in the Second Letter of Intent are 3.2 per cent in 1997 and 7.9 per cent in 1998, respectively.[157] Short-term interest rates will be maintained at a high level to support exchange rate stabilisation and restore investor confidence, but will be closely reviewed by the IMF and 'progressively' reduced once foreign exchange stabilises and investor confidence is resumed.[158]

The IMF conditionality measures, particularly the tight fiscal measures, have been widely criticised as too severe and to a certain extent inappropriate under the view that Thailand had not engendered unsustainable budget deficits as in the case of Mexico in 1994–5.[159] Therefore, the severe limitations imposed on government expenditures by the IMF were held as simply aggravating the liquidity crunch in Thailand. The Thai government

151 *See* the Second Letter of Intent, Table 1.

152 The Second Letter of Intent, para.17.

153 Ibid. at 2.

154 *See* Second Letter of Intent, para 10–11 and Annex C.

155 *See* Second Letter of Intent, para 3 and table 1.

156 Board of Investment, *Business Focus,* above n 138, at 3.

157 *See* Second Letter of Intent, table 1.

158 Second Letter of Intent, para 8.

159 BIS, above n 51, at 12.

attempted to further renegotiate these conditionality measures and other measures required by the IMF. The IMF, notwithstanding the status of the East Asia crisis and its prior position adopted with Korea that conditionality measures were not subject to renegotiation, agreed on the relaxation of certain austerity measures.[160] In January 1998 IMF Executive Director Michel Camdessus guaranteed the IMF's flexibility in reviewing Thailand's restructuring package. He further stated that '[the IMF] does . . . [not] want to impose artificial constraints on the economy of Thailand. What we want is the success of the program'.[161] Following approval of the second quarterly review of performance criteria for December 1997, conducted by the IMF in February 1998,[162] the IMF Executive Director endorsed certain key modifications to IMF austerity measures to the First and Second Letters of Intent in a Third Letter of Intent dated 24 February 1998.

The major change set forth in the Third Letter of Intent was the reduction of the fiscal target requirement from a fiscal surplus of 1 per cent of GDP to a deficit of 2 per cent of GDP. The change was the result of declining public revenues and the need for increased public spending to reinforce the social safety net.[163] Additionally, the impressively positive shift in current account positions provided leeway for the more lenient fiscal policy.[164] The macroeconomic framework was also readjusted according to the 'sharper ongoing decline in domestic demand and output' and reduced capital inflows due to the regional scope of the crisis. Real GDP growth targets were revised from 0.6 per cent to –0.4 per cent in 1997, and from –1.0 per cent to –3 to –3.5 per cent in 1998, respectively.[165] Nonetheless, an impressive achievement was the massive adjustment of current account positions estimated to be in surplus of around 4 per cent of the GDP.[166] The Third Letter of Intent further reiterated that monetary policy targets were intended to stabilise the exchange rate. Thai authorities now must provide 'symmetric flexibility to interest rate policy'. In other words, interest rates will be permitted to increase whenever there is pressure on exchange rate. If the exchange rate shows 'sustained stability in a more realistic range', however, interest rates will be reduced in cognisance of 'the potential

[160] Joseph Kahn, 'IMF Eases Terms for Thailand', *The New York Times*, 11 Feb. 1998.

[161] IMF, *IMF Survey*, above n 147, at 19.

[162] *See* 'Press Release Regarding Third Letter of Intent', *Ministry of Finance News*, No 15/1998, at 1.

[163] Memorandum on Economic Policies, Third Letter of Intent, para 16–20.

[164] Third Letter of Intent, 24 Feb. 1998 <http://www.imf.org/external/np/loi/ 022498.htm>, para 4.

[165] *See* Table. Thailand: Macroeconomic Framework, 1996–8, Memorandum on Economic Policies of the Royal Thai Government, Third Letter of Intent, 24 Feb. 1998.

[166] *See* Memorandum on Economic Policies of the Royal Thai Government, Third Letter of Intent, para 1 and Table on Thailand: Macroeconomic Framework, 1996–8.

damage that a prolonged period of tight liquidity conditions' that may incur to corporate and banking sectors.[167]

C. *Banking and Financial Sector Restructuring*

The cornerstone of the IMF conditionality measures is the fundamental reorganisation of the Thai banking and financial systems. The significance of financial restructuring with respect to sustainable economic development was reflected in three Letters of Intent executed with the IMF, the Letter of Development Policy submitted to the World Bank, and the Memorandum of Understanding with the Asian Development Bank (ADB). As required by the World Bank and the ADB for the provision of their respective credit facilities as part of the IMF assistance package, Thailand additionally needed to submit so-called 'Letter of Development Policy' to the World Bank and sign a 'Memorandum of Understanding' with the ADB. The IMF macroeconomic adjustment programme and Letters of Intent nonetheless played the central role in the restructuring process to be implemented by Thailand.[168] The restructuring of the Thai banking and financial sectors represents an 'integral part of achieving broader macroeconomic stability and sustainable economic growth'.[169] The basic restructuring principles and objectives 'agreed upon' between the Thai government and the IMF, as broadly set forth by the Thai Finance Minister, are (1) to restore investor confidence in the Thai banking and financial systems; (2) to restore the solvency, profitability, and liquidity of the broader financial system; (3) to enhance foreign ownership in domestic financial institutions; (4) to effect medium-term reforms in legal, regulatory, supervisory, and public disclosure practices, in order to strengthen the structure of the financial system and enhance incentives for increased market discipline; and (5) to require shareholders and creditors of subordinated debts to bear the burden of their losses.[170] The Finance Minister reiterated that government bailouts will be 'minimised and be tied to strict conditions to avoid moral hazard'.[171]

In October 1997 Thailand's comprehensive banking and financial sector restructuring package designed with the technical assistance from the World Bank and the IMF was announced. The restructuring measures contained 'fundamental reforms' to Thailand's financial system.[172] The Thai restructuring measure were highly received by the IMF as representing 'full

[167] Memorandum on Economic Policies, Third Letter of Intent, 24 Feb. 1998, para 13. On the Fourth Letter of Intent, *see* n 268, below.

[168] Bank of Thailand and Board of Investment, above n 36, at 12.

[169] Statement of HE Dr Thanong Bidaya, the Finance Minister, at the 1997 IBRD/IMF Joint Annual Meetings.

[170] Ibid. at 2.

[171] Ibid. at 3.

[172] *See* 'Joint Statement by the Ministry of Finance and the Bank of Thailand, Re: Thailand's Financial Restructuring Package', *Bank of Thailand News*, No 70/1997, at 1.

commitment of the Thai government to the economic program[me] supported by a stand-by arrangement with the IMF. It should go a long way toward resolving remaining market uncertainties about the implementation of financial sector restructuring and other elements of the economic program[me]'.[173]

As part of the implementation of the banking and financial sector restructuring requirements, the Thai government amended and will amend relevant laws to effect the financial system restructuring. For example, the Commercial Banking Act, the Act Regulating the Finance and Securities Businesses, and the Civil and Commercial Code have been amended as a result of the IMF conditionality measures. The Bankruptcy Act was also revised in March 1998 according to the dateline commitment of the end of March set forth in the Second Letter of Intent[174] to enhance readiness in foreclosure and asset liquidation. Bankruptcy trials were directed to proceed in a 'speedy manner' and without any 'undue postponement'. The Thai government also introduced rehabilitation and reorganisation programmes to preclude lengthy bankruptcy proceedings when a juristic entity is determined to be insolvent. In addition, the bankruptcy revisions mandate that during the reorganisation procedure civil charges cannot be separately raised.[175]

Indeed, certain measures had already been implemented by Thai authorities on a piecemeal basis prior to the comprehensive IMF reform package. In early 1997, the adverse impact of declining property values on the banking and finance sectors clearly manifested. Finance One Limited, the largest finance company in Thailand, became severely distressed as a result of becoming overexposed to the ailing property market.[176] As a result of this specific situation, the Thai authorities were forced to realise the seriousness of systemic overexposures to the property sector and initiated a series of measures aimed to enhance the stability in the financial system. In March 1997, the Thai authorities required nine finance companies and one credit foncier company to recapitalise in an attempt to address declining collateral values in the ailing property sector. The Thai authorities stood ready to assist the recapitalisation process via the Financial Institution Development

[173] 'Camdessus Endorses Thailand's Strategy for Restructuring the Financial Sector', *IMF News Brief* No 97/20, 14 Oct. 1997.

[174] The Second Letter of Intent, Box B, Implementation of the 14 Oct. Announcement Regarding the Banks and Remaining Finance Companies.

[175] Bank of Thailand, 'Bankruptcy Act B.E.2541 (AD 1998) and its implication on financial sector restructuring', <http://www.bot.or.th/Act/BkrupAct.html>; *see also* Bankruptcy Act (No 4) of 1998, s 90/12.

[176] In response to the problem, the authorities attempted to facilitate the merger between Finance One Ltd. and Thai Danu PLC., a medium-sized bank. *See Bank of Thailand News*, No 15/1997 and 29/1997. However, the attempt failed eventually and the Finance Company was suspended its operation in June 1997. The Company was lastly closed on the 8 Dec. in the same year after its rehabilitation plan was not approved.

Fund (FIDF), an arm of the Bank of Thailand established in 1985 in the wake of 1980s financial crisis.[177] The Bank of Thailand additionally required depository institutions to enhance loss provisioning for low quality assets.[178] The Thai authorities further encouraged domestic mergers and consolidations of financial institutions, with an emphasis on distressed finance companies. The Thai authorities also facilitated mergers of finance companies or credit foncier companies with foreign financial institutions by permitting relaxation of the shareholding circumscription and foreign ownership and directorate restrictions on a case-by-case-basis.[179]

In June 1997, the Thai government passed two emergency decrees which amended the Commercial Banking Act and the Act Regulating the Finance, Securities and Credit Foncier Businesses, respectively.[180] The first decree was designed to facilitate recaptalisation[181] and to stipulate the authorities' intent to relax existing foreign shareholding restrictions respecting domestic commercial banks if a need existed to improve the condition of the Thai bank in question.[182] The decree also relaxed cross-directorate prohibitions that had been introduced to reduce the concentration of power in the banking and financial sectors. The decree in effect authorise a person to hold a directorate position for two or more financial institutions upon the permission of the Finance Minister and with the recommendation of the Bank of Thailand.[183] The second emergency decree effectively facilitated the mergers

[177] *See Bank of Thailand News*, No 10/1997. To maintain public confidence in the country's financial system, the Bank of Thailand stated no more financial institutions to be ordered to recapitalise, and the authorities will stand ready to aval promissory notes from those depository institutions. *See Bank of Thailand News*, No 11/1997.

[178] Commercial banks were required to provision 15 per cent, finance companies and credit foncier companies 20 per cent, against sub-standard assets. *See Bank of Thailand News*, No 10/1997.

[179] *See Bank of Thailand News*, No 21/1997. *See also* Bank of Thailand Circular Letter, Tor Por Tor. Ngo Por.(Wo) 953/1997.

[180] At the time, four emergency decrees were passed. However, here only two relevant decrees are dealt with. The other two decrees concern the establishment of 'Special Purpose Vehicle (SPV)' for securitisation and the secondary market for housing loans. *See* Emergency Decree on Special Purpose Vehicle for Securitisation of 1997, and Emergency Decree on Secondary Market for Housing Loans of 1997, *Royal Gazette*, vol 114, part 29a, 28 June 1997.

[181] *See* Note, Emergency Decree (No 2) of 1997 Amending the Commercial Banking Act of 1962, 28 June 1997.

[182] Foreign ownership of more than 25 per cent of shares in a Thai commercial bank can be done upon the permission of the Finance Minister with recommendation from the Bank of Thailand, possibly subject to certain conditions. *See* Emergency Decree (No 3) of 1997 Amending the Commercial Banking Act of 1962, s 3, *Royal Gazette*, vol 114, part 29a, 28 June 1997.

[183] Such permission may be subject to certain conditions and cannot last longer than three years. Nonetheless, exceptions are given to legal advisers or positions of no involvement in the operation of a commercial bank. *See* Emergency Decree (No 2) of 1997 Amending the Commercial Banking Act of 1962 (28 June 1997), s 4.

of finance companies and credit foncier companies.[184] The second decree primarily addressed issues relevant to mergers and acquisitions[185] and amended the existing laws regulating finance, securities and credit foncier businesses.[186] Under the second decree, transfers of claims need not to be informed of outstanding debts as normally required by Thai laws.[187] The decree also waived the requirement that finance companies or credit foncier companies be public companies under Thai laws,[188] as well as the requirement for minimum registered capital and paid-in capital where it is deemed that a merger or acquisition,[189] capital write-down, and/or recapitalisation of an ailing company is necessary.[190] Finance companies or credit foncier companies were immunised under the decree from bankruptcy charges during the mergers and acquisitions process.[191] In addition, the Thai authorities suspended the operations of sixteen distressed finance companies viewed as unsafe and unsound. These finance companies were required to submit rehabilitation plans to the authorities for approval.[192]

The aforementioned measures were implemented by the Thai authorities prior to the eruption of the currency crisis and were separate and distinct from the IMF conditionality measures. The following section considers the measures implemented as a part of IMF conditionality requirements announced and/or implemented during or after August 1997. The Comprehensive Financial Restructuring Package jointly announced by the Ministry of Finance and the Bank of Thailand is also discussed in this section. The measures designed to revamp Thailand's financial system are stipulated in the three Letters of Intent with the IMF, the Letters of Development Policy with the World Bank, and the Memorandum of Understanding with the ADB regarding Thailand's proposed financial markets reform program and representing the commitment of the Thai government to their implementation.

184 *See* Note, Emergency Decree (No 3) of 1997 Amending the Act Regulating Finance Business, Securities Business, and Credit Foncier Business, *Royal Gazette*, vol 114, part 29 a, 28 June 1997.

185 The Emergency Decree added Part 5 *bis* (including sections 67 *bis.*, 67 ter., and 67 quarter.) regarding mergers and acquisitions to the Act Regulating Finance, Securities, and Credit Foncier Businesses of 1979. *See* Emergency Decree (No 3) of 1997 (28 June 1997), s 4.

186 Act on the Undertaking of Finance, Securities and Credit Foncier Businesses of 1979.

187 *See* Emergency Decree (No 3) of 1997 Amending the Act Regulating the Finance Business, the Securities Business and Credit Foncier Business of 1979 (28 June 1997), s 4 (s 67 ter.). The legal obligation to inform debtors in the case of transfer of claims according to the Civil and Commercial Code section 306 was waived.

188 Emergency Decree (No 3) of 1997 (28 June 1997), s 4 (s 67 quarter, para 2(1)).

189 Ibid.

190 Ibid. s 3.

191 Ibid. s 4 in connection with s 67 quater para 4.

192 Announcement of the Ministry of Finance and the Bank of Thailand, 27 June 1997, *Bank of Thailand News*, No 41/2540.

1. Separation of Sound Financial Institutions from Unsound Institutions

The Thai authorities initiated measures to revamp the banking and financial systems in March 1997. The implementation of the IMF restructuring measures began in earnest on 5 August 1997, however.[193] The principal objective of the IMF restructuring measures was to separate the distressed financial institutions from the healthy institutions, and to enhance investor confidence in the Thai banking and financial systems.[194] As of August 1997, the financial crisis clearly overwhelmed the meagre domestic measures introduced previously by Thai authorities, and certain financial institutions were encountering a serious liquidity problems that were far beyond the resolution capabilities of the FIDF.[195] To this end, the Thai authorities ordered forty-two additional finance companies facing serious foreign exchange liquidity concerns and holding low-quality loan portfolios to suspend operations.[196] Similarly to those suspended in June 1997, the suspended finance companies in August 1997 were required to complete due diligence reports within sixty days and thereafter to submit rehabilitation plans to the Thai authorities.[197] Holders of promissory notes and certificates of deposit, and bona fide creditors of the suspended institutions, however, would be protected from default.[198]

These measures unfortunately failed to enhance investor confidence in the Thai banking and financial systems, and instead caused wide-spread panic among investors with respect to the banking system. In the immediate period after the announcement, deposits in the billions of baht and promissory notes were withdrawn or redeemed from Thai financial institutions.[199] The loss of public confidence was considerably attributable to the

193 Despite its occurrence prior to the Thailand's signing of the first Letter of Intent on 14 Aug. 1997 and the IMF approval for the Letter of Intent on 21 Aug. 1997, the measures were a part of IMF advising restructuring package, as implicitly stated in the Joint Statement by the Ministry of Finance and the Bank of Thailand *Re: Measures to Strengthen Confidence in the Financial Institution System on 5 Aug. 1997. See* 'Joint Statement by the Ministry of Finance and the Bank of Thailand *Re: Measures to Strengthen Confidence in the Financial Institution System*' (5 Aug. 1997) [hereinafter 'Joint Statement 5 Aug. 1997'], *Bank of Thailand News*, No 51/1997.

194 Ibid. at 1–2. 195 Ibid. at 1. 196 Ibid. at 2.

197 'Details Supplement to the Joint Statement by the Ministry of Finance and the Bank of Thailand *Re: Measures to Strengthen Confidence in the Financial Institution System*'[hereinafter 'Details Supplement'] , *Bank of Thailand News*, No 51/1997.

198 The holders were permitted to exchange their existing promissory notes or certificates of deposit with Krung Thai Bank Ltd., a government owned commercial bank. Bona fide creditors were also permitted to restructure their loans with Krung Thai Bank. *See* 'Joint Statement 5 August 1997', above n 193, at 2. *See also* 'Details Supplement', above n 197, at 3.

199 Deposits withdrawn from Siam City Bank, a medium-sized bank, alone amounted to 600 million bahts within two days after the announcement of the closure of fifty-eight finance companies on 5 Aug. 2997. *See* 'Premier tries to stop panic by investors', *The Nation*, 7 Aug. 1997.

capricious stance of the government. In June 1997 following the suspension of sixteen finance companies, the Thai government declared that there would be no more suspensions of financial institutions.[200]

In response to the widespread disintermediation, the Bank of Thailand and the Ministry of Finance announced unconditional guarantees for all deposits and other debts of the suspended finance companies.[201] The Bank of Thailand also established a liquidity fund in order to 'recycle' money from the 'safer and sounder' financial institutions that were obtaining new funds from the disintermediation to provide liquidity to those institutions losing deposits as a result of disintermediation. These *de facto* recycling effort were conducted through the FIDF.[202] The initiation of the 'liquidity fund' did not receive sufficient support from large banks and was regarded as 'impractical' due to concerns regarding their inherent exposures from participating in the recycling process and the moral hazard risks involved in providing additional funds to unsafe and unsound financial institutions. Unfortunately, the recycling measures proved to be unsuccessful in coping with the volume of disintermediation from banks and finance companies.[203] In sum, all but two of the fifty-eight Thai financial institutions were eventually ordered to close down on 8 December 1997 when their rehabilitation plans were not approved by the Thai authorities.

2. Recapitalisation of Existing Banks and Other Depository Institutions

The currently existing Thai depository institutions[204] were required to recapitalise and to enhance loan loss provisioning.[205] Thai financial institutions were further required to 'arbitrarily suspend' payments of dividends for one year beginning in mid-October 1997. In order to facilitate the recapitalisation, the Thai authorities encouraged shareholding by foreign investors[206] by relaxing restrictions on foreign shareholdings of Thai financial institutions for a period

200 'Mathematics of "Chavalit government",' *Econnews,* vol 304, 18 Aug. 1997, at 15–17. 'Suspension of 58 finance companies', *Econnews*, vol 34, 18 Aug. 1997, at 18.

201 Ibid.

202 The established liquidity fund was operated in collaboration with foreign bank branches in Thailand and the five largest Thai domestic banks. The institutions whose funds are 'recycled' to weaker institutions will be compensated with a special rate on the amount recycled (150 points above the seven-day repurchase rate). *See* 'Bank of Thailand set up liquidity fund to recycle money', *Nation Breaking News* <http://www.nationgroup.com/nation/breaking/NWs803.HTML>.

203 'BOT to boost money supply', *The Nation,* 9 Aug. 1997.

204 The existing depository institutions include thirty-five finance companies and credit foncier companies, and fifteen domestic commercial banks.

205 *ee* 'Summary of Important Measures in the IMF Package Outlined in the Letter of Intent', *Bank of Thailand News*, No 56/1997, at 2.

206 *See* 'Future Supervisory Measures', ibid. No 57/1997.

of up to ten years.[207] The 'major' foreign shareholding liberalisation measures were undoubtedly encouraged by the IMF as a crucial measure in recapitalisation of financial institutions still in operation.[208]

3. Establishment of Financial Sector Restructuring Authority (FRA)

The FRA was established by Emergency Decree in October 1997 simultaneously with the announcement of the Financial Restructuring Package. The FRA was established to address the fifty-eight finance companies whose operations were suspended in June 1997 and August 1997, respectively. The FRA was empowered to stipulate criteria and procedures for the rehabilitation plans required to be submitted by the suspended finance companies.[209] Accordingly, the FRA established four types of proposals to be set forth in such rehabilitation plans: (i) recapitalisation either by internal measures or through investment by new partners; (ii) mergers between the suspended finance companies; (iii) mergers with other domestic financial institutions whose operations were not suspended; or (iv) mergers with commercial banks.[210] The FRA also required that capital adequacy, sources of capitals, debt repayment plans, liquidity management, and the quality of the management be addressed in such rehabilitation plans.[211] In December 1997 the FRA ultimately considered rehabilitation plans of all fifty-eight suspended finance companies and disapproved all but two of such plans.[212] The two finance companies whose rehabilitation plans were approved were permitted to open and to conduct business by the FRA under the condition that they maintain strict compliance with their rehabilitation plans, and that such compliance be monitored by the FRA. The assets of the closed finance companies are to be liquidated by auction, which was set to be completed by the end of 1998.[213]

4. Establishment of the Asset Management Corporation (AMC) and the Radhanasin Bank (RAB)

Both institutions were established to participate in the auction with other private bidders. The AMC was established by the Thai government to

207 'Joint Statement by the Ministry of Finance and the Bank of Thailand *Re: Thailand's Financial Restructuring Package*,' ibid. No 70/1997.
208 IMF News Brief No 97/20.
209 Royal Decree on the Financial Institution System Restructuring of 1997, *Royal Gazette*, vol 114, part 60 Kor, 24 Oct. 1997, 16(1).
210 Speech of the FRA chairman on 8 Dec. 1997 <http://www.mof.go.th/fra/frachai.htm>, at 1.
211 Ibid. at 1.
212 *See* Financial Sector Restructuring Authority (FRA), Announcement of Decision on the Rehabilitation Plans submitted by the fifty-eight Suspended Finance Companies, 8 Dec. 1997.
213 *See* Memorandum on Economic Policies, Third Letter of Intent, 24 Feb. 1998, Box 1.

address the portfolios of 'bad' assets of the closed finance companies. The AMC primarily focuses to purchase 'lowest quality' assets in the FRA-induced liquidation/auction, manage, restructure the assets, and 'maximis[e] asset recovery over the medium term'. The AMC will function as 'a buyer of last resort'.[214] On the other hand, The RAB will focus on bidding for the 'highest quality assets and be guided by the strictest commercial principles'.[215] The RAB was established 'to ensure a transparent and efficient bidding process' and is designed to 'play an important role in bidding process'.[216]

5. Enhancement of the Powers of the Bank of Thailand

The Bank of Thailand was given enhanced powers by legislative amendments to the banking laws to more readily address the distressed financial institutions. Pursuant to these new amendments, the Bank of Thailand is empowered to immediately remove the management of financial institutions whose sustained condition or continued operation is deemed to be detrimental to the public interest.[217] In addition, the banking laws were amended to render the 'minimum value' limitations of shares under the Civil and Commercial Code inapplicable with respect to distressed financial institutions. In effect, the Thai authorities can further 'write down' the capital of distressed financial institutions and can force the shareholders of the institutions in question shoulder the incurred loss.[218]

6. Reduction of Moral Hazard Risks

Moral hazard risks represented serious problems in the Thai banking and financial sectors and clearly contributed to excessive risk-taking by financial institutions prior to the crisis. The perception of implied government liquidity support, most probably, contributed to the magnitude of moral

[214] *See* ibid. para 4; *see also* Emergency Decree on the Asset Management Corporation of 1997, *Royal Gazette,* vol 114, part 60a, s 7, at 15; 'Thailand's Financial Restructuring Package', above n 207, at 5.

[215] Memorandum of Economic Policies, Third Letter of Intent, 24 Feb. 1998.

[216] 'Establishment of New Financial Institutions', Ministry of Finance Press Release No 4/1998, 20 Jan. 1998. The Ministry of Finance is a major shareholder and initial capital of 4,000 million baht came from the Structural Adjustment Loan of the World Bank and the Asian Development Bank. At a later stage, 'strategic alliances' will participate in shareholding of the Bank, and the Bank will be listed in the Stock Exchange of Thailand.

[217] *See* Emergency Decree (No 3) of 1997 Amending Commercial Banking Act of 1962 (24 Oct. 1997), s 4; *see also* Emergency Decree (No 4) of 1997 Amending the Act Regulating the Finance, Securities, and Credit Foncier Businesses of 1979 (24 Oct. 1997), s 3.

[218] *See* Emergency Decree (No 3) of 1997 Amending the Commercial Banking Act of 1962 (24 Oct. 1997), s 3; *see also* Emergency Decree (No 4) of 1997 Amending the Act Regulating the Finance, Securities, and Credit Foncier Businesses of 1979 (24 Oct. 1997), s 4.

hazard problems. Conditions for the government 'bailout' support were not clearly defined and (in certain situations) 'soft loans' were granted to well-positioned Thai banks, finance companies, and businesses on a massive scale.[219] In order to reduce the moral hazard risks, the Thai authorities have clearly emphasised that they will not initiate government bailouts of distressed financial institutions 'as a matter of course'. In addition, the requirement for Thai financial institutions to contribute funds to the FIDF was set to be increased 'beyond the highest deposit rates in the financial system'.[220] The exposure of the FIDF will be limited, however, as borrowings by distressed financial institutions that reach or exceed 75 per cent of Tier 1 capital will be subject to certain conditions. The relevant conditions include the 'immediate cessation' on dividend payments, bonuses, compensation, or other types of financial benefits. Also officials from the FIDF may be appointed as directors of a Thai financial institution to monitor 'future asset growth' and the suspension of dividend payments.[221] Finally, in the medium-term, a deposit insurance mechanism will be established to balance the moral hazard risks with necessary government intervention to offer limited protection to the Thai banking system.[222]

D *Evaluations and Critique*

1. Thai Reaction to the Crisis

The reaction of Thai authorities to the crisis was initially ambiguous and indecisive due primarily to political instability exacerbated by corrupt politicians and competing vested interests. Upon acceptance of the IMF assistance package, however, Thailand has fully committed to the conditionality measures required to obtain access to stand-by credit facilities of $17.2 billion. The Finance Minister made clear, at the Summer 1997 IMF/World Bank Annual Meeting in Hong Kong, that Thailand remained fully committed to the restructuring measures in order to 'restore stability, confidence, and prosperity domestically, regionally and globally'.[223]

The reaction of the Thai public was interesting as the public generally supported the IMF financial assistance as a means to reinstating investor confidence.[224] Nonetheless, after the acceptance of the IMF financial assistance as

219 Policy Conditionality Matrix, Thailand: Loans For Restructuring Finance Companies, proposed to the World Bank, 16 Dec. 1997, at 4.

220 Interest rates on FIDF loans will be at a minimum of the repurchase agreement rate (RP) plus 1 per cent in case of collaterised loans, and plus 2.5 per cent in case of uncollateralised loans. *See* Ibid.

221 Ibid.

222 'Future Supervisory Measures', above n 206, at 3.

223 Statement by HE Dr Thanong Bidaya, the Finance Minister, at the 1997 IBRD/IMF Joint Annual Meetings.

224 'Government turns to IMF for help', *Bangkok Post*, 28 July 1997.

implementation measures were introduced, the public sentiment changed considerably. As a result of the failure of the United States to contribute to the IMF package, the public sentiment in Thailand in the wake of the crisis arose against the United States[225] and increased dramatically in consideration of the long-standing diplomatic relations the US has maintained with Thailand. The pessimistic view was that the United States had continuously and hypocritically pressured Thailand on bilateral and multilateral bases via the GATS forum to increasingly liberalise domestic financial markets at the time when the Thai banking and financial systems were not prepared for liberalisation. The view presumed that liberalisation measures introduced in Thailand substantially increased its vulnerability to the latent risks of volatile capital flows. The role of the United States as the organising principal of the IMF assistance package pressed for liberalisation of domestic financial markets similarly to the bilateral and multilateral pressure to liberalise domestic financial markets organised principally by the United States in the first instance. It appeared that Thailand had no choice but to liberalise further its financial markets and to open its doors for 'foreign occupation' by foreign investors (primarily US financial institutions), one way or another, at the behest of the United States.[226] Thus, US diplomatic manipulations were viewed strongly as contributing factors to the crisis.

2. IMF Reaction to the Crisis

The IMF predictably came under criticism as the financial crisis manifested in Thailand and East Asia in general, and the institution took venerable steps to defend itself from such criticism. The IMF repeatedly asserted that its staff was well aware of the emerging crisis with respect to the vulnerability of the fixed-exchange rate regime, the increasing current account deficits, and the more fundamental problems inherent in prudential supervision and regulatory enforcement within the banking and financial sectors. The IMF further claimed to have warned Thailand on various occasions of conditions suggesting an impending crisis[227] either by informal visits or telephone conversations. The IMF claimed that such warnings could not have been disclosed to the 'public', however, as any predictions may not have been perfectly precise and the IMF staff was limited by the policies

[225] According to Mr Sura Sanittanont, an investment banker and adviser to the Deputy Prime Minister Supachai Panichapakdi, 'we will have to think about whether it is worth it to open ourselves up as demanded by the West, and find ourselves in a state of complete bankruptcy'. Paul Sherer, below n 266.

[226] 'The imperialism of free finance', *The Nation*, 14 Aug. 1997.

[227] Michael Mussa, 'The IMF Approach to Macroeconomic Policy', IMF Seminar 'Asia and the IMF', 19 Sept. 1997, at 3.

voted upon by constituent member nations.[228] IMF policymaking is dominated to a significant degree by the United States, which effectively controls approximately 18 per cent of the constituent vote and provides policy guidance through the US Department of the Treasury. Thus, the IMF failed to develop preemptive policies to address the onset of crisis, and the IMF staff was precluded from publicly disclosing that crisis in Thailand or East Asia was imminent. The Thai authorities also provided little disclosure of the severity of the situation, and stated in hindsight that 'all we can assure you is that the major decisions were made when things were deemed right and necessary at the time—although with the benefit of hindsight, it may seem otherwise'.[229] At the same time, the Thai authorities admitted that certain measures were insufficient or untimely, but also stated that certain warning signs were ignored such as those pertaining to short-term capital flows and excessive lending to the property sector. In addition, the Thai authorities claimed that the dramatic weakening of exports and speculative attacks on the currency were simply 'unexpected'.[230] In short, neither the IMF nor Thai authorities willingly stepped up and assumed responsibility or accountability in part or in whole for the onset of crisis.

3. US Reaction to the Crisis

The financial and economic crisis in Southeast Asia was widely claimed to have resulted from ill-timed responses to liberalisation pressures from the United States both in the WTO and bilateral fora. In response to the criticism, the US Department of Treasury predictably argued on behalf of the Clinton Administration that liberalisation of domestic financial markets was not the cause of the crisis. The Treasury Department asserted that an 'unsustainable macroeconomic policy mix' consisting of 'relatively open capital markets, independent monetary policy making, a fixed exchange rate and a current account deficit of 8 per cent of GDP' was the main cause thereof.[231] Treasury officials opined that sustained liberalisation policies were essential in order to achieve efficiency in Thai financial markets, and that a 'strong and efficient financial sector . . . [in turn would help an economy] to achieve the growth it is capable of'.[232] In addition, the Treasury officials asserted that 'modern well-regulated foreign participation in the financial sector can spur domestic markets to address their deficiencies'.[233]

228 'The IMF Assesses Its Hits and Misses in Asia', an interview with Stanley Fisher, Deputy Managing Director of the IMF, *Wall Street Journal*, 10 Feb. 1998, at A14.

229 Bank of Thailand and Board of Investment, above n 36, at 11.

230 Ibid.

231 Lawrence Summers, 'Building a Global Financial System For the 21st Century', address before the Congressional Economic Leadership Council in Washington DC, 12 Aug. 1997, at 7.

232 Ibid. at 2.

233 Ibid. at 4.

Thus, the Treasury Department largely shielded the Clinton Administration from political fallout with respect to the crisis and placed responsibility for the crisis almost entirely upon Thai economic policymakers.

The United States did not contribute funds to the IMF financial assistance package, but was nonetheless the organising principal of the IMF package.[234] The United States planned and endorsed the credit facilities and conditionality measures of the IMF, World Bank and ADB packages. The United States further 'supported the recent favo[u]rable review of Thailand's IMF program[me]' and the provision of 'additional IMF financing in the form of a Supplemental Reserve Facility, if needed'. The US Export–Import Bank expressed intent to 'increase short-term trade financing by up to $1 billion' to support bilateral trade flows into Thailand, and the United States executive branch pressured other G7 nations to make export credit facilities available to Thailand. Moreover, the US Overseas Private Investment Corporation (OPIC) expressed intent to provide financial support for two Thai electric power projects and equity investments. The United States will also sponsor the feasibility studies for the privatisation of a department of the State Railway Authority of Thailand.[235] Thus, the United States response to the Thai financial crisis was premised on 'dollar diplomacy' that effectively shielded the Clinton Administration from any accountability for policymaking in the IMF, GATS and bilateral trade arenas that effectively contributed to the crisis.

V. CONCLUDING OBSERVATIONS: A 'SILVER LINING' IN THE CRISIS CLOUDS?[236]

Amidst the crisis clouds there may well exist opportunities to resolve certain fundamental problems in Thailand.

A. *The Thai Constitution and Restrictions on Money Politics*

The political instability of Thai governance both caused and aggravated the financial crisis. As previously stated, prevalent vote buying practices in elections and subsequent corruption as a form of recouping costs incurred in vote buying rendered democratic governance in Thailand as a dysfunctional

[234] Hubert Neiss, the head of the IMF team in Thailand, stated so during a press conference with Thailand's Finance Minister in Bangkok. *See* 'US blasted for refusing to give Thailand aid', *The Nation*, 15 Aug. 1997.

[235] Fact Sheet: White House 3/13 on US–Thai Relations (visited 24 Mar. 1998) <http://www.inet.co.th/org/usis/pr/nrot063.htm>.

[236] *See* Joseph J. Norton, 'IMF Package Could be Catalyst for Positive Change in Korea: Expert', *The Korea Times*, 6 Dec. 1997: 'Crises invariably entail not only challenges but opportunities'.

concept. Political reform is not included in the IMF restructuring package, as such conditionality would clearly infringe upon the sovereignty of Thailand. Political reform is implicitly required, however, to sustain IMF economic growth targets in the medium and long term, and to implement conditionality measures in restructuring the Thai banking and financial sectors.[237]

One of the most positive fruits borne from the crisis was the adoption of the new Constitution of Thailand in October 1997.[238] The crisis gave considerable pressure in the passage of the New Constitution. The new Constitution was designed *inter alia* to eliminate prevalent vote buying practices and corruption, and represents a major reform in the history of Thai democracy. The Constitution mandates that Members of Parliament (MPs) cannot hold a cabinet portfolio simultaneously.[239] This measure separates legislative functions from executive functions and is intended to enhance the stability and the unity of the government.[240] Certain new measures which were designed to reduce vote buying were initiated.[241] Those include mixed electoral system where Members of Parliament are elected from constituencies and from party list.[242] To ensure fair election, independent Election Commission was established to supervise elections.[243] Further, vote counting will be done in public and at only one place in each constituency.[244] Politicians are now required to disclose all of their assets prior to and after holding their office.[245] In addition, the National Corruption Commission was established to investigate and prosecute alleged corruption cases.[246]

B. The End of Government Bailouts and Mitigation of Moral Hazard Risks

The Thai banking and finance sectors of Thailand were for long pampered by the Thai government and closed to foreign competition for more than

[237] 'Ailing Tiger', *Financial Times*, 6 Aug. 1997.

[238] The constitution is viewed as the first 'people's constitution', which ushered in a new political era and k[eep] money politics to a minimum.' *See* 'Country steps into new political era', *Bangkok Post*, 11 Oct. 1997.

[239] *See* Constitution of the Kingdom of Thailand BE 2540 (1997), s 118(7) and 110(1), *Royal Gazette*, vol 114, part 55, 11 Oct. 1997.

[240] John Laird, 'New Constitution: Can it overcome vested interest', *The Nation*, 21 June 1997.

[241] *See* Constitution Drafting Assembly, 'Constitution of the Kingdom of Thailand: What benefits people can gain', in Constitution Drafting Assembly, *Constitution of the Kingdom of Thailand B.E. 2540 (A.D.1997)* (1997), at 178–9.

[242] Constitution of the Kingdom of Thailand of 1997, s 98–99.

[243] Ibid. s 136, 138 and 144.

[244] Ibid. s 104. This measure is designed to make more difficult for canvassors to check whether those who sell votes really vote for them. *See* Suvicha Pouaree, 'Imperfections within the constitution', *Bangkok Post*, 31 Aug. 1997; *see also* Paitoon Boonyawat, above n 14, at 163.

[245] Constitution of the Kingdom of Thailand of 1997, s 292.

[246] Ibid. s 301.

twenty years. These sectors also long enjoyed generous and repeated government liquidity injections at the expense of taxpayers. As a result, the Thai banking and financial systems were inefficient as well as unsafe and unsound. The onset of financial crisis and adoption of IMF conditionality measures hopefully represent the end of such practices or at the very least raised them into public debate in Thailand. The Thai government has clearly stated that there will be no more guaranteed bailouts 'as a matter of course'.[247] In addition, the long-awaited deposit insurance scheme is soon to be established by the end of 1998.[248] These measures should reduce considerably the risks of 'moral hazard' that were all too prevalent in the Thai banking and financial systems.

C. *Restructuring the Banking and Financial Sectors*

Notwithstanding the end of government bailouts, the Thai authorities initiated serious and tough measures respecting domestic financial institutions. Unsafe and unsound finance companies have been closed, and the commercial banks and finance companies permitted to remain in operation are subject to strict prudential conditions and supervision. The Bank of Thailand has used its enhanced powers to order changes of management in three Thai commercial banks and one of the existing finance companies,[249] viz. Bangkok Metropolitan Bank, First Bangkok City Bank, Siam City Bank,[250] and Mahatun Finance Company,[251] respectively. The orders were aimed to enhance the efficiency of management and to strengthen investor confidence in the Thai financial system.[252] The Bank of Thailand also ordered these commercial banks to substantially recapitalise with the time limit in order to mitigate the ongoing liquidity problems and low quality property and equity portfolios.[253] Nonetheless, these banks failed to successfully recapitalise themselves, as investment deals with foreign finan-

[247] Statement by HE Dr Thanong Bidaya, the Finance Minister, at the 1997 IBRD/IMF Joint Annual Meetings.

[248] Dateline of 31 Dec. 1998 was set to 'finalise plan for introduction of deposit insurance scheme to replace the current blanket guarantee in the medium term', *see* Third Letter of Intent, Box 2, No 11.

[249] *See* Author's Postscript, below n 268.

[250] Bangkok Metropolitan Bank, First Bangkok City Bank, and Siam City Bank were ordered the change of management on 31 Dec. 1997, 23 Jan. 1998, and 6 Feb. 1998, respectively. *See* 'Change of directors of Bangkok Metropolitan Bank PCL', *Bank of Thailand News*, No 89/1997; *see also* 'Change of directors and management of First Bangkok City Bank PCL', Ibid. No 5/1998; *see also* 'Additional Measures to Strengthen the Financial System', ibid. No 8/1998, at 1.

[251] 'Change of Directors and Management of Mahatun Finance Company', ibid. No 80/1997.

[252] *See* ibid. No 89/1997; *see also* ibid. No 5/1998; ibid. No 8/1998.

[253] *See* ibid.

cial institutions did not materialise.[254] Therefore, the Thai authorities ordered the commercial banks and one additional bank[255] to write down capital,[256] to undergo recapitalisation via the FIDF, and to submit operational control to the authorities themselves.[257] For instance, in the case of Bangkok Metropolitan Bank, the Bank of Thailand considerably wrote down the commercial bank capital for approximately ten billion baht, and further recapitalised the bank in the amount of twenty-five billion baht by the FIDF[258] partly by means of equity swap with loans extended to the institution as liquidity assistance.[259] As a result of the recapitalisation measures implemented by Thai authorities, the commercial banks in question have maintained capital adequacy of approximately 10 per cent measured according to the two-tiered capital standard set forth by the Basle Committee in the 1988 Capital Accord.[260] In addition, the commercial banks referenced above became *de jure* public enterprises according to amended Thai laws, but the Thai authorities will privatise these banks in due course[261] as stated in the Third Letter of Intent of February 1998.[262]

The Thai authorities have initiated criminal prosecutions against the bank and finance company management involved in violating Thai banking and financial laws. The prosecutors included charges against the management of Chao Phaya Finance and Securities Company, one of the fifty-six finance companies closed by the authorities. The charges involved alleged dishonest acts resulting in damage to the Company, embezzlement and fraud. The persons charged are prohibited from leaving Thailand and their personal assets were seized and attached.[263] Prosecutors have also rendered charges of fraud against management of the Mahatun Finance Company[264]

[254] Citibank was very cautious with due diligence with First Bangkok City Bank. And ING Bank lost interest in obtaining 10 per cent of shares in Siam City Bank as a result of weak baht. *See* William Barnes, 'Thailand: State takes over two banks', *Financial Times*, 9 Feb. 1998. Foreign participation from a group of Taiwanese banks also failed in case of Bangkok Metropolitan Bank. *See* 'Central bank to take up BMB's reins', *The Nation*, 23 Jan. 1998.

[255] *See* Author's Postscript, below n 268.

[256] This additional commercial bank is the Bangkok Bank of Commerce which has been a problem since 1996. The Bank of Thailand at the time injected the capital with the absence of prior write-down of capital.

[257] In case of Bangkok Bank of Commerce, the Bank capital was written down in the amount of 33.7 billion bahts. In case of First Bangkok City Bank, nearly 10 billion bahts, and in case of Bangkok Metropolitan Bank approximately 5.5 billions. *See* 'Additional Measures to Strengthen the Financial System', *Bank of Thailand News*, No 8/1998.

[258] *See* 'Order to Write-down and Recapitalise Bangkok Metropolitan Bank Public Company Limited', ibid. No 6/1998.

[259] William Barnes, above n 254.

[260] *See Bank of Thailand News*, No 6 and No 8/1998.

[261] Those banks may need to be merged to attract foreign investors according to the Governor of the Bank of Thailand. *See* William Barnes, above n 254.

[262] *See* Third Letter of Intent, para 4. *See also Bank of Thailand News*, No 8/1998, at 4.

[263] 'Bank of Thailand filed charges against executives of Chao Phaya Finance and Securities Co. Ltd.', ibid. No 86/1997.

[264] Ibid. No 80/1997.

in connection with the falsification of promissory notes and the use of falsified promissory notes as collateral for loans from the FIDF.[265]

The measures set forth above and particularly the closure of more than half of all Thai finance companies are simply unprecedented in Thai prudential supervisory practices and regulatory enforcement. Under normal circumstances, when Thailand's banking and finance sectors were exceedingly powerful both economically and politically, such measures were highly unlikely or nonexistent. The IMF intervention proved to be a significant source of leverage for the Thai authorities. The IMF conditionality measures also may provide significant leverage for the Thai authorities to impose such measures on their banking and finance 'crony capitalists' that still remain as influential business elites because they had no other alternative but to do so.

D. *Elimination of Banking Sector Control by Limited Groups of Business Elites Concentrations of Economic Power*

As previously discussed, the Thai banking and financial systems were traditionally controlled by a limited group of business elites from prominent family groups. The implementation of recapitalisation requirements has functioned metaphorically like 'shooting two birds with one stone'. On the one hand, the recapitalisation measures have directly enhanced the stability of Thai financial institutions and the financial system in its entirety. On the other hand, the recapitalisation measures have tended to dilute control of a Thai financial institution by a single family interests.[266] The movement towards dilution of undesirable concentrations of banking and economic power in turn may resolve various other problems caused by the factor of single-family control, such as problems of favoured and connected lending, outright fraud, and the absence of effective prudential supervision due to crony capitalism. Additionally, enhanced opportunities for foreign shareholding in Thai financial institutions should facilitate competition and efficiency within the Thai banking and financial sectors, which should improve internal controls and risk management practices at Thai financial institutions.

E. *Environment for Prudential Supervision*

The dilution of concentrations of power in the banking and finance sectors, and enhanced opportunities for foreign shareholding in domestic financial

[265] 'BOT takes over finance company', *Bangkok Post,* 24 Nov. 1997.

[266] *See* Paul Sherer, 'Bangkok Bank Family Faces Dilemma of New Capitalism, Market Forces May Force Thai Dynasty to Cede More Control to Outsiders', *Wall Street Journal,* 18 Feb. 1998, at A17.

institutions, should provide a more conducive environment for prudential supervision. The problem of reaching compromise between vested interests of Thai influential families that own or control domestic financial institutions should considerably abate, assisted by the inherent leverage of IMF conditionality requirements. As previously discussed, the massive recapitalisation measures implemented by Thai authorities within the IMF restructuring programme have effectively diluted the concentrations of control and power in the banking and finance sectors. The recapitalisation programmes resulted in larger capital bases and more shareholders in Thai financial institutions and mitigates the possibility for an individual or small group to own or control sufficient shares.

Hitherto, four commercial banks, viz. Bangkok Metropolitan Bank, First Bangkok City Bank, Bangkok Bank of Commerce, and Siam City Bank, failed to recaptitalise and were acquired by Thai authorities. The former controller lost both control of those banks and their capital resources, and bank shares were substantially written down. Although the authorities will privatise these de facto 'nationalised' banks in due course, it is unlikely that any person or small group will resume control of a domestic financial institution during this time of economic and financial crisis. The financial bases of banking and finance elites have been considerably undermined *inter alia* by the closure of fifty-six finance companies[267] as well as the considerable writing down of shares in five commercial banks. As foreign ownership restrictions have been significantly relaxed, foreign institutions are likely to invest in Thai institutions and become more effective and prudent counterparts therein. The introduction of foreign investment and competition in the banking and finance sectors would likely facilitate the implementation of international standards of bank supervision and regulation as developed by the Basle Committee and made part of the IMF conditionality measures. The ultimate practical question in this respect is how long the financial sector structural improvements will last once implemented. The former owners of distressed domestic financial institutions may successfully regain control of their financial institutions in the medium-term. In the absence of continued IMF leverage, the sustained implementation of difficult prudential measures will be extremely difficult to achieve. Will the amended laws again become like a 'paper tiger'? Will the zealous prosecution of corrupt management of financial institutions continue? It is worth noting here that the change of laws or the initiation of an impressive government policy in Thailand does not by any means guarantee their implementation. As history well demonstrates the amended provisions and enhanced powers of supervisory authorities in the 1980s were barely implemented and enforced in

[267] *See* 'Thailand's wealthiest take a beating in finance sector', *Bangkok Post,* 8 Dec. 1997. *See also* 'Big families stare at losses as finance firms close', *The Nation,* 6 Dec. 1997.

practice; and this deficiency in implementation and enforcement turned into one of the major causes of the current crisis. Thus, it remains to be seen whether the same story will be revisited.[268]

F. The Nukul Commission Report on Policy Failures: Move Toward Greater Transparency?

The Nukul Commission was established by the Ministry of Finance in December 1997 to investigate the judicial bases behind the 1997 Financial Crises and to make recommendations for improving the efficiency and management of Thailand's financial system.[269] The Commission comprised seven members of high integrity, including the former Governor of the Bank of Thailand, the former Rector of Thammasat University, and the former Chairman of the Thailand Development Research Institute (TDRI), Thailand's think-tank. In conducting its investigation, the Commission interviewed various key related people including former Governors of the Bank of Thailand, the former Deputy Prime Minister, the former Minister of Finance, and the former Secretary General of the Ministry of Finance. The Report (the 'Nukul Report') that the Commission issued was the first formal, government-commissioned report on investigating financial crises. Clearly it was also the first government report ever to go into the specific details of what happened 'behind the scene', and clearly was the first such report ever to be made available to public (including an English translation of the full report).[270]

There arose a question as to whether this Report was politically motivated, as it clearly pointed out who actually were in charge of what inside the Bank of Thailand, and whether the Report needed to go into such

[268] *Author's Postscript:* Since the date of writing of this article, Thailand submitted the Fourth Letter of Intent to the IMF. Briefly, this Fourth Letter of Intent provided for the following: (1) Further cautious reductions in interest rates, (2) Proposed fiscal deficits to be 3 per cent of GDP instead of 2 per cent, due to significant current account surplus, (3) The auction of 'more complex' assets by the FRA, (4) Further reform of legal and institutional framework such as bankruptcy law, foreclosure procedures, and (5) Further liberalisation of restrictions on foreign participation. *See* Fourth Letter of Intent, 26 May 1998, available at the websites of the IMF, the Bank of Thailand and the Thai Ministry of Finance. In addition, on 18 May 1998, the Bank of Thailand ordered the change of the management of additional seven existing finance companies. The finance companies were also ordered to write down their capitals and to recapitalise through the FIDF. As a result, hitherto four commercial banks and eight finance companies have been intervened by the Thai authorities. *See* 'Order to write down capital, recapitalise, and change the management of distressed finance companies', *Bank of Thailand News*, No 25/1998; *see also* 'Comments by the Thai Minister of Finance on Today's Intervention in Seven Finance Companies', *Ministry of Finance News*, No 42/1998.

[269] *See Nukul Report,* above n 67.

[270] The author cannot overemphasise, particularly given the Thai historical tendency toward non-public criticism of government, that this Report represents a true milestone in terms of a new (and first) era of government transparency.

detail. Taking into account of the integrity and reputation of the Commission members, the Report should be presumed to be accurate and fair. Also, judging from the subject-matter of the Report itself, the Report appears, in most parts accurate, to make a fair evaluation. Having said that, the macroeconomic policies and prudential supervision decisions are highly complex, and subjective in nature.[271] Further, in other parts of the Report, such personal specificity does not seem entirely to be constructive and may amount to excessive 'BOT-bashing'.

What is helpful about the Nukul Report is that it makes various substantive recommendations, which raise basic policy issues for government consideration. For example, the Report recommends that the Bank of Thailand be deprived of bank supervisory power, and such power be placed in a the new separate organisation (possibly the 'Office of Financial Institution Supervision and Examination') formed in a manner similar to the 1992 formation of the Thai SEC (the power to supervise securities was removed from the Bank of Thailand to the newly formed SEC in 1992). Such recommendation means the separation between the prudential supervision duty and the monetary policy determination of the Bank of Thailand.[272] In this context, the Report sets the parameters for the current governmental and Parliamentary debate on who is to conduct prudential supervisory responsibilities, a policy itself directly at odds with the Bank of Thailand's suggestions that it be given full and independent powers in this area.[273]

As monetary policy can be highly politicised, the Report suggests that the management system of the Bank of Thailand be restructured. Specifically, the Bank should establish two Boards.[274] An Executive Board would be

[271] Looking in hindsight is always much easier. Moreover, in a politicised institutional structure such as the Bank of Thailand can be, at times, anyone in such a situation may be unable to do any better than those actually involved. In this context, identifying individual 'scapegoats' is not entirely helpful.

[272] The Thai Securities Exchange Commission (SEC) comprises the Finance Minister as the Chairman, Governor of the Bank of Thailand, Secretary General of the Ministry of Finance, and Secretary General of the Ministry of Commerce, as members, and another four to six experts appointed by the Cabinet upon the recommendation of the Finance Minister. *See* Securities and Exchange Act of BE 2535 (1992) s 8. In addition, the Ministry of Finance is responsible for the overall supervision, control for implementation (in consultation with the government and Cabinet) and is responsible for the enforcement for the Act. The Ministry is also to receive the annual SEC audit. The recommendation of the *Nukul Report* to organise a separate bank supervision entity managed by a commission like the SEC is arguable. The structure of the SEC, perhaps, is no better (and perhaps worse) than the existing Court of Directors structure of the Bank of Thailand in terms of vulnerability to politicisation.

[273] In light of the substantial organisational changes for the Bank of Thailand, most recently implemented and suggested by the Bank's new Governor, this author suggests that such a separation of supervision may not be necessary, nor desirable at this stage in the development of the Thai banking system. Again, this is a fundamental policy issue of options the government will need to address in the near-term. See n 106 above.

[274] *Nukul Report,* above n 67, at para. 454.

responsible for Bank management and internal policy. A Monetary Policy Board would be responsible for monetary and foreign exchange policies. This latter Board would be comprised of a number of outside directors. Also the Report suggests that the terms of the Bank Governor be fixed, and that the selection process for the Governor's appointment be broad-based to help ensure that the Governor will be independent and 'widely accepted by the public'.[275]

Similar to the Joint Mission Report, the Nukul Report suggested the abolition of the FIDF and the establishment of a deposit insurance scheme.[276] The Nukul Report also was highly critical of the FIDF and its lack of independence, vision and proper planning and monitoring.[277]

From a functional perspective the Nukul Report took the Bank of Thailand to task on what it saw as three major failures of the Bank. First, was the failure of the Bank to move sooner from a narrow trading band for the baht to a more managed flexible exchange rate policy, once the Bank had made the long-term commitment in 1990 to liberalise the Thai capital market (which commitment it was recognised had broad political support).[278] Secondly, the Report suggests that the Banks decision to vigorously defend the bank once the crises erupted (e.g. by the use of high-risk swap transactions) proved enormously costly to the country and, in fact, led to a further worsening of market confidence.[279] Thirdly, the Report is highly critical of the Bank in its long-term indecision and ineffectiveness in dealing with the Bangkok Bank of Commerce crises, which emerged in late 1994 and dragged on into 1998.[280] It is suggested that this highly visibly failure in bank supervision severely undermined the Bank of Thailand's 'image and credibility' in dealing not only with that crisis but the other ensuing institutional crises in the 1997–8 period.

G. *Looking to the Future*

Putting matters in a positive context and in looking forward, this author suggests that Thailand stands at a true historic 'crossroads' in terms of the future of its financial system. The prior system, based (in part) on patronage, politicisation, accommodation, nontransparency, and excessive concentrations of economic power, did produce significant economic bene-

[275] *Nukul Report,* at paras 454–5.

[276] Ibid, at ch V, paras 319–425.

[277] While the Report does not suggest the details of an appropriate deposit insurance scheme. Further, this author suggests that a properly structured and operated FDIF could serve as a complement to a viable insurance scheme.

[278] In addition, the Report criticises the Bank of Thailand for not heeding the advice of the IMF and others in 1996 to move to a more flexible exchange system.

[279] *Nukul Report,* above n 67, at ch.II, paras 66–209

[280] Subsequent to the Report this bank was restructured through merger in August 1998.

fits for Thailand—at least until the 1997–8 financial crises. However, if the government's and the IMF's current analyses of the Thai situation is correct, a major cause of the 1997–8 crises was the existence of a fundamentally deficient financial system. The extent of whether and in what manner the 'old Thai ways' in fact contributed to the current crises will certainly be debated, for sometime, within Thai society. But, at minimum, what seems clear is that the 'old ways' did serve as an impediment along with other factors, such as the Thai penchant for coalition governments, to instituting substantial, timely and effective financial sector reform. Without such reform, the Thai governmental goals of a modernised, more open and competitive, non-corrupt, and 'safe and sound' financial system (consistent with internationally accepted 'best practices') cannot be attained. Thus, the choice for Thailand is not so much between 'old' and 'new' ways, but in how Thailand, using 'Thai ways', wishes its financial system (and economy, for that matter) to be as it moves into the twenty-first Century.

The author is not a seer so he cannot 'crystal ball gaze' into whether Thailand's current efforts at financial sector reform are sincere and long-term or will be short-term with an eventual drifting back to the 'old ways'. What the author can conclude, though, are the following:

1. For the base of the economy to grow and for the base of the Thailand people to experience a sustainable and increasing betterment of their economic position, a robust financial sector must be developed and sustained.
2. For such a sector to be developed and sustained, it will need a more open, transparent, rule-based and competitive system.
3. Yet, in a parallel sense, this needed type of financial sector will require a sound prudential supervisory base that will reflect international best practices.
4. To have this 'safe and sound' financial system will, in turn, require a clear legal setting-out of supervisory and enforcement authorities within a clearly identified independent and depoliticised governmental structures.
5. To have a non-corrupt system, there will need to be greater transparency, public accountability, and good governance in the governmental administrative, legislative and judicial processes.

In looking at the above preconditions, this author remains optimistic for the future viability of the Thai financial system and economy. The Thai situation has been so dissected and analysed, internally and externally, that all those in responsible positions within Thailand have a relatively clear grasp of the causes and dimensions of the 1997–8 crisis and of what an effective and robust financial system should entail. In this context the recent

IMF/World Bank Joint Mission Report adds little to what the Thai authorities already have been considering in terms of needed policy reform.[281] However, the Joint Mission Report and, even more, the IMF assistance package itself provide the Thai authorities with a 'window of implementation' for the needed reforms and with a base of 'political leverage' for brining these reforms into reality.

Yet, in the Thai economy moving forward, this author has the following selective and modest recommendations:

1. While Thailand's financial sector reform efforts should seek consistency with international 'best practices', Thailand should devise a total reform package that is 'Thai compatible'. The lesson of recent years in the area of economic law reforms is that there is not one universal model, but country-specific models. Failure to recognise this can only result in an eventual systemic rejection (or even an initial non-acceptance) of an externally imposed reform package by Thai society.[282]
2. Developing new policies and laws is the easiest part of the reform process. The difficult part goes to effective implementation and

[281] After taking position in 1998, the new and current Governor of the Bank of Thailand, MR Chatu mongol Sonakul, also the former Secretary General of the Ministry of Finance, issued a Manifesto on restructuring the Bank of Thailand called 'Thoughts on the Bank of Thailand'. The Manifesto recommends restructuring the Bank of Thailand in various respects. First, the Manifesto suggests the establishment of a Litigation Department, as separate from the Legal Department in the Bank of Thailand. The separate Litigation Department will be solely and especially responsible for prosecuting wrong-doers in relation to banking and finance business. This is designed to make a 'clear accountability'. An additional Assistant Governor in charge of the litigation matters was also appointed.

Secondly, the Manifesto also addressed the problem of the FIDF being under the control of the Bank of Thailand in connection with the Fund's management. It also addressed the enormous burden that the FIDF has shouldered in injecting capital into troubled financial institutions. The Manifesto explicitly expressed disapproval in such implicit bailout policy. As stated, such a way 'does not teach the owners and executives to behave responsibly', in the case of failure due to financial institution mismanagement. It further suggested the establishment of a deposit insurance scheme and the abolishment of the FIDF.

Thirdly, a Monetary Committee was suggested to be established to advise the Governor of the Bank of Thailand in monetary policy matters. The Committee includes the Governor of the Bank of Thailand as the Vice Chairman, TDRI Chairman, Director General of the Fiscal Policy Office of the Ministry of Finance, as members, and Director of the Economic Research Department of the Bank of Thailand as the Secretary. However, such establishment under the current institutional framework cannot reduce politicisation of the Bank of Thailand.

Last but not least, the Manifesto acknowledged the need for good governance. It recognised the significance of the new Constitution in creating better governance in the governmental level. The Manifesto suggested that 'good governance' in the private sector and the civil service is needed as well. *See* Bank of Thailand web page <http://WWW.Grt.or.th/govnr/publ. . . WS2541/othernews/concept-e.html>.

[282] Cf. J Norton, 'International Cooperative Efforts and Implications for Law Reform', in H Shiffman and R Lastra, *Bank Insolvencies in Emerging Economies* (Kluwer International) (to be published early 1999).

enforcement.[283] To have effective implementation and enforcement will require a broad enhancement of the education infrastructure in Thailand—as to legislators, bureaucrats, the judiciary, the private financial and business community and the broader Thai population. A shared understanding and appreciation of the long-term benefits of meaningful financial sector and other key economic reforms needs to be developed within Thai society, over time.

3. As part of this educational enhancement, a better, more open and critical evaluation of the 'old Thai ways' needs to be understood—both as the positive and negative aspects and also as to the 'subtle hazards' of continuing blindly with the 'old ways' in a wholesale manner.
4. Financial sector reform should not occur in isolation but should be viewed as a component of broader economic reform in Thai society. As such, it needs to be meshed coherently with related monetary, trade, investment, fiscal accounting and commercial/business policies of the government.
5. While Thai economic and financial sector reform should be Thai-based, Thailand should continue to recognise that its economic and financial sector fate is interconnected with those of its East Asian neighbours. Thus, more meaningful regional and subregional collaborative efforts, on an ongoing basis should be sought and participate in by Thailand. At minimum, a better and more meaningful regional exchange of relevant economic and monitory information and surveillance should be sought.[284]

283 *See generally*, Joseph J Norton, 'The Thai Financial Crises: Delving Behind the Façade of Financial Sector Reform and the Need for an Interdisciplinary Law-Based Approach', *Thammasat Law Journal* (Sept.1998).

284 eg *see*, Web page for Asian Pacific Economic Cooperation Forum at <http//www.apec-sec.org.sg>. As regards regional cooperation, hitherto, the Bank of Thailand has joined the South East Asian Central Banks (SEACEN), the Executive Meeting of East Asia and Pacific Central Banks (EMEAP) and the Central Banks of South-East Asia, New Zealand and Australia (SEANZA). The EMEAP functions as a forum for central bankers to share their views and experiences, and to update themselves of financial developments. The SEANZA's main activity is training of senior bank officials. *See* Bank of Thailand, *Financial Institutions and Markets in Thailand* (1997), at 5–6.

Chapter 7

Indonesian Banking Reform after the Crisis

Joseph J. Norton and Mamiko Yokoi-Arai

I. INTRODUCTION

Indonesia was labeled an 'emerging market' and much investment entered its economy seeking higher returns until the crisis in 1997. Any investor in finance, natural resource development, or manufacturing would name the essential factors in Indonesia to be the political stability of the Suharto government, rich natural resources, and a vast supply of cheap labour. Even these three elements did not immune Indonesia from the financial crisis of 1997. Capital flight was rapid and the rupiah depreciated over several months at rates neither the Indonesian authorities nor the international financial institutions expected.[1] The sharp loss of confidence in Indonesia not only exhibits how easily investors can turn their backs in the wake of a crisis, but also reverse their appraisal of the economy. Thus, it is necessary to look into the underlying economics and structure of Indonesia and evaluate what conditions made Indonesia more susceptible to the financial crisis.

The Asian financial crisis broke out in Thailand in July 1997. After repeated attempts by the Thai monetary authority to defend the currency failed, Thailand abandoned the currency peg on 2 July 1997. Like other ASEAN countries, Indonesia had a currency peg to a basket of currencies and an accumulating short-term foreign currency debt, but these were not of prime concern when Indonesia was considered one of the growth centres in Asia. Previously, the currency peg had given investors added confidence with no inherent foreign exchange risk, but after the Thai experience, countries with currency pegs were subject to capital outflow. Although herd instinct did occur, it is difficult to imagine sophisticated investors who deal with large sums of money to simply reverse investment decisions due to currency depreciation. It was more the banking sector weaknesses and other struc-

1 On several occasions, the Indonesian government had to review its target exchange rate after realising that previous targets were not realistic. These reviews were conducted in Letters of Intent and Memorandum of Economic and Financial Policies from Indonesian government to the International Monetary Fund (15 Jan. 1998, 10 Apr. 1998, and 24 June 1998).

tural rigidities that were inhibiting the foundation of the economy, which were similar in Thailand, and the underlying problems began surfacing once the Thai crisis erupted. We can see two countervailing views of the same element in the economy, pre- and post-crisis. These were on the one hand the source of attraction to investors pre-crisis and then became the source of scepticism *post facto*. Hence, it is not sufficient that economic growth is high, but that appropriate safeguards are taken to foster a safe and sound economy in the long-run.

We will explore the measures taken by the Indonesian government in collaboration with the international financial institutions and bilateral sponsors, and how it has overhauled various areas and structures of the economy. This paper first takes a brief overview of the Indonesian economy from the 1970s up to the financial crisis. The second part examines how the financial crisis that erupted in Thailand triggered a crisis in Indonesia. The third part addresses the fundamental problems that were present in the Indonesian economy and how the economic and financial policies are being formulated to resolve those fundamental problems. The analysis of this paper has been based on information available from the publication of the Letter of Intent of 14 May 1999. The next Letter of Intent is to be released in July 1999 by the Indonesian government. Finally, the concluding remarks summarise the nature of reforms and suggest what direction could be contemplated to prevent another crisis.

II. ECONOMIC OVERVIEW: POST-SUKARNO TO THE FINANCIAL CRISIS IN 1997

Indonesia is an archipelago consisting of 13,500 islands. It has the world's fifth largest population, nearly 200 million people. The population is 95 per cent Malay, and the remainder consisting of various ethnic groups, Chinese is the predominant minority comprising 2 per cent of the population. Although the population is overwhelmingly Muslim (85 per cent), Indonesia is well known for its diversity in religions which vary depending on the island. Also, as in many South-East Asian countries, a great part of the commercial sector is owned by the minority Chinese notwithstanding their low percentage of the country's population.[2]

The Indonesian economy has maintained an astonishing average growth rate of 6 percent, from 1970 up to the crisis in 1997, which notches up to 8 percent for 1996. In spite of the ongoing debate, the long-term high

[2] The Chinese are said to own 70 per cent of all corporate assets. *See* WING THY WOO ET AL., MACROECONOMIC POLICIES, CRISES, AND LONG-TERM GROWTH IN INDONESIA, 1965–90 7 (1994).

growth was dubbed by the World Bank as 'the Asian Miracle' and remained an attractive investment for those seeking higher returns. The economic growth made possible the many poor Indonesians to rise above the poverty line.[3] The government's investment in education also enhanced the supply of skilled labour which fed into increased growth.

The path that Indonesia followed was not readily available at the time of independence from Japan in 1945. The era started when Suharto took over the leadership from Sukarno in 1967. Until Suharto resigned in May 1998, he was the sole leader of the country holding the casting vote. It is essential to recall the policies that were implemented, especially in terms of the banking sector prior to the financial crisis.

While focusing on development of the banking sector, this section gives a brief overview of the development of the Indonesian economy. The background of the policies implemented and the factors influencing them that are essential to understand the turn towards the crisis from the investors' perspective. It is clear that, excluding the banking sector weaknesses, causes of the crisis were often sources of economic growth as well.

A. *Beginning of the Suharto era: 1967–73*

Suharto came into power after an attempted communist coup in 1965 which overthrew his predecessor and founder of Indonesia, Sukarno. He was formally elected as President in 1967 and introduced his 'New Order'. The coup occurred out of economic disorder where annual inflation was 250 per cent between 1962 and 1965. The annual growth rate was 1 per cent over the same period accompanied by a highly unstable exchange rate.[4] Suharto's New Order government emphasised the importance of economic and social development, and welcomed the expansion of the private sector as well as foreign investment. This was the opposite of the previous government's anti-Western policy.[5]

In its first five-year development programme, the government's objective was economic growth and stabilisation. The key policies were tight monetary control and high interest rates to obtain control of the economy.

[3] The proportion of the population living under the poverty line made a dropped dramatically from 60 per cent to an estimated 11 per cent between 1970 and 1996. Each citizen who has one dollar per day to spend is considered to be above the poverty line. *See* WORLD BANK, COUNTRY BRIEF: THE WORLD BANK AND INDONESIA (1999).

[4] The effective exchange rate swayed from Rp17 per dollar in 1957 to Rp30 per dollar in 1958. From the beginning of the 1960s the rupiah was made an explicit depreciation. In 1960 the effective exchange rate was Rp37.52 per dollar. By 1962 it became Rp136.70 per dollar, but 1965 marked the exchange rate at Rp2,683 per dollar with increasing political stability.

[5] Suharto is well known for employing many US educated technocrats in his emphasis on economic development. Among these were the 'Berkeley Mafia'. They had 'influential foreign constituency', 'lack of ideological aversion to foreign investment', and many had degrees from the University of California. WOO ET AL., above n 2, at 152 n 12.

Nominal government expenditure was rising with increased subsidies to public utilities, state and other enterprises. The high inflation had led the economy back to barter trade to evade tax. Thus, fiscal discipline was introduced and selective credit programs were implemented.

Banking institutions were restructured through a number of Presidential Decrees in 1965. The central bank, three state commercial banks, one state savings bank, and state pawnshops were consolidated into one single institution, Bank Negara Indonesia. In 1967, the Commercial Banking Act was enacted drawing the legal basis of commercial bank activities, and in 1968, the Central Bank Act was implemented setting the principles of central bank operations and bank supervision, thus disintegrating Bank Negara Indonesia into separate banks: one central bank, one development bank, one savings bank, and five state-owned commercial banks. Foreign banks were only permitted to open branches in Jakarta.

To implement the government objectives, six measures were taken.[6] First, the interest rate on time deposits was raised to eliminate the real negative interest rate. Secondly, state-owned banks were subsidised to cover part of their interest payment on deposits. Thirdly, saving accounts were insured. Fourthly, transfers were made from the government development budget to state banks to make long-term loans. Fifthly, the central bank was allowed to participate in financing of long-term loans and offered substantial central bank credits to state banks to finance the import of aid goods.

B. *After the Oil Shock: 1973–82*

As a result of rice price increase caused by a drought and increased oil prices in line with Middle Eastern oil producers, Indonesia experienced a resurgence of inflation from 2 per cent in 1971 to 26 per cent in 1972. To control credit expansion of banks, a policy of 'moral suasion' was introduced in 1973. However, inflation did not subside, thus leading the government to introduce a package of measures in April 1974 to control credit expansion of financial institutions, foreign borrowing by the private sector, and stimulate time and savings deposits to reduce the rate of reserve money growth.[7]

As a result, the central bank had to return to direct monetary control. It used a number of instruments. First, credit ceilings were set for each individual bank and for Bank Indonesia's own credit. These ceilings were set not only on net domestic assets, but also on new foreign assets provided by the growing private capital inflow that was gaining significance in the banking sector. Secondly, maintenance and even extension of rediscount or

[6] *See* ANWAR NASUTION, FINANCIAL INSTITUTIONS AND POLICIES IN INDONESIA 10 (1983).
[7] *See* WOO ET AL. above n 2 at 58–62.

refinancing mechanism to allocate credit and subsidies to priority sectors in economy were reestablished. Thirdly, Bank Indonesia gained control of state-owned banks' interest rates, while private banks were free to set their own interest rates.

In 1975 the state-owned oil company, Pertamina, was unable to rollover short-term loan of 40 million dollars denominated. This led the governments to contain over-borrowing by its state enterprises and reduce its external debt. Pertamina was significant in its sheer size which amounted to 70 per cent of the government budget revenue and was the largest corporation in Asia outside Japan.[8]

With continuing inflation and depreciation of the US dollar, income from exports decreased which led to the rupiah devaluation on 15 November 1978. Prior to this, the rupiah had been fixed to the US dollar but after this date, it was pegged to an undisclosed basket of currencies.

C. *Measures for Economic Takeoff: 1982–8*

After a relatively stable period following the rise of oil prices of 1979, and increased prices of other export commodities, the world recession hit Indonesia in 1982. Indonesia had been achieving impressive GDP growth between 1979 and 1981; in 1979 GDP was 6 per cent, rising to 8 per cent in 1980, and 7 per cent in 1981. But there was a strong contraction in 1982 when the world slump hit, drawing back growth to –0.3 per cent. This undermined the balance of payment and fiscal position, requiring the government to make macroeconomic adjustments. In March 1983 the government devalued the currency by 38 per cent bringing the value of the currency back to the 1978 level.

When the price of oil started to fall in 1982, fiscal adjustment was made by cutting expenditure on state-owned enterprises. Bank Indonesia sought to reduce liquidity credits to state banks which resulted in a squeeze on the profit of state banks. In place of the decreased subsidies to state enterprises, it became necessary for the government to mobilise savings to support investment in a tight monetary stance.[9] Also, the credit allocation to priority sectors was not efficient since state banks rarely met their targets, and this inefficiency was aggravated by ceilings on deposit and lending rates.

The financial reform package of 1983 was implemented under this economic situation. The reform started with Bank Indonesia cutting back

[8] *See* D. P. HANNA, INDONESIAN EXPERIENCE WITH FINANCIAL SECTOR REFORM 9 (World Bank Discussion Papers, No 237, 1994).

[9] *See* Anwar Nasution, *An Evaluation of the Banking Sector Reforms in Indonesia, 1983–1993*, 1 ASIA-PACIFIC DEVELOPMENT JOURNAL (1994).

on its credit to lower priority sectors in 1982. In June 1983 direct control on interest rates on most credit and deposits was removed, most subsidised credit programs were eliminated, and the central bank's funding of state-owned banks curtailed.[10]

D. *Growth and Financial Integration: 1988–1997*

In 1998 the Indonesian government undertook another financial deregulation package, known as Pakto. Together with the plunge of oil prices and appreciation of yen since 1985, the Indonesian economy was losing its primary source of income, oil revenues. It became necessary for the Indonesia government to pursue new measures to stimulate the economy. With the success of the 1982 financial reform, the government was prepared to implement further policies to deregulate the economy and increase competition in the banking industry for greater efficiency.

The Indonesian banking sector was highly concentrated in the hands of five state-owned banks and the state development bank which accounted for 'approximately 80 per cent of total assets, total deposits, and total loans of the deposit money banks'.[11] These banks precluded other participants in the financial sector and amounted to 90 per cent of gross assets of the financial system in 1991.[12] State banks were able to obtain their strong credit position through the instruments Bank Indonesia used to disburse credit to targeted groups. State banks received 'liquidity credit' from Bank Indonesia at very low interest rates and re-lent them at higher rates. This was an economic rent to the state banks and inhibited the competition with private and foreign banks. Thus the 1988 financial reform promoted competition by allowing the growth of private banks and containing state bank business based on counterproductive incentives.[13] New entrants were allowed into the banking sector and expansion of activities was coupled with greater autonomy in decision-making.

Entry barriers to financing were lowered through a number of measures.[14] Banking licenses were made available to new banks that could meet the new minimum capital requirement. The process of obtaining a foreign exchange licence was simplified. Foreign joint-venture banks were

[10] WOO ET AL, above n 2 at 100.

[11] *See* ANWAR NASUTION, THE BANKING SYSTEM AND MONETARY AGGREGATES FOLLOWING FINANCIAL SECTOR REFORMS: LESSONS FROM INDONESIA 3 (Research for Action 27, UNU/WIDER 1996).

[12] It has been noted that state banks rarely met their credit targets, a result that may have been due to the large bribes these banks made which raised the cost of their credit above that of private banks. *See*, Wing Thye Woo and Anway Nasution, *Indonesia's Economic Policies and their Relation to External Debt Management*, *in* VOL. 3 DEVELOPING COUNTRY DEBT 17, 83–95 (Jeffery Sachs and Susan M. Collins, eds., 1989).

[13] *See* HANNA, above, n 8 at 10.

[14] *See* NASUTION, above, n 11 at 2.

authorised with extended branching network. Openings of domestic branches were permitted without prior approval as long as they adhered to the standard of prudential soundness.

Efforts to promote competition were coupled with improvements in prudential supervision of banks. Lending limits to persons, firms, or groups, set at 20 per cent, were increased to 50 per cent of equity. New minimum capital requirements forced greater level of equity for banks.

The Pakto led to an immense growth of the banking sector in terms of volume. However, it was not accompanied with prudential safeguards necessary to shift from a controlled financial arena to a market based system. This led the banking operations in Indonesia to be less regulated and supervised for more than two years until the new regulations were introduced in 1991, allowing free expansion of credit until this.[15]

The number of banks sharply rose from 111 in 1988 to 240 in March 1994, with each of the large business conglomerates having at least one bank. The number of foreign banks in Indonesia rose to 29 in 1991 after the reform from the eleven foreign banks which had been operating since the 1960s.[16] However, the increase in competition led to the lowering of credit standards of banks to attract more business opportunities. Banks continued to operate on outdated principles while the market was protected by numerous government controls. Banks need time to build their internal capability to select customers to make sound credit evaluations and control risks. The old practice did not pay much attention to the market value of loans and collateral.[17]

Prudential regulation aimed at monitoring credit risk of banks was introduced in March 1991. The new regulation required banks to reexamine the foundation of their operational basis, and strengthen their structure adhering to risk based evaluation of their capital base. First, professionally standards were set for bank directors. Secondly, the loss loan provisioning standard was based on analysis of the customers' financial condition rather than simply conducting a check of whether their payments were current or not. Thirdly, quantitative evaluation of bank soundness was implemented, using the CAMEL system for bank supervision instead of the former system, where focus was placed on compliance rather than risk evaluation.[18] Fourthly, risk-based capital adequacy ratios were introduced, requiring banks to achieve 8 per cent minimum ratio by end-1993.[19]

[15] *See* ibid. at 9 (referring to table 2, *Structure and Growth of the Financial Sectors, 1969–1994*).

[16] Ibid.

[17] Ibid.

[18] *See* HANNA, above, n 8 at 12.

[19] *See* J. D. Djiwandono, The Banking Sector in Emerging Markets: The Case of Indonesia, *in* BANKING SOUNDNESS AND MONETARY POLICY: ISSUES AND EXPERIENCE IN THE GLOBAL ECONOMY, PAPERS PRESENTED AT THE SEVENTH SEMINAR ON CENTRAL BANKING 347 (C. Enoch and J. H. Green, eds., Washington, DC, 27–31 January 1997).

To formalise these banking reform regulations, the legislation enacting the new Banking Law was effected in February 1992. This law contains elements of banking reforms that have been implemented since October 1988 and unified various issued regulations. The traditional functional specialisation between various types of banks and major areas of specialisation for state-owned banks was removed. All specialised banks became commercial banks. Also, stiffer penalties for fraud were included. The partial privatisation of state banks through public issuance of shares was also envisaged. In 1993, legal lending limits were implemented.

An interesting development of Indonesian banking reform may be the policy issued by Bank Indonesia in 1994 and 1995. Bank Indonesia encouraged banks to strengthen application of self-regulatory principles for prudential purposes which included banks' internal regulations, systems, standards, procedures and policies. As well, Bank Indonesia has explicitly used moral suasion programmes to influence banks in their lending activities in place of direct controls.[20] This banking regulatory culture reflects the strong emphasis policy makers placed on banks operating for community interest, expecting banks to fulfil social needs. Embedded in this culture were bilateral negotiations for monetary operations. Bank Indonesia consulted each bank to purchase or sell central bank certificates (SBIs) instead of using the conventional market auction system.

III. INDONESIAN ECONOMY AND FINANCIAL CONDITIONS LEADING TO THE FINANCIAL CRISIS

A. *Weaknesses of the Indonesian Economy Leading to the Crisis*

The financial crisis that started in Thailand in July 1997 not only shook the region, but it affected the international financial community. The globalisation rapidly taking place in finance has proved the saying that, a butterfly's flutter in Hong Kong can cause a storm in New York. Even the most mature and deep economies such as that of the United States experienced some credit squeeze, primarily after the Russian debt default in August 1998, when there were sharp increases in spreads of financial assets and volatility in the dollar-yen exchange rate.[21] But the hardest hit were clearly the Asian

[20] INTERNATIONAL MONETARY FUND, WORLD ECONOMIC OUTLOOK AND INTERNATIONAL CAPITAL MARKETS: INTERIM ASSESSMENT 17 (1998).

[21] Contagion is defined as 'co-movement of markets not traceable to a common co-movement of fundamentals.' H. C. Wolf, Regional Contagion Effects In Emerging Stock Markets, *in* WORKING PAPERS IN INTERNATIONAL ECONOMICS, (G-97-03:1–18, Department of Economics, International Finance Section, Princeton University). There are said to be three channels of contagion in financial markets. The first is herd behaviour which is attributable to asymmetric information and a failure of investors to discriminate among different fundamentals across

economies. South Korea and Indonesia's economic and financial condition deteriorated rapidly, necessitating a support package formed by IMF and bilateral donors. The sudden downturn in these hardest hit countries was great, but unlike Thailand, it was not evident from the outset that Korea and Indonesia would eventually resort to international support. It is thus necessary to look into the economic and financial nature that made Indonesia subject to the crisis. In this section, the economic and financial characteristics of Indonesia prior to the crisis are analysed. There are some features which are similar to the other crisis hit economies, which explains the contagion that occurred.[22] Then there are features of the Indonesian economy unique or more pronounced than others.

1. Common features with other crisis-affected Asian economies

South East Asian countries had been experiencing an exceptionally high growth period. During the past 20 years, East Asian crisis countries[23] achieved 6.9 per cent real GDP growth in 1981–90, and 7.2 per cent in the 1991–7 period.[24] Some common factors existed among these countries that enabled this rapid economic upsurge: low inflation, competitive exchange rates, conservative macroeconomic policies, balanced or surplus fiscal positions, higher public expenditure on education as an investment in human capital, high saving rates, and transfer of foreign technology.[25]

a. Short-term foreign debt

The policies that were implemented in the crisis-affected countries created similar vulnerabilities. Most of these countries had recently started to liberalise their financial markets in order to attract foreign capital to fund further economic development. Indonesia had opened its capital account in 1970, allowing free inflow and outflow of capital. In addition, banking reforms had been taking place since 1988 to remove obstacles to business

markets. Secondly, in portfolio allocation a change in one emerging market portfolio will lead to a review of investments in another emerging market. Thirdly, portfolio interdependence results in a sell-off will in one emerging market to regain the losses incurred in another. In this case, the contagion is subject to herd behaviour where investors see emerging market as a single asset class. *See* World Bank, Global Economic Prospects 1998/1999: Beyond the Financial Crisis 52 (1998).

22 The East Asian crisis-affected countries referred to here are Indonesia, Republic of Korea, Malaysia, Philippines, and Thailand often referred to as the 'East Asia 5'.

23 *See* World Bank, Global Economic Prospects, above, n 21 at 6 table 1–2.

24 *See* International bank for Reconstruction and Development, World Bank, East Asia: The Road to Recovery 3 (1998).

25 *See* ibid. at 7–9.

expansion and improve efficiency. This spawned the availability of foreign capital from private sources that had a matching interest for higher returns.

The current account of these countries had been in deficit, although the extent of the deficit differed among countries (Table 1), and these were financed through short-term foreign credit (Table 2). East Asia had been absorbing nearly 60 per cent of all short-term capital flows to developing countries. The large proportion of capital came from Japanese banks whose corporate borrowers had been expanding their manufacturing throughout Asia, and the European banks trying to gain market share where possible in Asia. European banks had actually outperformed the Japanese banks by 1996. The outstanding bank loans from Japanese banks were USD261 billion, EU banks USD318 billion, and US banks had USD46 billion.[26]

This build up comprised primarily of private decisions of financial institutions and corporations instead of foreign direct investment which has the advantage of longer-term lending. This led to credit booms. The ratio of short-term debt to foreign reserves, a rough measure of a country's ability to meet its current obligation from its own liquid resources, rose sharply from 1994 to 1997, except for Indonesia where it remained high. But in June 1997, the short-term debt to reserves ratio of Indonesia, Korea, and Thailand reached above 150 per cent, significantly higher than the 100 per cent ratio of Malaysia and the Philippines.[27] Credit growth was also common among the East Asia 5 (Indonesia, Korea, Malaysia, Phillippines, and Thailand) where broad money (M2) expanded at nearly 20 percent annually in 1996 and 1997.

Table 1 Current account balance of Asian financial crisis affected countries

	(USD billions)		
	1995	1996	1997
Indonesia	–6.8	–7.6	–3.9
Thailand	–13.2	–14.4	–3.0
Korea	–8.5	–23.0	–8.2
Ref: HK SAR	–5.5	–1.6	–5.5
Singapore	14.3	14.6	14.8

Source: IMF, *World Economic Outlook*, Oct 1998, pp. 63.

[26] *See* ibid. at 8.

[27] Ibid. at 34.

Table 2 Private capital flows of Asian financial crisis affected countries

	(USD billions)							
	1990	1991	1992	1993	1994	1995	1996	1997
Affected countries' net private capital inflows	24.9	29.0	30.3	32.6	35.1	62.9	72.9	–11.0
Net foreign direct investment	6.2	7.2	8.6	8.6	7.4	9.5	12.0	9.6
Net portfolio investment	1.3	3.3	6.3	17.9	10.6	14.4	20.3	11.8
Other	17.4	18.5	15.4	6.1	17.1	39.0	40.6	–32.3
Affected countries' net external borrowing from official creditors	0.3	4.4	2.0	0.8	0.7	1.0	4.6	25.6

Affected countries include Indonesia, Korea, Malaysia, the Philippines, and Thailand.

(*Source:* IMF, *International Capital Markets: Developments, Prospects, and Key Policy Issues*, Sept. 1998, 13.)

b. Pegged foreign exchange regimes

The countries which were most severely affected by the financial crisis all had a currency peg with a basket of undisclosed currencies, but heavily weighted with the US dollar. The pegged exchange rate worked to fuel the crisis in three ways. First, the implicit government guarantee of a fixed exchange rate provided banks an incentive to borrow off-shore without due consideration to foreign exchange risk. Consequently, this led to capital inflows. However, as a result of the perception of reduced foreign exchange risk of pegged currencies, external borrowing was typically unhedged. Also, narrow exchange rate movements encouraged short-term borrowing which had lower interest rates.

Secondly, because the currencies of the ASEAN nations were anchored heavily with the US dollar, the high interest rates of these countries created interest rate differentials with the US that made arbitrage transactions a relatively lucrative business.

Thirdly, the yen depreciation against the US dollar throughout much of 1996 caused the pegged currencies to lose their competitiveness. This spurred export growth slowdown and current account deficits because Japan is both a major market and a competitor in export markets.

c. Institutional weaknesses

Despite the rapid growth of the East Asia 5, their institutional structure was not sufficiently developed to keep apace with the rapid financial integration that was taking place in the international financial market bringing in large amounts of capital into these countries. The Asian economies had been liberalising their economies since late 1980s. These economies took advantage of capital available in the international market. However, they neither strengthened prudential regulations nor the supervision of financial markets. The existing prudential regulations, such as tighter loan classification and loan loss provisioning, were not adequate. Minimum capital requirements were not sufficient. Deposit insurance did not exist in Indonesia and Thailand but considered implicit by the government and central bank liquidity support. Information disclosure and transparency of operations were poor, and monitoring by regulators was not conducted adequately. The environment for moral hazard was readily provided.

The result of these policies were 'misallocation of resources, over-exposure to risky sectors, risky liabilities structure, and poor institutional development'.[28]

The banking sector's other problem was that it lacked an enforcement mechanism of prudential regulations. The supervisory authorities did not have sufficient power to enforce the results of supervision, and as a result, banks had low capital adequacy ratios, and connected party lending and legal lending limits were not strictly enforced.[29]

The lack of institutional development of banks' internal governance was also a source of risk. Lending was usually based on collateral rather than cash-flow, undermining sound credit judgments based on profitability and riskiness.

There was a high degree of indirect financing which was the result of government policy to concentrate resources to strategic industries through banks but left capital markets underdeveloped (Table 3).[30] Asian governments have commonly followed this Japanese model of fostering the banking sector to lend out their resources at lower interest rates to key industries. Where bond markets did develop, banks often guaranteed bond and other corporate securities and secondary trading was limited. The lack of securities markets hampered the necessary corporate governance of

[28] Krugman was one of the first critics of the Asian Miracle. He pointed out that the growth rates achieved were not a result of improved productivity but of higher use of resources and a failure to accept civil liberties. *See generally*, Paul Krugman, *The Myth of Asia's Miracle*, 73 FOREIGN AFFAIRS 62, (1994).

[29] *See generally* Masahiko Aoki and Hugh Patrick, eds., THE JAPANESE MAIN BANK SYSTEM: ITS RELEVANCE FOR DEVELOPING AND TRANSFORMING ECONOMIES (1994) (providing a brief description of main-bank and Anglo-American finance systems with a favourable view of the main bank system); and *Market-Based (Arm's Length) Versus Relationship-Based (Insider) Finance*, *in* US GOVERNMENT, ECONOMIC REPORT OF THE PRESIDENT 230 (1999) (Box 6.2, providing a critical view of the main bank system).

[30] WORLD BANK, EAST ASIA: THE ROAD TO RECOVERY, 34 (1998).

Table 3 Financial system composition of Asian financial crisis affected countries

(number of financial institutions)

	Private domestic commercial banks	State banks	Merchant banks security	Finance or institution	Foreign financial	Total
Indonesia	144	34	0	0	44	222
Korea	26	8	30	53	52	169
Thailand	15	5	0	108	14	142

(*Source:* World Bank, *East Asia: The Road to Recovery*, 1998, pp.36.

firms, leaving banks responsible for the monitoring of firms.[31] Also, insufficient risk diversification exposed firms to banking sector shocks which would directly translate into corporate sector financing difficulties in times of financial distress.

Another institutional weakness that crisis hit countries have in common is the lack of central bank autonomy. Massive central bank liquidity infusion to support troubled commercial banks was not justified as a lender of last resort facilities to help illiquid banks. Beginning in December of 1996, Thailand started to inject large amounts of central bank reserves to combat the intensifying pressure on the exchange rate. Eventually, the Thai government allowed the baht to float. The resources spent on fighting the depreciation of the baht reached 2 per cent of Thailand's GDP at the end of 1996 and 15 per cent by the end of 1997. In Indonesia and Korea, central bank credit rose immediately before the sharp declines of their currencies.[32] These credits were intended to help illiquid banks being severely affected by the high interest rates applied to maintain the currency peg.

d. Credit boom

The robust economic growth of the East Asian economies led them to be bullish in their borrowing attitudes leading to a lending boom in the 1990s. This was accompanied by high saving rates, affluent capital inflow, and lower reserve requirements allowing financial liberalisation.[33] Several East

[31] *See* World Bank, Global Economic Prospects 1998/1999: Beyond the Financial Crisis 74 (1998).

[32] *See* ibid. at 68.

[33] *See* Nasution, above, n 11 at 20.

Asian countries experienced private credit growth relative to GDP increase in their income levels.

As a reflection of high bank credit, corporations were highly leveraged which makes them more vulnerable to fluctuation of cash flows resulting from external shocks. The hardest hit countries, Indonesia, Korea and Thailand, can be explained in this context since their corporate sectors had a debt to equity ratio two to three times that of other affected countries. Cyclical factors also contributed to the vulnerability, eventually damaging the real economy.

Credit boom also means that once an external shock hits the economy, nonperforming loans increase. A credit or investment boom generally occurs during time of economic prosperity and rising asset prices were used for collaterals to overcome the information asymmetry in lending. This allowed credit extension to risky projects. Recently liberalised financial systems lack the expertise of screening and monitoring loans and were strained by the increased competition in the market place. Once the economy turns sour, lax lending makes it prone to bad loans. As long as the economy is robust and asset prices continue to rise, the risky loans do not surface. When the downturn arrives, inadequate loan classification, loan loss provisions and bankruptcy rules the turnaround becomes dramatic.

2. Economic features unique or pronounced in Indonesia

a. Bad loans and insolvent banks

The most notable feature of the Indonesian economy prior to the financial crisis is the accumulation of nonperforming loans and the number of banks which were already insolvent. Despite the economic growth, nonperforming loans were a big problem of the banking sector, especially among state-owned banks. The high proportion of poorly performing loans suggest that undercapitalised banks were making poor credit decisions. State-owned banks exacerbated the situation since loan decisions were not made on a commercial basis. Also, many private banks were affiliated with conglomerates as a result of the 1988 banking sector reform which removed entry barriers into the banking sector.[34]

In retrospect, the closure of sixteen banks immediately after Indonesia started negotiations with IMF for a standby arrangement became a signal to investors that there were several insolvent and undercapitalised banks in

[34] *See* ibid. *See also* J. Montgomery, The Indonesian Financial System: Its Contribution to Economic Performance, and Key Policy Issues 16, Working Paper of the International Monetary Fund (WP/97/45, 1997).

Table 4 Indonesia's Commercial Bank Non-performing Loans, 1993–5

	1993	1994	1995	1996*2	1997*2
(In per cent of total credits)					
All banks					
Non-performing	14.2	12.1	10.4	9.3	19.8
Bad*1	3.3	4.0	3.3	N/A	N/A
State banks					
Nonperforming	19.8	18.6	16.6	14.2	24.2
Bad	4.2	5.9	5.3	N/A	N/A
Private banks					
Non-performing	7.3	5.4	4.9	20.5	32.7
Bad	2.1	1.9	1.4	N/A	N/A
Memorandum items: (In trillions of rupiah)					
Total credits	177.5	217.0	267.8	N/A	N/A
State banks	99.1	104.1	120.9	N/A	N/A
Private banks	79.8	108.5	141.3	N/A	N/A

(*Source:* J. Montgomery, *The Indonesian Financial System: Its Contribution to Economic Performance, and Key Policy Issues*, Working Paper of the International Monetary Fund, WP/97/45, Apr. 1997, 14, and Bank Indonesia, *Report for Financial Year of 1997/8*, Sept 1998.
*1: Bad loans are lowest quality of three categories of non-performing loans.
*2: For 1996 and 1997 data is only available for ratio of non-performing loans.

business, making risky investments and eventually becoming nonperforming. Few suggested an exit policy for undercapitalised banks,[35] but Indonesia's central bank lacked the authority[36] and resources to conduct recapitalisation or credit assistance for mergers.[37]

Another problem in relation with loan classification was the lack of disclosure and accurate statistics in Indonesia that contributed to the difficulty in assessing non-performing loans.[38] Further, accounting adjustments may have been made to enable undercapitalised state banks to continue their operations.[39]

[35] *See* WORLD BANK, EAST ASIA: THE ROAD TO RECOVERY, above, n 24 at 19.
[36] *See* NASUTION, above, n 11 at 22.
[37] *See* Michael Walton, *The Maturation of the East Asian Miracle*, FINANCE & DEVELOPMENT, Sept. 1997, at 7, 9.
[38] *See* MONTGOMERY, above, n 34 at 17.
[39] *See* WORLD BANK, EAST ASIA: THE ROAD TO RECOVERY, above, n 24 at 16–17.

b. Corporate sector debt accumulation

Unlike foreign debt crisis in other countries that are caused mainly by borrowing by banks, the foreign debt crisis in Indonesia was caused by the private sector. As discussed above, the leverage ratio of corporate debt to equity was two to three. Therefore, corporations were more vulnerable to shocks. Before the crisis, it was difficult for authorities to monitor debt to equity ratios because of insufficient disclosure.[40]

c. Dominance of state owned banks

The banking sector of Indonesia was dominated by state-owned banks. Their role had been ebbing since the 1983 reform, but their presence was still dominant (Table 3, Table 4, and Table 5). The 1983 reform eliminated ceilings on lending rates of state banks. The 1988 reform permitted public enterprises to deposit 50 per cent of short-term funds with private bank,

Table 5 Indonesia: Composition of the Banking Sector, 1991–5

	1991	1992	1993	1994	1995
Assets (in trillion of rupiah)					
State commercial banks	78.0	93.3	100.6	104.5	122.6
Local government-owned banks	4.7	5.3	6.5	7.9	9.8
Private national banks	58.5	66.3	88.2	113.8	147.5
Joint banks	5.6	7.5	11.8	14.3	17.9
Foreign banks	7.4	7.5	7.9	9.2	12.3
Total	154.2	180.0	215.1	249.8	310.0
Assets (per cent)					
State commercial banks	50.6	51.8	46.8	41.8	39.5
Local government-owned banks	3.0	2.9	3.0	3.2	3.2
Private national banks	38.0	36.8	41.0	45.6	47.6
Joint banks	3.6	4.2	5.5	5.7	5.8
Foreign banks	4.8	4.2	3.7	3.7	3.9
Total	100	100	100	100	100

(*Source:* J. Montgomery, *The Indonesian Financial System: Its Contribution to Economic Performance, and Key Policy Issues*, Working Paper of the International Monetary Fund, WP/97/45, Apr. 1997.)

[40] A Nasution, *The Banking System and Monetary Aggregates Following Financial Sector Reforms: Lessons from Indonesia*, Research for Action 27, UNU/WIDER, at 20 (1996).

rather than exclusively with state-owned banks. The amendment to the 1992 Banking Law removed special categories of banks. After the amendment state-owned banks were no longer subject to subsidised interest rates or special liquidity support from Bank Indonesia. Despite the decline of state banks' assets, the seven state banks still held 39.5 per cent of total assets of the banking sector in 1995.

The problem with state banks is that their credit decisions are not commercial based, which often equates to the lack of adequate risk appraisal and inefficient operation. State banks are able to make riskier loans due to the implicit government guarantee that they will be bailed out in case of insolvency.[41] As Table 4 indicates, state banks have historically had higher rates of nonperforming loans. In addition, state banks have traditionally been undercapitalised,[42] making their credit evaluation even less credible.

Also, the role of state banks as the main provider of financing for companies that do not have access to capital markets or international financial markets further eroded their balance sheets.[43] This does not necessarily translate to risky investments, but unless appropriate risk evaluation is conducted to quantify expected return of the investments as the companies, loans may be given at a considerably lower interest rate.

Another problem associated with state banks is connected party lending to risky projects, outright fraud, widespread corruption by high ranking government officials, and credits between state owned enterprises.[44]

d. Noncompliance of prudential regulations

With regard to prudential regulations, Indonesia has had more problems with enforcement than implementation. Bank Indonesia has requirements for statutory reserve requirement, loan to deposit ratio (LDR), net open position (NOP), capital adequacy requirement (CAR), and legal lending limit (LLL). The non-compliance rates of prudential regulation for various banking institutions in 1995 are shown on Table 6 and Table 7.

This lack of compliance is induced by the weak law enforcement and lack of Bank Indonesia's independence.[45] There was little incentive among banks to strictly comply with prudential regulations since there seems to have been a consensus that connected lending was required.

41 Ibid. 42 Ibid. 43 Ibid.

44 Bank Indonesia, *Report for Financial Year of 1997/98* (Sept. 1998).

45 Japanese FY ends in March, F. GODEMENT, *THE DOWNSIZING OF ASIA* 45 (1999).

Table 6 Indonesia: Number of Banks Not in Compliance with Prudential Rules in 1995

	Total no.	CAR	LLL	LDR
State banks	7	0	2	1
Private banks	166	18	56	11
Local development banks	27	2	3	0
Foreign/joint venture banks	40	1	9	6
Total	240	21	70	18

(*Source:* J. Montgomery, *The Indonesian Financial System: Its Contribution to Economic Performance, and Key Policy Issues*, Working Paper of the International Monetary Fund, WP/97/45, April 1997.)

B. *Outbreak of the Crisis*

1. *Factors triggering the crisis in Indonesia*

The triggering factor of the financial crisis was Thailand's devaluation of the baht on 2 July 1997; however, there are a few background economic conditions that led to the devaluation. Japanese banks that had been rolling over short-term credit began to withdraw their assets towards the end of 1997.[46] Thai exports had contracted –1 per cent in 1996 from the previous 20 per cent growth. Indonesia export also slumped from 12 per cent in 1995 to 9 per cent in 1996. Equity investors were the first to start their

Table 7 Indonesia: Compliance with quantitative prudential regulations

	1996	1997	1998
Violation of reserve requirement (of 240 commerical)	72	111	120
Violation of LLL (of 240 commercial banks)	46	51	N/A.
CAR of commercial banks (required 4 per cent*1)	12.0	12.2	4.3
LDR of commercial banks	80.6	79.6	83.2
NOP of commercial banks	11.7	10.6	36.4

(*Source:* Bank Indonesia, *Report for Financial Year of 1997/98*, Sept 1998.)
*1: 8 per cent CAR will be required by end 2001.

[46] *See* above n 21 for contagion.

withdrawal after the Thai stock market peaked in February 1997, falling by more than 30 per cent by the year-end.

After the depreciation of the Thai baht on 2 July 1997, the search began for economies which had similar weaknesses. The herd instinct of investors led them to Indonesia. This herd instinct causes contagion[47] and makes panics self-fulfilling.

Indonesia's pegged currency was probably the first factor to contagion. External pressure made Indonesia lose its wage competitiveness, and export slowdown accompanied by rising current account deficit made the currency value seem overvalued.

The next weakness was the undercapitalised banks which had been well known in the market. Nonperforming loans were accumulating on a disclosed basis which led investors to believe that the real amount must be great. One state banks, Bank Summa, closed in 1992, had not yet been liquidated, leaving USD180 million debt to Bank Indonesia, and action against another state bank, Bank Pacific which is partly owned by Bank Indonesia, had not been decided.[48] The central bank straddled with troubled banks and large debts posed questions on its ability to act against more problem banks.

Connected lending was a widespread phenomenon in Indonesia. Suharto had been in power for 30 years; the Suharto family and his friends compelled inefficient credit decisions on banks.[49] Connected parties, who were usually investors in projects, were granted concessions and licenses enabling lucrative monopolies. (This also induced contagion since the economy was likely to be operating inefficiently.)

2. Response to the Crisis

a. *Initial response to the Thai crisis*

The crisis did not initially affect Indonesia after the Thai baht depreciation. The Indonesian rupiah started its decline in July 1997. Unable to maintain the rupiah trading band, it was abandoned on 14 August 1997. Bank runs occurred throughout August 1997 caused by loss of confidence in the banking sector by depositors. In hindsight, there was a moment of optimism after this initial downturn during the summer of 1997 in Indonesia. Then

[47] McDermott and Wessel, *Financial-Sector Weaknesses Are Rolling Asian Currencies*, Wall St. J., 6 Oct. 1997, at A1.

[48] The most widely known government action to assist projects conducted by the Suharto family which are economically unjustified is when the government ordered a consortium of Indonesian banks to offer US$690 million start-up loans to a controversial national car project led by Suharto's son.

[49] Box 1.4: Your money or your exchange rate?: Indonesia's monetary dilemma at end-1997. World Bank, East Asia: The Road to Recovery 13 (1998).

what made Indonesia susceptible to external pressures in October 1997? Indonesia did exhibit many potential economic and financial weaknesses; only this came into focus when investors realised that government action was not proactive and somewhat superficial. By October 1997 Indonesia turned to IMF for financial assistance resulting in a USD23 billion support package at the beginning of November 1997. At that time, the rupiah to dollar rate was approximately 3500 to 1 compared to 2450 to 1 in June before the financial crisis.

However, as interest rates were raised to stop capital flight, which rose as high as 75 per cent in October 1997, the market became illiquid causing difficulties for troubled banks to obtain cash in the interbank market. Also, as part of the October 1997 IMF programme, the government was required to close sixteen private banks; and although the government had announced guarantees for small depositors, depositors panicked and several private banks experienced crippling bank runs.

b. Loss of Market confidence

The rupiah depreciation did not halt throughout 1997, and market confidence towards Indonesian assets deteriorated. The loss of market confidence was the greatest problem that Indonesia faced and the most difficult to overcome. Financial intermediation terminated when interbank markets became highly illiquid. Bank Indonesia had to respond by extending a large amount of emergency credit to banks. Bank Indonesia provided 150 per cent of the base money in the final months of 1997 or five times the amount prior to the onset of the crisis.[50] Emergency liquidity continued to be extended, and by February 1998, it was double the amount of year-end 1997. Base money also expanded and together with the loss of the rupiah value, inflation was turning into hyperinflation.

Foreign capital ebbed rapidly. The net private capital inflow to the East Asia 5 which was USD97.1 billion in 1996 reversed more than USD100 billion to USD–11.9 billion in 1997.[51] This added to the credit crunch of financial institutions. The sheer size of capital outflow is a sign of herd instinct, which is the opposite phenomenon of what Alan Greenspan once commented as 'irrational exuberance', and this heightened the loss of confidence. Information asymmetry of the actual banking sector condition also played some part to exacerbate the problems.

[50] *See* above table 2 for changes in private capital inflow of East Asia 5.

[51] WORLD BANK, EAST ASIA: THE ROAD TO RECOVERY 27 (1998).

c. Transmission to the real economy

The contagion in Indonesia did not halt at the financial sector. The trade Indonesia had with other Asian economies were weakening. Intra-regional trade among East Asian countries amounted for almost 40 per cent of total exports in 1996. A total of 58 per cent of Indonesian exports were directed to East Asian countries in 1996,[52] of which 27 per cent was to Japan. This proportion is high in Asian standards as well.

Indonesia was also affected by the fall in the international oil prices with currency depreciation adding to the problem.

d. Political and social transitions

Indonesia was unfortunate that it faced its worst drought in 50 years during the financial crisis. The forest fires could not be extinguished because insufficient rainfall caused by the El Niño effect. This devastated rice production in 1997 causing a 4 per cent decline and riots. Unemployment rose causing social tension. Children stopped going to school in order to work. Poverty that Indonesia had been fighting for years, unfortunately, worsened from 21.9 million people under the poverty line in 1995 to 38.9 million people in 1998, an increase of 17 million.

Political transition also occurred in Indonesia. Political stability had been a hallmark of Indonesia since Suharto took power in 1967. However, the riots in May 1998 led to the resignation of Suharto. The political transition is still taking place with their fairest general election in four decades held in April 1999, nevertheless the political uncertainty has only added fuel to the lack of market confidence in Indonesia.

IV. ECONOMIC AND FINANCIAL RESTRUCTURING PROGRAM[53]

The Indonesian government requested the assistance of the IMF on 8 October 1997 as a result of its sharply declining rupiah against the US dollar. Since its first Letter of Intent (LOI) was published in 31 October 1997, Indonesia has published several LOIs and supplementary economic and financial policy documents. The IMF programs that were agreed upon

[52] This section mainly refers to the Letter of Intents and Supplementary Memorandum of Economic and Financial Policies which the Indonesia government have issued until May 1999 on the IMF website <http://www.imf.org/external/np/loi/mempub.htm>. All will be referred as 'LOI of Oct. 1997'.

[53] The changes in the fiscal balance and other items of the government budget are charted in 'Table 7. Sources of Changes in the Fiscal Balance', in T. Lane *et al.*, *IMF-Supported Programs in Indonesia, Korea and Thailand: A Preliminary Assessment* 58 (Jan. 1999) <http://www.imf.org/external/pubs/ft/op/opasia>.

by the three hardest hit countries (Indonesia, Republic of Korea, and Thailand) are unique from previous LOIs in that they include wide-ranging structural adjustments. Since the crisis was not caused from large current account deficits or government deficits, different remedies were taken from conventional treatment.

There have been many discussions on the validity of the IMF programmes, especially with regard to Indonesia, which faced serious bank runs following the first LOI. The structural reforms implemented are explored to consider whether the programs were adequate to stabilise the economy and to consider what reforms may be beneficial for the Indonesian economy.

It is worthwhile to note the fluctuation of the rupiah exchange rate since the beginning of the crisis. The rupiah underwent a turbulent period which necessitated the review and reinforcement of many aspects of the program. It also sent a strong message to the Indonesian government that it must be serious and proactive about reforming the economy to regain market confidence. Social and political tension also negatively affected the economy. This section discusses the macroeconomic policies, structural reforms and social safety net measures taken by Indonesia.

A. *Macroeconomic Policies*

1. Fiscal policy

The government's target for fiscal balance was reduced drastically from the original program due to the downturn in economic conditions in Indonesia. The program initially targeted for a balanced budget from a 0.3 per cent of GDP surplus in 1997/8, whereas the revised targets for 1997/8 and 1998/9

Table 8 Foreign exchange middle rates against rupiah at Bank Indonesia

	Jan	Feb	Mar	Apr	May	Jun
1997	–	–	–	–	–	2,450
1998	10,375	8,750	8,325	7,970	10,525	14,900
1999	8,950	8,730	8,685	8,260	8,105	–
	Jul	**Aug**	**Sep**	**Oct**	**Nov**	**Dec**
1997	2,599	3,035	3,275	3,670	3,648	4,650
1998	13,000	11,075	10,700	7,550	7,300	8,025
1999	–	–	–	–	–	–

(*Source:* Bank Indonesia, Statistics at <http://www.bi.go.id/intl/stats/T21301.rep>).

are –2.2 and –10.1 per cent of GDP, respectively.[54] The present problem of Indonesian fiscal position is underspending, especially for social development. Indonesia has been subject to corrupt practices at all levels of the government, and there is fear of public spending being used for private interests. Enhanced monitoring is being coordinated to prevent corruption and to encourage spending for social welfare.

Financing of Indonesia's deficit is mostly by foreign assistance. 84.2 per cent of the deficit is financed by foreign sources while revenue from privatisation will contribute to 15.8 per cent.[55] The balanced budget law dictates that deficit should be entirely financed externally, which lessens the crowding out of the private sector for credit.

a. Bank restructuring cost

Bank restructuring is the greatest expenditure item on the budget. The nonperforming loans are estimated at –17 per cent of GDP, implying a cost of up to 30 per cent of GDP to the government.[56] When it became clear that bank insolvency was worse than initially estimated, bank recapitalisation cost also increased.

The cost of financial sector restructuring includes compensation to the central bank for past support of failed banks, recapitalisation of banks, payment to small depositors, and operational costs for the bank restructuring agency (IBRA). The annual cost of Indonesian financial restructuring is estimated at around 2 per cent of GDP.[57]

b. Review of subsidies

Subsidies were a big part of economic life in Indonesia prior to the crisis. State enterprises were given subsidies to maintain their monopoly positions, costing the government dearly in terms of fiscal expenditure and economic inefficiency. Subsidies on essential imports[58] were eliminated in September 1998. Subsidies on fuel and electricity for large volume users were eliminated. However, some subsidies for basic commodities were maintained to protect lower income groups. To strike a balance between removing subsidies and protecting the poor, Indonesia is developing a price adjustment mechanism with a transparent criteria for regular and more automatic changes in prices of subsidised items in April 1999.

[54] T Lane *et al.*, Ibid. 59 (Jan. 1999) <http://www.imf.org/external/pubs/ft/op/opasia>.

[55] WORLD BANK, EAST ASIA: THE ROAD TO RECOVERY 49 (1998).

[56] Lane *et al.*, *IMF-Supported Programs in Indonesia, Korea and Thailand: A Preliminary Assessment* 58 (Jan 1999) <http://www.imf.org/external/pubs/ft/op/opasia>.

[57] Ibid.

[58] This includes sugar, wheat and wheat flour, corn, soybeans, soybeans meal, and fishmeal.

c. *Fiscal reform*

Following a review of expenditure, the government is reforming its tax system and decentralising its fiscal budget. Tax review is being conducted to strengthen tax collection and will take place by the end of October of 1999. As for fiscal decentralisation, a fiscal decentralisation legislation was approved by the Parliament in late April of 1999. This enables various regions to have greater autonomy and authority in all matters except defense, foreign policy, judicial reform, fiscal and monetary policy, and religious affairs.

2. *Monetary policy*

With a turbulent foreign exchange market, the prime objective of the Indonesian programme has been to keep a firm monetary policy to control inflation. In the foreign exchange market, the rupiah underwent periods of extreme downward pressure. This caused import prices to sore, inducing high inflation which had been kept to a single digit for the past decade prior to the crisis

a. *Money supply*

The program was initially targeted to limit the growth of the base money which eventually included net domestic assets of Bank Indonesia (NDA).[59]

b. *Interest rates*

To limit the growth of NDA, the interest rate of Bank Indonesia certificates (SBIs) were increased substantially. This was also intended to stabilise the capital flight from the rupiah occurring at an alarming level. Nominal interest rates on one-month SBIs were increased from 11.5 per cent to 30 per cent on 19 August 1997. The LOI of April 1998 indicates that the SBI rate rose from 22 to 45 per cent on 24 March 1998, accompanied by rise in commercial rates rise.[60] There is much debate on the interest rate hike the Asian countries took to restore the exchange rate. They had the negative effect of raising the burden on the debt laden corporate sector as well as increasing the nonperforming loans. Some have criticised the IMF for continuing to incorporate high interest rates into the structural adjustment

[59] Base money was the monetary target in the LOI of Oct. 1997, but in the LOI of Apr. 1998, it was shifted to NDA. This shift is due to a large growth of central bank emergency liquidity support provided to banks facing a severe credit crunch.

[60] Appendix I of LOI of Apr. 1998 <http://www.imf.org/external/np/loi/041098.htm>.

programmes implemented despite their failure to contain exchange rate movements.[61]

c. *Money market operations and liquidity support*

The problem that affected the implementation of the monetary policy was the bifurcation of the financial system. Despite the government guarantee for depositors and creditors, when sixteen insolvent banks were closed in December 1997, depositors shifted their deposits from state to foreign banks or fled the banks altogether. This led to concentration of liquidity in some banks while the other group of banks faced severe credit crunch.[62] Bank Indonesia (BI) provided liquidity to banks with funding difficulties to narrow the gap of interest premium. However, this liquidity support continued for a long period threatening the financial position of BI.

The liquidity support that BI provided was indiscriminate because it was difficult to determine whether banks were illiquid or insolvent. Base money grew by an alarming 126 per cent, well above the programme target of 10 per cent by March 1998. Also, banks on the brink of collapse received liquidity support and there was uncertainty whether the money would be repaid. Thus, in the LOI of April 1998, a clear criteria was introduced to the Bank Indonesia liquidity support facility where interest rates were set to discourage banks from resorting to BI liquidity too easily, but not too high as to push troubled illiquid banks into insolvency and limiting the gross credit facility by shifting the money supply target to NDA. The lender of last resort facility was explicitly established incorporating the conditions of a conventional lender of last resort facility.[63] In the course of bank restructuring, the repayment of BI liquidity support is incorporated as a term to receive recapitalisation.

d. *Monetary policy facilities*

To develop more effective monetary policy, various measures were introduced. In July 1998 a system where the interest rates of SBIs are determined

[61] Radelet and Sachs, *The East Asian Financial Crisis: Diagnosis, Remedies, Prospects*, Harvard Institute for International Development, at 36, 20 Apr 1998.

[62] The small number of banks which had sufficient credit traded among themselves at a relatively low rate of 15 per cent above the JIBOR (Jakarta interbank offer rate), while other banks could not obtain sufficient funds in the interbank market in spite of offering 75 per cent above the JIBOR. In LOI of Jan 1998. <http://www.imf.org/external/np/loi/mempub.htm>.

[63] The new liquidity support facility has the following features; interest rate are 150 per cent of JIBOR renewable monthly with increasing prudential sanctions, initial high penalty rates of interest on shortfall of reserve requirements to encourage banks to apply at early stage of difficulty, and flexibility to BI to determine the pace of imposition of sanctions after special on-site examination and reporting to management. Appendix I of LOI of Apr 1998.

by auction, rather than administratively, was introduced. This enabled open-market operations on a market basis rather than by the discretion of authorities which may not always be an effective rate. Further, the issuance of government bonds for bank recapitalisation on May 1999 became a useful benchmark for the domestic bond market, since a government bond market providing such benchmarks did not exist before. Previously, smaller enterprises in Indonesia were disadvantaged because they had no alternative to bank financing.

3. Foreign exchange policy

At the outset, the objective of the adjustment program was heavily focused on the stabilisation of the rupiah exchange rate. Unless the exchange rate was stabilised, with Indonesia's large private foreign debt and dependence on external financing, it was difficult to forecast the direction of the economy and set targets for the programme. As Table 8 indicates, the rupiah experienced an extended period of turbulence due to capital flight and political uncertainty. The monetary policy was kept tight to support the exchange rate. Intervention in the foreign exchange market also had to be controlled to avoid depletion of international reserves which occurred in Thailand and Korea.

The LOI of October 1997 used an exchange rate of Rp3,275 per US dollar. However, by the LOI of Jan 1998, the rupiah depreciated to Rp10,000 per US dollar, making previous projections invalid. Thus the program was revised at Rp10,000 level until the exchange rate stabilised. The essence of the exchange rate policy is that the Indonesian government no longer attempted to achieve certain target ranges, recognising that only market determined rates would be stable in the long term.[64] Although Indonesia did consider adopting a currency board to stabilise the exchange rate and restore confidence, concerns over its credibility and sustainability led to its rejection.

B. Structural Reform

Many have criticised the IMF programmes that were implemented for the countries affected by the Asian financial crisis.[65] Nevertheless, IMF defends its policy reasoning that the reforms were necessary since the structural rigidities of these economies were the cause of the crisis.[66] In any case, the

[64] In the LOI of Mar. 1999, the Indonesian government states that the exchange rate will remain market determined in the para 6 <http://www.imf.org/external/np/loi/ mempub.htm>.

[65] M. Feldstien, *Refocusing the IMF*, 77 Foreign Aff., No 2, at 27, Mar./Apr. 1998, which is the main critic of the structural reforms imposed on the Asian countries.

[66] S. Fischer, *In Defense of the IMF*, 77 Foreign Aff., No 3, at 103–6, July/Aug. 1998.

structural reforms that are taking place in Indonesia have become progressively comprehensive. Indonesians themselves are willing to transform their economy to health and return to growth again.[67]

The structural reforms cover banking, financial sector, and corporate sector. It is the first attempt by international financial institutions to reform the financial and corporate sector simultaneously opposed to the financial sector reform being reformed first.

1. BANKING AND FINANCIAL SECTOR REFORM

As explained in the previous section, Indonesia's financial sector suffered from serious nonperforming loans before the crisis broke out. The LOI of Oct 1997 reports nonperforming loans to be 8 per cent of total assets. However, the reality could be as high as 80 per cent considering only part of loans were classified, and capital and income may have been significantly overstated. This was enhanced by connected party lending and poor loan classification and loss provisions. Poor disclosure of bank performance also exacerbated the situation. The inability of the supervisory authorities to enforce prudential regulations against powerful parties allowed this to occur more readily. Financial and banking sector restructuring is taking place to address these issues and transform the Indonesian financial sector. Given the heavy reliance on bank financing, reform of the banking sector was probably necessary to regain robust economic growth whether or not the crisis occurred, although how and when might have been a choice for Indonesia.

a. Banking Law amendment

The new Banking Law was amended on 10 November 1998 (Banking Law), replacing the Banking Law of 1992.[68] The greatest changes the amendments brought were the establishment of the Indonesian Bank Restructuring Agency (IBRA) and permitting foreign ownership of financial institutions.

(i) Foreign ownership

Amendments to Article 26 of the Banking Law allow foreign individuals

[67] The political chaos which overthrew the former President Suharto is one sign of the Indonesians' will to change their corrupt system, and another is the initiative that Indonesians themselves made to implement structural reforms when IMF programs were being designed according to the US Executive Director of IMF, Karen Lissakers in a presentation made on 5 May 1999.

[68] Amendment to Law No 7 of 1992 on the Banking System, concerning Commercial Banking Law No 10 of 1998 (hereafter 1998 Banking Law).

and corporations to hold shares of commercial banks without limitation (*i.e.* up to 99 per cent ownership[69]) whereas the 1992 Banking Law limited foreign ownership to 49 per cent. Also, Article 26(2) of the Banking Law clarifies that shares can be obtained directly or through the stock exchange, permitting banks not listed on the stock exchange to have access to foreign investors.

(ii) Establishment of IBRA

Article 37A of the Banking Law was set in relation to the handling of troubled banks, promulgating the establishment of IBRA and its Asset Management Unit (AMU). IBRA was established in January 1998 to recover troubled assets. However, it did not have the legal authority to enforce asset recovery from debtors. The amendment strengthened its legal power as a temporary agency. Conditions to establish a bank restructuring agency are that banking sector difficulties endanger the national economy,[70] Bank Indonesia has judged that bank restructuring is necessary, and the government has consulted with the Parliament.[71] Banking Law Article 59A gives IBRA, which was established prior to the legislation of the Banking Law, the authority to be the bank restructuring agency.

IBRA has the authority to obtain all information on their businesses and explanations from banks put under restructuring and to examine the books of those banks.[72] The powers of IBRA are stipulated in Banking Law Article 37A(3). They include: take over of shareholders' rights in general meetings; acquire rights of directors and commissioners of a bank; review, terminate and amend a contract binding a bank; sell or transfer assets belonging to a bank or its directors or shareholders by private treaty or public offering; and to collect banks' debts by issuing enforcement letters which have the legal status of a court judgment.[73]

IBRA is accountable to the Ministry of Finance; however, this may not serve the Indonesians well[74] given the recent revelation that Rp904 billion (US$128 million) provided for bank restructuring is missing.[75] The

[69] Foreign parties can acquire a total of 100 per cent of shares on the stock exchange, but the maximum bank shares listed on the stock exchange is 99 per cent of total bank shares. Bank Indonesia, *The Publication of Banking Regulations as Guidelines for the Implementation of Law No 10 of 1998*, 14 May 1999.

[70] Endangering the national economy is when the crisis of public confidence affects all people in Indonesia according to Elucidation of 1998 Banking Law of Art. 37A paras (1) and (2).

[71] Art. 37A(1) 1998 Banking Law.

[72] Art. 37A(5) 1998 Banking Law.

[73] Elucidation of 1998 Banking Law of Art. 37A(3) letter i.

[74] Art 37A(7) 1998 Banking Law.

[75] On 6 Aug. 1999, reports were made that Indonesian Ministry of Justice opened an investigation into the disappearance of Rp550 billion from Bank Bali which was nationalised in July 1999. Bank Bali was acquired by Standard Chartered but made Standard Charter pay an extra Rp1000 billion to cover the gap. There are allegations against the ruling Golkar party and investigations are currently being carried out.

transparency of its reports may need to be made public to ensure accountability.

(iii) Bank secrecy

Bank secrecy in the 1992 Banking Law pertained to all information regarding the financial situation of their customers with exception to cases stipulated.[76] The 1998 Banking Law set out a definition clause in Article 1(28) stating that bank secrecy shall be provided for any information excluding depositors and their accounts. Thus disclosure of information on borrowers and other users of bank services can be made, and exception to depositor secrecy is made to assist the operation of Agency for State Receivership and Auction Affairs[77] and for tax authorities.[78]

(iv) Prudential regulations

Banking Law Article 29 states that banks must maintain their soundness according to prudential considerations of capital adequacy ratio, quality of assets, quality of management, liquidity, profitability, solvency. This covers the CAMEL criteria. The 1992 Banking Law did stipulate prudential considerations, but was not specific in the concerns to be taken into account.

Legal lending limits (LLL) are set out in Article 11. Bank Indonesia retains the authority to specify the limits but the significance is the additional Article 11(4A) which clearly prohibits banks from exceeding the LLL. Strict sanctions against non-compliance are provided in Articles 50 and 50A.

(v) Bank Licensing

A major shift has occurred in the regulator responsible for bank licensing from the Ministry of Finance to Bank Indonesia.[79] Bank Indonesia now has the authority to issue licenses and sets out the requirements and procedures to obtain a banking license as well as allowing opening of branch offices.[80] The requirements will be stipulated by Bank Indonesia in line with the prudential considerations set out in Article 29.

Deposit insurance is also stipulated in the Banking Law introducing the concept for the first time. Article 37B states that every bank must guarantee funds deposited with them to ensure that the funds are safe and the 'Agency for Guaranty of Deposits' is established as a legal entity.

(vi) Sanctions

The problem of Indonesia's banking system is the lack of enforcement. Thus sanctions promulgated in the 1998 Banking Law are pecuniary and can

[76] Art. 40(1) 1992 Banking Law. The cases of exception were Art. 41–4.
[77] Art. 41A 1998 Banking Law.
[78] Art. 41 1998 Banking Law.
[79] Art. 16(1) and (3) 1998 Banking Law.
[80] Art. 18, 19 and 20 1998 Banking Law.

entail imprisonment. If a commissioner, director, or an employee of a bank destroys, alters, hides or erases a record, report or account, or makes a false record, he may be imprisoned for five to fifteen years and fined between ten to 200 billion rupiah.[81] Also, shareholders who have intentionally ordered directors and employees to take measures that are not in compliance with the provisions of the Banking Law will be punished most harshly.[82]

b. Central Bank Law amendment

The Central Bank Law was enacted on 17 May 1999 strengthening the independence of Bank Indonesia (BI).[83] Some functions of BI were already been under review: the divestiture of its commercial banks since November 1997[84] and review of its lender of last resort facility. The divestiture was clarified in Article 64 and 77 with clear time limits.[85]

The Central Bank Law comprehensively stipulates the autonomy of BI to ensure their operations are based on the considerations stated in the preamble. The principle objective of BI is to achieve and maintain the stability of the rupiah value[86] with other subordinate objectives. Some of the objectives are to: prescribe and implement monetary policy, regulate and safeguard the smoothness of the payment system, and regulate and supervise banks. However, another prime objective many central banks state, soundness of the financial system, has not been included as one of the objectives of the Indonesian central bank.

(i) Autonomy and accountability

The principle independence from the government is stated in Article 4(2) that BI is an independent state institution free from any interference from the government and/or other parties except where prescribed in the Law. Further, Article 9 ensures non-interference in the implementation of its tasks, permitting to refuse and ignore any form of interference.

A key provision in relation to the independence of BI is Article 10(1)a which allows BI to set the inflation target itself. Many central banks with inflation targets usually agree on a contract with the government stating the target zone of inflation.[87] BI can set the target itself which may be more

[81] Art. 49 1998 Banking Law.

[82] Art. 50A 1998 Banking Law states that such contravention is subject to imprisonment of 7–15 years, and fines of Rp10–200 billions.

[83] Act of the Republic of Indonesia No 23 of 1999 concerning Bank Indonesia (hereafter Central Bank Law).

[84] LOI of Oct 1997 <http://www.imf.org/external/np/loi/mempub.htm>.

[85] BI must divestiture all its investments not in line with Article 64 of Central Bank Law by 23 Nov. 2000.

[86] Art. 7 of Central Bank Law.

[87] According to the Reserve Bank of New Zealand Act of 1998, a written contract, the Policy Targets Agreement, is exchanged between the Reserve Bank Governor and Treasurer,

flexible to the economic situation, but considering monetary policy is said to effect the economy in two years, BI needs to clarify the rationale of its target to remain accountable.

Whereas the former central bank law stipulated in Article 8 that BI will implement the policy determined by the government with assistance from a Monetary Policy Council chaired by the Minister of Finance, the 1999 Central Bank Law Article 38(1) prescribes the task to its Board of Governors.[88] Board members are required a high degree of qualifications to be nominated.[89] The Governor and Senior Deputy Governor are nominated and appointed by the President upon approval of the Parliament,[90] and the Deputy Governors are nominated by the Governor and appointed by the President upon approval of the Parliament.[91] The Governor, Senior Deputy Governor, Deputy Governors, and official of BI cannot be punished for any decision made in accordance with his tasks and authority as long as it was in good faith.[92] Board of Governors are prohibited from serving private enterprises or being a member of a political party.[93] Only if he violates the prohibitions[94] or evidence that he has committed a crime[95] can a Board of Governor member be dismissed from his office. This provides a great amount of freedom to Board members to conduct monetary policy in the interest of the principle objective, to maintain the stability of the currency, and not be concerned with political interference.

In return for this autonomy, BI is required to be accountable on its internal governance and transparency. BI must report annually to the House of Representatives an evaluation of its monetary policy of the previous year propose monetary policies for the following year.[96]

To enable a coherent economic and financial policy, the government must request the opinion and participation of BI in cabinet meetings discussing economic, banking and financial matters.[97]

Another aspect of the autonomy is the prohibition of BI to extend credit to the government.[98] BI cannot purchase government securities which will translate as credit to the government. This can limit monetary operations if the government bond market develops unless it is permitted to deal in the secondary market for government bonds.

publicly binding the central bank to an inflation target of 0 to 3 per cent. In Article 11 and12 of Bank of England Act of 1998, while the inflation target is set by the Chancellor of Treasury at 2.5 per cent, BOE has the operational freedom to achieve this. The ECB's prime objective is also price stability as stated in the Treaty of Amsterdam Article 105 and ESCB Statute Art. 2. The target is decided by the Governing Council of ECB which makes its more independent than its national central banks.

[88] Central Bank Law, above n 82, Art. 38(1). *See generally* ibid. Art. 1(1), defining the Board of Governors as management of BI.

[89] Ibid. Art. 40.

[90] Ibid. Art. 41(1).

[91] Ibid. Art. 41(2).

[92] Ibid. Art. 45.

[93] Ibid. Art. 47(1).

[94] Ibid.

[95] Ibid. Art. 48.

[96] Ibid. Art. 58(1) and (2).

[97] Ibid.

[98] Ibid.

(ii) Monetary instruments

Monetary instruments are stipulated but not limited to them which gives BI flexibility to develop future instruments to accommodate changes in the market environment.[99] Clear conditions are provided for the lender of last resort to avoid the excessive liquidity facilities extended to banks at the outset of the crisis.[100] This is in line with the criteria for lender of last resort stated in the LOI of April 1998.[101]

(iii) Foreign exchange rate policy and operations

BI is given the authority to determine the foreign exchange rate policy which is often vested to the Ministry of Finance.[102] The principle objective of BI is the maintenance of the rupiah value, the articles make it clear that this refers to both the internal and external value of the currency.

(iv) Bank supervision

The Central Bank Law states the authority of BI to grant and revoke bank licenses, implement bank supervision and impose sanctions[103] as promulgated in the 1998 Banking Law. Specific regulations on the criteria are to be promulgated by BI Regulation.[104]

Also, Article 34 stipulates that an independent supervisory authority will be established by 31 December 2002 as a legal entity with laws enacted for its establishment. This clause was incorporated despite the opposition within the Parliament to separate the supervisory power from BI.

C. Prudential and Supervisory Revision

The inadequacy of Indonesian prudential regulations are a result of the financial sector rapidly being integrated into the international financial market, although regulators were incapable of monitoring and enforcing necessary safeguards to cope with the development. Thus the Indonesian structural reform has largely incorporated prudential regulations and supervisory functions to ensure their compliance. The non-compliance of banks prior to the crisis was notorious, so the authorities' regulations include enforcement and penalties when non-compliance is discovered.

(i) Loan classification and loan loss provisions

It is quintessential that loan classification reflects the riskiness, and likely

99 Ibid. Art. 10(1)b.

100 Ibid. Art. 11. A maturity date of the credit facility is 90 days and necessitates a high quality and liquid collateral with a sufficient value.

101 LOI of Oct. 1997, above n 52.

102 Central Bank Law, above n 82, Art. 12 and 13.

103 Ibid. Art. 24.

104 Ibid. Art. 25(2).

and orderly repayment of loans to assess the true financial condition of a bank. Loose loan classification distorts the proportion of nonperforming loans, blurring the amount of recapitalisation as well.[105]

The loan classification of Indonesia was based on the delinquency of payments and provisions were determined after collateral had been taken into consideration. This delayed the realisation of bad loans and window dressed the amount. Hence, loan classification was revised to incorporate the international standard. The Decree of the Board of Managing Directors of Bank Indonesia (No 31/147) Concerning Earning Assets Quality of 12 November 1998 establishes loan classifications based on the business prospect and financial condition, including the borrower's cash flow and repayment capacity.[106] Accordingly, loans are classified into Pass, Special mention, Substandard, Doubtful and Loss.[107] In addition, a separate decree is stipulated for the provisioning of loan losses.[108]

(ii) Legal lending limit

The problem of legal lending limit is not that of regulation, but of enforcement. Article 11(4A) of the Banking Law now stipulates that sanctions will be imposed in case of a violation. The LLL to non-connected parties is 30 per cent of bank capital until the end of 2001.[109] The LLL to connected parties both to an individual and group is maximum 10 per cent of the bank capital and the total of lending to connected parties must not exceed 10 per cent of the bank capital.[110] If there is a LLL violation, the bank must submit an action plan to correct this.[111] Sanctions are set out for non-submission of report on LLL,[112] non-submission of action plan,[113] and non-compliance with the LLL itself.[114]

(iii) Capital adequacy ratio

Given the high insolvency rate of banks when the crisis erupted and the low capitalisation of banks in general, the Indonesian government has graduated the stages to reach an adequate capital adequacy ratio (CAR). Banks will be

105 The total of classified loans according to the reports of banks dropped to 7.2 per cent in Dec. 1997. This was due to the small coverage of loans (38.4 per cent of total classified loans).

106 Art. 3 of Decree of the Board of Managing Directors of Bank Indonesia Concerning Earning Assets Quality of 12 Nov. 1998.

107 Art. 4 in ibid.

108 Art. 2 of Decree of the Board of Managing Directors of Bank Indonesia (No 31/148) Concerning Allowance for Earning Assets Losses of 12 Nov. 1998

109 The maximum LLL for non-connected parties is phased to 25 per cent during 2002 and 20 per cent from 2003 according to Art. 7 of Decree of the Board of Managing Directors of Bank Indonesia (No 31/177) Concerning Legal Lending Limits of Commercial Banks of 31 Dec. 1998.

110 Art. 9 of Decree of the Board of Managing Directors of Bank Indonesia Concerning Legal Lending Limits of Commercial Banks of 31 Dec.1998.

111 Art. 15 and 16 in ibid.

112 Art. 18(1) and (2), and Art. 19 (2) in ibid.

113 Art. 18(3), and Art. 19 (2) in ibid.

114 Art. 19 (1) in ibid.

required to reach CAR of 4 per cent as a result of recapitalisation. They would then be required to reach 8 per cent by the end of 2001.[115]

The calculation of CAR was also amended so that only up to 1.25 per cent of risk-weighted assets equivalent of general provisions of earning assets can be computed into supplementary capital (Tier II).[116] The limitation of provisions which may include amounts reflecting lower valuation for assets is in line with the 1988 Basle Accord[117] due to the likely provisioning from loan losses.

(iv) Supervision

Supervision is the sole responsibility of BI, meaning that BI is the sole enforcing institution against prudential violations. Thus it is essential that BI has clear coordination, internally and externally, to detect any deterioration of banks' financial condition.

Off-site monitoring has been enhanced by liquidity monitoring. Indonesia has enacted a decree concerning liquidity monitoring.[118] This will enable BI to obtain information on the liquidity position of banks for the upcoming three months.[119] As for foreign exchange, banks are now obliged to report their foreign exchange exposure to the Bank Supervision Department of BI. Monitoring foreign exchange has also been promoted by broader coverage of data collection, improved transparency, and better assessment of short-term exposure of corporate and banking sectors. In this relation, Indonesia has enacted the Foreign Exchange Flow and Exchange Rate System Law.[120] This law allows BI to collect information on foreign exchange transactions.[121]

On-site supervision is strengthened by risk based appraisal based on international standards. IMF is training supervisors both in BI and IBRA.

[115] Art. 9(2)g of Joint Decree of the Ministry of Finance (No 53 of 1999) and Governors of Bank Indonesia (No 31/12) Concerning Implementation of the Commercial Bank Recapitalisation Program of 8 Feb. 1999.

[116] Art. 3(2B) of Decree Amending Decree of the Board of Managing Directors of Bank Indonesia (No 31/146) Concerning Changing Bank Capital Adequacy Requirement of 29 May 1993 (No 26/20), of 12 Nov. 1998.

[117] Basle Committee on Banking Supervision, *International Convergence of Capital Measurement and Capital Standard (Basle Accord)*, July 1988, updated to Apr. 1997, para 18–21.

[118] Decree of the Board of Managing Directors of Bank Indonesia (No 31/180) Concerning Liquidity Monitoring of Commercial Banks of 31 Dec. 1998.

[119] Art. 1b of Decree Concerning Liquidity Monitoring of Commercial Banks of 31 Dec. 1998.

[120] OFFICIAL INDONESIAN NAME OF ACT IN LARGE AND SMALL CAPS [ACT OF THE REPUBLIC OF INDONESIA NO 24 OF 1999 CONCERNING THE FOREIGN EXCHANGE FLOW AND EXCHANGE RATE SYSTEM] (Indon.) <http://www.bi.go.id/intl/press/act2499.pdf> [hereinafter FOREIGN EXCHANGE FLOW AND EXCHANGE RATE SYSTEM LAW].

[121] Ibid. Art. 3.

(v) Information disclosure
BI has amended the Decree Concerning the Annual Financial Statement and Published Financial Statement of Commercial Bank of 9 June 1998. Banks are now required to publish quarterly financial statements including information on CAR and asset quality.[122]

d. Financial sector reform and IBRA

(i) Establishment of IBRA
In an effort to resolve the worsening bank problems, IBRA was established on 27 January 1998. It was recognised as the special agency in the Commercial Banking Law of 1998 where Article 37A identifies the establishment of a special agency to resolve troubled banks and enables IBRA to transfer assets from them. A presidential decree has been issued to state the specifics of it[123] including its five-year term.

The main task of IBRA is to take over claims deriving from BI emergency support and the cost of guaranteeing deposits, and undertake close surveillance, monitoring and assessment of weak banks to resolve banking problems. By separating loss loans, banks can continue operation on a sound basis.

The cost of bank restructuring and IBRA are financed by the issuance of bank restructuring bonds. Total restructuring is estimated to be 15 per cent of GDP including the operating cost and interest payment of bonds. A total of Rp322 trillion of bonds have been issued, of which indexed bonds of Rp218 trillion are bought by BI, Rp80 trillion used for recapitalisation of four BTO banks, Rp1 trillion for twelve regional development banks, and Rp22 trillion for the government's contribution to recapitalise eight private banks. For the eight private banks taken over in 1999, an additional bond issue of Rp14 trillion will be needed. It is expected that Rp248 trillion of bonds will be issued to recapitalise state banks. The bonds are mainly bought by BI and banks, and are expected to be traded on a secondary market in the future.

The AMU was established in IBRA to maximise the recovery of assets. AMU has been reorganised in the Asset Management for Investments (AMI) and Asset Management for Credits (AMC) where AMC takes over the operations conducted by AMU and AMI recovers shareholder assets.

Loan recovery efforts are being strengthened. The government has

[122] Art. 5(2) and 1 of Decree Amending Decree of the Board of Managing Directors of Bank Indonesia (No 31/179) Concerning Amendments to Decree of Annual Financial Statement and the Published Financial Statement of Commercial Bank of 9 June 1998 (No 31/40), of 31 Dec. 1998.

[123] Regulation of Government of the Republic of Indonesia Indonesian No 17 Year 1999 regarding Indonesian Bank Restructuring Agency of 27 Feb. 1999.

instructed not only AMU but also state banks to accelerate their asset recovery. Appropriate legal actions will be taken against recalcitrant borrowers. Delinquent borrowers are being invited to participate in debt negotiations. Non-cooperative borrowers are being published.

(ii) Bank restructuring

The process of bank restructuring began on 1 November 1997, when sixteen insolvent banks were closed and owners lost their shares. The operation of the sixteen banks was terminated, banking licence revoked and a caretaker team sent to takeover management. Since then, the focus of the programme has been to categorise banks into viable and non-viable banks, taking appropriate measures for each. Banks with low capital are prone to make riskier investment. A cycle of moral hazard occurs because with nothing to lose, these undercapitalised banks will place bets on risky loans with larger returns. This process of categorisation identifies which banks need to be isolated from the banking system and which need to be preserved to maintain financial intermediation. Categorisation needs to be taken on a uniform and transparent basis. Appropriate loan classification is therefore essential to enable this.

Not only private but state and regional development banks are all subject to review of their financial condition and required to propose a rehabilitation plan. Private banks must have a special portfolio review conducted by an international accounting firm to be categorised. Large state banks are being merged and privatised.

Fifty-four banks including state banks were taken over by IBRA on 14 February 1998, receiving greater liquidity support than their capital base from BI (these banks are called BTO banks). All terms and conditions for restructuring of private, state and BTO banks are examined.

(iii) Private banks

The restructuring plan for private banks was announced on 29 September 1998 by the Governor of BI. All banks are subject to a due diligence report and external audit which is the basis of categorisation. The criteria of categorisation are in Table 9.

As a result of immediate action, some banks have been moved up to a higher status. All 'A' banks are subject to recapitalisation. In early March 1999, there were 73 A-banks (5 per cent of bank deposits), 38 B-banks (12 per cent of bank deposits) of which 9 are eligible for recapitalisation and 7 will be taken over by IBRA, and 21 B-banks and all C-banks which will be closed effective 13 March 1999.

The primary condition of eligibility to recapitalisation is repayment of liquidity support from BI.

The business plan of A-banks will be subject to comprehensive review in

Table 9 Bank categorisation for bank restructuring of Indonesia

Category	Criteria	Immediate action	Condition for survival	For re-capitalisation
A bank	CAR of at least 4%	Provide business plan.	If business plan approved: re-capitalisation conducted.	
B bank	CAR less than 4% but better than –25%	Provide business plan.	If status is improved: moved to A banks status. If remain in B category: – business plan accepted: qualify for re-capitalisation. – business plan fail to be accepted: will be treated as C bank.	– If business plan approved and compliance with criteria: recapitalised. – If non-complicance and business plan not approved: closure.
C bank	CAR worse than –25%	One month to raise status	If not improved, closure.	Transfer of deposits to designated bank.
D bank	C banks but offering interest above limit	BI monitor to mitigate any additional moral hazardous acts.	Subject to same conditions as C banks.	

April 1999, but do not need to participate in the recapitalisation programme. If additional capital is injected, a fit and proper test of owners and management, and regular audits every six months to ensure compliance with prudential regulations will be conducted.

In addition to the requirements and conditions imposed on A-banks, the business plan of B-banks will consist of plans to inject capital to a certain threshold from unborrowed sources. They will also need to have an investment contract with the government. B-banks need to resolve connected lending to LLL to be approved for recapitalisation.

The seven B-banks which have been taken over by IBRA (BTO banks) remained open due to their large deposit base of 2.5 per cent. The ownership rights were effectively revoked and management replaced by IBRA. As mentioned below, BTO banks are subject to amending their connected lending obligations with IBRA.

The banks closed amounted to 5 per cent of bank deposits. All deposits were fully protected and transferred to designated banks. The owners must settle connected lending with IBRA as well.

(iv) State banks

All seven state banks are subject to restructuring and privatisation. All are thought to be insolvent but since they hold a major part of the banking sector, 40 per cent of total deposits, the government has opted for downsizing and reform. Capitalisation of Bank Mandiri and recapitalisation of other banks will follow operational restructuring to downsize staff, branches, functions, and intensify asset collection. Deadlines have been set to sequence and accelerate the process while ensuring compliance with the agreements. Efforts against large delinquent borrowers have also intensified. It is important that bad loans are isolated from good loans so that the operations can be conducted on a clear balance sheet. Only after that should capital be injected into the state banks.

Four state banks (Bapindo, Bumi Daya, BDN and EXIM Bank) are to be merged into the newly created Bank Mandiri. Bank Mandiri will comprise of 30 per cent of bank deposits. The portfolio review of each bank was carried out in March 1999. Loss loans were transferred to AMU, and non-loss and performing corporate loans were sold to IBRA at net book value. Non-loss loans are anticipated to be collected by Bank Mandiri under a servicing contract with AMU. Performing loans were transferred to Bank Mandiri in May 1999. Bank Mandiri and the four component banks are planning to merge in July 1999 after redundant staff and branches are separated.

Other state banks are subjecting their largest delinquent borrowers to scrutiny for loan recovery or bankruptcy filing. They have appointed international banks to assist in preparing a business plan. Loss loans will be transferred to AMU and bankruptcy filings are already taking place.

(v) BTO banks

Ten private banks were frozen in April 1998 and subsequently transferred to AMU in August 1998. The license of banks not listed were revoked and liquidated. Those that were publicly traded requested for delisting and shareholder meetings were held to initiate liquidation.

Four large private banks taken over by IBRA in April 1998 (Bank Central Asia, Danamon, Tiara Asia, and PDFCI) are being restructured. Their restructuring plans have been put together with the assistance of international banks and financial advisers in March 1999.

Bank Central Asia (BCA) and Bank Danamon are to be nationalised and recapitalised to be bridge banks for closed banks. Owners of Bank Tiara and PDFCI are given an opportunity to restructure or be merged with Bank Danamon. It is envisaged that PDFIC will be delisted and made operational into an export credit agency owned by the state. BCA will merge with one BTO bank and an initial public offering will be held in 1999. Bank Danamon is being merged with a total of eight BTO banks which IBRA will divest its majority interest in 2000.

(vi) Bank recapitalisation

The amount of recapitalisation into each bank is the sum of negative net worth plus 4 per cent of risk weighted assets for insolvent banks, and difference between 4 per cent of risk weighted assets and actual ratio for undercapitalised banks. In sum, the amount necessary to achieve 4 per cent CAR will be injected into each bank. All capital infusion should be in tier 1 capital and paid in cash by the owners and with bonds by authorities.

The government will supply 4 : 1 to every capital the owner puts in until the bank capital reaches 4 per cent risk weighted assets. The government will take stake in the form of common stock but have a limited role in strategic decision making, not being involved in day-to-day business. After one year, the owners of the banks will have the option to buy back the shares.

e. Deposit Insurance

A blanket guarantee on all depositors and creditors excluding those related to bank owners was introduced on 27 January 1998. This guarantee was for a minimum two-year period with a six-month notification of termination. The scheme envisaged will be an explicit guarantee, aimed to minimise moral hazard and protect deposits up to a specified amount. However, with the banking system still in the midst of restructuring and CAR not amounting to 8 per cent for most financial institutions, it may be premature to have the blanket guarantee removed at this stage and it may cause a reverse effect.

2. Corporate sector reform

The corporate sector is debt burdened as a result of cheap foreign exchange borrowing that became available as a result of financial liberalisation. However, even if these debts were not to be recovered, Indonesia had neither a debt workout mechanism nor an adequate bankruptcy law to cope with the situation. As a result of debt negotiations between international creditors and debtors with the intermediation of the Indonesian government, IMF, World Bank and Asian Development Bank, they have been able to reach an interim agreement on debt workouts.

Insolvency procedures are also taking place as a result of the bankruptcy law amendment and commercial court promulgation. Here the progress in these fields are investigated.

a. Corporate debt reform: INDRA

On 26 February 1998, the first meeting between the Steering Committee for Foreign Bank Creditors and Contact Group of Debtors and Private External Debt Team (PED) was held. There, the four principles of negotiation was established: participation in scheme is voluntary with precise terms of any restructuring to be worked out between creditors and debtors, commercial risk will remain with creditors, maximum potential cost to the government will be capped at a manageable level, government support will only be provided in return for restructuring of obligations on specified minimum terms, and negotiations between creditors and debtors should begin as soon as possible. Accordingly, on 2 July 1998, Indonesian Debt Restructuring Agency (INDRA) was established by the Presidential Decree Concerning Establishment of INDRA.

The Frankfurt Initiative was agreed in June 1998 on corporate debt with foreign banks. This agreement allowed terms to be consistent with the external payment capacity of Indonesia and allowed much needed cash flow for domestic corporations. On 9 September 1998, the Jakarta Initiative was announced. It complemented the new Bankruptcy Law and INDRA, establishing principles to guide and streamline out-of-court corporate restructuring. Interim financing during workouts will be maintained to preserve viable corporations, and adequate information by debtor corporations necessary for creditors to evaluate business plans will be made available. Jakarta Initiative is currently handling US$17.5 billion of foreign currency debt and Rp8 trillion of domestic debt.

b. Insolvency law reform

The overhaul of the bankruptcy system and establishment of a special commercial court for fair, transparent, and expeditious resolution of commercial disputes is being carried out. The new Bankruptcy Law was ratified on July 1998 and the Special Commercial Court was established on August 1998. The Bankruptcy Law allows qualified private sector professionals to act as receivers and administrators. Procedural rules to ensure certainty and transparency in proceedings are being established to prevent unjustifiable delay of adjudication and a number of substantive rules are updated for greater protection against insider and fraudulent transactions and limitation on the ability of secured creditors to foreclose collateral during proceedings with requirement of adequate compensation and protection.

The Special Commercial Court has been established with jurisdiction in bankruptcy proceeding and general commercial disputes by a government regulation in April 1998. Judges have been specially trained to ensure rules of summary proceeding are strictly applied and render written decisions as legal basis for ruling. Bankruptcy filing against debtors who are non-cooperative is being initiated by state banks.

c. Accounting reform

Accounting has been raised to international standard by improving the loan classification from delinquency of the loan to the risk and orderly repayment of the borrower. Also, provisioning has been clarified to levels that reflect the level of riskiness involved. This will prohibit any cosmetic accounting of nonperforming loans.

d. Corporate governance

Corporate governance in Indonesia has been poor with board members being typically those who are well connected. The well connected have had an untouchable status in Indonesia allowing monopolistic and fraudulent practices to be common. Ownership has been concentrated, with the state holding a majority interest of the main industries in the form of state enterprises. Monitoring by shareholders have been weak as in many other East Asian economies.

To improve corporate governance, the Indonesian government is divesting its majority stakes in most of its state enterprises and transforming them to be commercially viable. This will create a broader investor base and encourage competition in the market.

The relaxation of limitation on foreign investment will also exert pressure on corporations to reform. The limitation of foreign investment in corporations listed on the stock market was banned on September 1997. This will support the effort to make corporations efficient and competitive.

C. Social Safety Net

The severity of the financial crisis has most affected the poor. Not only do they suffer through the effects of the financial crisis, but also the worst drought in half a century and forest fires that could not be extinguished because of the El ñino effect. The poor are the most vulnerable to shocks and the poverty level in Indonesia has risen. While an aggregate decline of 12 per cent of GDP is estimated for 1998, the increase of poor is estimated to drop from 11 per cent in 1996 to 14 per cent in 1999.[124] Efforts are being taken by the government and international financial institutions to assist those who face food shortage and unemployment.

1. FOOD SECURITY

As the rice production dropped in 1997/8 as a result of the drought, food supply became a serious concern for all, causing riots throughout the country. BULOG is a state enterprise for food distribution and holds a monopoly over essential foods.[125] The dismantling and privatisation of BULOG was scheduled as parts of the deregulation scheme, but the plan has been reviewed to enable sufficient food and energy supply[126] to the poorer households at a subsidised price. Food subsidies were in fact increased to secure food for the poor. The government allocated a substantial amount of budgetary resources to finance this.

Rice being the staple food of Indonesia and most severely affected by the drought, BULOG increased its import of rice to 3.1 million tons for 1998/9 from 2.85 million in the previous period. The rice programme which makes a monthly 10kg delivery of highly subsidised rice to poor households is also being carried out. The distribution of food supplies has also been damaged from social disturbance. Some riots attacked the warehouses and trucks of traders. Thus, physical protection and monitoring was provided to encourage traders to continue business. Importation of food was also freed to traders.

The UN has also set up a World Food Programme in Indonesia which is a food-for-work programme to drought affected regions. The Indonesian government has also included a supplementary feeding programme for children and pregnant woman into this programme.

The present problem is to prevent social safety measures currently implemented from falling into corrupt hands. Monitoring arrangements are being established with the World Bank and the Asian Development Bank to assist the process. To reform the food distribution system, the government has recently agreed with the World Bank on policy initiatives which include the

[124] WORLD BANK, EAST ASIA: THE ROAD TO RECOVERY 84 (1998)

[125] BULOG holds a monopoly of supplies such as rice, soybeans, sugar, wheat, flour, corn, soybean meal, and fishmeal which the government was subsidising to maintain its market advantage.

[126] Those which the prices were frozen are kerosene, gasoline, diesel, electricity, and essential medicines.

elimination of exchange rate subsidies for rice, public procurement floor price policy to keep rice price in line with world price levels, and unhindered importation of rice by the private sector.

2. Job creation

The unemployment in the urban area is more serious than the rural areas where people are engaged in agriculture. Urbanisation has been accelerated by the industrialisation of the Indonesian economy during periods of high growth, but when manufacturing halted, the uneducated were most affected. The result has been increased activities in the informal economy.

Fiscal measures are being taken for job creation. The Padata Karya Programs to raise benefits to poor are being redesigned to increase labour sharing, better targeting activities, stricter control on selection of workers, and special initiative to address unemployment in women.

3. Education

When poverty worsens, the education of children is no longer a priority of the household. Children are currently being pulled out of school to work as labourers.[127] In an effort to keep children in school, the government has implemented various fiscal measures. Block grant programmes are expanded, school lunch program is strengthened, and scholarship for poor students is being increased.

V. CONCLUDING REMARKS

Those that have been most severely affected by the financial crisis in Indonesia are clearly the poor who have no means to protect themselves against external shocks. It is essential that these issues are addressed, but simultaneously, Indonesia needs to reform the structural rigidities that have been the source of great social, economic, and political disruptions. This crisis has proven that capital mobility enables easy capital flight and advanced information technology strengthens the tide of herd instinct. Thus, it is necessary to adopt a regulatory framework that ensures the soundness and stability of the financial system in volatile market situations.

Although some blame the damage inflicted on Indonesia 'hot money' seeking higher profit opportunities, the lack of social safety nets enhanced the vulnerability of Indonesia. Establishment of such mechanisms would enable the economy to return to a sustainable growth path. Also, public

[127] Box 5.3 of World Bank, East Asia: The Road to Recovery, 1998, 83.

confidence will not be restored unless these have been removed, since the financial system will be subject to scrutiny of international investors who are now more aware of the problems which exist in Indonesia.

From the examination of events, we are able to see that it is necessary to diversify the economy in many aspects. The concentration of economic power in the hands of few well connected parties is economically inefficient. Subsidies to enterprises are being eliminated, monopolies abolished and cartels prohibited. Compliance with the legal lending limit is mandatory for all banks that receive financial assistance. Capital markets are being developed to diversify financing. State enterprises are being privatised to become commercially viable and to enhance competition.

Safety nets need to be placed with adequate enforcement mechanisms ensure compliance. Corruptive transactions are being criminally prosecuted and anti-fraud laws are strengthened. Prudential regulations are being reviewed so that banks are sufficiently capitalised and have a sound operational basis. Loan classification and loan loss provisioning have been reformed, and capital adequacy ratio has been brought in line with international standards applying risk weighted assets. Non-compliance with prudential regulations can result in both pecuniary sanctions and imprisonment. The bankruptcy law has been amended with the new Special Commercial Court set up to deal with commercial disputes. Supervision is being strengthened with training of examiners carried out and the establishment of a financial regulator is envisaged. Deposit insurance will be established replacing the blanket guarantee that the government placed in January 1998.

The current issue is to isolate the problem loans to terminate risky investments and create an environment which generates confidence in the economy. The greatest endeavour is being made in bank restructuring. State banks and private banks are both subject to scrutiny and are being restructured and recapitalised, merged, or closed. Disclosure is being encouraged to correct information asymmetry which led banks and investors to make bad investment judgments. Bad loans are being transferred to the AMU of IBRA and asset recovery effort strengthened to make a greater contribution to the budget deficit borne by the restructuring. Corporate debt restructuring is also taking place through the Jakarta Initiative framework where INDRA provides guarantees for bank debt to be rolled over.

The events in East Asia have prompted the question of whether there is a greater role for the Asian Development Bank in the region. ADB is involved in many aspects of the Indonesian reform, but has not taken a leading role. It has recently promoted its new slogan to fight poverty in the region which needs to be addressed as the Indonesian crisis is presented to us. A specific problem which could be addressed is prevention of systemic elements which could lead to worsening poverty as the financial crisis has exhibited. Surveillance and early warning is a function which should be considered.

The international environment is constantly evolving and once an economy has opened its doors to international investors, path dependency makes it difficult to reverse the wave of capital flows. Thus it is necessary to adopt a system which identifies associated risks. Indonesia liberalised its economy during the 1980s and 1990s, but did not establish an adequate structure to evaluate and avoid the risks. An economy is evolutionary and there is no one regulatory model which perpetually fits. Indonesia's experience has emphasised the importance of constant legal and structural enhancement.

Chapter 8

Korea's Search for a Viable Social Safety Net: Pension Reform and the Financial Market

Sungchul Shin[1]

I INTRODUCTION

Starting from the collapse of the Thai Baht in July 1997, financial crises swept through most Asian countries including Korea. Great depression and the massive impact of this financial crisis[2] consequently caused a high level of unemployment and threatened the fragile foundation of social protection.[3] For example, the large Korean conglomerates, commonly known as *Chaebol*[4], fostered a life-long employment culture, which in turn was

[1] I am greatly indebted to Professor Joseph Norton for providing me with essential viewpoints and significance of this issue and also to Ms Ruth Lane for her numerous comments and support.

[2] For a social impact, see Pak Po-Hi, *Responding to the Economic Crisis in the Republic of Korea* (A working paper prepared for the United Nations Development Programme, May 1988), at 7 <http://www.undp.org/rbap/program/ROK.html> [hereinafter PAK].

[3] *See* ILO, *The Social Impact of the Asian Financial Crisis*, available at <http://www.ilo.org/public/english/60empfor/cdart/bankok/index.htm>. *See also*, Tamar Manuelyan Atince and Michael Walton, *World Bank*, Resp*onding to the Global Financial Crisis; Social Consequences of the East Asian Financial Crisis* (last modified Sept. 1998) <http://www.worldbank.org/poverty/eacrisis/library/ socconsq/>.

[4] There are two different Acts governing Chaebol. The one is the Monopoly Regulation and Fair Trade Act, to control a concentration of economic power, and another is the Banking Act, to prohibit industrial capital from entering into a financial capital by owning a bank. Under Monopoly Regulation and Fair Trade Act, a conglomerate, *Chaebol,* is defined as a 'large interlinked business group' based on the size of assets. *See* Monopoly Regulation and Fair Trade Act ss 2(2), 9 and Presidential Decree on Monopoly Regulation and Fair Trade Act s 9,17. And according to the Banking Act, the interlinked business groups, any group with an aggregate volume of assets that exceeds 250 billion Korean won is classified as *Chaebol. See* Banking Act ss 30(2), Regulations Concerning the Supervision of Banking Institutions s 32. *See also*, Seung Hwa Chang, *A Probabilistic Approach to Multi-market Mergers: Proposed Merger Policy Against Economic Concentration Under the Korean Antitrust Act and Section 7 of the* US *Clayton Act*, 32 CLMJTL 43, at 48 II.A. *Chaebol* is very similar to the Japanese word *Zaibatsu* or *Keiretsu*. There are, however, several differences between *Chaebol* and *Zaibatsu*. '(i) *Chaebol* management are still family-centered, while *Zaibatsu* have moved to professional corporate leadership; (ii) *Chaebol* have not had unrestricted access to credit, because, unlike

viewed by the government and Korean society as a primary social protection shield for employees. In effect, over a four-decade period, the *Chaebols* effectively became a fundamental social institution for ensuring long-term employment of *Chaebol* employees and employees of a network of medium and smaller sizes of enterprises which dealt with the *Chaebol*. However, with the recent crisis, *Chaebols* have been unable to provide this 'social commitment' and economic necessities compelled them to unilaterally lay off and cut compensation and benefit schemes for employees.[5] The unfortunate result has been exposure of great numbers of workers to economic and social instability. As a result, it is anticipated that the middle class will shrink from the pre-crisis 70 per cent to 40–50 per cent of the population over the next several years[6], and that the impressive trends in poverty reduction achieved over the past twenty years may be reversed[7].

The financial crisis apparently agitated the social safety net concerns. Unfortunately it was shown that the recent financial crisis harshly affected the safety network through the existence of few social cushion devices. The social safety net needs to uphold social stability, and to protect social members from being damaged by economic insecurity and harmful impacts. The most significant role of a social safety net is to systemically provide stable economic security when threatened, and a major program in the social safety network is a pension scheme.

This chapter will examine that pension system in Korea. In doing so, we must first recognise how the pension scheme fits into the social dimension and the role of a pension scheme in association with the financial market. Section II of this chapter will look at what is meaningful pension reform in connection with financial reform. Section III will articulate the current regulatory framework of the National Pension scheme in Korea. As a part of the pension reform and to mitigate the social impact of from the financial crisis, a series of regulations have been revised, which entail some issues to be discussed in Section IV. The recent revision, neverthe-

the *Zaibatsu*, which have been organised under the controlling power of the banks, individual *Chaebol* have been prevented from acquiring controlling shares in privatised banks by the banking law; and (iii) *Chaebols* tend to form their own subsidiary companies to provide components of their major exports, rather than use outside contractors, as is common in Japan.'

[5] *See* PAK, above n 2. Discharge from employment was supposed to be decided by agreement between management and the labor union. But the agreement of the tripartite Labour–Employment–Government Committee was inactive at the financial crisis. Overall public opinion during the crisis turned against the radical labor force, urging them to undergo a nationwide hardship all together. *See* ibid. n 14.

[6] Ibid. at 12.

[7] *See* ILO press releases (ILO/98/15), *ILO calls for new policy responses to the crisis in Asia* (15 Apr. 1998). <http://www.ilo.org/public/english/235press/pr/1998/15.htm> (visited on 3 Nov. 1999)

less, did not address such crucial issues as the clarification of rights and liabilities between trustees and pensioners. Therefore Section V will offer suggestions for establishing the rule of law in pension management. Application of fundamentalgoals and innovative parameters will eventually move forwards, not entirely but in part, to privatising the public pension scheme. Section VI will explore privatisation issues, and briefly glance at Chile's experience in order to find an actual illustration that can be adopted in the reform process.

II. SOCIAL SAFETY NET AND PENSIONS

A. *Terminology*

It appears difficult to find the origin or history of the term, 'social safety net', while the term 'social security' has established a solid background and has been the subject of many studies. At first sight, both are broad enough to be regarded as twins, which makes it useless to try to single out differences. They both have in common the fundamental potential to keep the whole society sustainable during economic downturn, financial shock, or major risks. Social security is defined as 'programs providing cash payments to those whose income from earnings has ceased or diminished'.[8] Social security system has been developed to alleviate poverty and protect citizenry from conditions such as unemployment, old age or sickness[9], since Bismarck introduced first the social insurance system in the early nineteenth century.[10]

Introducing insurance to social security[11] was justified because of its broad wealth pooling mechanism that can be readily utilised within overall social security systems.[12] Sufficient funding via the insurance mechanism was considered to be an appropriate starting point to initiate socioeconomic stability. Framers believed it was through economic security that was the most effective way to achieve the goal of social security

[8] See ROBERT J. MYERS, SOCIAL SECURITY 6 (4th edn. 1993) [hereinafter MYERS].

[9] *See generally,* ibid. at 5–20; RICHARD A. MUSGRAVE, SOCIAL SECURITY; PERSPECTIVES FOR REFORM 56–90 (Joseph A. Pechman *et al* eds, 1968) [hereinafter MUSGRAVE].

[10] *See* Ruth Ben, *Social Security in the Year 2000: Potentialities and Problems*, 16 COMP. LAB. L.J. 139, 141 n 3; J. DOUGLAS BROWN, THE PRINCETON SYMPOSIUM ON THE AMERICAN SYSTEM OF SOCIAL INSURANCE: ITS PHILOSOPHY, IMPACT, AND FUTURE DEVELOPMENT 23 (1967).

[11] *See* MUSGRAVE, above n 9, at 24–30. As a rationale of a social insurance concept, he stressed first the humanitarian objective demands that no one should suffer economic distress, and accordingly calls for the assurance of minimum income. Secondly he referred to the egalitarian objective which demands that the coefficient of inequality should not exceed a certain level, and calls for general measures of wealth redistribution. Lastly he emphasised these two objectives should be properly balanced between two views.

[12] *See* MYERS, above n 8 at 12.

or safety net. In other words, society is the most vulnerable when economic instability prevails, which has been shown throughout the financial crises of the last decades.

This perception is also reflected in the 'social safety net'. Social safety net is understood as the term 'encompassing various transfer programs designed to play both a redistributive and risk reduction role in poverty reduction'.[13] The most distinguishing difference from social security is that the social safety net involves a less systemically institutionalised network than social security, which is generally inscribed into the system by its substantial enactment. Therefore social safety net implies not only cash arrangements but also provides transfer mechanisms of various resources such as human capital, natural resources etc.[14] In this chapter, because the economic and financial aspects of the pension system to be discussed overlap with similar aspects of the social safety net and social security, there is no need to differentiate between these terms.

B. Social Safety Net and the Role of Pensions

In Korea, the social safety net is composed of three major elements[15]: Social Insurance (national pension insurance, health insurance[16], worker's compensation insurance, and unemployment insurance[17]), Public Assistance (livelihood protection[18], medical aid[19], veterans relief, disaster relief[20]), and Social welfare Service for the disabled, the elderly, children, women, etc. Among them, the Social Insurance programme is the main buttress to the social safety net in Korea, and National Pension Insurance

[13] *See* World Bank, *Safety Nets—What are Safety Nets?* <http://www.worldbank.org/poverty/safety/whatare.htm> (visited 20 Jan. 2000).

[14] For example, private assistance or the informal protection is not dealt in the social security. *See* ibid. The use of social safety net is endorsed by many international organisations that pay a close attention to the development of developing countries.

[15] *See* Korean Ministry of Health and Welfare [hereinafter MoHW) <http://www.mohw.go.kr/html/e0003080101.html> (visited on 3 Nov. 1999).

[16] The health insurance scheme is mandatory for all individuals, so all 100 per cent nation are covered. The main source of financing is contributions. Employees and employers each pay half of the contribution to the Medical Insurance programme for industrial workers. The government pays a half of the contributions for its own employees, and 20 per cent for private school teachers. *See* MoHW <http://www.mohw.go.kr/html/e0003060102.html> (visited on 3 Nov. 1999).

[17] National Insurance covers 47.4 per cent, Industrial Injury Insurance covers 61.5 per cent, and Employment Insurance covers 32.3 per cent of the population.

[18] This service provides those who have no physical power and persons with low income in accordance with the Livelihood Protection Act enacted in 1961.

[19] Medical Aid has been operated separately by the Medical Aid Act from 1977 and now covers 3.8 per cent of the total population.

[20] Supporting through the Disaster Relief Act, the government offers the victims funeral costs, consolidation money, livelihood subsidies and house reconstruction costs to the members.

is posited at the pinnacle of the insurance programs in terms of its social importance.[21] Along with this national pension, there are important occupational pensions. Those are the Public Employee Pension, Military Personnel Person Pension, and the Private Teacher Pension. Those pensions are basically designed to soothe certain professions that each respective pension scheme covers.[22] These public pension schemes[23] have been an income maintenance programme in Korea providing their members with lifetime pensions against the economic and social distress caused by retirement or substantial reduction of earnings due to old age, disability or death.[24]

C. Meaningful Pension Reform

The further a modern theory of social security develops[25], the more a pension scheme comes into play with other sectors of a society. Since the insurance mechanism was favoured, the huge pooling mechanism has been put into place and pension funds contribute to the accumulation of social property.[26] The social security funds became susceptible to being used by government for purposes other than the original social security objectives.[27] For example, the accumulation of such mass funds might appeal to government officials for use in meeting other governmental or political objectives related to labour policy, infrastructure investment, or indirect market intervention into a financial market. Such uses, diverting from and exploiting the social security system, are often justified by politicians on a superficial level based on grounds of societal wealth redistribution. For various reasons, the accumulated assets are being invested in different sectors such as the public sector, the financial sector and the welfare sector.[28] Among them, the portfolio of the fund's investments in the financial sector is composed of national bonds, corporate bonds, individual

[21] For Latin Americas, see Sarah M. Brooks, *Social Protection in a Global Economy: The Case of Pension Reform in Latin America*, 4-SPG NAFTA: L. & Bus. Rev. Am. 91 at 92.

[22] Those professions are generally in a lower salary scheme compared to the private sector professions.

[23] The three occupational pensions have own sets of benefit formulas and contributions rates and are not combined with the national pension scheme. But a 'pension' is generally considered to comprise all four pensions, and is treated in the bundle.

[24] National Pension Act [hereinafter NPA] s 1.

[25] *See* Ruth Ben, above n 10 at 142–4 (classifying the evolution of the Social Security Model into four stages, first, the social charity era, the social insurance era, the social security era, and the social protection era).

[26] *See generally* Paul P. Harbrecht, *Pension Funds and Economic Power*, (the twentieth century fund, 1959). The author conceives the growth of pension trusts as the matter of shift of control over the social assets.

[27] *See* Lawrence H. Thompson, *ILO, Predictability of Individual Pensions.*

[28] *See* below Part II. 4.

stocks, and the other financial products.[29] It is evident that the pension system is heavily related to the financial market, considering the fact that the National Pension fund investments in the financial sector increased 25 per cent at the beginning of the scheme to recently about 40 per cent[30]. More recently, the financial crisis has shown the fact that pension funds are very much involved with the financial market. The collapse of the stock market caused a massive loss of pension funds[31], and those pensions were not able to collect their credits from the bankrupt financial institutions.[32] This indicates that a pension system can dampen the growth of a capital market.[33] On the other hand, it can also enrich the overall capital market if it is effectively invested and managed, since pension assets represent of

[29] *See* NPC, Monthly Statistics of a Pension Operation <http://www.npc.or.kr/data/e_aa_03_9904.html>(in Korean) (visited on 3 Nov. 1999) [hereinafter NPC, *Statistics*].

Financial sector investment

%	National bond	Corporate bond	Trust cash fund	Beneficiary certificate	CP	Stock	Short term money
total	41.83	4.73	12.36	14.01	0.77	10.40	15.90
'99.1–4	–41.79	25.42	–25.46	57.73	7.24	–3.81	80.67

For the portfolio of a financial investment in Latin America, see Queisser, *The Role of Pension Funds in the Stabilisation of the Domestic Financial Sector*, tbl.2 at 6 [hereinafter Queisser].

[30] *See* NPC, *Statistics* above n 29.

(100 million Won, per cent)

	Total	Public sector	Financial sector	Welfare sector
Amount (total)	395,538	282,550	100,705	12,283
%	*100*	*71.43*	*25.46*	*3.11*
Amount ('99.1–4)	20,891	14,599	8,394	–2,102
%	*100*	*69.88*	*40.18*	*–10.66*

[31] Public employee pension fund lost 4,000 billion won in the stock investment. *See* Korea Economic Daily Newspaper (in Korean), 19 Oct. 1998; And public employee pension management corporation bears a loss from a stock investment about 4,000 billion as of Aug. 1998. *See* Korea Economic Daily newspaper (in Korean), 18 Oct. 1998; And according to the report submitted before the congressional investigation committee, military personnel pension lost 200 billion won from a stock investment. *See Korea Economic Daily* newspaper (in Korean), 21 Oct. 1998.

[32] The public pension reportedly invested approximately 5,267 billion won in bankrupt financial institutions. *See* Mae Il Economic Daily Newspaper (in Korean), 15 Oct. 1998. *See also*, National Pension Corporation [hereinafter NPC], Press Release, *Improvement of pension management corp. because of the adoption of management evaluation system* (in Korean), 24 Nov. 1998.

[33] *See* Queisser, above n 29 at 5.

large portion of GDP.[34] For example, the pension assets of Chile, which privatised its pension system in 1981, have reached levels close to those in Malaysia and Singapore which established their pension systems in the 1950s.[35]

Therefore meaningful pension reform is necessarily related to financial infrastructure reform.[36] The financial institutions, for example banks, play a key role not only in mobilising savings and making them accessible to borrowers[37], but also most pension funds hold a significant amount of bank bonds or stock.[38] Trust investment companies and mutual funds are also managing a great part of pension assets.[39] Pension reform would benefit from having a sound and well-regulated stock market.[40]

Therefore, securing a pension system, more broadly a social safety net, cannot be separated from finding an economic and financial solution, especially while dealing with a financial crisis. On the other hand, efforts to redress the known financial distress have to generate a certain type of social consequence.[41] It is very important to look into how those consequential necessities can be facilitated into a system that uses the pension scheme. It seems that there is no single, universal magic potion determining which should be reformed first. The best approach to this is to take advantage of reform opportunities when feasible, then work incrementally as conditions permit.[42]

34 *See* ibid. table 1. *See also* Hans J Blommestein, *Pension Funds and financial Markets*, the *OECD Observer* No 212 June/July 1998 < http://www.oecd.org/publications/observer/212/Article6_eng.htm> (visited on 3 Nov. 1999).

35 *See* Queisser above n 29 at 2.

36 *See* Olivia S Michell, *Building an Environment for Pension Reform in Developing Countries* (World Bank, Jan. 1998) at 9 [hereinafter Michell]. The author intends to use 'financial infrastructure' as 'legal and accounting procedures, the organisation of trading and clearing facilities, and the regulatory structures that govern the relations among the users of the financial system'.

37 This will be more likely applied to Defined Contribution scheme.

38 *See* Michell above n 36.

39 *See* ibid. at 10. In Korea, the congressional investigation committee revealed that since 1993, NPC had a consulting contract with private investment consulting company about 3,230 billion won for five years. The companies recorded 20 per cent ~47 per cent loss yearly, but NPC renewed the contract although they were not able to keep even the principle from 95 to 1997. See *Korea Economic Daily* newspaper (in Korean), 3 Nov. 1998.

40 Some argue that a strong stock market need not necessarily be a precondition for successful pension reform. *See* Michell above n 36 at 10–11.

41 *See* ILO, *The Social Impact of the Asian Financial Crisis*, 2–1. < http://www.ilo.org/public/english/60empfor/cdart/bangkok/chapter2.htm> (visited on 3 Nov. 1999).

42 *See* Michell above n 36, IV at 13–14.

II. NATIONAL PENSION REFORM

A National Pension in Korea is a publicly mandated scheme. This scheme is relatively immature and there is a surplus of more than 1.5 per cent of GDP.[43] However, the Korean government recognised that a pension system would not be fiscally sustainable in the long run with an ageing population and the decline of fertility.[44] For example, the four major pensions are known to have 'very generous benefit' schemes for long periods.[45] The traditional, Defined Benefit ('DB'), Pay-As-You-Go ('PAYG'), pension schemes, therefore, drew a fundamental concern not only in Korea but also throughout the world, that possibly undermines their role in upholding a social safety network.[46] Thus on 1 Apr. 1999, a series of Acts concerning

[43] *See* World Bank, *Pensions in Korea* <http://www.worldbank.org/eapsocial/ countries/ korea/pen1.htm>.

[44] *See,* e.g., Peter S. Heller, *IMF, Aging in the Asian 'Tigers': Challenges for Fiscal Policy* (Oct. 1997) <http://www.imf.org/EXTERNAL/PUBS/CAT/longres.cfm?sk&sk=2369.0> (visited in Oct. 1999) (demonstrating that the East Asian countries are furthest advanced in terms of population aging). *See also* Nicholas Vanston, *The Economic Impacts of Aging, Observer* (OECD, No 212), June/July 1988 <http://www.oecd.org/publications/ observer/212/Article3_eng.htm> (visited on 3 Nov. 1999).

[45] *See Four major pensions' problem*, Mae Il *Korean Economic Daily* (Newspaper in Korean), 13 Jan. 1999.

(a) Public Employee Pension: Since introduced in 1960, it has yielded profit until 1993. The benefit level is determined by 50~75 per cent of a final monthly income. By contrast, since the contribution rate is still low 5.5 per cent in 1995, 2.3 per cent in 1960. Also the deposit on public sector yields a low leverage, and it is reported that an investment loss was 3 trillion won in 1998.

(b) Military Personnel Pension: Among four major pensions, this scheme holds the biggest problem. It has never produced a profit since 1973. Losses is 5,581 billion won in 1997, 4,100 billion in 1998, and it is estimated that the loss will be increased up to 6,400 billion won in 2002, and 7,500 billion won in 2005. The main cause is that, the beneficiary has already come up in 1963 long before the scheme reaches an optimal balance point. Also a benefit term is generally longer than the actual contribution according to the special official ranking system. It is said that the average benefit term is 12 years for a public employee, 10 years for a private school teacher, but 19 years for the military personnel.

(c) Private School Teacher Pension: The asset size is 3 trillion 6,600 billion won. This is the only profitable pension. But the profit size is gradually decreasing, because the retirement age changed from 65 to 62, which causes a sharp increase in the number of the retired. The main design problem here is that the contribution rate has been fixed at 11 per cent for last 20 years, in contrast, the benefit and the benefit term have been increased.

[46] *See* Karl Borden, *Cato inst., Dismantling the Pyramid: The way and how of privatising social security* (SSP No 1, 14 Aug. 1995) <http://www.socialsecurity.org/pubs/ ssps/ssp1es.html> (visited on 3 Nov. 1999) (commenting that Social Security in US violates basic principles of financial economics). Therefore, in US, for instance it is reported that social security will begin paying out more in benefits than what it collects in revenue by 2012, and the system will be insolvent by 2029 [hereinafter BORDEN]. *See also,* Empowering People: Testimony before the Subcomm. On Sec. of Senate Comm. Banking, Housing and Urban Affairs, 105th Cong. (26 June 1997) (Testimony of Josè Piñera) <http://www.socialsecurity.org /pubs/testimony/ct-jp062697.html> (visited on 3 Nov. 1999) [hereinafter Testimony of Josè Piñera]. In an effort to keep the traditional scheme viable, an enormous innovation has been

the National Pension scheme became effective. The revision focused on three major objectives as follows:

(1) To ensure funding resources, the scheme extended compulsory coverage to the self-employed (estimated at approximately 8.9 million persons). The benefit level was downgraded from 70 per cent to 60 per cent[47] of the monthly income while the pensionable age will be gradually increased from the current 60 to 65 by 2013[48].
(2) To facilitate long-term financial stability, the, so-called, financial calculation system was adopted[49], which will check the change of existing benefits levels and the pensionable age by requiring a consideration of the financial standing of the scheme.
(3) To ensure the transparency of fund operation, the number of the fund operation committee members was increased and the committee reorganised.

A. *Financing*

The National Pension scheme is an unfunded, PAYG/DB system.[50] The National Pension Scheme is mainly financed through contributions (pension insurance premiums) paid by the insured.[51] The contribution of the employed is charged half each from the employee and employer. The government supports a part of the administrative costs of the National Pension Corporation (hereinafter 'NPC') and a part of the contributions of farmers and fishermen.

1. Imposition Standard of Contributions

Standards determining contribution vary according to the types of coverage. The basis for the employee's contribution is the standard monthly

carried out across the globe. *See* Jean-Victor Graut, ILO, *Adequacy and Social Security Principles in Pension Reform,* No 3 [hereinafter GRAUT]; Joseph J Norton, *Privatization in Developing Nations*, 64 Brook.L.Rev.817, at 822 [hereinafter Norton]; David W. Kalisch and Tetsuya Aman, ILO, *Retirement Income Systems: The Reform Process Across OECD Countries* <http://www.oecd.org//els/pdfs/SocialPolicy/ENG4.PDF> (visited on 3 Nov. 1999); Hans Blommestein, *et al.*, *OECD, Retirement-Income Reforms in the Context of OECD Work on Aging* <http://www.oecd.org//els/pdfs/SocialPolicy/ENG10.PDF> (visited on 3 Nov. 1999).

[47] National Pension Act [hereinafter NPA] s 47.

[48] Ibid. app. s 3.

[49] Ibid. s 4, National Pension Enforcement Decree [hereinafter NPED] ss 11(2).

[50] *See* Peter S. Heller, *IMF, Rethinking Public Pension Reform Initiatives* (Apr. 1998) at 5 <http://www.imf.org/EXTERNAL/PUBS/CAT/longres.cfm?sk&sk=2582.0> (visited on 3 Nov. 1999) (observing that Korea has a DB/PAYG public pension system with substantial coverage of the work force unlike the other countries in the region which lack the type of primary pillar of flat or means tested benefits). [hereinafter HELLER]

[51] NPA s 74.

income, that is an annual wage income divided by twelve months. The standard monthly income of the self-employed, farmers and fishermen is calculated by dividing an annual income including agricultural income, forestry income, fishery income, business income, and wage income by twelve months. The standard contribution for voluntary coverage, e.g. housewives and students, is a median of the standard monthly incomes of all other insured persons in workplaces and in other areas.

2. Contribution Rates

The employed and the employer now each pay half of the contributions, 45 per cent of the monthly income, compared to the previous system where the employed, the employer and the retirement reserve each paid 30 per cent[52]. In order to mitigate the sudden increase in contributions, the contribution rates of the self-employed, farmers, fishermen, voluntarily insured persons and voluntarily and continuously insured persons will be increased by 3 per cent until June 2000 and shall be increased 1 per cent every year beginning in July 2000, resulting in a total increase of 9 per cent by 2005.[53] On the other hand, the government subsidises one-third of contributions for farmers and fishermen who are included in the lowest of forty-five grades of the standard monthly income from July 1995 to December 2004.

B. Scope of Coverage

The coverage of the National Pension Scheme extended to the workers of small firms that employ less than five and the urban self-employed after 1 April 1999.[54] There are two types of coverage. One is the compulsory insurance, such as coverage of employees in workplaces with five or more workers, farmers, fishermen and the self-employed[55], including foreigners.[56] The other covers the voluntarily insured persons, such as the self-employed in urban areas, housewives and students, and elderly persons whose insured term is less than twenty years and whose age is between 60 and 64.[57]

C. Benefits

The amount of benefits is calculated by the principle of income redistribution among the social strata, and the real value of all benefits is also secured through a sliding-scale system by price index.[58] Due to the adjustment, the level of benefit can be reduced from 70 per cent to 60 per cent.

52 Ibid. ss 75(2).
53 NPED ss 4(2).
54 Ibid.
55 Ibid. s 8.
56 Ibid. s 102.
57 Ibid. s 7, 9, 13.
58 Ibid. ss 47 (2).

1. Calculation of Benefits

The pension amount is composed of a basic pension amount and an additional pension amount.[59] The basic pension amount is a calculation basis for Old-age Pensions, Disability Pensions and Survivors Pensions, and it consists of the average amount of the Standard Monthly Income of all insured persons (equalised part), the average amount of Standard Monthly Income of an insured individual (earnings-related part), and additional part in proportion to the insured term of the insured.[60] The calculation formula is:

Basic Pension Amount = $1.8\ (A + B) \times (1 + 0.05n\ /12)$[61]

On the other hand, the additional pension amount, for dependants, varies according to the type and the number of dependants.[62] The additional pension is similar to family allowances, and the beneficiary is the spouse of a pensioner, a child (up to two children) less than 18 years old or with the disability of the second degree or higher, or a parent (including spouse's parents) 60 years old or more or with the disability of the second degree or higher.

2. Benefit Adjustment against Inflation

A price index system is adopted for the amount of pension benefits.[63] It is

[59] Ibid. ss 46 (2).

[60] Ibid. ss 47 (1).

[61] Ibid. app. s 3. **1.8** expresses the constant that determines the level of benefit when the insured has been covered for 40 years (for 480 months). In the case of the insured with the same as the average of the Standard Monthly Incomes of all insured, the level of benefit is about 60 per cent of his or her average Standard Monthly Income during the insured term.

A (An Average Monthly Income) means the average amount of the Standard Monthly Incomes of all compulsorily insured persons in the previous year of the year that the pension is first paid (equalised part).

An average monthly income shall be obtained annually by dividing the aggregate amount of the standard monthly incomes of all insured persons into the number of insured persons as of 31 Dec. of the year before the pension is first paid.

B means the average amount of Standard Monthly Income during a person's insured term (earnings related part). **B** shall be obtained by dividing the re-evaluated aggregate amount of standard monthly incomes of an insured person during the insured term by the numbers of insured years, in year before year the pension is first paid, after converting the standard monthly incomes of the insured during the insured term into the current value, using the revaluation rate which is determined annually and announced, based on annual rate of change of an average standard monthly income of all the insured during the insured term.

0.05 is the additional rate of the level of annual benefits per year at greater than twenty years.

n is the number of years in excess of 20 of an individual insured term.

[62] *See* NPA s 48

[63] Ibid. ss 47(2). This system is to protect the pensioner from the risk of inflation. Some countries, e.g. Chile, are using instruments to back the indexation, normally 'CPI-indexed government securities' to secure pension assets in a public investment sector. *See* cf., Queisser above n 29 at 4.

applied to both the basic pension amount and the additional pension amount. The basic pension amount shall be adjusted by the rate of change of the national Consumer Price Index. The period considered is from April to March. The additional pension amount is 150 thousand won for a spouse and 100 thousand won for each child or parent, and is also adjusted annually by the rate of change in the national consumer price index.

3. Qualification and Level of Benefits

The National Pension Scheme is classified into pension benefits and lump-sum benefits according to manner of payment. Pension benefits include Old-age Pensions, Disability Pensions and Survivors Pensions, while lump-sum benefits include Lump-sum Refund, Lump-sum Death Payment and Lump-sum Disability Compensation.

a. Old-age Pension

The Old-age Pension benefits can also be paid to a divorced spouse, 60 years or older who was married five or more years, and whose former spouse has an old-age pension right. The divorced spouse may receive up to half of the pension amount depending on the length of the marriage. The types of old-age Pension benefits are classified as Full,[64] Reduced,[65] Active,[66] Early[67] and Special[68] old-age Pensions.

[64] Ibid. ss 56(1). Full old-age Pension is paid to a person, 60 years old, whose insured term is twenty years or more. This pension is 100 per cent of the basic pension amount and the additional pension amount. In case of miners and seamen, it can be paid from the age of 55.

[65] Ibid. ss 57(2). Reduced old-age Pension is paid to a person, 60 years old, whose insured term is from ten to nineteen years. This pension is from 47.5 per cent to 92.5 per cent of the basic pension amount according to the insured term, and the additional pension amount can be added to it

[66] Ibid. ss 57(3). Active old-age Pension is paid to a person with a job, whose insured term is 20 years or more and whose age is from 60 to 64. The level of this pension depends on payment rates according to the insured term (47.5 per cent–92.5 per cent) and pension recipient age (50 per cent–90 per cent) added to the basic pension amount. Miners and seamen can receive this pension benefit from the age of 55

[67] Ibid. ss 57(4). Early Old-age Pension is paid to a person without a job whose insured term is ten or more years and whose age is from 55 to 59. The level of this pension is calculated by multiplying payment rates different according to the insured term (47.5 per cent–92.5 per cent) and pension recipient's age (75 per cent–95 per cent). The additional pension amount can be added to the basic pension amount.

[68] Special old-age Pension is paid to a person whose insured term is five or more years and whose age is 60. For this pension, the age should be from 45 to 59 as of the day when the Scheme should be applied compulsorily for the employed (1988) or rural areas (1995), or from 50 to 59 as of 1 Apr. 1999. The level of this pension is from 25 per cent to 70 per cent of the basic pension amount according to the insured term, and plus the additional pension amount, if applicable.

b. Disability Pension

The Disability Pension is paid to a person who becomes sick or injured during the insured term and who is physically or mentally disabled. The level of this pension is from 60 per cent to 100 per cent of the basic pension amount according to the degree of disability. The additional pension amount, based on revaluation, can also be added.[69] The amount depends on the per centage of remaining working ability after termination of medical treatment.[70] If more medical treatment is required two years after the first treatment day, the pension amount is re-evaluated at that point.

c. Survivors' Pension

The Survivors' Pension is paid to survivors of an insured person when he or she dies, survivors of a former insured person whose insured term is ten or more years, or survivors of a person entitled to the old-age pension or the disability pension of the second degree or higher[71]. The level of this pension is from 40 per cent to 60 per cent of the basic pension amount according to the insured term of the deceased, and the additional pension amount can also be paid. In this pension, survivors are defined as a spouse (if a husband, he must be at least 60 years old or disabled at the second degree or higher), children and grandchildren (less than 18 years old or disabled at the second degree or higher), and parents and grandparents (at least 60 years old or disabled at the second degree or higher).[72]

d. Lump-sum Refund[73]

The Lump-sum Refund is paid to survivors of an insured person, when the insured term was less than ten years, and is also paid to an insured person or a former insured person, 60 years old and whose insured term is less than ten years. It is also paid when the insured, with a term of less than ten years, loses his or her nationality or emigrates from our country. The level of this benefit depends on the contributions and legally fixed interest rate.

e. Lump-sum Death Payment[74]

The Lump-sum Death Payment is paid to a spouse, child, parent, grandchild, grandparent, sibling, or cousin, when an insured person or a former insured person dies and survivors' pension or lump-sum refund is not paid because of survivors' age limit, etc. The level of this benefit is equivalent to

[69] *See* NPA s 59. [70] Ibid. s 59. [71] Ibid. s 62.
[72] Ibid. s 64. [73] Ibid. s 67. [74] Ibid. ss 69(2).

lump-sum refund. The ceiling amount is within four times as much as the deceased's standard monthly income.

f. Lump-sum Disability Compensation[75]

Lump-sum Disability Compensation is paid when an insured person meets the qualifications for a disability pension and his or her disability is of the fourth degree. The level of this benefit is 225 per cent of the basic pension amount.

In addition, the relevant adjustment has been ensued including, an increase of the lump sum refund (the temporary pension benefit),[76] an introduction of the pension separation for spouse.[77]

D. Pension Fund

The pension assets should be invested, based on the decision of the National Pension Fund Council, to maximise profits as much as possible[78], while considering public interests and the fund security.[79] The National Pension Fund Council advises the Minister of Health and Welfare on such matters as the National Pension fund scheme, the payment of benefits, and contributions, etc.[80] The membership of the National Pension Fund Council is composed of individuals from each of the following groups; three employers, three employees, three insured persons in the rural area, and five persons representing public interests.[81] To ensure the long-term financial stability of the fund, the benefits level and contribution rate of the National Pension will be adjusted according to the results of periodical financial projections.[82] According to the result of the computation, an overall plan regarding the National Pension scheme will be redesigned, reported to the National Assembly, and publicised.

1. Resources of Fund

The resources of the Fund are contributions of the insured and all profits accrued from the fund management, a reserved fund and a surplus in the account of NPC.[83] Contributions are the principal source of funds.

[75] Ibid. ss 59(2). [76] Ibid. s 48. [77] Ibid. ss 59 (2),(3), app. s 10.
[78] NPA ss 83(2),(3), NPED s52(2). [79] NPA s 84, NPED s 54.
[80] NPA s 5, NPED s 12. [81] NPED s 13. [82] NPA s 4.
[83] Ibid. s 82(2).

2. Investment Sectors

The sectors of the Fund investment are public, finance and welfare.[84] Investment in the public sector is mainly used for public finances. That of the financial sector is for the purchase of public bonds, beneficiary certificates, and money in trust and securities. That of the welfare sector is loans for construction or renovation of facilities for children and elderly persons' welfare, and for establishment and operation of welfare facilities, and loans for the insured.[85] In order to assure a safe level of fund yield invested into the public sector, the yield of the fund deposited into the Public Capital Management Fund[86] will be determined under consultation with the National Pension Fund Operation Committee and it shall be more than the interest rate of five-year fixed government bonds.[87]

3. Management of the Pension Fund

For the efficient administration of the programme and for the purposes set fort in section 1 of the NPA, the NPC is empowered by the Minister of Health and Welfare with authority relating to the national pension management.[88] To develop transparent and specialised fund operations by allowing involvement of more insured persons, the number of the National Pension Fund Operation Committee members will be increased from the current fifteen to twenty, including an increase in the number of the representatives of employers and workers from two to three respectively.[89] This National Pension Fund Operation Committee decides guidelines for the pension fund operation relating to the ratio of fund assets to be used for public projects and the priority of fund allocation to public projects, etc.[90] To enhance the review function over pension management, the Working Committee for the Fund Operationhas been organised. It reviews the asset portfolio and the result of fund operations.[91] In light of the goal of fostering the nation's confidence in fund operations, the expenditures of the fund deposited into the Public Management Fund account will be reported to the National Assembly via the review of the National Pension Fund Operation Committee, and will be disclosed to the public.[92]

In addition, NPC now recruits a contractual executive director for the fund.[93] To encourage public involvement in NPC management, the number of *ipso facto* directors is increased from three to seven.[94]

[84] Ibid. s 83(2).
[85] NPA s 42, NPED ss 28(2).
[86] The fund was established by the Public Capital Management Fund Act [hereinafter PCMFA]. PCMFA was enacted to collaterally manage surplus of various funds and to utilise those funds for public purposes such as monetary financing. See PCMFA §1.
[87] NPA ss 83(3).
[88] Ibid. ss 22,83(5).
[89] Ibid. ss 84(2).
[90] Ibid. s 85.
[91] Ibid. s 84–2.
[92] Ibid. ss 87(2).
[93] Ibid. s 28–2.
[94] Ibid. s 28.

III. ISSUES AT THE RECENT REVISION

A. *Deposit Clauses for Fund Mobilisation*

1. A MANDATORY DEPOSIT

A government is entitled to raise public funds in order to achieve the public purposes such as monetary financing, job creation, and boosting market infrastructure,[95] and accordingly, a greater part of four major pension funds is invested in the public sector.[96] The major resource in this public mobilisation mechanism is so-called Public Capital Management Fund that includes the deposits from other funds.[97] The surplus of a certain fund shall be deposited to this Public Capital Management Fund. The surplus is defined as a remainder of a fund excluding the essential amount to achieve its own core purpose.[98] In addition to that, any other funds not listed in section 5(1) of the PCMFA can voluntary deposit at their discretion.[99] In the voluntary deposit, the funds under the PCMFA are to be managed by the management fund administration plan.[100]

The National Investment Fund Act (hereinafter 'NIFA')[101] also delineates the deposit clause. The NIFA is designed for issuing national investment bonds. The government can organise the necessary funds not only by issuing the bonds, but also by using the optional deposit, an alternative resource for this investment fund[102]. This option is given to those funds appointed by the National Investment Fund Presidential Decree (hereinafter 'NIFPD'), despite conflicting contexts in the regulations of the 'baby' funds.[103] Major public pension funds belong to this category. That is, unless a certain fund underwrites the national investment bond, the same deposit rule of PCMFA applies even to funds under NIFA.

Besides those funds directly governed by said regulations, there are also several credit associations to be mentioned. These organisations are rooted in a native mutual aid tradition among those who belong to a certain profession.[104] These organisations have been granted legal status and can

[95] *See* PCMFA s 1–2.

[96] *See* above n 29.

[97] *See* PCMFA s 3. Besides the deposit, the other resources are the amount transferred from a general account, interest accrued from both a re-deposit and a national bond or a local government bond, and a profit from managing the fund.

[98] Ibid. ss 5(1),(2).

[99] Ibid. s 6.

[100] Ibid. s 9.

[101] This Act was enacted to promote major industry and export by financing and supplying investment capital, and by establishing the national investment fund. See NIFA s 1.

[102] *See* NIFA s 8–1 provides creditors with the option either to underwrite the national investment bond or to deposit to the national investment fund.

[103] *See* NIFPD s 3.

[104] The number of public fund such as the Public Employee Pension Fund reached thirty-three in 1988. Other funds such as the Private School Teacher Pension Fund reached thirty-nine in 1997. *See* Mae Il *Korean Economic Daily* (in Korean), 13 Jan. 1999.

run their own funds primarily for members' welfare and support of livelihood. Their funding comes from member's contributions and government support when necessary.[105] Since they have funds to run, their funds are also subject to indirect influence, not only because each relevant Ministry is the supervisory authority[106], but also because of those broad regulations described above.[107] These funds have not created significant public interest due to the very limited number of beneficiaries. They lacked management know-how over their funds' transparency and they had difficulty reaching the funds' operational objectives It is unquestionable that those funds in a 'dead angle' also suffered serious financial problems, especially during the financial crisis.[108] In short, most public funds are directly or indirectly subject to PCMFA sections 5 and 6, FMMA section 3 and NIFPD section 3.

2. Deposit Rate

The funds which deposited a surplus were paid interest at the rate determined by the public capital management funds administration committee[109] taking into consideration both the rate of a national public bond in a given capital market and the earning ratio of the public capital management fund[110]. However, the rate has been decisively affected by the long-term national bond with a maturity of no more than seven years, of which issue rate is very low. Consequently it has caused a wide gap between the

105 Policemen Mutual Aid Act ss 17(1), Korea Educational Employee Mutual Aid Act ss 12, Korea Fire Officer Mutual Aid Act ss 18(1), Military Mutual Aid Act §§15(1).

106 *See* MoHW, <http://www.mohw.go.kr/html/e0003080102.html> (visited on 3 Nov. 1999). Funds governed by the Central Government include: the Ministry of Finance and Economy; Planning, budgeting, and coordinating of overall social security programme the Ministry of Home Affairs: directing and supervising of local governments, which implement the resident's welfare, program with commission of central government the Ministry of National Defense: pension for military personnel the Ministry of Education: pension for private school teachers the Ministry of Labour: Insurance for workers and laborers for industrial accident compensation and labour welfare services the Ministry of Patriots and Veterans Affairs: welfare services for the patriots and veterans the Ministry of Government Administration: pension for government employees.

107 The Fund Management Model Act ('FMMA') provides management guidance to those who manage funds such as, funds under the control of a head of central government offices, funds with resources are based on private subscription by law and with publicly important business, and those funded by a government with publicly important business. *See* FMMA s 3.

108 *See* above n 103. For example, the teacher associations lose 514 billion won from a stock investment, and the local government association lost 68 billion won. *See* Joong Ang Ilbo (in Korean), 19 Oct. 1998.

109 *See* PCMFA ss 7 (1).

110 Ibid. ss 7 (2). Base Rate = mid/long term national bond issuing rate + earning ratio of a financial asset portfolio/2. In the event that there is a difference between the base rate and the deposit rate of more than 5 per cent, the base rate becomes the deposit rate.

deposit interest and actual market interest rates.[111] Another important factor is, when the earning ratio of a financial asset is determined, the actual earning ratio of a fund was not accounted for, but instead the determination reflected the market-earning ratio of financial products announced by Bank of Korea.[112] In fact, during recent years, the profit from the public sector investment has diverged by approximately 2 per cent from the profit in the financial sector.[113]

For those deposits, the government has issued the Deposit Certificate.[114] This cannot be easily cashed because it is not clear when the Certificate is

[111] *See* MoHW Press Release, *Due to the increase of the deposit rate of a public investing fund,* Department of pension fund finance (in Korean), 13 Sep. 1998 [hereinafter MoHW, Press Release-*Due to*].

<Comparison between the deposit interest and the corporate bond>

	4th quarter/95	1st quarter/96	4th quarter/96	1st quarter/97
Deposit interest	11.57	10.37	10.37	10.37
Corporate Bond Earning ratio	11.38	11.29	11.78	12.31

[112] Ibid.

[113] *See* Kil Hoon Jang *et al.*, *The Korea National Pension Research Center Devise of the National Pension Fund management improvement* (in Korean) [hereinafter KIL] 4 at 7.

<Profit Discrepancy between a public sector and a financial sector > (100 million Won, per cent)

	1988	1989	1990	1991	1992	1993	1994	1995	1996
Public Sector	11.0	11.0	11.0	11.0	11.0	1.67	10.25	11.64	10.30
Financial Sector	12.95	14.35	13.83	14.04	14.07	13.87	13.91	13.11	11.86
Discrepancy	1.95	3.35	2.83	3.04	3.07	4.20	3.66	1.47	1.56
Opportune Cost	20	133	218	345	511	1,056	1,582	1,208	1,916

[114] Public Capital Management Fund Presidential Decree ss 8(1).

redeemable.[115] This did not need the approval or restraint of congress, because the Minister of Finance and Economy issues the Deposit Certificate at a time when the funds are deposited in the public capital management fund. Therefore, most pensions have such a serious liquidity problem that may not be capable of giving benefits.[116] Undoubtedly the limitless issuance of Deposit Certificates impairs the reliability of a government by increasing the liability burden. The mandatory deposit causes a distortion of capital flow because of its manipulative capital distribution mechanism.

B. *Immediate Response*

From fiscal year 1999, the interest rate paid for the public sector investment has been changed, so it is expected that the new rate will approach 12 per cent.[117] The deposit rate is determined by the transactional earning ratio of the National Housing Bond (1st class in five-year maturity), or the National Treasury Bond.[118] The increase of the rate by approximately 1 per cent is expected to take effect. In case there is a discrepancy between the actual earning ratio of the fund and the base rate, a compensatory interest is paid in the amount of the discrepancy to prevent the financial aggravation of a national pension fund[119]. Also the deposit certificates issued so far will be gradually converted into a national bonds, starting with 10 per cent of all certificates issued in 1999 and finally reaching 100 per cent by 2001.[120]

Although the revision attempts to redress some short-term fiscal problems without changing fundamentals at the pension system, it only addresses parametric issues of the traditional pension scheme; the revisions do not comprehend what else is involved in managing pension a system or what fundamentals should be addressed.[121] For the long run, the reform should recognise how the system can be sustained in an ageing society. It is also obvious that the public funds have been the biggest 'donors' to the public financing mechanism. In fact, it is shown that a greater part of the

115 Ibid. ss 8(2). Regarding the redemption of the deposit, the redemption of the deposit principle clause in the Monetary Investment & Financing Special Accounting Act shall be applied. *See also* PCMFA ss 7(1),(2).

116 Persons requesting unemployment benefits during 1–12 Feb. numbered 11,650 per day up to 204 in the second half of 1997 and 1,199 in Jan. 1998. *See* PAK, above n 2 at 11.

117 *See* NPC Press Release, *Improvement of NPC management system due to the adoption of a management evaluation system* (in Korean), 24 Nov. 1998.

118 NPA s 83, NPED s 52

119 *See* MoHW Press Release-*Due to,* above n 111.

120 *See* MoHW, Press Release, *The national pension fund management plan of 1999* (in Korean), Bureau of pension insurance, 7 Oct. 1999.

121 Some countries have shown good examples of a parametric pension reform, such as, changing the earnings base for pensions, reducing the replacement rate, making inheritability provisions less generous and increasing pension age. *See generally*, E. Philip Davis, *OECD, Private Pensions in OECD Countries The United Kingdom* (OECD/GD(97)113) <http://www.olis.oecd.org/OLIS/1997DOC.NSF/LINKTO/OCDE-GD(97)113> (visited on 3 Nov. 1999).

public pension has drastically surged into the public sector since PCMFA was enacted in 1993.[122] The Korean government views those surpluses as unmarked funds that can be mobilised in the name of the public policy at any time with little restraint. But, a surplus ought to be used to dissolve public debt rather than leading to higher 'government consumption'.[123] Furthermore the rate back up for those deposits by the public bond is an 'accounting illusion'[124] which does not reflect the actual value of the pension liability. It is, therefore, necessary to institute bold regulatory reform by recognising fundamental principles and parameters in the pension scheme, in line with enhancement of an efficient and sound financial market.[125]

IV. PRINCIPLES IN A MODERN PENSION MANAGEMENT

A. *Premise of the Pension reform: Recognition of Pension as a Right*

An adverse response came from the notion that the pension right has not been considered a fundamental right. The legal authority of a series of Acts regarding social security including pension schemes stems from the Constitutional Law.[126] Under constitutional theory, social insurance is generally perceived as one type of social right upon which each individual can actively request social benefits.[127] This right is distinguished from the other fundamental rights in that it coerces the government to take on a more positive attitude. Thus any individual is entitled to claim an adjustment based on the rationale of a protected social right.[128]

In Korea, one Constitutional Court decision is worth noting.[129] In it, the majority concluded that the mandatory deposit clauses[130] are not unconstitutional because the general regulations would be upheld as in accordance with public interest and a national economy. The mandatory deposit is not to be viewed as a probable infringement of the pension right. In contrast, the minority opinion rebutted this, stating that the mandatory deposit clause deteriorates the funds' profits rather than contributing to public welfare development, and that it could impair the pension right in the

122 *See* Kil, above n 113, table 2 at 5.

123 *See* Heller, above n 44 n 6

124 *See* Borden, above n 46.

125 *See* World Bank, *Pensions in Korea* <http://www.worldbank.org/countries/korea/pen1.htm> (visited on 20 Jan. 1999).

126 *See* Constitutional Law §34.

127 Social Security Reception Right. *See* Young-Sung Kwon, *Constitutional Law: A Textbook* (1994) (in Korean) at 652–9.

128 Ibid. at 653.

129 *See* 96HeonKa6 Entire Court (Korean Constitutional Court Decision), The 6 Oct. 1996; Ja 95Kagi 6548, Decision (Seoul District Court Decision), 15 Feb. 1996.

130 *See* PCMFA ss 5(1)–2, (2)–1.

future or the expectation of that right in the present.[131] The Court recognised the superiority of the public policy to the individual right. Interestingly, a new case has been filed very recently at the Constitutional Court to examine the constitutionality of NPA sections 75 and 76. Plaintiffs claim that the new expansion of a pension contribution is unconstitutional because it violates Constitutional Law section 59 which articulates that the item and rate of tax shall be determined by Law. [132]

In determining whether a public policy prevails over a personal right, the ultimate criterion lies somewhere between individual equity and social adequacy, which are in a direct conflict.[133] Although the tendency is usually more toward social adequacy than toward individual equity[134], the public attitude regarding pension assets should be constrained to the extent that a transparent, objective law identifies its scope and range. The social adequacy tendency is advocated by the claim that government investing would allow the government to reap the benefits of higher returns available in private capital, and would allow the government to spread the risk of poor investment performance.[135] As briefly mentioned earlier, the actual authorities that control the pension funds in Korea are the Fund Management Administration Council, the Working Committee for National Pension Fund Operation, and NPC.[136] Nonetheless, those Committees have not provided clear rules or principles for pension asset management, whereas some pension systems in the US, for example, have prohibitions against investment in specific types of companies, and restrictions on investment in companies that fail to meet certain principles.[137] In Korea, FMMA provides guidance for public funds in terms of fund's

131 With regard to whether this social right is acceptable as a personal right, US Supreme Court once decided that the contributor has no right to demand the benefit for which he has become eligible, denying the concept of 'accrued property rights' concept. *See Flemming v Nestor*, 363 US 603 (1960) 611–12. A dissenting opinion stressed that it is an earned right based upon the contributions and earnings of the individual. Ibid. at 623. But, later on, many cases have challenged this out-of-date decision and finally several regulations manifest a substantial recognition of the pension right. *See*, e.g., *Sherbert v Verner*, 374 US 398 (1963); *Professional Air Traffic Controllers Organization v Bond*, 477 F.Supp. 62 (1979); *Artway v Attorney General of State of N.J.*, 81 F.3d 1235 (1996).

132 *See National Pension to be examined by the Constitutional Court*, Joong Ang Ilbo (in Korean), 30 June 1999.

133 *See* MYERS, above n 8, at 10.

134 *See* ibid. At the recent National Pension Fund Operation Committee meeting, there was controversy over the philosophy and the basic frame of the pension system. The Committee noted that it is fallacy to see Korean social security system as one of social democracy. *See* NPC, Minutes, 31 Mar. 1999.

135 *See* Michael Tanner, *CATO INST., THE PERILS OF GOVERNMENT INVESTING* (No 43, 1 Dec. 1998) at 3 <http://www.cato.org/pubs/briefs/bp-043es.html> (visited on 3 Nov. 1999).

136 *See* above Part II.4.

137 *See* Tanner, above n 135 n 6 at 6. *See also* Steven L Willborn, *Public Pensions and the Uniform Management of Public Employee Retirement Systems Act*, 51 Rutgers L.Rev. 141 n

management, but it only depicts the general direction. For example, NPA states only that the Minister of Health and Welfare shall maximise the interest of fund for the sake of a long term stability,[138] and that the rate of profit of the fund shall be higher than that of one year time deposit in a given year.[139]

Therefore, setting aside the social adequacy tendency of a pension, we need to redefine the clear boundary not only to avoid high political behaviour in pension management, but also for a government not to unreasonably infringe upon personal property rights. Recognition of the pension right as a personal property right necessarily entails recognition of potential liability based on the relationships among relevant parties including, a pensioner, and pension asset management authorities, such as NPC, and the Committees. It is necessary to embody standard principles in the particularised pension asset management rules.

B. *Principles of Modern Pension Management*

Since a complicated regulatory framework does not provide enough legal principles and rules in pension management, it needs to be reinstated and reinforced by immediate regulations that govern the pension system. In 1977 the US enacted the Uniform Management of Public Employee Retirement Systems Act ('UMPERS Act') to standardise some aspects of public pension fund management. Although significant principles are derived from the Employment Retirement Income Security Act of 1974 ('ERISA'), it deliberates more public aspects of a pension and also encourages the use of so called 'Modern Portfolio theory' which reflects a modern investment experience.[140]

1. Fiduciary Duties[141]

The key component is an explicit articulation of fiduciary responsibility. It

68. 'We define social investing to mean excluding the securities of certain otherwise attractive companies because the companies are judged to be socially irresponsible, and including the securities of certain otherwise unattractive companies because they are judged to be behaving in a socially laudable way.' *See also*, Joel C. Dobris, *Argument in Favor of Fiduciary Divestment of 'South African' Securities,* 65 Neb.L.Rev. 209, 210; James D Hutchinson and Charles G Cole, *Legal Standards Governing Investment of Pension Assets for Social and Political Goals,* 128 U.Pa. L.Rev. 1340, 1341; Maria O'Brien Hylton, *'Socially Responsible' Investment: Doing Good Versus Doing Well in an Inefficient Market,* 42 Am.U.L.Rev. 209, 210.

138 NPA ss 83(2).

139 *See* ibid. ss 83(3), NPED s 52(2),(3).

140 Diversification is the essence. *See* Unif. Prudent Investor Act s 2, 7 ULA 61 (Supp. 1998). *See also*, UMPERS Act s 8, 7A ULA at 30, ERISA 404(a)(1)(C), 29 USC. s 1104(a)(1)(C). But this is basically a more sophisticated definition of the 'prudent man' standards. *See* Michell, above n 36 at 4. Some argues that this prudent man rule will be enough.

141 *See* Umpers Act. s 7–10, 7A ULA at 347.

should embrace a clear indication of the general duties of trustees and other fiduciaries as well as special duties that apply to where trustees invest and manage the assets of a pension fund. In the case there is, for example, a termination of the plan, the Model ought to also provide special applications of those duties. A certain type of a guideline would be needed for courts to deliberate. Additionally, fiduciary provisions need to provide trustees with the authority necessary to ensure that they can fulfill fiduciary duties.

2. Liability[142]

The manifestation of the location of liability is also crucial where there is a fiduciary violation. But because of pension's strong public tendency, it preferably has to protect the pension fund against losses resulting from fiduciary violations. [143] Even under the current authority system where several Committees are posited in a key position, it is essential to outline certain legal obligations for them. So as to disperse the liabilities or risks, it may be useful if it provides the various options to select the insurance arrangement, ranging from, for example, risk retention groups to commercial liability insurance.[144]

3. Disclosure[145]

The NPA gives a public notice of the operation results of the Fund annually after the deliberation by the Committee as prescribed by the Presidential Decree[146]. The UMPERS Act requires a similar disclosure of a Summary Plan Description, Annual Disclosure and Actuarial Status, and Annual Report to ensure that information sufficient to permit a thorough review of the system's operation is available to those with an interest in monitoring.

142 *See* UMPERS Act. s 11, 7A ULA at 355.

143 Measuring the pension value may be needed to allocate the pension liability. *See*, e.g., Robert, J. Ryan, Jr., *Corporate Pension Fund Management: Measuring the Pension Liability*, 25 Ga.L.Rev. 117 at 127–31 (trying to measure the value of the pension liability in a corporate pension).

144 Not only to reduce risks inherently carrying liability, but also to secure the pension system, development of this insurance as security needs to take place such as purchase trustee insurance in US, government guarantees in US and Canada, risk-pooling employer solvency funds in Germany. *See* Michell, above n 30 at 5.

145 *See* ibid. s 13–18, 7A ULA at 357–64

146 NPA s 87, NPED s 64.

4. Proper Relief

The NPA concedes in section 88 a certain right to request an examination in the event that there is any objection as to an assessment of monthly income, contribution rate, benefit level, and management of the NPC. The National Pension Examination Board is installed to screen cases upon request.[147] Any person who does not acknowledge the decision can call for the re-examination by the National Pension Re-examination Board[148]. That is to say, a complaint has to go through two administrative boards before it has standing in the Judiciary Court. This is not only unusual, because an administrative judgment generally takes place as a legitimate alternative for Administrate Court before the Appellate Court in a judiciary system, but also unclear because it provides few legal standards for the judgment. By contrast, for example in the US, ERISA recognises an important right by empowering the interested parties to bring a civil action against the pension fund as an entity.[149]

C. *Improvement of Role of the NPC*

The NPC's role is critically important in reforming pension management, not only because it is the actual manager of pension assets of the National Pension Insurance, but also because NPC can generate potential effects on the financial market as follows:

1. Norm Effect

If the NPC is equipped with good examples of pension asset management, all the other pensions, mutual aids, even private institutions would likely adopt the management rules and principles[150], as occurred in Chile when AFPs were introduced.[151]

2. Governance Effect

As the largest institutional investor, NPC will encourage improved corporate governance[152], especially in the Asia where many countries lack systemic governance structure.[153] In the United States, the ownership share

[147] NPA s 89. [148] Ibid. s 90,91.
[149] *See* 29 USCA s 1132. *See generally*, Annotation, *Right of Pension Plan, As Entity, To Bring Civil Enforcement Action Under §502 of Employee Retirement Income Security Act of 1974* (29 USC.A. s 1132), 69 ALR Fed. 947. *See* cf., UMPERS Act s 19, 7A ULA at 364.
[150] This is so called 'herding behaviour'. *See* Queisser above n 29 at 30.
[151] *See* below Part V.4.
[152] *See* Willborn, above n 137 nn 3, 4.
[153] *See* Queisser, above n 29 at 10.

of corporate equities held by pension funds rose sharply following the passage of ERISA in 1976.

3. FILTER EFFECT

It will be then possible to indirectly manipulate the capital market, as Central Bank of Korea does in the monetary issues. So, if the NPC functions with a clear and objective rule it can minimise the impression that it is controlled directly by the government. At the same time, a government or NPC must devise alternatives to the fund mobilisation that has been used for a government debt consumption scheme.[154] Thus the NPC will encourage public pension systems to engage in modern investment practices.

V. Road to the Privatisation

Adoption of these principles will benefit modern pension management practices and also increase the sustainability of pension assets. But we need to note that, despite all these efforts to innovate parameters in a public pension scheme, the current reform can only serve to extend the timing of the depletion of the pension fund.[155] The traditional DB/PAYG pension scheme arguably holds an inborn defect,[156] and public pension finances still remain unsustainable.[157] Rooted in the mere insurance concept, the financing system would collapse when the demands of increasing numbers of expectant recipients confront the limited resources of decreasing numbers of new participants.[158] Privatising the public pension gets substantial credit for addressing this defect.

A. Privatisation

One rationale for this privatisation is derived back from classical concepts of liberty, such as respect for individual rights and the liberty to decide one's

[154] *See* cf. Norton above n 46 at 857.

[155] It is predicted that the public pension in Korea will be insolvent by 2033. *See* MOHW Press Release-*Due to*, above n 111.

[156] *See* William G. Shipman, *Cato Inst., Retiring with Dignity: Social Security vs Private Markets* (SSP No 2), 14 Aug. 1995 <http://www.socialsecurity.org/pubs/ssps/ssp2es.html> (visited on 3 Nov. 1999).

[157] See Richard Hemming, *IMF, Should public fund be funded?*, Mar. 1998, at 7 <http://www.imf.org/EXTERNAL/PUBS/CAT/longres.cfm?sk&sk=2532.0> (visited on 3 Nov. 1999) [hereinafter HEMMING].

[158] *See* Borden, above n 46 (stressing that the current system is like that created by a Ponzi scheme. Known also as a pyramid financing scheme and illegal in all fifty states, this scheme creates no real growth but accounting data can create the illusion of wealth as long as the base of investors keeps growing).

own destiny.[159] In a social security system, privatisation is simply replacing the current traditional unfunded DB scheme with DC scheme of individual accounts held in individual's name.[160]

The essential advantage of privatisation lies in the reasonable assumption that better performance of assets could solve the deterioration of the DB/PAYG pension funding system. Proponents of privatisation hold that the return in the stock market has been higher than a low yielding DB/PAYG system.[161] A privatised pension scheme is also known to generate some additional benefit such as a higher savings rate[162], the avoidance of political risk, less microeconomic distortion, greater transparency, smaller government, improvement of corporate governance[163] and productivity of the financial market.[164]

In order to create those benefits, however, the process of privatising the traditional pension scheme requires numerous technical issues to be noted. Chile, as we know, has shown how a system can successfully transform into a privately managed, funded pension system, and accordingly how the privatisation induces positive effects on the financial market. This shows the intimate interrelation between the pension system and a financial market in a certain economy. Since the new Pension Saving Account ('PSA')[165] began to operate, it has begun to increase the productivity of capital and thus the rate of economic growth in the Chilean economy. The

159 *See* Daniel Shapiro, *Cato Inst., The Moral Case for Social Security Privatisation* (SSP No 14), 29 Oct. 1998, at 2 <http://www.socialsecurity. org/pubs/ssps/ssp-14es.html> (visited on 3 Nov. 1999). 'Privatisation is defensible not only from the classical liberal or libertarian perspective but from virtually every perspective in political philosophy. Egalitarians, who frame their arguments in terms of fairness, welfare theorists who frame their arguments in terms of economic security, communitarians who frame their arguments in terms of community, and anyone who frames an argument in terms of whether average citizens understand the institutions or programs which they are asked to support, should all support privation [hereinafter SHAPIRO'. *See also*, MYERS, above n 8 at 111. 'the question is raised why people should not be allowed individually to decide whether they which to participate in the social insurance program, especially those who are financially well off and who can take care of themselves'.

160 *See* John Geanakoplos *et al., Pension Research Council, Would a Privatized Social Security System Really Pay a Higher Rate of Return?*, 3 Aug. 1998, at 1 <http://prc.wharton.upenn.edu/prc/prc.html> (visited on 3 Nov. 1999)[hereinafter GEANAKPOLOS].

161 *See generally*, ibid.

162 *See* Mack Ott, *World Bank, Capital Market Implications of Pension and Social Insurance Reform in the NIS*, Oct. 1997 Part 2, <http://www.worldbank.org/wbi/capitalmarkets/psprfsd/postcon/ott/> (visited on 3 Nov. 1999) (finding that three possible savings incentives created by a traditional DB/PYGP system; a wealth substitutions effect, a retirement effect, and a bequest effect) [hereinafter OTT].

163 *See* Ibid. Part 5. *See also* Queisser, above n 30 at 10.

164 *See* Heller, above n 50 at 7.

165 During a working life, an individual has 10 per cent of his or her wages automatically deposited by his/her employer each month in his/her own PSA. This contribution, including voluntary additional savings, is not taxed. Pension level is determined by the amount of money the worker accumulates during his working years. *See* Testimony of Josè Piñera, above n 46.

PSA system has made the capital market more efficient and influenced its growth. The vast resources administered by the private Pension Fund Administration companies ('Administradoras de Fondos de Pensiones', AFPs) have encouraged the creation of new kinds of financial instruments.[166] Chile's pension reforms also contribute to sound operation, transparency of capital and to the improvement of corporate governance. As a result, the private pension system has had very important political and cultural consequences. The pension savings accounts now represent real and visible property rights for Chileans, and the new pension system gives Chileans a personal stake in the economy.[167]

B. Concerns in Privatisation

In studying Chile's reform, various empirical studies have drawn attention to the fact that rates of return on AFP portfolios have far exceeded what would have been achieved under the old system; that the national savings rate is probably exaggerated or may be misleading; and that it seems theoretically irrational that both the cost of labor and net wages could improve under the new system.[168] If portfolio growth rates decrease, the taxpayers will eventually be responsible for the minimum guarantee because the government provides a safety net.[169] There is also a requirement that at least half of portfolio assets be held in government securities. But the longer AFPs hold this position, the smaller rate of returns is, which would be the same even under the current public pension scheme. The requirement also imposes responsibility on taxpayers. That is why some critics prefer not to call the Chilean pension reform a genuine privatisation model.[170]

Besides, opponents of privatising the public pension scheme point out that a market-based privatised system will require pensioners to have greater financial knowledge in order to cope with such volatile market risks, compared to the current system where the pensioner expects to receive the benefit, which is already determined based on his/her contribution. They

[166] A worker chooses one of the AFPs to manage his/her PSA. Each AFP operates as the equivalent of a mutual fund that invests in stocks and bonds. The AFP makes investment decisions, and the government sets only maximum per centage limits both for specific types of instruments and for the overall mix of the portfolio. There is no obligation whatsoever to invest in government or any other type of bond. Since workers are free to change from one AFP company to another, there is a competition among companies to provide a higher return on investment and it generates self-regulating principles. *See* ibid.

[167] *See* Shapiro, above n 159 at 8.

[168] *See generally*, Borden, above n 46.

[169] The governments' role is a safeguard to guarantee a basic minimum pension. If an individual had not accumulated enough capital during his or her working life (minimum 20 years) the government would increase the account to the point where the retiree could purchase the minimum annuity. *See* Testimony of Josè Piñera, above n 46.

[170] *See* Borden, above n 46.

claim that a privatised system would be attractive only to a high-income class while it would hurt the low-income workers. Additionally, a market-based system would be expensive with administration costs such as, brokerage fees, consulting fees or management fees, all of which may mitigate the all the benefits earned by a privately managed pension scheme.[171] More fundamentally, there are deep-seated risks associated with a privatised market. This points out a dilemma about whether a privately managed pension system can be free from such risks and how it can then secure pension assets, if the market risk is not reduced, but just shifted, and if the market risk it is truly present.

Another important factor to consider in the course of privatisation is whether the public pension should be pre-funded before the full-privatised financing scheme. More often than not, the proponents of a privatised pension scheme encourage pre-funding of the current pension.[172] Pre-funding is considered to reduce the implicit and explicit debt of the scheme[173], and therefore takes the role of 'tax smoothing' to avoid the sharp increase of payroll rates in the future.[174] To finance the transition, funds from taxes and/or savings would pay benefits, would be invested for future, and would amortise the 'bridge-financing' debt incurred during the transition.[175] But this projected effect would theoretically apply only to the future generation by the time that all past accumulated debt is dissolved at the expense of higher taxes for the current generation.[176] In other words, the pre-funding inevitably entails a transitioning cost in the course of moving into the privatised, market-based system.

In Korea, expansion of a mandatory subscription could be considered the pre-funding to compensate accumulated pension liability. Until the new

[171] *See* Mellisa Hiegar and William Shipman, *Cato Inst., Common Objections to a Market-Based Social Security System: A Response* (SSP No 10, 22 July 1997) <http://www.socialsecurity.org/pubs/ssps/ssp10es.html> (visited on 3 Nov. 1999).

[172] The World Bank states that the principle of pension fund reform should derive from a well formulated, public DB scheme, with a significant amount of a pre-funding for especially the developing countries. *See* Heller, above n 50 at 4.

[173] *See* Geanakoplos, above n 160 at 4.

[174] *See* Heller, above n 50 at 14. For instance, US is known to bear $9 trillion in unfunded present value as of 1988. *See* Geanakoplos, ibid. In Korea, there seems to be no precise estimate of the unfunded value, but it would be the sum of a total opportunity cost and the total loss from asset management. *See* above n 99 table.

[175] Supporters of the market based system, commonly propose that the funds' surplus would not be earmarked but used to dissolve public debt. *See* William Shipman, *CATO INST., Facts and Fantasies about Transition Costs* (SSP-13, 13 Oct. 1998), at 8 <http://www.socialsecurity.org/pubs/ssps/ssp13es.html> (visited on 3 Nov. 1999). *See also*, HELLER, above n 50 n 4 at 6.

[176] *See* Heller, above n 50 n 5. To materialise desirable effects, 'effort[s] can be made to defer the age for pension eligibility, reduce the generosity of indexation provisions, change the formula used for determining the initial pension benefit, restrict eligibility for disability or survivor's benefits, and modify the tax treatment of pension contributions or pension incomes. These are consistent with the general parametric reform methods.'

system makes it viable, and even afterwards, the unfunded liability accrued from the present PAYG system represents a cost to be paid off, and it will offset advantages of privatising a pension scheme such as the extra returns attainable from the higher profitable stock market.[177] The sheer expansion of a mandatory subscription to the national pension scheme would be attractive to the government as a convenient injection of funding to the chronic fund deficit, but would, however, have the same effect as increasing the payroll tax.[178] The higher the payroll tax is for the pension participants, the less likely will people be to work 'on the books', and the more likely tax evasion becomes.[179] Moreover increasing payroll tax is empirically proven to promote steadily growing deficits.[180] It is, therefore, apparent that problems will result unless obstacles as such a lack of methodology on contribution collection, or contribution base determination are removed. [181]

VI. CONCLUSION: TOLERABLE PARTIAL PRIVATISATION

Chile's model is comprised of multi-layered pension provisions combining the traditional DB scheme and a privately managed voluntary pension scheme similar to that of the U.K.[182] Both countries also provide government back up or insurance for certain situations. To some extent, even in

[177] *See* Geanakoplos, above n 165, at 24.

[178] *See* Norton above n 46 n 37 at 829. The payroll tax is the standard source of financing for PAYG systems.

[179] *See* Michell above n 36 at 10. Upon the enforcement of the new extended coverage, it turned out that especially the self-employed have reported income levels far lower than that is believed to be accurate. If the contribution level is determined based on this incorrect amount, a whole indexation system could likely be distorted. *See Dispute flares up over pension system,* Korea Times, 21 Feb 1999. *See also, Opposition lawmakers urge government to postpone new national pension system, Korea Herald*, 24 Feb. 1999

[180] See Neil Howe and Richard Jackson, *CATO INST., THE MYTH OF THE 2.2. PER CENT* (SSP No 11, 15 June 1998) <http://www.socialsecurity.org/pubs/ssps/ssp11es.html> (visited on 3 Nov. 1999). Shifting from advance funding to pay-as-you-go financing will cause problematic rates of return for future generation. *See* Sylvester J Schieber, *Social Security: Past, Present and Future*, Social Security Brief No 5, Mar. 1999 <http://www.nasi.org/SocSec/Briefs/ssbr5.htm> (visited on 20 Jan. 2000)

[181] This transition process in Chile is very distinguished. The government guaranteed that old pensioners wouldn't be affected by the reform, and gave the choice of either staying with the PAYG system, or moving to the new system, to workers already contributing to PAYG system. All future pensioners were to enter the new system. In doing so, a fraction of the difference between a contribution and the current payroll tax was used as a temporary transition payroll tax without reducing net wages or increasing the cost of labor to the employer. Through using recognition bonds as a bridge debt financing, the transition cost was shared by future generations. *See* Testimony of Josè Piñera, above n 46.

[182] *See* Ian Tonks, *Pension Policy in UK*, 14 Nov. 1999, <http://www.bris.ac.uk/Depts/CMPO/abstract2.htm#99/012> (visited on 20 Jan. 2000). Pension in UK comprises of three tiers, first mandatory public, unfunded pension; second, SERPS (in which the benefit is related to the earning ratio); and third, voluntary private provisions.

the market-based pension scheme, there may be still a role for the government to play as a safety back up. It would probably be appropriate for the government to respond when the privatised system calls for proper regulation and prudential supervision over, a fund manager or a private managing company; ensuring transparency for participants as to the value of their assets and the performance of operators; setting quantitative limits on portfolio selections; and encouraging transparent policy disclosure.[183]

Regardless of all the feasibility of pension privatisation, we should bear in mind that one of the fundamental functions of a pension has been to serve as the income redistribution device of a social protection system.[184] A pension system is essentially a set of legal rules that govern that redistribution mechanism.[185] If it were voluntary, some low-income persons for whom coverage might be financially advantageous would opt out because they need the money now.[186] The basic idea that we cannot simply overrule is the need for collective provisions against economic insecurity. Neither can we abandon the wealth redistribution premise, which has been in a substantial part bolstered by a compulsory contribution of the public pension scheme. This still remains popular despite the rise of the ideology of privatisation.[187] In this respect, compulsory coverage seems to be one basic distinguishing principle and feature in the pension system.[188]

Therefore a pension reform realistically requires focus on partial privatisation as a transitioning approach.[189] Because the first tier of a partial privatisation can function to keep pension system's original rationale, wealth redistribution, where the pubic policy can be distilled in. It also can cushion probable adverse effects, as we see above, in carrying out wholesale privatisation all at once, The second tier benefit is facilitated in a local financial market. That is why multidisciplinary organisations endorse the partial privatisation approach in a pension reform especially for developing countries.[190]

[183] *See* Heller, above n 50 at 12. He, further, attempts to define a certain type of liability of a government such as a contingent liability or a conjectural liability by considering that a minimum guarantee, in Chile's pension scheme, implies the contingent public liability. *See* Ibid. at 8, 12–15. He also warns that this tight structure may cause especially 'moral hazard' of the private pension managing companies. *See* ibid. at 14.

[184] *See* Kathryn L Moore, *Redistribution under Partially Privatized Social Security System*, 64 Brooklyn L.Rev. 969 at 988–92 (stressing that Social Security should remain a 'floor of protection on which private-sector economic security measures can be built'): *see also*, Heller above n 50 V. (DC/Fully Funded solution is left distributional and poverty issues to be noted).

[185] *See* graut, above n 46 at 41.

[186] *See* Myers, above n 8 at 17–18. Also they may buy a mortgage or invest into the real estate or a high-risk mutual fund. *See* OTT, supra n 167.

[187] *See* E J Dionne, Jr., *Why Social Insurance?* Social Security Brief No 6, Mar. 1999. <http://www.nasi.org/SocSec/Briefs/ssbr6.htm> (visited on 20 Jan. 2000).

[188] *See* Myers, above n 8 at 10.

[189] *See* Norton, above n 46 at 825.

[190] *See* Hemming, above n 157 at 6.

In conclusion, the privately managed/publicly regulated pension scheme will be an affordable scheme in a sense that it can keep wealth redistribution viable, and harmonise government's role in a market oriented pension system. How to reform in the public pension scheme should be based on how the cause and effect of the reform will come into play in the financial market, and how the market can accommodate this transition. Since a social role of a pension system is moving towards a system that makes more economic and financial sense, 'financial affordability' becomes very much essential in the success of a pension reform, and it can not be separated from the development of a financial market at large. Therefore not only by adjusting parameters to redress fiscal problems in the current public pension scheme, but also by establishing set of legal rules and a regulatory system to accommodate modern pension management into the financial system, the pension should be able to function as a core social safety net to keep the society sustainable and endurable. As it happened in Chile, the anti-reform forces would gear up to defend the status quo.[191] The pensions in Korea have so far been considered politically untouchable and morally sacrosanct. However Korea should remember that it had to painfully witness the collapse of the legend that the Chaebol and banks never collapse.

[191] *See* José Piñera, *El Cascabel al Gato: La Batalla por la Reforma Previsional (The bull by the Horns: The Battle for Chile's Social Security Reform)* (Tom Jonney trans. and abridged) <http://www.pensionreform.org/articles/bull.html> (visited on 3 Nov. 1999).

Chapter 9

Are Hong Kong's Economic Fundamentals Really Sound? A Call for Reform and Transparency

Berry Hsu

The Hong Kong Special Administrative Region (HKSAR) is entering the new millennium with stronger economic fundamentals. Selected economic and financial indicators show that the HKSAR is on the road to recovery following the Asian financial crisis in 1998.[1] Amid globalisation, the rapid growth in importance of high technology and the impending admission of China to the World Trade Organisation (WTO) the economy of the HKSAR needs to undergo major restructuring.[2] Being a special administrative region of China has enabled it to maintain its status as an international financial centre, and it has the added advantage due to its past of having inherited a common law tradition.[3] There are, however, many outstanding issues, inspired by the Asian financial crisis, that the HKSAR must address. This chapter discusses the fundamental problems arising from the Asian financial crisis that the HKSAR has now to tackle, and the measures taken by the HKSAR Government to defend the Territory's financial markets from damage. It will also discuss some of the defects that require immediate attention.

I. THE FINANCIAL CRISIS IN THE CONTEXT OF THE HKSAR

Many factors contributed to the HKSAR becoming one of the most successful city-states in the world.[4] Major among them were the low interest rates,

[1] 'IMF concludes Article IV consultation discussions with the People's Republic of China in respect of the Hong Kong Special Administrative Region', *Public Information Notice (PIN) No 00/15*, Washington, DC: International Monetary Fund, 6 Mar. 2000, 3–4.

[2] Ibid. 2.

[3] The *Basic Law of the Hong Kong Special Administrative Region* (Basic Law) provides that the common law system will remain unchanged for 50 years after 30 June 1997.

[4] See D Roche, 'Hong Kong's troubles aren't over', *Time Asia*, Hong Kong, 3 Nov. 1997, 23.

low labour costs and the high value of assets in the capital market. These factors were supported by the negative interest rate and high land prices. As the Hong Kong dollar is pegged to the US dollar, so are Hong Kong dollar interest rates. It follows then that as the US rate of interest reflects the US rate of inflation, the HKSAR's interest rate should therefore do the same. The rate of inflation in the HKSAR, however, was higher than the rate of inflation in the US. In fact, the HKSAR's prime interest rate was lower than its rate of inflation.

Up until the Asian financial crisis, land sales income in the HKSAR had long been an important source of government revenue. As it is the end purchaser who has to carry the cost of the high value of the land, the high price policy is in effect an equivalent form of indirect taxation. Historically, the Hong Kong Government followed a high land price policy, which it implemented by limiting the supply of land. In addressing the Chinese Government's concern about the future supply of land in the Territory, Annex III (Land Leases) to the 1984 Sino-British Joint Declaration[5] provided that only 50 hectares of land could be granted by the then Hong Kong Government each year until 30 June 1997. However, land granted to the Hong Kong Housing Authority for public rental housing was excluded in order to encourage the administration at the time to release more land for public housing.

The high land price policy naturally resulted in a high book value for assets in the form of share prices and mortgages. This problem was aggravated by banking institutions in the HKSAR, which were lending up to 90 per cent of real estate values for mortgages, until the Hong Kong Monetary Authority (HKMA) issued guidelines restricting the upper ceiling to 70 per cent of the value of a piece of real estate.[6] The inflow of capital assets from overseas, taking advantage of the Hong Kong currency link to the US dollar, helped the economy of the HKSAR during the period of transition in 1997 develop into a bubble economy.

The first signs of the Asian financial crisis appeared in Thailand where large capital inflows, particularly in the form of short-term loans, were handed out through a structurally unsound banking sector.[7] Some of the money was invested in the real estate market, which resulted in inflated property prices.[8] The crisis spread from Thailand to the financial and currency markets in the HKSAR, Indonesia, Malaysia, the Philippines, and

[5] *Joint Declaration of the Government of the United Kingdom of Great Britain and Northern Ireland and the Government of the People's Republic of China on the Question of Hong Kong* (Sino-British Joint Declaration), 19 Dec. 1984.

[6] 'HKMA gives stern warning on mortgage rules', *South China Morning Post*, Hong Kong, 29 July 1997.

[7] S. Sugisaki, *Address to Symposium on Capital Flows and Financial System Stability in Asia*, Washington, DC: International Monetary Fund, 8 Dec. 1997.

[8] Ibid.

South Korea.[9] The fundamental health of the economies of these countries suffered, in varying degrees, the same problems as Thailand. All had inflated real estate markets and problems in the structure and governance of their financial sectors.[10] Banks that had lent money out imprudently eventually had to pay their dues.[11]

As a player in the global economy, the HKSAR, was not immune. However, it was better off than most Asian countries, as its deficits were not clearly visible. Under the Sino-British Joint Declaration the former Hong Kong Government was required to place half the proceeds from its land sales in a Land Fund. At the end of 1997, the foreign currency assets in the Land Fund amounted to US$17.59 billion. Together with the foreign currency assets of the Exchange Fund at US$76.19 billion (the net assets of the Exchange Fund at the end of 1997 were actually US$24.39 billion),[12] which placed Hong Kong third in the world in terms of foreign currency assets.[13]

The financial fate of the HKSAR is inevitably linked with that of mainland China. Ratings agencies have echoed this view. Moody's Investors Services currently links the economies of the HKSAR and China in its evaluation of the outlook of the HKSAR.[14] This has also been made apparent by the minimisation of contagion effects of the crisis that the HKSAR has been able to achieve on the backcurrents of positive reports on China's own economic situation: that China has little short-term debt with foreign lenders and has cooled its overheating economy—inflationary asset prices, rapid credit expansion, the tightness of the labour market.[15]

Prior to the crisis, HKSAR banks had rapidly expanded their lending and financed imprudent investments—such as speculation in taxi licences, securities, and real estate—which resulted in highly inflated asset prices. Hong Kong's foreign exchange reserves were a fundamental factor in the Territory's ability to better weather the effects of the crisis. The Basic Law provides that the 'issue of Hong Kong currency must be backed up by a 100 per cent reserve fund'.[16] Further support is offered by the Hong Kong dollar's exchange rate link to the US dollar under a currency board system.

9 Ibid.

10 Ibid.

11 'Most Asian bourses plunge, some fall on intel news', *The Wall Street Journal*, New York, 5 Mar. 1998.

12 *Annual Report 1997*, Hong Kong: Hong Kong Monetary Authority, 1998 77, 86, and 97.

13 'Hong Kong's latest foreign currency assets figures released', Press Release, Hong Kong: Hong Kong Monetary Authority, 26 Feb. 1998.

14 'Linking China fate to Hong Kong, Moody's lowers outlook for both', *The Wall Street Journal*, New York, 20 Feb. 1998.

15 'IMF Article IV concludes consultation discussions held in 1997 with the People's Republic of China in respect of the Hong Kong Special Administrative Region', *Press Information Notice No 98/5*, Washington, DC: International Monetary Fund, 16 Feb. 1998.

16 Art. 111, Basic Law.

A long-standing problem of the HKSAR banking system has been operating along the lines of the theory of moral hazard. During an earlier banking crisis, the former Hong Kong Government bailed out three troubled depositors; the Hang Lung Bank, the Overseas Trust Bank, and the Bank of Credit and Commerce,[17] the intention being to avoid bankruptcies, layoffs, and a possible economic downturn. On the other hand, it was equally the case that the depositors and bankers relied on the Government to come to their rescue. A further form of moral hazard is created by the currency board system. Overseas lenders able to lend money in the HKSAR for a higher interest rate than at home do so without fear of foreign exchange risks. The large part of the money attracted into the HKSAR through this channel turned out to be hot money.

On 29 October 1997 Moody's Investors Service downgraded the outlook for banks in the HKSAR, giving them a negative rating. It also reviewed the financial strength ratings of two of the HKSAR's leading banks, the Hang Seng Bank and The Hongkong and Shanghai Banking Corporation, for a possible downgrade.[18] The concerns expressed by the ratings related to the high level of exposure in real estate of the banks in the Territory and the impact of currency pressures and market volatility. Despite the ratings, the HKSAR Government issued a statement declaring that the local banks were in fact well capitalised and robust.[19] Although Moody's rating, which together with Standard & Poor's rating, has been recognised by the *Banking Ordinance*,[20] its accuracy is to a degree debatable as while it expressed a certain pessimism among the international financial community, the agency failed to forecast the crisis in Asia.[21]

On 12 November 1997 Standard & Poor's warned that the Asian financial crisis could have a negative effect on global banking.[22] Moody's rating was supported by another leading bank rating agency, Capital Intelligence, which also gave a negative report for HKSAR banks.[23] Standard & Poor's, however, was more positive, stating only that the volatile nature of the real estate market and stock market in the HKSAR would strain bank earnings and asset quality.[24]

[17] B. Hsu, *Law of Banking and Finance in the HKSAR*, (Hong Kong: Hong Kong University Press, 1998), 160–1.

[18] 'Rating action', *Global Credit Research*, New York: Moody's Investors Service, 29 Oct. 1997

[19] 'China joins critical barrage of US ratings agency as blue chips placed on review–bankers rally against Moody's downgrade', *South China Morning Post*, Hong Kong, 31 Oct. 1997.

[20] Sched. 4, *Banking Ordinance*, chap. 155, Laws of Hong Kong.

[21] 'Rating the raters', *South China Morning Post*, Hong Kong, 31 Oct. 1997.

[22] 'Market turmoil taking toll on global financial institutions', *Credit Week*, (New York: Standard & Poor), 12 Nove. 1997; 'S & P warns of global spread of Asian banking malaise', *South China Morning Post*, Hong Kong, 12 Nov. 1997.

[23] 'Capital follows in Moody's negative-rating footsteps', ibid. Hong Kong, 2 Nov. 1997.

[24] Ibid. 'Market turmoil taking toll on global financial institutions', *Credit Week* (New York: Standard & Poor's), 12 Nov. 1997.

The banks had for a while been granting mortgage loans for purchases of real estate with no consideration of the Territory's economic fundamentals. Banks simply evaluated property value from its technical aspect. Basing future performance on experience, bankers were able to count on such a practice. At the end of September 1997, the average outstanding principal for a property mortgage was HK$1.3 million and the average loan-to-property value ratio was 52 per cent.[25] Property acquired for investment purposes accounted for only 7 per cent and the delinquency ratio of all mortgage loans, i.e. loans overdue for more than 90 days, was 0.1 per cent.[26] These figures were compiled before the Asian financial crisis spread to the HKSAR and shortly after the Government's apparent determination to reverse the high land price policy of the former administration was made known.[27] The long-term plan of providing adequate housing to all HKSAR residents was announced on the first day of the establishment of Hong Kong as a Special Administrative Region of China.[28]

The Chief Executive of the HKSAR, Tung Chee-hwa, acknowledged that the HKSAR had inherited an economy from the former administration that was plagued by soaring real estate prices, high inflation and negative interest rates.[29] He stated that these problems had to be addressed. For the HKSAR to be competitive in the global markets as a value-added-service-based economy, real estate prices must be adjusted and stabilised. As a result of the HKSAR Government's stated desire to provide adequate housing to its residents, and the Asian financial crisis, real estate prices were expected to fall 55 per cent from their peak in June 1997[30] (this was a conservative forecast, as real estate prices increased by 50 per cent between February 1996 and September 1997.[31])

Mr Tung admitted that any further abrupt drop in real estate prices might adversely affect the banking system.[32] In reality, the banks could count on the Government to take measures to ensure their survival at the expense of the public interest. The HKSAR Government has taken a series

25 *Survey on Residential Mortgages in Hong Kong*, Hong Kong: Hong Kong Monetary Authority, 25 Feb. 1998.

26 Ibid.

27 'Housing blueprint sets high targets', *South China Morning Post*, Hong Kong, 2 July 1997.

28 'Speech by the Chief Executive', *Daily Information Bulletin*, Hong Kong: Information Services Department, 1 July 1997.

29 'CE's letter from Hong Kong', *Daily Information Bulletin*, Hong Kong: Information Services Department, 14 Feb. 1998.

30 'Hong Kong property issues falling to attractive level', *The Wall Street Journal*, New York, 27 Jan. 1998.

31 *Survey on Residential Mortgages in Hong Kong*, Hong Kong: Hong Kong Monetary Authority, 25 Feb. 1998.

32 'CE's letter from Hong Kong', *Daily Information Bulletin*, Hong Kong: Information Services Department, 14 Feb. 1998.

of measures which may cushion the steep fall of real estate prices, including designating certain prime land for government offices,[33] providing greater flexibility in the land sale programme to provide 85,000 flats each year,[34] implementing mortgage relief in the tax system,[35] and introducing fixed-rate mortgages.[36] These measures were not intended to boost real estate prices; rather, they were designed as a means by which the Government could monitor a possible collapse in real estate prices. In addition, the HKSAR Government has taken measures to improve the liquidity of the banking system and relaxed anti-speculation measures on real estate one day after the HKMA gave a negative outlook for asset quality of banking institutions.[37]

The global effects of the Asian financial crisis already have caused unavoidable damage to the banking sector of the HKSAR. The first casualty was the merchant banking arm of Peregrine, Asia's largest independent finance house, which lent US$350 million unsecured to an Indonesian taxi company controlled by a daughter of former President Suharto, without assessing the political risk.[38] In January 1998 the Securities and Futures Commission (SFC) restricted Peregrine's business pending clarification of its position. In early 1988, the majority of HKSAR banks began to report bad debt provisions as a result of their exposure in Asian countries during their financial crises.[39] The HKMA was also forecasting lower growth in bank lending and interest margins amid high interbank rates.[40]

However, the HKSAR also shared some problems with other Asian countries. It might have been able to fend off speculative attack on its currency peg to the US dollar in the short term, but its financial markets would have suffered severe damage, as demonstrated during the October 1997 currency crisis.[41] With the depreciation of other Asian currencies, particularly the

[33] 'Tamar selected for government offices complex', *South China Morning Post*, Hong Kong, 17 Jan. 1998.

[34] 'Exco backs 'flexible' land sale', ibid. Hong Kong, 11 Feb. 1998.

[35] *Budget 98*, Hong Kong: Government Printer, 18 Feb. 1998.

[36] 'HK Mortgage Corp. to proceed with fixed-rate mortgage plans', *The Wall Street Journal*, New York, 26 Feb. 1998.

[37] 'Financial Secretary's transcript', *Daily Information Bulletin*, Hong Kong: Information Services Department, 29 May 1998; D Carse, *Review of the Banking Sector First Quarter 1998*, Hong Kong: Hong Kong Monetary Authority, 28 May 1998.

[38] 'Last-ditch bid to rescue beleaguered Peregrine Asia's largest independent finance house in dire straits after bailout effort collapses', *South China Morning Post*, Hong Kong, 10 Jan. 1998; 'Peregrine loan pact with Steady Safe put at US$350m', ibid. Hong Kong, 16 Jan. 1998.

[39] 'Banks begin to measure depth of crisis', *Hong Kong Standard*, Hong Kong, 8 Feb. 1998; 'HSBC's growth of 10 per cent is lower than expected', *The Wall Street Journal*, New York, 24 Feb. 1998; 'Standard Chartered sees soaring bad debt ahead', *South China Morning Post*, Hong Kong, 26 Feb. 1998.

[40] Ibid. 'Goldman sees tough year for bank industry', *South China Morning Post*, Hong Kong, 16 Jan. 1998.

[41] 'The HKMA shapes up for showdown with speculators', ibid. Hong Kong, 27 Oct. 1997.

Japanese yen, the Hong Kong currency came under increasing pressure. Since the beginning of 1998, 'speculators' had begun to borrow substantial amounts of Hong Kong dollars through the debt market at low interest.[42] With a rising risk premium, real interest rates rose rapidly and asset prices suddenly plummeted dropping by half.[43] At the same time, stock and futures prices adjusted sharply downwards by more than 50 per cent.[44]

II. INTERVENTION OF THE FINANCIAL MARKETS

This downward adjustment led to a major speculative attack on the Hong Kong dollar in August 1998.[45] Finally, on 15 August 1998, the HKSAR Government intervened in a counterattack. Official justification for the move cited pressure and persistent attack on the currency.[46] The Government claimed it had evidence that there were speculators double playing; on the currency market and the futures market.[47] This allegation was not difficult to prove; an attack on the currency market would force up interest rates, and this would be followed by profit-taking through short-selling of the futures index. Free market economies have no regulatory controls for the use by investment banks of hedge funds to attack the Hong Kong dollar. Accordingly, the logic of free trade simply could not be applied to currency convertibility.[48] The Government alleged there were clear signs that the aim of these speculative attacks was to make quick profits in the futures market.[49] Taking no action risked a 50 per cent surge in interest rates and the a substantial drop in the Hang Seng Index.[50] This would further lower property prices, and impose enormous pressure on the banking system.

In order to restore investor confidence in the financial markets, the HKSAR Government decided to deploy its Exchange Fund to deal with this very exceptional circumstance.[51] As a result of its two-week intervention in the financial markets, speculative attacks were at last fading. The total cost of the share acquisition by the HKSAR Government was US$15.2 billion.[52] As a consequence of such a colossal injection of funds, the Government

[42] *LC Paper No CB(1) 534/98–99*, Hong Kong: Legislative Council, 7 Sept. 1998, 3.

[43] 'Transcript of Financial Secretary's press briefing', *Daily Information Bulletin*, Hong Kong: Government Information Services, 14 Aug. 1998.

[44] Ibid. [45] Ibid. [46] Ibid. [47] Ibid.

[48] J Bhagwati, 'The Capital Myth', *Foreign Affairs*, May/June 1998, 77:3, 7.

[49] 'Transcript of Financial Secretary's press briefing', *Daily Information Bulletin*, Hong Kong: Government Information Services, 14 Aug. 1998.

[50] *LC Paper No CB(1) 534/98–99*, Hong Kong: Legislative Council, 7 Sept. 1998, 4.

[51] Ibid.

[52] *Statement by Mr. T.L. Yang, Chairman of Exchange Fund Investment Limited*, Hong Kong: Hong Kong Monetary Authority, 26 Oct. 1998.

became the largest shareholder in HSBC Holdings PLC, which owns The Hongkong and Shanghai Banking Corporation and Midland Bank, with 8.80 per cent of issued shares.[53] This meant that the HKSAR Government could demand a seat on the Board of Directors of HSBC Holdings PLC. A legal barrier also arose; this substantial shareholding was barely short of the 10 per cent ownership threshold, which required regulatory approval in the United Kingdom. The British Financial Services Authority naturally would be most concerned whether the HKSAR Government was a desirable substantial shareholder in a major British banking institution.[54]

In addition to this unprecedented governmental intervention in the financial markets, the HKSAR Government also adopted seven measures to strengthen the currency board arrangements.[55] It also proposed some thirty measures to strengthen the order and transparency of the securities and futures market.[56] Although belatedly, the Government also tightened the rules on short-selling and settlement and streamlined the automatic trading systems that in the past had enabled speculators to take advantage of the delay in the settlement process.[57] However, it was concerned that if too many restrictions were imposed, the market would be unduly disturbed.[58] Speculator tactics were difficult to predict, the HKSAR had one of the most open financial markets in the world, there were no hard and fast rules in place that could prevent attacks on the Hong Kong dollar.[59] Accordingly, the HKSAR Government has to balance the need to grant the Chief Executive wide discretionary powers to direct the financial markets in emergency situation with the rule of law, which the rule-based financial markets of the HKSAR pride themselves on.[60]

The nature and the suddenness of the Government's action took many by surprise.[61] Economists were divided as to whether this move would effectively stabilise the Hong Kong dollar. The intervention drew the wrath of the financial sector; as most of the major investment bankers were counting on the success of the attack of the Hong Kong currency to make some quick money. While the HKSAR Government argued that it had to maintain a level playing field, its intervention was roundly criticised as illegal

[53] 'Authority has most shares in HSBC', *South China Morning Post*, Hong Kong, 2 Sept. 1998.

[54] 'Monetary authority's HSBC Holdings approaches British hurdles on ownership', ibid. Hong Kong, 3 Sept. 1998.

[55] *LC Paper No CB(1) 534/98–99*, Hong Kong: Legislative Council, 7 Sept. 1998, 4.

[56] Ibid. [57] Ibid. [58] Ibid.

[59] 'Measures to strengthen the currency board system', Press Release, Hong Kong: Financial Services Bureau, 21 Oct. 1988.

[60] 'Front Section', *The Wall Street Journal*, New York, 30 Sept. 1998.

[61] 'Hong Kong Investors Play Guessing Game', *The Asian Wall Street*, Tokyo, 19 Aug. 1998.

manipulation of the stock market.[62] The subsequent refusal of the HKSAR Government to disclose its shareholdings was considered by some a breach of the *Securities (Disclosure of Interests) Ordinance* and the *Code on Takeovers and Mergers*.[63] Critics suggested that the HKSAR Government was obliged to abide by the *Securities Ordinance* by 'necessary implication' of the *Interpretation and General Clauses Ordinance*.[64] Leading members of the Legislative Council attacked such intervention as lacking in transparency and a conflict of interests,[65] but it was an argument that was more political than legal.

During the crisis, the HKSAR Government alleged that share prices, interest levels and interest rates in the HKSAR were dictated wholly by manipulators,[66] yet it was unable to identify the manipulators, being disguised as they were by many different channels.[67] In reality, the HKSAR is struggling to keep up with the latest developments in financial technology, as is its currently inadequate regulatory framework. The HKSAR Government did not have the emergency powers to suspend the relevant laws while the markets were under attack. In an emergency situation, it could hardly be expected that the Government reveal its strategy in order to comply with legal provisions on transparency. Therefore, short of imposing marshal law, its options while it faced a meltdown of the financial system in the HKSAR were limited. Without addressing the merits of intervention, the HKSAR Government's legal position as regards it intervention may be better than was apparent at the time for the following reasons:

- There is a statutory provision in the HKSAR, which codified the long-established common law, that the state is not bound by a legislative provision unless such is expressly stated.[68]
- The intended purpose of the *Securities Ordinance* is primarily the protection of the investing public through the regulation of the stock markets, control of trading in securities and the investment advisory business, and protection of investors.[69] The intended purpose of the *Securities (Disclosure of Interests) Ordinance* is to provide a level

62 K. Lynch, ' The temptation to intervene: Problems created by the Government's intervention in the Hong Kong stock market', paper presented in Challenges for the New International Financial Architecture: Lessons from East Asia, Hong Kong: Asian Institute of International Financial Law, June 1999, 13.

63 Ibid. 15–16.

64 Ibid. 13–14.

65 *LC Paper No CB(1) 534/98–99*, Hong Kong: Legislative Council, 7 Sept. 1998, 5; Lynch, op cit, 16–18.

66 'Financial Secretary's transcript', *Daily Information Bulletin*, Hong Kong: Government Information Services, 8 Sept. 1998.

67 *LC Paper No CB(1) 534/98–99*, Hong Kong: Legislative Council, 7 Sept. 1998, 6.

68 Section 66, *Interpretation and General Clauses Ordinance*, ch 1, Laws of Hong Kong; *Bombay v Bombay Municipal Corporation* [1974] AC 58.

69 Long title, *Securities Ordinance*, ch 333, Laws of Hong Kong.

playing field by requiring certain persons to disclose their shareholdings.[70] Intervention into the financial markets in defence of the Hong Kong dollar had never been the mischief these ordinances intended to address.

- The Hong Kong dollar would not have survived the speculative attack had the HKSAR Government not so quickly and decisively intervened. The issue is whether breach of the law would avert a greater evil. Such a departure from legislative norms could be justified on common law grounds of necessity, which would render an unlawful act lawful.[71]
- The HKSAR Government was performing its public duty to protect the Hong Kong dollar under the Basic Law, which gives it the mandate to provide an appropriate economic and legal environment for maintaining the HKSAR as an international financial centre,[72] and requires the issue of Hong Kong currency must be backed up by a 100 per cent reserve fund.[73] It could have argued that the intervention was necessary to and essential in carrying out these provisions of the Basic Law. The common law doctrine that any legislation that is inconsistent with the constitutional document is invalid was incorporated into the Basic Law.[74]
- The Secretary of Justice could always exercise the prerogative power of *nolle prosequi* in the unlikely event that there would be a private prosecution, or a prosecution initiated by the SFC, when all these legally based justifications fail.
- The proper forum for addressing possible wrongdoing by the Executive Government is the Legislative Council, which has the power to impeach the head of the Executive.[75] There is little doubt that the HKSAR Government was acting in the public interest when it intervened in the financial markets. According to Blackstone, 'no human laws are of any validity, if contrary to' the law of nature.[76] In the case of *Dr Bonham*, Chief Justice Coke said that no legislation should contradict common right and reason.[77]

While the HKSAR Government could legally and morally defend its intervention in the financial markets, there were doubts about the fairness and soundness of the intervention. The Government may have extrajudicial grounds to justify its intervention to correct the failures and improve the

[70] Long title, *Securities (Disclosure of Interests) Ordinance*, ch 396, Laws of Hong Kong.
[71] J. C. Smith and B. Hogan, *Criminal Law* (London: Butterworths, 1992) 245–52.
[72] Art. 109, Basic Law.
[73] Art. 111, Basic Law.
[74] Art. 11, Basic Law.
[75] Art. 73(9), Basic Law.
[76] W Blackstone, *Commentaries on the Laws of England*, vol. 1 (Chicago: University of Chicago Press, 1979) 41.
[77] (1610) 8 Co. Rep. 114 at 118.

efficiency of the financial markets.[78] However, the general consensus remains that this type of intervention could well have the effect of hindering the efficiency of the financial markets.[79] In December 1998, the WTO raised concerns about the preference shown towards companies listed on the Hang Seng Index by the HKSAR Government.[80] This had to be so in the Government's defence action against the attack as speculators were short-selling the futures index. The WTO also expressed its concern about the holding of HSBC shares by the HKSAR Government, as it perceived a conflict of interest between the Government regulator and the bank it regulated.[81] The Government has since established, and appointed the directors of, Exchange Fund Investments Ltd, to manage and dispose the shares at arm's length. In the event, this concern has yet to be justified.

In retrospect, the intervention proved an aversion of the greater evil; repelling the speculative attack on the Hong Kong dollar, which might have caused the total meltdown of the HKSAR's financial markets. On 6 March 2000, the International Monetary Fund (IMF) praised the HKSAR Government for having successfully defended and even strengthened the linked exchange rate. It attributed this to its skilful economic management and credibility of policy making.[82]

III. FINANCIAL MARKET REFORM

Although the HKSAR was successful in defending its currency, this success may well be attributable to a combination of external factors and sheer luck rather than the infallibility of the measures that the Government took. In response to the 1997 Asian financial crisis, in April 1998 the HKSAR Government released its *Report on the Financial Market Review*.[83] While the report recommended rules on increased financial disclosure by listed companies, enhanced market rules on derivatives, and the regulation of brokerage-related finance companies, it showed a general satisfaction with the transparency of the banking system.[84] The report did not address the overall negative rating of HKSAR banks from Moody's and Standard and Poor's. In January 2000, Moody's rated the financial strength of six

78 *World Economic Outlook: Financial Turbulence and the World Economy* (Washington, DC: International Monetary Fund), Oct. 1998, 101.

79 Ibid.

80 'Hong Kong, China's free market system will help facilitate economy recovery', *Press/TPRB/95* (Washington, DC: World Trade Organisation), 4 Dec. 1998, 6.

81 Ibid.

82 'IMF concludes Article IV consultation discussions held with People's Republic of China in respect of the Hong Kong Special Administrative Region', op cit, 2.

83 Hong Kong: Financial Services Branch, 23 Apr. 1998.

84 Ibid. 42.

HKSAR banks, including a leader, D (or 'adequate').[85] However, it stated that strong recurring profits, a thick capital cushion, ample liquidity and strict supervision all work to ensure a stable outlook for the rated HKSAR banks.[86]

The regulatory framework of the financial markets in the HKSAR is scattered across twelve pieces of legislation, including the *Companies Ordinance*.[87] As a result of the April 1996 recommendation by the Securities Review Committee, the SFC published *A Consultation Paper on a Draft for a Composite Securities and Futures Bill*, consolidating and rationalising eight of these ordinances, and updating certain provisions.[88] The objective was to provide a modernised, simplified and user-friendly ordinance for regulation of the financial markets. After a few revisions,[89] this bill was introduced into the Legislative Council as lower priority.[90] As at 1 April 2000, this bill is still on the shelf.

In March 1999 the HKSAR Government announced its *Policy Paper on Securities and Futures Market Reform*.[91] It aimed at unifying and de-mutualising the Stock Exchange of Hong Kong (SEHK), the Hong Kong Futures Exchange (HKFE), the Hong Kong Securities Clearing Company Ltd, the SEHK Options Clearing House Ltd, and the HKFE Clearing Corporation Ltd. This is merely one step towards breaking the old boys' clubs and eliminating conflicts of interest in these organisations.[92] At about the same time, the SFC also released its *Proposed Amendments to the Securities (Disclosure of Interests) Ordinance*.[93] These long overdue amendments aim at promoting more transparency in the market. On 24 February 2000, the Legislative Council enacted the *Exchanges and Clearing Houses (Merger) Ordinance*.

Market volatility, caused by inefficient and imperfect financial markets, inevitably has a major impact on the banking sector.[94] The rating of banks

[85] *Banking System Outlook*, (New York: Moody's Investors Service), Jan. 2000.

[86] Ibid. 7–9.

[87] Ch 32, Laws of Hong Kong.

[88] Hong Kong: Securities and Futures Commission, 1996.

[89] *Main Proposed Revisions to a Draft for a Composite Securities and Futures Bill*, Hong Kong: Securities and Futures Commission, December 1996; *Overview Guide to The Proposed Securities and Futures Bill*, Hong Kong: Securities and Future Commission, 5 July 1999

[90] According to the Secretary General of the Legislative Council: 'The Bill (*Securities and Futures Bill*) was introduced into the Legislative Council last year. A subcommittee on the Bill has been subsequently formed and held its first meeting on 10 Sept. 1999. So far, 4 meetings have been held. However, the Bill is held in abeyance for the moment since the priority has been given to other Bills. Thus, we cannot tell when the subcommittee will resume its meeting for the time being.' (e-mail to this writer from the Legislative Council <pi@legco.gov.hk> dated 14 Feb. 2000).

[91] Hong Kong: Financial Services Branch, Mar. 1999.

[92] Hsu, op cit, 249–51.

[93] Hong Kong: Securities and Futures Commission, Mar. 1999.

[94] 'Market volatility impacts global banking', *Credit Week*, New York: Standard and Poor's, 12 Nov. 1997, 10–13.

in the HKSAR has to take account of the volatile nature of the stock and the property markets. With an increase in the number of financial products on the market and in off-shore subsidiaries, the Barings incident in 1995 illustrated the need to supervise the banking institutions and the whole range of their financial operations very closely. At the minimum, all the HKSAR's regulatory agencies should be rationalised into one super-agency. The overlapping of supervisory costs, as well as effort, may thus be avoided. The collapse of CA Pacific in 1998 demonstrates the urgent need for the establishment of a super-statutory body with powers to make rules.[95] As early as April 1991, the then Commissioner of Banking knew of the risk of authorised institutions extending credit facilities to stockbrokers against security over shares lodged by their clients.[96] Nevertheless, the HKMA and SFC failed to co-ordinate their regulation of the unregulated arms of stockbrokers. Even in 1998, the *Report on the Financial Market Review*, however belatedly, had recommended that all broker-related finance companies should be subject to regulatory control by the SFC.[97]

IV. TRANSPARENCY AND THE LEGACY OF HONG KONG'S ACCOUNTING STANDARDS

Although the HKSAR Government is revamping its regulatory framework of banking and finance, the legal infrastructure supporting this framework has to be enhanced in the long run. It is fortunate that the good regulation of HKSAR banks has mitigated some of the deficiencies in its corporate governance requirements.[98] The 1986 *Banking Ordinance* and its amendments are intended to establish a regulatory framework in accordance with global standards by requiring all banks to observe certain sound fundamental principles. Some of the recommendations of the Basle Committee on Banking Supervision[99] were adopted in the HKSAR. These included a capital adequacy ratio and a liquidity ratio as well as restrictions on loans advanced and interests held. The Banking Ordinance may have good intent, but it failed to take account of global flows of capital and the latest financial technology used to manage risk. Money can flow into the HKSAR in a split second, but it may also leave at the same speed. It is therefore the long-term economic fundamentals, rather than the short-term valuation of

[95] 'Lending loophole attached', *South China Morning Post*, Hong Kong, 21 Jan. 1998.

[96] 'Lending to stockbrokers', *Guideline No 5.4*, Hong Kong: Hong Kong Monetary Authority, 12 Apr. 1991.

[97] *Report on the Financial Market Review*, Hong Kong: Financial Services Branch, 23 Apr. 1998, 94.

[98] *Banking System Outlook*, New York: Moody's Investors Service, Jan. 2000.

[99] 'Prudential Supervision in Hong Kong', Hong Kong Monetary Authority, 1997.

assets, that should be given the greatest consideration. In evaluating the HKSAR's long-term economic fundamentals, banking institutions ought to make proper disclosure of their strengths and weaknesses. Transparency is essential to the strength of a country's economic fundamentals.

The weakness in the financial structures of most Asian countries during their own financial crises was a lack of transparency and accountability among the institutions involved and the financial system itself.[100] A transparent system will enable market participants to have sufficient information to identify the risks they assume.[101] On 15 March 2000, the *Securities and Futures Legislation (Provision of False Information) Bill* had its first reading in the Legislative Council. This bill addresses the absence of statutory provisions on the providing of false or misleading information to the SFC.[102]

This is just the 'tip of the iceberg', however. The HKSAR's banking and financial markets are far from transparent, in that the majority of participants in these markets do not have the ability to process information, and the availability to them of information on which they make their investment decisions is very much restricted. According to a 1993 study by Capital Information Services, in respect of bank accounting disclosure, including non-quantitative information, banks in the HKSAR were ranked just above their counterparts in mainland China, and below most East Asian countries, including Thailand, Malaysia, Indonesia, Taiwan (Republic of China), the Philippines and South Korea.[103] Since the report only very little change has occurred in the HKSAR's accounting system.[104]

The effects of globalisation mean that the HKSAR can be adversely affected by external factors beyond its regulatory control. According to a 1997 report by the IMF, the Asian financial crisis has significantly clouded the prospects for economic growth and financial stability in the HKSAR in the short term, and has left it with a degree of vulnerability.[105] As the HKSAR practises a free and open capital market with virtually instant liquidity, it is vulnerable to global shifts in investor mood.[106] However, it can minimise the risk by adopting internationally accepted accounting practices and disclosure rules as well as international banking standards. The

[100] *Report of the Working Group on Transparency and Accountability*, Washington, DC: International Monetary Fund, Oct. 1998, v.

[101] Ibid.

[102] 'Bill to criminalise provision of false information', Press Release, Hong Kong: Financial Services Branch, 2 Mar. 2000.

[103] P Delhaise, *Asia in Crisis: The Implosion of the Banking and Finance System* (New York: John Wiley & Sons, 1998), 48.

[104] This will be discussed later in this section.

[105] 'IMF concludes Article IV consultation discussions held in 1997 with the People's Republic of China in respect of the Hong Kong Special Administrative Region', op cit.

[106] Ibid.

IMF report subtly criticised the disclosure requirements of the HKSAR by suggesting that 'a further broadening of disclosure requirements could help reduce market uncertainty and limit the risk of unwarranted contagion'.[107] The full effects of the financial crisis on HKSAR banks cannot be fully analysed unless more information is disclosed. Unlike the retail and manufacturing sectors where sales volume counts, banks can always amend their balance sheets to give a rosy picture. These disclosures should therefore be highly specific.[108]

In August 1999, the IMF published another report. It stated the HKSAR had achieved a high degree of transparency in data dissemination, fiscal policy, monetary and financial policies, and banking supervision.[109] Nevertheless, it subtly mentioned that there was room to improve transparency.[110] In ensuring a level playing field, the financial markets must not be informationally impaired. In the HKSAR, poor accounting practices often conceal the weakness in the financial markets. Studies have shown that investors and creditors give issuers and borrowers the benefit of the doubt if they are not given adequate information about the firms' financial performance.[111] Without full, timely and accurate information, market participants are left to make investment decisions by drawing inferences from the limited information received.[112] That banking institutions may adopt their own accounting practices and methodologies in collusion with auditors to provide a rosy outlook is entirely legitimate in the HKSAR.[113] Had The Hongkong and Shanghai Banking Corporation adopted the 'benchmark treatment', as some banking institutions have adopted, instead of the 'alternative treatment', where investments are carried at fair market value at the date of the balance sheet, then its two interim reports on profits would have been higher by 72 per cent and 90 per cent respectively.[114]

In the HKSAR, auditors must conform to the auditing standards prescribed by the Hong Kong Society of Accountants (HKSA). The HKSA publishes auditing guidelines, e.g. *Statements of Standard Accounting*

107 Ibid.

108 'HSBC's growth of 10 per cent is lower than expected', *The Wall Street Journal*, New York, 24 Feb. 1998.

109 *Experimental IMF Report on Observance of Standards and Codes: People's Republic of China—Hong Kong Special Administrative Region*, Washington, DC: International Monetary Fund, Aug. 1999.

110 Ibid.

111 *Report of the Working Group on Transparency and Accountability*, op cit, 5.

112 Ibid.

113 'The Hongkong and Shanghai Banking Corporation Limited 1999 Interim Consolidated Results—Highlights', Press Release, Hong Kong: The Hongkong and Shanghai Banking Corporation Limited, 2 Aug. 1999, no 16; 'If adopted the same accounting treatment as the Bank of East Asia, Hong Kong and Shanghai Banking Corporation's interim profits would have risen by 72 per cent', *Ming Pao Daily*, Hong Kong, 3 Aug. 1999.

114 Ibid.

Practice. It also endorses some of the guidelines of the International Auditing Practices Committee of the International Federation of Accountants. However, the guidelines published by the HKSA are few and fall short of the *International Standards of Auditing* (ISA).[115] The *Companies Ordinance* requires every company to keep proper account books.[116] A company must present a 'true and fair' view of the state of its affairs and explain its transactions;[117] it must also prepare a balance sheet and profit and loss account in accordance with the Tenth Schedule of the Ordinance.[118] According to the *Consultancy Report on the Review of the Hong Kong Companies Ordinance*,[119] the information required by the Ordinance is no longer consistent with accounting practices.[120] The report recommended the adoption of generally accepted accounting principles (GAAP), which are to be set by an independent accounting standards body.[121] An IMF report published in August 1999 noted the HKSAR's finalisation of twenty-two new *Statements of Auditing Standards*, and which are compatible with the ISA.[122] However, a 1999 practice directive issued by the HKSA has stated that most securities, originally classified as long-term investments, can be booked through the profit and loss statement as 'benchmark treatment' or booked through balance sheet reserves as 'alternative treatment'.[123] The latter treatment follows the ISA standards.[124] This flexibility led to a jump in the interim profits of HKR International of some 33 per cent.[125] In any event, banking institutions should adopt conservative accounting practices to show steady profits in accordance with international standards.

Although the GAAP normally meet the 'true and fair view' requirement, there are always cases that escape coverage.[126] As a result, there is always the possibility that even compliance with the rules may not give a 'true and fair view'. In two cases, *Lloyd Cheyham and Co Ltd v Littlejohn & Co*

[115] For a comparison, see T. Chan and G. Chau, 'The Internationalisation of Accounting Standards Major Benefits for Hong Kong', *International Accountant*, 1999, 7, 24–5.
[116] Section 121(1), *Companies Ordinance*, ch 32, Laws of Hong Kong.
[117] Section 121(2), *Companies Ordinance*, ch 32, Laws of Hong Kong.
[118] Ibid.
[119] Hong Kong: Government Printer, Mar. 1997.
[120] Ibid. 100–1.
[121] Ibid. 100.
[122] *Experimental IMF Report on Observance of Standards and Codes: People's Republic of China—Hong Kong Special Administrative Region*, Washington, DC: International Monetary Fund, Aug. 1999.
[123] 'HKR profits from change in accounting', *South China Morning Post*, Hong Kong, 18 Dec. 1999.
[124] *Hong Kong Statement of Standard Accounting Practice* 2.124, conform with *International Accounting Standards* 39.
[125] 'HKR profits from change in accounting', *South China Morning Post*, Hong Kong, 18 Dec. 1999.
[126] G Macdonald, 'Substance, Form and Equity in Taxation and Accounting', *The Modern Law Review*, 1991, 54:6, 841.

Ltd[127] and *Prudential Assurance v Newman Industries plc (No 2)*,[128] the courts have shown that they are in fact not prepared to accept the standards as conclusive, although they are willing to give credence to the standards, the effect being that the standards are only of persuasive force.[129] The GAAP permit a departure in cases where adopting them does not give a 'true and fair view'; the auditor must, however, state the particulars and reasons for the departure.[130]

As the 'true and fair view' requirement is a matter of law rather than accounting,[131] it is necessary to consider what elements its legal definition should cover. 'True and fair view' implies that this definition should go further than compliance with accounting conventions, but accountants are unable to agree on what more it should involve. There has been much argument about the 'true and fair view' of balance sheets. The requirement of comprehensiveness is debatable because it is difficult to decide how much information should be revealed in each particular case.[132] Academic studies have consistently shown that auditors rely on precedent in choosing accounting standards. There is also a problem of what 'true and fair' is in a cultural context. The economic, historical, political and sociological background of the HKSAR's Chinese sub-culture should be considered in the formulation of such a view. Complexities may also arise if the nature of the concerned entity's trade is taken into account. If there is a difference between a precedent and a position that a company, or a particular trade, follows in adopting a certain accounting standard, the auditor would tend to rely on the precedent.

It has also been suggested that the legal test should concentrate on the effect of the accounts on users, rather than looking at the matter from the position of the company or of the auditors. However, this argument cannot be seriously presented unless some view is taken as to who the users are, or are assumed to be.[133] These different opinions on what is a 'true and fair view' mean that an investor may not be able to receive optimal information. Another difficulty concerning the 'true and fair view' is that, in many cases, those responsible for the accounts have no interest in making them helpful and informative because companies do not want to give full details of their financial position in a publication which may be read by their competition. Consequently, there is often pressure on auditors to accept the bare minimum of disclosure.[134] It is therefore necessary for auditors to maintain their independence. The *Companies Ordinance*[135] only requires the auditor to

127 [1987] B.C.L.C. 303. 128 [1980] Ch. D. 257. 129 McGee, op cit, 883–85.

130 'Foreword', *Statements of Standards Accounting Practice and Accounting Guidelines*, Hong Kong: Hong Kong Society of Accountants, 1997

131 McGee, op cit, 876. 132 Ibid. 879–81. 133 Ibid. 882.

134 Ibid. 883.

135 Para 43, Part III, Third Schedule, *Companies Ordinance*, ch 32, Laws of Hong Kong.

be a professional qualified under the *Professional Accountants Ordinance*[136] and to operate at arm's length from the company. However, there is no provision prohibiting the company from shopping around for the auditor that will produce the most favourable report.

Moreover, there is no provision in the HKSAR requiring an auditor to state which accounting rules it has used, or to expressly note and explain any departure from the *Companies Ordinance* or from the accepted professional standards. However, even if there were such a provision, it would not be of great help to non-accountants.[137] In *Caparo Industries plc v Dickman*,[138] the House of Lords held that auditors owed no duty to the investing public who relied on audited accounts to purchase shares, applying it also to existing shareholders who purchase further shares. There is no special relationship between the auditor and the investing public who rely on the auditor's report. Their Lordships do not seem to have considered the economic effect of such a decision on the securities markets.

Some auditors may manipulate accounting rules to circumvent or undermine the purpose of a regulation. This is known as 'creative compliance'.[139] Moreover, guidelines on the application of broad rules made by the regulatory authorities, e.g. the SEHK, the courts and legal opinion, etc. may lead to an even narrower application.[140] As a result, despite their purpose to thwart creative compliance, these regulations may themselves turn out to be a recipe for the creation of new avoidance devices—effectively, the tighter the controls, the more the ways around them that can be created. The present accounting standards of the HKSA allow depreciation to be computed by the straight-line approach or declining-balance method. A company is free to change the rates and period of depreciation. In August 1995 Cathay Pacific reported a 22 per cent interim growth in profit as a result of switching to a straight-line basis over 20 years.[141]

A company that wishes to list its shares on the SEHK must comply with the *Rules Governing the Listing of Securities of the Stock Exchange of Hong Kong Ltd*. The company applying to list, must normally provide audited accounts for at least the three financial years immediately preceding the listing.[142] The audit report is required to include the specified basic information, including assets and liabilities.[143] The auditor must certify

136 *Professional Accountants Ordinance*, ch 50, Laws of Hong Kong.

137 McGee, op cit, 883.

138 [1990] 1 All ER 568.

139 D McBarnet and C Whelan, 'The Elusive Spirit of the Law: Formalism and the Struggle for Legal Control', *The Modern Law Review*, 1991, 54:6, 848.

140 McBarnet and Whelan, op cit, 860–4.

141 'Analysts wary on Cathay', *South China Morning Post*, Hong Kong, 11 Aug. 1995.

142 Rule 4.04(1), *Rules Governing the Listing of Securities on the Stock Exchange of Hong Kong Ltd*.

143 Rules 4.04 to 4.07, *Rules Governing the Listing of Securities on the Stock Exchange of Hong Kong Ltd*.

whether or not the relevant information given presents a 'true and fair' view of the results for the period reported and the assets and liabilities at the end of that period.[144] However, a company can choose an auditing firm that comes up with figures acceptable to the listed company, as each firm may have its own acceptable method.[145] This is a perfectly legitimate practice in the HKSAR. As a consequence, the investing public may be misled into believing that the information available to them in a prospectus is accurate and precise, since the prospectus has to be filed with the SFC and, for listed companies, the audit report with the SEHK, both reputable bodies. In any event, regulatory control alone may not be sufficient because by the time any wrongdoing is discovered, the company may have already gone into liquidation.

The fundamental problem is that auditing firms are reluctant to report on any negative findings they uncover.[146] It is immaterial whether these firms have an international reputation, as they play by the rules of the game in the HKSAR.[147] In ensuring leniency, some banking institutions have routinely bribed the senior management of these auditing firms after paying them a handsome service fee.[148] It is therefore desirable that legislation requiring auditors to report to the appropriate authority any illegal activities discovered in the course of their duties be enacted. However, some leading members of the accounting profession have actively resisted law reform that might compel auditors to report corporate misconduct to the authorities.[149] They argue, without acknowledging that an auditor owes his duty to the shareholders collectively and not to the corporate wrongdoers, that such a move is against the public interest.[150] On 24 March 1999, the HKSAR Government announced the inclusion of legislative amendments in the composite *Securities and Futures Bill* to grant immunity to auditors who report suspected fraud or malpractice to the regulatory authorities.[151] This was made after the discovery of auditing irregularities and material misstatements in eleven cases over a six-month period.[152] Some leading members of the accounting profession naturally expressed their displeasure over this proposal.[153]

144 Rule 4.08(2), *Rules Governing the Listing of Securities on the Stock Exchange of Hong Kong Ltd.*

145 *Case No D52/96*, Board of Review Decisions 554 at 569–70.

146 Delhaise, op cit, 51.

147 Ibid.

148 Ibid.

149 'Accountants slam graft-buster plan', *South China Morning Post*, Hong Kong, 5 Oct. 1996.

150 Ibid.

151 'Audit of the accounts of listed companies', *Press Release*, Hong Kong: Financial Services Branch, 24 Mar. 1999, 3.

152 Ibid. 2.

153 'Fraud case auditors gain immunity', *South China Morning Post*, Hong Kong, 25 Mar. 1999.

V. CONCLUSION

The Asian financial crisis was a 'blessing in disguise' for the HKSAR, as the Territory had become complacent about its regulatory framework for banking and finance. During the crisis, the Executive Government put forward a number of proposals for legislative reform of the financial markets. Notwithstanding these proposals and lessons from previous crises, the composite *Securities and Futures Bill*, which was first proposed in April 1996, is still on the Legislative Council's backburner. Amid globalisation and at the advent of the high-tech revolution, it is inevitable that the economy of the HKSAR will become a knowledge-based economy in which citizens will demand greater accountability. Accordingly, the demand for transparency will be key in obliging the financial markets to disclose clearer and more detailed information about their dealings. The new millennium marks the beginning of the legislative phase of financial reforms in the HKSAR.

PART III

International Contagion: 1995 and 1998–1999

Chapter 10

The Recent Systemic Crisis and the Management of the International Financial System: A Latin American Perspective

Manuela Tortora

1. INTRODUCTION

The development, the pace and the implications of the most recent systemic crisis—i.e. the one initiated in the Asian region in July 1997—are still unfolding in many Latin American countries. The good macroeconomic performance of 1996 and 1997, which represented a surprisingly quick recovery after the '*tequila*' crisis of 1995, will now be compared with the recession started in 1998 in the whole region. The impact of the Asian crisis in Latin America demonstrates that we faced an important systemic crisis, deeper and larger than all the 'post-Bretton Woods' crises.

The lessons to be drawn from the behaviour of the international economic system in the last two years are important not only for the domestic policies as such but also for the global ones. More than the national dimension, the international ramifications of the crisis lead to an inevitable discussion on the management of the global financial system as well as the way to tackle development issues. As Professor Gerry Helleiner noted recently,

> financial instability, banking system failures, exchange rates crises and consequent real macroeconomic disruption have increasingly been seen as a major (and in many cases, new) threat to the development prospects of poor countries. Highest priority has in recent years been reassigned by international development institutions from advice on project evaluation and 'development strategy' (which, in any case, often remains controversial) towards macroeconomic and financial sector policy reforms. (. . .) Moreover, the potential problems created by contagion of financial distress are now seen as threatening to whole regions, and indeed well beyond.[1]

[1] Gerry Helleiner. *Financial Markets, Crises and Contagion: Issues for Smaller Countries in the FTAA and Post-Lomé IV Negotiations*. Paper prepared for the Caribbean Regional Negotiating Machinery, Kingston, Jamaica, Jan. 1999, 1.

The vulnerability of Latin American countries (and many other developing and 'emerging' economies around the world) can not be treated as a limited regional problem. The globalisation puts the local vulnerabilities at the global level. Based on its own painful experience, the Latin American countries can contribute to the debate with their own analysis of the mechanics of current systemic crises, as well as with their own views on the changes needed in the management of the international monetary and financial system.

This chapter (in which the primary timeframe is the 1990s) does not intend to give a complete picture of the Latin American perspective of that topic. It is aimed more at provoking more reflection and additional research, because this new kind of crises which may be 'the first of the XXIst century'[2] needs a serious strategic response, based on a careful assessment of the regional political and development needs. In this sense, the reader will find here some contributions more than solutions and partial descriptions more than prescriptions.

II. THE IMPACT OF THE ASIAN CRISIS IN LATIN AMERICA

Following a pattern which was already visible during the Mexican crisis of 1994–5, the impact of the distress that originated in Thailand in July 1997 for the Latin American economies unfolds in three main stages. First, the monetary (on the exchange rates) and the financial (on the investment flows) impacts, which are seen in the short-term immediately after the collapse of the Asian financial policies and which affect the access to capital markets. Second, the impact on trade flows, which becomes evident only in the medium-term, i.e. six to eight months after the first stage. Finally, the third stage is the one related to the recession in the aftermath of the crisis, which evolves like a deeper wave, with a more perverse but slower impact.

Each one of those stages deserves to be understood as part of an apparently irreversible sequence of events. They all demonstrate the vulnerability of the Latin American region *vis-à-vis* a crisis where it has no responsibility. Each stage reiterates the systemic features of the Asian crisis.

A. *The First Stage: The Impact on the Access of International Capital Markets*

The days and weeks following the devaluation of the Thai currency, the *bath*, were the days of panic among the new determinant actors of the

[2] The term was first used by Michel Camdessus, Managing Director of the International Monetary Fund, referring to the Mexican crisis of 1994–5.

international financial system. The 'institutional investors' and the 'money managers' who were relying on the high and quick rentability of the emerging economies started a generalised retreat, looking for more stable destinations, particularly in the case of the short-term financial operations. The 'flight to quality' became a global behaviour among investors all over the world in the last quarter of 1997. It continued the following months, particularly affecting the Latin American countries because they suffered not only the unfair impact of being assimilated to the Asian victims but also, in August 1998, the impact of the Russian crisis.

The 'flight to quality' is a confidence crisis with unpredictable consequences on the capacity of all emerging economies to maintain their credibility in the international capital markets. In other words, all emerging economies are viewed as integrating the same basket, in spite of their objective differences. Therefore, the good Latin American macroeconomic performance in the aftermath of the '*tequila*' crisis was not sufficient to compensate the fear of the contagion in the region—which in fact occurred, fed by the fear itself, in a typical vicious circle.

The Latin American stock exchanges were 'contaminated' by this general movement as early as September 1997. The exchange rates trembled, and the spreads of many Latin American bonds soared (mainly those of two key economies of the region: Brazil and Argentina), while the risk assessment by the rating agencies also deteriorated. Nowadays, the systemic impact of the new financial crises for the 'emerging economies' can be clearly visualised through those two indicators: the spreads of the debt bonds and the agencies' rating, determining the flow of international investments. In fact, as was observed during the last year in the region, the contagion affects both short-term and long-term capital (i.e. the foreign direct investments). In addition to the contagion effect, the retreat of some Asian investments in the region, or the suspension of some new projects that were being prepared (including some Japanese investments), can be explained by the lack of liquidity in the Asian banking system after the crisis.

All together, these macroeconomic elements constitute the 'configuration risk' of Latin American economies, established during the first stage of the impact by the international capital markets before any official reaction by the affected governments and by the multilateral financial institutions as the IMF. The time factor appears to be the most important driving force explaining the behaviour of the main actors of this stage; the accelerated pace of the contagion, helped by the new electronic devices, is now counted in terms of days or even hours. It is worthwhile to remember that in 1929, the financial collapse of Wall Street also had large ramifications in many European stock markets and banking systems, but at that time, the contagion was measured in months or years.

B. *The Second Stage: The Medium-Term Impact on Trade Flows*

The impact on the trade flows may not appear as impressive as the impact on the exchange rates or the flows of capital, because it evolves in slow motion and does not occupy the headline news. However, from the point of view of the Latin American strategies of development, the second stage may be even more negative than the first one, because it has perverse implications on the region's productive capacity, on its competitiveness in the global markets, and therefore on its rates of employment and growth. Since 1997, before and more severely after the Asian crisis, the main Latin American exports (raw materials, agriculture commodities, and oil) have been affected by four negative factors in the international markets:

The fall of the international commodities' prices, implying significant earnings' losses, particularly for Peru, Colombia, Chile, and Venezuela: this decline, which is part of a trend initiated in the 1980s, increased in the second half of 1997;

The fall of the Asian demand of Latin American exports, affecting more specifically Peru and Chile, whose shares of export to Asia represented, in 1997, 38.1 per cent and 25.3 per cent of their total exports[3];

The increased competitiveness of the Asian products in the international and regional markets, due to the devaluation of Asian currencies, implying that 57.8 per cent of Latin American exports to OECD countries face new Asian competition[4].

The decreasing global demand of commodities as the world economy enters a recession.

Therefore, as stated by the United States' Secretary of Commerce, W. Daley, 'the 1998 global financial crisis may be a global commercial crisis in 1999'. Obviously, the impact on the Latin American trade flows became more sensitive at the end of 1998, as a consequence of the Brazilian financial crisis and then in January 1999, with the devaluation of the Brazilian *real*. In fact, the medium-term direct and indirect impact of the Asian crisis in Latin America also includes: (i) the Brazilian monetary and financial crisis started one year later; (ii) the changes originated by this devaluation on the interregional trade flows; and (iii) its paralysing effect on the Mercosur.

One of the conclusions of the UNCTAD *Trade and Development Report, 1998*:

Since the debt crisis of the 1980s the major challenge in Latin America has been to

[3] See SELA, *The Impact of the Asian Crisis on Latin America*. Caracas, Feb. 1998.

[4] R. E. Saez, *Latin American Exporters to the OECD markets potentially more exposed to the Asian Crisis: A First Look*, Washington, DC, Inter American Development Bank, Mar. 1998, mimeo.

reconcile growth fast enough to keep unemployment at acceptable levels and reduce poverty with a sustainable external payments position. The recovery that has taken place since the Mexican crisis suggest that this dilemma is still present, as the payments position has continued to worsen, although the deficits now involve a higher proportion of capital goods in total imports than in the past. These difficulties have been compounded by the impact of the East Asian crisis on commodity and petroleum prices. The heavy reliance on private capital inflows to finance the growing payments deficits has meant that Latin American countries are still subject to the risk of contagion.[5]

C. *The Third Stage: The Recession*

The financial impact of the Asian crisis, as well as the beginning of the medium-term impact on trade flows, produced a drop of more than 2 per cent in the 1998 average GDP growth rate of the region, which did not exceed 2.6 per cent (ECLAC estimates). Without the impact of the crisis, the Latin American countries would probably have repeated an average GDP growth rate of 5 per cent or more, similar to the rates attained in 1996 and 1997. The forecasts for 1999, made by ECLAC and the World Bank at the end of 1998—that do not include the assessment of the impact of the recent Brazilian '*samba*' effect—indicate a regional growth rate average of 1.5 per cent, with deeper recessions in Brazil and Venezuela. In addition to the economic significance of those figures, it is worthwhile to note that, according to the World Bank, Latin America needs to have a sustained annual growth of 5 per cent during 10 years to stop the increasing rate of poverty.

The impact of the Asian crisis in terms of growth rates for Latin American economies should be analysed in the larger context of the global economic recession that affects some of its main trade and investment partners such as Japan and the European Union.

III. THE LESSONS OF THE SYSTEMIC CRISES

From the Latin American perspective, the Asian crisis, as well as the '*tequila*' effect in 1995, the Russian default in 1998 and the recent '*samba*' impact, demonstrate that the systemic crises have three main characteristics.

All the 'emerging economies' are perceived as similar in the international capital markets because of the 'flight to quality'. Mr Michel Camdessus, the IMF Managing Director, deplored the 'unfair punishment' of the Latin American economies since the impact they suffered was a consequence of other countries' or region's troubles.

[5] UNCTAD, *Trade and Development Report*, 1998 (Geneva, United Nations, 1999), 14.

The new systemic crises affect all kind of investment flows, because they generate a sudden retreat of short-term (portfolio) investments from the emerging economies, and they induce a climate of regional and global recessions, which explains delays or suspensions in the long-term (direct) investments.

They have implications on the trade flows, by introducing changes in the traditional trends and by modifying the conquered positions in traditional markets, and they accelerate the impact of the decreasing prices of commodities, therefore deepening the deterioration of the terms of trade for developing countries. The long-term national and foreign investment flows linked to the trade flows are also modified. The slow-down in the plans of the integration schemes such as the Mercosur or the Andean Community has to be considered in that same context.

Therefore, the systemic crises show that Latin America shares the disease of all the 'emerging economies': vulnerability (which is not only 'porosity') and hypersensitivity to the international contagion.

This vulnerability is ignited when one or more mistakes are made in the domestic macroeconomic policies of developing countries, such as: a financial openness with weak banking supervision (that was one of the main causes of both the Mexican and the Asian crises); the mismanagement of the economic '*bonanzas*' (which may be one of the roots of the Southeast economies' collapse); the speculative investments and/or short-term foreign capitals together with a lack of productive investments (factors present in the Mexican and Asian cases); the deteriorating terms of trade (particularly obvious in the Latin American economies); the unsustainable monetary policies (as was demonstrated in the Mexican and the Brazilian episodes); the fiscal deficit (a common feature of Latin American countries).

IV. THE LESSONS FOR THE MANAGEMENT OF THE INTERNATIONAL MONETARY AND FINANCIAL SYSTEM

The amplitude of the systemic crises, and the ramifications for the whole monetary, financial, and commercial net of short-term and long-term flows, is now bearing high costs for the international system, costs to high to conclude that those crises are similar to some 'growth pains' linked to the evolution of the globalisation process. Inertia and improvisation cannot continue to be the only reactions to turmoil too deep and far-reaching to be considered amere transitional accident. The realistic possibility that the international system may have to face more crises of this nature in the future adds to the need to look at the management of the system: what can be done to prevent and then to minimise the contagion?

The debate on the reform of the institutional Bretton Woods scheme is one of the main topics in the current multilateral agenda. This paper cannot analyse the details of that issue, but the following comments highlight the main concerns raised by the recent systemic crises, specifically from the Latin American perspective. Four lessons seem to be particularly relevant in this framework:

The first lesson concerns the objectives and the role of the International Monetary Fund (IMF). In the Mexican as well as the Asian crises, the IMF did not comply with its original and fundamental function of 'watchdog' of the international monetary system, since it did not provide an early warning. Its access to the information on the domestic macroeconomic situation and its traditional role in the financial markets were not sufficient to allow this institution to warn and to prevent both the collapse of the 'successful' Asian economies and the global contagion. The globalisation of the monetary and financial flows, the increasing role of new actors outside the sphere of the States, and the interdependence of the national macroeconomic policies, all call for a warning mechanism more effective than the kind of supervision currently applied, on the developing countries only, by the IMF.

The second lesson is related with the 'unfairness' of the systemic crises. The large impact of the Asian events on the Latin American countries and many other emerging or transition economies has to be compared with the relatively limited costs bared by the industrialised countries. Here, the above-mentioned vulnerability and hypersensitivity *vis-à-vis* the systemic contagion is obviously different and greatly reduced in the case of industrialised countries. The multiplier (and perverse) effect of the crises on the decreasing investment flows is virtually absent for those countries, since they do not rely on external financing. The impact on some trade flows certainly has an effect on their economic performance. But even in the worst scenarios, the aggregate loss is measured in terms of 1 or 2 per cent of the GDP growth rate while in the developing countries the cost of the commercial and the financial turmoil can reach seven or eight digits of the GDP growth rate.

In the third place, the systemic crises stress the unsolved problem of the development financing. The access to the international capital markets (whose role has been determinant in all the recent crises), more than a need to complement the internal savings, is a vital instrument of the long-term development strategies. The terms of the debate on development financing may have changed since the external debt crisis of the 80s, but the essence of the issue is still the same, particularly for the Latin American countries. Therefore, any review of the management of the monetary and financial system must include the question of how to guarantee that the developing countries get access to stable and productive investments for their long-term development?

Finally, as far as the structure of the institutional Bretton Woods scheme is concerned, it seems that the concept of the 'triangle' (trade, monetary and financial policies) established in 1944 is still basically valid. The interdisciplinary aspects of the globalisation process need an integrated approach, linking the pillars of all domestic and international economic policies. The impact of the contagion in the monetary, financial and commercial areas are the recent evidence that the 'triangle' is a concept that reflects the international economic reality today as it did more than fifty years ago when the scheme was designed. However, the current institutional framework of the World Trade Organisation (WTO), the IMF and the World Bank needs to be updated to respond to the changes generated by the globalisation. When revisiting these institutions, the need for an effective warning mechanism and a sustainable development financing are probably the main priorities to put on the agenda, together with an effective link with the trade dimension:

> these 'new' financial issues have by now assumed such regional, and even potential global, importance that any negotiation of longer-term development or trade co-operation cannot be credible without full provision for co-operation in financial crisis prevention and management within a fully integrated trade-financial co-operation package. It is no longer plausible for some intergovernmental agencies to address purely trade issues (sometimes even trade in financial services) in one forum while totally different ones (often considerably more powerful) 'sort out' the financial issues separately in another.[6]

V. SOME CONCLUSIONS

The economic and political dimensions of the mismanagement of the international monetary and financial system, and the risks raised by its crises, lead to thinking in terms of 'good governance' of the system. The notion of governance as usually applied to the domestic level involves political and ethical values such as participation, transparency, equity, and stability.

Taking into account those basic values, and by extrapolating the notion of governance to the international economic dimension, the issue of a 'global economic governance' should be introduced in the multilateral agenda, which would mean that: Any attempt to revise the rules and the functioning of the institutional mechanisms governing the current financial and monetary system that does not include the issue of the development financing, and that is limited to tackling the volatility of capital flows, is inefficient a priori, as far as the developing countries are concerned.

Any effort by the international financial institutions to tackle the issue of the management of the system without a strong and broad international political consensus will produce only ephemeral results.

[6] Helleiner, above n 1, at 1.

There are many obstacles in the way of achieving a discussion on global economic governance.

First, there is the usual and easy tendency to 'slice' the international economic agenda into as many specific issues as possible, to separate them and to distribute their treatment in different *fora*. That is why it is easier to talk about banking supervision than to consider a broad and sensitive issue like the quality of foreign investments, for instance.

Secondly, the increasing dissemination of actors (institutional investors, money managers, governments, international and regional financial institutions, etc.), where both governmental and non-governmental entities play a role in the system, does not help the decision-making process or the formulation of rules of the game equitable for all. In the third place, the debate on the redesign of the current institutional financial and monetary architecture may have just started and is probably heading towards a tortuous road. As a 1999 article in *The Economist* mentioned,

> listing the problems may be easy; finding solutions is not. Should there be more or less global regulation, more or less public financial support, looser or tighter exchange rate regimes? There are no simple answers, because the problems of modern economic policy are maddeningly inter-linked. A policymaker trying to design the ideal financial system has three objectives. He wants continuing national sovereignty: financial markets that are regulated, supervised and cushioned; and the benefits of global capital markets. Unfortunately (. . .) these three goals are incompatible. They form the 'impossible trinity' that underlies the instability of today's global architecture.[7]

The fourth obstacle is related to the political driving forces needed to introduce new mechanisms and new criteria in the management of the international system. The main driving force, as was the one leading to the Bretton Woods scheme, is political leadership. Not the United States alone, nor the European Union or Japan, and unfortunately not the developing countries, have the political leadership required. Some new alliances may be have to be forged to change the way the systemic crises and the impact of the globalisation process are dealt with at the international level. It is even possible that the ghost of a generalised crisis, worse than what we witnessed, may become the incentive that was lacking to begin a transformation of the mechanisms for managing the global system.

This leads to the last—but not least—obstacle: do we have the conceptual tools needed to adjust and reformulate the global financial system in an equitable and efficient way? Since apparently, nobody has clear and viable answers, we may have to face, in the first place, that new ideological deficit.

7 *Global Finance Survey. Time for a Redesign?*, THE ECONOMIST, 30 Jan. 1999, at 4.

Chapter 11

Preventing and Containing International Financial Crisis: The Case of Brazil

Jorge Guira

I. INTRODUCTION

By the Autumn of 1998, financial crises requiring the intervention of the International Monetary Fund had taken place across Asia and in Russia.[1] The Fall Agenda of the Joint meetings of the International Monetary Fund-World Bank were no longer focused on individual country matters or on merely incremental ways to improve the financial system.[2] Rather, the clear new focus, as reflected in policy pronouncements from the IMF itself as well as leading figures, such as US Treasury Secretary Robert Rubin and Chancellor of the Exchequer Gordon Brown, was on sweeping international financial law and institutional reform.[3]

The threat of out of control financial crises' was the stimulus for the policymaker's focus on building what was emerging as the new international financial architecture. Such an edifice would ensure that domestic financial collapse did not have a 'domino effect' on other nations, and that crises could be prevented or contained. Since the meetings, over thirty-five proposals for strengthening the international financial architecture have arisen.[4] The core elements of transparency, internationally accepted standards,

[1] See <http://www.stern.nyu.edu/~nroubini/asia/AsiaHomepage.html> for an exhaustive collection of readings and documents on the topic (hereinafter Roubini). See also J J Norton (ed.) *Yearbook of International Financial and Economic Law 1997 and 1998* (Kluwer, 1999, and 2000).

[2] See Roubini, n 1, What caused Asia's crisis and its currency crisis and its' global contagion? IMF: *1998 International Capital Markets: Developments, Prospects, and Key Policy Issues* (Sept. 1998); IMF: *The October 1998 World Economic Outlook*; see also <http//www.imf.org> for meeting information.

[3] See <http://www.imf.org/external/am/1998/index.htm> for detailed Fall Meeting information.

[4] See <http://www.imf.org/architecture>, generally. IMF, Progress in Strengthening the International Financial Architecture, 30 Mar. 2000; Roubini, generally at Reform of the Architecture of the International Financial System: Alternative Views. *See also*, *Symposium: Law Based Nature of the New International Financial Architecture*, 33 International Lawyer (ABA, Winter 1999).

financial sector building, private sector involvement, and contingent credit lines are the new common ingredients required for reform.[5]

At the same time that the above reform agenda was taking shape, Brazil was engulfed in its' own full scale financial crisis.[6] Facing pressure on its' dollar reserves to uphold the value of the Brazilian Real, the Brazilian government soon after the meetings began the difficult process to devalue the currency by over 35–40 per cent versus the dollar.[7] This resulted in the need for the Brazilian Central Bank, the Federal Government, and the International Monetary Fund and other international financial institutions to work closely together to come up with a solution to restore certain fundamentals and to re-instil confidence in the Brazilian economy and financial system.

The resulting Brazilian crisis was important not just for the Brazilian's who had to face the ramifications of the financial instability on their native soil, but also for the Mercosur trading partners, such as Argentina, Uruguay, and Paraguay.[8] The United States, of course, was also substantially affected due to its considerable investment and trade position with Brazil. Because of Brazil's position as the eighth largest economy in the world, the economic security of much of Latin America, and North America, was seriously, and potentially gravely, affected.

This article is to examine the Brazilian crisis from the point of view of an international financial law policymaker. Specifically, the objective is to examine how the Brazilian crisis developed, how it was handled, and how the current focus of the IMF and other international financial institutions to further the international financial architecture reform process may be effective in helping contain the Brazilian crisis and preventing further distressing episodes.

The first section therefore sets out the broad parameters of the IMF architectural program. The second section examines the pre-cursers to the

[5] IMF: *A Guide to Progress in Strengthening the Architecture of the International Financial System* (Apr. 1999); IMF, *Progress in Strengthening the Architecture of the International Financial System*, 12 Oct. 1999 (a full updated report is expected April 2000).

[6] For the best general introduction to the topic, see Roubini at Brazil and Latin America, including all relevant IMF, IADB, Central Bank of Brazil <http://www.bcb.gov.br> and other relevant web sites. IMF-Brazil Letter of Intent, 13 Nov. 1998; R Waters, *Brazil debt roll-over sparks fears* (*FT*, 3 Nov. 1998); *See also* Norton, 'Reform of Latin American Banking Systems', in id., *Asian Contagion and Latin America* (Kluwer, 2000).

[7] Ibid. An official devaluation took place 15 Jan. 1999 with a decision to let the Real float, including the failure of a massive $41 billion dollar US led capital infusions.

[8] Mercosur has a provision that provides for macro-economic coordination as one of its core legal objectives although there are few if any institutional resources that have yet been allocated to this aspiration and intention. *See*, Guira generally, *Mercosur as an Instrument for Development*, Nafta L. Rev (Summer 1997). Institute of International Finance Regional Overview of Latin America—15 Mar. 1999 (excellent discussion of trade implications of Brazilian crisis).

Brazilian Real devaluation, and focuses on what was happening internationally as the incipient currency crisis of 1997 emerged into a full-fledged devaluation debacle. This section therefore provides a history of the events as well as suggesting what measures might have been taken that could have helped stem the impending crisis. The third section broadly reviews the nature of the Brazilian problem for 1998 on and the domestic and international response. The final section assesses the legal and institutional methods used by the IMF to address the issues, and poses the question whether the reforms in progress provide a sufficient intelligence gathering and response mechanism to minimise the potential disruptions of financial crisis.

II. THE CORE INTERNATIONAL FINANCIAL ARCHITECTURAL PARAMETERS

Whether the issue is economic or military security, the policymaker must first face the question of defining the problem, and devising appropriate strategy and tactics. This section reviews these issues, in turn.

A. *Definition of Crisis*

For a problem to be perceived as substantial enough to be a crisis, there is no commonly accepted benchmark or measurement. (e.g. what the actual percentage of obligations outstanding is that cannot be repaid). For purposes of this article, a crisis is defined as the private sector or sovereign's inability or impending inability to pay its foreign or domestic obligations.

The roots of such crisis events, of course, often vary. Certain objective criteria, however, exist. These include declining terms of trade (decline of oil prices in Venezuela and Texas in the mid-1980s), capital markets decline in valuation (the US great depression in 1929). Other events, involving bank failures (Argentina 1982, Chile 1985, Venezuela 1994), and currency drops (Mexican peso devaluation 1994), are further examples of different major causes of crisis.[9]

B. *The Brazilian Crisis Elements*

The Brazil crisis is primarily based on the devaluation of the currency. It is not a bank insolvency or liquidity crisis. Moreover, the period from 1997 before devaluation when concerns existed about the ability of Brazil to

9 See L. Rojas-Suarez and S. R. Weisbrod, *Banking Crises in Latin America: Experiences and Issues* (IADB, 1996).

maintain its' currency value-and therefore continue to attract foreign investment and pay off its' debts-certainly qualify as either a crisis or pre crisis 'crucible' period.

The specific roots of the Brazilian crisis are widely debated. Some take the view that there were specific structural imbalances based upon too high a public debt relative to the ability of the country to repay.[10] Other commentators, such as Paul Krugman suggest that Brazil's fiscal policies were not really the problem.[11] Rather, it was many factors-including the lack of confidence in Brazilian's to exercise self-control, stemming from a post 1960 history of 'stop and go' policies that had cheapened the currency repeatedly.

In addition to these specific, negative reputation costs, an international climate of doubt spilling over from Asia and Russia to the next weak currency target that speculators could punish for being out of line with market benchmarks was also a crucial factor.[12] Specifically, the Russian default on syndicated loans triggered a global climate of fear and psychological unrest that, following sharp falls in crucial Latin American commodity prices could not be sated.

Next, the Brazilian consolidation of all public debt, rather than accounting for it into state, municipal, and federal units was also held significant as overstating the true state of default risk for many investors.[13] This is important because investors were otherwise constrained in evaluating creditworthiness by these negative combined parameters. The confluence of these perceived weaknesses rather than any actual major problem, it is argued, led directly to the self-fulfilling prophecy of devaluation.

Although there is little doubt that there could have been certain structural and fiscal improvements to the Brazilian economic plan, this author is of the view that this is shortsighted in minimising the pre-eminent position of confidence in retaining market support for the currency. To the extent, that this more broadly defines the Brazilian crisis, the key issues to resolve are how the international financial architecture proposals can contribute to crisis prevention and management through addressing the above fundamentals and the underlying confidence factor.

[10] See Guira, British Institute of International and Comparative Law Conference On Mercosur, The Brazilian Financial Crisis: Operational Considerations, 19 Feb. 1999.

[11] P. Krugman, *Don't Blame It on Rio . . . or Brasilia Either. The real is caught in a confidence trap* (Slate Febr. 1999), and P. Krugman, *Alas, Brazil*, Slate, Feb. 1999. Cf J. Sachs NBER Session, Brazil Fever, First Do No Harm, 15 Apr. 2000. This argues the IMF overfocused on cutting the debt when the underlying problem was what everyone already knew: the Real was overvalued in 1997–8 and it was a matter of time before some adjustment would be needed. This was due especially to the short-term debt problem Brazil had lack of sufficient foreign debt—as well as exporter's inability to sell goods with Brazil's high rates.

[12] *See* Impact of the Asian Crisis on Latin America (ECLAC, 1999); *see also* Roubini, Contagion in Russia and Eastern Europe; In the Roubini Brazil section, *see* G. Calvo, Understanding The Russian Virus (with special reference to Latin America) (Oct. 1998).

[13] See P. Krugman at n 11.

C. *The IMF's Broad Strategy and Targeted Objectives*

The IMF strategy of prevention has primarily focused on maintenance of confidence through surveillance and monitoring, and on encouraging the adoption of certain international agreements and policy prescriptions in banking and securities law. Those policy positions articulate certain fundamental benchmarks that provide guidance as to how individual country finance should be undertaken. They are complemented by the work of rating agencies that price a country's debt based upon supposedly objective criteria or risk.[14] Acceptance of certain ratios determines the level of creditworthiness.

Conditional funding was also available under certain conditions, when crisis broke out.[15] The broad objective of most global efforts prior to the Asian financial crisis that took place from 1996 on was therefore remarkably similar to the ex ante proposals advanced in their approach. The major difference, in addition to the heightened sense of urgency precipitated by the threat of systemic collapse, was the choice of a new set of tactics to ensure that the above objectives could be successfully implemented. Reviewing the specific tactical elements is therefore important to assess the 'new parameters' or specifications for risk management in the new international financial architecture. The next section therefore articulates the core concepts and their limitations as confidence building measures in building the five pillars of the new international financial architecture.

D. *The IMF Confidence Building Tactics and Their Constraints*

The first objective, transparency, is not new. Indeed, transparency has been a hallmark of law reform proposals deemed essential to capital markets liberalisation and the attraction of foreign investment.[16] This is because US institutions are often more reluctant to become financial involved in foreign countries that do not adopt certain standards, such as generally accepted accounting principles.[17] The IMF' specific emphasis, therefore, was to encourage further cooperation with the Special Data Dissemination Service,

[14] *See* Roubini, 'Rating Agencies: Why Did They Fail to Predict the Asian Crisis'?

[15] The proper extent of how much funding should actually be permitted based upon a country's reserves with the IMF is, of course, at the core of the debate, rather than the decision to bail out a Brazil or any of the above countries. This reflects an 'orthodox' perspective on the need to provide such assistance. See IMF-Brazil—Technical Memorandum of Understanding, 2 July 1999 for specific terms.

[16] For a collection of articles see Roubini, The Debate on 'Crony Capitalism'. Is Corruption Bad for Economic Growth?; and Corporate Governance in Asia and Around the World: The Asian Model vs. the Anglo-Saxon Model. See Norton, n 6, *Asian Contagion* at 311–14; IMF—Progress in Strengthening the Architecture of the International Financial System, 12 Oct. 1999.

[17] Ibid. at Norton; Basle Committee review of international accounting standards (No 70, Apr. 2000).

and to publicly release internal IMF reports of country finance assessments to increase opportunities for understanding and standardisation.[18]

The problem of course, is that transparency does not-and can not capture problems that exist due to private sector mismanagement. Moreover, it may, ironically enough, unduly punish certain countries for wrongs that they have not committed. In the case of Asia, broadly speaking, the problem was not the public sector borrowings being unsustainable, but the closed nature of private institutions such as banks. In this sense, the only solution is tighter internal regulation of banking and investment houses, including less opaque reporting. The three major credit rating agencies and the IMF, however, largely failed to focus on this concern in Asia, and better information by public authorities, by itself, would not have prevented the Asia crisis from deepening.

Moreover, as to Brazil, Paul Krugman and others have stressed that the lack of sophistication and the psychology of self-fulfilling prophecies among investors were more responsible for the devaluation crisis, than the fundamentals. Specifically, the anomaly in Brazilian law whereby state accounts reflect a fiscal deficit that is accumulated with federal debt created the basis for an institutional investor misperception of the state of the health of the Brazilian economy. Standard measurements used by many private investors to judge Brazil, rather than the absence of any meaningful public benchmarks, was instead a core problem of perception. Still, there is no question that reducing opacity and raising disclosure standards, even if this introduces additional costs and transfers the playing field for creative use of financial information is highly desirable.

The second strategy is the development of internationally accepted standards.[19] What this means precisely is codes of general ethical conduct as well as specific regulatory and supervisory banking and securities practices. Additional work in accountancy (International Accounting Standards Board), corporate governance (OECD), securities (IOSCO), banking (Basle), and in social policy areas (the respective development banks and the World Bank) comprise the institutional support for these new developments.[20] There is little question that despite the sensitivity of this area in domestic political environments who do not like such 'soft law' imposed on them, that such institutional development serves a highly positive social purpose.[21] In addition, it may also have unanticipated consequences, such

[18] See Roubini, Sources of Official Data and Reports, IMF's Dissemination Standards Bulletin Board (DSBB); *see* IMF, n 16.

[19] See IMF, n 16.

[20] Roubini, Bank Supervision and Regulation and Reform of Basle Capital Adequacy Standards; specific web sites include <http://www.bis.org>, <http://www.iosco.org>, <http://www.ibrd.org>.

[21] See J. Gold, *The Rule of Law in the International Monetary Fund* (IMF, 1980) for the seminal discussion of this topic.

as allowing leaders of many countries to do the politically unpopular, because the IMF—and other standard setting bodies with market influence, require it.

The third strategy is complemented by the financial sector-strengthening programme of the IMF.[22] This consists of continuous country assessment, and Basle cooperation. Continuous country assessment did not prevent the last set of crisis from Asia. The rapidity of electronic international financial movements, opportunities for regulatory arbitrage in cross border transactions, off-balance sheet instrumentation that derivatives provide to embed risk in transactions to unwary investors, and the lack of an international lender of last resort present substantial challenges that assessment alone can not fix. Basle, to its' substantial credit has been working on many such issues in an inclusive manner with emerging economies rather than maintaining an aloof posture.[23] Such cooperation is vital to the implementation of rapid response monitoring systems for capital flows.

The fourth strategy is greater private sector involvement to mitigate the moral hazard problem, such as where banks or other financial institutions are too big to fail so they must be rescued.[24] There is no doubt that the proliferation of bond finance rather than syndicated loans as the mainstay of developing country finance make decision making regarding debt substantially more unwieldy than in the days when syndicated loan creditors could all be gathered in one room to take collective action.[25] Accordingly, appropriate reforms to adjust to this new reality are most urgently needed.

The fifth strategy of contingent credit lines is based on alleviating temporary balance of payments problems for countries with strong policies.[26] This of course builds on the special drawing rights facilities based upon the

[22] Ibid. at IMF, n 16. M. Goldstein and P. Turner, 'Banking crises in emerging economies: origins and policy options' (IIE, Oct. 1996) *See also* the work of Goldstein on Building Robust financial systems in <http://www.iie.org>; *see also* IMF, *Financial Stability in Emerging Markets* (Dec. 1997); *See also* at <http://www.bis.org>, n 20, Report of the G-10 Working Party on Financial Stability in Emerging Markets, Financial Stability in Emerging Market Economies: A Strategy for the Formulation, Adoption, and Implementation of Sound Principles and Practices to Strengthen Financial Systems (Apr. 1997).

[23] *See generally* Roubini, 'Do We Need an International Lender of Last Resort,' and also 'Hedge Funds and Derivatives and Systemic Risk,' sections; *see also* R. Lastra, *The International Last Lender of Resort*, British Journal of International and Comparative Law Quarterly (Oct. 1999); The Three Reports of the G-22 Group on International Financial Architecture Reform (Oct. 1998).

[24] See Roubini, Moral Hazards; *see also* J Olsen, *Banks in Distress: Misdirection in Public Policy and Law* (Kluwer, 2000).

[25] This is an observation made by Lee Buchheit of Cleary, Gottleib, Steen, and Hamilton at a CCLS/QMW Conference on Reform of the International Financial Architecture Conference (May 1999); see also Norton, *International Syndicated Lending and Economic Development in Latin America: The Legal Context*, Essays in International Financial and Economic Law (1997).

[26] See IMF at n 16.

IMF Article I confidence building to prevent 'mal-adjustments in the balance of payments . . . destructive of national or international prosperity' but is a new 'pre-emptive' measure. There is no dispute that strong legal, economic, and political risk management to avoid escalation of dangerous situations that threaten the public good of international confidence is a potentially helpful measure. The problem, of course, is determining standards and sophisticated country judgement as to when it is prudent to provide help, and when the IMF may merely be enabling destructive behavior that is market self-correcting.

III. HISTORY OF AND DEVELOPMENT OF THE BRAZILIAN CRISIS

A Precursors of the Crisis: The Brazilian Economy has a Stop and Go Pattern

The June 1994 Real plan stabilised the economy through the introduction of a new currency loosely tied to the dollar. The plan broadly consisted of combining tight monetary policy (M1 money circulation was 2.5 in 1994 compared to 3.8 in 1996) and loose fiscal policy, and incentives to attract portfolio foreign investment, such as privatisation.[27]

The plan succeeded in reducing inflation from 640 per cent annual rate to less than 18 per cent within one year.[28] This allowed for business and consumers to plan their budgets. The effect of increased certainty was greater spending on goods and services: a consumption and related credit boom, particularly in the purchase of foreign goods among the top 10 per cent of the population who control over 50 per cent of disposable spending.[29]

The economy was now in a clear '*go*' stage. Indeed, *too much* of a '*go*' stage: the banking authorities became concerned about over heating of the economy, and cut back on credit in 1995. The overall inflation rate was 23.2 per cent in 1995 and 16 per cent in 1996.

B. Liberalisation Moves Forward

The Finance minister who introduced the Real Plan, former California Berkeley Sociology Professor Fernando Henrique Cardoso, became President of the Republic. He implemented the liberalisation through privatisation of key sectors such as mining and oil, with telecommunications and ports to

[27] See IMF–Brazil Letter of Intent, 13 Nov. 1998 (available at Roubini, and at Brazil section, <http://www.imf.org>).

[28] Ibid. at 1.

[29] Euromonitor, Brazil: Retail Trends (1999) (proprietary research).

follow. The idea was that increased selling off of state owned enterprises would increase the competitiveness of such industries, and stimulate massive foreign investment flows. This has happened, with over $18 billion in new capital flowing in and substantially more on its way expected prior to the end of 1998.

Brazil is the key player in Mercosur, the regional customs union.[30] It is therefore wed to a common external tariff (CET) of 14 per cent, although many exemptions exist, and the auto and sugar sector is exempted.[31] A large and growing percentage of trade is developing regionally rather than globally as the relevant local economies benefit from harmonisation of legal and customs policies that reduce costs and promote other synergies.

The above tariff rate was expected to diminish over time, but a 1997 policy reversal meant that tariff rates rose to 17 per cent average. Mercosur member states, during 1997, continued to boom, although later economic shocks did take place.[32]

No major regional financial services liberalisation measures have been undertaken, either unilaterally or through Mercosur, although there are working groups in Mercosur (Financial System Commission of Sub-Group 4) to advance this end.[33] Some positive steps in linking the stock exchanges in each country through broad ranging cooperative agreements and setting regional supervisory standards has been made.[34] Brazil is involved in the GATS negotiations, as are the other Mercosur states.

The over $400 billion banking sector in Brazil is administered through the National Monetary Council (NMC), the Central Bank, Banco do Brasil (the federal government bank), the Securities Commission (the CVM), the National Development Bank (BNDES), and public and private financial institutions. The National Monetary Council is the key group, and is comprised of the Minister of Finance, the Planning and Budget minister, and the Central Bank president. The Central Bank follows the rules of the NMC. The bank is responsible for regulation and supervision of the banking system.

30 See T. O'Keefe, Latin American Trade Agreements (Transnational, 1997); *See* <http://www.intr.net/mercosur> for all relevant agreements including the initial Treaty of Asuncion, *see also* IMF–Brazil, n 27 at 2.

31 See in Norton, n 1, *Yearbook 1997*, J. Guira and M. Tavarone, *Mercosur: Consolidation Among Turmoil*, esp. 43.

32 See *Brazil Inflation Up, Output down* (Reuters, 12 Feb. 1999) and also J Diderich, *Brazil Debt Dispute Overshadows Trade Summit*, Reuters (12 Feb. 1999); Documents also available of trade summit meetings held in the Mercosur web site, n 30.

33 *See* E. Holz, *Legislative Asymmetry and the Integration of Banking in Mercosur: A Preliminary approach* (Sela, Oct. 1997).

34 *See* A. Stetson and A. E. Stolper (eds), *Reform and Renewal: Current Regulatory Developments in Latin American Capital Markets* (Bar Association of the City of New York, 1996); *see also* Mercosur web site at n 30 for an on-line listing of documents. The Mercosur Administrative Secretariat in Montevideo, Uruguay, is the repository for all documents.

Many banks were taken over after the Real plan was put into effect, due to poor management.[35] The most spectacular failure was the demise of Banco Nacional, which was riddled with fraud; most of its' functions were transferred to another private bank, Unibanco, with the interim administration, and approval of the Central bank.

The privatisation of the state banking sector thereafter began to take place, with the Rio de Janeiro state bank sale, as well as one of the larger Minas Gerais banks. The state of Sao Paulo bank was scheduled to be sold, and was, before the end of 1998. This is an important trend because the state banks have sometimes been perceived as fonts of corruption for unscrupulous state politicians to reward political friends. (Indeed, this policy of 'patronage banking' has long historical antecedents going back to the nineteenth century.)[36]

Due to the above consolidation, many jobs were lost in the commercial banking sector, in particular. Because of low current valuations and an opening up to foreigners, these banks were viewed as a ripe target for mergers and acquisitions activity. The extent to which these purely foreign banks (as opposed to foreign participation in domestic banks) have been made welcome, is evidenced by the increase of over 100 per cent in the 1994–6 period in foreign assets.[37]

C. *The Crunch Commences: 1997*

The Real plan saw the monetisation of the currency to the dollar from other money substitutes; the end of indexation of currency; the slow increase of credit, other than overnight funds borrowing; the beginning of the privatisation process; and, the incipient flow of foreign funds.

But these positives did not and could not hide the surging current account deficit. By 1997 the government's deficit was taking up over 30 per cent of GDP (not to mention the large overall public sector debt of 32 per cent), soaking up domestic savings, effectively driving up interest rates, crowding out other investment.[38] The relatively high, albeit more relaxed degree of regulation which exists in the Brazilian capital markets, as compared to liberalising regimes like Argentina and Chile also contributed to distortions in capital flows.

In sum, the Brazilians were forced to find the right tools to maintain the value of their currency. Monetary policy restraint, exercised through tight

[35] IMF–Brazil Letters of Intent, n 27 at 1. Apparently more than forty banks were closed, according to Brazilian Central Bank sources, but the exact number could not be confirmed.

[36] T. E. Skidmore, and P. H. Smith, *Modern Latin America* (Oxford, 1992).

[37] See Brazilian Central bank web site, n 6, at Bulletin, Statistical Tables and Annual Report (1997).

[38] IMF–Brazil Letter of Intent, n 27 at 2–3 contains a good discussion of this period.

money growth, credit constraints, and relatively high interest rates were the tools available to help prop up the Real.

Fiscal policy problems relating to state government pensions and the size of the civil service in certain key states left the growing impression that Brazilian state creditors might not be able to pay their foreign exchange obligations, thus putting pressure on the federal government to devalue the currency. Bringing in record quantities of direct foreign investment in helped to alleviate this negative perception, but did not cover up the fundamental long-term perception of the problem. Indeed, only one year after launch, the IADB's review of IMF statistics showed the Real was now at 0.92 : 1, down significantly from a par value of 1 : 1 to the dollar, at launch.[39]

Under these conditions, the downside risk was that the Real was not only increasingly perceived as overvalued; absent strong government policy to address the fiscal issues, it seemed to have no other way to go, but down. Indeed, in the summer of 1997, noted MIT economist Rudiger Dornbusch said that Brazil's Real currency was in *real* trouble, owing to the disequibrilium in the above numbers.[40] The major positives were that foreign investment was coming in strong, the current account deficit was easily financed for six months based on existing international reserves (in contrast to Mexico's 1994 liquidity problems), and the US dollar upon which the Real was monetised was relatively steady.

For the next five months or so since Dornbusch's summer pronouncement, nothing much happened, at least in Brazil. Outside, of course, Thailand went into financial crisis, Indonesia and Malaysia were in clear trouble, and hints that Korea, and Japan might need reserves to prop up the value of their currencies drew the increasing attention and concern of international banking authorities.

Whether the causes were attributable to closed financial systems, a speculative bubble in the property market, corruption, lax accounting, and bank supervisory systems, one point was clear: an IMF bail out of these economies, with a substantial element of legal reform conditions seemed to be on its way-and needed.

Concurrently, stock markets, around the world, most importantly the US market, had reacted to the October 1997 drop in the Hong Kong Hang Seng Index, with a short, sharp, but ultimately modest correction of less than 10 per cent. The reason it seems is that the market did not perceive that massive collapse was in order in the US markets.

39 *See* <http://www.iadb.org>, Social and Economic Statistics, Statistical database section.

40 *See* Roubini, Brazil and Latin America, Brazil's Incomplete Stabilisation and Reform by Rudi Dornbusch (1997); *see also* R. Dornbusch, *Brazil and the IMF* (1998); Dornbusch's comments were widely publicised in various media, such as Business Week, and other influential mainstream and popular publications.

Confidence and calm were preserved as major US financial leaders pronounced the correction taking place as business as usual; earlier pronouncements that over allocation of assets in the stock market could result in a speculative bubble seemed to have inoculated the market from any psychological panic or distress.[41]

Without question, the US and the Brazilian market are highly linked. Unfortunately, for the Brazilian market, the leading exchange, the Sao Paulo Bolsa or the BOVESPA, dropped dramatically in response to every shift. In fact, the market dropped over 82 per cent from the beginning of the year.[42]

This event, on top of increasing pressure on the currency markets made it clear that serious asset allocation out of Brazil would result in hedge fund portfolios if corrective action was not taken to restore confidence in the Brazilian Real. The impending crisis was not arising from short-term liquidity problems or insolvency, but from the perception that its' currency value could not be sustained.

From the vantage point of 1997 the key elements precipitating crisis were fiscal or perceived fiscal overspending, the lack of political will to address the problem, and the perception of Real over valuation. The Brazilian and US stock market fall in October 1997, indirect contagion due to the psychological effect of Asian crisis, and the growing perception that unfavorable speculative pressure was building were other key negatives.

The fundamental issues to be addressed were ensuring broad government reform on key fiscal issues, and providing the political will to educate citizenry on need to absorb short term pain, to ensure long term gain. Reinstilling confidence in the domestic stock market and monitoring negative spillovers from the US stock market correction was also important. Defending the currency at an appropriate level after the Asian contagion dampened confidence in emerging markets was becoming a major problem without an easy solution.

D. *Response to Growing Crisis*

1. Denial

Shortly after the Sao Paulo stock exchange suffered drastic falls, there was public sentiment of confidence expressed in the overall need to take action to reform the economy drastically. This sentiment soon changed as the

[41] The statements and testimony of Chairman Greenspan can be seen at <http://www.federalreserve.gov> at Testimony of Chairman Alan Greenspan Before the Joint Economic Committee, US Congress 29 Oct. 1997.

[42] *See* <http://www.bovespa.com.br> generally for documents relating to price history of assets in various monthly Bulletins, and other official publications.

painful reality of stabilisation medicine, such as cutting public spending drastically, and raising interest rates higher, came sharper into focus.

2. CENTRAL BANK ACTION

The first public signal that Brazil recognised it was in a potential crisis was the Central Bank's decision to increase its interest rate from about 22 to 43 per cent.[43] It was now clear that something in the market persuaded the Brazilian authorities that strong and decisive corrective action was urgently needed.

3. PRESIDENTIAL ACTION

Throughout 1997 and beyond, President Cardoso rallied the country with a call to fiscal prudence, declaring that he would attempt to push through a civil service reform plan (and some other fiscal measures such as pension reform) to address the need to correct imbalances and restore international confidence in Brazil. Within a matter of days, the proposal was prepared and delivered to Congress, over the opposition of major Sao Paulo unions, and the leader of his own party who said that the party would not be *decreed* to on such a painful issue.

4. CONGRESSIONAL VOTING

350 votes in the lower chamber were needed for the proposed $9 billion reduction package to be approved. Brazilian politics does not flow along part lines since it has a strong personalist, local patronage component, such that the vote was expected to be close. Indeed, mustering the votes for this package or the less ambitious $3 billion package was also perceived as not so easy.

5. CO-ORDINATION WITH THE IMF

Through the end of 1997 the situation was one of consultation only. This approach, whether it was real or merely on the surface, seemed sensible, as further crisis avoidance rather than active involvement was the right dose of public diplomacy required to maintain still existing confidence levels. Given that the effective real (as opposed to nominal) exchange rate was perceived to be anywhere from 10–30 per cent less than its peg, further close consultation was clearly needed.[44]

[43] IMF–Brazil Letter of Intent, n 27 at 2–3; R. Waters, n 6.

[44] Ibid.

E. *Prevention of Deepening Crisis: Evaluation of Crisis Management Options and Lasting Reform Prospects*

1. Crisis Management

The sense of crisis appeared to have been seized upon as an opportunity to make needed correction before an even more *unreal* Real is perceived as the unit of exchange. For example, the Brazilian Central Bank November 1997 Bulletin reflects that the banking system appears sound, with no damaging capital surges which can be discerned—either into or out of the country.

2. Central Bank and Government Options

Obviously, guessing at what the Brazilian authorities, with or without the assistance of the IMF, would do next, was scenario specific. There were numerous scenarios that hedge fund managers could draw up in trying to decide whether, and in what proportion, to allocate their assets. Assuming, the reform of Brazilian fiscal policy takes place, a gradual devaluation could still be in order or it might be possible to 'buy time' using one of the instruments described below.

Assuming the fiscal/civil service reform plan either fully or partially did not go into effect, the increased pressure was likely to result in either further tightening of monetary policy (if possible), and further liberalisation.

It also seems that the Brazilian's agreement to raise the MERCOSUR CET to 17 per cent, would raise some additional revenues, to the extent the bulk of these goods are price inelastic and not subject to any other substitutions. Indeed, the widening trade deficit of over $5 billion represents a cause of concern which only increased competitiveness, not protectionism, will cure.

3. Lasting Reform Prospects

From the vantage point of 1997 crisis management, whether the current crisis yields to a process of reform depends heavily on the results of the congressional reaction to the proposed plan, the public mood, the degree of recession, including the outcome of the Presidential and other electoral contests. Brazil's President, is in a unique position to voluntarily ask citizens to accept pain *before* rather than after the election to maintain greater price stability over the long run.

Such a political position may work, because the alternative of a return to rampant *hyper*inflation seems worse, and is a prospect not so far away in memory. There also do not appear to be any creditable alternatives, who can carry the presidential banner. This is because Pedro Maluf is perceived by many to be the captive of the much more radical Socialists, and Cardoso is, by contrast, respected as a reasonably honest politician, who has not been dogged by any of the vote buying scandals which have afflicted other prominent politicians this year.[45]

To the extent banking law reform and related economic measures are contemplated, the next section discusses the specific approaches that could be used to prevent further crisis.

F. How Legal Technical Assistance Could Help Specifically and more Broadly to Reduce the Prospects for the Situation to Become Catastrophic

At the beginning of 1998, the following *legal and economic* advice represents some of the more salient coordinated policy options available to contain crisis.

1. Legal Options

The first step available to policymakers is to review opportunities to use various short-term facilities with the IMF in a confidential manner. Setting targets for key numbers can determine whether the currency appear to be sliding, in addition to the floating peg itself. For example, the ratio of M1 as a percentage of international cash reserves discloses much about the seriousness of the domestic authorities to their commitment to price stability.

A second step is to discuss possibilities for macroeconomic coordination with the United States and other major creditors. This should be done on an informal basis, tracking the APEC approach wherein the IMF is the lead player. Nevertheless, securing US support for such assistance may not be so easy, given the Republican's rebuff of Clinton's pledge to provide the IMF with additional capital suggests that legislative efforts to provide exchange stabilisation, if the situation worsens substantially seems currently unlikely.

The third step is to discuss possibilities for macroeconomic coordination with Mercosur. One of the key intentions of the 1990 Treaty of Asuncion is macroeconomic coordination. It seems reasonably clear that since the Argentine peso is likewise pegged to the dollar and that its economy turns in large part on the degree to which it can export products to Brazil, a regional partnership agreement, even if primarily symbolic, sends a signal of solidarity which is helpful. There is, however, no Mercosur Development Bank or other institution with reserve capacity to be of assistance. Chile, although an associate member could also be of help. The coordination of

[45] M. Reid, 'Brazil's Bright Future', *The Economist*, 26 Mar. 1999.

member states with the Bank of International Settlements (BIS) is possible, as took place after the Mexican crisis.[46]

The fourth step is ensuring that the central bank uses its authority wisely to ensure appropriate measures are taken. These include:

(i) Authorisation for a central pool of information about borrowers to monitor risk with release of this information to Brazilian banking supervisory authorities to outside regulatory and supervisory bodies for purposes of monitoring liquidity risk. The particular target here is monitoring the potential for capital flight through surveillance and disclosure requirements. Existing memorandum of understandings (mou) with the US SEC, Commodities Future and Trading Commission (CFTC), Argentina, and Paraguay already exist.

(ii) Training of staff who can understand consolidated accounting methods used in foreign branches and overseas offices; tighter enforcement of domestic accounting standard to ensure greater transparency. The purpose here is to ensure that the possibility of excessive loss of funds through various transfer mechanisms is provided for through innovative recharacterisation of transactions. This is important because valuation of banking assets is critical to any underlying issue relating to liquidity.

(iii) Strict tax enforcement. A specific concern here is enforcement of the 7 per cent entry tax on entry of short-term capital flows, with longer-term borrowings having tax reduced on a sliding scale. This tool is a means to deter flight and provide for a higher quality of funds to come in, in the first instance.

(iv) Interest Rate Setting at High Levels Relative to External Brady Bonds. The economic reasoning for this is to encourage arbitrageurs to come in and buy domestic Brazilian bonds, which rose dramatically in 1997, in line with the interest rate rise, rather than going out on the external Brady market. The importance of this sound policy is to keep the current account strong with strong currency reserves.

(v) Upholding the Basle requirements of at risk capital (implemented in 1994). This is needed in order to maintain capital requirements that help ensure public confidence in the banking system.

2. Economic Options

A first step is further maintenance of sophisticated information technology systems to track liquidity flows.

A second tool is for the Central Bank to buy dollars, such that currency

[46] D. Arner, generally, *The Mexican Peso Crisis of 1994–1995: Implications for the Regulation of Financial Markets*, 2 Nafta L. Rev (1996).

speculators have limited incentives to fight the Central Bank's pricing of the Real. Indeed, to the extent the international market is thin in Reals, this makes sense as part of a portfolio strategy; you can not sell short what you can not get. Specifically, this sends a signal to nervous international bankers that short-term foreign debt exposure can be covered, and that the government is taking places to support the Real. This may not help Brazil with any market interpretation that the currency value is truly unsustain-able-due to high budget deficits, market psychology, or short term debt and exporter's inability to finance goods due to the high value of the currency. However, more reserves, if corrective action is taken, is better than nothing,

The answer to whether the latter component of this strategy is feasible depends upon an empirical evaluation of the situation. If the market is a difficult one to become a major player in, gradually selling Reals makes more sense, so that, if a devaluation arises, it is much smaller than it would otherwise be because of the strength of the economic fundamentals.

In addition, another alternative for the government or central bank may be to fashion an OTC transaction(s) where as an undisclosed principal, they intervene with some novel products to protect their currency. There are a variety of bond based products, in addition to currency based products, which are highly correlated, and in which the Bank possesses superior information as to its own policy. Depending upon the degree of thinness in the market, this is another way for the Brazilians to possibly protect themselves, and even flourish.

3. INTEGRATED LEGAL AND ECONOMIC OPTIONS

The above suggestions are not addressed to problems of concentration of wealth (certain leading families dominate the private banking sector, for example). Nevertheless, the degree of independence of the central bank and key government agencies is of paramount importance.

Reducing the long-term possibility of corruption through true financial liberalisation with foreign parties, and increased international oversight is a long-term concern which also deserves some attention as the Brazilian banking sector modernises further. This is particularly true in the state banking sector in the federal regime, and the commercial sector overall, in the largest capitalised banks.

Likewise, the current situation is not one where the large Brazilian banking sector is confronting the specter of a high number of non-performing loans. Careful action, backed up by the government's response now and potential international assistance, can help anticipate the need for increased dollar liquidity, so that banks have prepared themselves for a worsening economic situation with greater dollar reserves.

IV. THE CRISIS UNFOLDS AND THE RESPONSE TO IT FROM THE INTERNATIONAL COMMUNITY

A. *The Political-Business Cycle in Brazil*

1998 was a presidential election year in Brazil. What this meant, of course, was that the party in power had a strong incentive to maintain itself with economic policies that were designed to keep the currency strong, the economy growing at a fast rate, and minimal inflation.

The international financial community had a slightly different agenda. While it also had a strong desire to see that Brazil remained prosperous, it's more focused concern was to protect it's direct and portfolio investments there.

The 1998 campaign was a show of contrasts. Cardoso promised that he would continue to push for reforms that would reduce the bureaucracy, and supported pension 'right sizing' in the larger Brazilian states. He promised, above all to keep the currency strong, and to serve as the voice of reason to the outside world of Brazil's seriousness in maintaining fiscal and monetary policies that promoted price stability. Even to his doubters, he positioned himself as not only the savior of Brazil through the formulation and implementation of the Real plan, but as the lesser of two evils compared to his socialist rival. With crisis looming but credibility, at home and abroad higher than his counterpart, Cardoso played the economic cards in a sufficiently skilful way to garner an easy re-election victory.

But the party was not to last long. The above-articulated problems of short term debt levels building up, had not been resolved and the central bank's interest rate tightening policies had not sufficiently reduced demand for borrowings. The fact of the primary surplus, when viewed against international fiscal standards—should have been impressive, but was ignored in light of state inaction to address under-funded pension and other liabilities to international and domestic creditors.

In sum, Brazil had an overall debt of 8 per cent of gross domestic product that, depending upon your point if view, either was too high or was perceived to be too high. Lack of confidence to pay back the debt had been growing as short term interest rates climbed, but these were the only sources to repay debt. Paradoxically, short-term interest rates would not be so punitive, if there was confidence in the ability to repay the debt.

The logic of investment in Brazil had now created a vicious circle. Cardoso's policy of increasing foreign investment, privatisation, and a real pegged to the dollar were intended to create a virtuous circle of stable, investment led growth. This effort, however, could not sustain confidence in the wake of an unforeseen Asian and Russian crisis that had seen currencies pummeled by speculators. Interest rate rises to prop the perception that the central bank had sufficient dollar reserves and that President Cardoso had the political will to sustain the real to its' pegged value could not hold, if confidence in the real fell on the international markets.

Indeed, only two weeks after his October re-election, President Cardoso ordered his finance minister to start the process leading to the devaluation of the Real. The virtuous circle had turned vicious and a new cycle-facing the harsh reality of devaluation—was about to begin.

B. *The International Dimension: The Capital Climate and the Problem of Speculation*

At the time of the Brazilian devaluation, confidence in the international financial system had been shaken. The IMF had embarked on an exhaustive program of conditional lending through 1997–8, and serious concerns were expressed that its' special drawing rights and other liquidity facilities could not cope with a crisis of this scale. Criticism of the IMF failure to spot the problem early was widely criticised.

But of course, the IMF was in a trap. If indeed it did indicate that it lacked confidence in an economic programme, such as that of Brazil, it could itself cause a crisis atmosphere. In addition it could not, short of advocating currency controls for country implementation, propose policies that constrained investors and corporate financial officers to—quite correctly—'vote with their currency hedging policies' when they lose confidence in the domestic governments ability to uphold price stability. Indeed, financial discipline via the market workings of the currency market actually encouraged prudent government policies.

But to some extent some of the problems extant were due to the overly positive perceptions of investors regarding the fortunes of emerging market financial products. For example, let's say a currency speculator decides that he wants to take a position on emerging markets currency, the Brazilian Real, in the Chicago Board of Trade, the Chicago Merc, Liffe, or any of a series of other exchanges. The trader knows that the option has been priced to anticipate expectations of certain events over time that reflect a pricing tend in the currency commodity. Indeed, if the price movement is perceived to be too one sided (eg everybody thinks the Real will drop) then no trades will be executed, because no market exists.

The same dynamic exists in the Over the Counter (OTC) market. This time, however, trillions of dollars of securities deals, far dwarfing the size of Wall Street and the City stock exchanges transactions, takes place between parties on an individual contractually tailored basis. Products are developed to sell to investors, based on black box proprietary formulas, seeking to capture market under valuations, growth curves, or tax advantages, and sometimes all three.

Emerging markets have benefited from these products because they have been used as methods to repackage sales of bonds and other financial items as linked to 'bets' on market behaviour, such as the degree to which a bond rises or falls during a given period. Sometimes, such products can be engineered as tax advantaged because they arise in an off shore jurisdiction in the Caribbean or Mauritius, and are executed by a charitable party, thus guaranteeing better tax treatment if not outright exclusion from one level of taxation.

Each of the above types of transactions can present the hypothetical investor with a higher yield curve with no greater degree of risk. This argument of an 'emerging markets free lunch' has in fact been used as a staple for investing in equities in emerging markets. The comparable argument for bond yields is more difficult to make, as the risk reward ratio curve relationship is more linear and straightforward.

All of these above products, unforeseen in the days of designing the Bretton Woods international financial system are not closely regulated. These products are responsible for a tremendous percentage of short-term capital flows in emerging and developed markets alike. For well-managed firms, they present rich trading opportunities. Major investment firms may make as much as 40 per cent of recent profits arise from proprietary trading activities, and no doubt much of this profit is embedded deep within the contract fine print of the over the counter trade.[47] And as long as both parties make money, who cares?

When a bet goes against the value of an emerging markets currency, like the Brazilian Real, such bets can cost a Central bank precious reserves. A Bank must therefore find some kind of money that can help stabilise the market, usually dollars or other high quality paper. It will then enact policies to show that it is not about to go out and print money; this robs the currency of more value, as it inflates its way out of the squeeze.

This type of scenario is not what took place in Brazil, but it was the case in Malaysia and Indonesia.[48] It ended up costing the IMF lots of money as it helps stabilise the economy, and directly costs taxpayers in all the major developed countries substantial sums of money, since they are the major underwriters of the Fund. In addition, the major developed countries can sometimes be called upon to underwrite exchange stabilisation pacts, as was the case with the US loans to Mexico, after the 1994 peso crisis.[49]

[47] See Roubini, Derivatives, Hedge Funds and Systemic Risk. A good overview of the post-LTCM landscape as to core risk management issues is Report of the President's Working Group on Financial Markets, Hedge Funds, Leverage, and the Lessons of Long-Term Capital Management, (29 Apr. 1999). The 40 per cent figure cited above is based upon F. Portnoy, *Fiasco* (1999); Compendium of documents produced by the Basle Committee on Banking Supervision, Volume Two—Advanced Supervisory Methods, includes detailed discussion of bank's disclosure and accounting for trading activities (Apr. 1997).

[48] Cf Roubini, 'Malaysia and Indonesia'.

[49] See US GAO Report, Mexico's Financial Crisis: Origins, Assistance, and Initial Efforts to Recover (GAO-GGD-(23 Feb. 1996).

The game of chance that the speculators are engaging in above is encouraged by the market, and has long been a staple of financial history in some form or another. (Rothschild supposedly made his initial fortune by capitalising on the fall of the French currency and rise of the British that would follow Napolean's defeat at Waterloo. John Maynard Keynes at Cambridge, and Harvard economist and prominent US economic advisor Martin Feldstein, are reputed to have made large fortunes on successful currency bets.)

What has changed is that currency or related bets on bonds, equities, interest rates, or proxy financial instruments can bring down an economy *quickly*. It is the speed of the financial transactions, along with their leveraged size, that kills. It is difficult to be responsive when you do not really see the calamity coming.

C. *The International Institutional Response and the Brazilian Stabilisation Program*

The IMF and Brazil jointly announced a support package on November 17, 1998. Brazil requested $18.1 billion dollars for three years, with $4.5 billion in special drawing rights reserve funds.[50] This was to be phased in various increments and was conditional upon the meeting of certain fiscal targets. The World Bank and the Inter-American Development Bank likewise stated their intention to commit over $4.5 billion towards social support programmes, priority public investments, and public administration, and small business credits.[51]

The justification for support was that the Real had come under significant pressure due to the Asia crisis. The 43.5 per cent interest rate set for overnight lending and the government's revenue raising measures, amounting to 2.5 per cent of gross domestic product were deemed ineffective in stemming the crisis.[52] The effect of such policies-causing the pain of higher unemployment rising from 6 to 7.5 per cent through 1998, and higher consumer prices had lowered incomes, without dampening consumer demand sufficiently.[53]

The mid-July figure of $70 billion in reserves had dwindled to just under $46 billion after the October 1998 elections and the IMF–World Bank meetings announcing the initiatives to formulate a new international financial architecture.[54] The announcement of devaluation was a foregone conclusion before the elections as sustaining the value of the Real at its' previous levels could not be maintained.

In sum, hindsight suggests that of the above policy prescriptions stated

[50] Brazil–IMF Letter of Intent, n 27.
[51] Ibid. [52] Ibid. [53] Ibid. [54] Ibid.

above as crisis management tools, none could have prevented the crisis, with the possible, albeit dubious prospect of massive speculation by Brazil on its' own behalf in the currency markets. Whether because of Real weakness or the perception that the reforms of pension trimming and such were not sufficiently satisfying, the conclusion is the same, that increased international and domestic coordination could not have prevented although they could have contained the devaluation crisis.

The policy reforms of cutting state pensions and various other measures that had begun in 1997 to ward off crisis had largely been enacted but had not been fully successful in restoring the loss of market confidence.

The Brazilian government's new 1999 program was comprised of front loaded fiscal adjustments, including planned reduction primarily at the Federal level.[55] Specifically, primary surplus targets were to rise from 1.8 to 3.0 per cent of gross domestic product.[56] The overall federal deficit was to fall from 5.6 per cent of gross domestic product in 1998 to 3.6 per cent in 1999.[57]

Taxes were to increase, including that on corporate transactions.[58] Moreover, the states were expected to do their share in reducing the deficit by agreeing to certain targets set by the government.[59] The Senate was to limit borrowing, such as new bond issues, and provide further limitation of deficit financing of the public sector.[60]

In addition to the above, a wide ranging set of fiscal and administrative support polices were proposed or enacted.[61] These included a new planned Fiscal Responsibility Act that would set debt benchmarks; a Social Security constitutional amendment that would cap state pension contributions; limits on the size of the state bureaucracy; tax reduction; and further privatisation.

On the monetary side, the objective of price stability was to be furthered with the above fiscal policies as well as the use of indirect monetary instruments. These include lengthening the public debt maturity, and other measures to reduce the cost of capital, especially since short-term dollar debt is oftentimes the most expensive burden that a country can face.[62]

As to banking policy, the previous policy of privatising state banks and further liberalisation in 1998, continuing the pre-1997 programme was listed as a positive confidence instilling achievement. Implementation of the Basle capital adequacy standards at higher levels than required by law (Basle recommends 8 per cent for tier one capital, the rule was 11 per cent in Brazil for 1999, and the top domestic banks had 15 per cent to back up their savings) was another positive development.[63] Moreover, a capital

[55] Brazil–IMF Letter of Intent, n 27. [56] Ibid. [57] Ibid.
[58] Ibid. [59] Ibid. [60] Ibid. [61] Ibid.
[62] Ibid. [63] Ibid.

charge against counterparty operations of derivative operations had been required since 1997, and other credit risk tightening had been undertaken.[64]

The Basle twenty-five principles of Banking supervision were adopted and the goal was year 2000 compliance.[65] The World Bank was involved with bringing more sophisticated technical banking supervision practices and a series of initiatives, resulting in better risk management and transparency were the result.

Further, the exchange rate band was to be widened with gradual devaluation of the Real.[66] Trade liberalisation with Mercosur with respect to tariff barriers was to be continued (it was in fact curtailed), and other broader liberalisation measures, consonant with the WTO, were pledged.[67] Finally, Brazil's statistical base was to be adjusted in line with international standards so that the degree of public sector debt was not over-reported.[68]

D. The 1999 Stabilisation Programme Takes Effect

By February 1999 there was reason to fear that Brazil was on the verge of collapse.[69] Inflation was rising, and industrial output was falling. Concerns that Brazilian banks might not have sufficient reserves had begun to be addressed, and soon thereafter contingent credit lines form private sources in the US were arranged.

By June 1999, a climate of scepticism regarding government policymaking began to take hold as it emerged that certain large capital outflows had taken place right before the devaluation.

But if the public news about the handling of the crisis was not completely positive, and the possibility of a liquidity crisis was being seriously prepared for, the confidence building process in Brazil was, remarkably, about to take a turn for the better.

The IMF, which had approved the use of $44.5 in conditional stand by funding in February had to be pleased with the economic performance of the country and its' decision to provide stand by assistance. This is because

64 Ibid. Counterparty risk is a subject of increasing concern among the Basle Committee as well. *See* Roubini, Prudential Supervision and Basle Committee on Banking Supervision for an extensive collection of reports on the above issues.

65 Ibid. at Brazil–IMF Letter of Intent.

66 Ibid.

67 Ibid. *See also* <http://wto.org, http://www.oas.org, http://www.iadb.org> section on regional integration, especially Periodic Notes compendiums.

68 Ibid. at IMF–Brazil letter of Intent.

69 See N. Yamaguchi, *Brazil's Former Foe, Inflation Creeps Back* (Reuters, 12 Feb. 1999); The best article this author has seen on understanding the core issues that give rise to a potential banking crisis, as opposed to a more generalised financial crisis, is DC Hardy, *Are Banking Crises Predictable?*, Finance and Development (IMF, Dec. 1998). Here the authors argue for greater credit lines, and other contingency measures. This is especially important as may be required to repay short term dollar denominated debt.

gross domestic product seemed to be on the decline to only 1 per cent rather than 4–5 per cent by July 1999.[70] Inflation that had been targeted at 11 per cent was only 7.4 per cent, and was expected to go to less than 5 per cent by end of 2000.[71] Fiscal performance in reducing the deficit was better than expected, and the measure to take prompt corrective action to reduce the state, federal, and municipal deficits were going significantly better than anticipated.[72]

Still, the Fiscal Responsibility Act had not been passed by mid-year, although this was expected to resolve itself by the end of the year. Streamlining of the pension system had helped contain expenses as had other administrative reforms enacted in 1998, and initiated seriously in 1997. (By December 1999, the Brazilian Supreme Court ruled that the above civil service reform was unconstitutional, although this did not seem to substantially negatively affect the economy.)

Monetary policy had shifted to a flexible exchange rate system as of January 1999, and the effect had been viewed, as positive from the IMF's perspective in diminishing inflationary expectations.[73] Specifically, the government instituted a formal inflation-targeting framework in March, and monetary aggregates were kept within a narrow range.[74]

The banking system had weathered the crisis well with adequate hedging of their Real positions vis-à-vis the dollar in advance of the crisis. Moreover, non-performing loans had risen only slightly from 7 per cent to 8.9 per cent owing to the recession, and the capital adequacy system instituted and recommended by Basle and adopted by Brazil had meant that a strong overall capital base was in place.[75]

The pace of foreign direct investment was high, flowing in at a remarkable $18 billion pace, notwithstanding the financial turmoil.[76] Remarkably, a balance of payments surplus was projected for the end of 1999, and the trade balance was expected to improve with the US, even as reports for the first two quarters seemed less than promising.[77] In short, the coordinated IMF and Brazilian government program (with some private sector and other international financial institutions assistance) was yielding positive results that were fuelling confidence in Brazil's ability to manage its' way out of the devaluation into a smoother stabilised future.

[70] IMF–Brazil Memorandum of Economic Policies, 8 July 1999.
[71] Ibid. [72] Ibid. [73] Ibid.
[74] Ibid. [75] Ibid. [76] Ibid.
[77] Ibid.

V. THE INTERNATIONAL FINANCIAL ARCHITECTURE AND THE BRAZILIAN REFORM PROGRAM: DO THE FIVE PILLARS OF THE NEW ARCHITECTURE REALLY MATTER?

From the vantage point of early 2000, the success of the IMF–Brazil programme seems even more remarkable. Positive economic growth is expected this year, in this, the second year of stabilisation—and no banking or liquidity crisis has taken shape. The November IMF review shows that the decline of 1 per cent of gross domestic product and only 1 per cent of inflation was substantially better than had even been predicted six months earlier.[78] Some setbacks had taken place, notably the unconstitutionality of social security reforms, but the government had responded to this, and other setbacks, uniformly, with prompt corrective action. In sum, it seems that the capability of the Brazilian policymakers to enact reform policies since the first Cardoso administration, and the ability to plan for and foresee that a devaluation crisis might hit the Real throughout 1997–1998, were valuable in preventing a deeper crisis and ensuring quicker recovery.

The stabilisation plan implemented represented the opportunity of crisis to engage in deeper reform than political might otherwise have allowed, and it was seen positively by the market. The Brazilian government was able to issue Euro-Bonds by November 1999.[79] Inter-bank credit lines were being rolled over at a 97 per cent rate, and were being supplemented by various private sources.[80] Progress was being achieved, it seems, amidst the pain of recession.

A. THE ELEMENTS OF THE NEW INTERNATIONAL FINANCIAL ARCHITECTURE IN THE BRAZIL REFORM PLAN

The core elements of the new international financial architecture are comprised of many details but are essentially comprised of transparency, international standardisation, financial sector strengthening, private sector involvement, and contingent credit lines support. This section reviews to what extent these concepts were part of the strategy and tactics involved in the Brazil crisis, the first post 'new international financial architectural' crisis.

[78] IMF–Brazil Economic Policies and Technical Memorandum of Understanding, 12 Nov. 1999.

[79] Ibid.

[80] Ibid.; See <http://www.imf.org/external/country/BRA/index.htm> for the most complete information as to the IMF's relationship with Brazil, including commentary on lessons learned by the Brazilian Central Bank Chief Antonio Fraga, as well as IMF Managing Director Stanley Fischer.

1. Transparency

As to the objective of transparency, a review of the IMF proposals in this regard, suggests that this was an issue of limited public concern for the IMF. Specifically, the IMF did not ask that any public sector accounts be opened up further to public scrutiny. Moreover, it did not request further clarification of bank or other financial sector reporting requirements *vis-à-vis* Brazil's letter of intent and memorandum of economic policies.

It did, however, demand that public sector spending be reduced, a problem caused by the patronage practice of rewarding supporters with jobs—and then pensions at which they really did not have to work. In this sense, the IMF was able to bypass the simple request for greater transparency and attack the greater evil of corruption, as a means of raising economic performance.

Likewise, the IMF did not have to set out transparency *per se* as an overriding policy objective as to bank supervision. This is because Brazil was extensively involved in such a programme with the IMF and was therefore required as a condition of participation in various aid programmes to maintain certain prudential standards, such as loss ratios for non-performing loans and capital adequacy generally. In other words, Brazil had plans in place and was operationally executing a cleaning up of its banking operations. The sale of many state banks to the private sector had required, as a pre-condition of sale, greater transparency than might previously have been required for the sales to be closed. In short, transparency as a process was well underway in banking as a by-product of liberalisation, and of cooperation with the World Bank and other institutions in implementing tough, new regulatory and supervisory safeguards.

2. International Standardisation

The impact of international standardisation likewise pre-dates the Brazilian reforms. Specifically, Brazil had adopted the Basle capital adequacy standards, the Basle off-balance sheet reporting requirements to minimise value at risk for derivatives. It was in the process of adopting the Basle 25 Principles for Effective Banking Supervision, as indicated in the IMF–Brazil memoranda.[81]

[81] See Roubini, Basle Committee on Banking Supervision (Sept. 1997); See J Norton, *Devising Bank Supervisory Standards* (Kluwer, 1995); Cf. E Holz, *La Integracion de Los Sistemas Bancarios* (1997) for a discussion of Mercosur systems. Also see the web site at <http://www.sela.org> for discussion of related issues related to Latin American banking; *See also more generally*, E Aguirre and J Norton, *Reform of Latin American Banking Systems*, J Norton, *The Experience of Developed Countries and the Possible Implications for Latin America and Other Developing Countries* (Kluwer, 2000).

Perhaps, more significantly the damage that Brazil had suffered by having its' consolidated public debt considered together rather than just the Federal debt as a percentage of gross domestic product was remedied. This meant that bond agencies assessing credit worthiness would not have to add a restricted rating that could raise interest rates or other risk premium, beyond that required by international standards. Brazil's return to the international bond markets in the second half of 1999 was no doubt helped by the wide spread recognition of and adjustment for this statistical reporting anomaly.

3. Financial Sector Strengthening

As the above has shown, a strong component of the IMF programme was geared toward enhancing the quality of services through improved supervision and reform. This was already underway, and although the IMF reports do not so indicate, there is little doubt that prompt corrective action measures and improved monitoring have resulted from the crisis. The fact that the banking sector has not suffered, in any substantial way, and remains robust, indicates that this area, was in any event, well prepared for devaluation, and not at the heart of the problem in the same way that fiscal and administrative reform was.

4. Private Sector Involvement

The obvious idea behind this was to eliminate or mitigate the problem of moral hazard so that if a banking or other important economic institution failed, it was not immune from the consequences. This is, due to the Asian system of close partnerships between private and public sector, an issue that is less important in the Brazilian context. Still, this is not to say that there are not some concerns about favouritism and the passing of inside information to selected depositors by the Central bank prior to the devaluation, resulting in the preservation of capital through capital flight.

5. Contingent Credit lines

There is little question that the IMF's provision of stand by credit, and the private sector commitment of contingent credit lines eased the way for Brazil to come out of the depths of its' crisis. The concept of public contingent credit lines is primarily focused on preventive measures. In the case of Brazil, it was private sector involvement for major US financial institutions that helped contain the crisis from turning into a possible collapse during the crucial January 1999 to July 1999 period. Paying off short term debt with private debt rollovers was required with Brazil and major commercial banks agreeing to help.[82] Contingent credit lines have not thus far been used in the exclusively public arena, and are based on legally and economically complex set of parameters that may make their potential use as a useful policy tactic, moot.[83]

B. *Assessing The Intelligence Gathering and Response Capabilities of the New International Financial Architecture in Dealing with the Brazilian Crisis*

The above snapshot does not, of course, capture the full range of proposals or all the dimensions captured by the new international financial architecture in leading to meaningful reform in Brazil. More importantly, we must measure the degree to which the Brazilian reform program has benefited from the conceptual focus on the above areas, and the operational execution of proposals consistent with this in preventing and containing crisis. In short, do these core elements provide a foundation for improved intelligence gathering and response to crisis?

The answer, of course, is mixed. The new financial architecture proposals are useful in heading off crisis but they do not address the problem of structural imbalances, such as investors perceived in Brazil's fiscal accounts. Moreover, they cannot control the outflow of capital that may arise in response to impending devaluation, further weakening a currency's downward spiral.

On the other hand, the improvement in information systems through implementation of better transparency, international standardisation and financial sector strengthening provide an improved early warning system to what was the case prior to the Asian crisis asset bubbles and private sector

[82] *See* Roubini, homepage—'Private Sector Involvement in Crisis Prevention and Resolutions: Market Views and Recent Exposure,' ch. 5.

[83] In a recent *Foreign Affairs* Spring 2000 article, The Council on Foreign Relations (CFR) Special Task Force on Strengthening the International Financial Architecture observed that setting firm standards as to the proper ratio of credit available relative to reserves in the IMF was an important issue. It also focused on the unwieldy nature of the contingent credit line process. The CFR task force recommended that more specific criteria be worked out for the percentage of lending facilities for a country relative to reserves and noted that Brazil had required substantially greater facility than prior practice and guidelines might suggest. For contingent credit lines, the same emphasis on setting standards was discussed, and it was indicted that the use of public credit seemed unlikely, absent processes that permitted quick response to crisis. For the full Special Task force report *see* C Hills and P Peterson, *Safeguarding Prosperity in a Global Financial System: The Future International Financial Architecture* (IIE, Sept. 1999); For a sweeping view of the above issues from the IMF perspective, M. Camdessus, Economic Prospects for the Americas Under a new Financial Architecture, June 2, 1999 conference remarks at <http://www.imf.org/external/np/speeches/ 1999/060299. htm>. The most recent summary of IMF effort's is the Acting Managing Director to the International Monetary and Financial Committee on Progress in Reforming the IMF and Strengthening the Architecture of the International Financial System, 12 Apr. 2000.

over-borrowing became apparent. They may therefore not have been as specifically useful to heading off crisis in Brazil as they might be in other parts of the world. But, that only means that this was a different type of crisis than that which struck Asia, not that the tools do not have some current and future utility.

As to responding to crisis, there is no question that the financial sectortrengthening program already underway was most helpful in containing the extent of the crisis. Likewise, contingent credit lines are, when moral hazard is properly accounted for and diminished, a potentially useful tool to be applied in responding to crisis.

C. *Concluding Thoughts*

In light of the above, it is therefore suggested that the international financial architecture proposals had a modestly positive effect on the ability of Brazil's decision makers to adopt legal and institutional reform measures that matter. Crisis prevention and management capabilities are significantly enhanced by the broad agenda proposed by the new international financial architecture proponents. Indeed, to do nothing means that countries like Brazil may lack the political cover, not to mention the risk management tools to prepare for market speculators and others that may seek to pounce on weakness.

Further continuation of this agenda provides a basis for the strengthening of international financial law and institutions.

Chapter 12

1995 and 1997: The Case of Argentina

Marcelo Rafael Tavarone

I. THE FINANCIAL SYSTEM IN ARGENTINA DURING THE 1990s

The Argentina's achievements in financial activity during the last decade have been related to three main points: (1) the Convertibility system; (2) the financial liberalisation; and (3) the 'Banco Central de la República Argentina' (BCRA)[1] independence.

A. *The Convertibility System*[2]

The Convertibility system was established in 1991 by Law No. 23.928 and it is sustained by three basic principles: (1) the convertible currency; (2) the prohibition of indexation, and (3) the possibility of using foreign currency for domestic transactions.

1. THE 'CONVERTIBLE PESO'

The BCRA must provide full convertibility between Pesos and US dollars and exchange controls have been eliminated. The strength of the system depends on the capacity of the BCRA to keep reserves in US dollars supporting the value of the Peso.

Articles 1 and 2 of Law 23.928 state that 1 Peso shall be equal to 1 US dollar and the state assumes the responsibility of free sale and purchase of both US dollars and Pesos[3], hence, to provide the above mentioned convertibility between Pesos and US dollars.

[1] 'Banco Central de la República Argentina' is the translation of 'Central Bank of the Argentine Republic'.

[2] For a narrower explanation of the convertibility system in Argentina, *see* Marcelo R. Tavarone, 'The Argentine Monetary and Financial Framework', *NAFTA: Law and Business Review of the Americas*, 1998 *and also* IMF Staff Report No. 98/38, 'Argentina: Recent Economic Developments', April 1998, prepared by Bob Tara, Luis Catao, Philip Gerson, and Paul Gruenwald, 4/9.

[3] For a narrower analysis *see* Carlos Gustavo Gerscovich, 'Derecho Económico Monetario', Depalma, Buenos Aires, 1991, 69.

According to Article 4 of Law No 23.928, the reserves in US Dollars and gold shall be—at least—equal to the 100 per cent of the monetary flow. This rule aims to fix the value of the Peso; otherwise whatever the value given to it by law, the reality would destroy confidence and value if the BCRA did not keep the necessary reserves.

2. The End of Indexation

Law No 23.928 prohibited the application of any kind of indexation to monetary debts after 31 March 1991.[4] The reason for this prohibition was a suspicion that indexation was one of the causes of increasing inflation rates. Furthermore, it was expected that after the stabilisation of the Argentine currency, indexation clauses would become superfluous because of the disappearance of inflation.[5] However, prohibition of indexation was not welcome by many authors[6] who mistrusted the success of the convertibility system. Nevertheless, the convertibility system gained wide consensus because of its successful implementation, and during the 1995 presidential election the three major political parties, representing 96.2 per cent of the popular vote, agreed to support it.[7]

Moreover, prohibition of indexation was also reinforced by Law No 24.283, which states that all indexation or application of interest to the value of any asset or credit shall not exceed the actual value of the asset or credit at the moment of the payment. The aim of this law was to avoid situations in which mechanisms for indexation, formerly aimed to keep the real value of the amount of payments, had actually produced a final amount that exceeded the real value of the asset. This law also received considerable criticism from authors who feared that creditors would suffer distortions in their expectations of reimbursement.[8]

[4] Arts. 7 and 8 CL.

[5] *See* Juan J Casiello, '¿El fin de la indexación? (Reflexiones sobre la llamada "ley de convertibilidad del austral")', *La Ley* 1991-B-1039, 1043.

[6] *See* Fernando R. Fravega, and Luis E Piendibene; 'Visión jurídica de la ley de convertibilidad', *La Ley* 1991-B-1076, p. 1078/1082. *See also* Marcos M Córdoba, Marina de Pasquale, María Laura Ochoa, and Néstor E. Solari, 'Reflexiones sobre el título II de la ley de convertibilidad del austral', *La Ley* 1991-B-1063.

[7] Steve H. Hanke, 'A Tale of Two Pesos: A Comparison of Currency Policies in Mexico and Argentina'; Heritage Lecture No. 552, the Heritage Foundation Lectures and Educational Programs, <http://www.heritage.org/heritage/library/categories/theory/lect552.html> delivered 12 Dec. 1995, 1.

[8] *See* Atilio A. Alterini, 'Aproximaciones a la nueva ley desindexatoria No 24.283', *La Ley* 1994-C-717.

3. The Possibility of Using Foreign Currency for Domestic Transactions

Article 11 of Law 23.928 modified Article 619 of the Argentine Civil Code, thereby allowing parties in a domestic transaction to agree to pay their debts with foreign currency. This represented an important change in Argentine legislation since the previous version of Article 619 of the Civil Code stated that where parties agreed to pay their obligations in amounts of foreign currency, they were actually allowed to extinguish debts by paying the amount of Argentine currency necessary to acquire the amount of foreign currency originally agreed. At the same time, foreign exchange controls were withdrawn as a coherent measure to achieve financial and economic liberalisation.

B. *Financial Liberalisation*

Financial liberalisation has been achieved through many different steps. One important path has been the change introduced in the Financial Institutions Law No. 21.526, removing all the restrictions to foreign capital in financial activity including the requirement of reciprocity with the country where the foreign bank comes from,[9] indeed, Article 3 of Presidential Decree No 146/94 states that rules imposing limitations to foreign financial institutions are descriminatory, thus foreign financial institutions are allowed to enter into the system through performing the requirements required of Argentine financial institutions. This allowed a renewed interest from foreign investors in financial activity and by the end of 1997 resulted in foreign banks purchasing several Argentine banking institutions.[10]

Other achievements came from a significant process of privatisation, which had a double effect: first, it increased the state reserves through the money obtained from the sale of large state-owned enterprises. Between 1991 and 1994, the Government privatised 90 per cent of all state owned enterprises for an amount equivalent to US$20 billion.[11]

Secondly, it reduced fiscal deficits which those large enterprises used to impose on the state. The Government also announced its decision to privatise Banco de la Nación Argentina in 1997,[12] the largest bank in

[9] Héctor Angel Benélvaz and Osvaldo Walter Coll, 'Sistema Bancario Moderno', Depalma, Buenos Aires, 1994.

[10] IMF Staff Report No. 98/38, op cit. 6.

[11] Ibid. 5.

[12] *Clarín*, 8 Nov. 1997, 'El Gobierno convocará a bancos del exterior para privatizar el Nación'; *Ambito Financiero*, 10 Nov. 1997; 'Sólo aspectos para privatizar el Nación opondrá el FREPASO'; and *La Nación*, 10 Nov. 1997, 'La venta del Nación, en el centro del debate'.

Argentina,[13] then owned by the state, and in the last years of the twentieth century other important financial institutions have been privatised, like the Caja Nacional de Ahorro y Seguro and the Banco Hipotecario Nacional.[14]

The Government has also recommended to the provinces the privatisation of their own provincial state-owned banks and some provinces have started with this process, eg the Province of Mendoza, which began with the 'Banco de la Provincia de Mendoza' and the 'Banco de Previsión Social'.[15]

The creation of a privately managed system of pension funds, following the Chilean experience has also been an important achievement.

C. *Central Bank Independence*[16]

Central Bank independence was established by the Central Bank Law No. 24.144, which states that the Central Bank will not receive Government instructions in relation to conduct of monetary policies, and has expressly established limits to the decision of printing money, which was a tool used by many Governments to address increasing state expenditures, loosing the control of inflation.[17] Law 24.144 has also strongly limited the capacity of the Central Bank to provide financial assistance to the Government, and other provisions complete the system preventing any Government from using the Central Bank and monetary policies for short-term aims.[18]

BCRA independence has been deemed to be a real safeguard of the convertibility system since it allows the BCRA to perform its role in keeping the value of the currency and protecting the economy from inflation, thus allow monetary stability to create the conditions for economic development.[19] At the same time, BCRA independence has its own safeguards in order to assure a binding legal and institutional framework.[20] These safeguards can be classified as organic, functional and central bank accountability.

[13] At the time, Banco de la Nación Argentina had US$9 billion in deposits and 526 branches. After the Argentine Government announced its privatisation some important banks like Merril Lynch, First Boston, Lehman Brothers, Goldman Sachs, and Deutsche Morgan showed interest in a possible acquisition. It has been said that the announcement had a political rather than an economic aim. For further details *see Clarín* 8 Nov. 1997, 'El Gobierno convocará a bancos del exterior para privatizar el Nación'.

[14] *Ambito Financiero*, 24 Nov. 1997, 'Hipotecario: otro avance en la venta más grande del año'.

[15] See Benélvaz and Walter Coll, op cit. 337.

[16] For further explanations on the BCRA independence, *see* Carlos G. Gerscovich, '¿Autonomía o aislamiento del Banco Central?', *La Ley* 1992-E-1102. *See also* Marcelo R Tavarone, op cit.

[17] *See* Benélvaz and Walter Coll, op cit. 50.

[18] *See* ibid. 58. *See also* Rosa María Lastra 'Central Banking and Banking Regulation', Financial Markets Group, London School of Economics, London, 1996.

[19] Benélvaz and Coll, op cit. 58.

[20] For a narrower analysis of Central Bank independence safeguards *see* Lastra, op cit. 25/59. *See also* Marcelo R Tavarone, op cit.

II. THE 'TEQUILA' CRISIS

Between December 1994 and April 1995, Argentina suffered the post Mexican Peso devaluation crisis effect. An initial shock produced a mini-domestic crisis which affected the confidence in bond trading houses with a re-evaluation of Argentinian exposure by investors. Stock and bond markets suffered large losses and increased risks produced deposit withdrawals. This led to a liquidity crisis in many banks and some of them failed.

Deposits fell further between January and March 1995, reaching a 16 per cent reduction.[21] The BCRA extended extraordinary liquidity assistance and an international package of assistance (from the IMF and World Bank) helped to restore confidence. Due to the legal reforms introduced during the 1990s, the BCRA lacked of any powers to assist troubled banks or to perform a role of lender of last resort. This legal gap was covered by immediate reform of Laws No. 21.526 (Financial Institutions Law) and 24.144 (Central Bank Law).[22]

At the same time, the state started to restructure the banking system through a trust fund, financed by US$2 billion of Government of Argentina bonds and a US$500 million loan from the World Bank.[23] Mergers and acquisitions of smaller and unhealthy banks were encouraged by the Government as well as privatisation of provincial state-owned banks.[24] This latter issue was aided by another special trust created for the assistance of troubled provincial banks subject to privatisation processes and funded by 70.559.999 shares of YPF SA, loans provided by the Inter-American Development Bank and other multilateral agencies.[25]

The BCRA provided assistance to the smaller banks for about US$2 billion and about US$2.5 billion was deemed necessary to spend to finance public provincial banks closures and privatisations.[26] In total, coping with its role of 'lender of last resort' in order to provide assistance to banks in trouble and providing full convertibility between Pesos and US dollars, the BCRA lost US$4 billion in reserves.[27]

21 *See* Gerard Caprio, Michael Dooley, Danny Leipziger, and Carl Walsh, 'The Lender of Last Resort Function Under a Currency Board. The Case of Argentina', The World Bank Policy Research Department, Finance and Private Sector Development Division, Policy Research Working Paper No 1648, Sept. 1996, 3.

22 Carlos G Gerscovich, 'Las crisis bancarias y financieras', *Jurisprudencia Argentina*, 24 June 1998, No 6095, 69/70.

23 *See* Mauricio Carrizosa, Danny Leipziger, and Hemant Shah, 'The Tequila Effect and Argentina's Banking Reform', *Finance & Development*, Mar. 1996, vol 33, No 1, 4.

24 *See* ibid. 2 and 5.

25 Bernardo E. Duggan, and Leonardo F. Fernández, 'Argentina Legal Report', *International Financial Law Review*, Special Supplement: Banking Yearbook 1997, available at <http://www.lawmoney.com/public/contents. . .supps/iflrsupp9707/iflrsupp9707.30.html>, 8.

26 *See* Caprio, Dooley, Leipziger, and Walsh, op cit. 4.

27 *See* ibid. 2.

The state created a limited and privately financed deposit insurance system [28] to restore confidence in the financial system at the same time that fiscal strengthening plans were announced. Commitments to restructure and privatise provincial banks were also announced.

Argentina successfully emerged from the Tequila crisis, with a consolidated financial system and deposits began to return at the same time that confidence was restored. However, Argentine's Government could not avoid the effects of recession, although the banking system remained strong after the crisis. Growth was negative in 1995 (3.5 per cent) and banks had to face an increase in non-performing debtors estimated 26.7 per cent of the net worth of banks in October 1995. Before the crisis the non-performing loans were 18.7 per cent.[29]

III. THE 1997 CRISIS

Although the 1997 crisis produced large losses in the Buenos Aires Stock Exchange[30] the banking system dids not yet suffer illiquidity or insolvency problems. Moreover, there were not deposit withdrawals: in fact, deposits increased a record amount of US$75 billion[31] while BCRA reserves were increased to the amount of US$23 billion.[32] However, the Government announced a plan of fiscal strengthening at the same time that the National Budget for 1998 was drastically reduced in order to build the State reserves to face a new crisis. The BCRA also proposed to increase the amounts

[28] Law No 24.485 created a deposit insurance system which can be described as limited, obligatory, private and not funded by the BCRA. The implementation of the system was done through Presidential Decree No 540/95 modified by Presidential Decree No 1292/96. It is limited since only covers deposits for less than 90 days up to the amount of US$20.000. It is obligatory, according to Art. 1 Law 24.485 and it is private since it is administered by a corporation called SEDESA ('*Seguros de Depósitos Sociedad Anónima*', which is the translation of 'Deposits Insurance Corporation'). SEDESA acts as trustee administering a Deposit Guarantee Fund, albeit according to Art. 2 of Presidential Decree No 540/95 modified by Presidential Decree No 1292/96 the BCRA will necessarily be a partner of SEDESA. Finally, the Deposit Guarantee Fund is composed by the contributions compulsorily paid by banks and others financial institutions since Art. 1 of the Law 24.485 clearly states that BCRA and the National Treasury shall not compromise their resources for deposit insurance funding.

[29] *See* Caprio, Dooley, Leipziger, and Walsh, op cit. 6.

[30] *See* Gerscovich, op cit. 68.

[31] The virtual disappearance of most of the unhealthy institutions during the 'Tequila' effect with a consequent consolidation of the strongest institutions as well as the existence of tighter requirements on capital adequacy and liquidity requirements are important reasons of this good performance of the Argentine banking system during the Asian crisis. (*See* Gerscovich, op cit. 71). However, this must not lead to the conclusion that the system is completely safe (no system could meet such a feature) and far from suffering systemic collapses.

[32] Georgina M Gómez, 'El sistema financiero batió dos records: reservas y depósitos', El Cronista en Internet, 6 July 1998, available at <http://www.cronista.com/DIA/htm/ml_fader.HTM>.

covered by the deposit insurance system in order to keep the stability of the banking system.[33]

International assistance (IMF) was received [34] and tax reforms were passed by the Congress during 1998,[35] albeit some obstacles were found at this parliamentary stage.[36] Some of these tax reforms are actually revenue neutral but are aimed to reduce corporate indebtedness, especially foreign borrowing as a response to the high indebtedness in foreign currency existing in the Argentine economy. Other reforms aimed to increase taxes on company and individual earnings.[37]

The Ministry of Economy also claimed for 'special powers' to create new taxes and reduce state expenditures [38] but the Congress was willing to give such an authorisation to the Ministry. Moreover, the Congress expressly refused to give such 'special powers' during the approval of the 1998 National Budget.[39]

On the other hand, the Argentine system showed some of its weaknesses during this crisis. With the creation of Mercosur, Brazil became the most important market for Argentine exports. Both markets—Argentine and Brazilian—are closely related [40] and the 1997 crisis had much stronger effects on Brazil than in Argentina. As a result of this close relation, all the losses produced in Sao Paulo were followed by strong losses in the Buenos Aires Stock Exchange and the cost of credit for Argentina suffered a considerable increase a few days after the crisis started.[41]

The Brazilian system, less consolidated and with a Real (Brazilian currency) which has been deemed to be over-valued seems to appeared weaker than the Argentine system. At the same time, the announcements of a Brazilian Government have strong effects on the Argentinea economy.[42]

33 *Clarín*, 19 May 1998, 'El Central propone subir las garantías de los depósitos'.

34 *La Nación*, 8 Nov. 1997 'La caída de las bolsas parece no tener fin' and 18 Nov. 1997, 'Acuerdo con el FMI por otros tres años'.

35 *Ambito Financiero*, 12 Nov. 1997, 'Lanzan aquí un plan con aumento de impuestos'.

36 *La Nación*, 28 July 1998, 'La reforma fiscal no conforma a sector alguno'. *See also*: Jorge Rosales, *La Nación*, 28 July 1998, 'El FMI reclamará al Gobierno una mayor austeridad fiscal'; Serra, Laura, *La Nación*, 26 July 1998, 'La reforma tributaria, sin acuerdo'; *Ambito Financiero*, 5 June 1998, 'Sebastiani: no van a votar esta reforma impositiva', Rabanal, Rubén, 'Es insostenible la reforma impositiva del gobierno', *Ambito Financiero*, 29 May 1998.

37 *Lawmoney News*, 'Argentina indebted to reform', available at <http://www.lawmoney.oyster.co.uk/public/news/hotnews/news9804/news980401.1.html>.

38 *La Nación*, 13 Nov. 1997, 'Se analiza un ajuste para enfrentar la crisis'.

39 *La Nación*, 17 Nov. 1997, 'Recortan el poder de Roque Fernández'.

40 *See* Jorge M. Guira 'MERCOSUR as an Instrument for Development', *NAFTA: Law and Business Review of the Americas*, Summer 1997 vol. III, No 3, 72.

41 The Argentine government had to pay an interest rate of 9.2 per cent for a bond issue of US$2.5 billion on 12 Nov. 1997. This interest rate was similar to rate paid during Feb. 1995, the worst moment of the 'Tequila Crisis' (*La Nación*, 13 Nov. 1997, 'Brusca alza del costo del crédito para el Estado').

42 *La Nación*, 31 Oct. 1997, 'Complica al país la crisis en Brasil'; 3 Nov. 1997, 'Con la vista puesta en el gran vecino'; and 12 Nov. 1997, 'Afectará a la Argentina el ajuste en el Brasil'.

The situation for Argentina seemed to be the following: first, if Brazil devalue the Real, international investors lose confidence in Latin American markets.[43] At the same time a devaluation of the Real might force Argentina to devalue the Peso in order to keep competitive conditions between both countries' exports. This would have been the first devaluation after 8 years of convertibility and it could have negative effects for the inflation rate. In the event, despite the Brazilian Government's assurancies that the Real would not be devalued (Governments always deny their intention of devalue the currency) Brazil in fact devalued—to its advantage and Argentina's detriment.[44]

Secondly, Brazil announced a plan of fiscal strengthening and deficit reduction.[45] This was deemed by Argentine businessman as a logical cause of recession for Brazil and, consequently, expected to produce a strong reduction in Argentine exports[46] to its principal partner in Mercosur.[47] This was shown by the car industry in Argentina, which reduced its production for 1998.[48]

Curiously, this plan of adjustment, was not initially supported through an agreement with the IMF in order to receive financial assistance. Moreover, the Brazilian Government initially refused to accept credits from the IMF and expressly denied a possible agreement with said organisation[49] and President Fernando Cardoso said that Brazilian Central Bank keeps reserves of more than US$50 billion and it would not need a credit from the IMF.[50] Consequently, without international assistance, interest rates had to be drastically increased in order to avoid a devaluation.[51] In the event, domestic pain eventually forced Brazil to enlist the aid of the IMF and to devalue.

[43] However, Brazilian President Fernando Cardoso kept in contact with Argentine President Carlos Menem and said that Brazil would not devalue its currency (*La Nación*, 31 Oct. 1997). This announcement seemed to be confirmed by the Central Bank of Brazil which sold a considerable part of its reserves in order to support the Real. (*La Nación*, 30 Oct. 1997, 'Wall Street sigue con dudas y preocupa Brasil').

[44] *See* Stephen Valdez; 'An Introduction to Global Financial Markets', Macmillan Business, 1997, 144. The author explains that devaluation is not an easy decision and Governments cannot announce a devaluation in advance because people would immediately sell their currency. Consequently, devaluation's are always denied by Governments although, some times, they finally devalue. Because of this reason the author suggests that announcements denying devaluation's may be disbelieved and this disbelievement can also lead to a massive sale of currency and to force a devaluation.

[45] *La Nación*, 10 Nov. 1997, 'Brasil defiende el real con un duro ajuste fiscal'.

[46] Brazil receives 25 per cent of Argentine exports. (*See* Carlos G Gerscovich op cit. 69).

[47] *Ambito Financiero*, 12 Nov. 1997, 'Lanzan aquí plan con aumento de impuestos'.

[48] *La Nación*, 13 Nov. 1997, 'Pánico en la bolsa de Brasil'; and *Ambito Financiero*, 19 Nov. 1997, 'Facilitarán las ventas de autos para detener una posible recesión'.

[49] *La Nación*, 13 Nov. 1997, 'Se analiza un ajuste para enfrentar la crisis'.

[50] (SCS) SUCESOS, 'Recurrir al FMI es "una cuestión fuera de época",' available at <http://www.mercosur.com/cgi-bin/htmlscript?articulos.hts+view+880742492>, 28 Nov. 1997.

[51] *Ambito Financiero*, 14 Nov. 1997, 'Cardoso duda: quiere ahora reactivación sin recurrir al FMI'.

At the same time, in order to avoid an 'invasion' of Asian manufactures after the East Asian countries' devaluations, Argentina proposed an increase of the common external tariff of Mercosur[52] to protect local industries, albeit Argentine businessmen are fearing an 'invasion' of imported Asian manufactures.[53] In addition, fears of Brazilian 'invasion' have in fact materialised.

IV. THE PROBLEMS AHEAD

The beginning of the East Asian crisis made many expect a serious recessional effect on the Argentine economy activity.[54] While growth decreased during the first months after the crisis and the economy started to accelerate and during the month of March of 1998 (industrial activity experienced a growth of 8 per cent),[55] the contagion from Russia and Brazil have forced Argentina into continued recession.

Further, growth was carefully assessed by the IMF since the explosive expansion of the economy was being followed by an alarming increase in the trade deficit and foreign indebtedness.[56]

High growth rates, an increase in foreign indebtedness and trade deficit might have been a warning of a crisis similar to the East Asian one. Moreover, there seems to be consensus to believe that the East Asian crisis was due to several key factors: (1) strong economic growth but only depending on domestic demand without enough expansion in exports; (2) aggressive expansion of loans provided by banks; (3) excessive increase in borrowing from the international interbank and in hard currency in the public and private sector leading to dangerous exposures.[57]

[52] (SCS) SUCESOS, 'Inminente aplicación del aumento del arancel externo común del Mercosur por parte de Argentina', <http://www.mercosur.com/cgi-bin/htmlsript?articulos.hts+view+880740978>, 28 Nov. 1997.

[53] Martín Boerr, 'Se acerca el aluvión de productos asiáticos', *La Nación*, 6 July 1998.

[54] *See* David Roche, 'Against the tide. Emerging banks: threat of systemic collapse?', *Euromoney Online: Euromoney Magazine*: Jan. 1998; available at <http://www.euromoney.com/contents/publi . . . romoney/em.98.01/em.98.01.20.html>. *See also* of the same author 'Against the tide. No escape for Latin America', *Euromoney Online: Euromoney Magazine*: July 1998; available at <http://www.euromoney.com/contents/publi . . . romoney/em.98/em.98.07/em.98.07/18.html>. The views expressed in these articles seem to be rather pessimistic on the chances of Latin American countries to avoid the effects of the Asian crisis.

[55] *Ambito Financiero*, 21 Apr. 1998, 'Ahora dicen que Argentina creció aún más en marzo: 8 per cent'.

[56] *Clarín*, 18 Mar. 1998, 'El FMI exige al Gobierno otro ajuste económico'. *See also La Nación*, 7 July 1998, Roberto García Lerena, 'Creció la deuda en 1997'.

[57] *See* Philip Suttle; 'Lessons from the crisis in Emerging Asia', *World Financial Markets*, Morgan Guaranty Trust Company, Economic Research, New York, 27 Mar. 1998, 10.

Some of these same factors continue to be observed in the Argentine economy and they represent a serious threat to the convertibility system, which materialised in 2000 and 2001 The IMF recommended an increase in interest rates and capital reserve requirements in order to prevent a potential financial crisis similar to that suffered by East Asian economies.[58]

The increase of interest rates and capital reserves requirements helped to stop these effects, but these measures had a negative and on-going impact on financial activity. In a convertibility system like Argentina's, governments face a choice to stimulate exports and decrease the trade deficit: (1) devaluation;[59] or (2) raise interest rates to hold the convertibility system.[60]

The effects of a devaluation would be disastrous for firms with foreign currency indebtedness at the same time that external confidence would be seriously damaged. It is enough to remember the case of the Mexican peso devaluation in 1994 to understand this last risk.

The choice of increasing interest rates, leads to difficult access to credit by firms, which ultimately lead to a recession in Argentina's case. At the same time, while an interest rate increase may lead bank borrowers to default on their obligations with a consequent deterioration of bank portfolios, this has not occurred. Nonetheless, this risk of deterioration, added to higher capital reserve requirements, may lead some banks to suffer illiquidity problems and the risk of a banking crisis would again appear.

V. CONCLUDING REMARKS

After the ' tequila-crisis', Argentina's system seemed to be strong enough to face a financial crisis and its situation was completely different from other countries involved in the East Asian crisis. Nevertheless, the question continued to arise as Argentina's economy deteriorated and foreign debt increased: Does the Central Bank keep enough reserves to provide full convertibility between Pesos and US dollars and, if required, to assist banks in case of a deposit withdrawals? While some of the measures adopted by the Government in order to reduce public expenditures plus the international help provided by the IMF [61] seemed to be good tools aimed to face

[58] *El Cronista en Internet*, 18 Mar. 1998, 'Frenarían la economía con más encajes', available at <http://www.cronista.com/Dia/Econ15/htm>.

[59] Philip, Suttle, op cit. 11.

[60] Ibid.

[61] The IMF compromised its assistance to the Argentine Government with a US$2.8 billion loan, with conditions related with achievements that the Argentine Government should obtain during the next 3 years. Some of these achievements are: (i) A reduction of fiscal deficit which will be of US$3.5 billion for 1998; (ii) An increase of tax collection to raise up to US$12.75 billion for Apr. 1998 and US$26.7 billion for August 1998; (iii) A reduction of commercial deficit which shall not be over US$5 billion for 1998; (iv) Limits for indebtedness; (v) An increase of banks liquidity requirements; (vi) The Government shall privatise all the enterprises

the new crisis, in 2000–2001, domestic deterioration in the context of international economic and financial instability eventually forced a restructuring of Argentina's foreign debt, albeit not an abandonment of convertibility.

Argentina's economy was the victim of both domestic and international problems and weaknesses: its macroeconomic balance suffers a high current account deficit and very high rates of unemployment.[62] Labour markets and labour law still need major modernisation since a considerable portion of the pre-convertibility system labour legislation is still in force and urgent reforms are being needed.[63] Current labour law does not allow flexibility in job assignments within an enterprise, makes part-time work contracts expensive and imposes additional costs in high redundancies to be paid in case of dismissal, increase costs in some sectorial areas through the existence of 'special statutes' and does not allow the re-negotiation between unions and employers. Also, labour law does not take into account serious differences in infrastructure existing in different regions of Argentina, since most of contracts of employment are negotiated at the central level in Buenos Aires (the most developed and productive region) and they are binding nationwide, with corresponding standards that are too demanding for the needs of employment growth in other less productive regions.[64]

At the same time, the 'shadow' of the 'big neighbour'[65] is still threatening the Argentine convertibility system and the future of Argentine economy will be closely related to the decisions adopted by the Brazilian Government.[66] At the same time, additional problems were produced by serious disputes generated by the presidential campaign of some candidates and the then-President of the country who insisted to be re-elected for the second time lead to an environment of political instability. This political instability (which became economic instability) clearly presaged later problems.

which are still Federal State owned; (vii) Labour law reforms; (ix) Implementation of controls for the judicial power, which is currently in a crisis of confidence; (xi) New structure for controls of public services companies. (*See* Marcelo Bonelli, 'El Gobierno pactó con el FMI un ajuste mayor por el préstamo de 3 años. Síntesis. Los puntos principales', *Clarín*, 4 Dec. 1997).

[62] IMF Staff Country Report No 98/38, op cit. 6. [63] Ibid. 7. [64] Ibid.

[65] The expression 'big neighbour' was used by *La Nación* in its publication dated 3 Nov. 1997. ('Con la vista puesta en el gran vecino') and it tries to describe the concern existing in Argentina about the future of Brazil's economy.

[66] Part of this concern may be easily understood by reading Argentine newspapers during the month of Feb. of 1998 when a devalutaion of the Real was feared (but had not yet taken place) after Brazil modified the margin existing between the Real and the US Dollar. (*See* Eleonora Gosman, 'Brasil amplía la banda cambiaria para el dólar', *Clarín*, 21 Jan. 1998. *See also Ambito Financiero*, 21 Jan. 1998, 'Brasil devaluó ayer 9 per cent'.

Chapter 13

Ten Years of Economic Reforms in Russia: Windows in a Wall

Christine Lang and Shlomo Weber***

The August crisis of 1998 had a devastating effect on financial markets in Russia. Russia announced a default on foreign debt payments for the three months period while the short-term debt was fully and unilaterally restructured towards long-term debt. In one year's time, the market volume of the Russian Trading System (RTS) stock market exchange plunged from US$70 billion to a mere US$5 billion.

The 1998 financial crisis is reminiscent of another crisis in 1989–1990 when Russia was still a part of the Soviet Union. Ten years of reform, first towards a 'socialist market economy' and then to a market economy, have aimed at an irreversible change in Russian economy and policy. In this chapter we try to assess some of the gains and losses of the first decade of transition. We argue that while democracy is still at risk in Russia, a Russian citizen has matured as a voter, a consumer and an investor. However, political and economic progress is still hampered by the poor and criminalised state of the business and political spheres. Russia badly needs a president, parliament, and government having the will and power to face the country's tremendous challenges. However, the maturation of the electorate provides for a better chance to reach a social contract now than ever existed a decade ago. Reforms and transition in Russia remain primarily a political challenge.

* C. Lang acknowledges the support of the Swiss National Research Foundation grant 8210–053488.

** S. Weber wishes to acknowledge the support of the Richard—Johnson Center for Economic Studies and the Dedman School of Law at SMU which enabled him to present a previous version of the paper at the conference 'The Reform of International Financial Architecture' held at the University of London, May 1999.

We wish to thank V. I. Danilov (CEMI, RAS), S. N. Gromov (FX Trader, Futurco Ltd., Moscow), R. Kueng (Rolcom Ltd.,) S. V. Ogluzdin (CBR), A. I. Sotskov (CEMI, RAS), V. Spivak (CEMI, RAS), K. A. Styrin (VESH), T. Troyanov (Secretan-Troyanov, Business Lawyers) for providing us with references and access to numerous sources. They also kindly shared their knowledge of business management, economics, finance, politics, and law in Russia since 1991. We are grateful to Cynthia Alcott for her contribution that went well beyond editing the manuscript. The authors are obviously responsible for the views presented in the chapter.

The Russian government's announcement on 17 August 1998, in which it conceded default on its sovereign debt, managed to surprise the international community. Indeed, indicators of macroeconomic stability had appeared strong in 1997 although somewhat undermined by ineffective policy implemented by the successive Prime Ministers Chernomyrdin and Kirienko and their governments. The Russian collapse could not have occurred at a more inopportune time. Many financial institutions around the world were still struggling with aftershocks from the Asian crisis, debt restructuring, and shifting speculation. Nonetheless, once the card was played, it was a formidable reality to be dealt with. Internally, the situation would be costly both in a literal and in a figurative sense. It would mean lawyers, conferences and evaluations of what assets might be salvaged and by whom. Where would surplus money materialise for the emergency rescue: from a different budget or from a camouflaged crisis account in some other part of the world?

Whether any such 'secret funds' existed or not, whether or not the government was brought to the figurative wall, is really beside the point. What matters is that Russian decision-makers chose the now documented 'mild' devaluation-restructuring of the GKO (Treasury bills) and OFZ (term-bond) markets package, proposing a planned three-month freeze-before-repayment arrangement. These ineffective decisions revealed to the world, in full light, the magnitude of Russia's malady. Reflexively, public and financial realms began trying to save what they could, which only led to a steeper downward spiral for Russia from mid-August until the end of September, followed again by a smaller peak in December 1998. Brazil followed Russia and defaulted only a few months later.

Russian citizens absorbed the news of the crash with disbelief. In a country synonymous with secrecy, they had believed some alternative would be found; some miracle would happen; the government would ultimately be able to avoid default. Prior to the collapse, percentages on savings accounts had been absurdly attractive, and GKO bonds were due to mature within the year. A deep-rooted conviction that special and hidden resources could invariably be relied upon was holy writ. Whether the public attitude was pure folly or credulity is difficult to say, but it speaks to some success on the administration's part in manipulating the aspirations of the ordinary population to acquire a better life.

What went wrong? How bad is it for the future? What are the lessons for the regulation of international economic activity?

First, we will discuss the post-crisis scenario, then proceed to analyse pivotal strategic decisions and events preceding the crash. This we do in an effort to speculate what the reverse direction, or any other strategically different direction, might have better encouraged Russian transformation to a market economy in its first decade of democracy. Having said this, even altering or reversing mistakes of the recent past will not provide a sufficient solution, for much weight rests on subsequent decisions and events. Of notable significance are the June 2000 elections, in which Vladimir Putin was named as President Yeltsin's successor. When considering how much new leadership and/or new policy will indeed affect Russia's second open decade, the timeless adage persists: *change occurs slowly*.

Post-crisis introspection is important notably in providing domestic incentives to improve the society as a whole, except that no Russian citizen can ignore the bleak scenario. The actual recovery of the Russian economy is pitted against a busy political agenda. One year after the crisis the main surprises were: a rather decent behavior of the ruble, a modest recovery of the financial market activity, some unexpected survivors in the banking sector and some signs of growth in industrial production. How, exactly, has this scenario evolved?

I. POST-CRISIS DEMOCRATIC RUSSIA: 1999–2000

The devaluation of the ruble and the exit or sharp cutting-down of Western firms' presence on the Russian domestic final consumption market has changed the structure of market demand which has switched back to local products (when they are available) or to lower-priced imports from Poland, Turkey, or other East European and Baltic States. Some modest import substitution has emerged, protected by the ruble barrier. Some enterprises are coming out on the visible market from the 'shadow market' (many enterprises in Russia prefer to remain obscure in order to avoid attracting too much attention from organised 'Robin Hood' crime). Also emerging are financial market players who have managed to wrest themselves from the GKO/OFZ market squeeze.

Some smaller individual investors have survived because their positions before the crash were insubstantial enough that they could back-peddle and reset their market position the instant indicators spelled certain loss. But many actors lost substantial amounts: *Kommersant Den'gi*[1], 36–7) points out that young institutional investors and portfolio managers held on until the very end, increasing their detrimental positions.

Some reports claim the average morale of the Russian population today is rather positive. This contingent supports that no matter the difficulties, Russians are ready to go back to the market and wager still more hope on the recovery of economic activity, although they adamantly believe *no*

[1] V. Arsen'ev, *Finishnaja Prjamaia (The Finishing Line)*, Kommersant Den'gi, 22 July 1998, 36–7.

credit for any recovery will be attributed to the actions of various governments. Others say a more accurate picture of Russian morale today can best be described by malaise and frustration, despite the fact that most citizens believe they would not turn back the clock even if given the chance.

With the volatility of day-to-day Russian events, certainly impatience has mounted to the point of sociological analysis. In other words, the notion of *tomorrow* is down-weighted in comparison to the notion of *today*. Naturally, instant gratification encourages greed and speculation—traits many older Russian citizens claim is even worse in their society today than during Soviet rule. Great hope exists that such mounting greed will bring about positive internal actions to redress this issue, especially since greed and corruption directly paralyse effective, constructive entrepreneurial activity. (It is prudent early in these discussions to point out that Russian citizens often expect and even anticipate calamity because they associate international embarrassment with subsequent national reform.)

All observers agree today that Russia has not exactly been equal to the task of successfully achieving the establishment of a market economy within its borders during the last decade. They worry about the democratic process. This consensus is quite *new*: prior to the 1998 collapse opinions were more diverse, if not optimistic.

Will history record the first decade of Soviet democracy as a success or failure? Doubtless the debate will be infinite because it is characteristic for opinions about Russia to be rather polar. Respective opinions are as numerous as dots on a graph, and their associated theories as subtle, yet obvious, as the difference between red caviar and Beluga. Today most Russian citizens, even cock-eyed optimists, are frustrated to the bursting point because rarely can one find employment or, if employed, expect to receive payment for months. The average male life expectancy is 52 years! Even military employees sell weapons on the black market to feed their families. For instance, in June 1999 the Russian military agency launched a massive 'employment shrinking' programme. This is both a direct result of the 1998 crisis, the further cutting of government military expenditures in the budget (Primakov's government was able to pass through Duma a drastic reduction of expenditures), and a result of the dismantling of many defence missile sites. The Russian defence sector had been affected minimally during the nine years of reforms, but was one of the biggest victims of the 1998 crisis.

Needless to say, the average Russian citizen feels that his living conditions have generally decreased during the last decade. This is correct in some respects. In practical terms most of the Russian population's living standards have worsened (real incomes fell by 55 per cent in 1992 after price liberalisation, and real wages by 42 per cent by the end of 1992 as compared to the previous year. The average dollar wage in Russia at the end of 1994 was $94 compared to $200 in Poland and $250 in the Czech

Republic. In 1999 the average dollar wage in Russia is believed to be around $60).

The worsening level of disparity creates mixed feelings of lassitude and malcontent, especially with regard to the subject of 'reforms' or 'reformers' and their promises of a better way of life. The mere mention of 'reforms' invites sniggers or outright vocal cynicism—*'here is yet another major farce'* —however this attitude should be considered with caution. Indeed it is fashionable to claim that no real reforms are on the way, that no reforms have been implemented, that any appearance of reform is only lip service—a showcase for the IMF. However, when asked point blank to recall developments of the decade and to assess whether or not they would prefer to go back, we reiterate that most reckon they would not. And this sentiment holds, notwithstanding other mixed feelings toward the new Russian society, including loss of security, shame, swallowed pride, disgust over widespread corruption, and international loss of position. President Yeltsin is both widely criticised and held responsible for an endless cortege of reforms that seems to go nowhere or, rather, that appears to profit some happy few, the weakened central power, the loss of prestige of the nation and its territorial and economic dismantling, the useless deaths in Chechnya, Dagestan, the chronic arrears in wages, pensions, the crisis and the routing of the banking system, and, above all, implementation of a personal agenda rather than action to promote the country's best interest.

In political terms, the media and public opinion agree that the former President is fully out of power, even before stepping down on 31 December 1999, in favour of Putin. And he seems to remain as unpredictable a player as in the past. One wonders however if this enigmatic behaviour of his final months in power was a carefully planned tactic or the result of capricious powerlessness. Even in the difficult situation (including the scandals around his personal and family affairs), Yeltsin maintained an even stricter commitment toward a general line of reforms than professed in the past. This exacerbates the belief that only a very strong presidential power can substantially deter the actions of counter-reform forces. Yeltsin's agenda created a high ministerial and governmental instability, which is not understood by the population, and negatively viewed by the entrepreneurial strata. (There is some movement towards modifying the constitution in order to attenuate disruptive economic consequences of rapid-fire economic changes.)

Recent money laundering scandals must stimulate reassessment, as the reappraisal of economic policies reveals some uncomfortable aspects of 'financial, advising and consulting arrangements made with Russia [in recent years]'.[2] What are the consequences for the international architecture

[2] As indicated in I. Y. Kozes and L. D. Nelson, 'Radical Reform in Yeltsin's Russia', *Political, Economic and Social Dimensions* (1995), p. 59: Private firms would come on the

of such 'outlaws'? On the other hand, is it fair to pawn off the whole 1998 disaster on Russian money laundering and other forms of self-serving forms of corruption? Is it fair to simply label Russia an 'outlaw'? (We shall later discuss the subject of Russian corruption.)

Placed in perspective, the changes in recent Russian culture have been rather rapid-fire, even if considered more gradual than radical. Such environmental changes have aroused grave uncertainty among Russian citizens about the future. Despite the negative forces in power during post-Second World War Soviet rule, the standard Soviet citizen's life was then characterised by a remarkable stability.[3] Prices, labour, and political structures remained practically unchanged. Today's blurred events are thus all the more difficult to accept. The stability of post-Second World War Russia exacerbates the current general perception that the newly formed Russian State cares even less about individuals and older generations than the former Soviet State (if that is possible). Many Russians question whether their restructured government even constitutes a democracy. A businessman from Perm encapsulates the general sentiment: 'Inflation, ruble instability, unpredictable price rises, political musical chairs all lead to the absence of any idea of what tomorrow brings and an inability to plan for the future.'

For example, housing rental agency business in Moscow is often closer to a virtual incarnation of Victor Hugo's 'middle-age miracle courtyard' than anything else. So caution is appropriate when assessing buoyant Russian urban businesses. Small entrepreneurial business *does* exist, even if the Mafia attempts to squelch it. Small business is as much alive today as in the early days of Perestroika, when it started booming, but the problem is getting hold of 'clean' credit sources (the few Russian banks in place still offer prohibitively expensive loans; to accept a 'clean' bank loan is about as precarious as borrowing money from the Mafia itself). Besides the need for 'clean' credit security, protective measures must be implemented to propagate any entrepreneurial activity.

A dirty money-laundering investigation is proceeding full scale, with the IMF and World Bank being the main targets. Sharp critiques about inflation-targeting programs and other monetarist solutions to crisis and structural

scene to offer expertise of various types to facilitate Russian economic reform. These activities would often be funded with US dollars—particularly from the US Agency for International Development (USAID). An interesting fact is provided in J. J. Fialka, 'Helping Ourselves', *Wall St J.*, 24 Feb. 1994, at A1: with so much aid money involved, there was a feeding frenzy in Washington. According to USAID, 1200 consultants applied to get into the programme, a record for the 33-year-old agency.

[3] Between 1960 and 1980 the retail price index (RPI) stayed almost constant, reflecting price controls (*see* M. I. Blejer and C. Cotarelli, *Forced Savings and Repressed Inflation in the Soviet Union: 1986–1990* (IMF Staff Papers, vol. 39, no 2, 1992) 256–86. Statistics indicate that between 1960 and 1985 prices grew by less than 0.25 per cent a year on average (*see* V. Popov, 'Central Bank Independence and Inflation in Russia', Address at the Conference on Central Banks in Eastern Europe and the NIS (1994).

transition programs continued to be voiced. The discourse expressed by Stiglitz on the necessity to go beyond the 'Washington Consensus' is evidence of the intensity of the debate.[4] Maybe Russia is in no worse shape than other CIS (*Commonwealth of Independent States*) countries or even some developing countries, although the ensuing reverse of development and industrialisation, that is in process, is disturbing. The fact remains that the international community cares about the fate of Russia, or perhaps is afraid of Russia (old fears die hard). More emphatically some just wonder why the 'market-economy jelly' did not set, a gripping problem for economists and politicians!

Whatever the new consensus is, it cannot be based in Washington. The Washington Consensus has advocated the use of a small set of instruments (including macroeconomic stability, liberalised trade, and privatisation) to achieve a relatively narrow goal: economic growth. The post-Washington Consensus recognises that a broader set of instruments is necessary and that Russian goals are also much broader. Russia seeks not just increases in measured GDP, but improved health and education. It seeks sustainable development, which includes preserving natural resources and maintaining a healthy environment. It seeks equitable development to ensure that all groups in society, not just those at the top, enjoy the fruits of development. And it seeks democratic development in which citizens participate on numerous levels, in making the decisions that affect their lives.

If policies are to be sustainable, then, developing and transition countries must claim ownership of their respective policies. A second principle of a newly emerging consensus is that a greater degree of humility is called for, an acknowledgement of the fact that no one has all the answers. Continued research and discussion, not just between the World Bank and the International Monetary Fund, but throughout the world, is essential if Russia is to better understand how to achieve its many goals.

As Earle and Estrin point out that long before the Russian Federation defaulted on Western bankers in 1990, 'It [Russia] defaulted on its own citizens, failing to pay wages and entitled social benefits.'[5] Yet an urban fringe of the population has had a taste of 'market economy' and found it savory. Although they sometimes have been carried away when the emerging Russian market looked so promising, and discouraged by the brutal wake-up call of August 1998, their hopes and dreams to grasp a better life have not lessened. The new diversity of brand preference appearing on Russian consumers' markets is appreciated for what it is (even if consumers cannot always afford what is available). Consumers are becoming more aware of

[4] *See* J. Stiglitz, 'More Instruments and Broader Goals: Moving Toward the Post-Washington Consensus', UNU/Wider Lecture (1998).

[5] J. Earl and S. Estrin, *After Voucher Privatization: The Structure of Corporate Ownership in Russian Manufacturing Industry* (CEPR Discussion Paper no 1736, 1998).

their rights, and sophistication for quality and comparison has begun to form. The average Russian may or may not believe there is much hope for a better future, but his/her conviction is still that Russia is wealthy, is a 'land of opportunities'. Cultural, educational, and scientific institutions are highly developed, and yet newspapers report that per capita GNP (around US$1000) is a little below that of Bolivia[6]. The Russian citizen believes Russia is an industrial nation, but reads in the newspaper that its current exports consist of almost entirely raw materials (oil, gas, nickel, etc.).[7] Media reports indicate that perhaps the most important Russian asset is its population, both massive numbers of impervious Russian residents who have remained, as well as the valued brainpower of those who have chosen and managed to leave the country.

History shows that, as Yeltsin came to power, radical economic and societal restructuring initially won out over a gradual approach much praised by G.Yavlinski and his followers. But, as earlier cited, the real chain of events was dangerously gradual. Thus the Russian civil society and economic landscape, at the end of the decade, had indelibly changed. Whether for better or worse, this is subjective. On the economic front, results are somewhat mitigated. On the civil society front, they seem more promising. Citizens might be winning a battle—that of getting hold of their rights. The question now is whether they might actually be able to express this victory.

II. PRE-CRISIS DEMOCRATIC RUSSIA (1990–8)

The path Russia followed throughout the 1990s has indeed moved it hesitantly toward a transition to both market economy and political harmony. But the chosen (gradual as opposed to the preferred radical) route has been costly. Russia has faced, and still faces, deep financial, economic, social and political difficulties. The Russian population has once again experienced a number of hardships: food shortages; hyperinflation (1992–4); a portentous default on western loans (1990); two financial near-crashes (1994–5) culminating with the 1998 sovereign default. This sequence is directly correlated to social and income inequalities gaping wider than ever. Other significant realities include a dizzying rise in unemployment; Mafia activity and political coups (August and December 1991, December 1993); what is perceived by many as 'territorial dismantling'; two wars (Chechnya and Dagestan); numer-

[6] *See* A. Koksharov, O. Leonov and E. Sherbinina, 'Don't Cry Argentina! Manipulation of Domestic Currency does not Guarantee a Way Out of Crisis', *Expert*, 16 Aug. 1999, at 12–14 which cites the Global Competitiveness Report (1999 World Economic Forum).

[7] *See* V. Arsen'ev, 'Structure of the Russian Industry: Ranking of the 150 Most Prominent Russian Firms', *Kommersant Den'gi*, at 33–4. The 1998 crisis strongly affected the developing telecom sector in Russia, as well as electrical giants adversely affected by the increase in import prices and the decline in domestic consumption.

ous border skirmishes (Tadjikistan); and a recent upsurge of blind terrorism directed at the civilian population. These are but some of the flashbulb montages straining Russia's framework, since the physical wall came down.

Indications of macroeconomic stabilisation were promising in 1997, but thwarted in early 1998 by hit-and-miss policies of the Chernomirdin and Kirienko governments. The state budget remained in deficit as a result of poor tax collection efforts, large expenditures and loose regulation over them. Simultaneously the administration continued financing its deficit by borrowing even *more* from internal and external markets. Since Russia's dependence on a consistent flow of foreign capital was heavy, it found itself almost powerless when the events of August 1998 put an abrupt stop to foreign lending while its other sources of foreign revenues were depressed on world markets (oil).

Many analysts also emphasise that the reforms undertaken during Perestroika (1985–1) made the task of 1990s reformers more difficult. Let us recall some vivid aspects of the Perestroika era. A legal framework for modifications of a fully centralised economy was created and, in part, implemented. In 1985–6 campaigns against alcohol and unearned incomes were waged in response to declining productivity of Soviet workers. In March 1986 a partial reform of agricultural structures was implemented, in effect decentralising decisions within state and collective farms (*kol-* and *sovkhozes*). In August 1986 a decentralisation of foreign trade decisions was also implemented. In January 1988 the Law on State Enterprises also decentralised decision processes for state firms (followed by a sharp increase in wages). This first set of legal reforms, then, mainly consisted of decentralising the decision-making process in the productive branches (agriculture, industry, services, handicrafts, and construction), in an effort to revive declining production and productivity. One must admit that the Russian Federation, emerging out of the collapse of the Soviet Union in the beginning of the 1990s, inherited a tough legacy—a large-scaled and ultra-concentrated industrial sector mostly tailored to satisfy defence objectives and the extensive road and railway network (qualification of the labour force was less emphasised). Many productive activities were focused on the large defence and military sector. Most sectors had been set up according to misguided economic objectives rather than those prevailing in market economies; location and technology choices did not satisfy market profitability criteria.[8] Neither was production quality a subject of concern.

[8] R. Ericson (['The Structureal Barrier to Transition Hidden in Input–Output Tables of Centrally Planned Economies', *Econ Sys* (forthcoming).]) notes: A structure of production location, capital, employment, materials and energy, etc., had been created without any regard for economic opportunity costs. This legacy of the Soviet system constitutes a structure of capital and economic activity that is fundamentally non-viable in an environment determined by market valuation, and hence requires massive transformation at its very roots.

J. Urinson, who served as the first deputy of the Russian Minister of Economy in 1994, says: 'We produced absurd men's coats with stupid astrakhan fur collars, which then remained 10 years in storage. Clearly our country does not need that kind of growth'[9]. One of the main issues surrounding August 1998 Russia and its shattered economy is whether the economic policy choices taken at the beginning of the 1990s were sound. The proponents of the implemented reform programme insist that reforms did not go far enough and that most of the industrial sector was irreversibly doomed. The critics emphasise that heavy weight on monetarist issues proved extremely destructive for the existing Russian potential, which they deem disorganised, dismembered, and subject to daylight robbery. Moreover, the latter claim the monetarist path solved none of the structural problems diagnosed at the end of the Brezhnev era. These analysts continue attacking monetarism as one of the main culprits responsible for unexpected features of Russia's actual international trade structure. Nelson and Kuzes[10] write:

> By 1994 Aslund was insisting that the structure of Russia's total exports will change towards larger exports of raw materials. With such statements as part of the public record, it should not be surprising that a widespread conclusion in the Russia of late 1994 was that the radical reform agenda included making the Western world safe from potential competition with Russian products while exploiting the country's natural resources.

But it is all the *more* surprising because the country is resolutely modern in a 'Western' sense. The infrastructure (even if ageing) is remarkable, the quality and education of the labour force in itself distinguishes Russia from developing countries, the capacity to adjust to new, imported technologies is excellent as is research and development of new products.[11] So the words of Nelson and Kuzes ring true for the 1995–9 period as well. One cannot, therefore, help wondering whether the actual policies will lead to a new structure of specialisation and whether the restructuring of industrial potential has started at all.

[9] J. Urinson, 'Kakoi rost nam nuzhen? (What Kind of Growth Do We Need?)' *Expert*, Mar. 1998, at 8.

[10] Op cit. 103.

[11] As Wilson 'Restructuring Large Enterprises in Preparation for Privatization: A Case Study', in *Creating Private Enterprizes & Effective Markets* (1995), 162) in his very interesting account of a rare successful restructuring of large Russian military-civilian enterprise, describes: Enterprise's hospital products, on the other hand, were in a rapidly growing segment of the increasingly important medical equipment industry. This relatively new product group offered good-quality products to both hospitals and patients, with lower costs to all. A few big international companies had come to dominate the world market and many more wanted to enter. The Russian market was quickly becoming important, and Enterprise, among a few local suppliers, became a target for acquisition itself. The transistor radio market was an easy target for cheap Eastern and Chinese consumer products. While some imports did not offer the *same technical quality*, their designs were more attractive, and rapidly gained market shares.

III. PRIVATE PROPERTY IN POST-COMMUNIST RUSSIA

The legalisation of private property and enterprise began with the four following steps: the November 1986 'Law on Individual Labor Activity'; the May 1988 'Law on Cooperatives'; the mid-1990 set of laws for 'joint stock companies and securities and banking activity in the USSR and small enterprises'[12] and the State Property Fund set to handle privatisation.

The May 1988 'Law on Cooperatives' ruling proved to be quite successful in stimulating business ventures. It stipulated that any private activity with at least three owners could qualify as a cooperative and, therefore, make decisions for (act on behalf of) itself (1988–9). Thanks to this law, the first wave of entrepreneurial activity was observed. Fifty to 100 banks were created as cooperatives. In the early 1980s, three 'specialist banks' had been created to channel credits to enterprises in the agricultural, construction, and social investment sectors and their subsidiaries extended all over the country: AgropromBank—APB; Pronstroibank—PSB; ZhilosotsBank—ZHSB. New cooperative banks served other branches. Finally, in 1990, the second wave of a banking establishment had become much linked to the specialised banks of the Perestroika period: over 800 banks emerged—700 of them regional banks of which 600 were ex-filials of specialised banks.[13] Many of these have been leading the banking sector throughout the past decade.

Aslund writes: 'However, these cooperatives became so dynamic that the law was amended several times in a restrictive direction', a fact that critical observers of post-Perestroika reforms stress as contrary evidence of the vivacity of small to medium to fully-new, private entrepreneurial activity at that time. Other analysts argue that existing state-enterprise managerial teams had successfully curbed these reforms.[14]

At the end of the 1980s the Soviet Union was plagued by significant industrial shortages and rising foreign debt (the Soviet State defaulted on its foreign payments at the end of the 1980s).[15] In the beginning of the 1990s,

[12] T. Troyanov (Secretan-Troyanov) describes how after arriving in Moscow to establish his Swiss-Russian law firm, he was offered many symbolic entrées to 'Russian joint-venture stock companies'—proof that a foreign stockholder could be availed of fast and uncomplicated registration.

[13] A. Aslund, *The Brookings Institution, How Russia Became a Market Economy*, 1–10 (1985).

[14] *See* ibid.

[15] *See* P. Aven, Problems in Foreign Trade Regulation in the Russian Economic Reform, Economic Transformation in Russia, 81–3 (Anders Aslund (ed.), 1984. 'During 1984–1991, exports from former USSR territories decreased: sharp decrease in oil extraction, collapse of COMECOM and the shift to mutual hard currency payments, and the overall depressed world conjuncture. 1991 sees a further slide in exports. On the other hand, the consumption of imported goods had increased in the USSR during the 1970s.'

a set of policy choices was rapidly implemented in the form of an installation manifesting the features of a market economy. These policies were mainly the result of economic expertise and brainstorming (J. Sachs, A. Schleifer, A. Aslund, and R. Layers were the main economic advisors at the time). However, financial aid that would have helped stabilise macroeconomic imbalances and allowed room to manoeuver conduct of monetary policy after price liberalisation failed to materialise. Russia, therefore, proceeded alone on the course of its first set of reforms: price and trade liberalisation, distribution of state property through the voucher scheme (privatisation), and a so-called legal apparatus that would specify private property laws. Many of the current problems, namely corruption, have also to do with this failed stretched hand policy from the international community.

IV. CHRONOLOGY OF EVENTS

The early phase of formation of the Russian market (1991–5) will be discussed in two sub-phases: 1991–2 and 1993–5, each phase initiating and/or concluding according to what we concur to be the starting point of a rather acute financial debacle. Price and international trade liberalisation characterise the first sub-phase, with the emergence of a Russian commercial banking system. The second sub-phase is connected with privatisation, the beginning of financial markets, and macroeconomic stabilisation attempts involving financial market structuring. This phase ends in the first market quasi-crash called 'Black Tuesday'.

The second phase (1995–7) characterises the next deeper wave of liberalisation, that of integration to the world financial markets. Russia becomes the booming emerging market of the decade and a recipient for 'hot money'.[16] This part of the story ends in the crash of 17 August 1998.

The third phase (1998–2000), is characterised by a slight distancing from policies adopted before 1998. With the August 1998 crisis, Russia has experienced a period of involuntary protectionism (capital market isolation and outflow of 'hot money'), and a relaxing of strict monetary targets (devaluation and controlled devaluation, i.e. the free-floating ruble is kept under control by open market operations). A restructuring of current short-term

[16] 'Hot money' is defined as 'excessive funds of short-term capital inflow' (*Handbook of Emerging Fixed Income & Currency Markets*, 199. Fabozzi and Alberto Franco (eds) 1999), 199). Liberalisation of capital and trade accounts and relaxation of foreign exchange controls can encourage the flow of hot money into a system. This scenario may be inflationary and cause authorities significant difficulties in achieving monetary targets. Further, short term capital tends to flow out of emerging economies during times of political or economic uncertainty, a process that is destabilising.

(GKO) debt has been forced upon national and international participants. The debt-servicing pressure has relieved due to restructuring, delivery of IMF tranches and boyant oil and gas world prices. There are even some positive signs in the economic landscape. For instance, there is a low-profile revival of financial markets (both stock and to a lesser extent fixed income) while the banking system is rallying. This is accompanied by an unexpected vitality of consumer-oriented industries, which seem to seize the opportunities resulting from ruble devaluation and lowered competition[17] to introduce newly designed Russian products (import substitutes). Tax receipts have increased relatively to 1998; capital flight is slightly more difficult because of foreign exchange controls. And, in fact, the economy *may* be growing modestly, an almost unprecedented occurrence in the last decades.[18]

It seems that the progression towards a Russian market economy has narrowly centered on working out the notion of private property and understanding its complexities. And in this regard, one must conclude that as of 1999 this aspect of the market had been significantly, if not fully, mastered. This progress is quite remarkable in a country where the tradition of private property weakly rooted before communism and was completely destroyed after. Formally, all the elements of the market were in place by 2000. It remains to be seen what the result of Putin's election will be on future developments.

V. CORRUPTION

'Russia's problem is that its reform program has not only been painful but, under Yeltsin, totally corrupt,' writes Thomas L. Friedman[19]. He correctly points out that 'Yeltsin has let business clans rip off Russia's gas, oil and minerals, and this wealth has gone to enriching individuals rather than cushioning the society in transition. That is why reform in Russia today has such a bad name.'

The Washington Post voices a similar view: 'Instead of a free-market model, Russia has become an oligarchy of competing financial, industrial and political clans, interlaced with criminality, all seeking to extract favors from a state that still clings to its overweening power.'[20]

We do not deny that corruption is crucial to understanding the Russian

[17] The significant downsizing of foreign presence in Russia is clearly due to depressed markets and ruble devaluation: Procter and Gamble, KPMG, Siemens, Hilti Distributions Ltd., Merrill Lynch substantially cut the number of their foreign and local employees.

[18] Only in 1997 do Russian statistics show a growth in GDP.

[19] T. L. Friedman, 'Those Funny Russians', *New York Times*, 14 Feb. 1996 at A21.

[20] A. Aslund, *Washington Post* (Moscow) (Feb. 1996).

reality. But the current trend is an almost obsessive focus on corruption, making only more delicate a genuine investigation and assessment of the outcomes (achievements and failures) of a decade of efforts to transform Russia into a market economy. At the expense of being naïve or optimistic, we shall concentrate some of our investigation on more positive aspects. Moreover, castigating corruption does not provide new solutions. Corruption may explain some dimensions of Russian economics and politics. However, the decrease in GDP, the emergence of the banking system, the building of financial markets, constitutional reform, dismissal of certain reformers, Yeltsin's apparent whims, and terrorism are not merely a story about corruption. Even in Russia one might seek deeper explicative schemes. The contemporary status of Russia's economy (and its corruption) is the direct result of political options and policy choices that were implemented when the magnificent '*window of opportunity*'[21] opened at the end of the 1980s. The general goal, upon which all agreed, was to improve the economy and the society, but this preliminary agreement left open numerous options for *methods* of implementation. Was improvement expected to come through radical or gradual change? What were the possible policies: Keynesian, monetarist, gradualist, idiosyncratic, none of these? Within the debate surrounding Russian transition, where did positive economy end and normative or ideological choices start? To say blithely that these are difficult issues is a platitude, yet they form the essence of the current domestic and international debate over Russia, the 1998 crisis and its general economic failure, a debate which remains sharply ideological. One cannot ignore this feature; therefore an objective assessment of the entire decade's achievements is flatly unreasonable.

Recently S. Bodrov, former executive for the Central Bank of Russia, declared that the commercial banks established were then formed by or 'closely connected with GOSBank circles', and that the main reason for their emergence was to enable more highly and less-highly ranked civil servants to conduct recently 'decentralised' foreign trade operations as well as businesses of their own.[22] Many in Moscow claim that this period coincides with the first wave of rapid accumulation of almost overnight fortunes in 1990–1, combining the framework and initial price liberalisation initiated by Y. Gaidar in the mid-1990s.

The initial capital for creating many such businesses was acquired from connections within both the 'Soviet banking sector' and industry connections (abroad, if possible). The principal mechanism was arbitrage.[23]

[21] Reference to the famous title of Allison's and Yavlinski's book, *Window of Opportunity: The Grand Bargain for Democracy in the Soviet Union* (1991: New York Pantheon Books).

[22] S. Bodrov, 'Mamai Has Not Left Yet: Offering an Insider View on the Problems of the Banking System', *Sovetskaya Rossita*, 14 Aug. 1999, at 2.

[23] Aslund, 'Russia's Collapse', *Foreign Aff.* (Sept./Oct. 1999) at 42.

The late Soviet State had implemented hundreds of currency coefficients —individualised exchange rates specific to goods and enterprises, with a central system of hard currency distribution. Further, a double accounting system existed for sovereign currency: there were 'cash rubles' (*nalichnyie*) and 'non-cash' accounting rubles (*beznalichnyie*) with an internal, informal, exchange rate of 2 : 1. Lastly, there was access to subsidised state production whose world price was substantially higher. Aslund offers the following theory:

For instance in early 1990, the Soviet wholesale price of a ton a crude oil was 30 rubles. This also happened to be the free market price of a package of Marlboro cigarettes. The black market rate of *nalichnyie* to *beznalichnyie* was 1 : 3. With the right connections it was possible to buy three tons of crude oil for one package of Marlboro cigarettes (less than $1), when the world market price of one ton of crude oil was in excess of $100.[24]

People allowed to 'exchange' non-cash rubles for cash rubles or who had licenses to get hold of hard currency cash (an extremely difficult coup at the time) or were well connected with a particularly interesting 'extractive' sector of the ministry (i.e. a specialised commercial bank), were privy to such arbitrage opportunities. One must mention however that not only purely speculative schemes were appearing: according to L. D. Weinberg, Russian businessman and CEO of the Siberian Ore and Mining Bank, many computer programming businesses, which were successfully sub-contracting to Western firms, made a nice and quick profit.

An interesting view on the Russian entrapreneurship has been presented by Vladimir Potanin, once considered the archetypal oligarch (robber baron). He clearly positions himself as a clear-sighted entrepreneur operating for the future of Russia's market economy and declares, in an interview entitled 'The Reform of the Oligarchs':

The Russian business elite should be open on two fronts: it should not only work with foreign capital, but also with the budding 'second wave' businesses. We should take them in our club, give them access to investment resources, give them, if necessary and needed, political protection (*prikrytie*). In two to three years from now, medium businesses—'Oneksim', 'Inkombank', 'Al'fa', 'Menatep', 'Most'—won't be needing us. They will have built their own financial networks with foreign banks, which will view them as interesting partners. We need now to succeed in our first step towards [assisting] these companies and as long as we are still useful to them—help them develop their businesses.[25]

As to an infamous recent money laundering scandal, it may never be untangled.

[24] Above n. 23.
[25] T. Lysova, 'The Reform of the Oligarchs', *Expert* (Mar. 1998), at 14–16.

> Elaborate shell games have become a dominant feature of Russia's post-Soviet economy. . . . Government officials are now looking into whether Menatep [Bank] was used to move funds through accounts at Bank of New York linked to Benex Worldwide Ltd., a Russian firm that investigators have already said has ties to a major alleged Russian mobster Y Now federal and international law-enforcement officials say they are looking into whether Mr. Kagalovsky [Menatep's first deputy chairman] helped construct a Byzantine network of offshore corporations that politically connected or mob-linked Russians may have used to siphon hundreds of millions of dollars out of the country. Included in that sum, investigators say, may have been many millions of foreign aid and funds pumped into Russia by Mr. Kagalovsky's old employer, the IMF, to shore up the reeling Russian economy.[26]

Interestingly, Mr Kagalovsky in his recent column for a Russian newspaper notes: 'It's high time now to remember two old truths: The end doesn't justify the means and a state based on corruption and theft is, as a rule, far less effective than an ordinary normal state.' He added, 'The IMF can't pull out of Russia, but should give it as little money as possible'.[27]

VI. CONCLUSION

Many either praise the patience of the Russian people or criticise their apathy. Whatever, this absence of sentiment is only apparent. The Russians' interest in building a new societal model was, and is, strong despite the fact that there seems to be little evidence yet of an emerging comprehensive programme for correcting the flaws of a 'dual' economy. It is hoped that the past decade of hardship has brought about a new political and social maturity. The process is slow, but persistent. Although many parameters have changed, the goals today are the same as they were over a decade ago: to achieve modernisation, conversion and growth. New political teams will be faced with achieving progress toward these ends, but the task may likely prove more difficult following the events of 1998–9 because Russia's credit market is tighter now than ever and the banking system, as a functional structure, is routed.

In the late Soviet system, the average non-dissident citizen was *infantilised.* A subtle system of mixing reward with penalty had been imbedded in the Russian's psyche that provided for a secure but somewhat decisionless, incentive-less social and working environment. How was anyone reasonably to expect, then, that in such a short period of time Russian citizens would seize the full right of their powers and duties?

In large towns modest, but firm, evidence hints of a change in mentalities, manifested by more active behaviour of a small segment of citizens.

[26] M. Allen *et al.* 'Brash Banker's Tangled Deals Become a Focus of Money-Laundering Probes', *Wall St J* (26 Aug. 1999).

[27] *See* ibid.

Consumers in Moscow have begun fighting for their rights by taking legal actions. These actions are cumbersome, but many cases have been successful. This is but another sign that alternatives to corruption exist in Russia as well.[28] It remains costly to the citizen, but feasible. Exposure to new concepts has persuaded the urban population that a well-functioning financial and banking system is quite useful in terms of life-cycle consumption and savings decisions. The notions of private insurance (life, health, etc.), pension funds, and their ability to smooth future consumption have been equally (more broadly) understood and awakened the interest of the Russian urban middle class (not talking about the 'new Russians'). *Expert*[29] discussed the fate of Vladimir Potanin's efforts to set up the first private insurance companies in Russia soon after the crisis: Renaissance-Straxovanie (insurance), Interros-Soglasie and the Interros-Doitsoinstvo (pension fund). The crisis has not been able to bring them down totally: 'here have been heavy losses but they are not dead'. Of course the confidence in such companies is not high. But the interest is still there, nonetheless. As soon as the legal framework will be able to guarantee some transparency in the working of financial and banking companies, there should be no difficulty in regaining the population's interest.

Because of the 1998 crisis, Russian consumers are less vulnerable to fraudulent schemes than in the past. For example the summer 1994 financial scandal of the AOA–MMM Moscow fund is still alive in people's memories. This 'fund' (directed by Sergei Mavrodi, who proved to be a masterful swindler) promised huge returns on what was later revealed to be unsound securities. The operation was successful. Mavrodi allegedly spent several hundred million to advertise his fund and was able to attract a considerable number of investors. The investors' gullibility may be softened by the fact that the AOA–MMM fund was betting on the similarity (a deliberate choice by Mavrodi) of its name with the MMMinvest fund that had set up a rather sound share fund and a GKO fund. Mavrodi was arrested, but then released and wound up being elected to the Duma. Stories of other fraudulent schemes abound: the Russkii Dom Selenga ('Selling') company, neither registered as an investment fund or licensed for securities, attracted 1.5 million depositors.[30]

[28] A similar attitude appeared in the young executive layer in Bogota, Colombia (another country where corruption is rather the rule than the exception): young lawyers, central bank economists, and young Colombian entrepreneurs are realising that the best way to fight corruption is to work within the legal framework. The results are encouraging and it becomes a challenge to win a case legally. Recent informal discussions with young Russian executives confirm that the formulation of the 'stake' is identical—indicating a love of the game, risk-taking, or perhaps a budding consciousness of one's right.

[29] *See* Lysova above n. 25.

[30] *See* M. Kazer, Privatization in the CIS, Challenges for Russian Economic Reforms, 81–97 (A. Smith (ed) 1995).

The reader might find these signs extremely tenuous (or even flimsy). And one cannot deny that anything can happen in Russia tomorrow or the next day or the next! But it seems the country seems more poised today for a new, more realistic and pragmatic social and political contract than it was a decade ago. The decade has in a way been won, although at a terribly high price and certainly not as triumphantly as participators and spectators would have hoped. Former US Treasury Secretary Lawrence Summers notes:

> It is certainly true that in this new global economy, the market punishment for bad policies comes more quickly and takes a harsher form. But the reverse is also true that good policies are rewarded much more quickly. That is the positive lesson for Russia that can be gleaned from experiences in Mexico and elsewhere.[31]

Russia faces tremendous challenges in the years ahead. But it is also an opportunity to address Russia's fundamental economical and political problems. It remains to the Russian voters to make their voices heard more loudly and clearly so that the country and its people do not miss the next *window of opportunity*.

[31] L. Summers, Russia and The United States: The Economic Agenda, Address at the US–Russia Investment Symposium (14 Jan. 1999).

Chapter 14

The Importance of Strengthening Regulatory and Supervisory Power over Financial Institutions: Lessons from the Failure of Guangdong International Trust & Investment Company (GITIC)

*Kai Chen**

In October 1998, Guangdong International Trust and Investment Company (GITIC), one of the largest trust companies of China, was closed by the central bank, the People's Bank of China (PBOC) due to insolvency. The bankruptcy of GITIC attracted much attention, not only because of the huge amount of outstanding debt it owed to more than 130 banks,[1] but also because it is the largest non-bank financial institution which has been officially declared bankrupt since the country's foundation. To many creditors' surprise, the Chinese central government announced that it would not bail-out GITIC, and would from then on, never again act as a guarantor for any commercial sector debt.[2] Moreover, the government declared that the

* The author wishes to express his thanks for the most generous advice of Prof Joseph J Norton of Southern Methodist University's Dedman School of Law and for the revision work contributed by Ms. Fallyme Guerrero from Southern Methodist University's Dedman School of Law.

[1] According to the report issued by PBOC on 10 Oct. GITIC's outstanding debt had reached 36.145 RMB Yuan with more than 130 foreign banks as the creditors, including Citibank and Bank of American. Japanese banks accounted for the top share of 31 per cent of the total US$1.41 billion in GITIC-related loans. *See* Matthew Miller, *GITIC debt decision dismays creditors*, S. CHINA MORNING POST, 11 Jan. 1999, at 1; Rone Tempest, *China Investment Trust's Woes Could Signal a Shakeout*, L. A. TIMES, 7 Mar. 1999 at C1. *See also Fallout from GITIC Closure Spreads to other China Firms*, ASIA PULSE, *available in* 1998 WL 19978964.

[2] China's officials notified all foreign lenders that Beijing would not bail them out on loans to failed Chinese financial institutions. Chinese premier Zhu Rongji also emphasised in his speech that the GITIC incident 'is of great significance because it has sent a message to the world that the Chinese government will not repay the debts for the financial institution or a financial firm if the debts are not guaranteed by governments at various levels in China'. *See*

procedure of the liquidation would not be arranged as most foreign creditors expected. This is to say, repayment to foreign creditors would no longer be prioritised.[3] Since more than half of the International Trust and Investment companies (ITICs) are in bad shape and could collapse at any time[4], disputes about the failure of GITIC and its aftermath have created various concerns regarding the future of the developing Chinese financial industry. Many people worried that the credit crunch created by GITIC would seriously jeopardise China's offshore borrowing. Some people even believed that if the problems were not tackled quickly and forcefully, GITIC's collapse would make China the last—but the largest—victim of the emerging market financial crisis.[5] This chapter discusses the bankruptcy of GITIC by examining the fundamentals of the Chinese financial market, the causes of GITIC's failure, the legal issues concerning the insolvency regime of China's financial entities, and suggests changes to the future development of the Chinese financial infrastructure.

I. INTRODUCTION: BACKGROUND OF GITIC

GITIC was established in 1980, at the outset of Guangdong Province's drive to promote investment, commercial and foreign trade interests overseas.[6] It was one of the 'window' financial entities that were responsible for offshore borrowings for the state.[7] By taking advantage of its unique location (adjacent to Hong Kong), the company and the province grew under the remarkable double-digit economic expansion of the period, which saw Guangdong's gross output increase nearly 400 per cent between 1978 and

Asian Region Starting to Feel Credit Crunch Efforts, ASIA PULSE, 27 Oct. 1998, *available in* 1998 WL 19979131 . *See also Chinese Premier on Bankruptcy of GITIC*, XINHUA ENG. NEWSWIRE, 15 Mar. 1999.

[3] In Feb. 1999, central bank governor Dai Xianglong announced that the foreign banks which had registered their loans with State Administration of Foreign Exchange (SAFE) would not be accorded priority over other creditors. He explained that if all registered foreign debts were paid off first, there would be nothing left for most domestic creditors such as banks and stated-owned enterprises (SOEs). *See* Mary Kwang, *China's Financial System Rocked*, STRAITS TIMES (Sing.), 14 Feb. 1999, at 27.

[4] After GITIC's closure, there were still about 240 ITICs with 3 per cent of the assets of the financial industry and foreign debts of about US$8.1 billion. With the same heavy short-term borrowings, most of these firms are facing financial difficulties. *See* Lana Wang, *Beijing Details Clean-up of Troubled ITICs Sector*, S. CHINA MORNING POST, 17 Apr. 1999, at 1.

[5] Gordon G. Chang, *GITIC Bankruptcy Signals China's New Debt Policy*, NAT'L L.J., 1 Mar. 1999, at B5.

[6] Matthew Miller, *Why Overseas Banks Kept Lending to the Trust Firm When Inconsistencies Surfaced Long Ago: Gitic Trouble Scars Country's Image*, S. CHINA MORNING POST, 26 Oct. 1998, at 5.

[7] Jerome A. Cohen and John E. Lange, *The Chinese Legal System: A Primer for Investors*, 17 NYL SCH. J. INT'L & COMP L. 345 (1997), at 357.

1986.[8] In 1993, when China's borrowings had reached approximately US$6.8 billion in world financial markets, a significant portion had been raised by GITIC and other ITICs, which were always considered 'large government agencies'.[9] Though China's sovereign debt carried an above-investment grade rating (BBB+/A3) at that time, the World Bank pointed out, however, that the firm did not attract enough long-term private debt capital (the average maturity of its 1993 borrowings was only about six years), and warned that lack of long-term financing could be an impediment to development because infrastructure projects require long-term debt in order to match debt service with revenues. In 1994, GITIC's assets were valued at tens of billions of Renmimbi (RMB—the Chinese currency or yuan). It became a financial consortium with an exceptional degree of autonomy. The consortium grew rapidly, with some 300 subsidiaries at home and abroad. In addition to its investments in finance, bonds, trade, hotels, tourism and investment consulting, it had over the years also become involved in several dozen industrial production fields, including transportation, energy, raw materials, communications, chemicals, textiles, electronics, medical equipment and high-tech industries. Unfortunately, GITIC had also put a huge amount of money into high-risk real estate development.[10] In 1995 the government instituted a 'one household, two

[8] In the autumn of 1980, Guangdong Province, at the forefront of China's reform and opening drive, set up the country's first local financing institution—the Guangdong Trust and Investment Corp. By Oct. 1983, with the approval of the central bank, the company became a SOE and obtained a licence from the State Administration Foreign Exchange for foreign exchange operation. In Dec. 1983, the Guangdong Trust and Investment Corp. changed its name to the Guangdong International Trust and Investment Corp (GITIC) and became a local 'window company' that was allowed to borrow and issue bonds overseas. That same month, GITIC signed loan agreements with twelve banks from various countries, including Japan, the United States and France, obtaining a credit line of US$136 million. In Aug. 1986, Document No 83 of the State Council confirmed GITIC as the Guangdong provincial government's 'window company' for issuing bonds, and one of the ten 'window companies' of China. By Sept. of that year, GITIC had earned an AA credit rating from the Japan Public Securities Research Institute. In the same month, GITIC made its first bond issue of 20 billion Japanese yen in 10-year Samurai bonds in Japan. In Aug. 1987, GITIC sold US$50 million in bonds in Hong Kong, and by May 1988, GITIC had issued 20 billion Japanese yen in bonds in London. Continuing at this breathtaking pace, during 1989–91, GITIC obtained US$70 million in loans from several Japanese banks, and by July 1992, GITIC entered the Japanese Samurai bond market once more, issuing 15 billion Japanese yen in bonds. *See The Spectacular Rise and Fall of GITIC*, ZHONGGUO WAIHUI, Apr. 1999, *available at* <http://www.chinaonline.com/industry/financial/newsarchive/secure/1999/may/fn_b2_99051423.asp>.

[9] In 1993 GITIC was granted a credit rating equivalent to China's sovereign credit by Moody's and Standard & Poor. In May of that year, GITIC entered the Eurodollar market, issuing US$150 million bonds. By Nov., it had entered the US market once more by selling US$150 million in Yankee bonds. *See The Spectacular rise and Fall of GITIC*, above n 8 and accompanying text. *See also* WORLD BANK PROJECT FINANCE AND GUARANTEES DEPARTMENT, RESOURCE MOBILIZATION AND CO FINANCING VICE PRESIDENCY, PROJECT FINANCE AND GUARANTEES, 1079 PLI/Corp 63,69 (1998).

[10] Ibid.

systems' paradigm.[11] The ITICs were delinked from the state banks.[12] Transactions had involved on-lending of bank deposits at longer (or unspecified) maturaties, with intermediation by these trust and investment companies and other non-banks, and with all-in lending rates well above approved levels. In this 'one household, two systems' paradigm, the ITICs have been the most widely used institutional format for 'non-bank banking' activities, serving as vehicles of the state banks at each level, local governments, and central government ministries and agencies.[13] By the same year, GITIC had enlarged its assets from its initial start-up capital of 200 million yuan (about HK$ 186.20 million or US$ 23.9 million) an estimated 100 times, while diversifying into a host of seemingly unrelated activities, including securities brokerage, equipment leasing, silk textiles, leather and plastics, investment, international trade, and industrial manufacturing.

To the world, GITIC, like other international trust and invest companies (ITICs), was 'unquestionably' a government company, wholly owned and controlled by the provincial government, and considered one of the most successful Chinese financial companies. Nevertheless, the development of the ITICs was largely overinflated and potentially threatened by world-wide financial market disorder in 1997–8. In October 1998, GITIC found itself buried in debt. When it was judged incapable of keeping up with debt service on domestic and overseas debts, it was closed by order of People's Bank of China (PBOC). GITIC's failure surprised all of its foreign creditors. For many years they had been told that GITIC was making money and that

[11] The 1995 Commercial Banking Law adopted a 'narrow banking' regime, with banks generally barred from trust, securities, and real estate investment business and prohibited from owning or investing in non-bank financial institutions. Consistent with these provisions, efforts have been underway to restructure ownership of the trust and investment companies and the securities firms. This task, difficult under any circumstance, must confront several stubborn realities. First, the shakeout of the past year has devastated many of the ITICs, and most off them are enmeshed in a vast web of financial 'triangular debt' that implicates their sponsor-shareholders, typically the state banks and various government agencies. Also largely as the result of the shakeout, the ITICs and securities firms have been deprived, if perhaps only temporarily, of revenue from various speculative activities, thus raising a question as to whether their legitimate 'core' business is adequate to support their typically overgrown operations. Finally, there is the practical problem of finding new shareholders, compounded in the case of the securities firms by the current limitation to financial institutions. *See* William D. Holmes, *China's Financial Reforms in the Global Market*, 28 LAW & POL'Y INT'L BUS. 715, 747 (1997).

[12] The 1995 action was called 'the fourth consolidation' of Chinese trust business. The Chinese central bank (PBOC) re-registered all the ITICs because of the financial market disorder. ITICs were totally disconnected from the four biggest commercial banks, namely Industrial and Commercial Bank of China, Bank of China, China Construction Bank and Agricultural Bank of China. *See* Borau Lu, *The Bankruptcy of GITIC Derived the Discussion Concerning Windows-company Credit and Sovereignty Credit*, PEL'S DAILY, 11 May 1999, *available at* <http://www.peopledaily.com.cn/zdxw/4/19990511/99051147.html>.

[13] *See* William D Holmes, above n 11, at 748.

Table 1. Loans by Trust and Investment Companies, 1986–96[14]

Year	1986	1987	1988	1989	1990	1991	1992	1993	1994	1995	1996
Loans *RMB billions*	22	44	66	65	89	121	183	205	203	241	234

its assets exceeded its liabilities[15], yet at the creditors meeting, they learned that the firm had been losing money since 1992 and that its debt ratio had reached 168 per cent.[16] While the financial crises in Asia did directly affect GITIC's business, the closure of GITIC is more accurately explained as the fruit of its internal problems rather than the external ones. As many economists have commented, these internal problems had existed not only in GITIC, but also in all of the other ITICs since the year of their foundation.

II. A REFLECTION ON THE ECONOMY: CAUSES OF FAILURE

GITIC's failure finally attracted the Chinese people's attention to ITICs' reckless way of doing business. For many years, ITICs were involved in banking, trust, bonds, and investments, etc.,—almost all kinds of financial activities. But the only available trust laws for these entities were two interim regulations that were promulgated in 1986.[17] Like other state-owned firms, these sectors were run under ambiguous ownership[18] and

[14] *See* Nicholas R Lardy, China's Unfinished Economic Revolution, 78, table 3–1 (1998).

[15] *See* Rone Tempest, above n 1.

[16] According to the report of PBOC, GITIC has 21.471 billion Yuan of assets, and 36.165 Yuan of debt. The debt/asset ratio reached 168 per cent. *See* Wang Hui, *The Warning by the Bankruptcy of GITIC*, <http://www.chinese yahoo.com/headlines/9904306 ... sheng_soc/922510799–19990326fztdtxtl.html>.

[17] They are *Interim Regulation for Financial Trust and Investment Institutions*, and *Interim Regulation for the Capital Management of Financial Trust and Investment Institutions*, promulgated in Apr. and Dec. of 1986.

[18] Before the economic reform, public owned enterprises were the only business forms of Chinese industry. The state, and only the state, had the right to make plans for the state-owned enterprises (SOEs) through different government departments, owned all of the SOEs' assets and had the exclusive right to dispose of these assets and make profits with them. The SOEs

very soft budget constraints.[19] First, many local governments shifted their bad loans to these trust firms to transfer out their liabilities. Secondly, the trust firms always preferred high-profit, but also high-risk business. In many cases, they provided loans to their subsidiaries. Thirdly, a money losing business could be shown 'profitable' on its auditing report.[20]

The direct causes of GITIC's failure can reasonably be summarised as: (1) politically-motivated decision-making; (2) cumulative burden of non-performing investments *vis-à-vis* the excessive short-term debts; (3) ineffective risk control and poor accountability; and (4) lax supervision. Each of these causes will be discussed in turn.

A. Politically Motivated Decision Making

Over the last two decades, China has made significant achievements in the economic transition from a central-planned to a market-oriented economy. Yet inconsistencies in parallel reforms such as fiscal reform, legal reform, and social security reform have kept the procedure of marketisation in its primary stage. Such inconsistencies have also affected the capital market integration for the economic stability. Like all the other ITICs, GITIC was created as a state-owned enterprise (SOE) to attract foreign capital to meet the needs of the state and provincial economy. Despite the central government's endeavour to corporatise and commercialise these financial entities,

themselves could not sell any of their assets, or use their profits to buy new equipment without the permission of the government agencies. With complete public ownership and state planned business activities, the SOEs had to accomplish the mission of production using assets with decreasing values. On one hand, the public ownership had to be shown in all levels of the society; on the other hand, SOEs themselves were actually performing most of the responsibilities that belong to the owner. Although China started its SOE reform in the 1980s—trying to liberalise the SOEs and make them self-decision-making entities—an inconsistent business environment and intervention from various classes of governments locked them in an ambiguous status.

[19] In China's ongoing financial reform and SOE reform, the effort to replace the hard budget constraint has never resulted in any sweeping improvement because of the ambiguous ownership. While most of the SOEs were money losing entities which generated a huge share of the non-performing loans to commercial banks, due to ambiguous ownership, the financial institutions were forced to keep on supporting these SOEs to keep them afloat. Furthermore, the government would normally bail out these financial institutions for the survival of the state financial industry. *See* David Eu, *Financial Reforms and Corporate Governance in China*, 34 COLUM. J. TRANSNAT'L L. 493 (1996); Joseph J Norton, *Receptivity of International and Domestic Capital Markets to SOEs: Criteria and Relevant Issues*, Address at the International Symposium on Capital Market and the Reform of SOEs in China in Haikou (21–23 Apr. 1997).

[20] With the soft budget constraint, trust firms even gave away new loans to many enterprises for repaying the interest they owned to the trust firms; such actions ballooned the unhealthy debts. *See generally*, Liu Borao, *GITIC's Bankruptcy Led to a Dispute Concerning 'Windows Company Credit' and 'Sovereign Credit'*, *available at* <http://www.peopledaily.com.cn/zdxw/4/19990511/99051147.html>.

the legacy of a central planned economy kept these companies' investment decision-making steeped in the political priorities of the province. As some critics described, many of the ITIC projects were developed not because they were financially viable, but because they reflected the demands of government officials who were more concerned about having impressive developments in their territories.[21] When the PBOC investigators entered GITIC to scrutinise its assets available for liquidation, GITIC's high-class officials could not even tell how many subsidiaries and how many accounts the company had.[22]

Such improperly functioning decision-making, arising out of an undeveloped management mechanism, was characterised by the companies' excessive expansion, reckless project setting, and irresponsible budgeting. As a typical case, GITIC's investment in Shantou Photo Materials Industry Corp. suffered a complete loss. In 1986, GITIC came to the rescue of Shantou Photo Materials Industry Corp., and with the blessing of the provincial leadership, GITIC provided US$400 million to buy color sensitising and finishing equipment from Fuji Film of Japan. The rescue was ill-fated. Lacking distribution channels and marketing skills, the Shantou firm foundered and the Fuji equipment lay idle after several tentative colour film manufacturing efforts.[23] Unfortunately, such losses are still happening to the other ITICs.[24]

B. *Non-performing Long-term Projects vs. Short-term Borrowings*

Unlike China's large state-owned domestic banks, investment trusts such as GITIC relied on foreign currency loans for some 70 per cent of their borrowing.[25] And before the onset of the Asian financial crisis, raising foreign funds was relatively easy. Yet as the central government permitted ITICs to tap foreign markets, these firms lost their purpose. They turned to risky investment practices, most notably borrowing short-term money for long-term projects.[26] In addition to the questions concerning massive derivative trading

21 *See* Tara Suilen Duffy, *Bad China Loans Could Mean Trouble*, ASSOCIATED PRESS, 1 Nov. 1998, *available in* 1998 WL 21782061.

22 *See GITIC Declared Bankrupt*, WORLD CHINESE BUSINESS NET, 14 Jan. 1999, available at <http://www.vipc.com/wcbn/topics/0119/topic011499.shtml>.

23 *See* Matthew Miller, above n 6.

24 In the cases concerning GITIC's insolvent sister ITICs such as Dalian International Trust and Investment Company (DITIC), it was found that these firms 'have piled up unmanageable debts due to poor management and the influence of local officials who steered investment decisions along political lines—often into doomed real-estate projects'. *See GITIC Liabilities May Rise as Officials Play Down DITIC Trouble (Incorporates China-Finance-DITIC, China-Finance-GITIC), available in* 1999 WL 2539757.

25 *See* Mark L. Clifford and Joyce Barnathan, *Red Chips No More: Beijing Learned a Costly Lesson from the Collapse of Two Investment Trusts*, BUS. WK, 26 Oct. 1998, at 48.

26 *See* Gorden G. Chang, *GITIC Bankruptcy Signals China's New Debt Policy*, NAT'L L. J., 1 Mar. 1999 at B5.

positions and personal misconduct surrounding its closure, GITIC's losses in core manufacturing and real estate investments were at least as responsible for the firm's demise. As was observed in little more than one year, the Asian financial crisis totally altered the economic landscape. The currencies of the East Asian countries depreciated, their financial and corporate sectors weakened and their dynamic economies plunged into recession.[27] As many economists noted, 'countries which were over-dependent on external borrowing, especially short-term borrowing, are more vulnerable to risk associated with reversal of capital flows'.[28]

Some commentators compared short-term capital flows to a 'double-edged sword'.[29] On one hand, short-term capital inflows fuel the burgeoning economic growth and produced economic welfare for the entire nation. On the other hand, serious reliance on short-term capital flows engenders significant latent hazards for funding current account deficits and ill-considered investment projects. The 'double-edged sword' paradigm clearly manifested itself in Thailand and other East Asian nations in 1997 and 1998. Korea, another victim of the crisis, exemplifies the paradigm. Subsequent massive and abrupt capital outflows in the face of falling international confidence was a direct triggering point of Korea's external liquidity crisis. The fundamental aspect of the crisis lies with excessive exposure to short-term external debt and the immaturity mismatch in the asset-liability portfolios of Korean financial institutions and corporations.[30] Commentators pinpointed that Korea's excessive exposure to short-term debt and its maturity mismatch problem resulted from a disastrous combination of ill-sequenced capital account liberalisation and lax supervision. Such combination was also found in GITIC's case.

The Asian Development Bank has concluded that a pattern of increasing vulnerability to external shocks emerged in all the region's economies prior to the crisis. First, short-term borrowing to finance long-term projects became increasingly important. Secondly, domestic banks lent to domestic firms in local currency, while borrowing short term in foreign currencies without hedging which created a significant currency denomination mismatch. Thirdly, the easy availability of credit fueled investment in increasingly risky assets.[31] To harmonise the nonconformity between long-term projects and

[27] *See* B. G. Lee, *Scenarios for Singapore's Future*, BUS. TIMES (Sing.), 13 Feb. 1999, at 3.

[28] William Crane, *Corporations Swallowing Nations: The OECD and the Multilateral Agreement on Investment*, 9 COLO. J. INT'L ENVTL. L. & POL'Y 429 (1998), at 454.

[29] Tull Traisorat, *The Thai Financial and Economic Crisis of 1997–98: An Opportunity to Re-address the Fundamentals*, this volume. *See also Foreign Debts of BIBF Business*, BANK OF THAILAND NEWS No 24/1997.

[30] *See* Chong Nam, *Corporate Governance in Korea* (presented at OECD 'Conference on Corporate Governance in Asia: A Comparative Perspective' in Seoul, 3–5 Mar. 1999).

[31] *See* ASIAN DEVELOPMENT BANK, ASIAN DEVELOPMENT OUTLOOK 1999: THE FINANCIAL CRISIS IN ASIA at 27.

short-term borrowings, financial firms need adequate capital, a well-developed management scheme, and a sound domestic banking and financial system which satisfies international financial criteria. Unfortunately, none of these needs have been served for GITIC or its sister ITICs.

In their summary of the Asian Crisis, Rajiv Kumar and Bibek Debroy point out that high short-term external debt by the corporate sector and high leveraging was only one example of a broader issue of financial sector fragility. Banking history is replete with examples of credit booms that led to speculative bubbles, aided by unwarranted optimism and mispricing of risk, especially with weak legal and supervisory structures. Between 1990 and 1996, the ratio of bank lending to GDP grew by more than 50 per cent in Thailand and 15 per cent in Hong Kong and China. Meanwhile, private credit to GDP ratio increased as per capita income increased.[32]

China was largely immune from contagion of the Asian financial crises thanks to its large foreign reserves, non-convertible currency, and low amount of short-term foreign borrowings.[33] However, the GITIC incident posted a warning to Chinese officials that the short-term borrowing situation was not as optimistic as they thought. Fearing the disapproval for long-term foreign loans that would have had to be registered with the State Administration of Foreign Exchange (SAFE), the ITICs had nonetheless taken out short-term foreign loans to service long-term investments.[34] Thus, even though the statistics show that short-term debts is less than 10 per cent of the state's total external debt[35], there could be many more short-term loans to those financial firms than the official number.

How could ITICs get loans from both domestic and overseas banks with such an unhealthy portfolio? First, in the absence of transparency and accountability, creditors had no way to fully understand the ITICs' financial status and their business activities. After the default, the creditors realised that much of what GITIC was doing did not show up on its balance sheet.[36]

32 In this summary, the cause of the failure of the affected states' financial industry were addressed as: (i) significant undercapitalisation, widespread insider connected or directed lending, weak credit appraisal and portfolio management capacities; (ii) non-observance of prudential norms and unsatisfactory asset classification; and (iii) inadequate loan loss provisions. *See* Rajiv Kumar and Bibek Debroy, 'The Asian Crisis: An Alternate View' (presented at Economics and Development Resource Center of Asian Development Bank in July 1999).

33 *See* Joseph J. Norton, 'International Financial Crises: Implications for Financial Stability in China' (presented at Conference of Asian Financial Crisis in Beijing in May 1998).

34 *See* Mary Kwang, above n 3 at 27.

35 In an interview with BUSINESS TIMES, China's director of the National Economic Research Institute, Fan Gang, said that China's short-term debt 'is less than 10 per cent of the total debts overseas', and insisted that the ITICs' condition would therefore 'still be manageable'. *See* Vikram Khanna, *ITICs' Problem Manageable, Says China Think-tank Chief*, BUS. TIMES (Sing.), 11 Feb. 1999, at 7.

36 Moody's estimates that off-balance sheet transactions, mainly loan guarantees such as those given by GITIC to the Guangdong–Shenzhen superhighway or the Shajiao C nuclear power plant, total some 15 billion yuan, or five times GITIC's capital. *See* Henny Sender, *Who's next? GITIC-Fueled Tempest Puts China's Investors Notice*, ASIAN WALL ST J, at 1.

Secondly, GITIC was not only founded as a SOE, but was also acting as a 'showcase' firm of the country, listed in Hong Kong's securities market with the 'red chip' stocks, even though the red chips had actually used much of their borrowed money to invest in speculative real-estate deals and the stock market. Foreign banks lent to the red chips 'without examining credit risks carefully'.[37] After GITIC's collapse, many creditors complained that GITIC's management was only encouraged by the support of international bankers who, convinced that the firm was too important within the province and influential offshore to fail, continued to extend lines of credit, even while complaining about the lack of transparency. Before GITIC's bankruptcy, no one would ever believe that in the case of an ITIC's default, the central government would not bail it out. Thirdly, after years of soft-budget constraints in the domestic market and illegitimate guarantees from the local (provincial) government[38], financial practice in China created 'bubble' credit with the foreign lenders.[39] Such 'bubble' credit shifted the foreign bankers from their safe-lending practices.

C. *Ineffective Risk Control and Poor Accountability*

GITIC's collapse revealed that China's attempts to install a safe and sound financial market are still hampered by insufficient risk control and poor accountability. Insufficient risk control arose largely from a lack of understanding of risk management technologies. Poor accountability, on the other hand, aggravated an already bad situation by providing incentives for self-enrichment and hiding serious weaknesses.

1. Lack of Understanding of Risk Management

In addition to being subject to politically motivated decision-making, GITIC's projects did not adhere to standard international practices for risk control. Financial regulation concerns itself with the control of systemic risk, which depends on the probability of the failure of individual institutions.[40] In recent years' international financial practice—and risk management technologies—especially after the regional crises in Europe and Mexico—such as models, stress tests and scenario analyses have been widely adopted by banks and non-bank financial institutions against both

[37] Philip Segal, *GITIC Bond Default Shakes China Creditors: Foreign Banks Move to Reassess Exposure*, Int'l Herald Trib. 28 Oct. 1998, at 13.

[38] In 1986, the central government regulated that no government levels except the central government should give any guarantees to private business firms. But since the ownership of the ITICs is relatively vague, the implementation of this rule has met tremendous difficulties.

[39] Such guarantee was also made by Guangdong provincial government to the overseas creditors until being stopped by the central government in Oct. 1998. GITIC was later closed by PBOC and declared bankrupt.

[40] Eddie George, Financial Regulation—Why, How and Where Now, ch. 5 at 73 (1998).

internal and contagious crises. As first lines of defence against systemic problems, internal risk-management and control mechanisms of private financial institutions are designed to prevent them from taking excessive risks that could threaten their capital positions and viability. In view of the extent of losses suffered by a number of large institutions, the degree of surprise associated with those losses, and the reaction of the equity prices for these institutions, these systems appear not to have worked well for many diverse and systemically important institutions, including internationally active commercial and investment banks, proprietary trading desks, and market makers.[41] When the crisis struck, it was evident that many market participants had not adequately anticipated or understood the risks. Several systemically important institutions appear to have made similar misjudgments in their risk association.[42]

After observing the bankruptcy of GITIC and Hainan Investment Bank[43] (the first commercial bank to become bankrupt in China), some Chinese economist still believe that the failure of these firms are coincidents of management mistakes and the Asian financial crisis. Such belief obviously neglects the inevitable relationship between internal mismanagement and external influences. As demonstrated in the affected countries, such as Indonesia and Korea, without prudential risk management, financial institutions are relevantly fragile to any possible crisis.

Table 2: Financial Institutions Closed Since 1996[44]

Financial Institution	**Closing Dates**
International Trust and Investment Corp. under the Bank of China	October 1996
China Rural Trust and Investment Corp	January 1997
Hainan Development Bank	21 May 1998
China New Technology Venture Capital Corp	22 June 1998
Guangdong International Trust and Investment Corp (GITIC)	6 October 1998

[41] Garry Schinasi, *Systemic Aspects of Recent Turbulence in Mature Markets*, Fin. & Dev., Mar.1999 vol 36 No 1 (an IMF publication), available at <http://www.imf.org/external/pubs/ft/fandd/1999/03/schinasi.htm>. [42] Ibid.

[43] Hainan Investment Bank was founded in 1993, and was closed by PBOC in 1998 after it enmeshed itself in high-risk property business and eventually became insolvent. *See* Chi Fulin, *Rise and Fall of the Hainan Development Bank*, TRANSITION NEWSL. (World Bank, Dev. Econ. Research Group), Oct. 1998, *available at* <http://www.worldbank.org/html/prddr/trans/oct98/cfulin.htm>.

[44] *See GITIC Bankruptcy Follows Four China Financial Institution Closure Since 1996*, CHINA ONLINE, 19 Jan. 1999, *available at* <http://www.chinaonline.com/industry/financial/NewsArchive/Secure/1999/january/fn_b9011326.asp>.

2. Aggravations Resulting from Poor Accountability

It is now notorious that the ITIC's calibre of management was wracked by malpractice, embezzlement and corruption[45] and that poor accountability technically assisted those crimes. Yet the dishonesty and opportunism should come as little surprise where the accounting system is substandard. A Guangzhou-based Eurpoean banker observed: 'It appears [GITIC] was a 'golden valley' for people to enrich themselves. When the accounting system is so chaotic, if you were to embezzle something, nobody would know.'[46] In the meantime, the financial accounting standard was just as questionable as the management accounting standard. In the proceedings of GITIC's liquidation, the accounting and disclosure practices that failed to accurately represent the company's liabilities made international lenders fear that similar problems could lie undetected in other Chinese corporations.[47]

Accounting standards clarify relationships and encourage investment, both domestic and foreign. In addition, internationally accepted accounting standards encourage investment because they provide transparency and comprehensibility[48] to the market as a whole. The Asian crisis illustrates the damaging consequences of deficiencies in the transparency and accountability of the private sector. In many Asian countries, the absence of consolidated financial statements for related companies and, more generally, poor accounting practice hid serious financial weakness—the result of bad lending and investment decisions—in the corporate and banking sectors and contributed to the misallocation of resources that led up the crisis. Accountability also enhances market efficiency. Accountability imposes discipline on management; firms that have to justify their actions publicly are less likely to take action of which their shareholders and creditors might disapprove.[49] Unfortunately, the undeveloped accounting standards have not yet been replaced in most of China's public and private firms.

3. Lax Supervision

GITIC's failure exhibited China's weak internal/external supervision respecting its financial sectors. First, the undeveloped financial legal infrastructure makes it too difficult for the central bank to officiate its supervision of the local financial institutions, especially over the firms located in

[45] *See* Mary Kwang, above n 3.

[46] Matthew Miller, *Questions of Felony Emerge in GITIC Crash*, S. China Morning Post, 23 Apr. 1999 at 3.

[47] *See Highlights of Recent Developments in Financial Markets*, Fin. Mkt. Trends, *available in* 1999 WL 16894419.

[48] *See* Joseph J Norton, above n 33.

[49] *See* Word Bank Group, Report of the Working Group on Transparency and Accountability (Oct. 1998).

the coast cities where the financial markets are more liberalised and more disorganised. Some creditors argued that GITIC was closed because of its, and Guandong Province's, frosty relationships with Beijing and that, if viewed from a commercial perspective only, GITIC could be resuscitated.[50] The fact is, the financial system has not yet been running separately from the intervention of either the central or the local governments. From the local side, the preliminary regulations that represent the primary stages of reform have also created legal uncertainty to the opened regions such as Guangdong. Such legal uncertainty and the legacy of the central-planned economy have deteriorated the environment of law enforcement on a local basis. From the state side, the macro-control of the state economy was found effective in maintaining financial market stability in the face of potential crisis for the moment. But over-reliance on the artificial means itself could also be a threat against the rules of the market economic criteria.

Secondly, ambiguous ownership generated a fatal obstacle to the full commercialisation of all the ITICs. On one hand, the selection of company officials and directors was not based on developed corporate law; rather, it relied—even if indirectly—on nominations of the central/local government which gave little space for the shareholders to enforce supervision of directors' performance of their fiduciary duties. On the other hand, politically-motivated decision-making and non-transparent business management made it too difficult for the lenders of the firms to externally supervise their rights.

III. TROUBLING ASPECTS OF GITIC'S BANKRUPTCY

A. *The Troublesome Chinese Financial Industry*

In recent years, China's economy has suffered from weak domestic demand and mounting deflationary pressure despite repeated efforts by authorities to cut interest rates and boost infrastructure spending.[51] The ongoing state-owned enterprise (SOE) reform has not yet brought the commercial banks out from their unhealthy portfolios[52], and hence, has restrained the

[50] *See* Gorden G. Chang, above n 26.

[51] *See* Anil K. Joseph, *S & P downgrades Chinese Fis*, INDIAN EXPRESS, *available in* 1999 WL 5579740.

[52] For a long time, most of the loans to SOEs performed negatively; the banks, however, were still forced to give policy loans to the SOEs so that the government could maintain social stability. Consequently, when the SOEs had too much debt, commercial banks were forced to deal with high risks and crisis. The periods for monetary circulation were gradually extended. To remedy the shortage of capital, commercial banks were forced to increase their interest rates for deposits in order to attract deposits from residents. Profits of these banks have been, as a result, significantly reduced because of the increase in costs that these higher interest rates represented. Furthermore, increasing deficits made the central bank over-issue currency notes, thus aggravating inflation.

commercialisation of the non-bank financial entities and the state financial system as a whole.

The obstacle of the money-losing SOEs was the legacy of the central planned economy. Although the central government began SOE reform in 1978[53], excessive debt ratios[54], heavy social burdens[55], poor management[56], and poor understanding of a market economy[57] resulted in an unsuccessful reform effort. Money-losing SOEs have become the biggest problem for the Chinese economy. During the 15th Party Congress which was held in September 1997, General Secretary Jiang Zemin emphasised that restructuring the inefficient SOEs would be one of the major tasks for the coming years.[58] As a solution, the state government planned to privatise most of the SOEs, and to reserve and restructure the thousand biggest ones. However, based on the experience of privatising SOEs in different countries, the World Bank pointed out that the proposed solutions could not be enforced without a healthy and sound banking system.

The bad debts of the SOEs are mostly the result of policy loans from commercial banks and other financial institutions.[59] With these non-collectible loans, the commercial banks were forced to deal with high risks and crises. The period of monetary circulation had been gradually

[53] During the last two decades, China has (1) replaced profit retention systems with a taxation system; (2) replaced the pricing system to encourage market transactions; and (3) begun to incorporate SOEs and give more power to their decision-makers.

[54] According to the statistics, the debt ratio in state enterprises was 18.7 per cent in 1980, 58.4 per cent in 1990, 60.5 per cent in 1991, 61.5 per cent in 1992 and 71.7 per cent in 1993. The general checkup on enterprises assets in 1994 shows that the debts ratio had increased to 75.1 per cent. *See* Gao Shang Quan, INSTITUTIONAL INNOVATION OF SOES AND THE DEVELOPMENT OF CAPITAL MARKET (July 1997).

[55] For a long time, SOEs offered cheap apartments and other social benefits, including pensions, free medical care, and financial support for low-income families. Since the number of the employees was growing rapidly and the performance of the SOEs was normally poor, neither the government nor the SOEs could afford these payments.

[56] The directors and managers of the SOEs acted as administrators, who were assigned by the government. The leaders had to follow instructions from the higher class officials of the government, all the while overlooking the bad performance of the enterprises. *See* Joyce Barnathan and Dexter Roberts, *Can Jiang Reform China's State-Owned Industries?*, BUSINESS WEEK (21 Apr. 1997).

[57] Most of the SOEs, especially the large-scale enterprises, were not allowed to change an item of their production. An enterprise which wanted to add or remove a production item normally had to make a long-term report and await approval from the relevant government department. Even when the power of decision-makers in the SOEs had been significantly liberalised in 1990s, without the necessary knowledge of the free market economy, these enterprises still suffered much from non-performing investments.

[58] *See* President Jiang Zemin's Report to the 15th Party Congress (12 Sept. 1997), *available at* <http://www.chinadaily.net/cndy/history/15/fulltext.html>.

[59] Based on the structure of creditors and credit amount, 66 per cent of the total debts of RMB 5812.63 billion were loans from financial institutions. Most of these are long-term loans from state commercial banks, other banks and non-bank financial institutions. Of the total debts of RMB 5812.63 billion in SOEs about 20~25 per cent, RMB 1200–1500 billion, are uncorrectable.

extended. To remedy the inadequate capital, commercial banks were forced to increase their interest rates for deposits in order to attract deposits from residents. Currently, China has the world's highest individual savings rate—40 per cent, and most of that comes from households that place the bulk of their earnings into banks, providing a much-needed cushion for the troubled banking institutions. Yet with profits of these banks significantly reduced due to the increasing costs that higher interest rates represented, Chinese commercial banks came to rely too much on the savings of individuals. By the end of 1994, the amount of the nonperforming loans of the four state-owned commercial banks had reached RMB 570 billion Yuan. This represented more than 20 per cent of the total loan amount, and 90 per cent of the nonperforming loans of the country. The capital adequacy ratio of these banks was far less from the '8 per cent capital adequacy standard' stipulated in the Basel Capital Accord.[60] Furthermore, increasing deficits made the central bank over-issue currency notes, thus aggravating inflation. Considering this situation, the need for well-managed non-bank financial institutions has been more urgent than ever. First, the country needs these non-bank firms to mobilise more funds for the ongoing economic reform and to reduce the pressure to the state banking industry, since the non-bank firms have a more liberal way of business. Secondly, if non-bank firms such as ITICs fail, the negative subsequence will spread the credit crunch to the commercial banks and aggravate their situation, which has already been critical.

B. The Nature of the Failure

Like other Asian countries that suffered in recent financial crises, China, with a high growth rate and a heavy burden on state financial institutions, is under the threat of the 'bubble economy'. Not affected by the other Asian countries in crisis, yet fearing the self-fulfilling crisis, China decided to 'break the bubble' as a temporary remedy, instead of blowing it up like Taiwan did.[61] The final result of the remedy remains unclear.

Money-losing ITICs have created large potential threats to the country's economy. The government worried that if it bailed GITIC out, the state would lack funds to rescue all the other ITICs. Without enough tools to

[60] The nonperforming loans at the end of 1997 made up 25 per cent of the banks' portfolios. The banks officially registered capital-adequacy ratio in 1998 at about 3 per cent to 5 per cent. The government issued 270 billion yuan of treasury bonds, trying to boost the four big state commercial banks. However, with the mono fund-raising measure and the huge NPL burden, the situation of the banking institutions is still critical. *See* Peter Chan and Mark O'Neill, *Asia Woes Spur Beijing to Act*, S CHINA MORNING POST, 14 May 1998 p1; *China's Hidden Timebomb*, EUROMONEY, 10 Mar. 1999 at 42; *In Bank We Trust*, FAR EASTERN ECON. REV., 10 Dec. 1998, at 58–9, *available in* 1998 WL 18230516.

[61] *See* above n 17.

defuse these 'time bombs', the central government attempted to extend the time to the explosion by separating the firms from their 'sovereign credit'. Compared to the capital flows in other Asian countries, most of China's foreign capital consists of direct investments. The government, therefore, believed that it would still be under control if the losing ITICs created a credit crunch in the financial market. Even if the purposes of the above strategies could be considered right, the authorities must realise that the 'side effect' of the closure could be much more destructive than what they assumed and success cannot be a certainty.

C. *GITIC's Closure to the Questionable Financial Market—Relief or Aggravation?*

The knock-on effect of the GITIC collapse has caused widespread market disenchantment. It terrified international bankers who had loaned US$10 billion to similar financial companies.[62] Furthermore, GITIC's default has accelerated the collapse of other ITICs.[63] Not surprisingly, attention has quickly focused on the effect of the GITIC bankruptcy and other ITIC exposures. Most listed banks do not have significant exposure to ITICs. The Hong Kong Monetary Authority (HKMA) estimates that, based on data collected on 30 September 1998, local banks have an exposure of HK$13.6 billion to ITICs, or 0.7 per cent of total assets (the percentage is similar for Authorised Institutions in Hong Kong as a whole). Based on statements made by listed banks' Chief Executives in their final results announcements, these exposures have been carefully examined and provisions made where necessary.[64] In many cases non-payment of interest or principal was due to technical reasons (eg awaiting approval from State Administration of Foreign Exchange to remit funds overseas), rather than a

[62] James Harding, *China's Closure of Guaangdong International Trust and Investment Raises Lager Fears*, FIN. TIMES-ABSTRACTS, 29 Oct. 1998, at 15.

[63] Many of the directors of ITICs complained after GITIC's closure; many foreign lenders urged their ITICs to repay their loans before the due date.

[64] According to the HKMA, the total direct exposure of the Hong Kong banking sector to ITICs (excluding GITIC) and their subsidiaries is around HK$30 billion. This represents a relatively small percentage of the total loans of the banking sector (0.9 per cent). In addition, there are about HK$14 billion of contingent and other contingent liabilities incurred on behalf of the borrowers. It should be noted that there could be double counting in the amount of direct exposure and contingent liabilities where ITICs have issued guarantees to the banks to support the banks' lending to their subsidiaries. But the HKMA does not have information on the amount of such guarantees involved. *See* Release from the Hong Kong Monetary Authority, The Hong Kong Banking Sector's Exposure to ITICs (excluding GIITIC) and their Subsidiaries (19 Oct. 1998) (available at <http://www.info.gov.hk/hkma/new/press/others/981019e.htm>). *See also* JOHN G. FERNALD AND OLIVER D. BABSON, WHY HAS CHINA SURVIVED THE ASIAN CRISIS SO WELL? WHAT RISKS REMAIN? (Board of Governors of the Federal Reserve System, International Finance Discussion Paper No 633, Feb. 1999), *available at* <http://www.federalreserve.gov/pubs/ifdp/1999/633/ifdp633.pdf>.

sudden drop in the borrowers' credit-worthiness. Also, uncertainties existed in respect to how the PRC government planned to tackle the debt ridden SOEs, in particular ITICs and window companies. As a result, many banks may have felt that it would be premature to treat Mainland China loans as non-performing, even if the above factors had affected their performance. A significant amount of work is currently being done to address debt-ridden state owned and 'window' companies.

After GITIC's closure, foreign lenders instinctively turned on the rest ITICs to avoid further losses, hence making the restructuring work of ITICs more difficult.

1. GZITIC

As GITIC was in the middle of its bankruptcy, another major financial firm in Guangdong teetered on the edge of failure. Guangzhou International Trust & Investment Corp (GZITIC), the investment arm of the Guangzhou Municipality, is struggling to stay alive.[65] About two weeks before GITIC's closure, GZITIC missed a payment on a US$30 million syndicated loan led by SocGan Asia. GZITIC blamed the State Administration of Foreign Exchange (SAFE) for failing to make a timely conversion of yuan into dollars so that payment could be made. Under GZITIC's own accounting the firm is solvent. However, the Guangzhou city government, which already had helped GZITIC raise three billion yuan to repay debt, has asked for a more complete audit.[66]

2. DITIC

As another fund-raising arm of the city, Dalian International Trust and Investment Corporation (DITIC) defaulted on millions of its loans to several banks overseas.[67] Although the official of the firm insisted that the firm was not in a net debt position, foreign creditors were haunted by GITIC's concealed proceeding of resolutions.[68]

[65] *See* Gordon G. Chang, *Watch Out for the Next 'GITIC'*, ASIAN WALL ST J, 10 Mar. 1999, at 8.

[66] *See KMPG Named GZITIC Liquidator*, ASIAN WALL ST J, 15 Feb. 1999, at 5.

[67] *See DITIC Fails to Meet Foreign Debt Repayment*, S. CHINA MORNING POST, 11 Nov. 1998, at 12; Henny Sender, *A Chinese Trust Defaults, Worrying Foreign Lenders*, WALL ST. J. EUR., 18 Jan. 1999, at 8; *Dalian ITIC Tries to Scotch Report of Default*, AGENCE FR.-PRESSE (18 Jan. 1999), *available in* 1999 WL 2530499.

[68] In Aug. 1999, DITIC announced plans to merge with four other trust and investment companies in the city. Talk of a joint-venture bank apparently has been shelved, as one DITIC official was quoted by state media saying: 'Different firms could take different approaches.' *See* Kate Pound Dawson, *GDE, Creditors Trade Proposals For a Revamp*, ASIAN WALL ST J. 16 June 1999, *available in* 1999 WL-WSJA 20525914.

3. SITICO

Shanghai International Trust & Investment Corporation's (SITICO) prospects have been in doubt since the closure in October of GITIC. In December SITICO acknowledged that its projected net profits for 1998 had plummeted 50 per cent to 350 million yuan. Unlike GITIC, SITICO was considered one of China's best-regulated ITICs and therefore more gun-shy about investing in the country. Its failure would be a devastating blow to Shanghai's prestige: SITICO is at the centre of Beijing's efforts to promote the city as an Asian financial hub.[69] If SITICO falls, the related social and economic problems will be unacceptable.

4. GDE, ANOTHER INSOLVENT 'WINDOW COMPANY'

Guangdong Enterprise (GDE) is not a financial institution, but its similar background and same huge amount of bad debts, make solution of its case very significant to China's future creditability. GDE is a massive holding conglomerate owned by the provincial government of Guangdong, controlling companies in fields such as real estate, food imports, and hotel operations. In December 1998, GDE defaulted on its loans and later revealed to its creditors that its debts outstripped its assets by US$1.6 billion. The outstanding debts of the firm were as critical as GITIC's; it currently owes its creditors US$2.94 billion.

The Guangdong government opted to restructure the company's debts rather than let it go bankrupt. An initial proposal called for the injection of Guangdong Investment (GDI) debts into GDE, allowing creditors to trade their bad loans for the new, higher-grade GDI debts as well as the preferred stocks of the restructured GDE. GDI is a subsidiary of GDE. The original restructuring proposal did not satisfy creditors. According to the *Far Eastern Economic Review*, the government also proposed to bolster GDE with the Dongshen Water Supply Project, a US$2 billion facility that supplies 75 per cent of Hong Kong's water.[70]

With the help of foreign banking expertise, a restructuring project was developed by the central government. The government explained that GDE is one of the biggest issuers of Red-chip Stock in Hong Kong's stock market.[71] Thus, GDE's future is tightly connected with Hong Kong's future

[69] *See* Trish Saywell, *Shanghai: High Water Mark*, FAR EASTERN ECON. REV., 11 Feb. 1999, at 56.

[70] *See* ibid. *See also GDE Creditors Want US$1.8 Bln More In Assets From Guangdong*, CHINA ONLINE, 1 July 1999, *available at* <http://www.chinaonline.com/industry/financial/NewsArchive/ Secure/1999/july/fn_c9070130.asp>.

[71] In the meeting with consular officials from sixteen countries, Guangdong's ViceGovernor Wang Qishan explained the different treatment between GITIC and GDE: First, GITIC was a financial institution, had more complicated background and more chaotic management;

prosperity. However, over-reliance on these administrative interventions has created more uncertainty to foreign investors, which might aggravate the existing credit crunch. Therefore, one important mission of the financial law reform is to create a financial legal environment and safeguard creditors' rights.

Despite the Chinese's government's endeavour to replace 'sovereign credit' with 'enterprise credit'[72], GITIC's closure might have set a negative example for all the other ITICs. Many of these firms' decision-makers have started to think about bankruptcy to escape their debt liability. Since China has not had a well-developed bankruptcy code, it could be another troublesome issue for the creditors to deal with the 'bad-faith bankruptcies' of these firms.[73]

It seems that what China really needs is a dose of market liberalism, not more financial morphine in the form of government bailout of insolvent state-owned financial institutions. Ultimately, the only way for China to build a strong financial architecture is to allow private ownership of capital and protect that right with the rule of law.[74]

Aside from the question of government bailouts, there remains the problem of deteriorated credibility. The GITIC incident has seriously eroded China's credibility by creating a negative precedent for the world, when central bankers at PBOC are increasingly concerned with leakage of precious foreign exchange. A country's creditworthiness is based on objective factors, such as external debt, inflation, growth and maintenance of international creditor support.[75] GITIC's closure is fueling fears over China's creditworthiness, largely because nobody knows the size of the

Second, GDE was registered in Hong Kong, and has five listed subsidiaries in Hong Kong's stock market. *See Wang Qishan Met with with Consular Officials from 16 Countries for Discussing the Bankruptcy of GITIC*, PEOPLE'S DAILY, <http://web4.peopledaily.com.cn/item/gxsj/A102.html>. The treatment of GDE will directly affect Hong Kong's market stablisation. Ibid.

72 In the meeting with consular officials from 16 countries, Guangdong's Vice-Governor Wang Qishan said that GITIC's bankruptcy 'marks the end of the mission of "showcase" companies and enterprises will have to establish'. Wang explained that At the early stage of China's reforms and opening up, they were given unprecedented authority, but the credibility of 'showcase' companies was not credibility in the real sense, nor was it the credibility of the local government, let alone state sovereignty. *See GITIC Bankruptcy Ends 'Showcase'*, XINHUA ENGLISH NEWSWIRE, 11 Feb. 1999, *available at* 1999 WL 7917910; *Wang Qishan Met with with Consular Officials from 16 Countries for Discussing the Bankruptcy of GITIC*, above n 71.

73 Some ITIC creditors complained that their ITIC borrowers were seeking bankruptcy models like GITIC to avoid their debt obligations.

74 James A. Dorn, *China's Financial Future*, CHINA ONLINE, *available at* <http://www.chinaonline.com/commentary_analysis/economics/currentnews/secure/c9091360e.asp>.

75 *See Emerging Market, China, Where have all the Reserves Gone?*, EUROMONEY, 10 Feb. 1999, at 16.

liabilities the ITICs and their Hong Kong subsidiaries really face.[76] Foreign banks claimed that they would cut back on lending in China following the collapse of GITIC. These banks are now re-assessing their risks, and in light of the GITIC bankruptcy will approach lending to other Chinese institutions backed by provincial governments more cautiously.[77] Several international service companies such as Moody's[78] and Standard & Poor's[79], have downgraded several other ITICs, reflecting worsening market sentiment toward the ITICs and other financial firms, and have thus created more funding difficulties for these firms.

Even if the government believes that the ITICs' condition is not yet a threat to China's macroeconomic stability, such a threat could arise from GITIC's non-transparent bankruptcy proceedings and closed-door government dealings.[80] First, the expiration of the 'windows function' could have been achieved in a way that was more rational and more legitimate. The denial of the central bank of the assurance from Guangdong provincial government has made the nature of assured loans relatively unclear. Secondly, since 80 per cent of GITIC's assets were in the Hong Kong subsidiary, confusion related to the one-country-two-system doctrine has turned into criticism of China's yet-undeveloped legal system. Thirdly, the less-than-transparent liquidation procedure with the largely untested bankruptcy law showed that in a shifting legal environment, decisions of law were often a matter of administrative fiat rather than black-and-white rules.[81]

D. *Summary*

From the day China started its de facto privatisation[82], the problems of systemic inconsistency between the former central-planning and market-

[76] *See* Henny Sender, *Who's Next? GITIC-Fueled Tempest Puts China's Investors on Notice*, ASIAN WALL ST J. 26 Oct. 1998, at 1.

[77] *See Less Capital for Chinese Companies,* WORLD TRADE 2426, 1 Mar. 1999.

[78] *See Moody's Downgrades Five Chinese ITICs Following GITIC Closure*, AGENCE FR.-PRESSE, 28 Oct. 1998, *available in* 1998 WL 16627581.

[79] Standard & Poor's Corp. downgraded the credit of CITIC. The Company insists that China's creditworthiness remains constrained by 'potentially high costs of industrial and banking sector reform and an inflexible political system'. *See* Thomas Crampton, *China's CITIC Lowered to 'Junk' Rating by S & P*, INT'L HERALD TRIB., 2 Mar. 1999, at 11. *See also* Standard & Poor's, China's BBB+ Foreign Currency Rating Affirmed, *available at* <http://www.standardpoors.com/ratings>.

[80] *See China's GITIC Liquidators Enlist Foreign Accounting, Legal Help*, AGENCE FR.-PRESSE, 8 Feb. 1999, available at 1999 WL 2542194.

[81] *See* Henny Sender, *GITIC Failure May Pinch Goldman Sachs*, ASIAN WALL ST J, 15 Feb. 1999, at 1.

[82] To implement privatisation in China and eventually deliver the SOEs from their crises, Chinese economists explained to the government that privatisation is a term used to describe the means by which a centrally planned economy can effectively make the transition to market

oriented economy have been inevitable. Foreign bankers now must learn that China has entered a key stage in its economic marketisation. The country is slowly, but significantly, losing its central-planning characteristics. Hence loans will no longer be made on personal or political relations; a more prudential pre-loan exam will be required for all borrowers.[83] The bright side of the story, however, is that GITIC's failure has accelerated China's movement toward a better bankruptcy law. Many issues arising from the bankruptcy of large state owned firms could only be noticed when actually confronted. In a recent effort, the Guangdong Higher People's Court froze US$97 million in assets of GITIC's debtors.[84] The best lessons are always given by the failures.

China has allowed GITIC to fail, and forced it to undergo bankruptcy proceedings. This might set an important precedent for managing other failures. In the short term however, it has had an immediate astringent effect on foreign lenders and investors, who have business with other Chinese companies. They are reassessing the new ground rules and revising the risk premiums for doing business in China.[85]

The multi-faceted nature of financial reform involving deregulation, liberalisation, globalisation, and privatisation complicates the measurement of its effects. In addition, reforms undertaken in each country have reflected the perceived problems of the pre-reform environment. Prior to reform, most countries experienced a period of mild or severe financial repression: intervention by governments in allocating and pricing credit, controlling

economy. They gave privatisation another interpretation—'*Min Ying Hua*', which means to make SOEs into privately managed businesses instead of private-owned businesses. These new concepts have somehow loosed the bonds of public ownership for the SOEs' reform. *See* Lan Cao, *The Cat That Catches Mice: China's Challenge To The Dominant Privatization Model*, 21 BROOK J. INT'L L. 97 (May 1996).

83 The banks cannot escape some responsibility for the debacle. 'They relied too much on the personal connections of their borrowers', says Merrill Lynch vice president, Jeffrey Lin. Adds Stephen Ching, head of syndication at Credit Lyonnaise in Hong Kong: 'Bankers were knocking on the doors of mainland companies on a daily basis to lend them money.' Local officials issued loan guarantees, but Beijing has said it will not honour these pledges unless the loans were registered with the national government. Most GITIC and GDE loans are backed by local-government guarantees, but are not registered in Beijing. *The Business of Bailouts: Lessons from Ailing Guangdong Enterprises*, ASIA WEEK, 11 June 1999, *available in* 1999 WL 7759204.

84 The court sent its GITIC panel to Maoming City and Dianbai County to freeze the assets of Zhongrun Group Company and four subsidiaries, Guangdong New Era Building Materials Industrial Co., Guangdong Pacific Ceramic Industrial Co. Ltd., Guangdong Chuangxin Machine-Building Co. Ltd., and Maoming Acrylic Fibers Chemical Industrial Co. *See Chinese Court Freezes US$97 Million in Assets of GITIC's Debtors*, CHINA ONLINE, 13 May 1999, *available at* <http://www.chinaonline.com/industry/financial/NewsArchive/Secure/1999/may/fn_c9051211.asp>.

85 *See* Fred Hu, *Probing for Weakness in China's Banking System*, ASIAN WALL ST J, 25 Feb. 1999, at 14.

what banks and other intermediaries could do, using intermediaries as tax collection devices, and often limiting competition, in particular from foreign institutions. These interventions varied by country, and in some countries included government ownership of financial sectors as a very direct way of influencing how they did business.[86]

In the wake of the ITICs' rescue, the government has to realise that artificial intervention can never be considered as a panacea, but only as one of the interim means before full market liberalisation. First, the government should be fully aware of the potential fiscal costs associated with genuine banking restructuring. The scale of the banking problem is huge relative to the size of the economy.[87] Secondly, bank restructuring should go hand in hand with SOE restructuring. The root cause of China's banking troubles lies with the country's grossly inefficient state industry.[88] Thirdly, re-capitalization and nonperforming loans (NPL) resolution, while absolutely essential, can only address the 'stock'[89] problem in China's banking system. It is also crucial that China pay close attention to the 'flow' problem—the quality of new loans, risk management, and operational efficiency of the banks and the non-bank financial institutions.[90]

IV. THE LAW-BASED APPROACH

A. *The Requirement of a More Mature Bankruptcy Law*

As a benchmark for China's continuing effort to transition from central-planned economy to the market economy, one factor determining whether a market economy exists is the presence of a bankruptcy code. Without a well-developed bankruptcy code, the insolvency regime that safeguards market competition would be without its fundament. Some—primarily, the United States, Great Britain, France, and Germany—believe the main goal of bankruptcy proceedings is to reallocate resources in a way that is most beneficial to the economy. By giving the debtor the opportunity for a new start, new business opportunities are created.[91] Banks and other financial intermediaries hold a special place in the economy, since they borrow from a broad base of depositors and make loans to a wide variety of economic

[86] *See* ORIANA BANDIERA, ET AL., DOES FINANCIAL REFORM RAISE OR REDUCE SAVING? (World Bank Policy Research Working Paper No 2062, Sept. 1999), *available at* <http://www.worldbank.org/research/projects/savings/pdffiles/sav9-12.pdf>.

[87] Ibid.

[88] Ibid.

[89] Which refers to the 'debt—equity swap', one of the major solutions to NPL problems.

[90] ORIANA BANDIERA, above n 86.

[91] Helmut Gerlach, *Bankruptcy in the Czech Republic, Hungary, and Poland and Section 304 of the United States Bankruptcy Code, Proceedings Ancillary to Foreign Bankruptcy Proceedings*, 22 MD J. INT'L L. & TRADE 81 (1998).

agents. Moreover, banks are highly exposed to each other through the inter-bank market. The main reason financial institutions in crisis need to be treated differently than enterprises is the potential systemic effect that the insolvency of a financial institution may have on the rest of the financial sector and the spill-over effect it can have on the rest of the economy.[92] In any particular circumstance, the bankruptcy of one financial institution could lead to the bankruptcy of another and potentially, to a meltdown of the whole system.

Though the insolvency of financial institutions poses a special problem for regulators, it is not clear that this requires a separate insolvency law. In the US, there is a separate law as well as a separate set of institutions to deal with financial institution insolvency; in Germany, France, and the UK, insolvency of financial institutions is governed by the same law that addresses general insolvency. For China, it may be preferable to add specific provisions relating to financial institutions to the existing bankruptcy law, rather than creating new and separate legislation. In either case, the key difference in handling bankruptcy in the financial sector is the important role that the regulator (supervisor) is required to play.[93]

China's brief bankruptcy law leaves many essential points uncovered. Perhaps as important, China's other bankruptcy rules conflict with that law in important respects. For example, the bankruptcy law assigns the highest priority to secured interests. Yet a 1997 regulation issued by China's State Council deprives creditors of their security interest in order to provide for the resettlement expenses of workers.[94]

But the problem in China is more political than economic. Chinese legislators realised that if they let all the insolvent state firms go bankrupt, major state banks would go bankrupt soon after. Thus, the government, wanting to encourage faith in the system and avoid social unrest, has a strong motivation to avoid liquidation. Their usual method of dealing with insolvent companies is to fold them into healthy companies. This has become more than a necessity. However, one result of the increase of a market economy

92 *See* OECD, Insolvency Proceedings for Financial Institutions in the Russian Federation (reporting on the OECD Corporate Affairs Division's Jan. 1997 informal experts meeting of the same title), available at <http://www.oecd.org//daf/corporate-affairs/insolvency/in-russia/insolvency1.pdf>.

93 Ibid.

94 China follows the general rule that bankruptcies are addressed by informal methods. Bankruptcy Law was last revised for state companies in 1986 and is currently under review. The procedure for non-state enterprises went into effect in 1994. Although modern laws exist, they are rarely used. Of the 20,000,000 businesses in China, probably fewer than 2,000 cases of bankruptcy have been resolved by the courts in the past nine years. *See Restructuring in Asia—A Brief survey of Asian Bankruptcy Law*, Emerging Market Vol. III, No 1 (Emerging Markets Strategies Company, Providence, R.I.), 25 Jan. 1999, available at <http://www.xensei.com/users/gamblet/RestructuringIII.htm>. *See also* Gorden G. Chang, above n 26.

has been the dispersion of economic power away from the central planning authorities. With the economic power has gone the political power. As a result, application of the bankruptcy laws can vary with the locality. With the variance in local conditions and the need to support the political system underlying the economic system, the Chinese process of reallocation resources will face more challenges in the foreseeable future.

The writer suggests that since the insolvency regime is the soul for vitalising the necessary competition, a more sophisticated bankruptcy code, with provisions mediating the market economic criteria and transition economy problems is needed to replace the current immature bankruptcy law. The new bankruptcy code should also have clauses concerning the restructure of SOEs and the detailed stipulation for the disposition of the internationalised financial firms such as ITICs.

B. The Need for an Anti-Corruption Code

While corruption may not be a direct cause of the financial institutions' failure, it is a vehicle for their fatal problems. It aggravates both systemic problems and policy improprieties. In GITIC's case, corruption was intertwined with all the embezzlement, mismanagement, and other wrongdoing.[95] Corruption makes it more difficult for governments to form and carry out coherent policies; to respond to citizens' needs, be they tangible or symbolic; and to use scarce resources in effective ways. Corruption poses fundamental questions about the relationships and boundaries between public and private interests. It directs our attention to the ways officials and institutions conduct public business, and to the age-old issue of 'who gets what'. But it also poses political questions about the ways private interests can be advocated and defended while protecting the rights of others, and about the legitimacy, creditability, and responsiveness of government itself.[96] Measuring corruption can help to establish priorities for reform by identifying activities and agencies where corruption is concentrated. It educates the public about the economic and social costs of corruption.[97]

At present, China still does not have an overarching anti-corruption law. Instead, it has a variety of regulations aimed at combating corruption. Included among them are the Interim Provision on Administrative

[95] In the Securities News, Executive Vice-Governor Wang Qishan declared that senior executives of GITIC were under judicial investigation for possible corruption and could be facing charges. *See* Cary Huang, *GITIC Executive in Graft Problems*, H K STANDARD, 9 Mar. 1999, *available at* 1999 WL 5641100.

[96] *See* Michael Johnston, *The Political Costs of Corruption* (presented at 'Primera Conferencia Latinoamericana de Lucha Contra La Corrupcion Administrativa', Colgate University, 17 Nov.1993).

[97] *See* Daniel Kaufmann, *New Frontiers in Diagnosing and Combating Corruption*, OECD PUBLIC MANAGEMENT FORUM, Vol IV, No 6 (1998).

Sanctions for Corruption and Bribery by the State Administrative Sanctions for Corruption and Bribery, and the Provisions Prohibiting State Administrative Offices and Personnel form Giving and Accepting Gifts. The Criminal Law was augmented with Supplementary Provisions Relating to the Punishment of Corruption and Bribery.[98] Despite intentions, China has found many of these regulations difficult to enforce. First, without a total separation between local government agencies and the business firms, the intervention form the local officials will continue to exist with the possibility of corruption. Secondly, the terms and conditions of existing rules are extremely ambiguous. A well-developed anti-corruption code will not only restrain corruption, but also help to turn market interests into anti-corruption forces. In recent years, the OECD's Anti-corruption Unit has upgraded anti-corruption law to an international basis by reviewing many countries' experiences, especially from the developing countries.[99] Many of its achievements should be adopted as the principles for the enactment of the law.

V. STRENGTHENING THE REFORM BY FOLLOWING INTERNATIONAL STANDARDS

Yet, the law-based approach to the economic regulation of the financial sector is not simply about laws and legal process: law is merely one of many societal means to achieve and legitimise appropriate policy objectives.[100] A law-based approach must also be an interdisciplinary approach: one where law is the thread that weaves together economic, political and social objectives with a transparent and fair implementation process and where the lawyers should work closely with the economists, policymakers, operational people and the accountants.[101]

In market economies financial institutions are not simply passive, responding to underlying changes in the real economy. Efficient financial systems contribute positively to economic growth. They do this through several means. Most obvious is their role in allocating funds to projects with the highest rate of return, thus increasing the marginal productivity of capital. What is less frequently noticed, however, is that more developed

[98] Criminal penalties for corruption include imprisonment and, where large sums are involved, death. Officials who participate in corrupt behavior can receive six different administrative punishments: a warning, minor demerit, major demerit, demotion, removal from position, and dismissal from the civil service. *See China's 1997 Investment Climate: Reforms Constrained by Concerns about Inflation and Stability*, 19 No 6E ASIAN EXECUTIVE REP, 20–1 (1997).

[99] *See* OECD, Combating Bribery and Corruption in International Business Transactions, *available at* <http://www.oecd.org/daf/noncorruption/20novle.htm>.

[100] *See* Joseph J. Norton, above n 33.

[101] Ibid.

financial systems, characterised by lower taxation and regulatory burdens, can allocate resources at lower costs.[102]

A. *The Importance of Following International Standards*

After GITIC's bankruptcy, the importance for financial sectors to follow international standards has been emphasised more than ever. The norms and best practices developed by the Basel Committee, IOSCO, the G10, and whatever other grouping gets to work to build a consensus on international standards are not 'international law'. The Report of the Working Party on *Financial Stability in Emerging Market Economies* is very clear on this point.[103] The Report describes the consultative process by which, in the financial area, norms of best practice are developed and then adds:

> A formal endorsement may give the recommendations greater weight. However, they have no legal force until national authorities adopt them. They derive their authority from the expertise of those that have formulated them and their wide acceptance from the consultative manner in which they are prepared. They come to be applied because they reduce risk, improve market functioning and foster a level playing field. If the conventions or norms are not observed, market participants exact a risk premium.

B. *Promoting Transparency and Accountability to Improve China's Credibility*

Transparency refers to a process ensuring that market participants have sufficient information to identify risks and to distinguish one firm's, or one country's, circumstance from another's. Moreover, transparency stabilises markets during periods of uncertainty and also contributes to the effectiveness of announced policies.[104] Accountability refers to the need to justify, and accept, responsibility for decisions taken. Accountability imposes discipline on decision-makers, thereby helping to improve the quality of decisions taken. Transparency helps to promote accountability by obliging decision-makers to make their decisions and the reasoning behind them known.[105] To reach this aim, a strong rule of law must be accompanied with the accordant legal environment with the contribution of the political reform.

[102] *See* NICHOLAS R. LARDY, above n 14, at 129.
[103] *See* BANK FOR INTERNATIONAL SETTLEMENTS, FINANCIAL STABILITY IN EMERGING MARKET ECONOMIES: A STRATEGY FOR FORMULATION, ADOPTION, AND IMPLEMENTATION OF SOUND PRINCIPLES AND PRACTICES TO STRENGTHEN FINANCIAL SYSTEMS (Apr. 1997), *available at* <http://www.bis.org/publ/gten02.pdf>.
[104] *See* WORD BANK GROUP, above n 49.
[105] Ibid.

C. *Prudential Regulation*

The case for prudential regulation and supervision is that consumers are not in a position to judge the safety and soundness of financial institutions. Prudential regulation is necessary because of imperfect consumer information and agency problems associated with the nature of a firm's business.[106] Prudential and systemic regulation are needed to protect not only consumers, but also those who finance the safety net or compensation scheme, especially when the premiums levied on the members of such schemes cannot be closely correlated to their relative risk.[107]

In the ITICs' case, prudential regulation requires a well-developed trust law. A new trust law would legalise and systemise the trust and investment business activity, encourage the private sector to participate in to the business, and eventually vitalise the dismal financial market. The trust law would also legally clarify all the rights and obligations of the trust business relationship to both domestic and overseas lenders. Lastly, the new trust law would be an important link to the expected financial legal infrastructure, and would harmonise the relationships among trust firms, banks and stock market. It is unclear whether China's new trust law will in fact achieve these objectives.

Prudential regulation should also guide financial institutions in the management of problem loans and improvement of credit origination and monitoring standards. Controls must exist to alert management when problem loans appear. A typical indication would be a missed payment on the due date. This trigger has come in some cases, too late to protect the bank from loss. Improvements could be made by changing the culture and procedures of the banks so that account officers are encouraged to come forward when they notice an adverse change in their customers circumstances or the industry in which they operate. Also, clear guidelines must exist to work out problem loans—particularly, in situations where liquidation or repossession of collateral may not be the most appropriate action.

Improved credit origination and monitoring standards can also be achieved with regulatory measures. First, better analysis of borrowers' credit-worthiness based on higher quality and more up-to-date financial and non-financial information. Secondly, lenders could conduct a closer examination of collateral and carry out more regular valuations. Thirdly, due care could be taken when granting foreign currency loans to ensure that natural or financial hedges exist to protect the borrowers from adverse movements in foreign exchange rates.[108]

106 Alain Jeunemaltre, FINANCIAL MARKETS REGULATION, Intro 7 (1997). 107 Ibid.

108 Announcements by Hong Kong listed banks showed declines in total asets and rising NPLs and provision. *See* KPMG, Listed Banks' 1998 Final results—asset quality, 22 BANKING NEWS 1, 22 Mar. 1999, available in Virtual Library: Newsletters at <http://www.kpmg.com.hk/>.

D. *Enforcing the VaR Based Risk Management*

The main regulatory problems in developing countries are still mostly the traditional ones, involving undue credit risk, lack of appropriate diversification, connected lending, politically directed lending, etc. The standard approach to such credit risks, developed over recent decades, involves the inspection of banks' loan books and the requirement of adequate capital as a protection against non-performing and impaired loans. This remains an appropriate approach, although it is often difficult to enforce in circumstances of weak external auditing and volatile macroeconomic conditions.[109] Internal risk management models and downside-risk measures such as Value-at-Risk (VaR) play an important role in contemporary banking practice. VaR measures the maximum loss born by a bank or other financial institution over a certain time period and given a certain level of confidence. Following the Basel guidelines for bank supervision, many supervisory institutions require banks to use such models and to report VaR measures on a regular basis.[110]

Yet VaR based risk management does not perform in a vacuum. Lessons and experiences from decades of financial practice, indicating that the VaR based risk measure must be supplemented by 'rigorous and comprehensive' stress testing programs, come as no surprise to risk professionals. VaR models are designed to estimate potential losses on given portfolios through fluctuations in interest rates, exchanges rates, equity and commodity prices. The value of any instrument in a portfolio will be influenced by one or more of these risk factors.[111] China's financial regulators must be proactive in installing the proper risk management regime before the financial system becomes more liberalised in the near future.

E. *Seizing the Advantages of Reunification with Hong Kong*

Hong Kong banks have experienced an unprecedented decline in profits as a result of the worsening economic conditions. While non-performing loans across the banking sector have increased substantially to levels that were inconceivable in previous years, even at these levels, the Hong Kong banking sector is showing significantly better performance than its counterparts in the region. Loan losses have eaten into operating profits, which were already under pressure from reductions in interest margins.[112]

109 *See* Eddie George, above n 40.

110 André Lucas, Testing Backtesting: an Evaluation of the Basle Guidelines for Backtesting Internal Risk Management Models of Bank (1999), ***available at*** <http://www.econ.vu.nl/medewerkers/alucas/default.htm> (author's webpage, Vrije Universiteit, Dept. of Finance & Financial Sector Management).

111 Ibid.

112 *See* Joseph J. Norton, above n 31.

Since China has entered into the key stage of its economic reform to full marketisation, Hong Kong will not only offer all of the former advantages, but will also help it accelerate the internationalisation of China's financial infrastructure, especially by giving ideas for rebuilding China's financial supervisory mechanism. The supervisory approach of Hong Kong Monetary Authority (HKMA) is based on a policy of 'continuous supervision', through on-site examinations, off-site review, prudential meetings, cooperation with external auditors and sharing information with other supervisors. It aims at detecting any problems at an early stage. The 'CAMEL' rating system (Capital, Asset quality, Management, Earnings, and Liquidity) is adopted to help identify those institutions whose weaknesses in financial condition, compliance with laws and regulations, and overall operating soundness requires special supervisory attention.[113] The strategic innovation will hopefully systematise and commercialise China's financial framework in banking, securities, insurance and other areas.[114]

VI. CONCLUDING REMARKS

On a worldwide basis, the economic reforms taking place in centrally planned economies have brought risks and challenges that require a constant effort to monitor experience and find new strategies. Meeting these challenges necessitates the development of new policy instruments, or modification of the existing ones, to make them suitable to the changing environments that arise as a direct consequence of the reforms.[115] China's economic reform, judged from the perspective of the financial system, is only half completed. China has abandoned the heavy reliance on budgetary financing of investment that was characteristic of the pre-reform era. Investment, particularly in the state sector, is now financed primarily through banks. But these institutions are state-owned and embedded in a financial system that impedes the efficient allocation of capital. The new system, moreover, has the additional shortcoming that it involves the build-up of enormous liabilities to households, the source of the savings that the banks channel to state-owned firms.[116] China's financial system threatens

113 Hong Kong Monetary Authority (HKMA), Banking Policy & Supervision: Supervisory Approach, *available at* <http://www.info.gov.hk/hkma/eng/bank/index.htm>.

114 Kai Chen, *Recent Developments in the People's Republic of China: The Process of Financial Reform in 1997*, YEARBOOK OF INTERNATIONAL FINANCIAL AND ECONOMIC LAW 1997.

115 VITO TANZI, TRANSITION TO MARKET, Ch 13 at 267(1993).

116 If China fails to complete the transformation of its financial institutions, the consequences are predictable. The intermediation of funds between savers and investors by banks would likely continue to be marked by the inefficiencies already evident. As the contributions to economic growth of various once-for-all factors wind down, one would be reinforced by the increasing physical constraints to growth that are evident—environmental deterioration, the

future growth and stability. Non-performing loans are mushrooming and may now be as much as 40 per cent of all loans; the four large state commercial banks are close to or at the stage of insolvency; interest rates are still determined by government fiat rather than market forces; and corruption fills the air. China's financial architecture desperately needs upgrading. At the heart of that process must be a move toward establishing a real private, competitive capital market—one in which profit-seeking entrepreneurs are the driving force, not government bureaucrats.[117]

China needs financial liberalisation now more than ever. But before it fully reaches the aim, a mature financial legal infrastructure including a better bankruptcy law must be preinstalled. To reap the long-term benefits of financial reform, China must endure the short-term pain of a severe credit crunch—just as it needs to support industry to curb labor unrest.[118] In a 1999 effort, the central bank (PBOC) approved a plan to merge twelve trust and investment corporations into two in Southwest China, starting a nationwide restructuring of the troubled sectors.[119]

While observing the results of the reform, investors are expecting a more sophisticated financial legal framework, which will create a safer and more attractive market. As a developing country, China will need more direct and indirect foreign investments to boost the state economy and strengthen the ongoing financial reform. Public sector infrastructure projects will be in ever-greater demand. Customary over-reliance on the domestic savings must be balanced by stabilised long-term foreign investment. To reach this aim and eliminate the credit crunch caused by GITIC and other ITICs, while cautiously moving forward to the market liberalisation, China will have to create a stable set of rights and responsibilities for the foreign investors.[120] Moreover, efforts to coordinate aspects of financial and regulatory policies can be advantageous to both sides to ameliorate the possible crises in the future,[121] and prevent repeats of failure that happened to GITIC and other ITICs.

challenge of sustaining an adequate rate of growth agricultural output, and growing an adequate rate of growth of agricultural output, and growing infrastructure shortages. *See* NICHOLAS R. LARDY, above n 14 at 17.

[117] *See* James A Dorn, above n 74.

[118] *See* Terry McCarthy and Jaime A. Florcruz, *China Hypocritical? No, Just a Bit Itic-al*, TIME MAG. Int'l Ed., 1 Feb. 1999, at 14.

[119] *See China Merges 12 Trust Firms, kicking off Industry Overhaul*, CHINA BUS. INFO. NETWORK, 30 July 1999, *available in* 1999 WL 17730269.

[120] National policies and regulatory institutions help foster a climate conductive to foreign direct investment by multinational corporations. Taking steps to clearly define the right and obligations of multinational investors will be a wise start. *See generally*, WORLD BANK, WORLD DEVELOPMENT REPORT 1999/2000: ENTERING THE 21st CENTURY, ch. 3 (2000) *available at* <http://www.worldbank.org/wdr/2000>.

[121] Ibid.

Chapter 15

Lessons of the Financial Crisis in Ecuador 1999

María Laura Patiño[1]

I. INTRODUCTION

This chapter is divided into three main sections: the first will deal with general background that surrounded the financial crisis in Ecuador 1999. The second section concentrates on specific characteristics that weaken state capability to deal with a financial crisis. The third concentrates on specific legal and institutional arrangements that underpinned the financial regulatory and supervisory bodies and the governmental intervention.[2] The crisis background provides good context to discuss ongoing concerns relevant to good governance in a developing country, in order to provide efficient regulation and supervision in a financial system

A. *Political Background*

The recent history of Ecuador is characterised by political, economic, and social distress. It comprises several presidential replacements in a few years (four, since February 1997), significant economic mismanagement, El Niño damage to key export sectors and a banking system collapse in 1999. Ecuador until 1999 had not faced a generalised banking crisis since the early 20th century. The most significant recent case of bank failure was overcome by the seizure of Banco Continental ('Continental') by the Central Bank of Ecuador ('CBE') in 1996, albeit through a controversial subordinated loan. In order to improve limited existent mechanisms to manage a systemic crisis, a controversial law enacted by the Congress in December 1998 created the Deposits Guarantee Agency ('DGA') and established an unlimited deposits' state-guarantee. Although Mahuad, President during 1999, also expressed interest in an IMF agreement, this was not

[1] Although the author acts as an official of Central Bank of Ecuador in Quito, Ecuador, the opinions expressed in it are strictly personal.

[2] The legal framework analysed for this purpose was that applicable in Ecuador as of 1 July 2000.

achieved on time. The major obstacles were political objections to reform and mismanagement of the emerging banking crisis.

Mahuad's government was short-lived. After an obscure intervention in Banco del Progreso ('Progreso') in March 1999, a one-year freeze on most bank deposits to try to save the banks and stem massive national currency depreciation, general discontent and dissatisfaction grew. This boosted macroeconomic instability and threatened to trigger hyperinflation in a country victim to inertial inflation reaching the highest levels in Latin America. Since 1998, fourteen banks accounting for about 65 per cent of the system's assets,[3] had to be seized by the State. This was done via the controversial DGA. Then, in September 1999, Ecuador became the first country to default on the Brady deal that restructured recently around US$6 billion of public commercial debt.

As an extreme and desperate measure to control inflation and regain exchange stability, in January 2000, Mahuad announced a Dollarisation program ('Dollarisation'), that is introducing the US dollar as legal tender for the country. This was the underpinning of an economic programme targeted to stabilise the out-of-control exchange rate and obtain the support of the IMF that the country needed desperately.

Before this was implemented, a military coup took place on 21 January 2000, forcing the presidential succession of Vice-President Noboa. Noboa immediately announced the continuation of the Dollarisation programme. On 31 March 2000 the Congress approved what is known as the *Trolebus* Law, introducing the Dollarisation scheme among other important economic reforms.[4]

The effects of this economic and political crisis have been catastrophic. After already poor results during most of the last two decades,[5] real GDP growth for 1999 was negative 7.3 per cent. In June 2000 inflation reached a record of 100.3 per cent.[6] Private sector credit in 1999 was reduced by 25 per cent in 1999, with a further 5 per cent decrease expected in 2000.[7] Non-performing loans averaged about 42 per cent of the total loan portfolio and external credit lines have dropped by more than a half to US$0.8 billion. Estimated fiscal costs of the banking crisis appear to be about US$2.7 billion, 24 per cent of GDP in 2000.[8]

[3] '*The Ecuadorian Recovery Program*', *IMF Representative Statement*, New York, 16 May 2000.

[4] Ecuador, 'Ley No 4 para la Tranformacion Economica del Ecuador', RO. Sup 34, 13 Mar. 2000.

[5] From 1990–1998, GDP growth has been 0.7 per cent. *See* PNUD (1999), 'Informe sobre Desarrollo Humano Ecuador'.

[6] Data published in newspapers on 1 July 2000.

[7] Goldman Sachs, *Latin America Economic Analyst*, 17 Mar. 2000.

[8] Above n 3.

B. Ecuador and Development Models I and II

This work will distinguish two trends of economic development. The first, called Development Model I, refers to what since the late 1940s, the Economic Commission for Latin America and the Caribbean have called the 'developmental model'. The second, Development Model II, is related to the 'Washington Consensus' recommendations from the late 1980s.[9] The last two decades have seen the spread and generalisation of Model II for emerging economies focused originally and principally on economic policies. It is implemented in these emerging economies with aid and funding subject to the 'conditionality' of structural adjustment programmes first applied after the 1980s debt crisis.

Development models I and II are characterised theoretically by opposite principles. In the first, the major elements are a state-planned and public-ordered economy that relies on extended public enterprises, pervasive economic regulation and closed economies with import substitution and industrial protection measures. Development model II, in contrast, relies on a market-driven and private-ordered economy. It requires privatisation of public enterprises and the actual deregulation and liberalisation of the economy.[10]

Development model II relies on market instruments. The market participants need transparent and explicit rules of the game, expressed in different kinds of legal norms and also through customary practices and proper information disclosure. An efficient dispute resolution system is also necessary, not only, but principally, through the judiciary. This creates the stability this system needs and generates fair and certain precedents. It is precisely this 'rule of the law' that permits generalised confidence in such a market system.

Many emerging economies are attempting to move from Model I to Model II. This move, however, affects the role of the law in the relationships between individuals and, especially, between individuals and the State. Legislation in Model I was used to weaken the institutions of private property and to endow the state with increased power. Relevant public law (public enterprise laws, foreign investment and currency control regulation, nationalisation decrees, price and financial regulation) was usually extensive, overlapping, and often contradictory and, thus, did not promote a transparent legal system. On the other hand, in Development Model II the focus is on the private and on the proper framework for market-driven policies.

[9] Terms are borrowed from J. Salacuse, 'From Developing Countries to Emerging Markets: a changing Role for Law in the Third World', 33 *Int'l Law* 875 (1999).

[10] Ibid and K. Davis, and M. J. Trebilcock (1999), 'What Role do Legal Institutions play in Development?', draft, IMF Institute Second Generation Conference, Washington, 8–9 Nov. 1999.

Primary is a well-defined and inalienable private property rights system and a formal system of contract law. Corporate law and tax regimes are means to attract capital investments. Finally, this Model requires insolvency regimes and bankruptcy rules as part of the framework.[11]

Ecuador has, since the early 1980s, been trying actively to adopt Development Model II. It has struggled to implement the stabilisation and structural adjustment programmes, however, according to its own timetable and specific economical, social and political characteristics.

C. *Deregulation in the Financial System in Ecuador*

The transition from Model I to Model II involves the 'deregulation' of the different economic sectors. Deregulation is the mechanism used by the state to 'retreat' from former practices of intervention in the private relationships and from over-regulating transactions that should be controlled by 'market forces' under Development Model II principles. Deregulation of the economy does not mean the absence of law, however. Rather, a legal framework for transparent and efficient market transactions is important. This is particularly true for emerging economies where underdeveloped markets are generalised, monopolies and oligopolies concentrate resources and information, and inequalities of wealth distribution do not allow extensive participation from new 'actors'.

The IMF and other multilateral organisations have used conditions precedent to the disbursement of funds to encourage emerging economies to adopt such deregulation programmes. Ecuador is no exception. Many of the major elements considered part of the deregulation process in the financial system have been required of Ecuador, including expanded and deepened financial intermediation activities and the development of capital markets. This was to be accomplished by: (a) fostering a more efficient and competitive financial system; (b) establishing adequate prudential oversight of financial institutions; (c) encouraging the emergence of new mechanisms to attract medium- and long-term savings, as well as developing the infrastructure and financial instruments needed to channel these savings toward private sector investment; and (d) expanding access to financial services, especially for small-scale savers and borrowers. These reform principles were introduced with the enactment of the new Monetary Law in May 1992,[12] the Banking Law in June 1994[13] and the country's first Securities

[11] Davis and Trebilcock (1999).

[12] Ecuador, 'Ley de Regimen Monetario y Banco del Estado', May 1992. For purposes of this work, together with subsequent ammendment it will be referred simply as 'Monetary-Law'.

[13] Ecuador, 'Ley General de Instituciones del Sistema Financiero', June 1994 and further amendments, referred to as 'Banking-Law'.

Law in 1993.[14] The bank supervisor and regulator, Superintendent of Banks ('SB'), lost many of its discretionary powers.[15] There were no major changes in the insurance and pension-funds fields.

Monetary and banking reforms reduced direct government control over basic banking practices, such as the setting of interest rates and the allocation of credit. The Central Bank of Ecuador ('CBE') discontinued direct allocation of credit. This task was mainly assumed by the financial system. Regarding allocation of credit, former Governor De la Torre, noted: 'The central bank *is not qualified . . . to assess the viability, efficiency and yield of thousands of investment projects. This task should be assumed by the financial system, including the banks and the capital markets . . .*'[16] Since January 1993 the Monetary Board fully liberalised interest rates.[17] Permitted 'operations' and transactions of banks were widened.[18] Also, early in the 1990s, the CBE introduced market instruments as its main tool to control liquidity and stability of prices. This kept the banking system as the major and main participant for monetary purposes, thus avoiding retail operations. These developments show that Ecuador has gone far down the banking deregulation trail in a short period of time.

The securities market reform was especially important. For the first time Ecuadorian law addressed relevantly its shallow market.[19] Regulatory responsibility was allocated to a separate entity, the Superintendent of Companies/National Securities Council.

The reader should not take the foregoing to suggest that this trail was a smooth one. This first stage of the 'deregulation' was very aggressive, resulting in many arguments and concerns about the impact of deregulation.[20] The state intervention in the financial system under Model I had been responsible for low volumes of saving and capital accumulation, and for stimulating inefficient and unprofitable allocation of investments. This had a corresponding effect on the possibilities for expanding productive capacity. [21] Indeed, because many find government intervention a major

14 Ecuador, 'Ley de Mercado de Valores', July 1993, and its ammendments referred as 'Securities-Law'.

15 About intervention disappearance, see Section 3.

16 *See* A De la Torre, (1999), 'El Banco Central y el Credito al sector productivo: analisis de una propuesta peligrosa e incongruente', Revista Cash Continental, Sept.

17 Reinserted in Mar. 2000.

18 See eg Ecuador, Banking Law, Art 51.

19 For an updated and complete analysis of Securities Markets in Ecuador *see* S. Pazmino, (2000), 'El Rol del Mercado de Valores en el Ahorro Interno', Apuntes de Economia No 10, Banco Central del Ecuador.

20 However at the same time of introduction of the deregulation process in the structural adjustment programs, there was already broad discussion about grounds and possible effects of the deregulation process. *See* for instance A. Hamilton, 'The Financial Revolution' (Viking, 1986) ch. 9–10.

21 R. Zahler, (1991) 'Financial Strategies in Latin America: The Southern Cone Experience' in P. Meller (ed), *The Latin American Development Debate: Neostructuralism, Neomonetarism, and Adjustment Processes* (Westview Press, Boulder), 102.

reason why the banking sectors of many developing and transition countries are so uncompetitive[22] there was emphasis on financial 'deregulation' as a means to correct deviations in the financial markets and to increase the competition of the banking system. These were the elements on which the initial legal reform efforts concentrated.

Notwithstanding the general reform process, the recurrence of banking crises in emerging economies during the last decade is not uncommon and has been analysed by scholars all over around the world, including those in Venezuela and especially the South Asian countries.[23] How effectively banks perform their specific functions depends, in turn, on competition in the banking system and the general state of the macroeconomy. Referring specifically to Ecuador there were also macroeconomic conditions that have to be taken into account in relation to the crisis. But this cannot disguise that the 'structural weakness of Ecuador's banking sector was exposed by the sharp deterioration of economic conditions in 1998 . . .'[24] As noticed by many analysts, a big reason for Ecuador's current mess is also its weak banks.[25]

It is interesting to note that there are some common conclusions and recommendations that are of particular interest when studying the banking crisis in Ecuador, particularly those related to the weak regulatory and supervisory institutions existent in the affected countries and problems in allocation of credit. Moreover, it was also noted that at the time of the reform all 'countries tried to improve prudential regulation and supervision, but progress in these areas was in all cases slower than expected and weaker than needed to ensure the safety and soundness of the financial system.'[26] There have been also incompatibilities of the model in a context of improper institutional framework and weaknesses in the political and economic structure of many emerging economies. As Lal and Mynt stated: 'The economic forces in the form of the world market demand, capital accumulation, population growth, and technological changes would oper-

[22] M. Knight, (1999) 'Developing and Transition Countries Confront Financial Globalization', in IMF Finance and Development, June 1999.

[23] *See* R. Krivoy, 'The Venezuelan Banking Crisis 1994–1995' in *Bank Failures and Bank Insolvency Law in Economies in Transition* (London, Kluwer, 1999); R. Cranston, 'Credity Security and Debt Recovery: Law's Role in Reform in Asia and the Pacific' in *Emerging Financial Markets and Secured Transactions* (London, Kluwer, 1998); T. Lane *et al* (1999), 'IMF-Supported Programs in Indonesia, Korea, and Thailand: A Preliminary Assessment', IMF Occasional Paper 178; and M. Bennett, (1999), 'Banking deregulation in Indonesia: An updated perspective in light of the Asian Financial Crisis' in UPJIEL, No 1. *See also* ECN 1997 'Banking in Emerging Markets Survey', 12 Apr. 1997.

[24] J. P. Morgan, Market Brief, 28 July 1999 'Ecuador, IMF facility alone may no avoid insolvency in the medium term'.

[25] ECN 99 20 Mar. 'Down but not out: Latin America's ills require several cures. For some countries, one may be to adopt the dollar' (761).

[26] V. Galbis, (1995) 'Financial Sector Reforms in Eight Countries: Issues and Results', IMF, WP/95/141-EA report that includes specifically Ecuador.

ate on our underdeveloped economy through the filter of its initial institutional conditions.'[27]

Some of these generalised concerns regarding the financial crisis have been faced by the official sector at the same time of discussion of the new financial architecture. It is in this context where it appears what has been called the necessity of a Second Generation Reform[28] that would include some of the old but also many innovative elements, specially those related to a deep institutional and legal framework reform. They are: (a) strengthening governance and the quality of government of institutions as an essential prerequisite for the continuation of stability in terms of the macroeconomic and growth policies and strengthening the capacity of Governments themselves; (b) enhancing the legal and judiciary systems, as it is very difficult to get protection for the poor on an equitable basis without it; (c) overturning the question of financial supervision and control through an appropriate framework in terms of bank supervision, supervision of capital markets, integrity, consistency and transparency; (d) fighting corruption, as it is something that pervades each of these former areas and might be able to create the environment for a virtuous economic circle; and, (e) reforming the social framework in a way that allow to deal with the people that fall out of the system.[29]

II. THE WEAKNESS OF THE STATE AND THE RULES OF THE LAW

Major reform, as previously described, occurred especially in the financial sector. This affected public and private participants in different ways. Multilateral organisations have recognised that these reforms have greatly reoriented the state's role in Latin American and Caribbean economies and are transforming governance in the region.[30] As crises of earlier periods are important in explaining the economic and political relationships that emerged and characterised the past several decades, so responses to this new era of crisis are the basis on which state-economy and State–Society relations in many countries will be constructed for the next several decades. Thus, it is important to understand the complex social and political components of the crisis, the quality of governments and the causes for Ecuador's

[27] Deepak Lal and H. Myint, *The Political Economy of Poverty, Equity and Growth* (Oxford: Clarendon Press, 1996), 190.

[28] The term is been adopted from the 'Conference on Second Generation Reforms' held by the IMF Institute in Washington, DC, on 8 and 9 Nov. 1999. See <http://www.imf.org>.

[29] Extracted from keynote Address at 'Conference on Second Generation Reforms' by James D. Wolfensohn, President of The World Bank Group, Washington, DC, 8 Nov. 1999.

[30] 'Latin America and the Caribbean in the Face of Globalization: Progress to Date and the Road Ahead', Statement by Enrique V. Iglesias, President of the Inter-American Development Bank (IDB) at the United Nations Conference on Trade and Development (UNCTAD X) Bangkok, Thailand—14 Feb. 2000. *See* <http://www.iadb.org/exr/s peeches/s14II00e.htm>.

ineffective implementation of reforms. It should be noted that 'government', for these purposes, should be understood as the State, in the legal sense.

For reform to work, each country has to design and implement its 'own' reform considering its political, economical and social context. It must also implement the reform at its 'own' pace. The new Ecuadorian banking law, however, was modelled on the Chilean law. This was a law introduced in the final stages of Chile's deep banking crisis, a crisis that required massive use of public resources. Thus, the Chilean law focused on the prevention of crisis and deterrence of public intervention (with public resources). De la Torre noted that, for reform to be effective in Ecuador it was necessary to count on certain macro and microeconomic conditions that have not characterised the Ecuadorian environment. In between macro conditions, it was desirable to have not only disciplined monetary and fiscal management, but also protection against exogenous shocks to decrease the general vulnerability of the banking system. As for micro conditions, first class supervision and regulation and transparent disclosure of information was indispensable. He also deemed necessary the existence of a basic institutional framework comprised of an efficient, independent and trustworthy judiciary to impede the offense of banking laws and frauds.[31] It is clear that these conditions were and are not present in Ecuador. They lead to another field of interest: the capabilities of any State to apply such reform and to what extent the arising weakness is merely the cost of implementing other core elements of the same structural adjustment: the desintervention of the state and the deregulation process.

The Ecuadorian financial reform process may be perceived as having been imposed from 'abroad'. It was closely related to the 'conditionality' of the multilateral financial institutions (IMF, World Bank, ADB, etc.) established in the arrangements and loan agreements executed by Ecuador during the last decade. This conditionality was widely applied in this context, not only in Ecuador.[32] These institutions are, however, actually very interested in the problems that confront the reform processes and have identified two major areas of concern: (a) an inadequate institutional framework; and (b) the absence of a domestic ownership of the reform (in a wider sense).

Usually the reasons given for this ineffective institutional framework relate to administrative constraints and corruption. The use of the term 'weakness' is preferred to corruption, as it broadens the scope of the analy-

[31] A. De la Torre, '*El Manejo de Crisis Bancarias: el Marco Legal Ecuatoriano y Posibles Reformas', Corporacion de Estudios para el Desarrollo*', (CORDES, 1997).

[32] V. Corbo, and S. Fischer, 'Adjustment Programs and World Bank Support: Rationale and Main Results' in P. Mosley, (ed), *Development Finance and Policy Reform: Essays in the Theory and Practice of Conditionality in Less Developed Countries* (1992).

sis, not confining it to the public sector, nor to individual behaviours. Let us assume that the weakness of the state, defined as the inability to implement its policy choices, creates the conditions for the failure of the institutional framework. Here, the problems that confront the public regulatory and supervisory bodies could be interpreted as a lack of institutional, political, technical, and administrative capability to perform effectively and efficiently their duties.

There is a renewed interest in state capacity and the relationship between state and economy. During 1999, the official sector referred to recent efforts to overcome the poor results of the prior process as 'second generation reform'. It has been noted that '[s]econd generation issues focus around the questions of the structure of the right institutions, of the improvement of the administrative, legal, and regulatory functions of the state, addressing the incentives and actions that are required to have private sector development and to develop *the institutional capacity for reforms* . . .'[33] These second generation reforms include financial, judicial, and public sector reform.

All this has encouraged scholars to pay greater attention to institutional structures and the way that such institutions affect the course of economic development:

> While the private sector correctly assumes a leadership role in the economy, it needs the support of strong state institutions, the rule of law, effective public and private market institutions as well as active political participation of civil society in democratic processes. Good governance is now recognised as a necessary and sometimes missing ingredient in the reform process . . .[34]

There is likely general agreement that the policy choices and implementation of the reform reside not only in its design, but also in the capability of the State to enforce it. Thus, how crises are played out in individual countries depends in large part on the strength and durability of existing institutions for conflict resolution and the skills and orientations of political leaders, using the expanded space available to them to define new strategies for economic development and to build new and durable coalitions of political support.[35] The first condition could be described as 'Responsiveness', the second, as 'Legitimacy'. But both of these conditions have to be applied in an appropriate framework that ensures transparent 'Accountability'.

33 Keynote Address at the IMF Institute Conference on Second Generation Reforms by James D. Wolfensohn, President of The World Bank Group, Washington, DC, 8 Nov. 1999.

34 Above n 30.

35 Merilee S. Grindle *Challenging the State: Crisis and Innovation in Latin America and Africa* (Cambridge: Cambridge University Press, 1996) 45–6.

A. Ownership of Reform

The problem of 'ownership' of reform may be manifest in two main areas: (a) inadequate adaptation of the legal systems to the requirements of the reform; and (b) insufficient legitimacy of the objectives and goals of the process with the ensuing lack of political and social consensus.

In Ecuador, the adoption of financial 'model' legislation that does not necessarily reflect the nation's own legal traditions, has not been accompanied by a relevant commercial law reform. This has kept in place major Napoleonic civil code traditions with characteristically complicated mechanisms to create security interests and especially to transfer them: proper assignments, duly notified to debtors. There also remains excessive taxation for transferring assets that considerably affects the efficiency of the financial system as a whole with regard to transparency of information and accurate determination of creditworthiness,[36] accompanied by the overcharging of debtors with non-transparent commissions added to active interest rates. 'Practical' solutions to the legal problems only added, therefore, to the lack of transparency of the financial operations.[37]

In contrast, English law provides a broader spectrum and greater flexibility for these matters. Some examples are: universal corporate floating charges; informal security over investment securities without registration of the pledgee in the books of the issuer; corporate non-possesory chattel mortgages; and self-help enforcement by possessory management through a receiver and private sale as opposed to a judicially-ordered public action. Rights of substitution, eg for collateralised investment securities, in English jurisdictions do not destroy the charge, but may demote it to a floating charge. In Franco-Latin countries, this dominion by the pledgor may destroy the security interest altogether.[38]

The accelerated pace of financial innovation has also forced bankers and practitioners to adopt 'innovative' legal instruments to overcome gaps, without analysing general implications for the legal system. An important example is the use of the commercial Common law trust, introduced together with the securities law, that has become rapidly and broadly popular as it provides a more flexible range of securities, transfers, securitisation of assets and avoids the requirement of judicial enforcement, generally felt inefficient.[39] However, this has brought new conflicts related to its enforcement, as judges were not appropriately prepared to accept

[36] Assets are kept undervalued for this reason.

[37] eg undervaluation or extensive use of 'Trusts'.

[38] Financial legal instruments in P. R. Wood, *Comparative Financial Law*, (London: Sweet & Maxwell, 1995), 62, absent in Ecuador, assessed as traditional Franco-Latin jurisdiction.

[39] Trust in other European Franco-Latin jurisdictions is still a matter of analysis, whereas in Latin America it is already common.

legal 'innovation' on financial matters, thus increasing legal uncertainty and credit risk. From the point of view of supervisors, these legal 'innovations' have brought also new challenges, as the regulatory framework has not been able to absorb all these 'new' legal institutions and forms.

Legal systems (the rules of the game) have to be carefully established, as they are supposed to last for a long period of time. Wood suggested that it is true that some legal systems do undergo great creative shifts and then 'settle down to stability, minor adjustments, occasional tinkering, the filling out of the detail'. He considers also that 'Stable change has its advantages: the law is a known quantity and is predictable, it does not overreact to an episode or to a transient political philosophy or to some fad or fashion of the day. There is time for reflection, for a *historical consensus to be reached.*'[40] (emphasis added). It is precisely the latter which accentuates the requirement of reform 'ownership' as a main quality for its ultimate success.

The reform has been permanently blamed as a major cause of fragility of Ecuador's financial system and the abuses of the bankers.[41] However, for others, 'Ecuador is in the process of a meltdown—not because it is fighting a war, but because it has avoided reform'[42] or lacked adequate reform[43] or even, because deregulation has been reversed.[44] But it is not possible to blame the reform itself, nor the 'lack' of it as the main cause of the crisis. First, there are other economic, political, and social conditions that affected its implementation. Secondly, it is impossible to have successful economic results by just transplanting the liberalisation 'recipe' from one country to another to pursue positive macroeconomic results. And last, reform requires a proper institutional framework in order to be successfully implemented.

B. The Capability of the State and the Legitimacy of Reform

The importance of ensuring efficient governance for implementing economic reform seems to be related directly to the spread of the social beneficial effects of the whole liberalisation process not only in the specific countries, but also in the globalised world.[45] Good governance is related to the roots of conformation of the States and the type of it. The social

40 Wood (above n 38), 55.

41 *See* eg A Acosta and J Schuldt, *La hora de la Reactivacion*, (ESPOL, 1999); Guayaquil and R Vallejo, 'Maridaje de la Politica y del Dinero', *El Comercio*, 23 Oct. 1999.

42 *Miami Herald*, 'Ecuador's problems not just "bum luck"', 25 Jan. 2000.

43 ECN 99, 'Deconstructing Latin ills: Not all of the region is in as bad a mess at it seems', 4 Sept. (741).

44 A Pachano, in 'Regular, no Imponer', *El Comercio*, 26 Nov. 1999.

45 The IMF Institute Conference (above 28) produced many interesting papers related to this field.

contract underlying such State conformation has been provided to societies, theoretically, as a means to achieve a general public welfare not attainable outside such form of organisation. Thus, good governance is expected to fill this objective, regardless of its political orientation. The communist and the market-oriented State concepts began to be discussed just at the end of nineteenth century, but the core objective of State conformation has never been completely different than the original. The lack of state capability might also be a cause for failure in the development process itself. However, measuring state capability to meet this objective is difficult. A *capable state* is one that exhibits the ability to establish and maintain effective functions in four main fields: institutional, political, technical, and administrative.[46]

When measuring rule of law, control of corruption, government effectiveness, and quality of the regulatory environment provided by States, Latin America ranks behind Asia and far behind the most developed countries. Opinion polls show that Latin Americans are dissatisfied with the quality of their governments and think corruption is getting worse. The IADB has also noted that inequality in Latin America is the most pronounced of any region in the world, and by most indications, getting worse. 'In Latin America, the top 20 per cent of the population earns 12 times what the bottom 20 per cent make'.[47] Often, economic stagnation or decline went hand in hand with widespread questioning of regimes in power and a generalised de-legitimisation of the state as an agent of economic growth.[48] Ecuador is immersed in this general concern about the region. It has engaged, also, during the last few decades, in muddling towards an economic stabilisation program and a structural reform process. Continually painful economic measures together with constant reductions in public money spent on social services and welfare in order to control public deficits, have increased wealth distribution inequalities instead of bringing an improvement in social welfare.[49] Deep frustration and dissatisfaction is a natural response to an exhausting programme of reform without improvement in social and economic standards. All of this suggests that there is decreased authority and legitimacy of governments to set authoritative standards for individual and group behavior, or, at least, increased challenging of the state policy choices, especially in the economic field.[50]

[46] State capability concepts are extracted from Grindle, (1996), ch. 1 and 2.

[47] Above n 30.

[48] Grindle, (1996), 2.

[49] PNUD 'Informe sobre Desarrollo Humano Ecuador 1999', (1999) ch 3 encompass an analysis about Poverty and Social Development in Ecuador during the 1980s and 1990s.

[50] This offers also one explanation for the political instability during 1999 and especially for the military coup in January 2000 in Ecuador, with active participation of the indigenous and other social movements.

There are two main models of State: *autonomous* and *factional*.[51] A regime or government having objectives of its own determines the autonomous state. The factional state, on the other hand serves the economic self-interests of the coalition of pressure groups that succeed in capturing it. Ecuador could be easily assessed as a factional state, in which not only the powerfully economic groups, in turn, have addressed the policy choices, but also other interest groups (like the public syndicates and, now, the indigenous movement) that have been 'allowed' to share 'pieces' of it. This is despite ongoing allegations by some coastal sectors, during periodic regional confrontations, about the maintenance of a 'centralist' model that serves only the capital public officials interests.[52] Rather than the implementation of calculated and centred policies with a long-term public welfare vision, the governments during the last two decades have been forced to shift decisions rapidly and readdress economic programmes and policy choices to contain and keep political support and avoid social confrontation.[53] With particular reference to the Ecuadorian financial and banking crisis, there is the perception by many national and international analysts of the existence of a 'commitment' from the former government to the banking sector, in order to manage financial crisis in 1999, without putting overall public welfare over particular economic interests.[54] A factional state could also be considered as a corruption-driven state. This because less evident corruption, but not less serious is the clandestine and undue influence by the economic power over the political power. 'Structural' corruption characterises factional-states.

Critics of Development Model I concentrated on the ways in which public action can distort markets and create disincentives for productive investment and behaviour, like financial repression. This supported even financial liberalisation and conformed major grounds for what could be called the 'minimalist-state' role. As a result, the naturally weak institutional framework prevailing in a developing country could have been directly and adversely affected not only because of a quantitative reduction, but mainly by a qualitative weakening and even some reversion of state powers. Indeed, desintervention and deregulation policies could have been underpinned by a wrongful perception of all developing countries

51 Theoretical support for state-models is provided by D Lal, and H Myint, *The Political Economy of Poverty, Equity and Growth* (Oxford: Clarendon Press, 1996), 260–73.

52 Indeed autonomous-depredatory state characteristic, which involves self seeking extraction of the maximum continuing flow of resources for the members of the government and its associates; Ibid.

53 eg several recent drawbacks in gas-price increase.

54 *See* eg ECN 99 'Chaos, continued: Ecuador', 20 Mar. (787) and ECN 99, 'Jamil's jam: Ecuador edges to an IMF deal', 19 June (547). *See* several editorials in Ecuadorian main newspapers from late 1999, eg from Vallejo, Andrés; Roldos, Leon; Acosta, Alberto; Vallejo, Raul; Herrera, Washington; Mauge, Rene; Hurtado, Oswaldo; and Espinosa, Simon.

being conformed as autonomous predatory states[55] and might not have taken into account the existence of factional states, like Ecuador.

Institutional capacity, or 'Legitimacy', is described as an ability to assert the primacy of national policies over those of other groupings. This is difficult to obtain in a factional-state. Often, economic stagnation or decline went hand in hand with widespread questioning of regimes in power and a generalised de-legitimisation of the state as an agent of economic growth.[56] In Ecuador, continually painful economic measures together with constant reductions in public money spent on social services and welfare in order to control public deficits, have increased wealth distribution inequalities instead of bringing an improvement in social welfare and economic standards.[57] All of this suggests that there is decreased authority and legitimacy of governments to set authoritative standards for individual and group behaviour, or, at least, increased challenging of state policy choices, especially in the economic field.[58]

Political capacity is considered to be effective and legitimate channels for societal demand making and representation. Unable to claim broad-based legitimacy due to the poor results of the reform or the loyalty of traditional support groups, political regimes demonstrated their inability to dominate and lead civic society as they had done in the past. Government responses to the crisis in Ecuador, such as decreased spending during most of 1999 and, especially, the freezing of bank deposits, have been undone by the popular anger. Moreover political parties have not given proper support for concrete actions of state leaders and hinder their effectiveness. Indeed, political parties are also distrusted by factional-driven perceptions about them.

Most of these demands will be reflected through the production of law. The absence of this political capability also turns into a conflictive and, even, contradictory legal system. The law exists in layers of conflicting legislation, reflecting very different conditions and political outlooks, and the interests of the groups that backed the political representatives in the Congress. It is very difficult for a State to put in place the necessary regulatory and supervisory infrastructure under such conditions. In the end, this disarrayed legal system could also be a cause for the financial crisis in Ecuador, due to the lack of proper instruments and tools for opportune state-intervention.

Technical capacity encompasses the ability to set and manage effective macroeconomic policies, through appropriately placed units for policy

[55] eg Mexico, controlled during almost all the century by an only political party.

[56] Above n 35, 2.

[57] *See* eg PNUD (1999), ch 3.

[58] The 2000 military coup in Ecuador has followed the announcement of the Dollarisation process.

analysis, and an important role for technical input and information in decision-making. This is important at the level of policy-makers that will have to design and introduce the reform, and of technocrats, which will implement and in some cases even administratively enforce it. Technocrats also take care of the 'institutional memory' that ensures implementation of long-term projects, without any direct link to a specific regime. This does not mean that technocrats eventually get directly involved in the selection of policy choices, but rather from a different and concentrated perspective. Ecuador shows increased numbers, visibility, and influence of economic and financial technocrats mainly during the 1990s. This includes increased presence of international technocrats in national policy-making. During the decade, technical analysis units became more important in national policy making, often to the detriment of cabinets, legislative institutions, party leaders, lobby groups, and traditional ministries such as interior, public works, and foreign affairs.[59]

Grindle also highlighted the surge of an evident tension between technocratic and participatory policy making.[60] In Ecuador, technocrats create a type of 'conflict of interest' between officials in the State who promote the factional state and those who are concentrated in building such a technical capability for the long term. Notwithstanding such technical capability, however, its technocrats have been isolated from major political decisions with the result that important projects and programmes ended uselessly wasting scarce economic and human resources. Moreover, the regional confrontation, accentuated during the banking crisis, has also affected the credibility of these technocrats, as their work has been naturally concentrated in and identified with one region, the capital, no matter their regional origin. On the other hand, there are also no proper and accurate channels to feedback design and implementation of technical programmes with societal results. This also hinders obtaining the political and social support fundamental for a successful implementation of any technical programme.

Administrative capacity is the ability to perform basic administrative functions essential to economic development and social welfare,[61] and will be extensively reviewed in Section 3.

Summing up, States must be 'capable' if they are to be effective in managing tasks of economic and political development and reform. This is especially true if they are to face the challenges that a factional state causes and to avoid a 'constituents interest economic groups' driven reform. Without proper development and maintenance of such capacities, the resulting changes in policies and the introduction of a reformed legal and institutional framework can result in further exacerbation of the natural

[59] Above n 35, 35–6. [60] Ibid. 7–10. [61] Ibid. 7–10.

weaknesses that are common characteristics in developing and emerging States.

2. *Allocation of Credit in Ecuador*

To produce the maximum benefit for society, credit funds would need to flow to projects offering the highest returns for a given level of risk. Resource allocation efficiency will determine the efficiency of the economy as a whole.[62] Defects in the operation of repressed financial systems hinder this market allocation of resources. State-driven allocation of credit policies benefited mainly restricted sectors of the society, with strong political connections. Post-stabilisation financial developments in Latin America did not imply changes in the oligopoly and segmented characteristics of the financial system that restrict the credit access to smaller enterprises and producers not related to the banks.[63] The impossibility of introducing any effective competition policies is another outstanding side effect of inefficient allocation of credit with devastating results on the confidence of the participants in the market.

In Ecuador, government intervention in the banking system was characterised, during the 1970s and the 1980s by prizing boards, such as the interest rate determination by the Monetary Board and especially by 'administrative' allocation of credit. In this period, the factional-state has driven allocation of credit mainly to sectors that have supported it, rather than to those more efficient for the economy as a whole. De la Torre also noted that there has been a pattern over the management of these resources, reorienting these policies with regard to the presently particular circumstances. During the 1970s, the major bulk of the available resources were governmentally driven not necessarily to the more efficient sectors of the economy. After the debt crisis in the early 1980s, central bank credit became the major source. In the 1990s, specifically after the major monetary reform that broadly restricted access to central bank resources and conferred central bank independence,[64] the main source of funding for the large economic groups came from the private banking system. [65] Somehow confirming this, Lasso, former Ministry of Economy, recently highlighted that Ecuadorian corporations have had higher availability of credit than other more developed Latin American countries. He considered decreases

[62] Above n 35.

[63] CEDES, *Estabilidad y Estructura: Interacciones en el Crecimiento Economico* (Buenos Aires, 1994), 38–47.

[64] Despite central bank independence only being introduced with the Constitution amendment in 1998, in practice independence was significantly increased after the 1992 monetary reform.

[65] *See* A. De la Torre, (1999).

in private corporation leverage levels and equity democratisation as a major means to achieve economic reactivation nowadays.[66]

While examining bank capital standards in Latin America, there are conclusions that the region's high levels of concentration of wealth and thin equity markets make it very unlikely that such standards can be effectively enforced. These conditions enable bank owners to dilute their real capital stake by making loans to themselves, either directly or by borrowing from each other.[67] Rodrik, in relation to effects of decision-making market discipline in emerging economies asserts: 'What goes under the name "market discipline" is not a neutral political force. It empowers financial markets—both domestic and foreign—over other constituencies in society. Hence it can be seen as serving the needs of particular social groups at the expense of others.'[68] Over time for well-known reasons, the inefficiencies associated with protection to those who supported the 'factional-state' will lower the efficiency of the economy.[69] De la Torre also observed that if allocation of credit in Ecuador is a function of the public entity that monopolises the issue of money, rather than the role of a professional banking system supported by market rules, and enhanced by transparent disclosure and efficient supervision, then there is no real market process, but a political process that will breed clientelism.[70] This could be applied extensively to the issue of state-driven allocation of credit and the supervisor 'difficulties' to control concentration of connected lending over the limits permitted by the law.[71] There is a vicious circle that structural adjustment and the financial liberalisation cannot easily break. Rather, as has been explained before, the deregulation of the banking sector and the fast pace of the implementation of reform has helped to increase the natural weaknesses of developing states, building up or accentuating incapability to supervise and regulate efficiently. And these conditions, instead of enlarging the market participants on the demand side, have restricted them as a consequence of the increase of poverty during the same period.[72]

At the end, in Ecuador, the costs of private inefficiencies have been transplanted to the public sector, through state-intervention in the banking system and to the society. The banking system overhaul by the DGA depended exclusively on Ministry of Finance funding. As there was not liquidity available at the time, the resources have been provided by the

[66] G. Lasso, 'Credito y Reactivacion', *Diario Hoy*, 30 May 2000.

[67] Liliana Rojas-Suarez, and Steven R. Weisbrod, *Towards an Effective Regulatory and Supervisory Framework for Latin America* (IDB, Washington, 1996).

[68] D Rodrik, 'Governing the Global Economy: Does one architectural style fit all?', (1999), 24 <http://www.globalarchitects.org/00005.pdf:>.

[69] Above n 51, 269–71.

[70] Above n 16.

[71] e.g., in Continental, Progreso, Filanbanco, Prestamos, etc.

[72] From 40 per cent in the 1980s to 80 per cent in the 1990s, *see* PNUD (1999).

direct discount of public bonds by the Central Bank or, indirectly, by the freezing of deposits declared in March 1999 after the bank holiday. As *The Economist* highlighted, 'depositors, saw themselves paying the cost of bankers' mismanagement and the government's reluctance to offend political allies by closing some banks that were near to collapse.'[73] It should be added that depositors have also paid the inefficiency costs of the private sector and high leverage permitted by a banking system without suitable risk assessment.

One way to overcome the situation is the strengthening of financial regulation, despite the strong political and interested interference. The case of external regulation depends on circumstances in which the private sector, left to itself, produces market failure, or at least sub-optimal results, which are arguably worse than public sector regulation, even with all the biases and failings that such regulation may entail.[74] Otherwise, without proper regulation in place, interested 'pressure' groups will be able to impose their own 'rules' over those that should attend to the society's general welfare. Financial reform's next steps will be forced to confront this allocation of credit reality and even the existence of this factional state. Indeed, re-regulation should not be confused with further 'financial' repression, as state-driven policies in a factional-state will not break the vicious circle. Orientation might rest mainly on proper responsiveness of the State, by enhancing its capability as a whole, in order to concentrate efforts on general public interest and to avoid efficiently such pressures.

Responsiveness will arise also through better assessment over personal, technical, and moral conditions of owners, managers, and directors of banks. This will have to be built under public, transparent and non-discretionary general rules to be efficient, perhaps through a public-registry with an opposition process, if necessary.[75] Indeed such technical and moral assessment should include the regulatory and supervisory officials and personnel.

Without proper regulation, the 'gridlock' could be boosted. Gridlock is explained as the moral hazard danger that good firms are induced to behave badly because they either see bad behaviour in others, or have no assurance that competitors will behave well.[76] The problem is enhanced in a competitive market where all the participants, in order to make profits, might adopt risky conducts with short-term time horizons and by lack of transparency. But the major cause for surge and persistence of gridlock is

[73] ECN 99, 20 Mar. 'Chaos, continued: Ecuador' (787).

[74] C. Goodhart, *et al* 'The rationale for regulation', in *Where, How and What Now?*, (LSE Financial Markets Group, 1998), 4–9.

[75] Ongoing bank secrecy rules deter this.

[76] The term 'grid-lock' is borrowed from D. Llewellyn, *The Economic Rationale for Financial Regulation*, FSA Occasional Paper (Apr. 1999).

the supervisors' inefficiency to enforce regulation. As 'competitors' cannot be sure about general regulatory compliance, they are encouraged to maintain risky behaviour in order to ensure their own profits. This is another way to explain generalised connected lending and bad credit-risk assessment in Ecuador.

D. *The Judiciary and the Financial System*

As a condition for enforcement of law, the disputes settlement core is comprised of a well-functioning judicial system, providing efficient and rational outcomes and adequate remedies. The absence of efficient enforcement mechanisms in a market-driven State raises legal uncertainty. The extent of judiciary deficiencies and, alternatively, the practical possibility to remedy them will directly bias the amount and extension of these costs.

The Ecuadorian judicial sector has suffered from a lack of financial and technical resources, administrative inefficiencies and a growing backlog of cases. On the other hand, strong political intervention has transformed many courts and judges into another instrument for managing the formerly described 'factional state'. In addition to systemic bribery, there is also the corruption of personal relations.[77] The enforcement of contracts, the enforcement of laws against rule breakers, and the ability to carry on economic functions without recourse to bribery and subornation became increasingly difficult under such conditions.[78] Inefficiency in execution of judgments has its own effects. Remedies can be incomplete, delayed until they are innocuous[79] and personal punishment is evaded by prescription.

The judiciary is important for the financial system, but the former has generally resulted in the sector's inability to meet requirements of the private and public sector. In the micro context, creditors are affected by the difficulties to ensure opportune or fair payment and application of proper insolvency mechanisms; and small weak debtors can be adversely affected by abuses of their creditors. In the macro context, enforcement of law and regulation in the financial system has been extremely poor. Most, if not all, cases filed during the 1980s by the banking supervisor against intervened financial institutions have ruled against the public sector, resulting even in damages and compensations being covered by the State and personal risks

[77] World Bank programmes and reports regarding judicial modernisation in Ecuador are major sources of information and background.

[78] Above n 51, 33.

[79] High inflation significantly affects economic remedies.

for the public officials.[80] Absence of trustworthy judicial review results in hidden costs for the financial system that could be classified in two types: first, purely economic costs that, due to uncertainty, are difficult to calculate. The second type is probably more important but less evident: the moral hazard costs.

Economic costs can be: (a) direct, such as bribery or even the necessity to access more costly alternative disputes resolution mechanisms, for instance, arbitration or submission to foreign courts, when possible; or (b) indirect, mainly the legal risk taken into account to assess credit risk, very difficult to determine, as uncertain results do not provide objective measurement tools. Indeed, legal risk is increased in the case of powerful and political influential debtors. These economic costs promote a subjective and non-transparent creditworthiness assessment over debtors. Risk managing has to introduce a subjective 'judicial risk' assessment that can make it inoperative. Without taking into account such risk, capital adequacy requirements might be insufficient to measure the soundness of the financial system, particular institutions or even particular creditors. The private financial institutions transfer these economic costs into the system, whether as a generalised increase in interest rates or as an unequal transference of losses to society, in the case of a banking failure. On the other hand, these economic costs are a burden difficult to overcome for public supervisors and regulators, in order to ensure efficient defence of the public interest. As rules of public funds use hinder any kind of direct bribery required by courts and judges, public lawyers confront a diminished position with regard to private practitioners. Foreign courts or arbitration, as a more efficient alternative dispute settlement tool, are restricted in the public sector also by institutional weakness and lack of economic and technical resources.

Moral hazard costs refer directly to the behaviour of the individuals, firms, and public entities in light of the non-existence of efficient enforcement of the rules of the game. Debtor and creditor behaviours in routine financial transactions are less transparent as legal uncertainty and inefficient enforcement of laws significantly encourage a non-payment culture[81] and boost the degree of tolerance in society for corrupt behaviours. This problem is more significant for supervisors and regulators of the system as inefficient and impractical litigation and defense tools have to be added to institutional and political weakness. It is noteworthy that the absence of an agile and trustworthy judiciary system can even boost financial fraud. The

[80] e.g. Fomamcoera de Los Andes, Banco Industrial y Comercial and Banco de Descuento, most of them judged during the 1990s.

[81] Defined as generalised social behaviour to pay as little as possible (or not pay) or just to delay compliance of duties. Delay is equivalent to non-payment in an inflationary environment.

shareholders of a nearly collapsed bank, encouraged by perception of little risk for financial frauds to be properly punished, might find fraudulent means to rescue their equity and avoid absorbing losses before depositors and other creditors.[82] Additionally, the gridlock problem formerly described will create the ideal environment for systemic financial fraud.

Ecuador's Continental case provides an empirical example of this 'judiciary' moral hazard. A criminal judicial prosecution in Ecuador, opportunely impelled by banking and monetary authorities against former managers and shareholders, shifted into a politically driven trial. Instead of determining responsibility of private bankers, the judge concentrated into the accuracy of the monetary policy[83] and the existence of cause for the adoption of systemic prevention measures by the regulators. Solorzano, the President of the Supreme Court at the time, even considered the accountability of the economical and human resources used by the Central Bank to support the legal procedures filed against former shareholders, rather than the fraudulent actions denounced by the authorities in detailed reports introduced in the discovery process. In 1997, imprisonment orders were issued against former Superintendent of Banks' and Central Bank authorities, together with some of the former shareholders and managers of the bank. Although the imprisonment orders and syndication of the authorities were removed a year later after a judiciary reform, there was serious damage to public confidence in the monetary and banking authorities. Former management of the bank and external auditors were called for definitive judgment in the criminal procedure in Ecuador, but restricted to the grounds of public documents and balance sheet forging and double gearing.[84] In this context the General Attorney role 'conflicted' with the other State officials. Rather then supporting legal actions against the bankers, he suggested imprisonment orders for the authorities. Paradoxically, but explainable under the conception of 'factional', the State prosecuted the State.

The Bahamian jurisdiction was selected by the Central Bank of Ecuador in 1996 as an alternative forum to impel the impartial treatment of a part of the financial fraud and to get some economic remedies. The defendants expressly alleged the 'laxity' of the authorities and the gridlock problem ('other Ecuadorian banks do the same') within their major defence exceptions. Furthermore, the bankers initiated a libel action in the Southern District of Florida, USA, alleging defamation and 'psychological stress' caused by the Central Bank's public exposure of the case. Resolutions about the criminal case issued by the Supreme Court of Justice in Ecuador,

82 Above n 31, 15.

83 Continental was seized by the Central Bank.

84 The decision does not consider most of the CBE observations with regard to fraudulent disposition of assets and mismanagement of liquidity credits granted by the Central Bank.

especially the imprisonment orders against the authorities, were an important defensive means further affecting the credibility of and weakening the regulators. There are no definitive results in any of the cases to date. Indeed the poor results of the more important recent banking case in Ecuador, may have induced the moral hazard and gridlock problem referred to above and generated the precedent for the 1999 banking crisis, as many analysts have observed. Effectively, many of the 1999 failed banks cases have had similar characteristics with the precedent, not only due to the poor judiciary treatment, but also because there is a pattern of behaviour between the different failed banks. Connected lending, double gearing, poor provisions, utilisation of foreign jurisdictions and off-shore banking for fraudulent purposes, conformation of special purpose vehicles, etc. are also common.

The Continental case shows that supervisory laxity is not only a question of lack of administrative capability, but also a result of political interference and judicial inefficiency and corruption. Financial regulation is difficult to enforce, even with the willingness of authorities and the existence of appropriate alternative litigation resources. Another problem that arose from judicial deficiencies in the Continental case is the public officials' extensive 'legal' risk, addressed in the next section, that might also affect efficient enforcement of regulation and accountability. However, the more dramatic threat is definitely the gridlock problem with its systemic risk implications. There is nothing as sensitive to public confidence as a financial system. The effects of loss of confidence in a bank have been duly studied in the context of bank runs and systemic risk. Sound banks can fail solely for this reason. Legal uncertainty generated by an inefficient judiciary is a major source of loss in confidence and judicial muddle can have important systemic resonance.

The evaluation of the relevance of the judiciary's problems in the financial crisis is that there is a need to determine the next steps of any judicial reform in Ecuador, in general, and, in particular, with respect to the financial system and its overhaul. Any serious judiciary reform takes time, to adapt its instruments, institutions and practices and to ensure independence from political influence. Capacitating programmes for judges and other officials, and the introduction of technology in courts also require reasonable terms to produce any beneficial results. Thus, it is important to establish a temporary regime to overcome the time mismatch, with politically independent bodies, which at the same time will encourage the rest of the strengthening process and avoid the present moral hazard and gridlock effect caused by diversion of justice.

Beyond a general strengthening programme, there are also some particular conditions related to the financial system. First, the independence of the judiciary from political intervention or even economical bribery is essential. Economic interests in the financial sector are very important, but so are the losses to the State and public. Secondly, the accountability of judges and recusal in cases of conflict of interests has to be carefully monitored by a technical and impartial forum. Thirdly, judiciary reform has to include also the General Prosecutor and Attorney institutional frameworks and other public entities that provide judicial services or support for any case in the financial field.

An urgent introduction of financial 'task' teams or financial courts, provided with proper endorsement through political, institutional, economical and technical support, could be a useful mechanism for the general restructuring of the financial system.[85] Another temporary solution might be to entrust banks, and in general, public entities involved in the financial sector matters, with broad extra-judicial procedures for enforcing and executing of financial obligations. Indeed, to accomplish these main objectives, it is necessary to implement an aggressive capacitating programme across the financial system, economic reform and deregulation.

Financial innovation and, moreover, financial globalisation raise another challenge for judges. Innovation causes any judicial review to have to confront not only natural existing judicial deficiencies, but also scarce technical, economic and human resources available for these purposes in the country. Access to foreign jurisdictions when possible could be not only a voluntarily choice, but also the only means to enforce and especially execute judgments. Deregulation has also facilitated international investments. For local investors, the necessity to access international jurisdictions is another hidden cost and risk, not necessarily transparent at the time of the investment.[86] How to evolve and access to an international efficient judiciary system is the future question for financial systems of emerging economies.

E. Balancing Public Accountability and Legal Risk

Disclosure and transparency are considered as main conditions to ensure efficiency in a market-oriented economy. Transparency could be understood as a type of accountability. It ensures that market participants and investors are provided opportunely with accurate information to duly assess their risk and costs, in order to take any efficient decision. Transparency also multiplies controllers over compliance with rules of the game and expels gridlock effects. Financial system regulators in Ecuador

[85] Procedural law reform can be implemented for ongoing cases.
[86] e.g., in Ecuador offshore investments related to Popular failure.

are public officials, thus such transparency is reached through public accountability.

Public institutions and officials are capable to make and enforce decisions that can affect individuals positively or negatively, communities, and in the broader sense, the public good. Evaluation of responsiveness of a State is only possible through fitting and efficient accountability. Public accountability can be defined as the compulsory duty of a public institution or official, to give account, justify or explain actions, decisions or omissions related to their public function. Accountability also relies on direct actions or omissions of public officials 'accountable' rather than third-party actions or even *force-major*. There are three major types of accountability: the judicial review of administrative resolutions, an administrative accountability (for instance, regular presentation of reports to Congress) and a general public accountability. [87]

Accountability implies an obligation to comply with certain standards in the exercise of power or to achieve specific goals. However, the more complex the activity, the more difficult it is to establish clear standards of conduct and specific outcomes. This is the case for financial regulation. Financial regulators have to exercise rule-making powers and set policies in a way that is compatible with the regulatory objectives: financial stability and consumer protection. A good example of accountability difficulties arises from banking bailout in order to contain systemic risk. Assessing justifications, intentions and costs can be subject to political considerations and multiple technical interpretations as well. In the context of a factional state, interested interference considerably increases personal and organisational risks and shuffles public accountability with bankers' and shareholders' sole responsibilities and actions.

Ecuador during the 1999 financial crisis, and even before, had a chronic problem of lack of public accountability. Problems arise from the difficulties to determine such standards and goals in the context of overlapping and conflictive legal and institutional arrangements or from inaccurate and an uncompleted banking-failure legal framework that forced 'legal-stretching' to cover several cases. Moreover, financial information is generally addressed to specialised recipients, so partial disclosure without acceptable interpretation could have also influenced a further lack of confidence in the system in general. Last but not least, judiciary inefficiency is another element that hinders confidence in fitting outcomes as the result of public accountability and creates moral hazard. Courts and the General

[87] Some theoretical concepts of accountability are borrowed from R. Lastra, and H. Shams 'Accountability: *Ex Ante* or Scrutiny, *ex Post* or Control and Transparency', Paper presented at London School of Economics Financial Market Group Seminar 'Rules, Incentives and Sanctions Enforcement in Financial Regulation', 26 May 2000.

Prosecutor's Office can provide a powerful tool for accountability. However, one of their key characteristics is that they are essentially reactive—to public pressure—and in such a contentious setting, the necessity of an objective public accountability has been shuffled with politics. Poor accountability also boosts inefficient defence of the interests of the State by the public officials.

Personal legal-risk can definitely affect the efficiency of responsiveness. Omission of responsiveness will result if the individual holder of the power considers that compliance with the standards will have a personal, more damaging effect than such omission. Systemic risk considerations and political implications overburden regulators and central bankers, especially in the presence of an inefficient or bribed judiciary. Therefore officials have to measure administrative decisions against the personal legal-risk involved. A supervisor will refrain to report detection of irregularities if the personal burden of such decision does not have an acceptable legal protection umbrella. Moreover, personal legal-risk is increased in the context of a factional State, where the judiciary and other public authorities can react adversely to the interests of the State, whether by bribery or just in accordance with particular economic interests of supporters of the government. This element has a special relevance in Ecuador for financial regulators and supervisors, including central bankers, as bankers might have financed political campaigns of higher authorities and congressmen.[88] Pervasive effects of personal-legal risk are not restricted to Ecuador and have been felt by several Latin American central bankers and supervisors.[89]

In Chile, under general principles, all public officials have a right to be broadly defended, in civil and criminal procedures that arise in the context of any public acts, by their institutions for 'official acts' in compliance of the specific public function. To balance this protective umbrella with private particular interests, Chilean public law also determined that public institutions are accountable for damages caused to private individuals in the exercise of their official duties. However, to ensure accountability, the institutions do have a 'right of repetition' against the public official, in the case of excesses in the exercise of their functions.[90] In Ecuador, the IMF has also confirmed the importance of the legal-risk protection umbrella for efficient responsiveness of the State. The introduction of an effective legal framework for this purpose has been included as a performance criterion

[88] e.g. Progreso.

[89] *See* e.g. papers of CBE Seminar CEMLA (Center for Latin American Monetary Studies), 'Crisis Financiero y Riesgo Legal para la Banca Central', Quito, July 1997.

[90] M. A. Nancrur, (1997) 'Responsabilidad Legal de los Consejeros del Banco Central Chileno y del Superintendente de Bancos e Instituciones Financieras-Principios de Derecho Publico Chileno', Off Print, CBE.

for the 2000 Ecuador Letter of Intent. This legal-umbrella, together with reasonable accountability, provides a better framework for institutions to perform their activities efficiently and achieve their goals, and for individuals to do their duties effectively.

The treatment of the Continental case previously described, is a good example of the legal risk incurred by central bankers, regulators and supervisors. The DGA Law introduced a special procedure restricted to criminal procedures against high-level officials and related essentially to compliance with the overhauling procedures determined in the DGA Law. However the protection was given by the requirement of a special previous report issued by representatives of the National Banks Association, the DGA and the General Prosecution Office, which did not actually ensure any kind of real legal protection.

A second and more general intent to introduce such kind of legal-umbrella came more recently.[91] It created Supreme and Superior Court special jurisdiction for high-level officials and for managers, interventors, receivers, and auditors of seized institutions. However, it still concentrates on criminal cases and does not cover medium and lower-level officials. As a 'protection' it requires the previous confirmation of financial experts qualified by the General Controller, about the material existence of the criminal offense before filing any action against them. However, this rule is also too restricted as it does not cover all the personal risk involved (specifically civil actions), all of the public staff that can be involved, or other financial supervisors, for example, the Superintendent of Companies and CBE. Because of these considerations, the 'umbrella' may be mostly ineffective. More effective might be the introduction of a Chilean-like scheme aimed to personal litigation protection, without hindering public accountability.

Another source for lack of transparency and personal legal risk for central bankers, regulators and supervisors arises from broad banking secrecy rules. Management of bank secrecy information generates another burden for regulators that can be used by the regulated institutions to impose pressure and threats about its disclosure. Although secrecy over banking liabilities can be justified in some circumstances, the grounds for secrecy over asset accounts ('banking reserve') determined in the Ecuadorian Banking-Law are not very clear. There are some jurisdictions where banks' asset-information is publicly available and commercially distributed, which can also contribute to further transparency between market participants: it gives clear signs of creditworthiness of individuals and allows other participants to duly assess credit risk in their transactions with financial debtors. Actual exceptions in Ecuador are too restricted to

[91] In Mar. 2000, with the Trolebus Law.

enhance transparency and in fact attenuate legal risk. They only provide for banking reserve and secrecy release in the context of a judicial procedure[92] and more recently a particular release for audit reports presented to certain other public bodies, provided the existence of previous requirement by and restricted to such institutions. It has to be highlighted that CBE information is not included in these exceptions, thus should be considered as subject to the general rules of banking secrecy.

The extent of discretion entrusted to the public official or institution is a final factor that can affect accountability. Objective accountability is feasible over non-discretional acts, whereas discretional performance is difficult to standardise. Accountability over discretionary powers can raise two main problems. First, the introduction of subjective elements for evaluation of compliance with goals and performance, such as the 'intention' of an institution or an individual, contradicts the essential objectivity that transparency requires. Secondly, it increases substantially the legal risk involved for the official, as the subjective elements will depend on third-party assessment, by judges and other 'accountees', rather than on duty performance and goal achievement. The problem is significant in the context of a complex technical field such as financial system regulation and supervision.

In Ecuador, the veto-power of the Superintendent of Banks, discussed later, adds another complex element for transparency and accountability in the field.

III. FINANCIAL SYSTEM REGULATION AND SUPERVISION: THE ADMINISTRATIVE CAPABILITY OF THE STATE

Banks perform key financial functions, allocating credit and operating the clearing and payments system and the foreign exchange market. Because of these diverse functions, a sound banking sector is the single most essential element of a healthy financial system. Banking regulation and supervision has a significant role to ensure soundness. This will require governments putting in place necessary infrastructure, in order to support and limit activities of institutions and individuals in the financial services marketplace. Essential elements of financial infrastructure are laws and regulations; accounting and auditing standards; transparency, disclosure and accountability; regulatory compliance supervision; and payments, clearing, and settlement systems.[93]

Financial markets can misbehave anywhere, but emerging economies

92 Indeed, this implies judicial files overburden.

93 Above n 51, 3.

like Ecuador are much more susceptible as result of the weak state capabilities previously described. Rodrik wisely observes that today's developed countries did not get their regulatory and legal institutions overnight. 'It would be nice if third-world countries could somehow acquire first-world institutions, but the safe bet has to be that this will happen only when they are no longer third-world countries.'[94] The Ecuadorian financial crisis showed how costly administrative weaknesses in institutions can be.

Laws and regulations ensure fair and equitable treatment of all players, be they owners, managers, borrowers, depositors/creditors, etc. In order to generate public confidence, the main asset of a financial system, the governmental role of financial supervision should ensure that financial institutions operate within the rules of the game and engage only in practices that are managed within reasonable tolerances of risk. Market discipline, even with good public disclosure and transparency, indeed not precisely characteristics of an emerging economy, cannot substitute for such role.

Probably the best period to assess the efficiency of regulators and supervisors is precisely in the aftermath of a systemic crisis. The organisational arrangements and legal framework have been tested at maximum stress. However, immediate reactions to solve particular cases, usually expressed by tightening regulation or amending the law, do not necessarily contribute to improving institutional-administrative capability. In May 1999 legal amendments with an impractical complete ban confronted the evidence of connected lending abuses, thus creating new conditions for laxity or overriding. On the other hand, discipline that markets exert in the aftermath of crises can be excessive and arbitrary.[95] To rebuild market confidence is not an easy challenge. However 'structural-accountability', an objective evaluation of the operation of the institutional framework, particularly the organisations with financial regulatory and the safety-net functions, constitute a good starting point to achieve such goal.

A. *Superintendent of Banks and Superintendent of Companies*

Ecuador has divided the regulatory and supervisory powers and functions respecting the financial system between two institutions. The Superintendent of Banks regulates banking and insurance business and, since 1993, the Superintendent of Companies/Securities Commission has had the control and regulation of securities houses and fund-companies administrators.[96] Institutional arrangements have to ensure compliance

[94] Above n 68, 13.
[95] Ibid. 22.
[96] Separation inspired by US 1933 Glass-Steagall Act model, reviewed in Nov. 1999.

with four major objectives of financial system regulation: systemic risk prevention, prudential regulation enforcement, consumer protection and prevention of fraud. The importance of each of these objectives is connected to the nature of the supervised business. This chapter is not oriented to discuss the general legal framework for financial supervision. It is important to note, nonetheless, several restrictions that surfaced during the crisis and hindered effective responsiveness.

There has been a blurring of the distinctions between different kinds of financial services business, including banks, holding societies, investment firms, insurance companies and others. This has added further to the complexity of financial regulation. On the other hand, financial conglomerates have become significant. The bulk of domestic securities houses and fund-companies have been closely related to the banking system and, indeed, acted with little independence of their parents. While these subsidiaries have been important for 'financial innovation',[97]some have used this innovation to defraud.

Another problem is the operation of 'offshore-banks within a bank' and, also, other companies regulated by local and foreign non-financial supervisors. Firms have taken advantage of limitations in coordination of the separate supervisory bodies, domestic and foreign. Provisions introduced by the Trolebus Law recognised the importance of properly coordinated and consolidated supervision over financial conglomerates. They tried to attenuate defects in information flows that arise with the extended bank secrecy rules. However, this did not overcome all the problems.

Domestically, in the context of a factional-state, the existence of separate institutions might be the source of conflicts between different agencies. On the other hand, the emergent Ecuadorian capital market and the lack of technical and human resources does not justify keeping the responsibilities and powers in separate institutions, especially if it does not ensure better quality of supervision. The great synergies between the roles of prudential supervisors of different financial activities increase the need for them to cooperate to improve understanding of the financial institutions they supervise and, hence, improve the effectiveness of overall supervision. This increasing need for cooperation and coordination may justify the establishment of a single prudential supervisor on the grounds of effectiveness.[98]

Single supervision is seen also as an appropriate response to the uneven quality of supervision and consumer protection across the various finan-

[97] e.g. trusts and adaptive forms of 'securitisation'.

[98] C. Hawkesby, 'The institutional Structure of Financial Supervision: A cost-benefit approach', in *Selected Issues for Financial Safaty Nets and Market Discipline*, ed L. Halme, *et al* (London: Centre for Central Banking Studies, 1999).

cial sectors' traditional lines of business: banking, securities and insurance. A fragmented regulatory structure might generate inconsistencies in approach, insufficient communication or an inadequate overview of regulated firms as more financial conglomerates emerge.[99]

Cross-border supervision creates challenges difficult to overcome. The legal framework is restricted to the domestic level and there exists no such system as a formal supervisor for international banking institutions. It, thus, requires effective coordination and harmonisation of regulatory and supervisory standards[100] and flows of quality information between regulators and the introduction of other tools like lead regulator arrangements and formal agreements between supervisors.

B. *Responsiveness of the State to Banking Failure: Restrictions on Administrative and Legal Instruments*

To provide adequate state capability to deal with individual banks, a legal framework has to establish clear and transparent rules over four major fields. They are lender of last resort—'LOLR', preventive measures, a clear treatment for institutions in the event of definitive closure and a deposit guarantee scheme.

Finally it requires accurate rules and efficient tools and powers for intervention of the State in potential systemic closures.[101] These include balanced coordinating mechanisms among different governmental agencies involved and transparency about allocation of public resources. This is significantly important for Ecuador, with a weak banking system and which has confronted periodical economic crisis that might boost financial instability.

At the same time, an intervention of the State, and specifically the use of public resources, require that the legal framework cope with three major criteria, in order to ensure its optimal use:[102]

(a) Those who benefited from risk taking in the banking activities, that is former shareholders and managers, should absorb, in the first place, any public intervention costs in order to avoid an 'unethical' benefit. Establishing this as a precondition for any public intervention and charging directly former shareholders' equity against the losses generated under their administration does this. Indeed, this needs clear and express legal provisions to divide the public and

[99] C. Briault, *The Rationale for a Single National Financial Services Regulator*, (FSA Occasional Paper Series 2, May 1999.

[100] Indeed, implemented through national legislation.

[101] The 'too big to fail' principle.

[102] De la Torre (1997) quotes these criteria extracted from Rojas-Suarez and Weisbrod (1996).

private interests on the matter and avoid the risk of counter-arguments or legal actions by former shareholders or managers that can weaken, even neutralise, the intended positive effects of a public intervention. This 'ethical' division must be 'eloquent and transparent' in order for any banking overhaul programme to bring discipline and to produce a sound and strong financial system in the long term.[103] However, this division is difficult to achieve as bankers significantly influence public opinion[104] and also have considerable political influence.[105] To avoid 'gridlock', there should be added to this criterion, proper accountability over previous corporate governance[106] including the establishment of criminal offenses and civil damages.

(b) The respective preventive measures should include severe restrictions on the operation of undercapitalised banks, with a special reference to increases in high-risk credit or restructuring of defaulted and moratorium interest through 'fresh' loans, taking advantage of public resources.

(c) Public commitment to opportune assignments for banking intervention, without the loss of control over inflation that such assignment might induce. Albeit, more important then the assignment of public funds might be the opportune intervention of the State endowed with proper failure-instruments. This is relevant for banks, because resource depletions can be overturned, for instance when there is an increase of equity, or with the proper management of the risky assets that caused such depletion; or can been further drained, in the event of a fraud. However, both require major and costly political decisions: First, because politicians are not aware that delay in governmental action only increases fiscal and even political and social costs[107] of the final resolution of the crisis.[108] Second, because the State should also allow some banks to fail. This is important for market discipline,[109] given the existence of practical and efficient mechanisms to avoid systemic risk (eg, LOLR, deposit guarantee schemes, etc.). Finally, there are

103 In Ecuador, e.g., complex 'secretisation' and 'compensation' procedures in the 1980s. These non-transparent bailing-out procedures, in the middle of an undetected banking crisis, did not show reality of financial system or supported opportunely necessary strengthening programmes at the regulatory and corporate level.

104 e.g., ongoing concerns about communications control by former failed bankers, eg, Filanbanco and Progreso.

105 *See* II.B. above.

106 Directors, managers, and even inferior officers.

107 e.g., Progreso in Mar. 1999.

108 Lastra (1996), *Central Banking and Banking Regulation* (London: Financial Markets Group, LSE, 1997), 125.

109 Ibid., 123.

> significant technical difficulties, at the time of the decision, to assess the soundness of a particular institution.[110] Indeed, the decision should be made independently of the existence or suspicion of fraud, which will enhance legal-risk. However, the practical impossibility at the time of the intervention to determine fraudulent conduct should be covered by the requirement of proper accountability, suggested in the first criterion.

After the enactment of the banking-law in 1994, there have been several amendments that affected banking restructuring in Ecuador. Analysis of the legal framework for the different fields requires some precise respect for its timing.

1. Financial Regulatory Function and the Lender of Last Resort: the Central Bank of Ecuador and the Superintendent of Banks

Typically three main reasons are put forward to justify regulation of the financial system: (a) to protect customers against monopolistic exploitation; (b) to protect smaller, retail, and, thus, less informed investors or depositors; and, (c) to ensure systemic stability. In the first two cases, is clear that the main interest of the regulators will be consumer protection, which is made through prudential regulation. Goodhart noted,

> both prudential and systemic regulation need to be distinguished, although both adopt similar approach. Systemic regulation is about the safety and soundness of financial institutions for purely systemic reasons (i.e. because the social costs of the failure of an institution exceed the private costs). On the other hand, prudential regulation is about the safety and soundness of financial institutions vis-à-vis consumer protection, in that the consumer loses when an institution fails, even if there are no systemic consequences.[111]

Systemic regulation concentrates on the potential runs that even solvent banks can suffer, derived from lack of confidence. A bank run might have contagion effects, which can throw other solvent banks into insolvency. This risk justifies systemic regulation:

> The probability that the failure of a single bank will induce a systemic problem may be low, but, if systemic failure were to occur, it could be serious and the costs could be high. Thus regulation to prevent systemic problems may be viewed as an insurance premium against a low probability occurrence.[112]

The low-occurrence probability and the high costs mean that determination of systemic risk might lack objective measurement. It will depend on the

110 Intervention timing relies on the technical and administrative responsiveness.
111 Above n 74, 2.
112 Ibid.

personal evaluation of the regulators. Illiquidity in a particular bank can be avoided with confidence recovery, provided opportune liquidity supply (through LOLR) and that professional and transparent banking governance has appropriately managed risks. This is precisely the engaging point between systemic and prudential regulation. Systemic regulation has been practically administered by central banks mainly through the LOLR function. LOLR implies, among other issues, that central banks should prevent temporarily illiquid, but solvent, banks from failing, through short-term lending and make clear readiness to lend freely, in advance, to the financial system.[113]

While the regulations imposed for systemic and prudential reasons may be similar (eg, the establishment of capital requirements), they do not need to be (nor should they be) conducted by the same agency. In the event of separate institutions, both will share common concerns about financial system stability but their approach will be different: systemic versus prudential; general macroeconomic concerns versus a strictly consumer protection bias (micro).

Although it is still most common for central banks also to be banking supervisors, over the last decade a number of countries have moved this function outside the central bank.[114] Many scholars count several advantages and disadvantages of both models but do not have definitive conclusions.[115] The recent developments in international and financial markets have forced consolidated financial regulation (over banking, securities and insurance) in one supervisory body outside central banks.[116] In the specific case of developing countries, however, there are suggestions to keep the banking supervision role as a responsibility of central banks. Lastra argues that the scarcity of economists and financial analysts in most developing countries could justify having the supervisory agency under the umbrella of the central bank.[117] The difficulties to create efficient and politically independent governmental agencies and their huge costs also confirm the rationale for consolidation of systemic and prudential capabilities in emerging economies in central banks. Hawkbesky[118] counts other factors determining the feasibility of the separate or single model of banking and systemic regulation. Among them are the extent of activity by financial conglomerates and

113 R. Lastra, 'Central banks as lenders of last resort: Lessons from the Asian contagion', in *Journal of Financial Regulation and Compliance*, 1999, vol. 7, No 3, quoting Thornton (1802) and Bagehot (1873).

114 For international practices *see* eg above n 98.

115 *See* e.g. C. Goodhart, and D. Schoenmaker, *Institutional Separation Between Supervisory and Monetary Agencies*, (Financial Markets Group, LSE, London, Apr. 1993).

116 UK Financial Services Authorities ongoing conformation has become a model. In this case, the Bank of England transferred bank supervisory functions and clearly kept LOLR and systemic regulation.

117 Lastra (1996).

118 Above n 98.

the size of the financial sector; objectives of supervision; degree of independence of the central bank, technical ability and eventuality of conflicts with monetary policy. Last are political considerations, like the degree of uncertainty that surrounds the economic costs and benefits of alternative regimes, which mainly depend on the recent history of the country in question. About this latter, Goodhart argues that, if there have been recent problems in the banking industry, for whatever reason, there may be a temptation for the government to make changes to supervisory responsibilities. By doing this, they are seen by the public to be addressing the problem, regardless of whether the reform redress any weakness there was in the old regime, and regardless of whether the old regime contributed to the original problems.

Kemmerer in the 1920s suggested the establishment in Ecuador of two separate institutions.[119] The Central Bank of Ecuador (CBE) was created in 1927, with stability of prices as a constitutional main goal. Until March 1999, monetary policy and the lender of last resort function have been CBE major instruments to duly perform its constitutional functions. Meanwhile, the Superintendent of Banks (SB) is responsible for prudential regulation and consumer protection. The separation, as noted, cannot evade strong boundaries between both institutions, thus the law has established mechanisms to 'coordinate' the 'separate' model: the Superintendent of Banks assists CBE Directorate sessions while the CBE Governor is a Banking Board member. The existence of the separation model, by itself, might even weaken regulatory and supervisory capability in the event that legal and institutional framework overlaps, distorts or even overrides the separate functions. This might be the case of Ecuador.

Until March 2000, LOLR legal provisions were contained in articles 24 and 25 of the Monetary Law. In order to be effective, LOLR has two operational principles: LOLR role is discretionary, not mandatory; and the central bank assesses not only whether the situation is illiquid or insolvent, but also whether the failure of an institution can trigger by contagion the failure or other institutions.[120] However, in Ecuador legally the SB was empowered with assessing the illiquidity or insolvency of the borrower, as a previous requirement for the loan concession, so that discretionality over LOLR assistance was extensively restrained. CBE opposition to this external 'interference' could be considered irresponsible, if not illegal. Additionally, under banking law provisions, the lender does not have the

[119] Whereas the separation model in South America was restricted to countries with Kemmerer performance in the Pacific coast, British missions visiting the Atlantic coast (eg, Argentina) encouraged the former 'Bank of England' model, with supervisors just as a unit, thus ensuring close coordination among monetary and financial policies.

[120] R. Lastra, 'Central banks as lenders of last resort: Lessons from the Asian contagion', in *Journal of Financial Regulation and Compliance*, 1999, vol 7, no 3.

authority to make any direct surveillance of the resource allocation and borrowers performance, and has to rely on *in situ* supervision made also, directly or through qualified external auditors, by the Superintendent of Banks. Other problems arose from the limited tools and legal instruments for the CBE to intervene in the banking overhaul and financial stability programmes, in particular from the 'veto-power' discussed later.

This is despite the evident interactions and boundaries between LOLR/systemic regulation and prudential supervision. Financial instability definitely threatened the independent monetary policy function. In other jurisdictions (the UK, for instance), the law provides not only that central banks effectively intervene in financial policy, but also *that the financial regulator is accountable to the central bank for their actions.*[121]

The consequence of overlapping and overriding operations is the definite weakening of *both* institutions. All this affects regulatory transparency and shuffles accountability. In March 1999, the SB assessed Progreso for LCLR credit, but the CBE did not grant them immediately but rather with an insistent requirement of further information. Taking advantage of the opportunity, Progreso underpinned by the SB report, publicly denounced CBE 'illegal' acts. Progreso unilaterally suspended payments, moreover, without an immediate intervention of the supervisory authority and seizure by the DGA, as the law expressly provided, thus boosting generalised concerns about the fairness of the regulators' procedures.[122] With uncertainty around the banking system already present[123], the weird closure of the largest bank in the country triggered a systemic problem that directly affected other institutions that were confronting stability threats. Systemic risk prevention, prudential supervision and consumer protection goals were not achieved. The public lack of confidence in the institutional arrangements triggered generalised financial panic.

The Trolebus Law and the dollarisation programme in March 2000 have eliminated the CBE's monetary policy capabilities and the old LOLR-function.[124] This has also introduced a 'liquidity fund', originally to be administered by the CBE. However at the time of concluding this chapter, it had not yet been implemented and there is still discussion about the proper administrator of the fund.

A bill in the US Congress, the International Monetary Stability Act of 1999, in order to encourage emerging-market countries to use the dollar as

121 Paradoxically recently the Superintendent of Banks 'intervened' Central Bank in order to override an administrative resolution of the CBE Board, despite the fact that the law provides that he does not have the right to vote in the Directory.

122 Formal intervention was delayed for almost three months.

123 Several banks have already failed and in early March, a deposits-freezing was ordered.

124 Dollarisation implies the CBE cannot issue 'domestic currency', so LOLR depends exclusively on fiscal sources.

their official currency[125] makes it explicitly clear that the United States *would have no obligation to serve as a lender of last resort to dollarised countries* or to *exercise supervision over their financial institutions*. This confirms that, even in the context of the dollarisation, efficiency with regard to the LOLR mechanism (whatever it is) and capable regulatory bodies are still essential to ensure financial stability. On the other hand, the CBE is still entrusted with the management of the system of payments. Thus CBE systemic-risk prevention responsibilities have not been removed. However, the Trolebus Law has not addressed the complexities regarding these arrangements referred herein.

2. Preventive Measures

There should be sufficient preventive measures, rules and powers to address: deficiencies in applicable capital adequacy standards, other corporate or administrative irregularities that can increase the failure risk of a financial institution, and the committing of fraud. These should be of a non-discretional nature, to eliminate abuses by the authorities, but also to give them an unquestionable legal support to enforce decisions.

Prior banking statutes provided broad discretionary rules, including the appointment of intervenors which deregulation restricted to a minimum. The SB was allowed to impose restrictions on investments and new credits, but only in the case of inadequacy of capital standards. Suspension of payments by a bank, until July 1996, was not even a cause for the SB to intervene or for liquidation.[126] SB powers were given only through the concession of short terms (90 and 30 days) in order for the institutions to properly adjust equity.

The creation of the restructuring programme by the DGA Law, in December 1998, reinserted some Banking Board discretion for preventive measures, but restricted it to restructuring-programme institutions.[127] In May 1999, another incomplete reform reintroduced the SB's capability to appoint broad-powered intervenors, albeit without improving the general preventive-measures framework.

The Trolebus Law (March 2000) has provided further and broader reform. It included discretionary measures and regularisation programmes to be exercised by the authorities, in particular, a duty to 'intervene' in any undercapitalised institution and, for the first time, a valuable mechanism to temporarily control bank stakes until the bank solves the problem. However, due to the range of discretion provided, it expands legal risk for authorities, as treated in section 2.5, and room for legal actions that might neutralise the same measures.

[125] *See* details in <http://www.rs9.loc.gov/cgi-bin/bdquery/z?d106:h.r.03493>.

[126] Clear insolvency warning.

[127] *See* III.C. above.

3. The Deposit Guarantee Scheme

It is necessary to count with clear treatment for institutions in the event of definitive closure, in order to ensure ordered and efficient liquidation and even winding-up procedures.

Until December 1998, the only mechanism supplied in the event of a failure was closure followed by an administrative winding-up of the institution. Despite the 1994 bank reform's introduction of a 'creditors-board' for its administration, the mechanism had been kept strictly controlled by the SB, which appointed liquidation-administrators and was even empowered to conform such creditor-boards. Historically, liquidations have generated long bureaucratic administrative procedures, which have not been publicly and transparently accounted. Nor have cost-benefit analyses been applied to evaluate results.

The expectation of negative results from the closure of a bank has permanently increased the lack of confidence in the system. For example, in 1996, if Continental, the fifth largest in the system at the time, had fallen, the opportunities to rebuild such public confidence would have been limited in the scope of the regular liquidations.

Thus, to give some comfort to customers and prevent instability caused by mass withdrawal, a proper deposit guarantee scheme is also required. This might take the form of a restricted state guarantee for small savers; a priority for depositors over other creditors; or a deposit insurance.[128] Its existence, at the same time, forces the improvement of regulation to avoid pernicious moral hazard. In Ecuador, over time, it has been coexisting or successively adopted in the three forms.

First, between 1994 and July 1998, there was a limited 'small-savers' priority over the rest of the depositors and other creditors, and up to 2000 UVC[129] were always paid in full. Then, a short-lived deposit guarantee scheme was enacted in July 1998. This scheme was not even initially endowed by the financial system, as was provided by the law. However, even if it had been duly financed, there was needed a longer period (up to 2 years) to fully capitalise the fund, long after the time the crisis arose. For small-savers the former priority scheme was retained.

The lack of a proper deposit guarantee scheme probably upgraded the uncertainty that already yielded the financially unstable environment of the last months of 1998. The consequences of the failure, closure and liquidation of another medium-sised institution, 'Prestamos', in September 1998, might have induced urgency for the authorities to fill the existing practical gaps. The result was the introduction of the DGA Bill to the Congress,

128 R. Cranston, *Principles of Banking Law* (Oxford: Clarendon Press, 1997), 78.
129 An account unit linked to inflation rates.

which originally considered a state-guarantee, which protected up to 3000 UVC and restricted its application to a 3-year period. The proposed guarantee was going to be initially and immediately covered with public resources, in order to attenuate the social impact of the 'forecasted' systemic crisis. The state, through an *independent* agency as conceived in the Bill, the DGA, was going to be repaid in full with the efficient and effective disposal of assets of the closed financial institutions. The law, enacted by the Congress in December 1998, broke this theoretical framework and may have caused even further financial instability and uncertainty.

First, Congress enacted an unlimited period and an unlimited amount for the state-guarantee. In the context of insolvency, no unlimited guarantee scheme could be properly financed, as the reason for such insolvency is precisely the existence of insufficient assets to cover all liabilities. Therefore, the losses (simply, the excesses of liabilities over assets) were transferred to the 'guarantor', in this case, the state. Moreover, the law introduced a central bank duty to discount fiscal bonds (DGA bonds) in order to ensure the availability of public resources at anytime. The latter created a significant distortion to constitutionally recognised central bank independence and forced the monetary authority to provide unrestricted resources to cover the 'losses' of the financial system in the context of a systemic crisis. Most international and national analysts now consider that this was the trigger for the inflation spiral and unstoppable exchange devaluation that was followed by dollarisation. At the same time, after natural restrictions imposed by the central bank, first voluntarily, and secondly, with the stringent rules of the dollarisation, the absolute inefficiency of such a scheme to protect consumers was proved. In March 2000, the Trolebus Law also moved back to the initial proposal, albeit this will be possible only within specific terms.

A second unexpected change, introduced by the Congress in the Bill, related to the independence of the DGA entrusted to perform specific functions related to the effective disposal of assets. The composition of its directory board was amended and the Superintendent was empowered with an unexplainable 'veto power' that surrendered the 'financing' members to the banking regulatory authority.[130] The third unusual element was the restructuring programmes not included in the original bill, to be discussed next.

4. Intervention of the State

Ecuador has not had mechanisms for intervention with public resources that fulfil the three above-referred criteria, even before the bank reform of 1994. These mechanisms have been the following:

First, until August 1998, subordinated loans were the only possible

130 *See* 3.4.

mechanism to intervene with public-funds. This was the case in 1996, when the Central Bank intervened Continental on behalf of the State. In order to frame this 'intervention' to meet first criteria, the loan was conditioned on the whole bank's stake to be transferred to a trust, for two main purposes: (a) to ensure the control of the bank by the state; and, (b) to make certain that losses caused by former management were going to be charged directly to shareholders, thus not affecing public-funds.

This 'legal-stretched' public intervention structure had several problems. First, the loan and the trust agreement had to be 'negotiated' forcedly with the administration involved in the failure. The law, at the time, did not contain any provision for authorities to take immediate control, nor even to impose an intervention (not even in the event of the suspension of payments). The state was overburdened by obtaining a 'voluntary' agreement from the shareholders, in order to avoid forecasted systemic risk. Secondly, after the intervention, central bank administration revealed that equity was already negative at the time of the state-intervention. It was forced to conduct further investigations in order to prepare and initiate effective legal actions for remedies. Although there was evidence of excessive connected lending and fraud was civilly prosecuted under the RICO Act in US courts, Ecuadorian law did not provide sufficient instruments, neither civil nor criminal, to impose proper penalties, without repeating damage to the concerned companies. Thirdly, and probably the most damaging for administrative capability of the state, was the shuffling of responsibilities of former managers and shareholders with public officials by the Supreme Court President in 1996. This promoted judiciary interference and conflict with the technical and discretionary powers of the authorities.[131] Fourth, the restricted period provided in the law for the subordinated-lender to own the resulting stake did not allow a proper overhauling of the bank.[132]

Secondly, the December 1998 DGA Law introduced two new forms of intervention: the first, contemplated in the original bill, was the overhaul-proceeding ('*saneamiento*'). The second, introduced by the Congress was the restructuring-programme ('*reestructuracion*').

In the first, the criterion about former shareholders assuming costs was met, as the state could immediately control the stake, even cancelling, if necessary. However, due to the distortions of the unlimited guarantee, there was no means to keep inflationary controls in place (third criterion). There was an excessive concentration of responsibilities over the Superintendent. More significant were the overlapping and overriding caused by the veto-power.[133] Other major difficulties were restrictions to proper management of

131 *See* II.D. and II.E. above.
132 A special law in 1997 allowed the CBE to keep this stake up to seven years.
133 *See* the following section.

assets and avoidance of banking closures, which deterred rapid and effective responsiveness in order to redress public confidence and spare public funds.

The conditions of restructuring-programmes have not varied, except for the non-compliance with first criterion: public funds were able to be 'invested', but former managers and shareholders have kept their rights to them and, unreasonably, even control. This was applied in practice to only one case: Filanbanco.[134]

Thirdly, in May 1999 Congress removed public resource allocation through restructuring-programmes. However there were no major changes to improve responsiveness in the case of failure except the reposition of the interventors appointment. In July, another Bill was prepared to strengthen supervision and ensure the existence of an independent agency and more effective instruments of intervention. But it failed and further legal-stretched interventions in the very next days (Previsora, Pacifico and Popular) were underpinned again on a subordinated loan, with the only difference that it was possible to appoint directly interventors.

In March 2000, the Trolebus Law broadened the conditions related to subordinated loans, and established clearer procedures to address damages from connected companies and former shareholders. However this evidently depends on the efficiency of the judiciary.

There are major problems derived from this 'legal-stretched' state-intervention framework. First, Ecuador shows several cases where delayed or weak intervention has allowed former managers/controllers to make 'adequate' accounting and legal documents and, even to divert resources. Secondly, further legal risk is added, especially because there is no clear division-line between the regulators and the bank-managers. Third, without an independent body to manage such state interventions, there is either lack of coordination or overlapping of functions. The objectives of a public intervention, to prevent systemic risk and regain public confidence are lost if the rules are not clear. The conflicts that the DGE law aimed to avoid, were not only kept, but increased through the introduction of three major changes: the unlimited guarantee, the restructuring-programmes and the veto-power.

C. *The Relative Powers of the State* vis-à-vis *the Superintendent*

The requirement of an individual favourable vote for the validity of a collective decision-making process is deemed as a veto-power. The Superintendent does have veto-powers in both major collective-boards entrusted with financial regulation and overhauling: in the Banking Board and in the DGA Board. Effects of a veto-power are:

[134] However the shareholders 'voluntarily' resigned their rights and consigned some personal assets in order to cover the losses of the Bank. This case has generated further controversies and legal actions during June 2000.

- It distorts democratisation of collective decision-making *vis-à-vis* individuals. Other board members are solely entitled to oppose, even if they have majority.
- It complicates the decision-making process and sometimes renders the reaching of a decision impossible.
- Impartiality and technicality regularly achieved through it is lost, as the veto-empowered personal opinion might deter a free decision-making process.
- Objective accountability and responsibility among board members is distorted, overburdened and shuffled. It will be necessary to account individual decisions to determine degree of responsibilities. A veto-empowered impartial negative-vote might be seen as an 'obstacle' for a majority-decision, instead of a mean to restrict personal responsibility. Vice-versa, veto-power implies that the majority cannot object unfair decisions, so that they might be accountable for the omission of the collective body.

The Ecuadorian framework offers a successful form of the collective decision-making procedure. The CBE Board decision-making process requires majorities, without any privilege for any member. On the other hand, monetary law distinguishes policy-maker's[135] from executor's capabilities.[136] The executor does not have a vote in the CBE Board, so that the board constitutes the real policymaker. This separation, on the other hand, ensures the existence of an impartial and technical 'accountee', in the event of non-compliance of specific policies by the 'executor'.

Meanwhile, the SB policy-maker is a five-member Banking Board, which includes a veto-empowered and executor Superintendent.[137] Then the Banking Board is not a real independent policy-maker body, nor a proper 'accountee', because the veto-power turns the Superintendent into judge of its own actions, in the context of routine financial system supervision.

The situation in the DGA is more relevant: the DGA was conceived as an independent body provided with tools to efficiently manage financial instability. This undoubtedly requires coordination of three different policymaking processes: monetary, fiscal and strictly financial. In the first case, because the system of payments might be affected by systemic risk or even by the closure of individual institutions, thus affecting monetary programmes especially due to the LOLR function. A banking crisis, on the other hand, forces use of public-funds or its reorientation, in order to restore stability. Moreover, the unlimited DGA guarantee formerly

135 Entrusted to the CBE Board.

136 Charged to the Governor and officials of the CBE.

137 This is nowadays shuffled, as the Trolebus Law entitled the Superintendent with many discretional policy-maker functions.

discussed, primarily depended on fiscal-sources. Finally, stability restoration evidently requires special financial regulation and strengthening of the supervision capability.

The introduction of the veto-power submitted monetary and fiscal policies to the actions and omissions of the Superintendent[138] and unfairly shuffles accountability among all institutions involved. This also deters impartial accountability over financial stability policies. Another practical effect is that in the event of a systemic crisis, state-responsiveness is confined to a solely non-accountable official. In the context of the factional-state largely discussed in this chapter, controlling a single public official is much simpler, than controlling multiple institutions and individuals.

IV. CONCLUSIONS

This chapter has dealt with the recent and to some extent ongoing financial crisis in Ecuador. It has analysed the institutional underpinnings surrounding the crisis and has evidenced weakness in the financial system in the country.

There are two readings of the origin of the crisis: one simple and superficial that blames a decade of macroeconomic instability and the 'lack' of economic reform. The second reading might be more realistic. General conditions of the economy prevailing during the last decade cannot be removed. Albeit the crisis origin lies beyond it, as structural weaknesses not restricted solely to the financial system, but also to political and economic interactions, have not allowed building public confidence. Poor macroeconomic results and financial instability might just be result of this. The ongoing dollarisation process is the recognition of the state failure in achieving political independent monetary control due to interminable interference by particular economic interests. The Brady default is also result of lack of structured and long-term governmental policy choices that might have ensured reliable economic growth and equitable wealth distribution.

Abuses in allocation of credit are not new in Ecuadorian history, however its effects have virulently surfaced in the context of open and globalised competitive international markets. At the time of crisis, rather than having a private sector assuming responsibilities about decision-making, further political pressures have been imposed in order to 'socialise' their losses at the expense of the whole society. In the context of the economic reform in Ecuador, building up capabilities and regulation enforcement cannot be taken for granted. Governmental responses addressed by political considerations and private interests have added complexities to the ongoing financial crisis, rather than redressing existing conflicts and strengthening regulator capacities.

138 This even infringed the constitutional central bank independence.

Financial regulator capability in order to ensure proper enforcement also requires other elements beyond just improving technical and economic resources or successfully introducing international financial standards. Judiciary deficiencies on financial matters imply huge, but hidden, moral and economic costs that might also be transferred to the society. Legal risk is increased in the context of a factional-state and extensive bank secrecy rules. Institutional overlapping and overriding is another way to increase factional-state deficiencies.

Complete and balanced accountability and disclosure of public and private actions is the best way to support the legal framework and to improve legitimacy and responsiveness of the State in the financial system. Without transparency and fairness it is not possible to bring improvement to the ongoing structural anarchy.

PART IV

Financial Reform following the East Asian Crises

Chapter 16

China's Financial Reform and its Implications

Chuanjie Li

China's financial system shares the same characteristics as those in most other Asian countries, such as Japan, Korean, and Thailand; which is to say, the financial system in China is banking-dominated. By the end of 1998, the total assets of China's financial institutions (excluding insurance companies and securities companies) were RMB15.03 trillion, among which the assets of four large state banks were RMB9.5 trillion, other commercial banks RMB1.68 trillion, three policy banks RMB1.38 trillion, urban and rural credit cooperatives RMB1.65 trillion, investment and trust companies RMB0.54 trillion and foreign banks RMB0.28 trillion.

It is worth noting, however, that the market share of banking assets in 1998 was the smallest compared to the shares in previous years. It is evident that banks, the four large state banks in particular collectively, play such a dominant role in China's financial landscape that it is justified to say that how successful the banking reform is should be the most important indicator as to whether the financial reform succeeds or not. Therefore, the focus

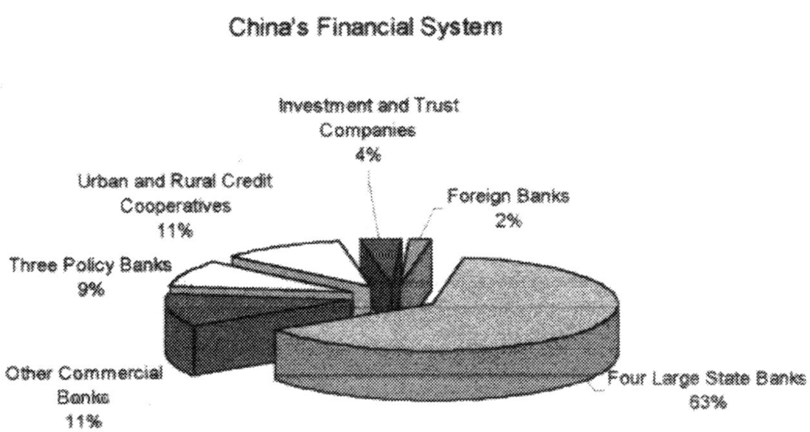

of this discussion is on China's four large state banks. This chapter reviews three stages of China's financial reform as carried out from 1978 through 1999, examines four major problems that the 1999 reforms will face, and assesses the implications of these reforms to the Chinese financial system. This assessment shows where more reforms are needed and how law-based reforms should be integrated with other reforms to support a market economy and social stability.

I. THREE STAGES OF BANKING SYSTEM REFORM

In 1978, China embarked on a gradual but far-reaching reform of its economic system. Since then, China's economy has been significantly modernised and opened to the rest of the world. The concept of reform underwent a dramatic change in November 1993 when the Third Plenum of the Fourteenth Central Committee outlined and approved a comprehensive reform strategy aimed at achieving a breakthrough in China's efforts to transform its economy into a socialist market economy.[1] In 1997, the Asian financial crisis posed a new challenge to China's economic reform. This chapter, coinciding with the broad economic reform phases, divides the banking system reform into the following three stages: from 1978 to November 1993, from November 1993 to November 1997, and from November 1997 to the present.

A. *Stage One: 1978–November 1993*

In 1978, under the leadership of late Deng Xiaoping, China began its economic reform and opening up to the outside world. China's central bank, the People's Bank of China was created out of the Ministry of Finance in November 1979. However, since its inception the People's Bank of China had assumed the responsibilities of both a central bank and a commercial bank until 1 January 1984 when a new bank, the Industrial and Commercial Bank of China was established to take over the People's Bank of China deposit-taking and lending functions. Soon the Industrial and Commercial Bank became China's largest bank (measured by assets). In March 1979, the Bank of China was separated from the People's Bank of China to become an independent entity. This bank was designed to support China's economic opening to the outside world. Currently it is the second largest bank in China (measured by assets). The third largest bank

[1] Central Committee of Communist Party of China, Decision of the Third Plenum of the Fourteenth Central Committee on Issues Concerning the Establishment of Socialist Market Structure (Nov. 1993).

(measured by assets), China Construction Bank, was set up in 1979. It specialises in supporting infrastructure projects and in long term fixed asset investment. The Agricultural Bank of China, which focuses on deposit and lending activities in rural areas, was reestablished in February 1979 as a separate bank. Now it is China's fourth largest bank (measured by assets).[2]

After the frame of China's financial structure was established, China continued forming more banks in the following decade. These banks are China Investment Bank (originally created in 1981 to control the disbursement of project funds provided to China by the World Bank and by the Asian Development Bank, but was acquired later in March 1999 by China Everbright Bank), the Bank of Communications (a joint stock bank created in 1986), Shenzhen Development Bank (created in 1987 with its shares listed on the Shenzhen Stock Exchange), Merchants Bank (created in 1987 with its headquarters in Shenzhen), Yantai Housing Savings Bank (created in 1987 with its headquarters in Yantai, Shandong Province to meet the needs of China's housing market development), Bengbu Housing Savings Bank (created in the same year as the Yantai Housing Savings Bank with its headquarters in Bengbu, Anhui Province), Guangdong Development Bank (created in 1988 with most business in Guangdong Province), Fujian Industrial Bank (created in 1988 with most activities in Fujian Province), Shanghai Pudong Development Bank (created in 1988 with head office in Pudong Economic Development Zone in Shanghai City), Huaxia Bank (created in 1992 with headquarters in Beijing) and China Everbright Bank (created in 1992 and converted to a joint stock form of ownership in 1995).

During this period, these Chinese banks, especially the four state banks, were major players in allocating relatively scarce capital and assisting unusually rapid economic growth. But because of their dual roles in policy lending and in commercial lending, many critical problems existed in these banks (and still exist today), such as a relatively low rate of capital adequacy, lower loan loss reserves as compared to assets, substantial share of non-performing loans and low rate of return on assets. Besides, the semi-governmental nature and the quasi-monopolistic position of these banks made them less diligent in improving management. As a result, operation costs climbed year after year while productivity dropped over time. These problems had deteriorated the financial health of these banks to such a great extent that they even threatened the survival and development of China's overall economy.

2 *See* NICHOLAS R. LARDY, CHINA'S UNFINISHED ECONOMIC REVOLUTION 62–63 (1998). According to a survey in 1995, the total assets of the Industrial and Commercial Bank of China, Bank of China, Agricultural Bank of China, and Construction of China were RMB8,056.3 billion, 3,107.5 billion, 1,995.1 billion, and 1,722.7 billion, respectively. *See* ibid. at 224.

B. Stage Two: November 1993–November 1997

In November 1993 China's ruling party formulated an important document, the Decision on Establishment of Socialist Market Economy. One month later the State Council instituted another important document, the Decision on Reform of Financial System. These two documents demonstrated China's determination to develop a market–oriented economy and to establish a modern commercial banking system.[3] For the next four years a series of measures were taken to achieve these goals.

First, in order to independently and prudently supervise, regulate and inspect China's banks and other financial institutions, in an unprecedented move, beginning in 1994 the People's Bank of China refused to lend money to the Ministry of Finance to cover the state's budget deficit.[4] Later, the People's Bank of China discontinued its practice of lending money to non-financial institutions. Then the head office of the central bank successfully gained full control of credit the People's Bank of China extended to financial institutions. Previously, provincial and lower-level branch offices of the People's Bank of China controlled about 30 per cent of all the bank lending. Since there is a close connection between these branch offices and local government (for example, the local government usually has say over the appointment of important bank positions), it is obvious that these branch offices are quite vulnerable to the influences of government officials. This abnormal situation was dramatically changed by the recentralisation of the authority for all lending and the allocation of credit quotas of the People's Bank of China. Furthermore, the People's Bank of China was stripped of running all its business subsidiaries. In March 1995 the Law of the People's Bank of China was enacted and made effective immediately, indicating the independence and authority of the People's Bank of China as China's central bank was legitimately established.

Secondly, as part of a long-term plan to convert the state banks to commercial banks, the State Council in 1994 approved the creation of three new policy banks, the State Development Bank of China, the Import–Export Bank of China, and the Agricultural Development Bank of China. These new institutions were to provide financing for policy-oriented projects identified in the state's development plan or in its industrial policies for specific sectors. The State Development Bank is the largest of these new institutions with registered capital of RMB50 billion. Its main purpose is to finance long-term infrastructure projects and strategic industries.[5] The second largest policy bank is the Agricultural Development Bank of China

[3] *See* ibid. at 180.

[4] *See* ibid. at 174.

[5] *See* State Council, *Notice Concerning the Establishment of the State Development Bank*, 10 BULLETIN OF THE STATE COUNCIL OF THE PEOPLE'S REPUBLIC OF CHINA 393–6 (June 1994).

with registered capital of RMB20 billion. Its primary role is to provide short-term credit to state agencies responsible for the procurement of agricultural products, but it also provides funds for projects that assist the poor in rural areas as well as general agricultural development projects.[6] The Import–Export Bank, with registered capital of RMB3.38 billion, is the smallest of the new institutions. It was created primarily to provide export sellers' credit to promote the international sale of Chinese goods, particularly electrical machinery and equipment. But it also provides guarantee of export buyers' credit and export credit insurance.[7] In addition, the bank has assumed responsibility for handling the concessionary loans that China receives from most industrialised countries and the concessionary loans that China makes primarily to countries in Africa and Latin America.[8] Despite the fact that at present the state banks act as agents to conduct most businesses for two out of the three policy banks (the other one is the Agricultural Development Bank of China), state banks are not responsible for any profit or loss associated with these businesses.

In the meanwhile, China made great efforts to strengthen its legal system in order to keep up with the ongoing financial reform. In 1995 four important laws were enacted: the Law of the People's Bank of China, the Commercial Bank Law, the Insurance Law and the Negotiable Instruments Law. The much stronger legal structure was designed to regulate the activities of banks along with the activities of other financial institutions, give banks operational independence and outlaw local political interference.

C. *Stage Three: November 1997–The Present*

The outbreak of the Asian financial crisis in 1997 was a wakeup call for China leaders. They realised that major problems that caused the crisis existing in Japan, Korea, Thailand, and Malaysia, such as the weak banking system, a large portion of policy loans and insufficient loan loss reserves, were not uncommon in China. Though China has not been involved in the crisis, the main reason is that its domestic currency is not convertible for capital account transactions. On 17 November 1997 a high level National Financial Work Conference was held in Beijing to discuss China's financial system and the possible solutions to fight crisis. It was at this meeting that China decided to take about three years to establish a Socialist market economy-compatible financial institution system, financial market system and financial regulatory and supervisory system. The goal was to improve China's financial institutions' management, bring back

[6] *See* NICHOLAS R. LARDY, above n 2, at 177.

[7] *See* YUAN CHEN, ALMANAC OF CHINA'S FINANCE AND BANKING (English edition) 47–8 (1995).

[8] *See* NICHOLAS R. LARDY, above n 2, at 176.

soundness and order to China's financial community and enhance China's immunisation from financial crisis. As discussed below, a series of reforms were immediately carried out right after the three-day meeting.

In January 1998, the People's Bank of China abolished the quota lending system that had been implemented in China for as long as half a century[9] and converted it to an asset/liability ratio management system.[10] The quota lending system had strict control over the maximum amounts of loans that could be made and the minimum amounts of loans that had to be disbursed to designated sectors and industries on an annual basis, while the asset/liability ratio management relates banks' permitted lending to their deposit base. According to the new system, banks may use new deposits to make loans on commercial principles after they set aside reserves, return borrowed funds to the central bank and subscribe for government bonds. The central bank outlined a basket of asset/liability ratios from the standpoint of risk control. The commercial banks are allowed to formulate their own ratio system based on the guidelines of the central bank. The most important ratios are: (1) overdue loans, doubtful loans and bad debt shall not exceed 8 per cent, 5 per cent and 2 per cent of total loans, respectively; (2) total loans shall not make up more than 75 per cent of total deposits; (3) the ratio of medium- and long-term loans denominated in domestic currency with a maturity of over one year to total deposits denominated in domestic currency with a maturity of over one year shall not be more than 120 per cent; (4) loans made to any single borrower and to the ten largest borrowers shall not exceed 10 per cent and 50 per cent of banks' net worth, respectively; (5) the assets denominated in domestic currency with residual maturity of 30 days or less or other marketable assets shall be at least 25 per cent of the liabilities denominated in domestic currency with residual maturity of 30 days or less; (6) current assets shall not be lower than 25 per cent of current liabilities; (7) interbank borrowing shall not exceed 40 per cent of total deposits and interbank lending shall not be more than 8 per cent of total deposits; (8) cash and reserves denominated in domestic currency which are placed in the central bank shall not be lower than 5 per cent of total deposits denominated in domestic

[9] *See* People's Bank of China, *Circular Concerning Improvement of Administration of Loan Scope of State-Owned Commercial Banks*, 41 BULLETIN OF THE PEOPLE'S BANK OF CHINA, 3–6 (13 Feb. 1998).

[10] As a matter of fact, as early as Feb. 1994, the People's Bank of China issued the Guidelines on the Regulation of Assets and Liabilities Ratio of Commercial Banks. In Dec. 1996, the People's Bank of China published the Monitoring Norms and Assessment Methods for the Regulation of Assets and Liabilities Ratio of Commercial Banks, which revised the Guidelines on the Regulation of Assets and Liabilities Ratio of Commercial Banks. PEOPLE'S BANK OF CHINA, MONITORING NORMS AND ASSESSMENT METHODS FOR THE REGULATION OF ASSETS AND LIABILITIES (Dec. 1996) [hereinafter MONITORING NORMS FOR ASSETS AND LIABILITIES]. One year later, the Instructions for Completing Reporting Forms for Off-Site Examination issued by the People's Bank of China amended the above two rules.

currency; and (9) the average maturity of securities purchased shall not exceed 5 years and those securities with maturity longer than 5 years shall not exceed 30 per cent of the total securities purchased.[11]

The asset/liability ratio management is a big step forward compared to the old quota lending system. However we can see that by nature it is a liability management, ie, a system about how to attract and manage deposits rather than how to manage assets and deposits dynamically. Therefore it is an early stage of modern asset liability management.

To improve Chinese banks' capital ratios, in May 1998 the Ministry of Finance issued RMB45 billion in special government bonds to give as capital to the commercial banks (excluding the four state banks).[12] On the 28 February 1998, the National Congress empowered the Ministry of Finance to issue special RMB270 billion to recapitalise the four state banks.[13] This paralleled the reduction of about the same amount of cash in the banking system as the deposit reserve ratio was lowered from 13 per cent to 8 per cent by the central bank in March 1998.[14]

The magnitude of non-performing loans of China's state banks was increasing in the mid-1990s,[15] and has since posed a crucial challenge for restoring the financial health of China's banks. Since 1994, China has conducted experiments in a new loan classification system called 'Five-Grade Credit System'.[16] In April 1998, the People's Bank of China issued Guiding Principles for Loan Risk Classification (trial implementation) to officially introduce the Five-Grade Credit System. The new method classifies loans based on their credit risk rather than on their payment status, which was the method used by the old system for a long time.

Before 1994 each of the major banks in China had its own system and standards for classifying non-performing loans. However, the biggest flaw shared by these systems was that there were ceilings on the portion of loans that could be classified, irrespective of the actual quality of a bank's loan portfolio. Then in 1995, the People's Bank of China set forth a universal—yet rather simple—loan classification system. Under this system, classified

11 MONITORING NORMS FOR ASSETS AND LIABILITIES, Arts. 2–10.

12 *See* Anthony Chan, *PRC Regulations Ministry of Finance Issues RMB45 Billion in Bonds* (26 May 1998) <http://www.lawmoney.com>.

13 National Congress, Resolution on Issuance by Ministry of Finance of Special Government Bonds to Supply State-Owned Banks' Capital (2 Feb. 1998) (PRC).

14 *See* People's Bank of China, *Circular on Reforming Deposit Reserve*, 43 BULLETIN OF PEOPLE'S BANK OF CHINA, 3–4 (6 Apr. 1998).

15 Western analysts estimate non-performing loans account for between 25 and 40 per cent of loan portfolios but central bank governor Dai Xianglong put the figure at under 10 per cent, with bad loans totaling just 2.9 per cent at the end of 1998. *See China: Three More Financial Debt Processing Corps to Be Set Up*, CHINA BUSINESS INFORMATION NETWORK (14 May 1999), *available in* 1999 WL 17728859.

16 *See* ZHAOLIANG JIANG, *et al*, A QUICK TEXTBOOK ON FIVE-GRADE CREDIT SYSTEM 5–6 (Jan. 1999).

loans were of three types. The first, called 'overdue loans', included loans not repaid when due or not repaid after the due date had been extended. The next category, 'doubtful loans', included loans that were past due two years or more or loans that had been extended to a borrower who had suspended production or whose project was no longer being developed. Finally, 'bad loans' included those that had not been repaid after the borrower was declared bankrupt and had gone through liquidations.[17]

It is generally regarded that China's loan classification system of 1995 was far more lenient than that prevailing in the banks of developed countries. First, regulators in developed countries require that reserves be established primarily based on risk assessment rather than on payment status, a practice then dominating in China's banking system. Second, China's banks were allowed to delay classifying loans as non-performing. This was both because the specified time periods during which delay of repayment was allowed were longer and because in China classification of loans is generally tied to failure to repay principle rather than interest.[18]

China's new Five-Grade Credit System classifies loan into five categories, which are normal, credit watch, substandard, doubtful and loss. The last three types represent non-performing loans.[19] The normal loans refer to loans that can be repaid in full amounts when due. Credit watch loans mean those loans that can be repaid based on borrowers' current financial capabilities, but which repayment may be affected by some unfavorable factors. Substandard loans are loans whose repayment cannot be made by borrowers' normal revenue, given the forecast of borrowers' future cash flow. Doubtful loans are loans that cannot be repaid in full amounts even if the pledged collateral or guaranties for the loans are taken into account. Loss refers to loans that cannot be repaid or can only be repaid in negligible amounts after banks have made all the possible efforts, even going through liquidations to recover the loss.[20]

The new classification system is also applicable to the direct credit substitution items on the off-balance sheets, such as stand-by letters of credit, guaranties and irrevocable loan guaranties.[21] In addition, commercial banks are required to classify their loan portfolios at least every 6 months[22] and they are subject to the on-site inspection by the People's Bank of China annually.[23] It is expected that the new Five-Grade Credit System will allow China's banks to be in a better position to monitor their loan quality and lower the share of non-performing loans.

17 *See* People's Bank of China, General Rules on Loans (1995), Art. 34.

18 *See* Nicholas R. Lardy, above n 2, at 115–16.

19 *See* People's Bank of China, Guiding Principles for Loan Risk Classification, Art. 3 (issued Apr. 1998).

20 *See* ibid. Art. 4.

21 *See* ibid. Art. 27.

22 *See* ibid. Art. 16.

23 *See* ibid. Art. 23.

In November 1998 the People's Bank of China promulgated its restructuring plan, which is believed to be modeled on the Federal Reserve System of the United States. Nine regional branches were set up to take over the operation of the old provincial level branches that were more than thirty by that time.[24] In provincial level regions where no People's Bank branch was operating, a financial regulatory office was to be established in the capital city of each of those regions.[25] These nine regional branches are Tianjin, Shenyang, Shanghai, Nanjing, Jinan, Wuhan, Guangzhou, Chengdu, and Xi'an.[26] All of these cities are economically and financially developed relative to China's other cities and six out of the nine cities are along the east coast, the most developed area of China in terms of GDP and population. These nine regional branches were authorised to regulate and supervise the financial activities in their surrounding provincial level regions, some as many as four or five. The new system was announced to take effect 1 January 1999.

Another big move China has made to improve its financial regulation and supervision is the establishment of the China Insurance Regulatory Commission in November 1998. This new commission, along with the already existing People's Bank of China and China Securities Regulatory Commission, would be separately responsible for the supervision, regulation and inspection of the insurance industry, banking and securities industry, respectively, from 1999 on.[27]

In March 1999 a voluntary acquisition took place for the first time in China's banking history. China Everbright Bank purchased China Investment Bank along with its 137 banking offices that used to be managed by twenty-nine branches of the China Investment Bank. After the takeover of China Investment Bank, China Everbright Bank doubled its assets, network branches and employees. This placed it as the sixth largest commercial bank in China with RMB150 billion in assets, 245 offices and more than 5,000 employees.[28]

In April 1999 China's first asset management company, China Cinda

[24] *See* People's Bank of China, *Implementing Plans for Reforming Provincial Offices of People's Bank of China*, 61 BULLETIN OF PEOPLE'S BANK OF CHINA 4–5 (10 Feb. 1999). China's central bank used to be a gigantic institution with branches in every provincial level and region and offices in all larger cities as well as most counties. However the provincial branches responded primarily to provincial level political leaders rather than central bank headquarters in Beijing. It is obvious that the structure of authority in the old central bank made it difficult to limit political intervention in loan allocation and in supervision of commercial banks. China tried to achieve its central bank's operational independence by setting up the new regional branch system.

[25] *See* ibid.

[26] *See* ibid.

[27] *See China's Financial Sector Restructured*, WORLD TRADE 24 (1 Dec. 1998), *available in* 1998 WL 17410565.

[28] *Ebank Completes Merger With China Investment Bank*, WORLD NEWS CONNECTION (17 June 1999), *available in* 1999 WL 19381429.

Asset Management Company, was set up to handle China Construction Bank's non-performing loans. The Ministry of Finance financed Cinda's registered RMB10 billion of capital.[29] Cinda would take over more than RMB200 billion in non-performing loans from China Construction Bank. These loans are one or two year old non-performing loans, but they do not include the overdue loans made after 1996.[30] Cinda would be permitted to re-lend, issue bonds, underwrite shares or bonds and securitise debt to liquidate those non-performing loans. Cinda would also be exempt from all business taxes.[31] This was China's first move towards resolving the non-performing loans in its banking system. More similar asset management companies have since been set up to handle the other three state banks' non-performing loans.

II. EXISTING PROBLEMS

Over the past two decades the Chinese government has made great efforts to reform the financial system. The splendid achievements have generally been acknowledged. However, the financial system is still problem-ridden with impediments such as non-performing debts, under-capitalisation, governmental intervention, lack of prudential regulation and supervision, and backward banking technology, among others. Four of the most significant existing problems, (1) lack of internal profit driven systems, (2) non-implementation of the separate operation separate regulation principle, (3) mismatch of finacial market shares, and (4) slow development of financial regulation and supervision, must be examined in turn before implications of the 1999 reforms can be assessed.

A. *Lack of Internal Profit-Driven Systems*

Since their inception, the state banks have operated on both policy-supporting and commercial principles, so the problem of conflict of interests exists from the very beginning. Strictly speaking, in terms of lending activities state banks are more policy-oriented than profit-driven, ie, they do not operate on commercial terms under most circumstances, although this unfortunate situation began to change in 1993 when China decided to transform the state banks into commercial banks.

[29] *China: Three More Financial Debt Processing Corps to Be Set Up*, CHINA BUSINESS INFORMATION NETWORK (14 May 1999), *available in* 1999 WL 17728859.

[30] *Cinda Asset Management Not to Acquire NPLs Created After End-1996*, WORLD REPORTER (16 June 1999), *available in* 1999 WL 20159431.

[31] *China's First Asset Management Company Established*, CHINA PRESS (21 Apr. 1999).

1. Overburdening of State Banks

State banks' lending activities were under great control by quite a few government ministries and agencies, such as the Ministry of Finance, the Ministry of Economics and Trade, the State Planning Commission and the People's Bank of China. Each year there were quotas regarding the caps of lending and the share to be allocated to different industries and sectors handed down to the banks. Even though the mandatory quota lending system was officially abolished in January 1998, the guided quota lending system is still in place. Thus it is too early to judge how effective the asset/liability ratio management system is in controlling the quality of bank loan portfolios. Despite the fact that three policy banks were announced to take the policy lending function from the state banks, given the size and capital adequacy level of policy banks, it is very difficult for them to take up even most of the policy lending in the country, much less all of the policy lending. As a matter of fact, not only have the original policy lending activities not been transferred to the policy banks (such as the pillar project loans made by China Construction Bank before 1994), but new policy loans are continually made by the state banks. For example, since 1994 the Industrial and Commercial Bank has continued lending the natural disaster relief loans, the payroll loans for enterprises in extreme difficulties and the cotton (or other materials) reserve loans to state-owned enterprises.[32]

On the other hand, even though the weight of state-owned enterprises in China's overall economy has fallen year after year for the past decade, the state-owned enterprises still contribute 65 per cent of China's GDP, support 60 per cent of the urban workforce in China[33] and control 65 per cent of the country's assets.[34] In order to keep these state-owned enterprises afloat, state banks have to extend most of their loans to them. It is estimated that, at the end of 1995, the loans made to state-owned enterprises made up about 83 per cent of the state banks' total loans outstanding.[35] Unfortunately, the average financial performance of these state-owned enterprises has been deteriorating over time. For example, China's state-owned enterprises' average debt/asset ratio, the single most important index that measures a firm's financial strength, was surprisingly as high as 85 per

32 This problem stems from the weakness of the Commercial Bank Law. The Commercial Bank Law provides that the state commercial banks issue loans for special projects approved by the State Council, and that the State Council makes restitutions for all losses incurred through such mandated loans. *See* Commercial Bank Law, Art. 41.

33 *See* Nicholas R. Lardy, above n 2, at 26.

34 *See ibid.* at 29.

35 *See* Lihong Wang, *Trial Project Targets Debt*, China Daily Business Weekly, 7 Oct. 1996, at 1.

cent by the end of 1995.[36] In other words, without banks' loans, many firms would have ceased to exist a long time ago. The severely indebted state-owned enterprises have been a huge burden for state banks and it is unrealistic to expect these enterprises to depend upon their own resources any time soon. As a result, banks' profitability has been greatly penalised by those loss-making state-owned enterprises.

2. The Control of Interest Rates

Until recently, interest rates had been officially set by the People's Bank of China, and state banks had been allowed to set their own deposit and loan rates only within a margin around the officially posted guidelines.[37] Since 75 per cent of state banks' operational income comes from interest income, the banks are left with very few choices when it comes to generating income. In addition, not only are banks' interest rate margins pre-set, but are further squeezed during periods of accelerating inflation. For example, from September 1988 through the end of 1997, the central bank adjusted rates on most time deposits eleven times, increasing them when inflation picked up and decreasing them when inflation was brought under greater control.[38] At times of rapid inflation the central bank instituted so-called value-guarantee deposits which were indexed to the inflation rate during the lifetime of the deposits. This programme was designed to insulate longer-term deposits from inflation. It was first instituted on 10 September 1988 and continued until December 1991. Then, when the inflation rate again rose sharply in 1993, the central bank reinstated the value-guarantee subsidy programme on 11 July 1993. The programme lasted until April 1996 when it was ended for new deposits. These adjustments raised the cost of funds to banks enormously. In the first inflationary period, state banks were forced to raise the base interest rate on three-year time deposits by 4.86 per cent and also to pay supplementary interest under the value-guarantee programme. In the second inflationary period, the banks had to raise the basic interest paid on three-year deposits by 3.96 per cent and paid extra interest under the value-guarantee subsidy programme. On the other hand, the central bank raised lending rates upward by much more modest amounts. For example, the People's Bank of China raised the rates they required banks to charge on one-year working capital loans by only 3.44 per cent and 3.42 per cent as inflation accelerated in 1988–9 and 1993–5, respectively.[39]

[36] *See* Jian Yu, *The Predicament and the Solution for State-Owned Enterprises*, Financial Daily, 29 Jan. 1996, at 3.

[37] *See* Commercial Bank Law, Arts. 31, 38 (PRC).

[38] *See* Nicholas R. Lardy, above n 2, at 107

[39] *See* ibid. at 109.

3. Lack of Effective Performance Measurement System

As mentioned before, since China's state banks are not operated on commercial terms, it is very difficult to set up an effective evaluation system to measure the performance of the banks and bank managers. Even today there is no standard and consistent performance measurement system in China's banking sector. Currently, China's banks are not evaluated by the most accepted international standard, ie profitability, but are measured by multi-objective indicators. This originates from the rationale that the state wants them to turn in as much profit as possible to cushion the budget deficit and directly finance the designated industries or projects, while at the same time maintain enough liquidity to meet their obligations. This multi-objective system gives bank managers both political and managerial challenges, but also provides them with perfect excuses for not being able to meet the objectives. If profits decline, bank managers can simply say that they have made too many policy loans or too many state-owned enterprises have defaulted on principal or interest payments. The managers can also claim that profits, operational costs, non-performing assets and fraud rates are not comparable with the historical data because of the intervention of local governments, the ongoing reform of state-owned enterprises, the value-guarantee deposit programmes and even natural disasters. Therefore the inadequacies of managers' skills are too easily buried in this multi-objective measurement system. This system is partially accountable for the overbuilt branches and offices, overstaffed organisations and out-of date facilities as well.

Since the financial reform began, the financial performance of China's state banks has deteriorated year after year. Taking the return-on-assets ratio for an example, one can see that this ratio is amazingly low. In 1996 the average return-on-assets ratio for four state banks was 0.3 per cent.[40] Even for Bank of China, with more than 500 overseas branches that are much more profitable than their domestic peers, the return-on-assets ratio has headed south on a yearly basis. In 1997 this figure was 0.53 per cent, down from 0.74 per cent in 1996, and 0.96 per cent in 1995.[41]

B. *Failure to Implement the 'Separate Operation, Separate Regulation' Principle*

In the mid-1990s, the People's Bank of China proposed that banking, securities, insurance, and trust industries should be operated separately, and equally important, that they be regulated separately by different regulators,

[40] *See* ibid. at 100.
[41] *See* Bank of China, 1997 Annual Report (1998).

a principle referred to as 'separate operation, separate regulation'. The Commercial Bank Law confirms this principle, prohibiting commercial banks from making trust investment, trading in shares, and making investment in fixed assets for non-self use.[42] This theory developed from the fact that China is now in its early development stage of Socialist market economy and banking, securities, insurance and trust industries are far from maturity and efficiency, therefore driven by conflict of interests; the involvement in more than one function makes banks, securities firms or trust companies hard to position themselves in the market, greatly increasing risks to themselves and to the market as a whole. Another rationale is that neither banks nor securities firms nor trust companies have sufficient capital or expertise to conduct activities beyond their own core business. This principle has been proven by nearly two decades of multifunctional practice at China's banks, securities firms and trust companies.

China began to sell treasury and other types of government bonds in 1981, and the first corporate bonds emerged in the market in 1986. Securities firms were first established in China in September 1987 and soon gained rapid development following the official opening of the Shanghai Stock Exchange in December 1990 and Shenzhen Stock Exchange in July 1991.

The trust and investment companies in China are of two broad types. The first are internationally oriented, of which the best known is the China International Trust and Investment Company (CITIC), established in 1979 and the parent of the CITIC Industrial Bank. Other international trust and investment companies were established beginning in 1980 by provincial governments in Shandong, Liaoling and Guangdong, by major municipalities such as Guangzhou, Xi'an and Dalian, as well as by small cities such as Changjiang in Sichuan Province. The second type is domestically oriented trust and investment companies which developed rapidly during the 1980s. Most of these companies were under the sponsorship of provinces or local governments. In 1988 the number of trust and investment companies reached a record high of 745.[43]

Since these securities firms and trust and investment companies embraced China's financial market, they have been entangled with China's banks. State banks started to create securities departments almost immediately after government bonds and corporate bonds floated into the market, and trust departments of state banks were authorised to undertake trust activities as early as 1980. Total trust lending of the four large state banks has been quite large. In 1990 and 1992, these loans totalled about RMB345 billion and RMB490 billion, respectively, equal to almost one-fourth of the

[42] *See* Commercial Bank Law, Art. 43 (PRC).
[43] *See* NICHOLAS R. LARDY, above n 2, at 73.

regular lending activity of these banks. Then trust lending declined sharply in the next couple of years, but still reached RMB550 billion in 1995, the equivalent of one-seventh of banks' regular lending.[44]

Over the past two decades, banks, securities firms, and trust and investment companies have tried to achieve economies of scale and economies of scope based on their own core businesses. Almost every branch and office has been involved in deposit-taking, lending and investment activities. Because no internal risk control systems exist in these institutions, these activities are in a pretty chaotic state. As was later discovered, it was not the branches or offices that made the loans and investments which were accountable for the risks, but their headquarters that knew nothing about what their subordinates were doing which undertook the responsibilities. Because a large portion of lending and investment went to the favorite projects or enterprises of provincial or local governments, it is quite doubtful that this lending and investment ever stimulated the local economy. To make things worse, it has been disclosed that much corruption and fraud was associated with this lending and investment. For example, many securities firms used the margin deposits placed by their clients to make commercial loans without their clients' authorisation. Some went even further to make loans to those enterprises that were about to go public, hoping that they could get access to these enterprises. In order to increase their lending many firms had to borrow heavily. The excess borrowing problem in 1993 and the abuse of repurchase agreements in 1995 spread to the entire securities industry. As a result, many firms threw themselves into debt triangles or debt chains with other financial institutions, making liquidity a real threat to the industry for the first time.

Because China's capital market is rather underdeveloped, a substantial portion of the trust and investment companies' funds go to enterprises or specific projects rather than flow into the capital market. Shortly after their inception the trust and investment companies engaged in businesses beyond what they were entitled to do. While in principle, the major source of trust and investment companies should be trust funds and entrusted funds, in reality, most trust and investment companies have participated in the activities of taking deposits from the public and using these deposits to make loans. The sizes of the loans have far exceeded the authorised limits and the scope of the loans has been much broader than the allowed exposure. Some companies even used money they borrowed from the interbank markets to finance long-term projects or investments. Not surprisingly, interest income, rather than agency commissions, is the major income source of most of the trust and investment companies.

It was not until mid-1990s that the state council and central bank

[44] *See* ibid. at 79.

realised how serious these problems were. In the first half of 1996 the People's Bank of China formulated a scheme that required the four state banks to break up with the trust and investment subsidiaries which they set up in thirty-five major municipalities throughout the country. By the end of 1997, the separation of state-owned commercial banks and their subsidiary trust and investment companies was complete.[45]

C. *Mismatch of Financial Institutions' Market Share in Rapidly Changing Financial Environments*

The allocation of capital is dependent on banks to an unreasonable degree, and the potential of the capital market has yet to be fully developed. China's capital market, currently in its primitive development stage, is dwarfed by the banking industry. According to published statistics, the total assets of banks, city and rural credit cooperatives and trust and investment companies represent 131 per cent of China's GDP, while the total market value of stocks and the total nominal value of bonds that have been issued is only 25 per cent and 31 per cent of China's GDP, respectively.[46]

Even though China's leaders, in their public speeches and formal documents, have emphasised the importance of developing the capital market more frequently than ever, given the fact that China's economy is still dominated by state ownership, state-owned enterprises are always automatically given privileges when it comes to who can get access to the capital market first. Among 868 companies that have been listed on the Shanghai and Shenzhen stock exchanges,[47] the majority are state-owned enterprises. However, the performance of state-owned enterprises has been disappointing for quite a long time, which is no exception to those public companies that are considered to have relatively stronger balance sheets than non-listed enterprises. For example, in 1998 the overall performance of China's public companies was worse than that of the 772 listed companies in 1997. Among the 868 companies that have disclosed their annual reports, the average earnings per share were RMB0.2, RMB0.05 less than that in 1997 and the average return on assets was 7.97 per cent, down 2.18 per cent from 1997 while the average assets per share were RMB2.50, RMB0.05 up from the previous year.[48]

On the other hand, the nonstate sector, which includes collectively owned enterprises, private firms, foreign-funded companies, and self-

[45] *See* YUAN CHEN, CHINA FINANCIAL OUTLOOK '98 33 (1998).
[46] *See* CHINA PRESS (13 May 1999).
[47] *See* China Statistical Information and Consultancy Service Center, *Report: To Look Over the Achievements of Listed Companies From Their 1998 Annual Report*, CHINA MONTHLY STATISTICS (April 1994).
[48] *See* ibid.

employed workers, has played a bigger role in China's economic development. Currently there are about 1.2 million private firms, 330,000 foreign-owned firms and joint ventures, and 31.2 million self-employed workers in China. The total products and services (measured monetarily) provided by private firms and self-employed workers accounted for about 25 per cent of China's GDP in 1997. In some coastal provinces such as Fujian, the nonstate economy has already comprised 80 per cent of the gross industrial products (measured monetarily) of the province and covered almost every industry that is open to competition.[49] According to the State Statistics Bureau of China, in 1998 more than RMB418 billion tax revenue was generated from the nonstate sector, which was almost 50 per cent of China's total tax revenue in 1998. Yet the percentage taken by the state sector has been shrinking over the past twenty years, dropping from 75 per cent in 1978 to 54 per cent in 1998. Since 1994, China's foreign exchange reserve has accumulated at an accelerating rate. With USD51.6 billion worth in 1994, the foreign exchange reserve jumped to USD73.6 billion in 1995, to USD105 billion in 1996, to USD140 billion in 1997[50] and then slowed down a little bit to USD145 billion in 1998.[51] This achievement is undoubtedly largely attributed to foreign-funded firms because these firms make up almost 75 per cent of China's total exports.

Despite the fact that the nonstate sector has a significant presence in China's economy, due to three reasons the credit resources available to it remain very limited. First, the state banks dominate China's financial landscape. Because of their state nature, they mainly respond to the financial needs of state-owned enterprises. It is estimated that the loans made to state-owned enterprises account for 83 per cent of state banks' outstanding loans.[52] Secondly, in order to compensate state banks' high operational costs (such as inflation-indexed deposits and policy loans), state banks tend to charge these nonstate firms higher loan interests than what they are willing to pay, which leaves state banks a small pool of nonstate customers. Thirdly, although the nonstate sector has mushroomed since the 1980s, due to its firms' shorter proven history, smaller sizes and lack of implicit government subsidy and support, state banks are very reserved in exposing themselves to the risks associated with lending to these firms.

Fortunately, China's authorities have realised how difficult it is for the nonstate sector to continue developing without access to the capital market

49 *See The Development Environment for China's Private Enterprises Expected to Improve*, CHINA PRESS (23 April 1999).

50 *See* INTERNATIONAL MONETARY FUND, INTERNATIONAL FINANCIAL STATISTICS (YEARBOOK) 317 (1998).

51 *See* INTERNATIONAL MONETARY FUND, INTERNATIONAL FINANCIAL STATISTICS 204 (Mar. 1999).

52 *See* Jian Yu, above n 36.

and bank loans. Since it will take quite some time for state banks to increase their lending to the nonstate sector, more aggressive development of the capital market and allowing these nonstate firms to directly raise capital seems a feasible approach. Just as the Vice-Chairman of China Securities Regulatory Commission, Mr Chen Yaoxian, disclosed at the '1999 China Investment Forum' held on 12 May 1999, from now on as long as firms have proved to be profitable and prosperous, operated in conformity with the Company Law and met the criteria for going public, they can apply for initial public offerings. This message means that the ownership of a firm will no longer be considered in the entrance to the capital market process.

Another notable problem that cannot be overstated is the all-too-limited role played within the banking sector by other commercial banks and foreign banks. As mentioned before, the nonstate economy has gained substantial weight since China began its economic and financial reforms. The market shares of banks with different ownerships, however, are not compatible with this change. It has become urgent for China to encourage other commercial banks, such as shareholding banks (with some voting shares owned by the private sector), private banks and foreign banks to compete with the state banks. Interestingly, these commercial banks have demonstrated exceptional strength compared to China's state banks. Minsheng Bank, for example, is one of the top players.

Minsheng Bank is China's first private national commercial bank. It was established with registered capital of RMB1.38 billion in January 1996 by the All-China Federation of Industry and Commerce. The initial fifty-nine shareholders, almost entirely nonstate enterprises, are members of the Federation.[53] Currently more than 65 per cent of Minsheng's clients are small and medium-sized enterprises and more than 60 per cent of its RMB13.9 billion loans are granted to private enterprises.[54] Because of the bank's tightened risk control and successful business expansion plan, it has accumulated RMB640 million pre-tax profits since its inception.

China first opened up its banking sector to foreigners in 1982 when Nanyang Commercial Bank from Hong Kong established a branch office in Shenzhen. Then in September 1990 Shanghai opened up to foreign banks as well. In 1992 seven more coastal cities were added to the list. They are Dalian, Tianjin, Qingdao, Nanjing, Ningbo, Fuzhou, and Guangzhou. In August 1994, eleven more inland cities were opened to foreign banks, such as Beijing, Shenyang, Xi'an and Chongqing. After

[53] *See* NICHOLAS R. LARDY, above n 2, at 69.

[54] *See* DELOITTE & TOUCHE, EXPRESS CHINA NEWS, No 99–2 (Mar./Apr. 1999).

Hainan became China's 31st province, it soon allowed foreign banks to set up branches and representative offices there. By the end of 1998, 150 financial institutions from forty counties had established 173 branch offices and 283 representative offices in 23 cities and one province. The total assets of these foreign banks were USD34.18 billion, representing 2.58 per cent of China's total financial assets (excluding assets of insurance companies and securities companies). The total foreign currency assets of these foreign banks were 16.4 per cent of China's total foreign currency assets. Their foreign currency loans were USD26.05 billion, equal to 23 per cent of China's total foreign currency loans. And their foreign currency deposits were USD4.55 billion—an amount equal to 5 per cent of China's total foreign currency deposits.[55]

The role of foreign banks in China is quite limited due to two factors. First, their geographical locations are restricted to thirty-three cities and one emerging province. This strictly limits their business scope and customer base. Secondly, most foreign banks are faced with the restriction on conducting local currency business. In 1996 seven banks were granted permission to conduct local currency business in Pudong Economic Development Zone in Shanghai. These banks include Citibank, Hongkong and Shanghai Banking Corp, Bank of Tokyo-Mitsubishi, Industrial Bank of Japan, and Daichi Kangyo Bank. Then in 1998, foreign banks got permission to do local currency business on an experimental basis in Shenzhen. By April 1999, there were altogether twenty-three foreign banks permitted to conduct local currency business in China. Although these foreign banks can carry out local currency business, they are not allowed to take deposits from households or Chinese firms, nor can they offer loans to them. They can only deal with foreign-owned companies or joint ventures.[56] Besides, there is a limit on the working capital of each foreign bank, which is set at RMB100 million.[57]

Obviously all of these restrictions have put foreign banks into a very disadvantaged situation, which greatly limits foreign banks' impact and development.

[55] *See* Runxiang Feng, *The Opening up of China's Banking Industry Must Follow a Conservatively Developing Principle*, 58 FINANCE REV. (5 May 1999).

[56] *See* PEOPLE'S BANK OF CHINA, TENTATIVE PROCEDURES ON ADMINISTRATION OF PILOT OPERATION OF RENMINBI BUSINESS BY FOREIGN INVESTMENT FINANCIAL INSTITUTIONS IN SHANGHAI PUDONG NEW ZONE (DEC. 1996), Art. 6; SHENZHEN BRANCH OF THE PEOPLE'S BANK OF CHINA, GUIDELINES FOR PILOT OPERATION OF RENMINBI BUSINESS BY FOREIGN INVESTMENT FINANCIAL INSTITUTIONS IN SHENZHEN (Aug. 1997), Art. 6.

[57] *See Foreign Banks Expand the Scope of Renminbi Business*, CHINA DAILY (Overseas Edition), 24 Aug. 1998, at 15; SHENZHEN BRACH OF THE PEOPLE'S BANK OF CHINA, GUIDELINES FOR PILOT OPERATION OF RENMINBI BUSINESS BY FOREIGN INVESTMENT FINANCIAL INSTITUTIONS IN SHENZHEN (Aug. 1997), Art. 5.

D. *Financial Regulation and Supervision Lags Behind the Financial Market Development*

Since the mid-1990s China has implemented a series of measures to improve its central bank's independence in order for the bank to effectively carry out monetary policy and prudently regulate financial institutions. These measures include ending the practice of extending loans to the state, forbidding the central bank to run any business, establishing nine regional branches to replace the old provincial level branches and enacting the Central Bank Law to protect the central bank on a legitimate basis. However, China's central bank system has still fallen short of the needs of rapidly developing financial markets.

1. Central Bank's Regulation and Supervision Are Inconsistent with International Standards

Objectively, reforms in the financial sector in China over the past few years have helped create a legal framework for the central bank's regulation and supervision. China has adopted over 200 laws and regulations directly related to financial supervision since 1995.[58] At the highest level, the National Congress promulgated the Law of the People's Bank of China, the Commercial Bank Law, Insurance Law, Negotiable Instrument Law and Securities Law. At the lower level, the State Council and the People's Bank of China issued a number of regulations and rules to bring bank regulation and supervision into a legitimate orbit.

But there are apparent weaknesses in this legal framework. A major deficiency is that it is, in varying degrees, out of keeping with international standards and practices. For example, the current practice with respect to capital regulation is to combine specific rules and prescriptions with a system of general principles for sound and prudent management. In many situations, bank management is granted freedom to determine its capital adequacy. By contrast, the Commercial Bank Law in China ignores the part bank management plays in the determination of capital adequacy, only stipulating that capital adequacy is not less than 8 per cent.[59] Other deficiencies such as non-transparency and political intervention also impede the effectiveness of bank supervision.

The authority of the central bank is faced with challenges in practice as well. For example, trust and investment companies have boomed in China since mid-1980s. By 1993 the total number of trust and investment

[58] *See China: Banking Reform in Line With Basle Core Principles in China*, China Business Information Network (4 June 1999), *available in* 1999 WL 17729256.

[59] *See* Commercial Bank Law, Art. 39 (PRC).

companies reached an all-time high of 795, much more than what the market could absorb. One of the most important reasons that these companies were granted permission in the first place and were not regulated strictly enough later on is that most of those trust and investment companies were established by the provincial or municipal governments or governments' agencies or the direct subsidiaries of governments. Only when these companies seriously disturbed the financial order and stability by heavily lending to enterprises, extensively borrowing at the interbank markets, abusing the repurchase agreements and burying huge amounts of money in commercial real estate investment, did the central bank begin to stop these violations and clean up the mess. After the cleanup, by the end of 1995 there were only ninety-seven securities firms and 394 trust and investment companies in existence, only half of the previous level. In 1996 the People's Bank of China instituted the rule that from that year on, no more new trust and investment companies would be approved for quite an extensive time and the existing trust and investment companies would be more strictly regulated.

2. Lack of Integration of Financial Institutions' Internal Controls and Central Bank's External Regulation

With ever-changing financial markets and ever-complicated financial instruments, banks' internal controls must be in place in order to effectively prevent risks. However, over a long period of time internal controls have been ignored in the Chinese banking field. At the level of both supervisors and bank management there is an idea that implies that the stability and soundness of banks are the supervisors' responsibility rather than bank management's responsibilities. As a result, internal controls are not in place, internal audit departments are not established or are understaffed, and general managers often override the board of directors.[60] Even after the People's Bank of China issued the Guiding Principles for Strengthening Internal Controls in Financial Institutions in May 1997, many banks did not establish internal control committees and internal audit departments.

In addition, there is a loose connection between financial institutions' internal auditing and the central bank's supervision. This has already been responsible for many hidden risks in China's financial markets. The increasing banking frauds and crimes are a prominent example. Similar problems exist in other industries as well. When repurchase agreements were first introduced into China in 1994, it did not take long for securities firms to make false repurchase agreements with one another. The motive behind this

[60] *See* Yun Wei, *An Analysis of the Inefficiency of China's Financial Regulation*, 10 HAINAN FINANCE 15–16 (1998).

was to borrow money to cover their unauthorised lending and excessive investment in commercial real estate. Because there were no efficient audit departments in the securities firms and no accurate documents and timely records could be found to track these illegal activities, within only a couple of years there were extensive debt chains among financial institutions. By June 1996 the value of debt chains among Tianjin Securities Trading Center, Wuhan Securities Trading Center and their affiliated members was as high as RMB45.6 billion.

3. Lack of Equal Competition Between Domestic Banks and Foreign Banks

There are several discriminatory measures with regard to foreign banks in foreign bank regulations. These measures take the form of discriminatory barriers to entry and discriminatory operating constraints. The Regulations for the Administration of Foreign Investment Financial Institutions require that foreign bank applicants must be financial institutions.[61] This requirement runs afoul of the General Agreement on Trade in Services (GATS), which requires that Member States neither maintain nor adopt limitations on the number of service suppliers in the form of exclusive service suppliers.[62] Limitations on the location of foreign banks have existed since foreign banks were allowed access to China. Now only twenty-four cities and Hainan province are open to foreign banks. In contrast, domestic banks are free from the applicant and location limitations. Foreign banks are also required to employ at least one Chinese citizen to be senior management[63] and accountants registered in China.[64]

With respect to discriminatory operational constraints, those related to sources of funds are conspicuous. Foreign banks are restricted to solicit deposits from foreign investment enterprises, foreigners and approved domestic enterprises, and to lend these types of borrowers. When dealing with non-foreign-investment enterprises, foreign banks are subject to external debt ceilings of non-foreign investment enterprises. In addition, foreign banks cannot offer the same line of banking activities permissible for domestic banks. Among these, the notorious one is the domestic currency restriction. Although some foreign banks have obtained licenses to engage in Renminbi banking business since December 1996, foreign banks are stymied by a number of requirements.

[61] State Council, Regulations for the Administration of Foreign Investment Financial Institution (Apr. 1994), Arts. 6, 8 (PRC).

[62] *See* General Agreement on Trade in Services [hereinafter GATS], Art. XVI(2)(a).

[63] *See* Regulations for the Administration of Foreign Investment Financial Institution, Art. 33 (PRC).

[64] *See* ibid. Art. 34.

Besides the *de jure* discrimination, *de facto* discrimination still exists. The People's Bank of China applies an economic needs standard in considering foreign and domestic applications.[65] The approval standards lack transparency, and may lead to potential inequality between foreign and domestic applicants.

4. The Partially Implemented 'Separate Operation, Separate Regulation' Principle

China officially announced that beginning in 1999 the People's Bank of China, China Securities Regulatory Commission and China Insurance Regulatory Commission would separately regulate and supervise China's banking industry, securities industry and insurance industry. This is to say that theoretically the China Securities Regulatory Commission will be responsible for the regulation and supervision of the primary and secondary markets of the securities industry. However this is not what is going on now. Despite the fact that China Securities Regulatory Commission was established as early as in 1992, until today the People's Bank of China is still accountable for granting licenses for securities firms and regulating securities firms' daily operation. Given the current situation, it is very important that cooperation be created in the relationship between the People's Bank of China and China Securities Regulatory Commission. There is no doubt how profound and lasting an impact an independent securities industry regulator may have on the healthy development of China's securities markets, and consequently on the healthy development of China's banking industry.

III. BANKS' REFORM IN 1999 AND ITS IMPLICATIONS

Since the financial crisis broke out in Asia in October 1997 and until very recently, the economies in Japan, Korea and Thailand have seemed to be getting back on track. Despite the fact that China escaped the crisis, the substantial shrinking of its exports to these surrounding countries has hindered the momentum of China's economic growth. This adverse situation, coupled with the deepening reforms of state-owned enterprises, made people wonder if China could meet its 7 per cent growth rate objective for 1999. As of April 1999, the Retail Price Index in China had posted negative growth rate for consecutive 19 months and the Consumer Price Index negative growth rate for consecutive 13 months.[66] In the meantime, the

65 *See* Commercial Bank Law, Art. 12 (PRC).

66 *See* Dahua Li, *A New Challenge Facing China: Anti-deflation*, China Press (23 May 1999).

household deposits have climbed steadily even though the central bank cut interest rates six times within two years. By the end of January 1999, the savings deposits of urban and rural residents reached RMB5,400 billion.[67] Within the first two months of 1999 alone, banks pulled in an extra RMB330 billion household deposits. In order to meet the planned growth rate objective, China decided to encourage consumption as a major means to stimulate the economy. This policy, coupled with the current stage of banking reforms, makes promoting consumer credit—home mortgage loans in particular—the new focus. In the long run this reform is absolutely inevitable and correct because it can diversify banks' loan portfolios and lower banks' risks while at the same time upgrade households' consumption level and improve their living standards. However under China's current circumstances, it is unpredictable whether and to what extent this goal can be met.

A. *New Moves In 1999*

Historically, consumer credit in China has been extremely limited. By the end of 1998 the total household deposits in China's banks were as high as RMB5,000 billion,[68] while the total consumer credit amounted to only RMB90 billion, less than 1 per cent of China's total consumption, in contrast to the 20 per cent–30 per cent typically observed in industrialised countries.[69]

Since the Bank of China issued China's first Chinese credit card, the GreatWall Card in 1986, each of the four state banks and the Bank of Communications has had its own credit card business. For example, the Industrial and Commercial Bank issues the Peony Card and the China Agricultural Bank has the GoldenSpike Card. Yet, for three reasons these credit cards provide little credit to households. First, most of the cards have been issued to firms, which use them as a means of payment. Secondly, almost all the cards issued to households are debit cards rather than credit cards, which means that the households who use these credit cards to buy goods and services actually use the money they deposit in advance with the banks rather than credit.[70] Thirdly, the scale of credit card business is negligible. If we look at the transaction volume (including fund transfers and cash withdrawal) and direct retail purchase of the GreatWall Card holders in 1998, we will find that they were only RMB246.5 billion and RMB10.2

[67] *See* China Statistical Information and Consultancy Service Center, *Report: Prospect for the Economic Operation of 1999*, CHINA MONTHLY STATISTICS (Jan. 1991).

[68] *See* Yuanlong Wang, *Some Issues of Developing China's Consumer Credit Business*, 5 INTERNATIONAL BANKING RESEARCH (1999).

[69] *See Try Consumption Credits*, CHINA COMMODITIES DAILY, 14 Mar. 1999, at 2.

[70] *See* NICHOLAS R. LARDY, above n 2, at 82

billion, respectively.[71] Yet during the same year, the total deposits of Bank of China were RMB730.2 billion and the total lending was RMB657.4 billion.[72] A similar pattern exists in other banks as well.

Car loans in China are quite new, almost exclusively on a trial basis. China's first car loan, made by the Industrial and Commercial Bank, came into the market in late 1998. Within two months, the bank extended car loans to more than 1,000 car buyers in forty cities. About 70 per cent of those vehicles are passenger cars.[73] Bank of China has cooperated with Dongfeng-Citroen Automobile Corporation, a joint-venture carmaker in China, to offer consumer credit to its customers and car dealers as well.

Chinese banks introduced home mortgage lending in the 1980s, but the sums extended so far are minuscule, relative to total bank lending and to household savings deposits. By the end of 1998, the home mortgage loans made by the four state banks and by all the banks combined were approximately RMB50 billion and RMB69.1 billion, respectively. However the total loans outstanding were RMB8,678.8 billion and the total household savings deposits were RMB5,000 billion.[74] So by 1998 the total home mortgage lending accounted for only 0.8 per cent of total bank loans outstanding and 1.4 per cent of total household savings deposits. In China's largest and most crowded city, Shanghai, the mortgage business did not get started until 1992.

Apart from the credit card, auto finance and home mortgage lending, bank loans to individual consumers for other purposes, such as education, durable goods and home improvement, are almost non-existent.

Faced with such situations under which consumer credit is seriously paltry and bank loans unreasonably concentrate on state-owned enterprises, since 1998 the People's Bank of China has adopted a new policy to promote the development of consumer credit, which is reflected in the following documents and regulations. The Individual Housing Loan Regulations allowed all of the commercial banks in China to conduct individual home mortgage lending and extending loan terms up to 15 to 20 years.[75] The Notice on Increasing Lending and Supporting House Construction and Consumption encouraged banks to increase lending to residential house construction and purchase.[76] The Car Loan Regulations

[71] *See* Yuanlong Wang, above n 68.

[72] *See* BANK OF CHINA INSTITUTE OF INTERNATIONAL BANKING, THE ANALYSIS OF CURRENT INTERNATIONAL AND DOMESTIC ECONOMIC AND FINANCIAL SITUATIONS (1998).

[73] *See* DELOITTE & TOUCHE, above n 54.

[74] *See* Yuanlong Wang, above n 68.

[75] People's Bank of China, *Individual Housing Loan Regulations*, 47 BULLETIN OF THE PEOPLE'S BANK OF CHINA (20 May 1998).

[76] People's Bank of China, *Notice on Increasing Lending and Supporting House Construction and Consumption*, 47 BULLETIN OF THE PEOPLE'S BANK OF CHINA (20 May 1998).

allowed more banks to engage in car lending activities.[77] The Guide to Developing Individual Consumer Credit proposed consumer credit as a new focus and requested banks to conduct durable goods loans, education loans, tourism loans and credit card business on an experimental basis. It was in this document that the down payment rate for home mortgage loans and car loans was lowered from 30 per cent to the current 20 per cent and the lending ratio was raised to up to 80 per cent of the house or car value.[78]

B. An Analysis Of The New Moves

After China's authorities and the central bank raised green lights to permit banks to boost consumer credit business, the four state banks suggested that they would put the consumer credit business on the top of their priorities for 1999. For example, the Bank of China announced that it would allot 10 per cent of its new loans to individual consumers and increase its lending in home mortgages, car purchasing and big-ticket items.[79] However, later development of consumer credit business in China has shown that the achievements have not lived up to the authorities' expectations. Not surprisingly, this disappointment originates from the lower level of consumers' disposable income, the dilemma faced by banks as creditors and the insufficiency of consumer credit-related institutions.

Firstly, the Chinese savings rate is one of the highest around the world, somewhere around 40 per cent of their annual income. Apart from Chinese tradition of thrift spending and current unwillingness to consume due to the upcoming medical insurance reform, education reform, pension and retirement plan and housing reform, the low household income is one of the most important reasons that restrict consumers' consumption level. Between 1993 and 1998, the real income growth rate per urban resident was 27.2, 35.6, 11.2, 3.4, 2.9, and 5.8 per cent, reaching RMB5,425 in 1998. The real income growth rate per rural resident was 17.6, 32.4, 29, 8, 4, and 4.3 per cent, hitting RMB2, 160 in 1998.[80] Had the goods prices not declined over the past two years, the real income growth rate per capita in China would have dropped more sharply.

While due to the declining prices and interest rates, it may be possible to stimulate consumers to use credit cards to purchase durable goods, computers and large entertainment instruments such as pianos, it is very difficult to boost home purchasing since the house price is far beyond the level that the

[77] People's Bank of China, *Car Loan Regulations*, 54 BULLETIN OF THE PEOPLE'S BANK OF CHINA (2 Nov. 1998).

[78] *See* People's Bank of China, *Guide to Developing Individual Consumer Credit*, 63 BULLETIN OF THE PEOPLE'S BANK OF CHINA (31 Mar. 1999).

[79] *See* DELOITTE & TOUCHE, above n 54.

[80] *See* CHINA STATISTICAL BUREAU, STATISTICAL YEARBOOK OF CHINA 1998 (1999).

average household can reach. Usually, in order for a housing market to be effective, there should be a stable relationship between the average house price and the average annual income. In Tokyo, the price/annual income ratio is 12 : 9. In Hamburg this ratio is 7 : 2. In New York, Los Angeles and Paris, this ratio is 9 : 2, 8 : 2, and 4 : 3, respectively. Presently, the World Bank determines this ratio to be in the range of 3–6. Currently the average house price in China's major cities is close to that in the major cities of industrialised countries, but the annual income in China is not even comparable to what people earn in industrialised countries. For example, in 1996 the house price in Shanghai's prime locations is forty-two times annual income of a Shanghai resident and the house price in suburban Shanghai is twenty-one times the annual income of a Shanghai resident. Similarly Beijing's price/annual income ratio also falls into the range of 30 to 42.[81] This means that households will have to set aside a down payment six times their annual income if they want to purchase a house, even though the down payment rate currently stays at 20 per cent.

Here we present a few options for China's authorities to reconsider their policy. First, they could postpone their request for banks to spread home mortgage lending activities for the time being. Secondly, they could substantially increase the salary level, but this would pose tremendous inflation pressure. Thirdly, the government could give subsidies to consumers for the purpose of house purchasing, or give subsidies to house developers to lower house prices, or establish special agencies to provide guarantees to help consumers to get access to bank loans. But this would broaden the government's budget deficit and discourage developers from making market profits.

Secondly, state banks do not share the authorities' opinion that for the time being the consumer credit business is a profitable business. As we can see, the current policy regarding the expanding of consumer credit is somehow administrative in nature. If commercial banks implemented such a policy, ie extended credit to individuals, the banks would have incurred another category of policy lending, rather than achieved the diversification of loan portfolios and the improvement of their loan quality. For example, guided consumer lending rates put banks at a disadvantage. The home mortgage lending rate is one grade below the rate of commercial loans with the same maturities, and the car loan rate is equal to the rate of commercial loans with the same maturities.[82] This rate schedule is in contrast to the standard practice, ie, the consumer lending rate is higher than the commercial lending rate, other terms being equal. From the perspective of banks, if the interest margin

81 *See* Xiao Jing, *The Risks of Developing China's Housing Market and Its Management*, 7 INTERNATIONAL BANKING RESEARCH (1998).

82 *See* Yuanlong Wang, above n 68.

is too thin and the lending scale is too small to offset the risks associated with the consumer lending, banks will have no incentive to conduct consumer lending activities. This has been proved by the practice of Yantai Housing Savings Bank and Bengbu Housing Savings Bank. Since their inception over 10 years ago, in order to survive these two banks have had to operate in the same way as the regular commercial banks would. Both banks have already deviated from their commitment to residential house lending, as statistics show that the residential house lending business is only 20 per cent of their total business.[83]

Thirdly, the individual credit rating system, consumer credit guarantee system and the corresponding consumer credit laws and regulations are incomplete or nonexistent. Currently there is no standard and consistent individual credit rating system in China, which is one of the major reasons that banks set up harsh lending terms and are overcautious about consumer lending. It is inevitable that the consumer credit business is going to expand in China sooner or later, and the proportion of consumer lending to total bank lending will undoubtedly increase. If China does not set up an efficient individual credit rating system, and institutions or banks have no way to consistently monitor individuals' credit records, then the default rate of consumer lending will not stay at the current level of 1 per cent forever.[84] Therefore consumer credit risk management should be the first priority for both authorities and banks. The development of consumer credit guarantee systems, especially the system for long-term consumer lending, should be addressed as soon as possible, too. For the time being, it is a common practice for China's banks to request that borrowers provide a third party guarantee when banks offer credit cards and extend car loans or home mortgage loans to individuals. These third parties are usually none other than the borrowers' employers. Since the financial situations of many of China's enterprises are not encouraging and changing jobs is becoming more and more commonplace, most employers are not willing to provide guarantees for their employees anymore. It is therefore up to the government to come up with an effective proposal to ease banks' nervousness about consumer credit business. Laws and regulations that cover how to resolve problems after defaults occur should be formulated to support the consumer credit system as well. In China free housing or the payment of a nominal rent while living in a residence permanently has existed for about half a century. There are no laws to instruct banks how to cover losses through legal procedures if defaults do happen. Despite the fact that in the loan agreements banks are entitled to dispose of borrowers' property to cover the unpaid loans if they cannot meet the payment, in practice it is very difficult to carry this out. Will the banks really chase the borrowers out of their houses after

83 *See* Xiao Jing, above n 81.
84 *See* Yuanlong Wang, above n 68.

they fail to repay the loans? Is there any kind of social security system to prevent borrowers' lives from falling apart due to their defaults? The answer is not only in the best interests of banks, but it is also crucial to the stability of society as a whole.

IV. CONCLUSIONS

The financial reform in China is needed not only to create a modern financial system, but also part of an integrated approach to creating a market economy. Two decades' financial reforms are beginning to show results, with financial institutions, particularly state-owned banks, starting to act on a commercial basis. However, the problems with China's financial system are still comprehensive and structural. Often, old problems have not been solved while new problems are emerging. As a result, reforms and re-reforms occur simultaneously in response to broad-based problems. So that the financial reform does not exist as a patchwork, it is paramount to overhaul the country's financial system across the board. Furthermore, such an overhaul is closely interlinked with reforms in other fields such as state-owned enterprises and the tax system.

The issue of sequencing will also require attention. The Nordic bank crisis of the late 1970s, the Mexican crisis of the 1990s and the recent Asian crisis all underscore the importance of financial reform sequencing. Financial reform sequencing is country-specific. In China, for example, the issue of non-performing loans is not only a result of banks' imprudence but also is rooted in structural problems. So priority should be given to solving structural problems. In addition, prudential regulation and supervision should always be emphasised concurrently with other reforms in progress.

Critically, financial reforms in China should be law-based.[85] Not only should laws and regulations with regard to reforms be in place, but also these laws and regulations should be in line with the international standards and practices in order to avoid the award situation that a new law is out of date as soon as it is promulgated. Furthermore, it should be noted that the law-based approach to financial reform is not simply about laws and legal processes; it must also be an interdisciplinary approach, where law is the thread that weaves together economic, political and social objectives with a transparent and fair implementation process.[86] The latter will be particularly important to China's financial reform.

[85] Professor Joseph J. Norton has argued that all of the problems in the Asian crises are law-based failures; correspondingly, financial sector reform should be law-based. *See* Joseph J. Norton, *Financial Sector Reform and International Financial Crises: The Legal Challenges*, Paper of the W. G. Hart Workshop 1998 on Transnational (Corporate) Finance and the Challenge to the Law (7–9 July 1998).

[86] *See* ibid. at 3.

Chapter 17

Evaluating China's Banking Reforms Post Asian Crisis

Zhongfei Zhou

I. INTRODUCTION

Due to the absence of capital account convertibility, a strong trade and foreign exchange reserve position, and using foreign direct investment as a main form of capital inflows, China was relatively unscathed from the Asian Crisis. However, the Asian Crisis gave the Chinese government a wake-up call. China shared similar vulnerabilities with those crisis-hit Asian countries. The central bank was subject to political interventions and was unable to exercise adequate prudential regulation and supervision. Commercial banks were not immune from government interference. They had excessive lending in specific industries. Financial systems were heavily bank, particularly state-owned bank, dominated. The four biggest state-owned banks accumulated huge amounts of non-performing loans. A rough estimate was 25 per cent of total loans.

The Chinese government recognised those fundamental vulnerabilities and the risks associated with delaying further reforms. On 17 November 1997, China's State Council convened an unusual high-level National Financial Work Conference in Beijing to discuss the problems of China's financial and banking system. At this conference, China decided to take about three years to establish financial institutions, financial markets, and a financial regulatory and supervisory system compatible with the Socialist market economy. Subsequent to the conference, a series of reforms were carried out to achieve these objectives. In the area of banking industry, these reforms consisted of strengthening the independence of the central bank (People's Bank of China, PBOC) through restructuring the central bank system; strengthening sound and safe operations of banks and corporate governance in banks through the injection of capital, introduction of a new loan classification system, and establishment of supervisory boards; and setting up asset management companies within the four biggest state-owned banks. This chapter is intended to evaluate these reforms, review the achievements, and discuss the remaining reform issues and obstacles.

II. RESTRUCTURING OF THE PEOPLE'S BANK OF CHINA (PBOC)

The branch offices of the PBOC used to be established in accordance with the administrative structure of the government at provincial and county level. This structure was considered a source of interference by the local governments with the central bank.[1] Even if the State Council vested the PBOC with the formal legal authority to exercise central banking functions in 1983, the provincial branches of the PBOC were relatively subordinate to local government and party officials. The PBOC had to consult with the provincial governments and party committees when they appointed, transferred and promoted personnel of banks operating within their geographic jurisdictions. In order to acquire the independence of the PBOC, the PBOC promulgated its restructuring plan, approved by the State Council in 1999. The plan was believed to be modeled on the Federal Reserve System of the United States. More than thirty PBOC branches were replaced by nine regional branches.[2] A financial regulatory office was established in the capital city of each of the regions where no PBOC branch was operating.[3] These nine regional branches are Tianjin, Shenyang, Shanghai, Nanjing, Jinan, Wuhan, Guangzhou, Chengdu, and Xi'an.[4] In 1999, all nine branches had been set up. The main responsibility of these regional offices is to regulate and supervise the operations of banks and non-bank financial institutions. The new structure helps minimise local interference as these regional branches are accountable directly to the PBOC headquarters.

As a matter of fact, the Law of the People's Bank of China (PBOC Law) in 1995 established a fair degree of operational autonomy for the PBOC. The PBOC Law gives the central bank all the features of a legal entity, although it does not refer to the notion as such. Under Article 8, the PBOC is endowed with paid-up capital and, in accordance with the provisions of Article 40, has to complete an annual balance sheet and a profit-and-loss account, to be published in an annual report. Articles 37 and 38 confer a reasonable degree of budgetary independence on the PBOC. The Law vests the PBOC with all the functions of a modern central bank, including the conduct of monetary policy; the issue of the currency; the centralisation and administration of the foreign reserve; the supervision of financial institutions and financial markets; and oversight of payments and clearing systems.[5]

[1] *See* Yuan Mu, 'Actively and Steadily Establishing the Commercial Banks', *The People's Daily*, 16 Feb. 1994, at 5.

[2] *See* PBOC, Implementing Plans for Reforming Provincial Offices of the People's Bank of China, *Bulletin of the People's Bank of China*, iss. 61, at 4–5. (10 Feb. 1999).

[3] Ibid.

[4] Ibid.

[5] *See* PBOC Law, Art. 4.

Notwithstanding the efforts to restructure the PBOC and to create relatively modern central bank legislation, it might be an extravagant wish to look to the full independence of the PBOC. The political system and the compromise nature of the central bank law determine that it is impossible for the PBOC to acquire full independence. Although the PBOC Law stipulates that the PBOC shall be free from intervention by local governments, other administrative organs at all levels, social organisations, and individuals,[6] it fails to prohibit any interference by the central government. The Law clearly indicates that the PBOC remains an institution under the leadership of the State Council. The leadership encompasses the formulation and implementation of monetary policy, supervision of the financial industry;[7] the nomination of the Governor and Deputy Governors of the PBOC,[8] and the operations of the monetary policy committee.[9] The absence of a management board allows for a more direct participation of the State Council in the decision-making process of the PBOC because there is no intermediary body between the Governor and the State Council.[10]

The independence of the PBOC is further undermined by the provisions on Governor and Deputy Governors in the PBOC Law. In many western countries, legislation clearly provides for the term of office of central bankers which is normally sufficiently long in order to safeguard independence and prevent politicisation and short-term perspectives.[11] By contrast, the PBOC Law is silent on the term of office of the Governor and Deputy Governors of the PBOC. It is unclear whether the term of office of those central bankers is concurrent with that of the Premier of the State Council or not. As a result, there is possibility that the term of office of the Governors would terminate with the expiry of the Premier of the State Council. Under the PBOC Law, the Governor of the PBOC is nominated by the Premier, approved by the National People's Congress and appointed by the President of the country.[12] But, under the current Chinese political regime, the nomination and removal of the Governor of the PBOC is determined by the Party committee and the State Council. The National People's Congress only plays a procedural role.

The independence of central banks depends heavily on qualified central bankers and their sophistication. Although the PBOC has a large staff, most of them have not been adequately trained in the past, especially on central

6 Ibid. Art. 7.

7 Ibid. Art. 2.

8 Ibid. Art. 9.

9 Ibid. Art. 11.

10 Hassanali Mehran *et al.*, *Monetary And Exchange System Reforms in China: An Experiment in Gradualism*, (Sept. 1996) at 19.

11 Rosa M. Lastra, *Central Banking and Banking Regulation*, (1996) at 30. For example, in the Bundesbank, the president, the directorate and the presidents of the land central banks are appointed for a term of eight years (which is renewable). Within the Federal Reserve System, the members of the Board of Governors are appointed for fixed terms of 14 years. *See* ibid.

12 PBOC Law, Art. 9.

bank functions under market economic conditions.[13] The PBOC's supervisors lack experience in financial business, and do not understand the financial reports submitted by financial institutions; as a result, they cannot detect material problems from the financial reports and are at the mercy of the regulatees' interpretations.[14] It is questionable whether the PBOC staff is able to exercise independent judgement when supervising financial institutions.

Although the restructuring of the central bank and the central bank law may enhance the independence of the PBOC, it is naïve to think that the intervention of the government will be eradicated. The source of the PBOC's authority, combined with the government's habitual involvement in the financial system, would most likely reduce the independence of the PBOC. As a result, the PBOC would often yield to the government as a tool of carrying out the government's policy. For example, in 1999, the government attempted to support the medium and small sized state-owned enterprises. The PBOC, accordingly, issued several circulars to the effect that commercial banks should extend credits to the medium and small sized state owned enterprises. Although these circulars were not legally mandatory, they exerted *de facto* mandatory effects on commercial banks' lending policy.

As a matter of fact, in the Chinese political and institutional setting, an autonomous entity separate from the State Council would have been inconceivable. Creating such an institution would have amounted to establishing an entity separate from the State Council without any authority because the state, as represented by the State Council, is the source of all authority.[15] Against this background, an appropriate legal framework for the independence of the PBOC is an essential step, but it will not by itself entirely eradicate political pressures. The PBOC's activities therefore need to be sufficiently transparent so that the PBOC can be seen as effectively exercising its powers. One way of achieving such transparency is to provide for periodic reports to be published describing the actions that have been taken by the PBOC to achieve its objectives. In this way the PBOC's performance can be monitored by the supervised banks and by the public at large, which in turn helps prevent possible government's interference and facilitates the PBOC's effective and fair performance of its functions. In addition, without sufficiently qualified staff, the supervisory authorities cannot fulfill their mandate. The PBOC should adopt adequate personnel policies to recruit and retain qualified staff. The PBOC should make great efforts to develop its staff's capacity with respect to all central banking activities.

[13] Yangxin Huang, 'Revamping the Legal Framework for the Chinese Banking System: A Critical Examination', *Studies in International Financial & Economic Law*, (1996) at 34.

[14] Yun Wei, 'An Analysis of Causes for Low Efficiency of Financial Regulation in China', *Hainan Finance*, at 17 (Oct. 1998) (Chinese).

[15] *See* Mehran, above n 10, at 19.

III. RECAPITALISATION OF STATE-OWNED BANKS

The paid-in capital of China's four largest state-owned banks had been declining relative to bank assets. Between 1985 and 1996 their assets grew almost six times more rapidly than their paid-in capital. Thus, the ratio of paid-in capital and their assets fell by five-sixths, from 12.1 per cent in 1985 to 2.2 per cent in 1996.[16] Declining capital adequacy was unlikely to be reversed without an injection of new capital into the state-owned banks. On 28 February 1998, the National People's Congress empowered the Ministry of Finance to issue RMB270 billion of special government bonds to recapitalise the four biggest state-owned banks.[17] This paralleled the reduction of the deposit reserve of the state-owned banks. This recapitalisation process involved three steps:[18] (1) the PBOC lowered the legal reserve requirement from 13 to 8 per cent freeing up about RMB377 billion of bank liquidity (roughly RMB270 billion from the state-owned banks and RMB107 billion from other financial institutions); (2) the state-owned banks used the additional liquidity to purchase bonds issued by the Ministry of Finance; and (3) the Ministry of Finance injected the entire proceeds into the state-owned banks to strengthen their equity capital. The PBOC indicated that the recapitalisation plan would bring the average capital adequacy ratio of the state-owned banks to 8 per cent.[19]

However, no official channels have confirmed that the capital adequacy ratio of the Big Four has reached the target of 8 per cent. Someone estimated that the ratio was only 6 per cent as in 2000 the PBOC required the Big Four to boost their capital adequacy ratios from the current average 6 per cent to the 8 per cent.[20] A more reliable conclusion is from Mr Xiaochuan Zhou, president of the China Construction Bank (one of the Big Four) and former deputy governor of the PBOC. In an article, he disclosed that the capital adequacy ratio of the China Construction Bank at the end of 1999 was 5.37 per cent, and that other three state-owned banks were facing the same problem of not reaching the target of capital adequacy.[21]

Perhaps, the four state-owned banks are even weaker than the data suggest. One reason is that large quantities of nonperforming loans are still

16 Nicholas R Lardy, *China's Unfinished Economic Revolution*, (1998) at 92.

17 National People's Congress, Resolution on Issuance by Ministry of Finance of Special Government Bonds to Supply State-Owned Banks' Capital (2 Feb. 1998).

18 Y. K. Mo, 'A Review of Recent Banking Reforms in China', in *Strengthening the Banking System in China: Issues and Experience*, (BIS Policy Papers No. 7, October 1999) at 93.

19 *See* ibid. at 94.

20 Yiping Huang, 'It Takes More Than Recapitalisation to Fix China's Banks', 8 Sept. 2000, available at <http://www.chinaonline.com/commentary_an...treform/currentnews>.

21 Xiaochuan Zhou, 'How do State-Owned Banks Replenish Capital?', *Xinhua Digest*, iss. 8, 2000, at 50. At the end of 1999, the net capital of the China Construction Bank was RMB94.5 billion and the risk-weighted assets were RMB1,760 billion. *See* ibid.

carried on bank balance sheets as assets. Newly created asset management companies can only resolve the stock problem but not the flow problem of nonperforming loans. The experience of transition economies in eastern and central European has shown that injecting capital without solving the flow problem of non-performing loans could easily lead to an additional capital injections.[22] Writing off these nonperforming loans requires capital as the loan loss reserves in the Big Four are too small to serve this purpose. Another reason is that China's risk weighting system diverges significantly from international standards. For example, under the Basel Committee on Banking Supervision's 'International Convergence of Capital Measurement and Capital Standards of July 1988' (1988 Capital Accord), all claims on banks incorporated in OECD countries and short-term claims (ie up to one year) on banks incorporated in non-OECD countries may be risk weighted at 20 per cent.[23] Under the Basel Committee on Banking Supervision's 'A New Capital Adequacy Framework' of June 1999 (New Capital Framework), whether adopting the approach based on risk weighting of sovereign in which the bank is incorporated or that based on the assessment of the individual bank, claims on banks would, at a minimum, receive a 20 per cent weighting.[24] By contrast, according to the PBOC's Instructions for Reporting Forms for Off-Site Examinations, lending to or purchasing bonds of domestic debt-ridden banks only carries a 10 per cent weighting.[25]

The recapitalisation of the state-owned banks was criticised as leading to moral hazard by increasing risk-taking by banks and by reducing market discipline by depositors. Recapitalisation of banks can undermine the incentive of banks to adopt prudent lending criteria and foster the expectation that, having bailed out troubled banks once, the government would do so again.[26] In my opinion, the issue of moral hazard is often misunderstood. In theory, as the owner of the state-owned banks, the government has a duty to provide capital to state-owned banks as other owners do in private banks. Recapitalisation of banks does not necessarily lead to banks' excessive risk-taking. Furthermore, depositors' inactivity to discipline banks is concurrent with banking regulation, and would not become deteriorated only because of recapitalisation of banks by the government. Depositors tend to regard bank regulation and supervision as government certification

[22] Mo, above n 18, at 101. For example, the Hungarian government had to recapitalise the country's state banks four times between 1991 and 1994 as little had be done to tackle the flow problem before mid-1994. ibid.

[23] 1988 Capital Accord, annex 2.

[24] New Capital Framework, at 28–9.

[25] PBOC, Instructions for Reporting Forms for Off-Site Examinations, Art. 5.

[26] Nicholas R. Lardy, 'The Challenge of Bank Restructuring in China', in *Strengthening the Banking System in China: Issues and Experience*, above n 18, at 32.

of an individual bank's safety and the stability of the banking system.[27] They always have a perception of being protected. As a result, currently, market discipline is not yet at the stage where it could play a critical proper role in monitoring banks. Moreover, depositors do not have sufficient information and skills to evaluate properly the soundness of the bank in which they place their funds. All these require us not to look to market discipline too much, at least at the current stage.

Without doubt, the recapitalisation of the state-owned banks has positive effects. More or less it increases the capital base of the Big Four. However, the issue is whether this top-down approach to recapitalisation is cost-effective. As the depth and sophistication of financial markets increase, governments show no ability to keep up with new developments; as a result, governments find it harder to determine how much banks need. 'Too much' would waste resources while 'too little' would not be working to solve banks' problems. By contrast, some large foreign banks have developed their own models to track and evaluated some risks on a quantitative basis. They are able to set limits on risk-taking, evaluate the return and risks of specific activities, and allocate capital accordingly.[28] Since the Basel Committee has allowed banks to use their own models for market risk capital adequacy requirements in the 1996 Market Risk Amendment and welcomes the use already made of credit risk models at some sophisticated banks under the New Capital Framework, it is expected that in the future capital regulation will be based less on specific rules and prescriptions and more on a system of general principles for sound and prudent management.[29] So I argue that it is the Chinese state-owned banks themselves who should determine the capital charges rather than the government. Of course, the task that the Chinese banks face is how to improve their skills in order to develop their own internal capital adequacy models.[30]

[27] Gillian Garcia, *Deposit Insurance: Obtaining the Benefits and Avoiding the Pitfalls*, at 8 (Aug. 1996); *see also* Charles Goodhart *et al., Financial Regulation: Why, How, and Where Now?*, (1998) at 15 (When a regulatory authority is created and established regulatory requirements, an implicit contract is perceived as having been created between the user of financial services and the regulator, ie the consumer assumes that, because there is an authorisation procedure, specific aspects of regulation are established, the supplier of financial services is authorised and supervised, and the institution is therefore safe.). Professor Dale also argues that the very presence of regulators responsible for ensuring the soundness of banks and preventing bank failures may induce both equity investors and depositors to rely on regulatory protection rather than on their own independent analysis of banking risks. Richard Dale, *The Regulation of International Banking*, (1984) at 57.

[28] *See* General Accounting Office of the USA, *Risk-Based Capital: Regulatory and Industry Approaches to Capital And Risk* (July 1998) at 75.

[29] William J. McDonough, 'Conference Overview: Major Themes and Directions for the Future', *Federal Reserve Bank of New York Economic Policy Review*, (Oct. 1998) at 5. McDonough, above n 116, at 5.

[30] The Basel Committee implies that in the future full credit risk models will be used. *See* New Capital Framework, above n 24, at 38 (stating that an internal ratings-based approach

IV. OPERATIONAL INDEPENDENCE OF COMMERCIAL BANKS

With a planned economy tradition, credit allocation in China was based on a mandatory quota system under which the PBOC set lower limits on new loans to be made annually and their allocation to specific sectors. The government was directly involved in the formulation of the credit plans. Under this system, banks were often asked to allocate credits to support the operations of loss-making state-owned enterprises.[31] In January 1998, the PBOC abolished the quota system and replaced it with an indicative, non-binding, target. Banks have freedom to extend lending provided that their total lending is in line with asset/liability ratio management[32] and the central bank's monetary policy targets.

On 21 September 2000, China took the first major step in liberalising its rigid interest rate system, allowing the market to set rates for foreign currency loans and large deposits. The move is part of a three-year central bank plan to free interest rates now set by administrative decree. Foreign currency lending rates and deposit rates for sums of more than US$3.0 million are set by banks. Rates for deposits of less than that amount are decided by the China Association of Banks.

There is also a legal guarantee from the Commercial Banking Law of 1995 for the operational autonomy of commercial banks. The Commercial Banking Law enables commercial banks including state-owned banks to act as an independent legal person, that is, to have paid-up capital, to own assets, to enter into contracts, and to sue and be sued. They conduct business according to laws, free from interference from any organisations or individual.[33]

While China has made great progress in freeing commercial banks from administrative interventions, there are still some obstacles to banks operating on fully commercial principles. Article 41 (2) of the Commercial

could provide incentives for banks to further refine credit risk management techniques, paving the way for a transition towards full credit risk models in the future). In April 1999, the Basel Committee published a report on credit risk modeling. William McDonough, the chairman of the Basel Committee for Banking Supervision, said that if the hurdles discussed in the report could be overcome, it may also have a role in the determination of regulatory capital requirements. *See* Anonymous, 'Basle Committee Seeks Refinement of Credit Risk Models', *Dow Jones International News*, 21 Apr. 1999, available at <http://www.lawschool.westlaw.com search>.

31 Lardy, above n 26, at 99.

32 Asset/liability ratio management system has undergone several changes since it came into force in 1994. In Dec. 1996, the PBOC published the Monitoring Norms and Assessment Methods for the Regulation of Asset and Liabilities Ratio of Commercial Banks, which revised the Guidelines on the Regulation of Assets and Liabilities Ration of Commercial Banks of 1994. In 1997, the PBOC's Instructions for Completing Reporting Forms for Off-Site Examination amended the above two rules.

33 Commercial Banking Law, Art 4(2).

Banking Law clearly provides that state-owned banks should extend loans to specific projects approved by the State Council and the State Council would make restitution for all losses incurred through such mandated loans, although the same article prohibits any organisations and individuals from forcing commercial banks to extend loans.[34] It indicates that state-owned banks still have to assume responsibility for issuing policy loans. If this is to happen, the process of commercialising these banks will be hampered.[35]

As regards local commercial banks, administrative interference is more serious as their establishment requires local governments' approval and their existence depends on the blessing of local governments. When local governments have strong interests in developing their local economy, often characterised by huge commercial centres, office skyscrapers and luxury apartments, they will exert pressure on local banks to fund projects in their locality.

Notwithstanding our efforts, political interference with banks never disappears. In my opinion, the cause for this is that we never solve the issue of banks' accountability. In theory, banks, due to the nature of state-ownership, should be accountable to the government as a sole or major investor. Increasing the value of their investment in banks is only one of the governments' targets, however. They have many other targets, economic, social, and even political. In some cases, the government would sacrifice its value-increasing target for other targets. For example, in the mid-1990s the response of the local governments to the demonstrations by the workers who were furloughed from their jobs in state firms was just to require local branches of state banks to extend additional credit so that back wages could be paid and urban unrest defused.[36] In 1998–9, the Ministry of Finance spent RMB200 billion on infrastructure projects in order to achieve the government's growth target. Commercial banks were called to provide RMB400 billion of policy loans on companion projects.[37]

More importantly, in my opinion, the problem is that banks have established inappropriate performance accountability.[38] In other words, they do not know what they should be accountable for. According to the Company Law, banks, like other companies, should achieve the objective of maintaining and increasing the value of assets.[39] However, the long practices of applying administrative means to economic activities have formulated such a value that the relation between government and banks is that of superiority and

[34] Ibid. Art 4(1).

[35] Mehran, above n 10, at 23.

[36] Lardy, above n 16, at 128–129.

[37] Huang, above n 20.

[38] 'Performance accountability' is borrowed from Dr Lastra's term when she discusses the issue of central bank accountability. Performance is generally measured with relation to the statutory goal/s to be achieved. The governing bodies of the central bank, particularly the governor should be held accountable for failing to achieve such objectives. *See* Lastra, above n 11, at 51.

[39] Company Law of People's Republic of China of 1993 (amended 1999), Art. 5(2).

inferiority. As a result, banks are accountable to the government for obeying orders and regard as a duty fulfilling satisfactorily the government's tasks (sometimes the government's tasks would be called political tasks). The performance in this regard has much to do with the promotion of bank officials, in particular when the governments at various levels maintained authority over bank personnel within their localities. So it is understandable that banks may focus on how to satisfy the government rather than on how to increase the value of state-owned assets at banks.

V. ASSET MANAGEMENT COMPANIES (AMCs)

Each of the biggest four state-owned banks had major asset quality problems. It was estimated that at least 25 per cent of their loans were non-performing loans. Apparently, only banks themselves were unable to solve the non-performing loan problems. In October 1998, Premier Zhu Rongji decided to set up an AMC for the China Construction Bank as a pilot project to acquire non-performing loans from the China Construction Bank. Following this, the other Big Four banks followed suit with their own AMCs. During the period from April to October 1999 four separate AMCs were set up within the four biggest state-owned banks. They are; the Cinda AMC for the China Construction Bank, the Dongfang AMC for the Bank of China, China Great Wall AMC for the Agricultural Bank of China, and China Huarong AMC for the Industrial and Business Bank of China. AMCs are wholly owned by the central government, and not by the respective Big Four banks. The Ministry of Finance capitalised them with RMB10 billion each.

These four AMCs only deal with the non-performing loans issued before 1996. Banks themselves are required to handle the non-performing loans created after the beginning of 1996. By the end of June 2000, the four AMCs had taken over RMB1.3 trillion from the Big Four.[40] Taking over bad assets from banks is only the first step. The second step is that banks take on a debt-for-equity swap deal with state-owned enterprises. Under these debt-for-equity swaps, the AMC acquires from the bank at its face value a loan made by the bank to a state-owned enterprise. The AMC then forgives the debt of the state-owned enterprise in exchange for equity of the enterprise. The AMC will at some time sell the equity. The state-owned enterprises selected for this program must be those among the 512 key enterprises, or industrial state-owned enterprises established during the periods of the 'seventh plan' (1986–90) or the 'eighth plan' (1991–5), or

[40] Anonymous, 'Asset Management Cos Receive US$157bn of Bad Assets from Banks', 3 Aug. 2000, *available at* <http://www.chinaonline.com/issues/econ-new/currentnews/ secure>.

during the first two years of the 'ninth plan' (1996–2000). They must demonstrate that they have the potential to be profitable after debt-for-equity swaps.

AMCs are authorised to conduct a wide range of activities which involve both commercial and investment banking activities. Under the Regulation on Financial Asset Management Companies promulgated by the State Council in November 2000, AMCs may undertake listing sponsorship as well as bond and stock underwriting for companies within the scope of their asset management. They may also enter other areas, if approved by the PBOC and the China Securities Regulatory Commission. They are also allowed to lease, transfer or reorganise assets formed by bad loans they have purchased. They may transfer enterprise equities in their holding to domestic and overseas investors or have the equities repurchased by firms whose debts have changed into equities according to law. After AMCs transform financial claims into equities, they may dispatch personnel to the firm's board of directors and board of supervisors to exercise their rights as shareholders.[41]

Different from the practices in other countries, AMCs in China are required to achieve three objectives. The first objective is to facilitate state-owned banks to change their operational mechanism and turn them into 'good banks'; the second is to help restructure state-owned enterprises and turn them into 'good enterprises'; the third to recover non-performing loans to the fullest extent possible, reduce the financial burden of the government, and maintain 'good finance'.[42] It is understandable that without solving the state-owned enterprise problems, it will be impossible to solve the non-performing loan problem at state-owned banks, because in China banks are intertwined with state-owned enterprises. However, the problems in state-owned enterprises are so comprehensive and deep-rooted that alone AMCs are unable to deal with them. In my opinion, the triple tasks may make AMCs unable to accomplish each of them.

Another problem with AMCs is the lack of a solid legal infrastructure for the operations of AMCs. The Regulation on Financial Asset Management Companies was not promulgated by the State Council until 19 November 2000. Before this Regulation, only a proposal issued jointly by the PBOC, Ministry of Finance and China Securities Regulatory Commission governed the AMCs. This proposal is neither law nor regulation. Moreover, the authority of AMCs to conduct the wide range of activities is easily challenged. In China, there is a very strict policy on the separation of banking,

41 *See* Anonymous, 'Regulations on Asset Management Companies Released', 21 Nov. 2000, *available at* <www.chinaonline.com/industry/financial/currentnews/secure>.

42 *See* Xuebing Wang, 'Three Objectives, Three Risks and Three Measures in Setting Up Asset Management Companies in China', *Studies on International Finance* (Chinese) (iss. 6, 1999).

securities, insurance and trust, which is laid down by the laws enacted by the National People's Congress. The Securities Law clearly provides that securities, banking, trust and insurance are operated and regulated separately, and securities companies are set up separately from banking, trust and insurance institutions.[43] Under the Chinese legislative system, regulations made by the State Council are junior to laws made by the National People's Congress and its standing committee, and are not allowed to contravene the basic principles laid down by the latter. Apparently, the Regulation on Financial Asset Management Companies contradicts the basic principle of 'separate operations'. In my opinion, there is no legal basis for AMCs' broad scope of business.

There are several practical obstacles to invigorating the large amount of static assets. China's undeveloped capital market restrains AMCs from innovating new products to deal with the non-performing loans. AMCs are restricted from selling equity rights in certain domestic sectors to foreign investors. Because many of the non-performing loans are loans to rusty state-owned enterprises which generate little or no cashflow, there will be much possibility that no one would like to buy the banks' compromised assets. Without cooperation of local governments, AMCs would not win success in solving state-owned enterprise problems. However, many local authorities are unwilling to give tax rebates to companies carrying out debt-for-equity swaps, nor are they willing to take responsibility for any resulting worker lay-offs or unprofitable assets from the companies.

VI. PRIVATISATION: A WORKABLE APPROACH TO IMPROVING CORPORATE GOVERNANCE IN STATE-OWNED COMMERCIAL BANKS

Given that the changes in laws and regulations do not eradicate problems inherent in corporate governance, many people have urged the privatisation of wholly state-owned commercial banks. Privatisation or corporatisation which China prefers to use,[44] means restructuring ownership at the largest four state banks and making them shareholding companies with listings on

[43] Securities Law, Art. 6.

[44] The terms 'privatisation' and 'corporatisation' reflect the difference in ideology. Corporatisation which is the conversion of a state-owned enterprise into a shareholding company is regarded as ideologically compatible with 'socialism with Chinese characteristics' while privatisation, stemming from the word 'private', is identified with the institution of private ownership without necessarily ensuring the preservation of the state as the agent of the whole people. *See* Lan Cao, 'Chinese Privatisation: Between Plan and Market', 63 *L. & Contemp. Problems*, at 14 (Autumn 2000).

domestic or overseas stock markets.[45] The basic consideration is that under a shareholding system there are several sanctions and incentives being used to induce bank management to maximise the value of shareholders' investment. Since investors can withdraw their assets by selling stock (vote with feet), the market for shares gives owners a means of pressure while the absence of a share market would remove such a sanction for bad management performance. The threat of bankruptcy and takeovers, which lead to dismissals of managers, may also discipline managers.

It was reported that the Big Four are planning to list some time over the next three to five years.[46] It seems that only restructuring state banks into shareholding banks can solve the structural problems in corporate governance.[47] However, even if the Big Four state-owned banks can be privatised, they will remain with government holding the majority share. The Governor of the PBOC, Dai Xianglong, claims that wholly state-owned commercial banks which meet the requirements may be restructured to be joint stock banks with the state retaining a controlling share; and when conditions are ripe, those joint stock banks can be listed.[48]

Under a bank with the government holding a majority share, however, corporate governance cannot be expected to be improved critically, although those banks, as joint stock companies or probably listed companies, have to comply with statutory requirements on protecting minority shareholders and have greater transparency, which represents an improvement over the governance of banks. As in wholly state-owned commercial banks, the government will still have the power to appoint the board of directors. The government's will will still be carried out by its appointed board and the board appointed management. Supervisory boards will be

45 The Chinese Academy of Social Sciences, the government's top think-tank, called for listing part of the state banks' shares on the domestic stock markets, placing shares with non-state Chinese firms or selling some stakes to foreign investors. Reuters, 'China: China's WTO Deal Heralds Radical Banking Reform', *Reuters English News Service*, 16 Nov. 1999, <http://web2.westlaw.com/shared/search>.

46 R. J. Michaels, Bullish over Big Four: Experts Favor Top Banks' Plans to List, 17 Oct. 2000, <http://www.chinaonline.com/topstories/001017/1/c0001101751.asp>.

47 For example, Fang Xinghai, general manager of the Construction Bank of China's group coordination committee, said: 'I see no better way than listing the banks on the stock market to improve the banks' corporate governance.' *See* Reuters, 'China: China's Big Four Banks Eye Stock Listings', *Reuters English News Service*, 23 Apr. 2000, <http://web2.westlaw.com/hared/search>. The last ten years has witnessed a massive surge in the size and number of firms being sold to private investors by governments around the world. The cumulative value of privatisations passed US$1 trillion during 1999. Almost all published empirical research has strongly suggested that privatisation is associated with significant performance improvements in enterprises. William L. Megginson, Corporate Governance in Publicly-Quoted Companies, Paper on the OECD Conference on Corporate Governance of SOEs in China, at 15, 17 (Beijing, 18–19 Jan. 2000).

48 *See* Dai Xianglong, 'Do Our Best at All Types of the Central Banking Activities in an All-round Way with an Emphasis of Financial Regulation', *China Finance*, at 6 (iss. 2, 2001).

still confronted with the problem of conflict of interests as they are authorised by the government to supervise the government appointed board and management. Ambiguous property rights will not become clear-cut with the emergence of joint stock banks because in such banks real owners of property will be still unable to exercise their ownership rights and the government will still exercise *de facto* ownership rights without bearing any residual risks.

As a matter of fact, even in typical joint stock companies, there is the chronic principal-agent problem arising from the separation of ownership and management. Market systems provide three corrective mechanisms to mitigate the problem.[49] One method is to induce managers to carry out efficient management by directly aligning managers' interests with those of shareholders, eg management compensation and direct monitoring by boards. The second solution involves the strengthening of shareholder's rights so shareholders have both a greater incentive and ability to monitor management. This approach enhances the rights of investors through legal protection from expropriation by managers, eg protection and enforcement of shareholders rights and prohibitions against insider-dealings. The third approach is to use indirect means such as takeovers. The takeover market is widely recognised as a potentially important mechanism by which capital markets ensure management discipline.[50]

However, the above three approaches might not be workable. The role that management compensation currently plays as a mechanism of corporate control may be overemphasised.[51] There is a possibility that the initiatives of managers to maximise shareholder value would be reduced if managers can benefit more from rent-seeking behaviours than from management compensation. In addition, the board of directors often performs their monitoring function either passively or ineffectively.[52] As regards the second approach above, as a matter of fact, corporate laws and relevant regulations have already clear stipulations on these issues. Apparently, the reason why the approach may not be workable is effective implementation of these laws and regulations. Implementation of law is

[49] Maria Maher and Thomas Anderson, 'Corporate Governance: Effects on Firm Performance and Economic Growth', at 7 (1999) <http://www.oecd.org>.

[50] Stephen Prowse, *Corporate Governance in an International Perspective: A Survey of Corporate Control Mechanisms Among Large Firms in the United State, the United Kingdom, Japan and Germany*, at 46 (BIS Economic Papers, No 41, 1994).

[51] Ibid. at 45.

[52] Benjamin T. Lo, 'Improving Corporate Governance: Lessons from the European Community', 1 *In. J. Global. L. Std.* at 223 (Fall 1993). The reasons are that first, board members are often nominated by chief executives to serve on corporate boards; second, directors usually do not have adequate time to carry out their assigned duties; third, directors may be poorly informed about corporate matters; fourth, boards are unable to work as a cohesive group for the corporation; and finally the chief executive officer also often assumes the role of the chairman of the board of directors. Ibid.

forever a sticky problem. For takeovers, there are a number of impediments for them to be an effective mechanism of corporate control.[53] The first is the free-rider problem in making a successful tender offer for a firm.[54] The second impediment is the inability to keep a tender offer secret, which implies that the original bidder who expends resources to identify the target will have a negative expected profit, and will therefore have little incentive to undertake such research in the first place.[55] The final impediment is that current managers are often well placed to take strategic action to deter takeovers.[56] In particular, under a rather concentrated ownership structure, a bidder would find it difficult to attain a sufficiently large stake in a company to take it over without the consent of the largest shareholders, the government in a Chinese joint stock bank, for instance. In China, government approval for takeovers may pose an additional impediment to successful takeovers.[57]

In the absence of well-developed and efficient capital markets, privatisation of China's wholly state-owned commercial banks is not a workable approach to improving corporate governance in these banks. As a matter of fact, the existence of concentrated holdings by the government in China's state-owned commercial banks may constitute an important way to overcome the perennial problem of principal and agent in corporate governance. It has been argued that ownership concentration can overcome the problems with the monitoring of management that are associated with dispersed ownership. This is because if the equity of the firm is concentrated in the hands of a few investors, each investor will have sufficient private incentive to invest in information acquisition and monitoring of management;[58] and they are less able to sell their shares and take the 'Wall Street walk'.[59] In addition, large shareholdings also give them the ability to exert control over management either through their voting rights or through representation on the board of directors, or both.[60]

53 *See* Prowse, above n 50, at 63–4.

54 Shareholders in a company subject to a hostile takeover bid have an incentive not to accept the bid and will hope that others will sell out. Should the bid succeed the resistant shareholder can reap the full value of the equity arising from the reorganisation of the company, which may exceed the value of the bid. The shareholder will fee-ride on the eventual returns to the bidder. If all shareholders behaved in this way a bid would fail. Sanford Grossman and Oliver Hart, 'Takeover Bids, the Free-Rider Problem, and the Theory of the Corporation', 11 *Bell J. Econ.*, at 42–64 (1980).

55 Prowse, above n 50, at 63–4.

56 Ibid. at 64

57 Under the 1999 Company Law, the merge or division of a joint stock limited company must be approved by the government departments. 1999 Company Law, Art. 183. For a bank, its merger or division should be approved by the PBOC. Commercial Banking Law, Art. 69.

58 Prowse, above n 50, at 11.

59 John H Matheson, 'Corporate Governance at the Millennium: The Decline of the Poison Pill Antitakerover Defense', 22 *Hamline L. Rev.* at 735 (Spring 1999).

60 Prowse, above n 50, at 11–12.

In contrast, the Chinese government has paid attention to the role of the dominance of the state as equity holder in corporate governance. For general joint stock limited companies and limited liability companies, the state-authorised investment institutions or the departments authorised by the state hold state-owed shares and exercise the rights of state shareholder on behalf of the government.[61] These institutions or departments include holding companies, investment companies, parent companies of enterprise groups, and the Bureau of State Property Management when the state-authorised investment institutions are not clarified.[62] These institutions and departments enjoy the same rights as other shareholders.[63] However, this practice has been criticised as unsuccessful,[64] or at least we can say that corporate governance of China's companies has not benefited from the advantages associated with concentration of state ownership in companies. The main reason is that most of the state-authorised institutions were directly restructured from government departments and have not become true modern companies. Management of these institutions is in fact civil servants. Governmental bureaucratism still inherently exists. In addition, there are conflicts of interest between the Bureau of State Property Management (BSPM), as a special administrative agency for state-owned shares, the state-authorised investment institutions, and companies.[65]

Apparently, the idea of the state-authorised investment institution or the

[61] *See* Bureau of State Property Management and State Commission for the Reform of the Economic System, Interim Regulations on the Administration of State-Owned Shares in Joint Stock Limited Companies, Arts. 2, 16 (Nov. 1994); Bureau of State Property Management and State Commission for the Reform of the Economic System, Opinions on the Formalisation of the Exercising of the Rights of State-Owned Shares in Joint Stock Limited Companies, Art. 2 (Mar. 1997); and 1999 Company Law, Arts. 20, 21, 64.

[62] Interim Regulations on the Administration of State-Owned Shares in Joint Stock Limited Companies, Arts. 16.

[63] These institutions and departments have the following shareholder rights: (1) to delegate a shareholder's representative to attend the general shareholders' meeting and exercise his voting right; to participate in company election and being elected; (3) to increase purchase, receive, donate, transfer or mortgage shareholding according to rules; (4) to inspect company articles of association, minutes of general shareholders' meeting, and financial and accounting reports of the company; monitor the management of production, business and finance of the company, and make suggestions and enquiries; (5) to obtain dividend and other distributed benefits according to proportion of shareholding; and (6) to take legal action against any illegal and harmful behaviour of the company. *See* Opinions on the Formalisation of the Exercising of the Rights of State-Owned Shares in Joint Stock Limited Companies, Art. 6.

[64] Some authors asserted that the higher ratio of the state-owned shares, the worse the situation of corporate governance. *See* Junju Ma and Decong Nie, 'Recent Development of Corporate Governance Structure', 22 *Law Studies*, at 87 (in Chinese), (iss. 2, 2000); Xiaonian Xu and Yan Wang, 'Ownership Structure, Corporate Governance, and Firms' Performance: The Case of Chinese Stock Companies', at 23 (manuscript, on file with author, May 1997) (stating that the state as a large shareholder has negative or insignificant effects on firms' value).

[65] For example, when a company needs to raise new capital through rights offerings, the BSPM will force the state-authorised institution or through its representatives on the board to vote against it as the offerings will likely dilute state shares. *See* Xu and Wang, above n 64, at 24.

department authorised by the state as holders of shareholders may not be helpful to improving corporate governance of state-owned commercial banks. To make full use of the advantages arising from concentrated ownership, China should establish special, professional, and commercial-based Investment Companies for State-Owned Assets in Wholly State-Owned Commercial Banks (Special Bank Investment Companies). The government should delegate state-owned assets in the Big Four banks to these Special Bank Investment Companies. Under this structure, the government is no longer the shareholder of the Big Four banks. The banks do not have any relationship with the government.

The Special Bank Investment Company is a privatised company, whether joint stock limited company or limited liability company, with clear corporate objectives, strong economic incentives, and delineated lines of responsibility. For the purposes of diversifying risk and enhancing competition, a Special Bank Investment Company will be set up for each wholly state-owned commercial bank. The Special Bank Investment Companies are long-term investors in these banks. Their main business activity is to monitor management by the Big Four of state-owned assets. Their main income is the dividends associated with the investments in the banks, shared with the government. As a result, their own economic interests are closely interrelated with the performance of the banks, which would provide strong incentives to actively monitor the banks.

The Special Bank Investment Company specialises in asset management with possession of time, expertise, and monitoring skills. As the sole shareholder of a wholly state-owned commercial bank, the Special Bank Investment Company enjoys shareholder's rights stipulated in the company law. It will delegate day-to-day monitoring to the supervisory board (the two-tier board model will be adopted in state-owned commercial banks, see below). It can hire executive directors and non-executive directors to undertake bank-specific monitoring for it. It can also place its own representatives on the supervisory board. The representatives are likely to be more accountable to the Special Bank Investment Company which nominates them, and less to bank management.

In a state-owned commercial bank, the German two-tier board model should be adopted in order to create a clear institutional and personal separation of monitoring and management organs. The supervisory board will appoint managing directors and exercise day-to-day monitoring activities on behalf of the Special Bank Investment Company. Managing directors will be unable to influence or dominate the supervisory board meetings as they cannot be present or represented on the supervisory board. Thus, the supervisory board will act independent of the managing board and lead to effective monitoring of the bank.[66]

[66] *See* Lo, above n 52, at 241.

The Special Bank Investment Company would owe fiduciary duties to the government concerning state-owned assets in a wholly state-owned commercial bank. These duties include duty of care, duty of loyalty, duty of good faith.[67] Related to the issue is who will monitor the monitor. The issue in the Special Bank Investment Company is less serious that other cases. Due to the specifics of the business of the Special Bank Investment Company, ie, monitoring bank management of state-owned assets, the duties owed to the government and benefits produced to the company are interrelated. Its indolence in monitoring and thereby resulting in bad performance of a bank would directly affect its economic income. In addition, the government will have the power to withdraw its assets from a problem Special Bank Investment Company and delegate them to other Special Bank Investment Companies. Therefore, the Special Bank Investment Company will have limited incentives to breach fiduciary duties because it loses more if it is 'caught' than it gains if it succeeds.[68]

The idea of the Special Bank Investment Company would overcome some of the most common problems faced by institutional investors, such as institutional passivity,[69] conflicts of interest,[70] and free riding.[71] The primary function of a Special Bank Investment Company is to monitor bank management. Actively devoting itself to monitoring is its job. So for a Special Bank Investment Company institutional passivity does not exit. As

[67] *See* Julian Javier Garza, 'Rethinking Corporate Governance: The Role of Minority Shareholders—A Comparative Study', 31 *St. Ma. L. J.*, at 628–34 (2000).

[68] Fiduciary liability is a strong constraint on institutional investors. *See* cf Bernard S. Black, 'Agents Watching Agents: The Promise of Institutional Investor Voice', 39 *UCLA L. Rev.*, at 856 (Apr. 1992).

[69] If an institutional investor collects a large amount of one company's stock, it will no longer be sufficiently diversified. Unable to manage risk effectively, it will become less attractive to customers seeking to use it to mange risk. As a result, an institutional investor is unlikely to adopt the strong ownership role. Instead, the institution will remain largely passive investors. Thomas A. Smith, 'Institutions and Entrepreneurs in American Corporate Finance', 85 *Calif. L. Rev.*, at 5 (Jan. 1997).

[70] Many institutional investors face conflicts of interest. For example, money mangers who vote against a company's proposals are likely to lose any business that they conduct with the company. Money mangers who develop an anti-manager reputation may lose corporate business, or find it harder to gain new business. These conflicts lead some institutions to vote pro-manager even when doing so is likely to decrease company value. Black, above n 68, at 826. *See also* Mark J. Roe, 'Political Elements in the Creation of a Mutual Fund Industry', 139 *U. Pa. L. Rev.*, (1991) at 1503–4.

[71] Although an institutional investor that undertakes successful shareholder interventions may attract new clients, other fund managers also benefit from the successful intervention. Bernard S Black and John C. Coffee, Jr., 'Hail Britannia?: Institutional Investor Behavior under Limited Regulation', 92 *Mich. L. Rev.*, (June, 1994) at 2057. *See also* Monika Queisser, 'The Role of Pension Funds in the Stabilisation of the Domestic Financial Sector', in *International Financial Standard Setting* (Say Woo, Douglas Arner, and Zhongfei Zhou (eds), 2002 forthcoming) (stating that any gains a pension fund might reap from a more active participation in company management must be shared with the other investors in the company, including institutional investors competing with the pension or mutual fund mangers).

a matter of fact the Special Bank Investment Company is truly monitoring activism. As sole shareholder of a wholly state-owned commercial bank, only the Special Bank Investment Company and the government as the former beneficiary, will benefit from its successful monitoring. No other institutions will share the gains arising from its successful intervention. There are no 'free riding' rivals. What distinguishes a Special Bank Investment Company from institutional investors is that the former is a pure equity investor and its sole interest is in investment returns. They do not have any business relationships with the portfolio banks. Thus, Special Bank Investment Companies would not give rise to the problem of the conflicts of interest that would accompany active investments by commercial banks, pension funds, mutual funds or insurance companies.

VI. CONCLUSIONS

It is undeniable that China has made great progress in every aspect of banking reforms over the past four years. However, the problems with China's banking system are still comprehensive and structural. Often, old problems have not been solved while new problems are emerging. So, China's banking reform should not be a patchwork. It is paramount to overhaul the country's financial system across the board. For this purpose, Chinese banking reforms should be law-based. Not only should laws and regulations with regard to reforms be in place, but also these laws and regulations should be in line with the international standards and practices in order to avoid the awkward situation that a new law is out of date as soon as it is promulgated.

As a matter of fact, it is an easy process to transplant international standards and practices and other countries' laws into China, thereby superficially keeping in line with international standards. The difficult process is how banking reform legislation is established on an internationally accepted common values basis.[72] In my opinion, the first priority for the Chinese legislators and banking reformists is to cultivate those common values that should underpin the banking reform legislation, thereby ensuring that, on the one hand, legislation is in line with international standards and practices in various respects; and, on the other hand, legislation is implemented consistently.

72 For a discussion of internationally accepted common values in banking area, *see* Zhongfei Zhou, *Chinese Banking Law and Foreign Financial Institutions*, at ch. 1 (Mar. 2001).

Chapter 18

Taiwan and the Asian Financial Crisis—The Reasons for Stability during and after the Crisis and Related Lessons

Chunghsing Chou

One of the common nightmares for most East Asian countries before the end of twentieth century might be the financial crisis which occurred in 1997. The crisis not only terminated the rapid economic development of the East Asian area of the previous two decades, but also has had a serious impact on most of these countries.

The influence of the crisis was wide and deep, and not only limited to economic and financial aspects. The political situation of most East Asian countries also experienced dramatic alteration during the crisis. In Korea and Thailand, the then ruling party has shifted. In Indonesia, ex-president Suharto, was forced out. The unsteady economic and political situation in the region attracted international attention and assistance.

Under the effort of international organisations, most crises-effected countries have gradually recovered. Although the future economy of the region seems unable to enjoy the high degree growth of the past two decades, most effected countries have walked out of the crisis mud by the end of 2000.

Amid the turbulent period, the relatively steady economic condition in Taiwan presented a strong contrast to the turmoil suffered by its neighboring countries, and thus attracted the attention of the world. The success of Taiwan in surviving the financial crisis was regarded as a good model for all crisis-stricken countries.

However, Taiwan's survival in the turmoil seems not able to stand long-term trial. An article in *The Economist* at the end of 2000 predicting that Taiwan was going to experience a financial crisis before the Chinese lunar new year in 2001 placed the country under the shadow of financial crisis.[1] Although the predication of the financial crisis did not

[1] 'Taiwan's Financial System, Too many debts to settle,' THE ECONOMIST, 11 Nov. 2000.

come true then, the threatening of financial crisis has annoyed the country again. The comparison of the Republic of China's performance during and post the Asia financial turmoil might provide the international community with a good opportunity to explore the factors, which might affect Asian countries' liberalisation and internalisation of their financial system.

This article is first going to examine the improper policies and practices adopted by other crisis-stricken countries during the Asian financial turmoil and by contrast, the factors that sustain the stability of Taiwan. Next, the article will discuss the present economic situation in Taiwan and its influence on the country's financial system. The article will finally present the real lessons of the Taiwan during and post the Asia financial crisis, and conclude the potential risks threatening the country financial system in the future.

I. BACKGROUND OF THE CRISIS

Experiencing a decade of 'economic miracle', some of the high-performing Asian economies, including Indonesia, Malaysia, Thailand, and South Korea, faced drastically adverse changes to this economic growth since the beginning of 1997 with the onset of the Asian financial crisis.[2] The financial crises seriously devalued many of these countries' currencies[3], affected

[2] *See generally* Manuel F. Montesk, Kevin F F Quigley, and Donald E Weatherbee, 'Growing Pains: ASEAN's Economic and Political Challenges' (visited 31 Aug. 1998) <http://www.asiasociety.org/publications/asean-miracle.html>. It was not the first time that East-Asia countries experienced financial crises. In 1984, Thailand baht, with an over-extension of credit like that of 1997, experienced a drastic and controversial devaluation. In 1983, with international petroleum prices falling, Indonesia confronted an economic crisis that inaugurated four years of economic uncertainty. The sharp reductions in foreign investment inflows and the extreme drops in domestic property prices made Singapore face a major economic slowdown in 1985. In 1984–5, Malaysia, with its export revenues falling as a result of declines of oil prices, suffered a financial crisis when external financing for its current transactions disappeared as a result of financiers' loss of confidence about the country's ability to service its future debt obligations. However, the threat of the financial crises gradually reduced since Japanese companies began to relocate production facilities offshore as a result of the boost of the Japanese yen in 1985. Meanwhile, the Republic of China (Taiwan) and South Korea gradually move out labour-intensive industries to these East-Asian countries since 1988 enable these countries to recover from the financial crises. Moreover, the inflow of new production facilities from Japan, Taiwan, and South Korea also lead the recent economic growth spurt in Southeast Asia since 1988.

[3] *See also* Chong-yah, Lim, *The Solution to the Asian Currency Crisis,* before the International Conference on the New Role of Government in a Market Economy (5–6 Feb. 1998), Nanyang Technological University, Singapore. Between 1 July 1997 and 30 Jan 1998, the Indonesian rupiah fell, for example, from 2,432 per US dollar to 10,500 per US dollar, a fall of 77 per cent of the original value. The Thai baht fell by 53 per cent, the South Korean won 42 per cent, the Malaysian ringgit 40 per cent and the Philippine peso 38 per cent.

the stock markets[4], ended this rapid economic growth,[5] caused significant the social instability[6] and even resulted in political revolution.[7]

The crises started from the sharp devaluation of Thai baht in early 1997.[8] Because East Asian economies are closely tied together, the currency crisis of Thailand quickly spread into neighbouring countries[9] and lead to the so-called Asian economic or financial turmoil.

The Asian financial turmoil not only rapidly spread to neighbouring Southeast Asian countries, such as Indonesia, Malaysia, and Singapore, but also gradually affected most East Asian countries, such as South Korea, Japan, Mainland China, and Taiwan. Regional economic growth accordingly generally suffered greatly. Furthermore, this regional financial crisis diffused to other regions of the world. The Russian ruble collapsed in 1998 and more recently the financial crisis has threatened the historical reforms in Brazil and other Latin American countries.[10] As a result, the whole world has faced the dominant threat of a world-wide economic recession.[11]

[4] *See also* 'Asia Chronology 1998 Apr.–June' (visited 15 Aug. 1998) <http://www.stern.nyu.edu/~nroubini/asia/AsiaChronology 1998Q2.html>. The Hong Kong, stock market suffered its heaviest drubbing on 20 Oct. 1997. The Hang Seng index dropped 23.34 per cent from 13601.01 to 10426.30 in a day. By the end of June 1998, the Hang Seng index had dropped to 8543.10.

[5] *See also,* Stanley Fischer, 'The IMF and the Asian Crisis' (visited 19 Apr. 1998) <http://www.imf.org/exter . . . speeches/1998/032098. HTM>. After experiencing the crises, all affected countries had adjusted their GDP from 1 per cent to 3 per cent for 1997. *See generally* International Monetary Fund, *World Economic Outlook, Interim Assessment,* Dec. 1977, at 2. During 1992–5, the developing economies of Asia experienced average real GDP growth above 9 per cent.

[6] *See generally* Sidney Jones, 'Social cost of Asian crisis' (visited 20 Aug. 1998) <http://www.stern.nyu.edu/~nroubini/asia/socialcostFT198.htm>. In Indonesia, most reports revealed that a lot of sexual attacks on economically dominant ethnic Chinese occurred in the capital riot in June. When past economic downturns have led to expulsions of foreign works, the result has been physical violence against migrants. Both Malaysia and Thailand have started to send back migrant workers, mostly Indonesians, Filipinos, Burmese, and Bangladeshis. Meanwhile, martial law and other emergency legislation could look tempting to several leaders, especially as political dissent grows. In Indonesia, the Anti-Subversion Law have been used to detain critics and opponents.

[7] *See generally* 'Asia Chronology 1998 Apr.–June' (visited on 15 Aug. 1998) <http://www.stern.nyu.edu/~asia/AsiaChronology1998Q2.html>. Indonesian President Suharto, who had ruled since 1966, had been under escalating domestic and foreign pressure to step down amid the country's worst economic crisis since he came to power. A week before Suharto announced his resign decision on 21 May 1998, the country's capital, Jakarta, had occurred a widespread riot. Ethnic Chinese have become the political scapegoat in the riot.

[8] *See* LEE H HAMILTON, THE ASIAN ECONOMIC CRISIS, Congressional Record (28 Jan. 1998).

[9] *See* Lim Chong-yah, 'The Solution to the Asian Currency Crisis', Address before the International Conference on the New Role of Government in a Market Economy, 5 Feb. 1998, Nanyang Technological University, Singapore.

[10] *See* Special Report: The World Economy, *Los Angeles Times*, 16 Sept. 1998.

[11] *See also* International Monetary Fund, 'World Economic Outlook' (visited 7 Oct. 1998) <http://www.imf.org/external/pubs/ft/weo1098/index.htm> (the International Montertary Fund predicted that the average economic growth of the world was about 2 per cent for 1998, only half of the 1997 level.)

Nevertheless, the devaluation of these currencies was not the only reason for the crises in these East Asian countries. The economic and financial policies adopted and the underlying political conditions contributed to the problems which arose.

Encouraged by their great economic performance in the past decade, most East Asian countries over-optimistically estimated their future economic development before 1997. These unrealistic estimations led these countries to adopt aggressive economic policies, which were designed to continue the high economic growth and to increase the countries' competitive abilities. However, the economic policies, not supported by adequate financial control and a suitable political environment, resulted in economic crisis. Furthermore, most financial sectors and financial policies in these Asian countries were not then stable enough to support the countries' liberalisation of their financial markets.

Since the second half of the 1980s, most Southeast Asian countries accelerated the liberalisation of their trade and financial markets.[12] Almost all Southeast Asian countries, encouraged by the experience of Taiwan, Hong Kong, Singapore, and South Korea, followed outward-orientation economic policies[13] and trade liberalisation became a necessary condition to the successful enactment of the policies. As expected, the trade liberation not only created the Asian economic miracle but also gave a number of South-east Asian countries sufficient confidence in liberalising and internationalising their financial market from the beginning of the 1990s onwards.

However, the rapid liberalisation and internationalisation were not consistent with the internal political situations and financial systems. The cronyism, family run businesses, militarism and closed political structures already in place lead to the creation of an Asian style of capitalism that is essentially not suitable for financial liberalisation and internationalisation. Furthermore, most domestic financial systems were not stable and sufficient enough to manage the foreign investment that was attracted by the past brilliant economic performance and the US dollar-pegged exchange rate policies effectively. Since mainland China (the People's Republic of China) dramatically depreciated its currency in 1994, South east Asian countries have gradually lost their competitive advantage in most labour intensive

[12] *See generally* Manuel F. Montes, Kevin F. F. Quigley, and Donald E. Weatherbee, 'Growing Pains: ASEAN's Economic and Political Challenges' (visited 31 Aug. 1998) <http://www.asiasociety.org/publictions/asean-miracle.html> (trade liberalisation is a relatively new phenomenon in the regions. Before the late 1980s, most South-east Asian countries had followed classic industrial policies, such as protecting manufacturing activities from foreign competition).

[13] *See also* Shigemitsu Sugisaki, 'Economic Crises in Asia-Address by Shigemitsu Sugisaki' (visited 18 Feb. 1998) <http://www.imf.org/external/np/speeches/1998/013098.htm> (in order to promote the export policy, most countries took the following measures: export processing zones, tax breaks, and direct export subsidies).

products and have experienced increasingly heavy economic challenges. Concerned about the countries' future economic performance, foreign investment that was mostly short term was withdrawn immediately. The outflow of foreign investment triggered a confidence crisis and exposed many the defects that already existed in many Southeast Asian countries' liberalisation policies. The currency crisis not only resulted in financial and economic turmoil but also destroyed the Asian economic miracle created over the past two decades. Only a few fortunate countries suffered substantial damage, such as in Taiwan.

II. TAIWAN'S STABILITY DURING THE CRISIS

Despite the experience of fewer negative impacts, Taiwan did not entirely come out unscathed. The turmoil also caused the country's currency and interest rates, and stock prices to experience severe fluctuations.[14] Moreover, the turmoil also slowed the overall economic growth.[15] However, compared to its neighbour countries, Taiwan was luckily blessed with relatively strong economic and financial foundations and had relatively a better performance. There are several reasons behind Taiwan's safety in the turmoil: (a) high foreign exchange reserves and low foreign debt, (b) moderate financial internationalisation, (c) gradual liberalisation of the financial market, (d) the consistence of the conservative economic policies, productive structure and financial situation, and (e) pure luck.

A. High Foreign Exchange Reserves and Low Foreign Debt

High foreign exchange reserves and low foreign debt were among the main reasons that Taiwan avoided serious impact of the currency crises, while other Asian countries faced more costly losses.[16]

Taiwan started to have some foreign exchange reserves in 1965; five years before the United States ended its financial aid to the country.[17] Since

14 Shea Jia-Dong, 'The ROC's Experience in Addressing the Asian Financial Crisis,' Addressed to the ROC-USA and UAS-ROC Economic Council of 1998.

15 The Republic of China's economic growth rate in 1997 was 6.81 per cent. Influenced by the Asian financial crisis, the country's estimated economic growth rate has been adjusted to be lower than 5 per cent.

16 See Chung Hsing Chuang, 'Whether the Crisis is Coming—Financial System Challenge Taiwan', COMMON WEALTH MAGAZINE, Volume 201, 1 Feb. 1998, at 164.

17 *See generally* COUNCIL FOR ECONOMIC PLANNING AND DEVELOPMENT REPUBLIC OF CHINA, TAIWAN STATISCAL DATA BOOK 1994, at 227 and 228 (1994). Since 1951, the Republic of China started to receive financial aid from the United States. The aid included programme assistance and non-project assistance. In the 17-year aid, Taiwan received US$1,482.2 million from the US. The aid was mainly used for defence support, technical cooperation, and development loan fund.

then, Taiwan, accompanied with rapid export growth, enjoyed the accumulation of a huge foreign exchange reserve. In 1973, the total amounts of foreign exchange reserve for the first time exceeded US$1 billion. In 1983, the amount was over US$10 billion. By April of 1998, the country possessed about US$84 billion of foreign exchange reserves, ranking fourth in the world.[18] Meanwhile, the country has very few foreign debts.

There are several reasons for the accumulation of a huge foreign exchange reserve and a relatively small amount of foreign debt: the continuous trade surplus, long-term foreign exchange control, the particular political situation, and the special cultural background.

First of all, Taiwan's remarkable economic growth in the past three decades not only led the country to join the ranks of developed economies, but also to accumulate huge foreign exchange reserve. The rapid economic growth was based upon the export-orientated policy. From the agricultural and forestry products in the 1960s to the textile, leather wood, paper, and related products in the 1970s and mid-1980s, the country gradually upgraded its manufacturing structure. Since the mid-1980s, the country started to develop its high-tech industry of electrical machinery and components, with computers and related products becoming the main export products.[19] By the end of 1997, the country became one of the major computer-producing countries in the world. The successful export-oriented policy steered the country to enjoy a trade surplus, which stored an increasing fortune for the country.[20]

Secondly, Taiwan strictly controlled the flow of foreign currencies since the government moved from Mainland China to Taiwan. The purpose for the control was not only to steady the prices, but also to support the country's export-oriented policy. A multiple foreign exchange rate system was the main approach of the control. Under the system, lower exchange rates were applied

[18] *See also* Council for Economic Planning and Development, Republic of China, International Economic Statistics Index, NO 529 (4 June 1998). Japan, possessing US$2 trillion foreign reserves, was the number one country. Mainland China was number two, US$140 billion, and Hong Kong US$98 billion.

[19] *See also* Council For Economic Planning and Development Republic of China, Taiwan Statiscal Data Book 1994, at 192, 194; Bureau of International Trade Ministry of Economy, Foreign Trade Development of The Republic of China 1996, at 4. Before the mid-1960s, the agricultural products and processed agricultural products occupied 50 per cent of the total export and the total amount was about US$200 million. Since 1968, the textile and other light industry products replaced the agricultural products and became the main export products. The total export amount rapidly increased from US$1,481 million in 1970, US$19,811 million in 1980, US$67,214 million in 1990 to the US$122 billion by the end of 1997. The total export amount has increased over 100 times.

[20] *See also* Council for Economic Planning and Development Republic of China, Taiwan Statiscal Data Book 1994, (1994) at 190. Taiwan started to have a trade surplus in 1970. In the past 27 years, the country has had atrade surplus every year except in 1975 and 1976. The surplus reached the highest point in the 1980s. The average annual trade surplus was over US$10 billion. Most trade surplus were derived from trade with the United States.

to imported capital goods, raw materials, household necessities, while higher rates were applied to imports of other goods, unspecific outward remittance and exports of private enterprises.[21] The system also reflected the government's policy of encouraging exports and leading limited foreign exchange resources into productive activities. The control greatly limited the market-oriented function. Under such a control, the foreign exchange rate was decided not by market needs but by the government. The market could not reflect the real value of the country's currency. However, it effectively controlled the inflation of the country during the period.

The foreign currency market gradually recovered its normal function since the country amended the 'Statute Governing Foreign Exchange' in 1970. The amendment established the fixed-exchange rate system[22] and the centralised foreign exchange clearing system.[23] The purpose of the amendment was not only to regulate foreign currency transactions[24], but also to ensure the government effective control over foreign currencies.[25] Furthermore, the fixed exchange rate system was adopted by way of pegging to the US dollar.[26] The Central Bank decided the rate by evaluating the conditions of the global financial market. This system and the country's policies have provided a favourable environment for the development of foreign trade and investment.[27]

However, the collapse of the international fixed exchange rate and the pressure of inflation in the domestic economy forced Taiwan to abolish the

[21] Bureau of Monetary Affairs, Ministry of Finance, Republic of China, the ROC Financial System and Policy 81 (1996).

[22] *See also* Bureau of Monetary Affairs, Ministry of Finance, Republic of China, The ROC Financial System and Policy 80 (1996). The Central Bank decided the exchange rate on a daily basis. Authorised foreign exchange banks could only conduct transactions according to the rated listed by the Central Bank.

[23] *See generally* Bureau of Monetary Affairs, Ministry of Finance, Republic of China, The ROC Financial System and Policy 80 (1996). All authorised foreign exchange banks should record the types and value of foreign exchange trading and report to the Central Bank for clearance day by day.

[24] Under Article 5 of the 'Statute Governing Foreign Exchange Regulation, 1978', the foreign currency control authorities are responsible to (1) appoint banks to operate foreign currency, (2) review the inflow and outflow of foreign currencies, (3) the transaction of foreign currencies, bills and stocks, and (4) all other foreign currency related affairs.

[25] Under Article 17, 'Statute for Foreign Exchange Regulation, 1978', all approved foreign currencies shall deposit into or sell back to appointed banks when the reasons of holding foreign currencies disappeared. However, under Article 26-1, amendment of 1987, the Executive Yuan is authorised to cease this article when there is long-term trade surplus, huge foreign reserve and the dramatic change of international economic situation.

[26] See Bureau of Monetary Affairs, Ministry of Finance, Republic of China, the ROC Financial System and Policy 82 (1996).

[27] *See generally* Bureau of Monetary Affairs, Ministry of Finance, Republic of China, the ROC Financial System and Policy 82 (1996). Before 1979, the foreign exchange rate of the New Taiwan Dollar to the US Dollar was very steady. The change of the rate in 15 years was less than 10 per cent.

fixed rate system and adopt the floating rate system in 1978.[28] This change also triggered the country's liberalisation and internationalisation of its financial market. In 1979, the country officially instituted the foreign exchange market to accommodate the floating foreign exchange rate system.[29] Initially, the foreign exchange rate was still decided by the Central Bank and the five appointed foreign exchange banks. Since March 1980, the Central Bank was not involved in the process of determining the rate any more, and the Central rate system was adopted instead.[30] However, the fluctuation of the foreign exchange rate was still limited within a specific scope,[31] hence the country was still cautious in controlling the foreign currencies.

Because of the continuous and huge trade surplus since the 1980s, the country's foreign exchange reserves accumulated rapidly.[32] In order to carry out the policy of foreign exchange liberation, the country amended the 'Statute Governing the Foreign Exchange' in 1986[33] and remarkably deregulated the foreign exchange control in 1987.[34] Therefore, the capital flow increased its liberalisation.[35] At present, the foreign exchange control on

[28] See BUREAU OF MONETARY AFFAIRS, MINISTRY OF FINANCE, REPUBLIC OF CHINA, THE ROC FINANCIAL SYSTEM AND POLICY 82 (1996).

[29] *See generally* BUREAU OF MONETARY AFFAIRS, MINISTRY OF FINANCE, REPUBLIC OF CHINA, 1991 ANNUAL REPORT OF BUREAU OF MONETARY AFFAIRS MINISTRY OF FINANCE 12 (1992). The foreign exchange market was officially instituted on 1 Feb. 1979. Because of the lack of qualified brokers or dealers, the Central Bank appointed several banks to conduct the foreign exchange business.

[30] *See generally* BUREAU OF MONETARY AFFAIRS, MINISTRY OF FINANCE, REPUBLIC OF CHINA, 1991 ANNUAL REPORT OF BUREAU OF MONETARY AFFAIRS MINISTRY OF FINANCE 14 (1992). The 'central rate' system was adopted on 1 Sept. 1982.

[31] *See generally* BUREAU OF MONETARY AFFAIRS, MINISTRY OF FINANCE, REPUBLIC OF CHINA, 1991 ANNUAL REPORT OF BUREAU OF MONETARY AFFAIRS MINISTRY OF FINANCE 14 (1992). The daily rate change could not exceed or below 2.25 per cent of the central rate and every transaction could not exceed or below NTD5 cents.

[32] *See generally* COUNCIL FOR ECONOMIC PLANNING AND DEVELOPMENT REPUBLIC OF CHINA, TAIWAN STATISCAL DATA BOOK 1994, (1994) at 4. The Republic of China's trade surplus increased rapidly since 1981. In 1981, the total amount of surplus was US$1,412 million, US$4,836 million in 1983, US$10,624 million in 1985, and in 1987 reached the historical US$18,695. The foreign exchange reserve held by the Central Bank in 1981 was US$7,235 million, US$11,859 million in 1983, US$22,556 million in 1985, and US$46,310 million in 1987.

[33] *See* BUREAU OF MONETARY AFFAIRS, MINISTRY OF FINANCE, REPUBLIC OF CHINA, THE ROC FINANCIAL SYSTEM AND POLICY 105 (1996). To cope with the amendment of the Statute, the trade-related foreign exchange control was transformed from an approval system to a reporting system.

[34] Under the 'Statute Governing Foreign Exchange' Art. 26–1, the Executive Yuan suspended certain provisions of the Statute, including Art. 6–1, 7, 13 and 17. Since then, local residents could freely own and manage foreign exchange. *See* Executive Yuan No 2039 Meeting Resolution, 9 July 1987.

[35] *See eg* BUREAU OF MONETARY AFFAIRS, MINISTRY OF FINANCE, REPUBLIC OF CHINA, 1991 ANNUAL REPORT OF BUREAU OF MONETARY AFFAIRS MINISTRY OF FINANCE 13 (1992); BUREAU OF MONETARY AFFAIRS, MINISTRY OF FINANCE, REPUBLIC OF CHINA, THE ROC FINANCIAL SYSTEM AND POLICY 106 (1996). Since the relaxation of foreign exchange controls in 1987, the Central

the international payment/transfer regarding the current account has been completely abolished.[36] However, the accumulated foreign reserve has established a profound financial and economic foundation.[37]

Thirdly, the special political circumstance forced Taiwan to strictly control foreign currencies. Unlike other East Asian countries, Taiwan strictly controlled the foreign exchange reserves because the country was always under military threat from mainland China since the government retreated to Taiwan in 1949. In order to steady the country's financial situation, the country not only strictly controlled the flow of foreign reserves but also kept most foreign reserves in the hands of the central bank. The amount kept by the central bank was much higher than its ordinary international payment needs.[38] The huge foreign reserve not only attracted the international community's attention but also made the country strong enough to face unexpected economic and political challenges.[39]

Fourthly, the special cultural background and economic structure resulted in low foreign debt. Comparing to the amount of its foreign reserves, foreign debt was small.[40] One of the main reasons that the country has less foreign debt than other East Asian countries was the conservative economic and financial policy, and significant cultural and business background. One of the main differences of economic development policies between Taiwan and South Korea is that the former encouraged the development of small and medium businesses,[41] while South Korea intentionally raised large corporate

Bank adjusted the ceiling for private foreign currency outward and inward remittances for six times. In respect of foreign exchange control on capital account, each resident may make an outward or inward remittance up to US$5 million, and US$10 million for each corporation per year. This policy has actually released the foreign exchange control.

36 See BUREAU OF MONETARY AFFAIRS, MINISTRY OF FINANCE, REPUBLIC OF CHINA, THE ROC FINANCIAL SYSTEM AND POLICY 83 (1996).

37 *See generally* COUNCIL FOR ECONOMIC PLANNING AND DEVELOPMENT REPUBLIC OF CHINA, TAIWAN STATISTICAL DATA BOOK 1994, (1994) at 196 and 4. The huge foreign reserves are not an exclusivly beneficial factor for Taiwan. As the reserve rapidly accumulated since 1980, the country's currency faced strong appreciation pressure from the international community. Between 1986 and 1989, the foreign exchange rate of New Taiwan Dollar to US dollar rose from 39 : 1 to 26 : 1. The appreciation rate was over 30 per cent. The rapid appreciation of the currency strongly affected the country's productive structure. Many labour-intensive industries lost their competitiveness and moved to South East Asian countries.

38 *Author's note*: A country's reasonable foreign reserve is about 3 to 6 months of the country's international payments.

39 *Author's note*: The huge foreign reserves once supported the country to avoid the capital outflow crisis caused by the People Republic of China missile launch into the Taiwan Strait in 1994.

40 *See* Chung Hsing Chuang, *Whether the Crisis is Coming—Financial System Challenge Taiwan,* COMMON WEALTH MAGAZINE, Vol 201, 1 Feb. 1998, at 167. According to the OECD's data, Taiwan's foreign debt was about US$28 billion that occupied about 7 per cent of the country's GDP.

41 *See also* COMMON WEALTH MAGAZINE, Vol 204, 1 May 1998, at 44. In Taiwan, the small and medium business occupied 95 per cent of the country's business.

conglomerates and provided necessary financial support.[42] Taiwanese traditional business etiquette is to operate by owning capital.[43] The main encouragement approach that the government provided for the small and medium business was tax privileges.[44] These businesses always raised capital by themselves and with the help of relatives. Unlike the situation of South Korea and some Southeast Asia countries, the government of Taiwan did not actively participate in business operations and capital raising.[45] Furthermore, the country leaves the market to decide the fate of a private business. Any non-competitive company is given the freedom to collapse.[46] Under such an environment, the banking system was very careful in approving loan applications, thus the small and medium businesses were forced to be accustomed to raising capital by themelves. The average debt/capital ratio of most Taiwanese businesses is low.[47] In other words, most companies use their own capital to do business, so debt or foreign debt has less impact on normal operations. From the government's viewpoint, there was no big public construction in process in the past decade and the government did not borrow money from overseas. The country's US$80 billion foreign reserves can easily cover the current US$28 billion foreign debts that were mostly loaned by private enterprises.[48] Because of this situation, the scope of depreciation of the foreign exchange rate of the country's currency was limited and did not cause the currency crisis or economic crisis that Thailand, Indonesia and South Korea experienced.

In short, the successful export-oriented policy and the government's effective foreign exchange control contributed to the country's enormous foreign exchange reserves. The reserve was ever one of the pressures on the

[42] *See* e.g. Yua-Han Ku, *The Secret of Taiwan Avoid the Financial Crises,* WEALTH MAGAZINE, Mar. 1998, at 224. In Taiwan, the top six corporations only occupied 23 per cent of the total stock market); Hseng-Yuang Tsang, *The Collapse of the Economic Model of Japan and Korea,* GLOBAL VIEWS MONTHLY, 5 Mar. 1998, at 100. In South Korea, the top six corporate conglomerates occupied 58 per cent of the total value of the stock market.

[43] *See* COMMON WEALTH MAGAZINE, vol 201, Feb. 1998, at 166. Taiwan's businesses tend to not to loan for business.

[44] See Chi Schive, *Why Taiwan did not collapse?* COMMON WEALTH MAGAZINE, 1 Dec. 1997, at 214.

[45] *See* ibid. For example, the South Korean government deeply participated in the development of large corporate conglomerates. Besides tax privileges, the government provided these conglomerates with full financial support.

[46] *See also* Yua-Han Ku, 'The Secret That Taiwan Avoid the Financial Crises', WEALTH MAGAZINE, Mar. 1998, at 224. In East Asia, Taiwan has the highest business collapse rate. Under the market's competition, only competent companies can survive.

[47] *See also* Chung Hsing, Chuang, 'Whether the Crisis is Coming—Financial System Challenge Taiwan', COMMON WEALTH MAGAZINE, vol 201, 1 Feb. 1998, at 171. Of the top 1,000 Taiwan manufacturers, the average debt/capital ration is below 50 per cent.

[48] See Gustav Ranis, 'Miracles that don't cease', 19 Feb. 1998. Although the short-term foreign debt occupied 84 per cent of the total foreign debt, the country's huge foreign reserves could easily cover it. Foreign currency traders were unwilling to bet against a currency backed by US$86bn of reserves.

country's currency.[49] However, the abundant foreign reserves have become one of the important tools for the country to conduct its economic and financial policies. It also provided the country more resistance to escape the 1997 Asian currency crises that resulted in financial crises.[50]

B. Moderate Financial Internationalisation

The economy and financial markets of Taiwan were internationalised before liberalisation. Under the export-oriented policy, the country's economic situation had very close connections with the international community. However, the economic environment and financial market of the country were domestically oriented before the 1980s. Because the economic scale of the country was so small and the trend of 'liberal trade' had not started yet, this kind of economic environment and financial market did not capture the international community's attention. Moreover, because industry was mainly based on small and medium businesses,[51] it was unnecessary and not possible for most of these businesses to internationalise their operations. Furthermore, the strict control over the financial system and the special political situation[52] hindered international investment on the country. Under such an environment, it was not a crucial issue for the country to internationalise or liberalise its market.[53]

Since the rapid economic development accumulated huge foreign exchange reserves from 1980, the international community started to take notice of Taiwan's economic performance as well as its expanding market.[54] Because the trade surplus between Taiwan and the United States

[49] *Author's note*: The New Taiwan Dollar (NTD) exchange rate to the US Dollar appreciated over 30 per cent in two years since 1985. One of the main reasons for the appreciation was that the US believed that the abundant foreign exchange reserve reflected that the NTD had been under-estimated for a long time.

[50] As the result of the turmoil, the Korean Won depreciated more than 50 per cent by the end of first quarter of 1998. The Thai Baht depreciated more than 30 per cent by the end of the first quarter of 1998. Backed by the abundant foreign exchange reserve, the Republic of China's foreign exchange rate remained relatively steady. The New Taiwan Dollar had depreciated by 19.08 per cent against the US Dollar by the end of July 1998.

[51] *See also* 'Be Care of The Next Collapse', COMMON WEALTH MAGAZINE, 1 May 1998, at 44. The small and medium business occupied about 95 per cent of the country's businesses.

[52] *Author's note*: To confront the threatening of Mainland China, Taiwan even declared Martial Order in Taiwan for more than 30 years. Although the Martial Order did not delay economic development, the economic and financial policy during this time period could not provide a suitable environment for the internationalisation of private businesses.

[53] *See generally* COUNCIL FOR ECONOMIC PLANNING AND DEVELOPMENT REPUBLIC OF CHINA, TAIWAN STATISCAL DATA BOOK 1994 (1994) at 244. Private foreign investment in Taiwan increased slowly before 1980s. The annual amount of foreign investments did not exceed US$200 million. Since the 1980s, foreign investment gradually increased. In 1987, the annual amount of foreign investment exceeded US$1 billion.

[54] For example, the United States continuously requested the ROC government to open its domestic market in the annual USA–ROC and ROC–USA Economic Councils Conference that was held since 1977.

increased dramatically since 1976,[55] the United States started to urge Taiwan to reduce the surplus.[56] Under pressure from the United States, the rapid appreciation of the New Taiwan Dollar triggered the outflow of labour-intensive industries since 1985. It could be regarded as the beginning of the internationalisation of private enterprises in the past two decades. Those industries remaining in Taiwan were very competitive but domestic.

The private enterprises' large-scale internationalisation was later than the government's financial policy. Before Taiwan formally declared its financial internationalisation policy,[57] the government had promulgated the Offshore Banking Act in 1983.[58] Under the Act, both domestic and foreign banks may apply to establish an offshore banking unit (OBU) within the jurisdiction to operate offshore banking business.[59] Because the operation of OBU is exempted from the Act Governing Foreign Exchange, the Banking Law, and the Act Governing the Central Bank of China,[60] it attracted the participation of both domestic and foreign banks.[61] The promulgation of the Act was the beginning of the financial internationalisation of the country.

Taiwan did not expedite the process to internationalise and liberalise its domestic market until the pressure from the United States increased, and the trend of liberal trade gradually became the trend of the international economic system.[62] However, the speed of the internationalisation was slow to moderate[63] until the General Agreement on Tariffs and Trade concluded to establish the World Trade Organisation.[64]

[55] *See generally* COUNCIL FOR ECONOMIC PLANNING AND DEVELOPMENT REPUBLIC OF CHINA, TAIWAN STATISCAL DATA BOOK 1994, (1994) at 196. Taiwan had a trade surplus with the United States since 1968. The trade surplus increased fast but steadily before 1975. In 1975 the amount of the surplus was US$170 million. Since 1976, the amount increased dramatically: US$1.2 billion in 1976, US$2.6 billion in 1978, US$4.1 billion in 1982, US$10 billion in 1985, and US$13 billion in 1986. The amount increased tenfold in ten years.

[56] *Author's note*: One of the main purposes of the ROC-USA and USA-ROC Economic Council was to reduce the trade surpluses between Taiwan and the United States.

[57] *See* BUREAU OF MONETARY AFFAIRS, MINISTRY OF FINANCE REPUBLIC OF CHINA: THE ROC FINANCIAL SYSTEM AND POLICY 104 (1996).

[58] The Act was designed to develop the country to be a regional financial centre. *See* ROC OFFSHORE BANKING ACT, Art. 1.

[59] OFFSHORE BANKING ACT, Art. 3 (ROC).

[60] Ibid. Art. 5 (ROC).

[61] *See generally* STATISTICS OFFICE, BUREAU OF MONETARY AFFAIRS MINISTRY OF FINANCE, REPUBLIC OF CHINA, FINANCIAL STATISTICAS ABSTRACT, Nov. 1996, BUREAU OF MONETARY MOF 34 (Sep. 1998). At the beginning, only seven banks joined the OBU business in 1984. The amount increased rapidly after 1988. By the end of November 1996, sixty-five banks had established the OBU. Almost all domestic general banks operated the business.

[62] *See also* John H Jackson, *The World Trading System: Law and Policy of International Economic Relations* (Massachusetts Institute of Technology Press (1994).) It is the goal of 'liberal trade' to minimise the amount of interference of governments in trade flows that cross national borders.

[63] See Chung Hsing Chuang, 'Whether the Crisis is Coming- Financial System Challenge Taiwan', COMMON WEALTH MAGAZINE, vol 201, 1 Feb. 1998, at 165.

[64] In 1994, the Uruguay round of the General Agreement on Tariff and Trade came to an

In order to accede the Organisation, the country started to negotiate with the existing member countries.[65] The opening of the financial market was one of the main issues in most negotiations.[66] In order to help the financial market to face the coming challenge from the international community, the government more actively began to internationalise and liberalise the financial market.

Before the country allowed the establishment of new domestic commercial banks in 1990, there were already more than thirty foreign banks.[67] However, there were a lot of restrictions on these foreign banks.[68] In the procedure to eliminate these restrictions, these foreign banks also played the forerunner role in promoting the internationalisation and liberalisation of the country financial market and its economy as well.[69]

Since Taiwan set up the Economic Reform Committee in 1985 to undertake the review of the economy, the American Chamber of Commerce in Taiwan (ACCT) continuously submitted its recommendations to the country to reform its financial and economic system. In its 1985 Recommendation, the ACCT suggested to implement the transparency of the bank regulatory process and to nurture financial market development.[70] In its 1987 Proposals, the ACCT demanded to have a series of structural reforms in order to remove unfair trade practices.[71]

agreement establishing the World Trade Organisation. *See* GATT *Focus Newsletter*, Dec. 1993—Attachment 1.

65 *See generally* COUNCIL FOR ECONOMIC PLANNING AND DEVELOPMENT REPUBLIC OF CHINA, 'ROC's Financial Liberalization' (visited on 15 Oct. 1998) <http://cepd.spring.org.tw/Speak/870416/1.html>. There were twenty-six existing WTO member states that required Taiwan to have separate negotiations.

66 *See generally* COUNCIL FOR ECONOMIC PLANNING AND DEVELOPMENT REPUBLIC OF CHINA, 'ROC's Financial Liberalization' (visited on 15 Oct. 1998) <http://cepd.spring.org.tw/Speak/870416/1.html>. Twelve countries required the Republic of China to negotiate the service industry topic.

67 In 1989, the total number of the local branches of foreign banks was 38, 43 in 1990 and 47 in 1991. All these foreign were defined as commercial banks. *See eg* COUNCIL FOR ECONOMIC PLANNING AND DEVELOPMENT REPUBLIC OF CHINA, TAIWAN STATISCAL DATA BOOK 1994, (1994) at 133. *See* BANKING LAW. Art. 121(1985) (ROC).

68 The restrictions included deposit ceilings, additional branches, credit limit, ATM networks. See the AMERICAN CHAMBER OF COMMERCE IN TAIWAN, *Financial Services Reform in the Republic of China*, 5 June 1987, at 3, 4, 6.

69 *See generally* the BUREAU OF MONETARY AFFAIRS MINISTRY OF FINANCE REPUBLIC OF CHINA 1991 ANNUAL REPORT BUREAU OF MONETARY AFFAIRS MINISTRY OF FINANCE 24 (1992). Before the government lifted the ban on the establishment of domestic commercial banks in 1991, US banks occupied one-third of the total foreign banks. These banks submitted their inquiry of the improvement of the Republic of China's financial and economic system through the American Chamber of Commerce in Taiwan.

70 AMERICAN CHAMBER OF COMMERCE IN TAIWAN, *Recommendations of the American Chamber of Commerce in the Republic of China to the Economic Reform Committee*, 31 Aug. 1985.

71 AMERICAN CHAMBER OF COMMERCE IN TAIWAN, *Financial Services Reform in the Republic of China*, 5 June 1987, at 1.

The government had very positive responses to these recommendations, and took substantial steps towards the internationalisation of the financial services industry through the amendments of the banking laws and regulations and the conduct of financial policies.[72]

The country amended the Banking Law in 1989 and 1992. After the amendments, foreign banks were allowed to expand business scope[73] and to establish multiple branch networks.[74] New financial products[75] and international banking capital requirements[76] were introduced. The total number of local branches of foreign banks increased from 50 in 1992 to 65 by the end of November 1996.[77] The amendments provided a favourable environment for foreign banks, and also brought the domestic banking market into a period of competition.

The internationalisation of the financial market focused not only on the improvement of the domestic banking environment, but also on domestic financial participation in the international financial markets.[78] Since 1991, the ROC government took several policies to promote the internationalisation of domestic banks. The policies included encouraging domestic banks to strengthen communication with large foreign financial organisations, and the participation in international financial markets,[79] increasing the number of Taiwanese banks' overseas branches and subsidiaries,[80] and

[72] *See generally* BUREAU OF MONETARY AFFAIRS, MINISTRY OF FINANCE REPUBLIC OF CHINA, THE ROC FINANCIAL SYSTEM AND POLICY 104 (1996). Besides banks, other financial institutions such as insurance companies and branches of foreign securities firms were gradually allowed to enter into the Taiwan market. In 1986, foreign insurance companies started to make inroad into Taiwan. The branches of foreign securities firms began to emerge in 1991.

[73] Foreign banks were allowed to operate those business activities of the saving banks, and the trust and investment companies. *See* ROC Banking Law of 1992, Art. 121, 71, 78, and 101.

[74] *See generally* BUREAU OF MONETARY AFFAIRS MINISTRY OF FINANCE REPUBLIC OF CHINA, 1994 ANNUAL REPORT BUREAU OF MONETARY AFFAIRS MINISTRY OF FINANCE 38 (1992). The restriction of the establishment of branches was abolished by the revise of the 'Guidelines Governing the Screening of Application to Establish Branches/ Representative Offices by Foreign Banks' in 1994. Also, the criteria used in the screening of the application of the establishment of branch were being eased considerably.

[75] The amendment of the Banking Law in 1992 delegated the Ministry of Finance the legislative power of promulgating regulations to introduce new financial products in the money market. *See* BANKING LAW. Art. 47–1. (1992) (ROC).

[76] In order to improve the financial structure of banks, the amendment of the Banking Law in 1989 adopted the capital adequacy ratio (8 per cent) that was set by the Basel Capital Accord in 1988. *See* BANKING LAW. Art. 44 (1992) (ROC).

[77] *See* STATISTICS OFFICE, BUREAU OF MONETARY AFFAIRS MINISTRY OF FINANCE, REPUBLIC OF CHINA, FINANCIAL STATISTICAS ABSTRACT, NOV. 1996, BUREAU OF MONETARY MOF 24 (Sep. 1998).

[78] BUREAU OF MONETARY AFFAIRS MINISTRY OF FINANCE REPUBLIC OF CHINA, 1994 ANNUAL REPORT BUREAU OF MONETARY AFFAIRS MINISTRY OF FINANCE 44, (1992).

[79] *See* ibid.

[80] BUREAU OF MONETARY AFFAIRS MINISTRY OF FINANCE REPUBLIC OF CHINA, 1992 ANNUAL REPORT BUREAU OF MONETARY AFFAIRS MINISTRY OF FINANCE 18 (1993).

developing offshore banking business.[81] Through the establishment of overseas offshoots, local banks may learn international financial experience, and help cultivate and train international financial experts.[82] The internationalisation policy has since reached the expected goal. By the end of September 1996, the total overseas offices and branches of domestic banks amounted to 90,[83] 5 times of that in 1984.[84]

Since the government formally declared its financial internationalisation policy in 1984, it took more than 10 years for the country to reach the current situation. The experience reflected several factors that might affect a country's internationalisation: (1) the domestic economic development, (2) the international economic environment, and (3) the governmental policy. Although Taiwan has had great economic performance since the 1980s, the government undertook very conservative economic and financial policies. Under great pressure from the United States and the changing international economic system, it seemed that the country intentionally moderated the speed of internationalisation. Compared to its economic development, Taiwan's internationalisation was even slower than most East Asian countries that began their high economic growth from the mid-1980s. However, just because of the moderate internationalisation of the country, international capital did not largely rush into Taiwan immediately.[85] Because the country's financial market had the chance to be gradually accustomed to international competition,[86] it received less impact from the Asian financial and economic crises.

81 BUREAU OF MONETARY AFFAIRS MINISTRY OF FINANCE REPUBLIC OF CHINA, 1991 ANNUAL REPORT BUREAU OF MONETARY AFFAIRS MINISTRY OF FINANCE 45 (1992).

82 BUREAU OF MONETARY AFFAIRS, MINISTRY OF FINANCE REPUBLIC OF CHINA, THE ROC FINANCIAL SYSTEM AND POLICY 104 (1996).

83 The amount included forty-nine branch offices, 28 liaison offices, and thirteen overseas subsidiaries of domestic banks. *See* STATISTICS OFFICE, BUREAU OF MONETARY AFFAIRS MINISTRY OF FINANCE, REPUBLIC OF CHINA, FINANCIAL STATISTICS ABSTRACT, AFFAIRS NOV. 1996, BUREAU OF MONETARY MINISTRY OF FINANCE 26 (Sept. 1998).

84 *See generally* BUREAU OF MONETARY AFFAIRS, MINISTRY OF FINANCE REPUBLIC OF CHINA, THE ROC FINANCIAL SYSTEM AND POLICY 104 (1996). In 1984, only three local banks, International Commercial Bank of China, First Commercial Bank and Chiao Tung Bank, set up eighteen overseas establishments.

85 Until the crises occurred, Asia attracted almost half of total capital inflows to developing countries-nearly US$100 billion in 1996. However, only about US$1 million flowed into Taiwan. *See* eg Stanley Fischer, 'The Asian Crises: A View from the IMF', (visited 24 Feb. 1998) <http://www.img.org/external/np/speeches/1998/012298.htm>; Cheng-hsung Chiu, 'The Transparency of Legal System', COMMON WEALTH MAGAZINE, vol 201, 1 Feb. 1998, at 173. Mr Cheng-hsung Chiu, was then the Minister of Finance of the Republic of China.

86 By the end of Nov. 1996, foreign banks only occupied 3.23 per cent of the ROC banking market share. *See* STATISTICS OFFICE, BUREAU OF MONETARY AFFAIRS MINISTRY OF FINANCE, REPUBLIC OF CHINA, FINANCIAL STATISTICS ABSTRACT, NOV. 1996, BUREAU OF MONETARY AFFAIRS MINISTRY OF FINANCE 168 (Feb. 1997).

C. Temperate Liberalisation of Financial Markets

Liberalisation has become the trend for the international economic system. Under the trend, most East Asian countries, such as Thailand, Malaysia and Indonesia, accelerated trade liberalisation since the second half of the 1980s.[87] The substantial approaches taken by these countries included the release of the protection of the domestic manufacturing activities from foreign competition, the reduction of import tariffs, and other crucial measures to promote free trade.[88] This liberal trade policy resulted in the successful and strong economic growth in the area since the mid-1980s, and attracted the inflow of huge foreign investments to the area. In order to accommodate the needs of foreign investors for modern financial services, most of these countries started to liberalise their domestic financial systems since the late 1980s.[89] With greater confidence in the availability of international financing, these Southeast Asian countries eased the regulations over international movements of capital which accelerated after 1992.[90] The World Bank estimates that net inflows of long-term debt, foreign direct investment, and equity purchases to the Asia Pacific region were only about US$25 billion in 1990, but exploded to more than US$110 billion by 1996.[91] Comparing to the foreign investment flow into other East Asian countries, Taiwan did not attract too much foreign capital in the past decade. One of the reasons for this situation was that the country took very conservative and cautious policies to liberalise its financial system.

Although Taiwan started to release its strict control over the financial system in 1976, the full-scale liberalisation was not triggered until the late 1980s. The concrete measures adopted by the government to implement the policy of liberalisation included: (1) deregulation of interest rates and foreign exchange rates, (2) liberalisation of the establishment of financial institutions, and (3) encouragement of financial innovation.[92]

[87] Manuel F Montes, 'The Economic Miracle in a Haze, Growing Pains: ASEAN's Economic and Political Challenges, Asia Society', Dec. 1997 (visited 24 Feb. 1998) <http://www.asiasociety.org/publications/asean-miracle.html>.

[88] *See* e.g. Shigemitsu, Sugisaki, 'Economic Crises in Asia', (visited 18 Feb. 1998) <http://www.imf.org/external/np/speeches/1998/013098.HTM>; Montes, 'The Economic Miracle in a Haze, Growing Pains: ASEAN's Economic and Political Challenges, Asia Society', Dec. 1997 (visited on 24 Feb. 1998) <http://www.asiasociety.org/publications/asean-miracle,html>.

[89] Ibid.

[90] *See* ibid.

[91] Testimony of Chairman Alan Greenspan before the Committee on Banking and Financial Services, US House of Representative, 13 Nov. 1997 (visited on 17 Feb. 1998) <http://www.bog.frb.fed.us/boarddocs/testimony/19971113.htm>.

[92] BUREAU OF MONETARY AFFAIRS, MINISTRY OF FINANCE REPUBLIC OF CHINA, THE ROC FINANCIAL SYSTEM AND POLICY 90 (1996).

1. Deregulation of Interest Rates and Foreign Exchange Rate

The government exclusively decided both the deposit interest rate and loan interest rate before the amendment of the Banking Law in 1989. During the 1950s and 1960s, the interest rate of the country was flat and the government decided it. Later, the Central Bank of China was authorised to prescribe the ceiling rate for bank deposits, and authorised to approve the range of top and bottom interest rates of banking loans as proposed by the Bankers' Association in Taiwan.[93] The banking interest rates became a little more flexible than what it had been.[94] After the establishment of the money market in 1976, the Central Bank of China started to release the control over the interest rates of money market transactions. Since then, the interest rate could gradually be decided by the market. This policy also founded the further deregulation of interest rates. In 1980, the Central Bank promulgated the 'Guidelines Governing the Adjustment of Interest Rates of Banks'. Under the Guidelines, the Bank Association was authorised to play a more active role in deciding interest rates. Since then, the rate could gradually cope with the situation of money supply and demand. In 1985, the government abolished the 'Statute Governing Interest Rate' and financial institutions were given more flexibility in setting up the interest rates of loans and deposits.[95] In the Banking Law amendment in July 1989, the Central Bank control over the interest rate for loans and savings was totally removed.[96] The removal signalled the major step toward banking liberalisation and the initiation of a new era of the banking market.

Since the Bankers' Association participation in deciding the interest rate in 1975, it took the country more than 10 years to liberalise the interest rate control. From the government to the Central Bank, from Central Bank exclusive decision to Banker Association participation and finally market functional decision, the country released interest control step by step. Although the interest rate liberalisation was pushed by international pressure,[97] this step-by-step policy not only successfully adjusted the financial market through the exercise of free market function, but also raised the

[93] Banking Law (1975) (ROC).

[94] Bureau of Monetary Affairs, Ministry of Finance Republic of China, The ROC Financial System and Policy 90 (1996).

[95] *See generally* ibid. 91. Other financial institutions, such as the credit unions and credit departments of farmers and fishermen associations, were given more discretion to decide their interest rates.

[96] Banking Law. Art. 41 (1995) (ROC).

[97] *See generally* American Chamber of Commerce in Taiwan, *Recommendations of the American Chamber in the Republic of China to the Economic Reform Committee*, 31 Aug. 1985, at 8–9. It was one of the important issues that the American Chamber of Commence in Taiwan (ACCT) inquired the Republic of China to release the control over interest rate.

financial service quality and operational efficiencies based on fair competition and market integrity.[98]

The foreign exchange rate liberalisation experienced several stages: (1) the fixed foreign exchange rate system,[99] (2) floating rate system,[100] (3) central exchange rate mechanism,[101] (4) reference exchange rate system,[102] and (5) free exchange rate system. During the past two decades' foreign exchange rate liberalisation procedure, the government gradually adjusted its foreign exchange policies according to the country's economic situation.[103] The exchange rate was devolved from exclusive government control to the banks' participation and the market function. The release of foreign exchange transactions was step-by-step from the transactions between banks to the transactions between banks and public customers.[104] This long procedure of liberalisation has provided the country a stable environment for economic development.

2. Liberalisation of the Establishment of Financial Institutions

The liberalisation of the establishment of financial institutions was pushed by both external pressure and internal need. In 1984, the American Chamber of Commerce in Taiwan started to press the Ministry of Finance

[98] Bureau of Monetary Affairs, Ministry of Finance Republic of China, The ROC Financial System and Policy 90 (1996).

[99] *See generally* Council For Economic Planning and Development Republic of China, Taiwan Statiscal Data Book 1994, (1994) at 4. The system was established in 1965. Between 1965 and 1972, the fixed foreign exchange rate of the New Taiwan Dollar to US Dollar was NT40.5 to US$1. Between 1973 and 1977 the rate was 38 : 1.

[100] The floating rate system was established in 1978. Under the system, the exchange rate was negotiated by the Central Bank and five authorised foreign exchange banks. Although the rate was floating, the Central Bank actually controlled the rate.

[101] *See generally* Bureau of Monetary Affairs, Ministry of Finance Republic of China, The ROC Financial System and Policy 97 (1996). The central exchange rate system was setup in 1982. Under the system, the foreign exchange rate for bank customers was decided by a weighted-average foreign exchange rate of inter-bank US dollar transactions of the previous business day. The rate was negotiable. However, the fluctuation was limited within US$0.1 for bank-customer transactions, 2.25 per cent for inter-bank transactions, based on the central exchange rate. It was a custom close to a free market.

[102] *See generally* Bureau of Monetary Affairs, Ministry of Finance Republic of China, The ROC Financial System and Policy 97 (1996). Reference exchange rate system was started in May 1989 and ended in Feb. 1990. Bureau of Monetary Affairs, Ministry of Finance Republic of China, The ROC Financial System and Policy 97 (1996).

[103] See Bureau of Monetary Affairs, Ministry of Finance Republic of China, The ROC Financial System and Policy 55 (1996).

[104] *See generally* Bureau of Monetary Affairs, Ministry of Finance Republic of China, The ROC Financial System and Policy 55 (1996). Before the establishment of the central exchange rate system, the government and the few authorised banks had the discretion deciding the exchange rate. Since the establishment of the central exchange rate system, the authorised foreign exchange banks might negotiate the exchange rate with customers. However, the fluctuation of the exchange rate was limited in a narrow scope. (US$0.1 of the central rate for bank–customer transactions).

to grant foreign banks national treatment.[105] Furthermore, in order to join the World Trade Organisation (WTO), Taiwan was required to negotiate with twenty-six other member states of the organisation. By the end of February of 1998, Taiwan reached the conclusion with ten member states.[106] One of the important issues in the negotiations with twelve of these twenty-six member states was the liberalisation of Taiwan's financial service market.[107]

The internal need was another reason compelling the government to lift the ban on the establishment of financial institutions. After more than two decades' restriction on the increase of new financial institutions, the government discovered that the restriction had caused inefficiency of operation, and produced adverse effects on service quality. Since 1988, the country started the liberalisation of financial institutions. In 1988, the government announced to allow the new establishment of securities firms. In 1990, the amendment of the Banking Law opened the door to the establishment of commercial banks.[108] In 1992, the country allowed the establishment of new insurance companies.[109] In 1993, the government announced to allow the establishment of future commission merchants to engage in the brokerage service of foreign futures.[110] In 1994, the government relaxed the establishment of foreign bank or banking branches.[111] In the same year, bill companies were allowed to be established.[112] The establishment of these financial institutions not only resulted in the increase of financial institutions in the ROC, but also stimulated the positive development of the whole financial market.

105 AMERICAN CHAMBER OF COMMERCE IN TAIWAN, *Financial Services Reform in the Republic of China*, 5 June 1987.

106 *See Chi* Schive, 'The ROC Financial Liberalization' (visited 30 Sept. 1998) <http://cepd.spring.org.tw/Speak/870416/1.html>.

107 *See* ibid.

108 BANKING LAW. Art. 52 (1989) (ROC); RULES GOVERNING THE INCORPORATION OF COMMERCIAL BANKS. Art. 1 (ROC).

109 INSURANCE LAW. Art. 137. s 2 (1992) (ROC); RULES GOVERNING THE INCORPORATION OF INSURANCE COMPANIES. Art. 1. (ROC).

110 After the promulgation of the 'Law of Foreign Futures Transactions' in 1992, the Ministry of Finance formulated the relevant rules and regulations, such as the 'Guidelines Governing the Establishment of Futures Brokers', and the 'Administrative Rules Governing Futures Brokers' on 8 Jan. 1993. The futures operations began in Apr. 1994. *See* eg BUREAU OF MONETARY AFFAIRS MINISTRY OF FINANCE REPUBLIC OF CHINA, 1993 ANNUAL REPORT BUREAU OF MONETARY AFFAIRS MINISTRY OF FINANCE 15 (1994); BUREAU OF MONETARY AFFAIRS MINISTRY OF FINANCE REPUBLIC OF CHINA, 1995 ANNUAL REPORT BUREAU OF MONETARY AFFAIRS MINISTRY OF FINANCE 17 (1996).

111 The 'Guidelines Governing the Screening of Application to Establish Branches/Representative Offices by Foreign Banks' was revised on 9 Aug. 1994. *See* BUREAU OF MONETARY AFFAIRS MINISTRY OF FINANCE REPUBLIC OF CHINA, 1994 ANNUAL REPORT BUREAU OF MONETARY AFFAIRS MINISTRY OF FINANCE 21 (1995).

112 *See generally* BUREAU OF MONETARY AFFAIRS MINISTRY OF FINANCE REPUBLIC OF CHINA,

3. Enlargement of the Business Scope of Financial Institutions

Partly because of the suggestion of the American Chamber of Commerce in Taiwan in 1987, Taiwan gradually accepted the international trend of 'universal banking'.[113] The amendment of the Banking Law of 1989 gave the banking authorities more discretion to approve the business scope of various banks.[114] Foreign banks, after the amendment, were allowed to engage in more financial businesses, such as savings and trust.[115] The Ministry of Finance has gradually released the control over domestic banking business operations, such as credit card,[116] margin trading, bills trading,[117] non-discretion trust services in investing foreign securities, and financial derivatives.[118] The Ministry also relaxed the restrictions imposed on medium business banks regarding business district and foreign exchange operations.[119]

It took about 10 years for Taiwan to modernise its banking market. The enlargement of the business scope of banks not only allowed local financial institutions to compete on an equal footing in the international arena, but

1994 Annual Report Bureau of Monetary Affairs Ministry of Finance 22 (1995). To cope with the fast development in the bill market as well as to effectively monitor financial institutions conducting money market instruments, the Ministry of Finance revised the 'Regulations Governing the Operations of Money Market Instrument Traders' and renamed it as the 'Regulation Governing the Money market Instrument Trader's. Since then new bills finance companies are allowed to establish.

[113] *See also* American Chamber of Commerce in Taiwan, *Financial Service Reform in the Republic of China*, 5 June 1987, at 2. The concept of 'universal banking' was one of the important suggestions that the American Chamber of Commerce in Taiwan desired to persuade the ROC government to accept.

[114] Banking Law. Arts. 71. 78, 89, 101, and 121 (1994) (ROC).

[115] Ibid. Art. 121 (1994) (ROC).

[116] In 1993 the Ministry of Finance formulated the 'Regulations Governing Credit Card Business' which started the country's credit card era. *See* The Ministry of Finance Tal-Tsai-Yuang no 82248464 Executive Order, 30 June 1993.

[117] *See generally* Bureau of Monetary Affairs Ministry of Financial Republic of China, 1995 Annual Report Bureau of Monetary Affairs Ministry of Finance 18 (1996). In 1992, the Ministry of Finance allowed banks to operate as brokers and dealers of money market instruments. In 1995, the Ministry allowed banks to certify and underwrite money market instruments.

[118] *See generally* ibid. In order to strengthen supervision of derivative financial transactions handled by financial institutions, the Ministry formulated and promulgated the 'Essential Points Governing the Transactions in Derivative Financial Products Conducted by Banks' in Apr. 1995. Under the requirement of the Essential Points, all banks approved to conduct derivation products must establish a detailed and clear guideline on risk management and internal control mechanisms for transactions. The internal guideline must follow the principles listed in the 'Essential Points'.

[119] *See generally* Bureau of Monetary Affairs Ministry of Financial Republic of China, 1994 Annual Report Bureau of Monetary Affairs Ministry of Finance 34 (1995). Since 1994 the Ministry of Finance took two stages to allow regional banks to expand their operational territories. Regional banks are allowed to establish new domestic branch outside its own existing operation territory, if the regional bank's financial situation and operations reach a certain level.

also brought positive effects on the promotion of service quality.[120] However, this enlargement and other liberalisation measures mentioned above made all financial institutions face more competition and operational risk. Financial discipline became one of the important issues in the process of the liberalisation.

The government did not ignore financial discipline while it started to expedite the process of the financial liberalisation. Since 1991 the financial authorities gradually strengthened the supervision and examination of financial institutions.[121] The scope of examination and supervision expanded from domestic banks to their overseas branches.[122] Meanwhile, the authorities have established a nationwide financial early warning system designed to early identify problems in all financial institutions.[123] However, the authorities' efforts did not prevent the series of insider bank frauds occurred in 1994.

In short, although Taiwan took very conservative and cautious steps to liberalise its financial system, the country could not completely avoid the negative impact resulting from liberalisation. Taiwan's experience proves that liberalisation is really not an easy task. Purely administrative approaches seemed not enough to mold a liberal and safe financial system.

D. *Conservative Economic Policies, Productive Structure and Financial Situation*

Although its economic achievements are as brilliant as those of other East Asian countries, Taiwan has different economic development policies and productive structures than the others. Most of all, the economic policies and productive structures were consistent with the financial policies.

In order to seek continuously high economic growth, most East Asian countries encouraged investments in both domestic markets and foreign markets in the past several years. These countries have been some of the closest countries in the world to foreign direct investment.[124] In the three

120 BUREAU OF MONETARY AFFAIRS, MINISTRY OF FINANCE REPUBLIC OF CHINA, THE ROC FINANCIAL SYSTEM AND POLICY 101 (1996).

121 In 1991 the Bureau of Monetary Affairs drafted the 'Operation Guidelines for Financial Examinations'. *See* BUREAU OF MONETARY AFFAIRS MINISTRY OF FINANCIAL REPUBLIC OF CHINA, 1991 ANNUAL REPORT BUREAU OF MONETARY AFFAIRS MINISTRY OF FINANCE 16 (1992).

122 In order to improve international cooperation in banking supervision, the ROC started to dispatch examiners to undertake examinations on domestic banks' overseas branches. *See also* BUREAU OF MONETARY AFFAIRS MINISTRY OF FINANCIAL REPUBLIC OF CHINA, 1992 ANNUAL REPORT BUREAU OF MONETARY AFFAIRS MINISTRY OF FINANCE 23 (1993).

123 The warning system was designed by the Central Deposit Insurance Corporation and fully operated over all financial institutions in 1993. *See* BUREAU OF MONETARY AFFAIRS MINISTRY OF FINANCIAL REPUBLIC OF CHINA, 1993 ANNUAL REPORT BUREAU OF MONETARY AFFAIRS MINISTRY OF FINANCE 24 (1994).

124 *See* 'The text of Mr Severino's speech' (visited at 20 Aug. 1998) <http://www.smh.com.au/news/9806/17/pageone/pageone2.html>.

years preceding the crisis, Southeast Asia's growth spurts increasingly depended on the bidding of asset and property prices,[125] with a large portion of the investment from abroad. Since the Mexican crisis of 1994, the overseas portfolio and equity investments rapidly flew into South East Asian countries. Malaysia reported a total capital inflow equivalent to 20 per cent of its GDP in 1994.[126] In the same year, Malaysia had to manage US$30 billion in external capital buying into its stock and bond markets. In Thailand, the Bangkok International Banking Facilities (BIBF)[127] permitted local and foreign commercial banks in Thailand to take deposits or borrow in foreign currencies from abroad, and lend them both in domestic and overseas markets.[128] As a result, massive amounts of currency flowed into the country. In 1995, Thailand's external capital inflow peaked at 12.3 per cent of GDP.[129] Unfortunately, the governments did not make adequate economic policies and domestic financial institutions were not in a position to effectively intermediate these resources into productive use.[130] Most of these capitals flew into the construction industry and luxury spending that could not contribute to substantial national economic growth.[131] In order to absorb the rapid in-flow foreign capital, domestic banks were allowed to expand lending rapidly. The expansion of the credit market not only fueled imprudent investment, but also unrealistically increased asset prices.[132]

In South Korea, a series of bankruptcies of government-supported large enterprises[133] exposed that the country's economic policy of raising large

[125] Manuel F. Montes, Kevin F. F. Quigley, and Donald E. Weatherbee, 'Growing Pains: ASEAN's Economic and Political Challenges' (visited 20 Aug. 1995) http://www.asiasociety.org/publications/asean-miracle.htm>.

[126] *See* ibid.

[127] *See generally* The Straits Times Interactive, 'Nukul Commission Report: The main findings' (visited 20 Aug. 1998) <http://www.asia1.com.sg/straitstimes/pages/stfea2.html>. The Bangkok International Banking Facilities (BIBF) were established in 1993. One of the main functions of the establishment of the BIBF was to open the floodgates for offshore loans into the country.

[128] Kirida Bhaopichitr, 'Thailand's Road to Economic Crisis' (visited 20 Aug. 1998) <http://www.hartford-hwp.com/archives/54/113.html>.

[129] Manuel F. Montes, Kevin F. F. Quigley, and Donald E. Weatherbee, 'Growing Pains: ASEAN's Economic and Political Challenges' (visited 20 Aug. 1995) <http://www.asiasociety.org/publications/asean-miracle.htm>.

[130] Shigemitsu Sugisaki, 'Economic Crises in Asia' (visited 18 Feb. 1998) <http://www.imf.org/external/np/speeches/1998/013098.htm>.

[131] *See also The Economist*, 'Asia's Economic Crises: How far is down?' (visited 23 Feb. 1998) <http://www.stern.nyu.edu/~nroubini/asia/sf0983.html>. The banks of these East Asian countries convinced that demand for offices, hotels and luxury homes would continue to soar. They threw money at grandiose construction projects.

[132] Stanley Fischer, 'The Asian Crisis: A View from the IMF' (visited 24 Feb. 1998) <http://www.imf.org/external/np/speeches/1998/012298.htm>.

[133] *See generally* 'Chronology of the Asian Currency Crisis and its Global Contagion' (visited 23 Feb. 1998) <http://www.stern.nyu.edu/~nroubini/asia/AsiaChronology1.html>. At the beginning of 1997, one of the largest steel companies, Hanbo Steel, collapsed under $6 billion

domestic enterprises needed to be reviewed. In the process of rapid economic development, the limitations of South Korea's system of detailed government interventions at the micro level have become increasingly apparent.[134] In order to develop strategic industries, the South Korean government provided full support to large corporate conglomerates (*chaebol*), and the government's intervention in economic activities raised some large international conglomerates for the country. Some of these international conglomerates had the biggest scale in the world.[135] Nevertheless, the real investment yield of these conglomerates was not the same as their scale. In order to immediately occupy a market, South Korean manufacturers dumped their products to the market at a very low price or even without any profit. The total net profit of the top forty-nine Korean conglomerates in 1996 was only US$65 million, which was even less than some Taiwanese electronic companies' individual net profit.[136] Moreover, the excessive investment in certain sectors such as steel and autos, and a weakening in the profitability associated with the cyclical downturn not only caused the bankruptcy of a number of conglomerates, but also severely weakened the financial system.[137] The bankruptcies also spilled over into a sharp increase of nonperforming loans. By the end of September of 1997, the amount of bad loan reached 32 trillion Korea won.[138]

Moreover, South Korea is among the fundamental deficit economies in the region.[139] The country had a huge amount of foreign debts but less foreign reserves. By the end of 1997, the total debt of the country was US$155 billion, with US$60 billion short-term debt.[140] However, the country only

in debts. In 1 July South Korea's third largest car maker Kia suffered credit crunch and asked for emergency loans, but finally went bankruptcy later.

134 *See* 'Korea Letter of Intent, December 3, 1997, Attachment: Korea- Memorandum on the Economic Program' (visited 19 Feb. 1998) <http://www.imf.org/external/np/120397.htm>.

135 Samsung Electronics is the world's largest producer of computer memory chips. *See* Andrew Pollack, 'Corporate Fire Sale Seen for Korea' (visited 27 Dec. 1997) <http://www.nytimes.com/library/financial/122797Korea-takeovers.htm>.

136 If the bankrupted Hanbo Steel was listed in the top fifty enterprises, there was no net profit for all the top fifty Korean conglomerates. *See* Shen-yuan Tsang, *The Collapse of Japanese and Korean Economic Model*. GLOBAL VIEW MONTHLY, 5 Mar. 1998, at 103.

137 *See* International Monetary Fund, 'IMF Approves SDR 15.5 Billion Stand-by Credit for Korea', Press Release No 97/55 (visited 25 Nov. 1997) <http://www.imf.org/external/np>.

138 It equaled to 7 per cent of the country's GDP and about double that level at the end of 1996. *See* Shigemitsu Sugisaki, 'Economic Crises in Asia' (visited 18 Feb. 1998) <http://www.imf.org/external/np/speeches/1998/013098.htm>.

139 There are two broad groups of East Asian economies: the fundamental current account deficit economies and the current account surplus economies. The fundamental deficit economies are Thailand, Malaysia, Indonesia, the Philippines, and South Korea.

140 *See also* 'Chronology of the Asian Currency Crisis and its Global Contagion, 9 Dec. 1997' (visited 23 Feb. 1998) <http://www.stern.nyu.edu/~nroubini/asia/ AsiaChronology1.html>. According to an internal IMF document the country's short-term external liabilities, including 'debt contracted by residents, nonresident branches and affiliates of domestic financial institutions, and offshore banking debt contracted by domestic banks', were estimated at

possessed US$17 billion foreign reserves in the same period,[141] hence the country ran out of foreign-exchange reserves. No international businesses, calculated by foreign currencies, could proceed and the country almost went bankrupt.[142] These countries' failures could be regarded as the result inconsistent economic development and financial policies.

Despite the strong macroeconomic performance of these East Asian countries, a number of underlying weaknesses, including the financial policies and the health of the financial sectors, have made these countries vulnerable to adverse external shocks. The weaknesses gradually appeared as these East Asian countries started to liberalise their economic as well financial markets in the late 1980s.

Most Asian countries started to liberalise their domestic markets in the late 1980s. All these economies were clearly more open than most developing countries. Most economists agreed that the economic openness policies were essential for achieving the remarkable export performance.[143] The liberalisation policy included trade liberalisation and financial liberalisation. In Indonesia, prudent macro-economic policies, continuing structural reforms, and well-maintained economic balances kept Indonesia on a path of rapid economic development over the past several decades.[144] However, the relative stability of the foreign exchange rate of the rupiah during most of the 1990s, together with high domestic interest rates and high domestic investment, encouraged and facilitated high levels of overseas borrowing. By the end of 1997, the country's external debt stood at US$140 billion (about two-thirds of GDP), of which US$20 billion was short term.

Therefore, foreign countries lost confidence on the region,[145] and the sharp depreciation of the Indonesian rupiah immediately swallowed the economic harvests accumulated in the past several decades.

about US$100 billion at the end of Sept. 1997. This result contradicted the Financial Ministry's statement that South Korea's short-term foreign debt was US$65.6 billion at the end of Sept.

[141] *See* J. P. Morgan, *World Financial Markets*, First Quarter 1998.

[142] *See* Shen-yuan Tsang, *The Collapse of Japanese and Korean Economic Model*, GLOBAL VIEW MONTHLY, 5 Mar. 1998, at 103

[143] *See* Shigemitsu Sugisaki, 'Economic Crises in Asia' (visited 18 Feb. 1998) <http://www.imf.org/external/np/speches/1998/013098.htm>.

[144] *See generally* 'Indonesia-Memorandum of Economic and Financial Policies' (visited 19 Feb. 1998) <http://www.imf.org/external/np/loi/011598.htm>. Since the 1970s, the economic growth of Indonesia has averaged 7 per cent per annum and the economic structure has successfully become diversified. Meanwhile, macro-economic balance has been maintained: the budget has been balanced; inflation has been contained at relatively low levels; current account deficits have been kept moderate; and international reserves have remained at comfortable levels.

[145] The large depreciation reflected a severe loss of confidence in the currency, financial sector, and the overall economy. *See* 'Indonesia-Memorandum of Economic and Financial Policies' (visited 19 Feb. 1998), <http://www.imf.org/external/np/loi/011598.htm>.

Unlike that of most South East Asian countries and South Korea, Taiwan's economic structure is not framed by big enterprises but constructed by small and medium businesses.[146] In the past several decades, the main economic policy was to develop small and medium businesses. This policy not only successfully created the country's economic miracle but also properly diversified the business risk to all small and medium business.[147] This economic policy could not create international large enterprises as South Korea did. However, it could reduce the impact of international economic recession.[148]

There are several features of the small and medium business economic structure.

First of all, the business is very flexible and diverse. From the early economic development stage concentrating on labour intensive industries, such as umbrellas, shoes and clothes, to the later development in high-tech products, such as computers and accessories, the small and medium business always successfully transformed their business types at different economic stages. Taiwan was the kingdom of bicycles, yacht boats, and umbrellas. However, these intensive industries had been moved to Mainland China and South east Asia when the labour expense soared in Taiwan. The moving of labour intensive industries did not empty the country's economic structure, because the gap was immediately filled by various high-tech products. By the end of 1997, Taiwan had become one of the main computer export countries in the world.[149] The flexible feature of small and medium business allows the country to easily convert its economic structure to face new challenges and competition.

Secondly, operational risks were shared by all manufacturers. Because the small and medium businesses do not need much capital, the amount of loans from financial system to any individual manufacturer is limited. Furthermore, under such a situation, any individual manufacturer's failure will not cause fatal bad debts that may threaten the financial system.

146 In South Korea, the top six conglomerates occupied 58 per cent of the total amount of the stock market. In Taiwan, the number is only 23 per cent. The small and medium business constitutes 95 per cent of the country's business. *See* WEALTH MAGAZINE, Mar. 1998, at 225; COMMON WEALTH MAGAZINE, vol 204, 1 May 1998, at 44.

147 *See* WEALTH MAGAZINE, Mar. 1998, at 225, and COMMON WEALTH MAGAZINE, vol 204, 1 May 1998, at 44.

148 *See* COMMON WEALTH MAGAZINE, vol 201, 1 Feb. 1998, at 165

149 *See generally* BOARD OF FOREIGN TRADE, MINISTRY OF ECONOMIC AFFAIRS, *Foreign Trade Development of the Republic of China 1997*, 1st edn, June 1998, at 11. In 1997 the production value of computer related products reached US$30.40 billion with a growth rate of 21.4 per cent. This has placed the country the third largest producer of computer products worldwide. Among the different world leading products are monitors, main boards, notebook computers, image scanners, computer mice, and keyboards.

E. Luck

Luck was on Taiwan's side. Although the country was very proud of its performance in the Asian financial turmoil, the government did not afford any effective and direct approach to avoid the crises. Just like most East Asian countries facing the currency crises, the Central Bank tried to directly intervene in the foreign exchange market to steady the currency. However, when the market force was too strong for the Central Bank to defend the New Taiwan Dollar, the Central Bank was compelled to abandon the defense of the country currency exchange rate. In order to defend the New Taiwan Dollar, the Central Bank spent more than US$7 billion to defend the country exchange rate in four months.[150] However, the Bank's effort could not stop the depreciation of the New Taiwan Dollar exchange rate.[151] In order to avoid the adverse impacts on both the real sector and financial markets resulting from foreign exchange intervention,[152] the Central Bank allowed the market function to decide the New Taiwan Dollar exchange rate since mid-October 1997.

Besides the above reasons that the ROC could be free from the Asian financial turmoil, pure luck might be another reason.

In the past decade, the ROC economic development was not always smooth. It also experienced several potential crises that were sufficient enough to cause similar turmoil experienced by East Asian countries in 1997. The last economic crisis that threatened Taiwan occurred in the late 1980s.

The soaring of the stock market in 1987 triggered the country's money game. The stock market index rocketed from the 1000 point in 1987 to the historic 12,000 point in 1989. The rapid rise of the stock price not only attracted a lot of capital flowing into the market,[153] but also resulted in the

150 Taiwan's foreign exchange reserves shrank from US$90 billion at the end of June 1997 to US$82.9 billion ate the end of Oct. in 1997. *See* Jia-Dong Shea, 'The ROC's Experience in addressing the Asian Financial Crisis', Address at the ROC-USA Economic Conference (1998). Mr Shea is the Deputy Governor of the Central Bank of China.

151 The exchange rate between the US dollar and New Taiwan Dollar dropped from 1 : 28.5 in July 1997 to 1 : 34.23 in June 1998. *See* TAIWAN ECONOMIC RESEARCH INSTITUTE, *International Economic Data*, No 534, 4 June 1998.

152 *See generally* Jia-Dong Shea, 'The ROC's Experience in Addressing the Asian Financial Crisis', Address at the ROC-USA Economic Conference (1998). The Central Bank tried to stabilise the exchange rate by raising both the rediscount rate and the interest rate on accommodations against secured loans. However, both the loan interest rate and the stock market received severe impacts. The inter-bank call-loan interest rate rose above 10 per cent in early Oct. 1997 and the stock index dropped about 30 per cent in two months. Both these situations were disadvantageous for the country's macroeconomic development.

153 The capital apparently flew from the community financial institutions, such as the credit cooperatives, credit departments of farmers' and fishermen's associations, and the Postal Savings System between 1986 and 1989. During the period, the market value of the listed stocks in the public stock market increased from NT$548 billion in 1986 to NT$6 trillion in

change of the entire economic environment. When the investment of stock became the most convenient and profitable earning tool, many people devoted themselves to the market. Investing in the stock market became the national game, and seriously affected the country's normal economic and financial development.

The effect was unprecedented and tremendous. Many manufacturers and some fundamental construction companies could not find labourers, thus triggered the country's policy of importing foreign labour.[154] The real estate price rocketed,[155] with the country's wealth relocated through the money game. Foreign 'hot money', under native citizens' names, flew into the country for the high earning rate of the stock market and for the expected appreciation of the New Taiwan Dollar. Financial fraud increased. The numbers and losses of these frauds were huge enough to affect the public confidence in the whole financial system.[156] These factors constituted the 'bubble economy'.

Since the stock price slid down from the highest point in 1989,[157] the bubble economy burst not only destabilised the country economy but also the country's political sentiment.[158] However, the burst did not fatally hurt the economy just as most South-east Asian countries experienced in the Asian financial crises, because the financial market then was still under the government's control and foreign capital could not freely flow into the country.[159] On the contrary, the bubble burst provided the country a good opportunity to review its economic structure and financial system.

1989. It increased over tenfold in three years. *See* eg Statistics Office, Bureau of Monetary Affairs Ministry of Finance, Republic of China, Financial Statistics Abstract, Nov. 1996, Bureau of Monetary MFO 42–43 (Feb. 1997); Bureau of Monetary Affairs Ministry of Finance Republic of China, 1991 Annual Report Bureau of Monetary Affairs Ministry of Finance 13 (1992).

154 *See generally* Statistic Monthly, Table 12 (visited 30 Oct. 1998) <http://www.evta.gov.tw>. The Republic of China started to import foreign labour in 1990. The main labour resources are from Thailand, the Philippines, Malaysia, and Indonesia. By the end of Sept. 1998, the total amount of legal foreign labours allowed to work in Taiwan was 263,747.

155 The government income from property reached the highest period between 1987 and 1990. *See* Council for Economic Planning and Development Republic of China, Taiwan Statiscal Data Book 1994 (1994) at 39.

156 A lot of financial frauds, such as the Chang-Hwa Fourth Credit Corporation Fraud and International Bill Company Fraud, were related to the stock investments.

157 Man-pon, Diau, *Who Can Terminate the Financial Crisis?*, Common Wealth Magazine, 1 Mar. 1996, at 121.

158 Schive Chi, 'Asian Financial Crisis and Prospects' (visited 30 Sept. 1998) <http://cepd.spring.rog.tw/English/speak/980805.html>.

159 The country open its stock market to foreign investment institutions in 1990. The total amount of foreign investments Taiwa's stock market was then limited to US$2.5 billion. Although the restrictions gradually relaxed since then, foreign investments could not freely move in and out of Taiwan's stock market until 1996. *See* Schive Chi, 'The Financial Liberalization of the Republic of China' (visited 30 Sept. 1998) <http://cepd.spring.org.tw/Speak/870416/1. html>.

It took Taiwan two to three years to stabilise its currency and the stock market, and some investors are still affected. Moreover, it also compelled the country to expedite the changes to the economic structure and the reform of the financial system. Since then, the country's production structure has formally shifted away from labour-intensive to capital and technology-intensive industries.[160] The financial market gradually liberalised. Because this bubble experience has driven most non-competitive companies out of the country, the remaining companies were strong enough to face further challenges without too much competition. This successful restructuring of the economic environment distinguished Taiwan from other East Asian countries. While the South East Asian countries competed with one another in the field of traditional labour-intensive industries, Taiwan has become one of the main high-tech producing countries in the world. This made the country's competition ahead of most Asian countries, and thus received less impact of economic recession.

Furthermore, the bubble economy was caused by non-comparable economic development and financial control. It was a purely domestic problem and did not cause any chain reaction in the neighbouring countries.

In short, the timing of the bubble burst in the late 1980s was advantageous to Taiwan. Because the economic situation in the world was good during this period of time, Taiwan could resolve the crisis alone and had the opportunity to recover from the burst of the bubble economy. Moreover, the burst of the bubble economy provided the country a good opportunity to restructure its economy and to reform its financial system which in turn immunised Taiwan from the impending Asian financial crises in 1997.

III. PRESENT ECONOMIC SITUATION IN TAIWAN AND ITS INFLUENCE ON THE COUNTRY'S FINANCIAL MARKET

A. *Present Economic Situation*

Since the new government took over the regime in May 2000, Taiwan has experienced a series of political confrontations, which not only resulted in political chaos but also seriously affected the public confidence in the government.[161] As a result, the country's economy has experienced the most serious recession since the mid-1970s, and financial crisis threatens the country's financial system again.[162] The following factors and statistics may reveal the situation of economic recession:

[160] Ibid.

[161] 'The KMT hangs fire', THE ECONOMIST, 14 Nov. 2000.

[162] 'Taiwan's financial system: Too many debts to settle', THE ECONOMIST, 14 Nov. 2000. *The Economist* predicted Taiwan might experience a financial crisis around the Chinese Lunar

1. The Continuous Decline of Economic Growth

Taiwan's economic situation during the Asian financial crisis remained relatively stronger than all neighbouring countries. While all other East Asian countries struggled to get out of the crisis, Taiwan enjoyed steady economic growth before 2000.[163]

The country's economy sharply turned down since mid-2000. The country's economic growth rate of the fourth quarter of 2000 dropped from 5.97 per cent to 4.08 per cent. The adjustment made the annual economic growth rate decline from an estimated 6 per cent to 5.98 per cent. Furthermore, the 2001 prediction, considering all present factors, tends to be pessimism, and may be under 5 per cent.[164] The continuous decline of the economic growth rate signals that the country seems to face economic recession.

2. The Soaring Unemployment Rate

One of the statistics that may appropriately resonate the present economic recession in Taiwan is the soaring of the unemployment rate. The rate in the country was always kept under 3 per cent since the mid-1970s. The low unemployment not only reflects the prosperous economic development, but also cements the foundation of social security. However, this situation has gradually changed since the economic situation turned down in mid-2000. At the beginning of 2001, the rate reached 3.35 per cent, and is predicted to be over the record highs, 4 per cent, until the mid-2002.

B. Impact on the Financial Market

The economic recession has direct impact on the financial industry. Taiwan's financial industry has experienced the most difficult period ever. The difficulty seems not only a temporary phenomenon, but potentially tends to develop as a financial disaster, which may be signalled from following:

1. The Reduction of the Domestic Loan Rate

The economic recession made private enterprises and banks take a more conservative strategy toward the market. As a result, the growth rate of loans to private enterprises started to shrink since the end of 2002. By the

New Year in 2001. One of the main reasons of *The Economist*'s prediction is that the Chinese Lunar New Year is the traditional time for debts to be settled in Chinese society.

163 *See* interior Charter Economic Growth Rate.

164 'The turning point-private investment sharply reduced in the fourth quarter of last year', United Daily News, 17 Feb. 2001.

end of January 2001, the rate has fallen down to the historic low point –0.02 per cent. The major function of financial institution lending is almost frozen.[165] This situation not only substantially reflects the economic recession, but also increases the operational difficulties for both financial institutions and private enterprises. If this situation keeps on, both the economic development and the stable of financial system will face rigid challenge.

2. The increase of Past-Due Loan Ratio

The average past-due loan ratio in Taiwan before 1996 was below 2 per cent. The ratio increased sharply since 1996. By the end of September of 2000, the official past-due ratio of domestic bank was over 5.35 per cent.[166] In spite of the official claim that the situation is still within acceptable and controllable scope,[167] the continuous increase of the bad debt is a warning signal of the country's financial condition.[168]

As the result of the interaction of the increase of over-due loans and the reduction of the domestic loan rate of the financial system, the deficit of most financial institutions sharply increased at the end of 2000.

C. *Short Conclusion*

Most analysts attribute the present economic recession to the political chaos. It seems a good argument, because all the privileges that protected Taiwan from the Asian financial crisis have not changed. Furthermore, there is no exterior factor, such like those affecting Thailand, Indonesia and Korea in the Asian financial crisis, impacting the Taiwan's economic and financial situation. The difficulties that the Taiwan has experienced are the outcome of internal political chaos, and the chaos mainly resulted from the country's democratisation.[169]

[165] 'The annual growth rate of bank loan to private enterprise sharply reduced', ibid. 27 Feb. 2001.

[166] 'Taiwan's financial system-Too many debts to settle', The Economist, 14 Nov. 2000. Indicating that the real bad debt level might be two to three times of the official statistics, according to analysts.

[167] 'Central bank claims that the ROC does not have the symbol of financial crisis'. United Daily News, 27 Feb. 2001.

[168] 'Major commercial banks adjust the date of announcing the overdue loan ratio', United Daily News, 13 Mar. 2001. Reporting that the total amount of overdue loan of seven major domestic commercial banks by the end of February reached the historic high of NT$386 billion. The total amount of overdue loans of the whole banking system was over NT$773 billion by the end of 2000.

[169] *See* 'Taiwan's financial system—Too many debts to settle', The Economist, 14 Nov. 2000 at 109 and 'The KMT hangs fire', The Economist, 14 Nov. 2000, at 42.

IV. LESSONS OF TAIWAN'S EXPERIENCE DURING AND AFTER THE CRISIS

The Asian financial turmoil holds good lessons for the whole world. Both affected countries and non-affected countries could learn something from each other. Taiwan was one of the few countries that received relatively less pain and could be almost free from the crises. The country's experience certainly could be the model for other neighbouring countries. On the other hand, the affected countries' experience was also a valuable warning for Taiwan to consider future financial system developments. Furthermore, Taiwan's economic and financial performance at the end of the twentieth century provided the world with another reason to review other possible causes of a financial crisis.

A. *Sequencing Decided the Consequence of Liberalisation and Internationalisation*

Although there is no disagreement about the goal of a liberalised and internationalised economy and finance, the path and the sequence of taking measures make the great difference in success.[170] Taiwan may be one of the countries that has successfully transferred its financial system from a closed and monopolised one to open and internationalised one. The value of its experience to liberalise and internationalise its financial system was not the speed or scope of the liberalisation and liberalisation. What the experience provided was a model of liberalisation causing least negative impact.[171]

It took more than twenty years for the country to liberalise and internationalise its economic and financial system. Since the release of the control over interest rates in 1976, the country gradually started to liberalise the financial system. The scope and the speed of the liberalisation mainly depended on the country's economic development and financial need.

The main initial reason for the release of the interest rate control was that the control had interfered with the normal order of the capital

170 Schive Chi, 'Asian Financial Crisis and Prospects' (visited 30 Sept. 1998) <http://cepd.spring.org.tw/Englixh/speak/980805.html>.

171 *Author's note*: In Indonesia, the financial crisis caused a series of riots and resulted in the collapse of the 32-year Suharto regime in 1998. In Malaysia, the financial crisis triggered the political confrontation between the Prime Minister, Mahathir Mohamad and Deputy Prime Minister, Anwar Ibrahim, in Sept. 1998. In South Korea, the financial crisis helped the liberal reformer Kim Dae-jung win the presidential election in Dec. 1997. All these affected countries experienced similar troubles, such as the increase of unemployment, the depreciation of currency and the skyrocketing of food prices.

market and resulted in illegal underground financial activities.[172] The abolishment of the 'Fixed Foreign Exchange Rate System' in 1978 responded to unreasonable long-term high import prices.[173] It reflected the rapid growth of the country's international trade, in which the government encouraged domestic and foreign banks to establish offshore banking units since 1983. The opening of the domestic financial market since 1990 mainly resulted from the international and domestic pressures.

As a result of the cautious policies, the country's economic development was not as brilliant as that of its neighbouring competitors before the Asian financial crisis occurred.[174] The country's bankruptcy rate of small and medium-sized companies that dominated the country's economy ranked first in Asia.[175] The country's investment rate was lower than its neighbouring countries,[176] but most investments focused on low-risk production.[177] The allocation of resources was left more to the markets, and foreign capital was accepted cautiously. In addition, direct foreign investment outweighed the more footloose portfolio kind.[178] In short, the country's active economy was developed within a conservative financial environment.

The slow and cautious sequence of liberalisation and internationalisation were strongly criticised by Western countries.[179] However, the financial turmoil proved that the country's cautious attitude toward liberalisation and internationalisation not only successfully led the continuous and adequate economic growth, but also shaped a good economic

[172] BUREAU OF MONETARY AFFAIRS, MINISTRY OF FINANCE REPUBLIC OF CHINA, THE ROC FINANCIAL SYSTEM AND POLICY 55 (1996).

[173] Ibid. 59.

[174] The average Gross Domestic Product (GDP) of Taiwan in the 1980s was 7.6 per cent against South Korea's 9.6 per cent. Before the financial crisis occurred, the GDP of Taiwan in 1996 was 5.71 per cent against South Korea's 7.1 per cent and Singapore's 6.5 per cent. *See* eg COUNCIL FOR ECONOMIC PLANNING AND DEVELOPMENT REPUBLIC OF CHINA, TAIWAN STATISCAL DATA BOOK 1996, at 307~8 (1994); International Monetary Fund, 'IMF Approves SDR 15.5 Billion Stan-by Credit for Korea' (visited 19 Feb. 1998) <http://www.imf.org/external/np/loi/122497.html>.

[175] 'The Secret that Taiwan Escape the Financial Turmoil', THE ECONOMIST, Mar. 1997, at 224.

[176] For example, South Korea's investment rate has been considerably higher—at 38 per per cent compared with 21 per cent in Taiwan. *See* Gustav Ranis 'Miracles that don't cease', 19 Feb. 1998.

[177] Taiwan's large-scale investments were always processed through the government-owned enterprises and the investment risk was always low. *See* 'Seeing the Future from the Edge of the Turmoil'. COMMON WEALTH MAGAZINE, Feb. 1998, at 175.

[178] Consequently, Taiwan's reliance on foreign savings has amounted to less than 10 per cent of total investment over the past four decades in sharp contrast to 60 per cent for South Korea. *See* Gustav Rains 'Miracles that don't cease', 19 Feb. 1998.

[179] The American Chamber of Commerce in Taiwan (ACCT), in a 14-page recommendation to the ROC government in 1985, criticised Taiwan's financial system as an antiquated financial system that weakened the financial structure of the average large Taiwanese company.

circumstance. Under this circumstance, the small and medium business that seldom borrowed money from foreign countries had trained themselves to overcome operational difficulties. Unlike Japan and South Korea, Taiwan's economic structure was more flexible to face economic challenges.[180] The flexible economic structure and the moderate liberalisation made the country more able to bear the rush of liberalisation and internationalisation.

B. *Removing the Improper Links among Government, Business and the Banking Industry*

One of the important lessons from the Asian financial turmoil for Taiwan is that improper links among the government, business and the banking system are the biggest enemy of liberalisation and internationalisation.

Because of the political situation, capitalism that is known as the combination of a free political society and open economic system in the Western world has a different nature in almost every Asian country.[181] Almost every East Asian country's government holds a very close relationship with its financial institutions. According to the history of economic development of most East Asia countries, the Pacific Rim miracle could be regarded as the close link between the government, banking industry and businesses. In Indonesia, the former president Suharto governed the fourth largest country in the world for more than 32 years. His family substantially controlled the country's financial system. In South Korea, the government has treated the banks as tools of state industrial policy for years.[182] The government, *chaebols* (big business conglomerates) and the financial institutions composed a tight group. The group dominated the economy thanks to subsidised, government-directed, and implicitly government-guaranteed, bank loans.[183] In Malaysia, the Prime Minister Mahathir Mohamad substantially controlled the financial system.[184] In Taiwan, the former ruling party, KMT, once governed the country as well as the financial system for about 50 years. Even in Japan,

180 The manufacturing debt/equity ratios are estimated at 87 per cent in Taiwan, and at a massive 300 per cent in Korea. *See* Gustav Rains, 'Miracles that don't cease', 19 Feb. 1998.

181 *See* A. M. Rosenthal, 'Lessons of the Asian Collapse' (visited 23 Feb. 1998) <http://www,nytimes,com/library/financial/122397oped-rose-lessons.html>.

182 THE ECONOMIST, 'Asia's Economic Crisis, How far is down?' (visited 23 Feb. 1998) <http://www.stern.nyu.edu/~nroubini/asia/sf0983.html>.

183 *See* Hseng-Yuang Tsang, 'The Collapse of the Economic Model of Japan and Korea', *Global Views Monthly*, 5 Mar. 1998, at 100.

184 The Malaysian sort of capitalism has helped cement Mahathir's political control during 16 years as prime minister. *See* Seth Mydans, 'Malaysia Is Ready to Inflict Its Own Economic Medicine' (visited on 10 Jan. 1998) <http://www.nytimes.com/library/financial 121497 market-watch.htm>.

one of the largest economic powers in the world,[185] the successful economic performance in the past several decades was mainly based upon related enterprises[186] that always have very close relationships with the government. The government, industries and financial institutions constituted a firm economic development group. The government always arranged retired officials to some high-ranking positions of private enterprises not only for private interests, but also for the enterprise's conduct of governmental economic policies.[187] That is one of the reasons that these Asian countries hesitated to let the big companies and financial institutions enter into bankruptcy. These improper links also constituted Asian capitalism based on cronyism, familism or corruption.[188]

Under such a special political situation, the government's economic policies could be effectively conducted. However, the financial system, under long-term strict control, not only lost its normal market oriented function, but also reduced competition. The worst thing was that financial institutions bore the risk of the government's mistaken policies and the ruling level's corruption.

In South Korea, in order to encourage the development of the large cooperation conglomerates (*chaebol*), the government always guaranteed the large cooperation conglomerates loans. Furthermore, almost every conglomerate has been assigned to certain banks as the financial supporter.[189] This policy did raise some international conglomerates, such as Kia and Samsung. However, the full support from the government and financial institutions also promoted these conglomerates to borrow capital from the banking system negligently. In order to expand the business scope, some of the loans even flew into low profit businesses. When the profit could not support the conglomerates' operations, these conglomerates naturally sought more capital from the banking system. The

[185] Japan has the largest foreign reserve in the world. By the end of Apr. 1998, the amount was over US$205 billion. *See Japanese Economic News*, 11 May 1998.

[186] *See generally* Hseng-Yuang Tsang, 'The Collapse of the Economic Model of Japan and Korea', *Global Views Monthly*, 5 Mar. 1998, at 98. The 'Relative Enterprises' were formed by some independent companies. By the cross investments, these companies established long time cooperative relationships. The core of every enterprise is a financial institution. It is a custom that the government arranges retired officials to serve as high ranking officers in these companies.

[187] Another purpose of the arrangement was to assure that the private enterprises could match the government's production policies. *See* Shen-Yuang Tsung, 'The Collapse of the Japanese and Korean Economic Model', *Global Views Monthly Magazine*, Mar. 1998, at 100.

[188] Under this Asian Capitalism, the government, bank and business cliques that get together to decide who gets contracts and how they are split. Also who gets loans, at what rate, and with what collateral. *See* A. M. Rosenthal, 'Lessons of the Asian Collapse' (visited 23 Feb. 1998) <http://www.nytimes.com/library/financial/122397oped-rose-lessons.html>.

[189] *See* Schive Chi, 'Why Taiwan did not collapse?', COMMON WEALTH MAGAZINE, vol 199, Dec. 1997, at 213. Mr Schive Chi is the vice chairman of the Council for Economic Planning and Development and Professor of Economics, National Taiwan University.

debt/capital ratios of most South Korean conglomerates were even over 400 per cent.[190] The close link between the government, industries and banks seriously twisted the normal operation of the banks, and it also shaped a system of bribery, politically motivated loans and fiscal irresponsibility. The system has become a hotbed for insider frauds.[191]

In South East Asian countries, the financial system also has very close links with the bureaucrats.[192] Some of the links are to ensure the implementation of the government policy while others are to cement the ruler's political situation. In Indonesia, even privately owned commercial banks were approached to join a US$690 million loan to a 'National car' project involving former President Suharto's youngest son. And monetary authorities told state-owned Bank Negara Indonesia to assist Bank Yama, which was controlled by the former president's eldest daughter and widely believed to be illiquid.[193] It seems an Asian tradition that lending to friends-either of bank owners or of powerful politicians-means many loans will never be repaid. In some instances, the politically well-connected routinely move money from banks they control to industrial combines they own.[194] All these improper loans, as matter of fact, were frauds.

Taiwan has a similar pattern to other East Asian countries. The ruling party, KMT, exclusively controlled the country for 50 years. Under the ruling party's policy, some important fundamental productive industries have been monopolised by a few government-owned companies, such as the electric, water, and petroleum industries. Furthermore, the government substantially controlled all the domestic banks before 1991. The government's important economic and financial policies were conducted

190 The average debt/capital rate of Taiwan enterprises was 86 per cent, US 160 per cent, Japan over 200 per cent. The rate of some Korean conglomerates that went bankrupt in 1997 were even over 3,000 per cent. *See also* Shen-Yuang Tsung, 'The Collapse of the Japanese and Korean Economic Model', GLOBAL VIEWS MONTHLY MAGAZINE, Mar. 1998, at 102.

191 *See generally* Seth Faison, 'One Korean Certainty: No More Business as Usual', NY TIMES, 4 Janu. 1998. The scale of corruption and collusion resulting from the link of government, conglomerates and financial institutions was huge. After Hanbo Iron & Steel went bankrupt in early 1997, and investigation showed that the chairman had borrowed US$6 billion for the company, and used several hundred million dollars of that to bribe officials to keep authorising cheap bank loans, keeping some for himself. The executive of Korean Airlines had handed several million dollars to then-President Chun Doo-hwan to insure that the executive could keep his job after a Korean Airlines was shot down by a Soviet fighter in 1983.

192 Taiwan, Singapore, Indonesia, and Malaysia were somewhere in-between, but all borrowed in part from the Japanese development model. Bureaucrats in all those countries sometimes seemed to think that they were better at allocating capital and goods than markets were. Nicholas D. Kristof, 'Crisis Pushing Asian Capitalism Closer to US- Style Free Market' (visited 20 Jan. 1998) <http://www.nytimes.com/library/financial/011798asia-capitalism.htm>.

193 Darren Mcdermott and David Wessel, 'Financial-Sector weaknesses Are Roiling Asian Currencies', WALL STREET JOURNAL, 6 Oct. 1997.

194 Ibid.

through these government-owned companies and financial institutions. Therefore, these businesses and financial institutions unavoidably have very close relationships with the government. Just like the situation of Japan, many retired government officials were assigned to important positions in these companies. However, the links did not cause the same problems that other East Asian countries have experienced. The main reason was that the links were established not for any individual, family or specific businesses. Personal advantage created by the link was strictly prohibited before the 1990s.[195] Although direct or crony capitalism is not exclusively absent in Taiwan, it is much less pronounced.[196] Taiwan's experience indicated that the Asian variety capitalism did not necessarily result in financial turmoil.

However, Taiwan's financial environment has changed because of the altering of the political situation and financial policies. Since the ruling party gradually lost its exclusive political power and the country sped to liberalise and internalise its financial system in 1990, a series of bank frauds in fundamental financial institutions has occurred. Some of the fraud resulted from the improper links between the local political powers and the financial institutions, while others resulted from insufficient legal regulations. This criminal phenomenon, accompanied with the release of the establishment of new financial institutions,[197] gradually expanded from the regional financial institutions to the national banks. These frauds not only revealed that the country's legal system was not enough to control the new financial environment, but also exposed that political influence resulting from different reasons has become a potential threat to a country's liberalisation and internationalisation.

Moreover, as a part of the liberalisation, the country has scheduled to privatise the government-owned banks that occupied more than 50 per cent of the market.[198] This policy will substantially affect the country's

[195] In the 10 Credit Cooperative Unit fraud case, several high-ranking government officials who were suspiciously related to the fraud were withdrawn.

[196] *See* Hseng-Yuang Tsang, 'The Collapse of the Economic Model of Japan and Korea', GLOBAL VIEWS MONTHLY, 5 Mar. 1998, at 100.

[197] Besides the establishment of new domestic commercial banks in 1991, the Ministry of Finance stipulated the 'Guidelines Governing the Expansion of Operational Territories by Credit Cooperative Associations' and promulgated the 'Criteria and Guidelines Governing the Reorganisation of Credit Cooperative Associations as Commercial Banks' in 1995. Furthermore, the medium business banks were allowed to reorganise as commercial banks in 1996. Since then, the local financial institutions gradually expanded, both in geographic and business scope, to the national level. *See* eg BUREAU OF MONETARY AFFAIRS MINISTRY OF FINANCE REPUBLIC OF CHINA, 1995 ANNUAL REPORT BUREAU OF MONETARY AFFAIRS MINISTRY OF FINANCE 20 and 26, (1996); BUREAU OF MONETARY AFFAIRS MINISTRY OF FINANCE REPUBLIC OF CHINA, 1997 ANNUAL REPORT BUREAU OF MONETARY AFFAIRS MINISTRY OF FINANCE 43 (1998).

[198] Since the early 1990s, the Ministry of Finance pushed the policy of privatisation of government-owned financial institutions. Farmers Bank of China and Chiao Tung Bank are

banking market. As a result of the policy, the monopoly financial system will no longer exist, and a more liberal, international but competitive financial environment is going to appear. While Taiwan is shaping a new financial environment, the experience of other East Asian countries reminds Taiwan that cutting the improper links among the political powers, businesses and financial institutions is one of the crucial elements for the success of liberalisation and internationalisation.

C. *Reforming the Legal System*

Another lesson of the Asian financial crisis is that the success of a country's liberalisation and internationalisation of its financial system require a suitable environment. The suitable environment includes a health economic structure, a democratic political climate, and a proper legal system that may support the democratic capitalism.

Taiwan has developed a relatively better environment to liberalise and internationalise its financial system than its neighbouring countries. The country's significant small and medium business economic structure has been proved to be more flexible and compatible than Japan's and South Korea's large enterprises in the market.[199] The degree of the country's democracy is much better than that of most South east Asian countries, such as Indonesia, Thailand, and Malaysia. However, these prevailing factors cannot assure the success of Taiwan's liberalisation and internationalisation. The country has to further reform its legal system to prevent the defects that other Asian countries have experienced from occurring.

The Asian financial crisis exposed that the reform of the legal system for liberalisation and internationalisation should not be limited to the field of financial laws and regulations. Because the real advantages of liberalisation can only result from democratic capitalism,[200] the reform of the legal system must aim not only to liberalise the financial market but also to shape and maintain a fair and open financial system. A fair and open financial system means a system without control by government-business conspiracy and partnership.[201] The amendments of financial

among the first to considered. The privatisations were scheduled for two stages. By the end of 1996, the first stage for both of the banks was completed by raising capital from the public offering and listing of the shares on the Taiwan Stock Exchange. *See* BUREAU OF MONETARY AFFAIRS MINISTRY OF FINANCE REPUBLIC OF CHINA, 1996 ANNUAL REPORT BUREAU OF MONETARY AFFAIRS MINISTRY OF FINANCE 15 (1997).

199 *See* Gustav Ranis, 'Miracles that don't Cease', 19 Feb. 1998.

200 Democratic capitalism is the combination of a free political society and an open economic system, without control by government-business conspiracy or partnership. *See* A. M. Rosenthal 'Lesson of The Asian Collapse' (visited 23 Feb. 1998) <http://www.nytimes. com/library/financial/122397oped-rose-lessons.html>.

201 Ibid.

laws and regulations, without a thorough legal reform, could only result in an open but unfair market.

Most East Asian countries reformed their financial systems to match the trend of liberalisation earlier than did Taiwan.[202] However, most of the reforms focus on the financial laws and regulations. Other auxiliary legal approaches, such as criminal law and civil law, seldom have been updated or amended. As a result of the rapid liberalisation of the financial market, the existing loose financial system provided more criminal opportunities for frauds. From the viewpoint of Western world, the frauds, no matter committed by high-rank banking officials, middle and low rank clerks, or even co-committed by the government, banks and industries shall be strictly prohibited.

However, it is not an easy work for most Asian countries to thoroughly reform the legal system to combat bank fraud involving political powers, because the existing banking circumstance always mingles with corruption and political advantage sharing. The political consideration always prevails against the justice consideration in any legal reform. Nevertheless, the legal reform is the fundamental and the most important approach for a country to shape an environment that is suitable for financial liberalisation and internationalisation, if the country really desires to reach the goal of liberalisation.

Taiwan has gradually experienced the hurt of bank fraud which apparently increased since the country started to liberalise its financial system. In order to conduct the liberalisation and internationalisation policies, the country has started to reform its legal system. By the end of 1997, the country had amended or stipulated more than sixty laws and regulations. However, the legal reform mainly focused on the promotion of liberalisation and internationalisation before the occurrence of a series of bank frauds in 1993 and 1994. Even after these frauds, the legal reform concentrated on the reform of the administrative supervision and controls. Other legal approaches to combat financial institution fraud committed by insiders and created by the improper links among the political powers, financial institutions and business have not been addressed.

The Asian financial turmoil exposed that bank fraud, including the improper link among the government, businesses and financial institutions and insider bank fraud, would seriously weaken the financial sector. Financial liberalisation and internationalisation could not root in a weak

[202] *See also* Yu-may Kim, 'Evaluation of Taiwan's Financial Power', COMMON WEALTH MAGAZINE, Nov. 1995, at 68–9. According to a 1995 Asian Development Bank research about the Asian countries' financial system, Taiwan's financial system was tiered far behind Singapore and Hong Kong. Even in Malaysia and Thailand, the liberalisation of financial system had better performance than Taiwan did.

financial system. Therefore, a thorough legal reform is necessary for a country's liberalisation and internationalisation.

D. *Democratisation, Liberalisation, and Internationalisation—Stabilising the Political Situation*

Unlike most East Asian countries experiencing financial turmoil, the difficulties that Taiwan has experienced since mid-2000 have not resulted from internalisation or liberalisation, but from the shift of political regime, which is a part of democratisation.

When the world applauded the peaceful shifting of political regime in Taiwan in mid-2000 as the great democratic achievement in Asia, they seemed not able to foresee the reverse impact on the country's economy, which resulted from the chaos of the political regime shift. If the Asian style of capitalism, as discussed before, is one of the most unfavourable elements for Asian countries' financial liberalisation and internationalisation, and a real liberal and internationalised financial system shall be based upon a democratic political environment,[203] democratisation is undoubtedly a must for most Asian countries. However, Taiwan's experience post the Asian financial turmoil at the end of the twentieth century revealed the risk of liberalising, internationalising, and democratising concurrently.

Taiwan's experience exhibits that the procedure of democratisation is as important as that of the internationalisation and liberalisation. How to maintain the stable of political situation when a country proceeds with democratisation becomes very crucial for a country's financial liberalisation and internationalisation.

V. PROVISIONAL COMMENTS

The Asian financial crisis was potentially of value in at least one respect for the world. The affected countries, less-affected and non-affected countries have all been able to learn something from the crisis. Taiwan's performance in the crises provides a good example for these countries review their economic and financial policies. The affected countries' experience also exposed the importance of the important link between the political and financial environment in a country's liberalisation and internationalisation policies.

Taiwan's experience indicated that strict financial control was not necessarily a disadvantage and that liberalisation and internationalisation

203 *See* Gustav Ranis, 'Miracles that don't Cease', 19 Feb. 1998.

were not always a panacea for a country's economic development. For a country starting to open its financial market, the main consideration is whether the country's policy, both economic and financial, can adequately reflect the country's need. The proper sequence of liberalisation and internationalisation may decide the final consequence of the liberalisation and internationalisation.

These affected countries' experience disclosed that liberalisation and internationalisation of financial markets was not easy to achieve. If a country can not properly conduct a policy of liberalisation and internationalisation, the negative impact of liberalisation and internationalisation may appear before its benefits. Moreover, internationalisation and liberalisation were not only transplanting foreign countries' systems and regulations or to opeing its domestic markets to foreign countries. One of the important factors that affected the result of liberalisation and internationalisation was whether the country was ready to create an environment that was suitable for the liberalisation and internationalisation. This environment must include not only some modern financial transaction functions, but also some other effective legal mechanisms that may ensure that the financial activities are undertaken under normal market functions. Furthermore, the creation of a liberalised and internationalised circumstance is based on democratic capitalism. Without the establishment of a real democratic capitalism, the goal of liberalisation and internationalisation cannot be reached.

For most Asian countries, the main challenge in shaping a democratic capitalist environment is to break the traditional political culture of close and direct intervention in the financial system and financial activities. It is not the purpose of this chapter to discuss the possible conflict between political considerations and legal regulations. It is also not the purpose to predict if the legal reforms adopted can be successful in these countries. However, basic legal reform is necessary if these countries really wish to achieve the benefits of liberalisation and internationalisation.

The valuable experience provided by Taiwan in the Asian financial crises for other countries is the process of transferring a closed and monopolised financial system into an open and internationalised one. However, Taiwan's safety and stability in the financial crisis does not mean that the country has already established a perfect environment for the future financial liberalisation and internationalisation. Certain phenomena existing in most Asian countries, such as the improper and illegal intervention of bureaucracy and political power in the financial system, has also gradually appeared in Taiwan. The pure liberalisation and internationalisation of the financial system without the support of other legal controls have left some gaps for modern financial frauds. The occurrence of a series of financial frauds since the country gradually relaxed its control of the financial system in the late 1980s has demonstrated that the country's legal system, including the criminal and civil legal framework, is not adequate enough to support the country's financial liberalisation and internationalisation. A thorough legal reform is necessary for the country to continue to develop in a safe and stable manner.

Moreover, Taiwan's experience post the Asian financial crisis provides us with another aspect to consider the dilemma among liberalisation, internationalisation, and democratisation for Asian countries. A stable political environment is crucial for a country's financial liberalisation and internationalisation. However, how to maintain a stable political environment seems a very difficult task for Asian countries when they democratise their political environment.[204]

204 *Author Postscript:* Since the Democratic Progress Party won the President Election in March 2000, Taiwan has experienced a series of political confrontations. The cabinet has changed once in three months after President Chen Shui-bian took over the regime. A series of political and personal issues, such as the abolishment of the nuclear power plant programme, Taiwanese independence and President Chen's 'affaire de coeur', resulted in the public losing confidence in the government and the country's future development. The impact has appeared in the stock market as well as the economic development. The government tried to use the traditional ways, such as public funds, to save the stock market and stimulate the economy. However, all measures had not taken effect by the end of Mar. 2001. The worse situation is that the government can not yet display its ability to govern the country. Whether the current political chaos will destroy the country's economic achievement in the past three decades requires further observation. However, the continuous economic recession will undoubtedly result in the worsening of the financial market. That the Japanese model of economic and financial recession will occur in Taiwan might be the greatest concern for the government in its remaining term.

Chapter 19

Korea's Recent Financial Reform: Law-Based Banking Regulations in the Current Financial Crisis

*Byung-Tae Kim**

I. INTRODUCTION

Korea's economy was impacted severely and adversely by the recent East Asian financial crisis, which began in early 1997 in Thailand.[1] This crisis resulted in emergency financial assistance from the International Monetary Fund (IMF), the World Bank and the Asian Development Bank (ADB) in late 1997. To recover from the crisis, Korea is currently implementing legal and economic-based financial reforms in cooperation with international financial institutions (IFIs). While the reforms have resulted in restructuring of almost every sector of the Korean economy, the banking sector, which was the principal actor among those that contributed to the recent financial crisis, has been the main target in these reforms.

The recent financial reforms in Korea include economic, social and legal endeavours to recover from the financial crisis and to resolve its underlying problems. For the purposes of this chapter, however, the term 'recent financial reform(s)' is limited to include (1) Korea's law-based reforms (ie legislation of new laws and amendments) passed in December 1997 after the IMF's bail-out package and (2) a series of structural reforms in Korea's financial sector thereafter (ie government's bank restructuring).

As a result of the law-based financial reforms and active government-steered bank restructuring, Korean banks are now facing new developmental and competitive pressures. Under these financial reforms and the

* The author would like to thank Professor Joseph J. Norton for his helpful comments and suggestions, and Fallyme E Guerrero and Ellis R Reed for their valuable assistance.

[1] The East Asian economic crisis of 1997 became plainly visible with the spring and summer 1997 speculative attacks against the baht, the official currency of Thailand. For various aspects of Thailand's recent financial crisis, *see* T. Traisorat, 'A "Silver Lining" in the Crisis Cloud?: The Thai Financial and Economic Crisis of 1997–1998: An Opportunity to Redress the Fundamentals', *Yearbook of International Financial and Economic Law*, 1997.

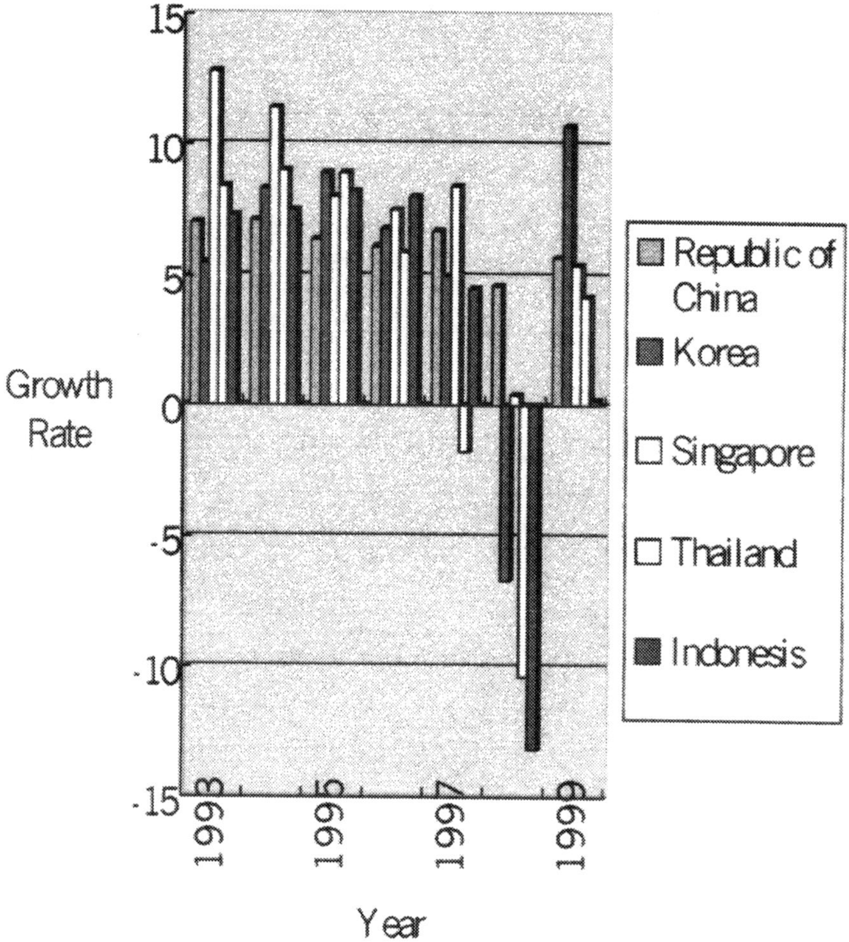

Figure 1: Real Economic Growth Rates of Selected Countries

conditions of the IMF programme,[2] the Korean government has been restructuring the financial and related sectors overall including banking, securities, insurance and even the corporate sector. This financial sector

[2] According to the 'Letter of Intent of the Government of Korea', the Korean government agreed to overhaul the financial sector and take 'belt tightening' measures in exchange for the IMF bail out loan. The government also agreed to allow the establishment of subsidiaries of foreign banks and security companies, and to extend the upper limit for foreigners acquiring per item shares. *See generally* Government of Korea, 'Letter of Intent of the Government of Korea 3' (3 Dec. 1997) (visited on Jan. 1998) <http://www.imf.org/ external/np/loi/ 120397.htm>.

restructuring has focused on compelling unsound financial institutions to exit the market, resolving the 'overhang' of bad loans, strengthening institutions' capital bases and ensuring the transparency of management.[3] The banking sector reforms, which play a pivotal role in supporting newly restructured financial institutions, are directed to make the banking system more open, competitive and transparent.

In furtherance of the reform principles and in fulfilling its commitment to the IMF programmes, Korea is incorporating internationally accepted standards such as the Basel Committee's 'Core Principles for Effective Banking Supervision' to address some of the current banking sector problems. These standards have now been extended to other financial and foreign bank regulations. For example, the former restrictions which existed on foreign investment and on foreign banks have been largely dismantled under the recent restructuring process. Adoption of these international standards creates a new environment for banks, one of increased transparency and prudential bank supervision.

Nevertheless, these financial reforms are imperfect solutions for Korea's financial problems. Korea is still engulfed with many fundamental problems in its financial sectors, particularly the banking sector, that must be resolved.

This chapter is concerned mainly with law-based financial reforms effected through the banking sector. The question is this: how should the Korean banking sector be regulated with the goal of providing an effective legal base and a well-organised infrastructure? To answer this question, this chapter will address, in turn, (1) the changes in regulations in the Korean banking sector during the current financial crisis, (2) efforts taken by the Korean government to adopt and implement new banking sector reform measures and (3) the determination of the best, or at least an alternative, financial reform package for successfully addressing Korea's financial problems without contravening the structural adjustment arrangement with the IMF.

Section II provides a brief overview of the Korean financial crisis, general problems of financial and banking sectors, and law-based reforms implemented after the IMF's intervention in Korea's financial policies. With this background, Section III discusses the new rules and regulations in the banking sector such as the new general banking system of Korea, the central banking system and its reshaping, the new bank supervision system, the bank deposit insurance scheme, and the regulation of foreign banks. As the recent banking sector problems are closely related to the corporate sector, any corporate implications from bank problems are separately discussed in

[3] The Banking Department of the Bank of Korea, *Bank Restructuring in Korea* (98–5), Dec. 1998, at 2.

Section IV under the '*Chaebol*' regulations. Finally, this chapter concludes with a few lessons from the current financial crisis and reforms and some recommendations for future reforms.

II. OVERVIEW OF THE KOREAN FINANCIAL CRISIS AND REFORMS

The recent financial crisis in Korea has resulted in significant reforms to the financial and banking sectors. To examine the cause of this crisis and to discuss the new banking regulations, the section addresses the following questions: (1) Why did the financial crisis occur in Korea? and (2) What has been the Korean government's response to the recent crisis, particularly on law-based reforms and bank restructuring?

A. *Recent Financial Crisis: The 'Why'*

In early 1997, after several decades of outstanding economic performance, Korea began to experience difficulty in its financial sector. The 'contagion' effects of the Thai financial crisis were affecting the financial and currency markets in East Asian countries such as Hong Kong, Indonesia and Korea, and magnifying fundamental political, financial and economic problems. By November 1997, Korea's financial and economic sectors had weakened to a point that Korea was forced to seek emergency assistance from the IMF,[4] just as Thailand and Indonesia had done earlier in 1997.[5] On 4 December

[4] The IMF was created to promote international monetary cooperation, to facilitate the expansion and balanced growth of international trade, to promote exchange stability, to assist in the establishment of a multilateral system of payments, to make its general resources temporarily available to its members experiencing balance of payments difficulties under adequate safeguards, and to shorten the duration and lessen the degree of disequilibrium in the international balances of payments of members. *See* Article I (Purposes) of the Articles of Agreement of the International Monetary Fund. The IMF came into official existence on 27 Dec. 1945, when twenty-nine countries signed its Articles of Agreement (its Charter); it was established at a conference held in Bretton Woods, New Hampshire, USA, from 1–22 July 1944. The IMF commenced financial operations on 1 Mar. 1947 and the IMF's membership now numbers 182 countries including Korea (David D. Driscoll, *What is the International Monetary Fund?*, External Relations Department, Publication Services International Monetary Fund, Washington, D.C. 20431 USA, Sept. 1998).

[5] On 4 Dec. 1997, the IMF Executive Board approved a US$21 billion stand-by credit for Korea in support of that country's economic adjustment programme [International Monetary Fund, *IMF Board Approves Record $21 Billion Stand-By To Support Korea's Adjustment Program*, 26/23 IMF Survey 385, 388 (15 Dec. 1997)]. Before the IMF's support to Korea, the IMF also approved, on 20 Aug. 1997, a US$3.9 billion package for Thailand supplemented by a US$12.7 billion support package coordinated with other interested countries and multilateral institutions [International Monetary Fund, *Thailand: Stand-By*, 26/17 IMF Survey 283 (17 Sept. 1997)]. Subsequently, the IMF approved a US$10.14 billion stand-by credit for Indonesia as a major element in international assistance totaling some US$23 billion on 5 Nov.

1997, after protracted negotiations, the IMF reached an agreement[6] with the Korean government to provide a total of US$55 billion (SDR 15.5 billion)[7] in emergency funds, including loans from other countries.[8] In exchange, Korea agreed to overhaul its financial sector, open its markets to foreign banking and investment institutions, and allow for increased foreign direct investments. The agreement proved to be the decisive catalyst for law-based financial reforms.

Prior to Korea asking the IMF for assistance, Korea's economic base had looked reasonably healthy. Economic forecasts had not been that unfavourable even in late 1996. Although Korea's financial problems did not seem serious enough to require IMF-intervention even during the first part of 1997, several distressing economic symptoms or warning lights already indicated a forthcoming financial crisis.

Korea was the eleventh largest economy in the world and had recently joined the major industrialised nations of the Organisation for Economic Cooperation and Development (OECD). GDP growth was about six per cent throughout the 1990s.[9] Korea was generally regarded as one of the world's 'economic miracles' over the past thirty years. Since Korea had kept

1997 [International Monetary Fund, *Indonesian Measures Welcomed As Important Step In Stabilising Southeast Asian Financial Markets*, 26/21 IMF Survey 353 (17 Nov. 1997)].

[6] Korea asked financial assistance from the IMF on 21 Nov. 1997 to overcome the country's difficulties in the financial and currency markets (*See* the Ministry of Finance and Economy Press Release, *IMF Program for Korea* (Dec. 1997). For a request of financial assistance, the 'Letter of Intent of the government of Korea' was drafted in a hurry with the help of IMF officers on 3 Dec. 1997. With this request letter, Korea has had to be under the IMF programme. (*See* Government of Korea, *Letter of Intent of the Government of Korea.*)

[7] This amount of US$55 billion consists of (i) an International Monetary Fund (IMF) loan decided on 4 Dec. 1997 to provide a total US$21 billion stand-by arrangement package (IMF Press Release No 97/55, 4 Dec. 1997), (ii) a World Bank ('IBRD') loan agreed on 21 Dec. 1997 for a total US$10 billion (The World Bank Group, News Release No 98/1553EAP; Ministry of Finance and Economy Press Release, 24 Dec. 1997), (iii) an Asian Development Bank ('ADB') loan decided on 19 Dec. 1997 for the total US$4 billion (Ministry of Finance and Economy Press Release, 20 Dec. 1997), and (iv) other loans ('Second Line Defense Loan') released on 4 Dec. 1997 by G-7 and other countries for US$20 billion (IMF Press Release No 97/55, 4 Dec. 1997; The IMF News Brief No 97/32, 24 Dec. 1997; Ministry of Finance and Economy Press Release, 24 Dec. 1997). In addition, as Korea's financial situation adversely affected overseas creditors' confidence, foreign banks started declining requests to 'roll over' maturing debts. As the month progressed, an understanding was reached among the Governments of countries with major creditor banks to encourage them to rollover Korean debts. As a result, 123 commercial banks of thirty-one countries agreed on13 Mar. 1998 to roll over the total of US$21.375 billion, which will be converted to medium or long-term debts with maturity terms of longer than one year (United Press International (UPI), 13 Mar. 1998).

[8] IMF Press Release No 97/55, 4 Dec. 1997; *The Korea Times*, 4 Dec. 1997; *Chosun Ilbo* (daily newspaper), 4 Dec. 1997.

[9] Kyung Shik Lee, 'Current Economic and Financial Situation' in Korea (July 1996) (Presentation for the first EMEAP Governors Meeting), at 2; Sang-Loh Kim and Won-Geun Kang, 'The Recent Trends and Forecast of Korean Economy', *KDB Monthly Bulletin* 1–2 (Feb. 1998).

its fundamental macroeconomic indicators generally in order, it was expected that the financial sector's problems would soon be resolved.

However, the reality was that by the end of 1996, the Korean economy had entered a period of economic deterioration. As of the summer of 1997, Korea has been struggling with a collapsing currency, diminishing foreign exchange reserves,[10] and with a plunging stock market.[11]

In addition, since the latter half of 1996 Korea had been experiencing unprecedented bankruptcies of highly leveraged corporate conglomerates (called '*Chaebol*' in Korean). Because these corporate bankruptcies have been related to banks' defaulted loans or policy loans and to weak financial supervision, the Korean government started to prepare new financial reform bills in early 1997 in order to reduce the impact of these financial difficulties, to stabilise and increase confidence in financial institutions and to restore market confidence. Unfortunately, none of the reform bills passed in the National Assembly at their first hearing in November 1997. The failure to institute these reform measures proved to be a perpetuating factor in the on-going financial crisis.

Thereafter, an unprecedented number of Korean banks, struggling in the face of accumulating nonperforming and bad corporate loans,[12] and the country's on-going poor financial situation, found themselves bankrupt.[13]

[10] In the case of usable foreign exchange reserves of Korea, these became reduced since the end of 1996 and their amount were getting lower during the financial crisis period of 1997. It continued to lower from US$29.4 billion in 1996 to US$25.3 billion in Jan., US$22.4 billion in Sept., and US$22.3 billion in Oct. 1997. The usable foreign exchange reserves finally lowered to US$7.3 billion in Nov. and US$8.9 billion in Dec. 1997. *See* Bank of Korea Press Release, *Official Foreign Reserves*, 8 May 1998, at 2.) In fact, it appears that this lack of foreign reserves was the immediate cause for Korea to request IMF assistance.

[11] Stock prices and the stock market also continued to fall from early 1997 due to the lack of domestic and overseas confidence in the Korean market and in Korean companies. Compared with the stock prices in 1996, stock prices in 1997 fell to less than half of their original value. The Korean Stock Market Index plummeted to 400 Korean Won by the end of 1997 from their 900 Korean Won value in early 1996. The uncertainty in the stock market has continued as of May 1998 with shares closing down at less than 400 Korean Won. (*See* Bank of Korea, *1997 Financial Crisis and its Process*, Jan. 1999.)

[12] Non-performing credit includes bad credit (which includes the credits classified as 'Doubtful' or 'Estimated Loss') and the credits classified as 'Substandard'. Substandard credit is the credit expected to be collected by selling collateral among total credit extended to customers who have been in arrears for no less than six months or to the issuer of dishonoured bills and cheques, or to the company which is under court receivership. Doubtful credit is the portion of credit in excess of the amount expected to be collected among total credit to customers classified as substandard that is expected to be a loss, but has not yet been realised as such. Estimated loss is the portion of credit in excess of the amount expected to be collected among total credit to customers classified as substandard that must be accounted as a loss, because collection is not possible in a foreseeable period. *See Bank of Korea News Brief*, 'Problem Credits of Korean commercial banks', 26 Feb. 1998.

[13] According to a report of the Bank of Korea, 'nonperforming loans' had sharply increased high during 1997. At the end of December 1997, the nonperforming loans of twenty-six Korean commercial banks including nationwide banks and regional banks, reached 22.6 trillion Korean won (approximately US$22.6 billion), and the non-performing credit ratio

For the first time in Korean banking history, disciplinary measures against troubled banks were taken. For example, the operations of nine troubled merchant banks were suspended on 2 December 1997 prior to the completion of the IMF's mission on 4 December 1997.[14]

Even after the IMF's bailout package decision was announced and implemented, as of 4 December 1997, several banks continued to face financial problems due to nonperforming loans to certain companies which later went bankrupt. In particular, 'Korea First Bank' and 'Seoul Bank', two of the largest banks in Korea, had been deteriorating in soundness since 1997 due to bad loans given to certain '*chaebols*' such as Hanbo and Kia.[15] Those two banks are now experiencing bank restructuring through the sale of their shares to foreign financial institutions by the government to protect domestic depositors and the Korean economy.[16]

The reason for the explosion of the financial crisis in Korea cannot be simply expressed. As discussed above, multiple factors combined under Korea's specific banking circumstances to cause the financial crisis. That is, one financial problem probably contributed to other problems, creating a domino effect. One can state, however, that on the whole, Korea's recent financial crisis has resulted from consecutive corporate failures and bankruptcies, financial sector difficulties caused by nonperforming loans, the

compared to total credits was 6.0 per cent. (Ibid.) This increase of the nonperforming credit ratio to 6.0 per cent, as of the end of Dec. 1997 from 3.9 per cent as of the end of 1996, was caused mainly by bankruptcies of large companies such as Hanbo, Kia, Halla, and Sammi, all of which had held large outstanding credits. These non-performing loans for commercial banks continued to increase to 28 trillion Korean Won as of May 1998, and the ratio of nonperforming loan over total loans increased to 7.7 per cent from 6.0 per cent. *See* 'Nonperforming Loan by Banks', *Chosun Ilbo* (daily newspaper), 13 May 1998. In the case of 'bad loans', (ie as of the end of Dec. 1997), the bad credits of twenty-six Korean commercial banks reached 10.1 trillion Korean won, and the bad credit ratio compared to total credit was 2.7 per cent. The bad credit ratio compared to total credit had steadily decreased to 0.8 per cent at the end of 1996 from 2.0 per cent at the end of 1990. However, the ratio has increased again during 1997 because of the bankruptcies of large companies. Bad loans with no prospect of recovery continued to increase to 12.4 trillion Korean Won as of May 1998 from 10.1 trillion Won of the end of 1997. *See* ibid.

14 'Closing Troubled Banks', *The Korea Times*, 3 Dec. 1997.

15 The 'Korea First Bank' and the 'Seoul Bank' tried to carry out their own self-rescue plans after the implementation of 'Management Improvement Advice' from the Korean Office of Bank Supervision in 5 Sept. 1997. (*See* the Bank of Korea Press Release, *Regulatory Guidelines for Provisioning in Fiscal Year of 1997 and Supervisory Measures to Problem Banks*, 22 Dec. 1997.) However, their sound management continued to deteriorate due to the increase of nonperforming loans and the sharp decline of the domestic stock market. In this case, the government and the central bank did not bail them out, but implemented a 'Management Improvement Order' to them following the decision of the Monetary Board according to the General Banking Act. Under the 'Management Improvement Order', these two banks were required to reduce their number of employees and to freeze their investments and loans. All this was indirectly related to the Korea's current financial troubles.

16 'Privatisation of Korea First Bank and Seoul Bank', *Chosun Ilbo* (daily newspaper), 31 Mar. 1998.

devaluation of the Korean won, the decline of stock prices, and the contagion effect from other Asian countries' financial crises. Subsequently, the ensuing financial situation based on these causes reduced market confidence. Other factors, including successive rating downgrades of Korean financial institutions by international credit rating agencies, government inaction, and reduced foreign reserves, all contributed to worsening an already deteriorating Korean financial condition.

Given these poor economic and financial sector conditions, Korea's 'new government'[17] has endeavoured to implement a series of structural reforms in its financial sector for the purpose of solving the problems and restoring market confidence. Some of these reform efforts were initiated prior to the current financial crisis, and others commenced after structural adjustment arrangement under the IMF Agreement since late 1997. The law-based financial reforms in Korea, which will be discussed in detail below, were structured according to the guidelines of the IMF after the agreement with the IMF on 4 December 1997.

B. *Recent Financial Reforms*

For the purpose of this chapter, the Korean financial reforms that were implemented through the banking sector during the crisis are discussed in terms of law-based reforms and bank restructuring.

1. Law-Based Reforms

a. Road to current reforms

For the last forty-five years, Korea's financial policy has been one of government control for the efficient accumulation of capital reserves. This policy proved successful in the early stages of the country's economic development, yet, during the 1990s, this policy of governmental control proved to be uncompetitive. It was also incompatible with guidelines laid out by the World Trade Organisation ('WTO') and the OECD because Korea's financial policy was against the deregulation principle of both organisations. Government control also led to mismanagement, which became even more apparent when the financial crisis set in.

A look back on the history of the financial sector reforms in Korea shows

[17] There is an ironic story that the former government created the financial crisis and the new government has been solving such crisis problems. When Korea was asking financial assistance from the IMF and other international institutions, Korea had a presidential election in 18 Dec. 1997, and Mr Kim Dae Jung was elected as the new President of Korea. Accordingly, the new government of President Kim Dae Jung has taken over the solution of the current financial crisis from the previous government that caused the crisis.

that the government's financial reforms since the early 1990s have focused primarily on financial deregulation and financial market liberalisation.[18] Financial reform measures to deregulate the market have included free floating of interest rates, expansion of powers of financial institutions and of their sources of funds, managerial autonomy of financial institutions, realignment of business scope, and lowering barriers of entry into the financial market for domestic and international institutions. The measures to liberalise the market have included allowing foreign investment into the domestic financial sector, opening the bond market, and permitting foreign financial institutions' entry into the domestic market.

Under these financial reform measures, Korea has been attempting prudently to strengthen its financial regulations, particularly since the 1990s. In an attempt to create stable financial institutions and a more competitive banking system, the Korean government instituted several financial reforms in the early 1990s. The two most important financial policies were the 'Five-Year Financial Reform Plan of 1993' and the 'Financial Market Open Schedule Under the Guidelines of the OECD of 1996'. These financial sector related reforms were to be the basis for further internationalisation and deregulation in the financial sectors.

While Korea was implementing these reforms, it was unexpectedly confronted with financial turmoil in 1996 and 1997. In 1997 as the Korean economy was vacillating and banks were feeling the effects of several recent large corporate bankruptcies, the Ministry of Finance and Economy ('MOFE') prepared and announced proposals for another financial reform, absorbing the previous ones and providing new regulations and policies. In June 1997, the MOFE submitted proposals for a more sound and safer banking system and a more effective bank supervisory structure to the National Assembly for legislation.[19] The proposals were summarised as the unified supervisory function on financial organisations including banks, insurance and securities, and the central bank autonomy over monetary policy.

In the general meeting of the National Assembly held on 17 November 1997,[20] the financial reform bill that included the merging of the three supervisory offices of banks, securities and insurance was postponed until the next session for political reasons.[21] The main political reasons were that

[18] Kang Nam Lee, 'Financial Reform in Korea: Its Impact on the Financial Sector and the Policy Implications' 2–3 (Nov. 1996) (manuscript on file with 12th Pacific Basin Central Bank Conference).

[19] *See Financial Reform Bills*, Ministry of Finance and Economy Working Paper (July 1997).

[20] Unfortunately, even at that time, the National Assembly did not take Korea's financial condition seriously. About 2 weeks later, however, Korea asked and agreed financial assistance from the IMF on 4 Dec. 1997.

[21] 'Postponing Financial Reforms', *Joongang Ilbo* (daily newspaper), 14 and 18 Nov. 1997.

national elections for a new president and government were only a month away and that partisan politics would likely polarise opinions on the bill because of their own self-interests. As a result, the National Assembly simply could not vote on the financial reform bill at that time. Thus, the Assembly left it to the new government to deal with such issues. Meanwhile, resistance to reforms was already surfacing. Officials of the Bank of Korea and the labour union of the central bank had both voiced opposition to the government proposal that would limit the Bank of Korea's supervisory power over banks through its single watchdog arm, the 'Bank Supervisory Committee'.[22] Even some financial experts protested the government's reform package.[23] Though most recognised that something had to be done, few could agree on a way to address the problems.

As the reform package lay dormant in the politicians' hands, the financial and economic situation was worsening. Only after the IMF's approval of the bail-out package to Korea in 4 December 1997[24] did the government take bold and decisive action to address the problem of troubled financial institutions and to open the financial sector to foreign investment. The financial reform bill was redrafted and revised. Some features reflected financial sector reform efforts staged by the government throughout the year, and others were dictated by the IMF as a precondition to the emergency assistance package fund. In addition to the current law-based financial reforms and in accordance with the IMF guidelines, prompt action was also taken to enact the necessary legislation to establish a strong and independent supervisory agency, to strengthen and consolidate prudential supervision, and to increase transparency.[25]

After many complications, the law-based financial reforms and other governmental actions enabling legislation were finally approved at an extraordinary meeting of the National Assembly on 29 December 1997. The Assembly dismantled the extensive powers of the MOFE and stripped it of its financial regulatory and supervisory functions. Those reforms marked the beginning of a new banking system and bank structure, quite different from anything Korea ever had before.

b. Recent law-based reforms

The new banking and financial sector reforms of Korea that were enacted on 29 December 1997 are similar, in some parts, to past financial reforms. Like the 'Five-Year Financial Reform Plan of 1993' and 'Financial Market Open Schedule under the Guidelines of the OECD of 1996', they focus on

[22] Bank of Korea Press Release, *Financial Reform by the Government* (July 1997).
[23] Bank of Korea Press Release, *Our opinion for the Financial Reform* (Aug. 1997).
[24] *See* above n 4.
[25] Government of Korea, *Letter of Intent of the Government of Korea* 5 (3 Dec. 1997).

financial deregulation and financial market liberalisation. However, new financial policies and reforms were put in place to effect better financial and corporate conditions in accordance with the IMF guidelines. In turn, based on the arrangements made with the IMF in December 1997, the government's overall economic recovery program, including law-based financial reform measures, focused on: (1) creating a strong macroeconomic framework designed to continue the orderly adjustment in the external current account and to contain inflationary pressures, thus involving a tighter monetary stance and further significant fiscal adjustments; (2) developing a comprehensive strategy to restructure and to recapitalise the financial sector and to make the financial sector more transparent, more market-oriented, better supervised and free from political interferences; (3) measures to improve corporate governance; (4) accelerating liberalisation of capital account transactions; (5) promoting further trade liberalisation; and (6) improving in the transparency and timely reporting of economic data.[26]

This fundamental restructuring and adjustment required that many legislative acts and regulations be amended, legislated and executed to provide an effective legal basis and a well-organised infrastructure for the financial sector. Among them, the 'Bank of Korea Act' and the 'General Banking Act' are the most important acts for the regulation and operation of the central bank, the general commercial banks and the foreign banks in Korea. Amendments of these acts or other new legislation were mainly concerned with overcoming the financial crisis and problems, making Korea's banking and financial institutions safe, sound and competitive, and adopting internationally accepted standards of bank supervision. The key changes and new policies and regulations on law-based financial reforms became effective on 1 April 1998.

Each amendment will be discussed in detail below. The 'Bank of Korea Act' was amended to give more independence to the Bank of Korea ('BOK'), the central bank of Korea, and the newly established bank supervisory system. The Bank of Korea Act also changed the organisation of the Monetary Board, the decision-making committee of the BOK. The amendment created a new committee replacing the existing Monetary Board of the BOK, the 'Monetary Policy Committee' or '*Keumyung Tongwha Wiyonhoi*' in Korean, gave it strengthened rights to create and execute monetary and credit policies, and made it independent from the government.[27] To facilitate the independence of the central bank, the Minister of Finance and Economy is now excluded from chairmanship or membership on the Monetary Policy Committee of the BOK, and the bank supervisory function of the BOK has been transferred to a newly established body, the 'Financial

[26] Ibid. at 3.
[27] Ministry of Finance and Economy, above n 14.

Supervisory Committee', leaving only limited supervisory functions to the BOK. Bank examinations and approval powers for the change of articles of incorporation of the BOK by the Minister of Finance and Economy are also excluded under this amendment of the Bank of Korea Act.[28]

The 'General Banking Act' was amended to provide bank restructuring and better bank management and operation of general commercial banks including foreign banks. This amendment strengthens the responsible bank management system through re-regulation of bank ownership. It also annuls the approval system in regard to the opening, closing and moving of a bank branch.[29] This act directly regulates the branch and representative office of foreign banks

In addition to these two main acts, the 'Act Concerning Establishment of Financial Supervisory Organisations' significantly changed the supervisory system for banks and financial institutions. This law deprived the Bank of Korea of its supervisory function over general and foreign banks, and created a new committee, the 'Finance Supervisory Committee' or '*Keumyung Kamdog Wiyonhoi*' in Korean as the sole watchdog.[30] Under this legislation, the supervisory functions over financial organisations, such as banks, securities companies, and insurance companies, have been centralised and given to the 'Finance Supervisory Committee' under the auspice of the Prime Minister.[31] As will be discussed in detail later, this single watchdog was necessary for independent and effective financial supervision although it consolidated supervisory entities and raised scepticism over how much the unified board will comprehend its duties.

Many changes occurred and new policies were implemented for general financial sectors other than for the banking sector discussed above.[32] Although these changes and regulations are not the topics in this chapter,

[28] *See* Research Department of the Bank of Korea, *Amendments and New Legislation of Acts concerning Financial Matters*, Research Paper 98–2 (Jan. 1998)

[29] *See* ibid. [30] Ibid. [31] Ibid.

[32] For the law-based reforms of other financial sectors, *see* Research Department of the Bank of Korea, *Amendments and New Legislation of Acts concerning Financial Matters*, Research Paper 98–2, (Jan. 1998). The important law-based reforms for them are as follows: The 'Bank Deposit Insurance Act' was amended to provide for the unification of the various channeled deposit insurance organisations into the Korea Deposit Insurance Company. It strengthens now the clearing power of the Deposit Insurance Corporation over troubled financial institutions. The Deposit Insurance Corporation may also request, under the Act, the Financial Supervisory Committee and the Financial Supervisory Board to conduct on-site examinations or joint examinations with it on its insured financial institutions. The amendment of the 'Financial Industry Restructuring Act' was carried out to reinforce the power of the Supervisory Board to enable it to take prompt corrective action and to execute management redress order to financial institutions. A trust business in Korea is regulated by 'Trust Business Act'. This 'Trust Business Act' was also amended to increase the capital requirements and the penalty provisions against all officers and employees, and to reshuffle the overall provisions according to the reorganisation of the new bank supervisory system. As for the amendment of the 'Act concerning Merchant Banking Company', it provides the credit ceiling for a major stockholder and inter-linked business group, and the management regulation of

some of the important and related issues to the banking sector will be referred to and reviewed later in various sections that are relevant to banking issues.

2. Bank Restructuring

a. Restructuring principles

Bank restructuring is another way to help troubled banks and the weakened banking sector. During the financial crisis, Korea's bank restructuring was implemented to dissolve unsound financial institutions as promptly as possible and in accordance with internationally accepted standards, to promote efficiency in viable banks and to ease the credit crunch. The banking sector restructuring, to a large extent, was based on the IMF programme set forth pursuant to the IMF's standby agreement in December of 1997, subsequent developments between Korea and the IMF, and Korea's pronouncements toward international standards.

The wisdom of bank restructuring has been debated. Some critics viewed the process as a heavy handed and premature act of government intervention that would not give enough time for self-restoration of each troubled bank or consideration to free market principles. In the end, however, Korea's bank restructuring has been regarded as an inevitable action. Each troubled bank was already deeply weakened and objectively could not

securities, real estate, etc., while it also reshuffles the overall provisions according to the reorganisation of the bank supervisory system. The amendment of the 'Mutual Savings and Fund Act', while reshuffling the overall provisions according to the reorganisation of the bank supervisory system, provides the application of the deposit insurance corporation to these institutions and increases the credit ceilings on single borrowers. The securities and insurance supervisory system have been also greatly changed according to the newly established Financial Supervisory Board in order to unify the Bank Supervisory Board, the Securities Supervisory Board and the Insurance Supervisory Board. The amendment of the 'Securities and Exchange Act', while reshuffling the overall provisions according to the reorganisation of a bank supervisory system, abolishes the debt ratio provision of the securities company and the preliminary authorisation of overseas branches of the Securities company doing business in the local market. The amendment of the 'Futures and Exchange Act', while also reshuffling the overall provisions according to the reorganisation of the bank supervisory system, abolishes the preliminary authorisation system for the overseas operation by the futures business companies. The amendment of the 'Insurance Business Act' reshuffles the overall provisions according to the reorganisation of the bank supervisory system and provides the new insurance program for insurance companies by the deposit insurance corporation. The amendment of the 'Act Concerning the External Audit of Corporations' was carried out to regulate the '*Chaebol*' (a large inter-linked business group in Korea) which has proved to be the direct cause of the current financial crisis of Korea. This new act also reshuffles the overall provisions according to the reorganisation of a bank supervisory system, and introduces the combined financial statement of the inter-linked business group. Lastly, for the transparence of a finance transaction, the 'Act Concerning the Real Name Finance Transaction and Protection of Confidentiality' was newly legislated. This new act provides an exceptional provision for the real name finance transaction, and fosters the confidentiality of a finance transaction.

survive. It was reasonable to believe that the impact on the country's economy would be much more severe if the banks' problems were not resolved in a more orderly manner.

Since other financial sectors, such as the securities and corporate sectors, stood to be affected by the bank restructuring process, a principled process was needed.

Bank restructuring in Korea has been guided by four fundamental principles,[33] which seem to originate from international experience.[34] First, bank restructuring should be swift and thorough to restore the financial market's intermediation function as soon as possible. The slower the restructuring process is, the longer and deeper the associated credit crunch will be. Secondly, the burden of fiscal support on taxpayers must be kept to an absolute minimum. Financial institutions should only be supported when they strive to cut costs and attract foreign investment for recapitalisation. Thirdly, to reduce moral hazard arising in the course of resolving troubled banks, shareholders, employees and managerial staff should share the pain and the responsibility. Fourthly, bank restructuring should be implemented in line with transparent and objective criteria to avoid the likelihood of subsequent disputes.[35]

b. *Restructuring process*

There are several different ways to restructure a bank: bailout, assisted mergers, recaptalisation and sale, restructuring, and liquidation and payoff. Each method has both advantages and disadvantages. For example, if the government is to bail out troubled banks by supplementing bank capital with public resources, the strategy has the advantage of speed, but it is at a high cost to the government treasury and low incentives for bank managers to improve performance. On the other hand, if the government is to recapitalise distressed banks and sell them later, this lowers fiscal costs, provides

[33] *See* Banking Department of the Bank of Korea, *Bank Restructuring in Korea* (98–5), Dec. 1998, at 4–7.

[34] International experience offers some principles for bank restructuring. First, only viable institutions should stay in business, and restructuring should allocate losses transparently while minimising the cost to taxpayers. Secondly, restructuring should strengthen financial discipline by allocating losses first to existing shareholders; and then to creditors, and perhaps large depositors. Thirdly, measures should be taken to maintain credit discipline for bank borrowers and to preserve incentives for the infusion of new private capital. Fourth, restructuring should be fast enough to restore credit, while maintaining confidence in the banking system. (*See* World Bank, 'East Asia: the Road to Recovery', Sept. 1998, at 49.)

[35] However, Korea's financial problems cannot be solved in the banking sector alone. The banks' problems are intricately linked with those of corporations. A solution for financial sectors in distress can only be considered after understanding the problems of the corporate sector. Korea's recent corporate restructuring must be understood in this regard. This will be discussed in detail later in respect to '*Chaebol*' regulation.

better incentives for bank performance, and raises confidence in the banking system, but at the probable cost of prolonging the process. Liquidating and paying off creditors and depositors provide a speedy solution, gives better incentives for bank performance, and entails relatively low fiscal costs, but this might severely undermine the confidence in the banking system.[36] In deciding which alternative to use, the government must consider the proper balance of these considerations in light of the country's specific economic and political environment.

The restructuring method which Korea has adopted in its bank restructuring is a complex mixture of several generally recognised methods. The Korean government, in close consultation with the IMF, has pressed ahead with the exit of nonviable banks, while helping the viable banks to recapitalise and dispose of nonperforming loans. The government has injected public funds but only on the condition that these banks make every effort to rehabilitate themselves through mergers, induction of foreign capital and improving the management.

(i) Liquidation and payoff (exit)

Due to bank restructuring, for the first time in Korea's banking history, nonviable banks were forced to close their doors. First, the Korean government revoked the foreign exchange licenses of eight merchant banks and imposed business suspensions on fourteen other merchant banks.[37] In all, eighteen merchant banks had their operations suspended, and sixteen out of these have since had their licenses revoked. Currently, only fourteen merchant banks are in operation.

As for commercial banks, orders or recommendations for management improvement measures were issued in early 1998 to twelve commercial banks not including Korea First Bank and Seoul Bank, which had BIS capital adequacy ratios of less than 8 per cent at the end of 1997. These banks were given until April 1998 to present management rehabilitation plans including those for capital enhancement. The Management Evaluation Committee, a group of twelve private sector experts appointed by the FSC, evaluated the plans to determine whether they should be approved.

On 29 June 1998, in a move unprecedented in modern Korean banking history, the FSC ordered the exit of five (Daedong, Dongnam, Donghwa,

36 World Bank, 'East Asia: the Road to Recovery' (Sept. 1998), at 49–50.

37 The government revoked the foreign exchange licenses of eight merchant banks (Gyongnam, Samyang, Hangil, Coryo, Yeungnam, Daehan, Samsam, Kyungil) which were unable to meet their current liabilities at the time the negotiations with the IMF began in 26 Nov. 1997. On 2 Dec. 1997, business suspensions were imposed on nine merchant banks (Samsam, Hansol, Gyongnam, Coryo, Hangdo, Ssangyong, Shinsegae, Chongsol, Kyungil) owing to their liquidity shortages, and then the suspension of an additional five merchant banks (Daehan, Central Banking, Shinhan, Hanhwa, Nara) was ordered on 10 Dec. 1997 following runs on them.

Kyungki, and Chungchong) of the twelve commercial banks deemed by the Management Evaluation Committee ('MEC')[38] to have little possibility of rehabilitation. The dissolution of these five banks was to be achieved through a purchase and assumption (P&A) formula, whereby the acquiring banks (Kookmin, Housing & Commercial, Shinhan, Koram and Hana) would purchase the sound assets and assume the liabilities of the distressed bank. In accordance with this decision, operations of the five banks slated for exit were suspended, and the green light was given to preparations for the acquisition of these banks, including the winding-up of their remaining affairs. In this 'liquidation and payoff' situation, it was advisable to liquidate the distressed commercial banks and merchant banks as a first step in the process of financial restructuring, rather than simultaneous closure of all the troubled financial institutions, which would have generated serious systemic risk.[39]

(ii) Recapitalisation and sale

Recapitalisation and selling distressed banks promotes confidence in the banking system and provides better incentives for bank performance. This method has been applied to two commercial banks.

Korea First Bank and Seoul Bank have been treated differently from other commercial banks because their problems were the most severe and posed the greatest threat to the whole financial system.[40] It was agreed in an agreement with the IMF that Korea First Bank and Seoul Bank would be sold back to the private sector following their recapitalisation by the government. Therefore, a privatisation process committee was set up in March 1998 to handle this transition and independent third agents were selected for a transparent and effective process. Coopers & Lybrand were selected as the accountants responsible for the due diligence evaluation of the two banks' assets, and Morgan Stanley was chosen as lead manager of the sell-off. During 1998, both banks were nationalised through subscriptions of 1.5 trillion won in government-owned securities by the government and the Korean Deposit Insurance Corporation (KDIC), bringing each bank's capital to 1.6 trillion won (approximately US$1.6 billion).

The rationale behind using public funds to rescue these two distressed banks, rather than forcing their exit, was to avoid the severe systemic risk liquidation would have created for the financial industry. As Korea had no previous experience of bank closures at the time, and the two banks were

[38] It consists of experts from the private sector and was set up by the FSC on 20 June 1998, to deliberate on the basis of the accountants' assessment as to whether the rehabilitation plans should be approved. So as to ensure the objectivity and professionalism of the evaluation, the MEC is made up of twelve members including accountants, lawyers, university professors, and researchers.

[39] *See* Banking Department of the Bank of Korea, *Bank Restructuring in Korea* (98–5), Dec. 1998, at 8.

[40] For the process of two banks, *see* n 13.

well known and established, a forced exit of these banks would have raised the very likely prospect of heavy bank runs.

By October 1999, the asset valuation by Coopers & Lybrand and the consultation with Morgan Stanley on the method of selling the two banks to overseas buyers were complete, and finalisation of the details of the sales procedure was underway.

(iii) Assisted mergers and capital increase

As for the other seven commercial banks whose turnaround plans were conditionally approved, they are currently carrying out their rehabilitation plans through mergers, capital increase by infusion of foreign capital, consolidation with subsidiaries, and partial limitation of their banking business activities.[41]

Amendments of the General Banking Act have accelerated the capital increase in banks, eased the limitations on bank share holdings by non-residents and thus encouraging investment of foreign capital.[42]

Also, those banks have been subject to government merger plans of banks that had been both sound and of substantial size.[43] To support the government plan, on 14 September 1998 the amended 'Act Concerning the Structural Improvement of the Financial Industry' was implemented, providing for the simplification of merger procedures and tax incentives for mergers between financial institutions.[44]

In addition to the merger between the conditionally approved CBK and Hanil Bank, Hana Bank, which had a BIS capital adequacy ratio of more than 8 per cent at the end of 1997, merged with Boram Bank, while Kookmin Bank paired off with Korea Long-Term Credit Bank. In merger procedures, the Korean government acted to improve the merging banks' BIS capital adequacy ratios through injection of public funds to prevent a possible deterioration of banks' status.

[41] By the end of Oct. 1998, non-performing loans with a book value of 9.33 trillion won had been cleared from the books of those conditionally approved banks which had actively pursued management rehabilitation plans and mergers. These non-performing assets were acquired at a discount by the Korea Asset Management Corporation (KAMCO).

[42] Non-residents may now hold up to 10 per cent of the overall equity of a bank without requiring the permission of the FSC and can own stocks in excess of 25 per cent or 33 per cent of the total voting stocks of a bank by obtaining approval from the FSC at each stage (Art. 15 of the General Banking Act).

[43] Its objectives are to hone the competitive edge of the Korean banking industry through economies of scale and remove the inefficiency caused by the presence of many relatively small banks.

[44] Major elements of the act are that the FSC is given the right to order mergers of distressed financial institutions and that the Minister of Finance and Economy can, if need be, grant exemptions from the corporation or personal income taxes payable on income arising from the liquidation of a financial institution. He may similarly waive or reduce acquisition or registration tax payable on real estate purchased in the course of the merger.

III. NEW BANKING REGULATIONS

The effects of the Korean financial crisis can be best seen in a study of the banking sector. As discussed above, Korean financial reforms are still ongoing and are changing the whole financial system and structure throughout the banking sector.

The changes which will be discussed in the following sections have already become a part of the current banking rules and regulations in Korea. Therefore, this section will begin with a discussion of the Korean banking system in general. The detailed new regulations and policies for central bank, bank supervision, bank deposit insurance, and foreign banks will be examined to determine the current banking regulations in Korea.

A. Restructuring of the Banking System

1. KOREAN BANKING SYSTEM IN GENERAL

The Korean banking system has been developed along with other financial systems for non-banking institutions since the 1950s. Korea's modern banking system and its regulations began from the time the National Assembly approved the drafts for the Bank of Korea Act in April 1950; a new central bank, the Bank of Korea, came into being on June 12, 1950; and when commercial banks were to be reorganised under the General Banking Act.[45]

Korean financial institutions consist of (1) banking institutions (eg commercial banks and specialised banks), and (2) non-banking financial institutions (eg investment companies and mutual savings and finance companies, credit unions, mutual credits, postal savings, trust accounts of banking institutions, insurance companies, securities companies, lease companies, etc).[46]

As the following table indicates, the hierarchy of Korean banking institutions is divided largely into three types according to the objectives and governing laws of each type—commercial nationwide bank, commercial local bank, and specialised bank. The principal difference between a commercial nationwide bank and a local bank is that a nationwide bank is

[45] Bang Shik Lee, *The Central Banking System* (July 1994), at 67. In history, there were old style financial institutions and systems (eg *'Kaegju,' 'Yeokaeg'*, or *'Kae'* in Korean language) in Korea before its modern banking and financial system. However, it is said that the modern banking system in Korea dates to the beginning of Japan's domination of the country. In 1878 the First National Bank, a Japanese bank, was established and engaged in modern banking practices, including the issuance of bank notes. Thereafter a bank called the 'Bank of Korea' was founded in 1909 to function as a central bank under the Japan's domination (ibid. at 68). However, they were all Japanese banks, not Korean banks.

[46] Research Department of the Bank of Korea, *Current Banking and Financial Institutions of Korea* 4 (Sept. 1997).

much more efficient than a local bank in scale of operation and level of profitability. A nationwide bank is more active in foreign exchange business, whereas a local bank relies much more heavily on investments in domestic securities for revenues. A foreign banking institution in Korea including its branch and representative office is included in the commercial bank category, which is governed by the General Banking Act. Foreign banking institutions in Korea are chartered or approved basically under the General Banking Act. In commercial banks, the formation of their new banks or branches is subject to Monetary Board approval under the Bank of Korea Act. Foreign exchange activities and trust activities by banks need Ministry of Finance and Economy ('MOFE') approval under the Foreign Exchange Control Act and under the Trust Business Act.[47]

Under the modern Korean banking system, the Bank of Korea ('BOK') acts as a central bank in Korea. It performs the usual functions of a central bank, serving as issuer of bank notes and coins, banker to the banking sector, banker to the government, controller of the money supply and supervisor of banking operations under guidance from the Monetary Board.[48]

Traditionally, the Korean government has been involved directly or indirectly in the banking system through the MOFE. Even though the BOK, the primary regulatory agency, has sought, in recent years, greater autonomy to become a central bank, the MOFE still has had the strongest voice over the functions of the BOK and the banking system. For example, its Minister has presided over the Monetary Board of the BOK which determines monetary policy. However, as will be discussed below, there have been great changes recently in the central banking system since the new Korean financial reform, which was passed at the end of 1997. These changes include several kinds of reforms for a more sound and competitive banking and financial

[47] Byoung Kook Min, Chang Hee Lee, and James M. West, 'Special Report', *International Financial Law Review: Special Supplement* 37 (Sept. 1992).

[48] The Bank of Korea consisted of four important bodies under the old Bank of Korea Act, which were (i) the Monetary Board, (ii) the Governor of the Bank of Korea, (iii) the Bank Supervisory Board and (iv) the Auditor. Under the old Bank of Korea Act, the 'Monetary Board' initially formulated monetary and credit policies, exercised other functions and powers explicitly granted to it, and was responsible for the general direction and supervision of the operation, management and administration of the Bank of Korea. The 'Bank Supervisory Board' was, under instructions from the Monetary Board, responsible for the supervision and periodic examination of banking institutions. The supervision for non-banking financial institutions such as securities companies and insurance companies was executed by a separate Board which was the 'Security Supervisory Board' and the 'Insurance Supervisory Board' according to each of its own acts. However, all financial supervisory functions are now merged into a single body, the Financial Supervisory Committee, since April 1998 according to the new financial reform of 29 Dec. 1997. Under the current Bank of Korea Act, the Bank of Korea consists of three important bodies, which are (i) the Monetary Policy Committee, (ii) the Governor of the Bank of Korea, (iii) the Auditor. (Art. 12, 33 and 43 of the new 'Bank of Korea Act'). The Bank Supervisory Board, one of the BOK's bodies under the old Bank of Korea Act, was transferred to the newly established 'Financial Supervisory Committee'.

Korean Banking Institutions[49]

*Competent Ministry	Ministry of Finance and Economy
*Bank Supervision Entity	Financial Supervisory Committee
*Central Bank	Bank of Korea
*Specialised Banks (Chartered by Special Laws and State-invested)	6 Banks as of July 1999 Korea Development Bank The Export-Import Bank of Korea Industrial Bank of Korea National Federation of Fisheries Cooperatives National Agricultural Coop Federation National Livestock Coop Federation
*Commercial Banks:	
*Nationwide City Banks (Chartered for nationwide operation under the Act)	11 banks as of July 1999
*Local Banks (Chartered for regional operational under the Act)	7 banks as of July 1999
*Foreign Banks (Korean branches and offices of foreign banks)	66 branches and 23 representatives offices from 19 countries as of December 1998

Source: the Bank of Korea, Current Banking and Financial Institutions of Korea (March 1994); the Bank of Korea, the Korean financial system (July 1999); Seog Roon Lee and Jung Soo Lee, Korean Banking Institutions (1997).

system and for the liberalisation and internationalisation of the financial system, focusing on independence for the central bank. According to the new Bank of Korea Act regarding the independence of the BOK and the Monetary Board, the Governor of the BOK serves concurrently as the Chairman of the Monetary Board,[50] excluding governmental intervention by the MOFE.

The supervision and guidance of banks are regulated by the Bank of Korea Act and the General Banking Act. Before this new financial reform was carried out, the Bank Supervisory Board of the BOK, which was subject to the instructions of the Monetary Board, was in charge of the supervision

[49] The number of these banking institutions is based on the data established as of July 1999. The exact number of banks during 1999 may vary because Korea is currently restructuring the banking and financial sectors.

[50] Art. 13(2) of the new 'Bank of Korea Act'.

and regular examination of banking institutions according to the old Bank of Korea Act. However, according to the new Acts, the newly established committee (the 'Financial Supervisory Committee') is now in charge of the supervision and regular examination of banking institutions.

The Korean banking system basically follows the 'US Glass–Steagall Act'[51] model with respect to separation of commercial and investment banking functions. Commercial banks accept deposits, issue loans and guarantees, administer trusts and perform limited money management and exchange risk-hedging services, but their ability to market bonds and commercial paper is restricted.[52]

On the surface, the Korean banking system resembles the banking system of the OECD countries, but behind the scene, government intervention through so-called window guidance and other informal channels remains important.[53] Historically, the Korean government has controlled many parts of banking activities, by holding of bank stocks or by appointing presidents of banks. In a major effort to liberalise the banking sector, however, the government has turned over the ownership of major national commercial banks to private hands. Along with the denationalisation of commercial banks, the General Banking Act was revised once again at the end of 1982 to give banks a freer hand in dealing with their own managerial affairs in order to boost their public accountability by establishing a ceiling on the ownership of bank stocks per shareholder.

Most importantly, Korea recently enacted a new law, the Bank Deposit Insurance Act, for a stronger bank deposit insurance scheme. In fact, whenever banks have carried large bad loans and had financial problems in the past, the government and the central bank have consistently bailed them out without any special insurance fund to pay for the bail-outs. However, under the Bank Deposit Insurance Act legislated at the end of 1995, bank depositors would be protected beginning on 1 January 1997 in case of any bank bankruptcies.[54]

2. New regulatory banking system

On the whole, modern financial and banking institutions of Korea have

[51] Under the Glass–Steagall Act of the United States, banks have limited securities powers. Banks can only underwrite government debt, but they can do brokerage. Banking affiliates (non-bank subs of BHCs) can do more. For example, they can underwrite corporate debt and equity securities through so called §20 subsidiaries, so long as they are not 'engaged principally' in these activities. [Hal S. Scott and Philip A. Wellons, *International Finance—transactions, policy and regulation*, 139 and 171 (1997)].

[52] Byoung Kook Min, Chang Hee Lee, and James M. West, ibid. at 38.

[53] Ibid.

[54] *See* below s D. 'Bank Deposit Insurance'. This Act was also amended in 29 Dec. 1997 along with other financial reform bills.

been developed and liberalised according to the implementation of government-steered economic development plans since they were created and reorganised with relevant laws by the government in the 1950s. Through various economic and political changes, the Korean banking system has been undergoing a slow transition from central control to a more market-driven order. Since the early 1980s, the Korean government has pursued a policy of deregulation designed to increase the efficiency of the local financial industry and to cope with the ongoing internationalisation of the domestic financial markets.[55] Keeping in step with the previous financial and banking reforms, the new reform measures are focusing on the banking restructuring and the new bank supervisory system, especially following the guidelines of the IMF and trying to avoid further difficulties in the banking and financial sectors.

As already mentioned, the Korean government proposed a bill, in the middle of December 1997, to revise the Bank of Korea Act in order to enhance the independence and autonomy of the BOK after many twists and turns. It also proposed another bill for the legislation of an act concerning the establishment of a Financial Supervisory Body in order to consolidate the existing financial supervisory bodies. On 29 December 1997, those bills were passed by the National Assembly, promulgated by the government on 31 December 1997, and they have been effective since 1 April 1998.

Even under this new regulatory framework for the financial sector, Korea's basic modern banking system is being maintained to ensure the existence of a central bank and general commercial banks in the banking sector and to maintain the MOFE as a competent Ministry which has direct and indirect powers over banks.

However, the Bank of Korea has been reshaped by the new financial reform. The new financial reform has granted total independence to the Bank of Korea in implementing monetary policy with price stability as its main mandate. Bank supervision is now governed by a single committee, the 'Financial Supervisory Committee', over banks, securities companies and insurance companies as the government has established a unified financial regulatory agency with operational and financial autonomy. The bank deposit insurance has been strengthened to protect depositors against recent bank bankruptcies or mergers. Another big change is that foreign banks can now establish their subsidiaries as well as participate in joint venture banks with Korean partners because regulations for the foreign financial institutions have been changed favourably for them.

One thing that was missed in the new banking sector reform was the

[55] Tae Hee Lee, 'Special Report', *International Financial Law Review: Special Supplement* (Sept. 1991), at 128.

'bank holding company' scheme.[56] Even though the Korean government has reviewed the bank holding company system,[57] it should have been included in this new financial reform package because Korea's strict restriction on entry into the banking business by a corporation may cause another problem: the likelihood of small domestic banks being unable to compete with large banking institutions of foreign bank holding companies.

B. *Reshaping of the Central Bank*

1. Bank of Korea as the Central Bank in Korea

The Bank of Korea was founded in 1909 to function as a central bank (named the 'Bank of Chosun' in 1911).[58] The National Assembly approved the drafts for the Bank of Korea Act in April 1950, and a new central bank, the Bank of Korea, came into being on 12 June 1950. Upon its establishment, the Bank of Korea initiated a number of policies to combat inflation and drafted the General Banking Act, under which commercial banks were to be reorganised. While many other countries' initial central banks, such as the Bank of Amsterdam, Banque Royal, Bank of England, Bank of Sweden, Banque de France, Bank of Prussia, along with the first and second Bank of the United States,[59] were created as national banks to achieve stronger, more reliable banking against the private banks, and some of them survive today, the new Bank of Korea was established to create a modern banking and financial system.

Under the new Bank of Korea Act, the BOK consists of three important bodies[60]: (1) the Monetary Policy Committee; (2) the Governor of the Bank of Korea; and (3) the Auditor.[61]

56 The US Bank Holding Company Act of 1956 defines the 'Bank Holding Company' as the company that owns or controls one or more banks or other bank holding companies. In the United States, such companies must register with the Board of Governors of the Federal Reserve System. Bank Holding Companies can do activities 'closely related to banking', §(4)(c)(8) of the Bank Holding Company Act. (Hal S. Scott and Philip A. Wellons, op cit. n 51 at 138.)

57 *See* Press Release of the Ministry of Finance and Economy, Strengthening the Responsible Management System of a Bank and Introducing Bank Holding Company System, 25 June 1997.

58 Bang Shik Lee, *The Korean Central Bank System* (in Korean) 67 (1994).

59 In the case of the United States, the Federal Reserve System is now regarded as the central bank of the United States. It was founded by Congress in 1913 to provide the nation with a safer, more flexible, and more stable monetary and financial system [Board of Governors of the Federal Reserve System, *The Federal Reserve System: Purposes & Functions* 1–2 (1994)].

60 Arts. 12, 33, and 43 of the new 'Bank of Korea Act'. The Bank Supervisory Board, one of the BOK's bodies under the old Bank of Korea Act, was transferred to the newly established 'Financial Supervisory Committee (FSC)'.

61 With comparison of the central bank of the Unites States, the Federal Reserve System of the United States is composed of the Board of Governors and twelve regional Reserve Banks

Historically, the objectives of the Bank of Korea have been to preserve the value of the currency with exclusive currency power and to maintain stability in the banking system. It performs the usual functions of a central bank, serving as issuer of bank notes and coins, as banker to the banking sector and the government, as controller of the money supply and as supervisor of banking operations under guidance from the Monetary Policy Committee.[62]

The central recurring policy issues for the central banking system have been the BOK's level of independence from the government and the level of supervisory control over the general banks in order to promote higher economic growth and to develop a better and safer financial environment. The recent central bank reforms and policies were implemented to reshape the structure of the Bank of Korea and to make it more independent from the government.

2. Reshaping of the Bank of Korea

The reshaping of the BOK was caused by its role in the recent financial crisis. Before the onset of the crisis, the BOK failed to notice/detect any sings of an inevitable financial crisis. To add to its inability to prevent a crisis or lessen the impact of a crisis, during the crisis itself, the BOK failed (1) to monitor the progress of the financial crisis, (2) to keep a check on local businesses' overseas borrowings, and (3) to properly respond to the change in the economic cycle. Critics have complained that the BOK's functions and practices were slow and outdated, that the BOK was more bureaucratic and exclusive than a government administration, and that its service record was unbelievably poor.[63]

Reshaping of the BOK under the new Bank of Korea Act has started with the independence of the central bank. Since the BOK was established in June 1950 as the Korean central bank under the Bank of Korea Act, the BOK Act has been amended many times. However, those amendments to the BOK Act contained various provisions which have restricted the BOK's independence and autonomy over its internal management.

(*see Board of Governors of the Federal Reserve System*, ibid. at 3–15). A major component of the System is the Federal Open Market Committee, which oversees open market operations by influencing the money and credit conditions in the economy. The System also has depository institutions and advisory committees.

62 Similarly, other countries' central banks are performing those functions. For example, the Federal Reserve System of the United States is also (1) conducting the nation's monetary policy, (2) supervising and regulating banking institutions, (3) maintaining the stability of the financial system and containing system risk, and (4) providing certain financial services to the US government, to the public, to financial institutions, and to foreign official institutions. (*See* Board of Governors of the Federal Reserve System, *The Federal Reserve System: Purposes & Functions* (1994).)

63 'Reorganising the Bank of Korea' (editorial), *Chosun Ilbo* (daily newspaper), 14 Mar. 1998.

The functions and operations of the BOK as reshaped under the new Bank of Korea Act are quite different from those of the old Bank of Korea Act.

First, the new Bank of Korea Act defines the BOK's objective as being solely concerned with maintaining price stability.[64] Under the old Bank of Korea Act, however, the BOK was to pursue the dual objectives of maintaining the stability of the value of money and strengthening the soundness of the banking and credit systems. This change means that powers and functions of the Bank of Korea have been greatly reduced.

Secondly, to increase the independence of the Monetary Policy Committee (the former Monetary Board), which is the supreme policy-making body of the BOK, the new Bank of Korea Act changes its composition. The Minister of Finance and Economy is now excluded from chairmanship of and membership on the Committee.[65] Instead, the Governor of the BOK serves as the Chairman of the Board.[66] The Monetary Policy Committee consists of seven members under the new Bank of Korea Act. They are the Governor (the Chairman), and six members who are individually recommended by the Minister of Finance and Economy, the Governor, the Chairman of the Financial Supervisory Commission, the President of the Korea Chamber of Commerce and Industry, the Chairman of Korea Federation of Banks, and the Chairman of Korea Securities Dealers Association.[67] The Governor is nominated by the President and confirmed by the State Council.[68] The remaining members are appointed by the President on the recommendation of each pertinent institution.[69] Each member is appointed for a term of four years, and except for the governor, others may have their terms extended for three to four years. Once appointed, no committee member may be discharged from office against his will. Therefore, the committee members' terms and activities are now legally protected from any political interventions.

Additionally, the provisions concerning the authority of the Minister of

64 Art. 1 of the new 'Bank of Korea Act'.

65 For example, under the old 'Bank of Korea Act' which was effective until 31 Mar. 1998, the Minister of Finance and Economy took the chairmanship of the Monetary Board, and five out of the seven non ex-officio members of the Board were appointed on the recommendation of the Government Ministers.

66 Art. 13(2) of the new 'Bank of Korea Act'.

67 Under the old 'Bank of Korea Act', there were nine members, which were the Minister (the Chairman), the Governor, one member recommended by the Minister of Finance and Economy, two members recommended by the Minister of Trade, Industry and Energy, two members recommended by banking institutions, two members recommended by the Minister of Agriculture and Forestry.

68 Under the old 'Bank of Korea Act', the Governor was appointed by the President on the recommendation of the Minister of Finance and Economy. The term was for four years.

69 Under the old Bank of Korea Act, the remaining members were appointed by the President on the recommendation of each pertinent institution. The term was for three years.

Finance and Economy to approve amendments to the Articles of Incorporation of the BOK and to carry out business examination of the BOK are abolished.[70] The budget for the BOK will be determined by a resolution of the Monetary Policy Committee. However, the budget for the operating expenses will require approval from the Minister of Finance and Economy.

Even though much of the government's interventions in the Bank of Korea have been reduced or abolished, the new Bank of Korea Act has not completely eliminated interference from the government. For example, the Act leaves the Minister with the right to request the Board to reconsider a resolution it has adopted while adding a provision which restricts potential abuse of this right. Under the provision, the Minister may ask for reconsideration only when the resolution is in conflict with the government's economic policies, and in such cases, the Minister should immediately announce this publicly.

During the period of the old Bank of Korea, even without written regulations, the BOK customarily consulted with the MOFE before planning or implementing a major monetary policy.[71] The new Bank of Korea Act does not comment on this. So it is uncertain whether similar government intervention will be required under the new Act.

Thirdly, as it will be discussed below in relation to bank supervision, the bank supervisory power is transferred to the newly established 'Financial Supervisory Committee' and the 'Financial Supervisory Board', which will supervise all financial institutions including banks, securities companies, and insurance companies.[72]

Under the initial Bank of Korea Act and the initial General Banking Act, the supervision and guidance of banks were carried out only by the Bank of Korea. Accordingly, the Bank Supervisory Board of the Bank of Korea, which was subject to the instructions of the Monetary Board (former Monetary Policy Committee), was in charge of the supervision and regular examination of banking institutions.[73] Other financial institutions, for example securities institutions, were supervised by the MOFE and the Securities and Exchange Commission, while they were examined by the Securities Supervisory Board. Insurance institutions were supervised by the MOFE and the Insurance Supervisory Board and examined by the Insurance Supervisory Board. Other specialised banks and most non-bank financial institutions were subject to the supervision of the MOFE pursuant

70 Under the old Bank of Korea Act, the Minister also had the rights to appoint the Auditor and to carry out business examination of the BOK.

71 *See* Research Department of the Bank of Korea, *The Main Points of Reshaping the Central Banking and Financial Supervision System in Korea* (Jan. 1998).

72 The change of bank supervision will be discussed in detail in section C 'Bank Supervision'.

73 Art. 28 of the old 'Bank of Korea Act'.

to the relevant statutes. However, the examination of those institutions was frequently undertaken by the Bank Supervisory Board of the BOK upon the delegation of authority by the MOFE.[74]

While the BOK's independence and autonomy were in debate, a fiercely debated issue was the BOK's policies and supervision of financial and banking institutions without the government's intervention. Responding to the BOK's request for independence, the new Bank of Korea Act eliminated the government's intervention in the BOK and, at the same time, it took the BOK's supervisory powers and gave them to a new commission. Therefore, the BOK's bank supervisory function, which was the fundamental power of the BOK, was transferred to another body, the 'Financial Supervisory Committee' (FSC).

However, the BOK still has indirect and limited supervisory powers. The BOK has rights to request all banking institutions and some non-bank financial institutions entering into agreements on current deposit accounts with the BOK to submit such materials as it may request. The BOK also may require the Financial Supervisory Board to conduct on-site examinations or joint examinations with the BOK on specific banking institutions and to send the BOK the findings of these examinations, on the basis of which the BOK may ask the Financial Supervisory Board to order banking institutions to take corrective actions. If the BOK extends emergency credit to banking institutions, non-bank financial institutions or other profit-making enterprises, it may check and confirm their operations and the status of the assets.[75]

In regard to the relationship between the Monetary Policy Committee and the Financial Supervisory Committee, the Monetary Policy Committee may, when it has a different opinion, request the Financial Supervisory Committee to reconsider a resolution it has adopted provided that the resolution is directly related to monetary and credit policies. When the request for reconsideration is made, the final decision shall require confirmation by a two-thirds majority of the Financial Supervisory Committee's members.

To promote autonomy and independence of the central bank, there was no dispute about the necessity to prevent government intervention and control over the central bank. However, there were many disputes between the Bank of Korea and the government regarding the bank supervisory body.[76] No matter what problems there are in the new bank supervisory

74 The Research Department of the Bank of Korea, op cit. n 71 at 4.

75 Art. 65(3) of the new 'Bank of Korea Act'.

76 The BOK wanted to keep the basic bank supervisory function, while the government wanted to hold the supervisory power over all financial institutions. More about disputes between the Bank of Korea and the government can be found in The Bank of Korea, *Our Opinion for the Financial Reform* (Aug. 1997) and *Financial Reform Bills*, the Ministry of Finance and Economy Working Paper (July 1997).

system, the separate supervisory body has already been set up and is operating according to the guidelines of the IMF.[77] Despite the operation of the new bank supervisory system, in fact, a question still lingers: how does the Bank of Korea function as a central bank and make policies over banks without the bank supervisory function or with limited powers? To solve this question, the cooperation, interconnection and harmony between the central bank and the 'Financial Supervisory Committee' will be required.

Fourth, under the new Bank of Korea Act, the BOK's accountability and transparency will be enhanced. This change has been caused by the critics saying that service records of the Bank of Korea are unbelievably poor and by the government's promise in the Letter of Intent to the IMF.

To enhance the BOK accountability and transparency in formulating and implementing its policies, the BOK will set a price stability target every year in consultation with the government and publicly announce an operational plan for monetary and credit policies.[78] Further, the BOK will, at least once a year, prepare a report on the implementation of its monetary and credit policies and submit it to the National Assembly. The Governor will attend and answer the National Assembly concerning the policy report by request of the National Assembly. The Act also obliges the Monetary Policy Committee to produce the minutes of each Committee meeting and to publish them.

C. *Bank Supervision*

1. Necessity of the new bank supervisory system

In consultation with the IMF, the government stated that prompt action would be taken to enact the necessary legislation to set up a strong and independent supervisory institution, strengthen and consolidate prudential supervision, and increase transparency.[79] According to this promise and to Korea's own financial reform plan, bank supervision has been greatly changed, and the new 'Act Concerning the Establishment of a Financial Supervisory Body' was legislated on 29 December 1997 for this purpose. Based on this Act, the new financial system has brought together the financial supervisory functions which were distributed among the MOFE, the BOK, the Securities Supervisory Board and the Insurance Supervisory Board, establishing a separate financial supervisory body for all of them.

So, why is this single watchdog for the financial supervision necessary in the Korean financial situation? First of all, under the previous complicated

[77] *See* Government of Korea, *Letter of Intent of the Government of Korea* (3 Dec. 1997).
[78] Art. 6(1) of the new 'Bank of Korea Act'.
[79] Government of Korea, at 5.

supervisory system, it was difficult for supervisors to investigate fully the details of financial scandals occurring among different financial sectors and to resolve problems arising from them. Looking back at the recent experience with financial supervision, there were many mistakes in supervising each financial institution by a separate supervisory body. Also, as the global economy tends toward universal banking and the development of complex financial products like financial derivatives, it is now necessary to establish an agency which supervises and examines all financial institutions with functions and products that are different from each other.

2. New bank supervision

The new bank supervision means change in the supervisory entity for banks. Before this new financial reform became effective, supervisory powers were distributed among the Ministry of Finance and Economy (MOFE), the BOK, the Securities and Exchange Commission, the Securities Supervisory Board and the Insurance Supervisory Board.

Under the 'Act Concerning the Establishment of a Financial Supervisory Body' in effect, a new financial supervision institution, the 'Financial Supervisory Committee ("FSC" "*Keumyung Kamdog Wiyonhoi*" in the Korean language),' merges the three supervisory offices of banks, securities and insurance established under the Prime Minister.[80] The Office of Bank Supervision of the BOK has been merged into the 'Financial Supervisory Board' (FSB) of the 'Financial Supervisory Committee'(FSC), which was established in 1999 as prescribed by the Presidential Decree.[81]

The FSC consists of nine members. Three of them are ex-officio members: the Vice-Minister of Finance and Economy, the Deputy Governor of the Bank of Korea, and the President of the Deposit Insurance Corporation. The other six members consist of the Chairman and Vice-Chairman of the FSC,[82] who are appointed by the President, and four general members, who are appointed by the President on the recommendation of the each of the pertinent organisations.

The duties of the newly established FSC are to deliberate and agree upon

80 Art. 3 of the 'Act Concerning the Establishment of a Financial Supervisory Body'. The issue where the Financial Supervisory Committee should be positioned was in high debate when it was legislated. After a long discussion, it was decided that it should be established under the Prime Minister because the government is the last entity responsible for the financial supervision.

81 From 1 Apr. 1998 on which the Act was in effect for an interim period until the Financial Supervisory Board was established, the Office of Bank Supervision had been separated from the BOK and established as a special juridical person with no capital.

82 The Chairman is appointed by the President on the deliberation of the State Council, and the Vice-Chairman is appointed by the President on the recommendation of the Minister of Finance and Economy (Art. 4 of the 'Act Concerning the Establishment of a Financial Supervisory Body').

the main aspects of financial supervision, such as enactment and revision of regulations concerning supervision of financial institutions, securities and futures markets, and authorisation of business-related matters for financial institutions. The FSC also directs and supervises the operations, administration and management of the FSB.[83]

The MOFE, however, undertakes the functions of proposing legislation and revision of finance-related acts and chartering financial institutions in accordance with each individual finance-related act.[84] Accordingly, under the new banking and financial reform, there is a contradiction of bank supervision being carried out by the FSC but the chartering of banking institutions being carried out by the MOFE. Considering that both functions are important in a banking-related matter, they should be carried out together by one responsible body.

On the one hand, the FSB is a special juridical person with no capital and performs the examination and supervision of financial institutions under the direction of the FSC and the Securities and Futures Commission.[85] Until the establishment of the FSB, its function had been performed by four supervisory bodies (the Office of Bank Supervision of the BOK, the Securities Supervisory Board, the Insurance Supervisory Board and the Credit Management Fund).[86] The FSB has as its executive officers one Superintendent, four Deputy Superintendents, nine Assistant Superintendents and one Auditor. The Chairman of the FSC serves concurrently as the Superintendent of the FSB.

D. *Bank Deposit Insurance*

1. In general

Before the Korean financial crisis of 1997, not only had there never been any bank bankruptcies at all in modern Korean banking history, but there also had never been a deposit insurance system for banks. Until then, there had been only deposit insurance programmes for non-bank financial institutions. Deposit insurance programmes for non-bank financial institutions

[83] Art. 3, 17, and 18 of the 'Act Concerning the Establishment of a Financial Supervisory Body'.

[84] Art. 8 and 55 of the new 'General Banking Act'.

[85] The Securities and Futures Commission (SFC) is established in the FSC. The SFC is in charge of investigation of unfair trading in securities and futures market, and the pre-deliberation of matters concerning the supervision of securities and futures market before the deliberation and resolution by the FSC.

[86] However, the Office of Bank Supervision of the BOK had been split off from the BOK and established on 1 Apr. 1998 as a special juridical person. (*See* Research Department of the Bank of Korea, op cit. n 71.) The Office of Bank Supervision performed the examination and supervision of banking institutions for a temporary period under the direction of the FSC.

in Korea have been in operation since the early 1980s through the Korean Non-Bank Deposit Insurance Corporation.[87]

Contrary to non-bank institutions, whenever banks had carried large nonperforming loans in the past, the government and the central bank consistently bailed them out without any special insurance scheme[88] to avoid bank bankruptcies and their ill-effects on the Korean economy. Bank depositors were therefore protected indirectly. However, the Korean government realised that this implicit bailout guarantee, though a feature of the Korean economy for several decades, was no longer sustainable in an era of financial liberalisation and internationalisation.

Accordingly, on 29 December 1995, the National Assembly of Korea passed the 'Depositor Protection Act' (Law No 5042, the 'DPA') which came into effect in January 1997, in order to regulate bank deposit insurance system and to protect bank depositors. Under this act, the 'Bank Deposit Insurance Corporation', which is in charge of managing bank deposit insurance, was established on 1 June 1996 and has conducted business since 1 January 1997.

The main goal of the DPA has been to protect depositors and create financial stability by means of a bank deposit insurance system designed to deal with the rare, but inevitable occasions when banks are unable to repay depositors in the event of bank insolvencies.[89] To further this goal, the DPA administers and operates the 'Deposit Insurance Fund', levying insurance premiums on member banks like the operation of the 'Federal Deposit Insurance Corporation' (FDIC) in the United States,[90] and extends financial support to participating banks seeking to merge with ailing banks or to assume the liabilities of failing banks.

Under the DPA, eligible participating banks are commercial nationwide banks, specialised banks, local banks and foreign bank branches in Korea, and the participation of all domestic banks except the Bank of Korea is mandator.[91] However, the DPA provides that although foreign bank branches are eligible to participate in the DPA, they may be exempt from

[87] Dong Won Ko, 'Korea Introduces Bank Deposit Insurance Scheme', *International Financial Law Review* 46 (Apr. 1997); *See also* Ministry of Finance and Economy Press Release, *Establishment of Bank Deposit Insurance Corporation*, 18 June 1996.

[88] Hee Seog Kim, 'Bank Deposit Insurance', *The KDB Monthly Bulletin*, 2–3 (1997); *See also* Dong Won Ko, above at 47.

[89] The Ministry of Finance and Economy, op cit. n 87 at 2.

[90] The 'Federal Deposit Insurance Corporation' in the United States established in 1933 guarantees funds on deposit in member banks and thrift institutions and performs other bank regulatory functions. Under the US deposit insurance system, the US insures deposits of up to US$100,000. This may minimise bank runs, and be a form of creditor protection, but raises a moral hazard issue: since creditors are insured, they do not police bank risk (Hal S. Scott and Philip A. Wellons, op cit. n 51 at 138.)

[91] Art. 2 (i) of the 'Depositor Protection Act'.

the mandatory deposit insurance system on the basis of a 'Reciprocity Principle' as set out in the Enforcement Decree of the DPA.

The Deposit Insurance Fund established under the Bank Deposit Insurance Corporation is financed by contributions from member banks[92] and the government, loans from the government and the BOK, premiums paid by participating banks, and profits from the operation of the Fund.

Under the DPA, the flat rate insurance premium can be imposed on all participating banks, forming a uniform premium structure. The initial premium rate is currently 0.02 per cent of insured deposits at the end of each quarter as set out in Article 17 of the Enforcement Decree of the DPA. However, according to government report concerning bank insurance premiums,[93] a flat-rate insurance premium will be used at the initial stage until the deposit insurance system is well established. Thereafter, a risk-based premium system may be introduced. Currently, in the event of a bankruptcy, the Enforcement Decree of the DPA has set the insured amount for each depositor at 20,000,000 won (approximately US$20,000).

2. New bank deposit insurance

Through the experience of the recent bank bankruptcies in Korea, the protection of depositors has become a real issue. Though the DPA took effect in January 1997, it was not yet ready to handle the problems which suddenly occurred in troubled banks at the end of 1997 because of a shortage in the deposit insurance fund and because of an ill-organised Bank Deposit Insurance Corporation. Therefore, it was necessary to reorganise the Bank Deposit Insurance Corporation to make it more effective and to make the bank deposit insurance system stronger in order to protect depositors from any unexpected financial crisis.

Accordingly, one of the financial reforms, the Depositor Protection Act, was revised on 29 December 1997. The new DPA was designed to merge the existing diverse deposit insurance funds into the Bank Deposit Insurance Corporation in order to form a single financial insurance system and to protect depositors from troubled financial institutions. Previously, the deposit insurance funds had been managed by the respective regulatory bodies in charge of banks, securities companies, insurance companies, and credit cooperatives. Under the new DPA, all deposit insurance funds from banks, securities companies, insurance companies, and credit cooperatives are managed by the Bank Deposit Insurance Corporation.[94]

[92] Mandatory contributions from participating banks is up to 1 per cent of the bank's capital under the Enforcement Decree of the 'DPA'.

[93] The Ministry of Finance and Economy, op cit. n 87 at 5.

[94] Arts. 1 and 2 of the new 'Depositor Protection Act'.

The other basic frameworks of the old DPA have remained in the new Depositor Protection Act. However, some functions of the Bank Deposit Insurance Corporation have been strengthened in the new Depositor Protection Act. Under the new DPA, the Bank Deposit Insurance Corporation may also request the FSC and the FSB to conduct on-site examinations or joint examinations on its insured financial institutions.[95] Once the request is made, the FSC and the FSB must respond to the request unless a special reason not to do so exists.

E. Foreign Bank Regulation in Korea

1. FOREIGN BANKS IN GENERAL

Modern financial and banking institutions of Korea have been developed and liberalised according to the implementation of government-steered economic development plans since they were created and reorganised with relevant laws and by the government in the 1950s. Through various economic and political changes, the banking system is presently undergoing a slow transition from central control to a more market-driven order. Since the early 1980s, the Korean government has pursued a policy of deregulation designed to increase the efficiency of the local financial industry and to cope with the on-going internationalisation of the domestic financial markets.[96] Many foreign banks entered Korea during this period since the first Korean branch of a foreign bank was established in 1967.[97]

Before the foreign banks were introduced in Korea in earnest, Korean domestic financial institutions were not ready to compete with foreign banks or international financial markets. That is why the Korean government has implemented policies to allow foreign banks to establish their branches in Korea, sometimes with and sometimes without limitations on their business practice. In order to motivate domestic banks into improving their banking practices and managerial skills, the government has allowed additional foreign bank branches to open in Korea since 1981, bringing the total number of foreign bank branches and representative offices to ninety-two by February 1998.[98]

95 Art. 21 (3) of the new 'Depositor Protection Act'.

96 Tae Hee Lee, 'Special Report', *International Financial Law Review: Special Supplement* 128 (Sept. 1991).

97 Seog Roon Lee and Jung Soo Lee, *Korean Banking Institutions* (in Korean) 230 (1997). The Korean branch of 'Chase Manhattan Bank' of the United States which was established in 1967 is regarded as the first foreign bank branch under the modern banking system of Korea, though there were several Japanese bank branches before the modern banking starting point of 1950 (ibid.).

98 Bank of Korea Press Release, *Policy for foreign banks during 1998*, Kongbo 98-2-12, 19 Feb. 1998, at 2.

Since their arrival in Korea in 1967, foreign bank branches have taken a large share of the domestic financial market and have realised high profits as a result of various privileges and of their competitive positions.[99] However, the continued relaxed and improved rules have eventually led to an altered environment and financial market in which Korean banks and foreign bank branches could compete. These changes will also improve existing unequal competitive conditions by reducing privileges for both domestic and foreign bank branches and relaxing cumbersome regulations.

Moreover, compared with the past financial reforms, the Korean government's recent reforms are to pursue a stronger and sounder financial system and to follow international trends. Some examples of those recent financial reforms follow. The government has already announced and has been engaging in the 'Five-Year Financial Reform Plan of 1993' for an internationalisation and liberalisation of domestic financial institutions. In addition, when Korea became a member of the OECD at the end of 1996, the government prepared the 'Banking and Financial Market Open Schedule' under the guidelines of the OECD. While only branches or representative offices could be established under the old General Banking Act, the subsidiaries of foreign banks, in accordance to this financial market open schedule, were to be allowed to operate beginning 1998. In early 1997, however, the government announced new financial reform proposals for the independence of the central bank and for the soundness and safety of all banking institutions. As stated above, these proposals, which also included the foreign banking sector, were completed under consultation with the IMF after the financial crisis in 1997.

Under the initial General Banking Act, foreign banking institutions could enter into Korea in the form of a branch or representative office. That is, the General Banking Act and the Foreign Capital Inducement Act[100] operated to bar foreign banks from either acquiring a controlling interest in national banks or establishing their subsidiaries. Therefore, a subsidiary or any other form was not allowed until the new financial reform was put into practice at the end of 1997.

In the history of foreign banking institutions in Korea, however, there was one exception for the limited forms of foreign banks in Korea. In 1983, after receiving the Korean government's blessings, 'KorAm Bank' was formed as a joint-venture bank between Bank of America of the United

[99] The Korea Development Bank, KDB Data Plaza: Foreign Banks in Korea (last updated on June 1995) <http://www.kol.co.kr/~kdbmst/focus/ for_bank.html>.

[100] The Foreign Capital Inducement Act formulated the possible business types by foreign investment and their procedures. Under this Act, foreign banks '*may*' request establishment of subsidiaries or joint venture banks to a competent Ministry or the Bank of Korea. However, foreign banks have not been allowed to establish their subsidiaries because of government restrictions. The General Banking Act also regulated only branch and representative office types according to the policy.

States and several of Korea's most renowned companies.[101] Being the first, and still the only joint-venture bank, KorAm Bank was intended to utilise the advanced banking techniques and strategies learned from Bank of America and to influence the Korean banking industry's development. This was, however, very exceptional and has not been regarded as a normal entry of foreign banks into Korea.

2. FOREIGN BANKS' ENTRY BY STAGE AND NUMBER

The expansion of foreign banks in Korea has been directly related to Korea's economic development and the government's rules and policies toward them. Over the last 30 years, the laws governing foreign bank entry and operation in Korea have been changed, and the number of branches and volume of business have expanded rapidly, reflecting their relatively advantageous business circumstance *vis-à-vis* domestic commercial banks.

Foreign banks seem to have entered Korea during four stages: preliminary, active, selective, and stagnant before the financial crisis of Korea[102]; the new stage after Korea's crisis in 1997 can be considered as another due to the recent increase in the number of foreign bank branches.[103] Each stage cannot be classified as part of an actual economic stage since the parameters for each stage were chosen based on the number of foreign banks opened under certain economic conditions at that time.

First of all, in the 'preliminary stage', from 1967 when Korea first opened its banking industry to 1975, foreign banks launched branches in Korea because government policies which were designed to attract foreign capital were favourable.[104] When foreign banks first arrived, Korea had neither a stable fundraising system nor the capital necessary for economic development on account of the deficit balance in international payments. During this period, nine foreign bank branches and nine representative offices were established in Korea.

101 KorAm Bank, KorAm Profile (visited on 20 Sept. 1997) <http://www.korambank.co.kr/profe.htm>; *see also* Byoung Kook Min, Chang Hee Lee, and James M. West, above at 38.

102 Korea Development Bank, op cit. n 97.

103 *Number of Foreign Branches and Offices in Korea*

Year	65–75	76–80	81–90	1991	1992	1993	1994	1995	1996	1997	1998	Total
Branches												
Opened	59	24	44	6	5	2	1	0	0	5	2	98
Closed	0	0	8	5	2	1	3	1	4	4	4	32
Total (A)	**9**	**24**	**36**	**1**	**3**	**1**	**–2**	**–1**	**–4**	**1**	**–2**	**66**
Offices												
Opened	9	17	40	5	2	4	0	2	1	3	2	85
Closed	2	5	35	6	2	3	1	0	2	4	2	17
Total (B)	7	12	5	–1	0	1	–1	2	–1	–1	0	23
Total (A+B)	**16**	**36**	**41**	**0**	**3**	**2**	**–3**	**1**	**–5**	**0**	**–2**	**89**

Source: Bank Supervisory Office, Statistics on Bank Management, 1999

104 Ibid.

'1976 to 1982' is classified as an 'active stage' in which foreign banks rushed into Korea even though the domestic economy had suffered harsh stagnation as a result of political disturbances and price increases brought on by the second oil shock.[105] In the early 1980s, when the major government policy was for stable growth, financial liberalisation was implemented on a limited scale and the financial policy focused on supporting the real economy. Foreign banks, consequently, entered Korea because the government had a favourable attitude toward them and because of Korea's economic and financial conditions. From 1976 to 1985, forty-four foreign bank branches and thirty-six representative offices were established in Korea.

During the 'selective stage', 1983 to 1990, there was a great increase in the number of foreign banks as a result of the 1986–8 economic prosperity fed by low interest rates and low raw-material prices.[106] During this period, foreign bank branches were considered rivals to the domestic banking industry, and various privileges accorded them were gradually reduced. At this time, foreign banks selectively branched into Korea in response to the government's proactiveness toward financial internationalisation and liberalisation rather than to take advantage of preferential favours. From 1986 to 1990, twenty-four foreign bank branches and twenty-three representative offices were established in Korea.

In the 'stagnant stage' from 1991 to 1995, only three new foreign bank branches were opened in Korea. The decline in the number of new branches was due to Korea's economic sluggishness and the improvement in domestic banks' competitiveness that had been the direct result of financial liberalisation, which had been detrimental to management conditions in Korea.[107] Thus foreign banks were no longer attracted to branch into Korea. During this period, fourteen foreign bank branches and ten representative offices were established in Korea.

However, since 1996 and in early 1997, the government announced several financial plans for internationalisation of the banking environment and has applied a more favourable policy for foreign investment and an unlimited open financial market policy following the guidelines of the WTO and the OECD. Due to those endeavours, the number of applications for foreign bank branches once again increased. During 1997, three representative offices were upgraded to branches, and a total of five branches were approved by the authority.

Since Korea has been implementing its new laws and rules related to foreign banks in response to the recent Korean financial crisis, foreign banks now have an opportunity to expand the number of their banks and business volume. This may be viewed as a 'second active stage' if Korea's

[105] Korea Development Bank, op cit. n 97. [106] Ibid. [107] Ibid.

recovery is successful in supporting and regulating foreign banks. While Korean banks have been struggling since the end of 1997, at which time the nation was afflicted with unexpected financial turmoil, foreign banks have continued to have better financial positions in the banking market. Even though three banks from Europe and the United States and five Japanese banks have pulled out of Korea or are in the process of withdrawing, this is a result of the respective banks' headquarters restructuring.[108] During this period particularly, shortly before the foreign exchange crisis erupted, depositors were rushing to foreign banks. This phenomenon was the result of widespread worries about the stability of domestic banks due to restructuring efforts in the wake of the foreign exchange crisis.[109]

By the end of December 1998, sixty-six foreign bank branches and twenty-three offices from nineteen countries had a business presence in Korea.[110] A review of the characteristics of each foreign bank branch shows that most foreign bank branches are located in Seoul, the capital city of Korea, and almost half of the foreign banks are from the United States (fourteen banks) and from Japan (eighteen banks) as of December 1998.[111]

The number of foreign banks is expected to increase steadily in the future in spite of the languid rate of increase in the 1990s. This prediction is based on the belief that there is infinite potential in the Korean economy, the fact that foreign banks can never ignore the importance of Korea if they are to form global networks, and the expectation that the North east Asian economic bloc will rise to the centre of the world economy.[112] In addition, relaxed restrictions on business operations and the allowance of foreign bank subsidiaries will also be an attraction to the Korean financial market.

As already mentioned, Korean banks' weak competitive position, caused by the constant growth of the real economy and chronic excessive capital demand, has been considered a big opportunity for foreign banks. When a foreign bank actually has made a decision to enter the Korean financial market, it has undoubtedly evaluated its superior competitive position over that of domestic banks and sometimes over other foreign banks in Korea. This fact cannot be disregarded by foreign banks entering Korea.

108 *Korea Times*, 16 June 1999. 109 Ibid. 6 Oct. 1998

110 However, the number of foreign bank branches and representative offices will be increasing continuously as the Financial Supervisory Committee (FSC) has reported that four foreign banks (Metro of the Philippines, First International of the United States, Mees Pierson of the Netherlands and Natexis of France) have expressed their intention to begin operations in Korea. (Press Release of the Financial Supervisory Committee, June 1999). If they get approval from the government, the number of foreign banks in Korea will increase still more.

111 *See* Bank of Korea Press Release, 'Policy for Foreign Banks', 19 Feb. 1998.

112 Korea Development Bank, op cit. n 97.

3. Business operation of foreign banks

As noted, while the Korean government has allowed foreign banks to establish their branches in Korea in order to promote the domestic bank industry and learn from high banking technology of foreign countries, foreign banks have opened their Korean branches for a variety of reasons depending on Korea's economic situation and the government's financial policies at any given time. The number of those foreign bank branches has fluctuated in response to the purpose. Therefore, after launching a new branch their management strategies tend to focus on a specific field based on the unique characteristics of the individual bank.[113] Although this may change, currently foreign banks have better business operations than domestic banks.

Fund-raising, activities and profitability of foreign banks have changed over the years. In the past, these banks focused on loans, but since 1994 they have emphasised profitable businesses like securities investment. Their foreign exchange business, however, is still one of their most profitable businesses. Their foreign liabilities, as sources of funds, have constantly increased since 1990, whereas their profits have dropped significantly since 1993.[114]

Formerly the main purpose for funds was to provide loans to customers. However, foreign banks' share of loans has declined sharply to less than fifty per cent, while the portion of funds dedicated to purchasing securities has risen gradually since 1990. The foreign banks' decrease in the loan market was caused by unfavourable domestic circumstances. Corporations were gradually becoming independent of banks, and loans by domestic banks to small and medium enterprises were mandated by law. Additionally, domestic banks were stronger because there was more latitude in the use of funds. Other reasons for the decline in shares were that most domestic banks had increased their capital, and several new domestic banks had recently been established.[115]

Net profit at foreign bank branches has constantly increased except in 1993 when it suddenly dropped sharply. Unlike the domestic banks, the decrease in net profits at foreign bank branches lasted until the first half of 1994.[116] The reason for this seems to be that since they had focused primarily on industry finance, they were hit harder by the change in financial circumstances than were domestic banks. That is, even though small foreign bank branches were concentrating on industry finance, they were burdened with an overall increase in bad loans because clients, hit by the nation's economic slump, went bankrupt.

[113] Bank of Korea, op cit. n 98 n.
[114] Korea Development Bank, op cit. n 97.
[115] Lee Ik Joo, *Foreign Banks in Korea, Monthly Review of the Korea Exchange Bank* (Vol XXV, No 7) July 1991, at 5.
[116] Ibid.

Even though, in the first six months of 1997, net profits at foreign bank branches consistently increased to 39.2 per cent as compared with the net profit in 1996,[117] by the second the effects of Korea's financial crisis were felt, and the net profit of foreign banks as of the end of December 1998 stood at only 577 billion won, while 1.12 trillion won had been recorded at the end of 1997.

The question remains as to what caused foreign banks, especially the American branches, known to possess advanced banking and credit appraisal skills, to record lower profits in 1998, when Korea's economic situation was generally on the upturn. The answer may be found in the drastic change in the Won-Dollar exchange rate over the last couple of years and the way foreign banks typically hedge their capital.[118]

Lastly, because of sound business operations of foreign banks, those banks could survive during Korea's financial crisis; their bad loan ratio was only one-tenth of that of domestic banks. According to the Office of Bank Supervision, bad loans of the forty-eight foreign bank branches operating in Korea amounted to fourteen billion won as of the end of 1996, or 0.08 per cent of their total outstanding loans. On the other hand, nonperforming debts of the twenty-five domestic banks amounted to 0.8 per cent of their total lending.[119] The sharply lower proportion of bad loans at foreign banks was attributed to the lack of outside pressure or illegal commissions given for loans at foreign banks.

4. New regulations for foreign banks

As mentioned above, even before the new financial reforms, the Korean government had implemented a detailed financial market open policy and had proceeded to allow foreign banks to do various kinds of businesses in Korea[120] through the 'Five-Year Financial Reform Plan of 1993' and 'Banking and Financial Market Open Schedule' under the guidelines of the OECD by the end of 1996. In fact, according to this plan, the new form of a Korean subsidiary by a foreign banking institution was to be allowed beginning in December 1998.[121]

117 The Bank of Korea, Report of Former Half Year of 1997 for Foreign Banks Profit (June 1997). In detail, Chase Manhattan Bank, NA made a net profit of US$37.2 billion, CitiBank NA US$12 billion, Credit Lyonnais US$10.5 billion, and Bankers Trust Company US$10.3 billion during the half year of 1997. To the contrary, several new branches such as Nations Bank and Matro Bank which began their businesses in early 1997 had losses in their business.

118 *Korea Times*, 'Foreign Banks' 98 Profits Misled', 4 Mar. 1999

119 *Korea Herald*, 'Foreign banks bad loan ratio one tenth of domestic banks', 17 June 1997.

120 Dong Won Ko, *Financial Circumstances and Regulations of Korea*, Korea Commercial Law Association 12 (July 1997).

121 Ministry of Finance and Economy, *Effect of OECD Membership and Future Tasks* 38 (Oct. 1996). The Government's other plans for the financial market open schedule including non-banking institutions are fully discussed at this book.

However, Korea's current financial crisis has caused this plan to take effect beginning with the date of the new financial reform. According to the letter of intent of the government of Korea, the Korean government announced it would allow foreign financial institutions to purchase equity in domestic banks without any restrictions.[122] This means that 100 per cent ownership by foreign merchant banks can now occur. Following the government's foreign bank-related policies, the General Banking Act was amended, on 29 December 1997, in order to allow a subsidiary or a joint venture by foreign banking institutions.

In addition, based on the agreement with the IMF, the government has been rapidly removing restrictions on mergers and acquisitions (M&A) activity in the financial sector to help relieve troubled banks.[123] In reality, there were many M&As of banks during 1998. Accordingly, foreign banking institutions can now merge with domestic banks.

With these new policies in place, most banking rules and policies may now be applied to foreign banks. One example of this is the supervision of both domestic and foreign banks by a single watchdog, the 'Financial Supervisory Committee'.

5. Treatment of foreign banks: national treatment

Banks in Korea, whether domestic or foreign, are generally regulated by the General Banking Act (Law No 139 of 1950 as amended), and the Foreign Exchange Control Act (Law No 933 of 1961 as amended). There are also various administrative rulings and orders issued by the Ministry of Finance and Economy, the Monetary Board, the Bank Supervisory Board, the Bank of Korea and other governmental authorities. Once foreign bank branches are established in Korea, they are generally regarded as financial institutions under the General Banking Act, and foreign bank branches in Korea are treated equally with domestic banks. In the past, it was true that foreign bank branches were treated unequally in some respects to domestic banks; however, foreign banks may have been treated favourably in other respects.

In the past, chronic shortages of funds in Korea have provided lucrative opportunities to induce overseas funds to finance local companies. In line with the government's objective to have foreign bank branches act as intermediaries to attract foreign capital, foreign bank branches were granted certain privileges.[124]

Since the mid-1980s, however, these privileges have been slowly phased out in an effort by the government to submit foreign banks to the same treat-

[122] *See* Government of Korea, op cit. n 77.
[123] *Chosun Ilbo* (Korean daily newspaper), 24 Dec. 1997.
[124] Bank of Korea, *Korean Financial System* (1993), at 84.

ment as that of national banks. For example, foreign banks' exclusion from the obligation to provide policy loans for strategic industries or small and mid-sized companies is being phased out. Also, foreign banks are now required to subscribe to the liquidity-absorbing Monetary Stabilisation Bonds issued by the government. Foreign bank branches' right to use a swap system with the Bank of Korea to exchange foreign capital with local currency is being reduced.[125] This swap facility was originally instituted as an incentive for the foreign banks and included a guaranteed spread, profit margin, on the exchange rate used in the swaps. For a long time, every foreign bank in Korea benefited from this arrangement.[126] As a result of the economic crisis, the Korean government has increased swap lines in order to generate needed foreign exchange. In July 1998, position limits were abolished for foreign exchange swap lines.

Under the current acts, a major impediment inhibiting the ability of foreign banks to compete in Korea is the Korean government's continuing use of local branch capital as the benchmark for determining a variety of funding and lending limits.[127] Korea requires foreign branches to be separately capitalised while other regulations are based on local branch capital.[128] For example, a foreign bank's prudential lending limits are based on its branch capital as opposed to its total capital, which would undoubtedly be much higher. Especially, while domestic banks face the same restrictions under the single customer loan limit (20 or 25 per cent of a bank's equity) but have the kind of broader branch coverage and local lending expertise to undertake this lending on a more prudent basis, the single customer loan limit constrains foreign branches' operations in 20 or 25 per cent of the branches' capital rather than of the parent bank's capital (Article 35 of the General Banking Act). The branch capital limits also affect foreign bank activity in the forward foreign exchange market. Even though the Korean government thinks that this treatment of branch capital limits is necessary for prudential regulatory reasons, foreign banks complain about this regulation because the United States and other industrialized countries base prudential limits on the worldwide capital of a foreign branch's parent bank.[129]

125 Ibid.; *see also* Tae Hee Lee, op cit. n 3.

126 Lee Ik Joo, *Foreign Banks in Korea, Monthly Review of the Korea Exchange Bank* (Vol XXV No 7) July 1991, at 8. The Swap facility allowed foreign bank branches to swap a certain sum of foreign exchange, usually in the form of US Dollars, for Korean won.

127 Department of the Treasury of the United States, *1998 Report on Foreign Treatment of US Financial Institutions*, 30 Nov. 1998, at 322.

128 When a foreign bank has two or more branches in Korea, all such branches are considered as one financial institution like branches of domestic banks (Art. 59 (2) of the General Banking Act). In this situation, a foreign bank's total Korean capital is calculated by adding together the capital of all the separate branches (Art. 11 (5) of the Rule of Bank Supervision).

129 With respect to a foreign branch's capital limit, currently there are no official reports or news releases that this regulation is under consideration for change by the Korean government.

Regulations imposed on foreign bank branches are gradually being eased. Under certain circumstances these branches are now allowed to purchase real estate and to engage in some of the financial services that were closed to them in the past. One example is the issuance of certificates of deposit ('CDs') and credit cards.[130]

As discussed above, effective April 1998, foreign banks are allowed to set up subsidiaries in Korea. Effective 26 June 1998, the government removed all restrictions on land ownership by foreigners. Foreign financial institutions are now allowed to participate in non-hostile and hostile mergers and acquisitions of domestic financial institutions. In the aftermath of the economic crisis, the Korean government has been encouraging increased foreign investment in the financial sector.

Legally, any branches of foreign banks which are authorised under the General Banking Act are considered as financial institutions under the Act, and the Act is applied equally to both domestic and foreign bank branches. A representative of a foreign bank in Korea is considered as an officer of a financial institution as prescribed by this Act.[131] In addition, if a foreign bank had two or more branch offices in Korea, each branch office was considered as a separate financial institution in the past. However, through the 1991 amendment of the Bank Act, when a foreign bank had two or more branch offices in Korea, all such branch offices were now considered as one financial institution like branches of domestic banks.[132]

Therefore, through several reforms for foreign banks, their national treatment in Korea has been getting stronger according to international standards. Under the recent financial reform, most regulations and policies are now applied to foreign banks except in very special cases.

IV. CORPORATE IMPLICATIONS FROM BANK PROBLEMS: 'CHAEBOL' REGULATIONS

A. *The* 'Chaebol' *in Korea and its Relationships with Banks*

The '*chaebols*' in Korea have undoubtedly affected Korea's financial crisis. The word '*chaebol*' in the Korean language depicts a large inter-linked

However, recently Korea lowered the single customer loan limit to 25 (or 20) per cent of a bank's equity from its previous 45 per cent limit.

[130] CD issuing business was allowed to foreign banks since Sept. 1985 (*see* Bank of Korea, op cit. n 58). Credit card business by foreign banks was operated at first by the Bank of America since July 1994; recently Citi Bank branch obtained preliminary authorisation from the Monetary Board for credit card business in June 1997 (*see also* Bank of Korea, Preliminary Authorisation of Credit Card Business to Citi Bank Branch, 20 June 1997).

[131] Arts. 37–3 (Application of Law to Foreign Financial Institution) of the General Banking Act.

[132] Art. 59 para 2 of the General Banking Act.

business group.[133] In other words, a *chaebol* is a conglomerate of many companies clustered around one holding company, with the various companies holding shares in each other. The parent company in a *chaebol* has usually been controlled by one family.

In reviewing the *chaebol* effect on the Korean economy, we find that thirty chaebols accounted for more than 15 per cent of the GDP at the end of 1997. One reason these *chaebols* have survived is that they have built their businesses through internal borrowings as well as external borrowings, and some of the *chaebols* are still surviving even under severe financial pressures brought on by their borrowings.[134] Moreover, the financial lending institutions believed that *chaebols* offered cast-iron guarantees of repayment, because the chaebols were 'too big to fail'.[135] The Korean government also controlled these *chaebols* for purposes of Korean economic development through its supervision of bank lending to *chaebols*.

Some economists point to the cozy relationships between the government and chaebols, as well as between banks and *chaebols* as a root cause of the Korean financial problem. They compare this situation to a feudal economy run by a handful of families. By the same token, *chaebols*' problems created non-regulatory agencies in Korean corporate culture.

During 1997, the string of *chaebols* or large corporate bankruptcies or near bankruptcies further aggravated the ongoing economic recession and severely damaged the entire industrial sector. As corporations played a major role in Korea's economic development, corporate failures or bankruptcies worked to the detriment of Korea's economy and became one of the leading causes of the country's current financial crisis.

Main causes of Korean corporate failures including *chaebols*' failures are considered as follows: (1) the companies' over-dependence on banks that were not forthcoming with additional credits due to the banks' nonperforming loan accounts, (2) the sudden depreciation of the foreign exchange rate, (3) the companies' historical 'conspiracy' with politicians and bureaucrats for their businesses, and (4) large unproductive investments by the *chaebols*.

First of all, corporate bankruptcies were related to the banks' inability to make further loans to the troubled companies due to previous bad loans or nonperforming loans. Large companies, especially *chaebols* such as Hanbo

133 Out There News, 'Asia's Economic Crisis' (visited on Mar. 1998) <http://www.megastories.com/seasia>. *See also* Kyung Shik Lee, 'Current Economic and Financial Situation in Korea', (24 Nov. 1997) (Presentation Paper of the Governor of the Bank of Korea).

134 'Mutual borrowing' is the practice of mutual payment guarantees to banks within interlinked business groups. In this mutual borrowing situation, if one company is trouble in financing, other companies in the business group may be also adversely affected because of a mutual payment guarantee, and finally all companies in the business group may go bankrupt together.

135 Kyung Shik Lee, op cit. n 84.

and Kia, borrowed money from banks, which later turned into bad loans. Additional loans by banks to the troubled companies were prohibited thereafter; thus, those companies had difficulty in securing further financing. Some companies even incurred losses and encountered cash flow problems in servicing debts accumulated during boom years to finance large investments. When new bank loans were no longer available, some of these companies, including some large conglomerates such as Hanbo Steel, Jinro and Kia went bankrupt.[136] Their bankruptcies had significant adverse effects on the economy of Korea.

Secondly, because interest rates on foreign loans were much lower than interest rates on local currency, won, many Korean companies and banks in previous years had borrowed excessively in US dollars as the economy boomed. The exchange rate of the won was pegged against the dollar, therefore, there were no apparent risks in having to earn won to repay loans in dollars.[137] However, from the middle of 1997, foreign exchange suddenly went up and the Korean won was devaluated. With this, four of Korea's *chaebols* either collapsed or nearly collapsed in 1997.

The 'conspiracy' between various large companies and politicians or bureaucrats for business purposes was another reason for the corporate failures in Korea. The failure of the Hanbo Group is a good case in point. The Hanbo Steel Corporation, one member of the Hanbo Group, secured large loans to finance investments. These loans combined with Hanbo Steel's expenditures on facility investment which far outstripped the original estimates led to an extreme shortage in cash flow. This gave rise to the assessment by bank creditors that normal operation by Hanbo Steel was extremely difficult, and that the insolvency of Hanbo Steel was inevitable.[138] However, during this procedure, the interrelationships between bureaucrats, politicians, the Hanbo Group and banks had created 'political' loans motivated mostly by political or non-business considerations. This led banks to lend excessive amounts of money to the Hanbo Group with little or no collateral. Subsequently, the loans to Hanbo Group became nonperforming loans. Eighteen per cent of the loans from the Korea First Bank were not collateralised. Because of the inability to repay the loans, the Hanbo Group went bankrupt, and the Korea First Bank was confronted with severe financial troubles.

To prevent further repetition of the same mistake, many Korean business groups are now vigorously engaged in restructuring their companies through sell-offs of unprofitable business units, merging and acquiring businesses, or simply down-sizing their operations.

136 Kunio Saito, 'Korea's economic adjustments under the IMF-supported program' (21 Jan. 1998) 2–3 (at Sogan Uni./Korea Economic Daily Conference).

137 Out There News, op cit. n 84.

138 *See* Ministry of Finance and Economy Press Release, 'The Hanbo Situation', Feb. 1997, at 1–3.

B. New Policies and Regulations for 'Chaebols'

As corporate failures had been a critical problem in the Korean economy, they weaken the rate of economic growth of Korea in the short-run. As previously reviewed, *chaebols* in Korea have affected the Korean economy both positively and negatively. Therefore, Korea cannot disregard the existence of any *chaebols* completely.

By the time Korea asked the IMF for assistance, Korea recognised the need to improve corporate structure and corporate governance structure. According to Korea's Letter of Intent[139] to the IMF, the transparency of corporate balance sheets (including profit and loss accounts) will be improved by enforcing accounting standards in line with generally accepted accounting practices, which include independent external audits, full disclosure, and consolidated financial statements for business conglomerates.

Under the Letter of Intent, the Korean government guarantees that it will no longer interfere in bank management and lending decisions (except for prudential regulations) and that it will fully support and respect banks' business decisions in group loans. Directed lending will be eliminated immediately. While policy lending to agricultural and small businesses will be maintained, the interest subsidy for policy lending will be incorporated in the government's budget.

To strengthen market discipline, the corporate bankruptcy provisions according to Korean law will be allowed to operate without government interference. No government subsidised support or tax privileges will be provided to bail out individual corporations. To ensure the transparency of financial transactions and reduce scope for corruption, the 'real name' system in financial transactions will be maintained, although with some possible revisions.[140]

To restructure the corporate sector during the current financial crisis, the Korean government has introduced some important measures to prompt restructuring of the business sector, especially for bankrupt or near-bankrupt conglomerates. These measures include the exemption of a capital-gains tax on real property sales for debt repayment purposes, and allowance of transferred payment of capital gains tax on the facilities and real property acquired through M&As. In addition, the government is considering relaxing the restrictions on hostile M&As to expedite reorganisation among private firms. This measure, if carried out, may apply to foreigners who have equity investments in existing local firms.[141]

[139] Ibid. The provisions regarding the corporate sector in the 'Letter of Intent of the Government of Korea' to the IMF can be found in paras 29, 30, 34, 35, and 37.

[140] Arts. 2 and 3 of the 'Act Concerning the Real name Finance Transaction and Protection of Confidentiality' legislated on 29 Dec. 1997.

[141] Sang-Loh Kim and Won-Geun Kang, op cit. n 9 at 6–7.

Until now, the government has prohibited *chaebols*' ownership of a bank by setting upper limits on the amount of shares a conglomerate could buy, while owning various financial organisations including securities, insurance, merchant, and finance companies, and managing them as if they were a source of their own pocket money. However, beginning with Seoul Bank and Korea First Bank, the government has decided to revise this regulation by raising the share ceiling to 50 per cent in order to prevent foreign financial institutions from cheaply purchasing domestic financial institutions.[142] This means that, from now on, conglomerates will be allowed to effectively manage a bank by becoming its major shareholder.

Allowing conglomerates with weak financial structures caused by their own unreasonable borrowing practices to own other subsidiary businesses including banks seems to be against wise reform policy. As there is no precedent in any other part of the world for industrial capital to manage financial capital, it will be advisable to enforce the condition that a conglomerate may take over a bank only when that conglomerate sells off all its other subsidiaries.

V. CONCLUSION

The Korean economy and financial system are currently surrounded by much uncertainty and many difficulties. In the past, Korean people have been through numerous hardships and have survived. This time, however, a huge financial disaster has fallen on them. Though Korea has received financial assistance from the IMF to overcome its crisis, its citizens have joined the government in facing the problems caused by the new financial system and policies.[143]

Analysis of the IMF programme in Korea suggests that help from the IMF can be a catalyst for Korea to eradicate various structural contradic-

142 'Banks and Conglomerates' (editorial), *Chosun Ilbo* (daily newspaper), 26 Feb. 1998.

143 Endeavours to overcome the current Korean financial crisis were not made only by the government and its regulations. There were also non-governmental endeavours by students and citizens as part of a national movement. Korean citizens including school students donated US Dollars to their government to help ease the government's economic pains. High school students burned effigies symbolising the high level of consumption they believe has worsened the economic crisis; they crushed imported school supplies as their fellow students showed placards reading 'No imported goods' during a campaign against anti-consumption. Further, gold was donated by citizens to the Korean government for it to sell in order to pay some of its debts. This gold collection campaign carried out by six financial organisations was participated in by 3.4 million people or 23 per cent of the total households in the country and raised US$2.17 billion. ('Gold collection campaign ends at US$2.17 billion', *Chosun Ilbo* (daily newspaper), 14 Mar. 1998) Among those taking part, 21,000 people donated 187Kg of gold and 1,700 people exchanged 131Kg for bonds. Of the total 225 tons collected, 196.3 tons (US$1.82 billion) has been exported with the balance being purchased by the Bank of Korea.

tions and resume its economic success[144] or that assistance can be a deterrent for positive change in the Korean financial sector as it has been in other countries.[145] Its success depends on how well Korea regulates its financial system, including adequate prudential regulation and supervision over financial institutions, removal of unlimited and unnecessary government control over the financial sector, and a fair lending system by banks.

Accordingly, a new financial system and its regulations are now being tested. It goes without saying that the current law-based financial reforms are far from perfect, but as they were developed following almost one year of discussions, including discussions with the IMF, they can be seen as the next best option.

While reviewing the causes of the recent financial crisis and reforms in Korea, one should consider the legal basis for a safe and sound banking system and market.

One of the most important factors in Korea's success in reforming its financial markets is the task of the Financial Supervisory Committee, which will carry out its supervisory functions independently from the Bank of Korea and the Ministry of Finance and Economy.

Until recent years, the local system was such that banks, whether local or foreign, had been made aware of unwritten government policies under which they had to operate. Thus, much of the regulatory structure in Korea may have been based on undocumented principles and policies which were frequently adjusted by the government in response to market conditions.[146] That will no longer be tolerated because transparent bank supervision is now being pursued and mandated in the new banking laws, and foreign banks are also regulated by their home countries' supervisory authorities.

Under new financial reforms, intense competition in the Korean financial market is expected in the near future among domestic banks, foreign banks, and domestic and foreign banks. The number of foreign bank branches as well as subsidiaries will be also steadily and greatly increasing in the future in spite of the languid rate of increase in the 1990s due to the government's present favourable financial reform for foreign banks and their fair competition with other banks. This prediction is also based on the belief that there is infinite potential in the Korean economy, the fact that foreign banks can

144 Joseph J Norton, 'IMF Package Could Be Catalyst for Positive Change in Korea: Expert', *The Korea Times*, 6 Dec. 1997.

145 *See* Martin Feldstein, *Refocusing the IMF*, 77 Foreign Affairs 22–33 (Mar./Apr. 1998). In his article, Professor Martin Feldstein indicates the adverse effect of the IMF's support to Korea's current financial crisis; he says that 'the IMF's fund called for reform of inefficient conglomerates and inflexible labor laws. However, beneficial in the long run, such changes are not needed to resolve the current crisis. By stepping in too far and too soon, the IMF discourages countries from seeking modest help. Even worse, it encourages bankers to undertake more riskly loans, making another crisis more likely'. Ibid.

146 Tae Hee Lee, op cit. n 3.

never ignore the importance of Korea if they are to form global networks, and the expectation that the Northeast Asian economic bloc will rise to the centre of the world economy. In addition, relaxed restrictions on business operations will attract competition in the Korean financial market. Moreover, authorities in the Korean government have announced their intention to open Korea's financial and banking markets without any special restrictions on foreign banking and financial institutions.

As already mentioned, Korean banks' weak competitive position was considered a big opportunity for foreign banks. When foreign banks decided to enter the Korean financial market, they undoubtedly evaluated their superior competitive position over domestic banks and sometimes over other foreign banks in Korea. Therefore, it is now imperative for Korea to help its domestic banks to become competitive against foreign financial institutions. The recent M&As among domestic banks is one approach to help domestic banks become competitive to protect themselves from potential future financial crisis.

In addition, Korean banks and bank supervisors must completely understand the new financial environment and culture and change the outdated practices of bank supervision that was in place prior to and during the financial crisis.

The Korean government has had unique experiences in the past with controlling not only the corporate sector, but also the financial sector. Government controls were largely in the form of (1) the government's unlimited control over the banking industry,[147] (2) the government's intervention into bank corporate lending or 'policy' lending and bank management,[148] and (3) the government's bail-out practices of both financial institutions and the chaebols, thus creating a broad environment of moral

[147] Under the old Bank of Korea Act and the old General Banking Act, the supervision and guidance of banks was to be carried out by the Bank of Korea ('BOK'). Accordingly, the Bank Supervisory Board of the Bank of Korea, which was subject to the instructions of the 'Monetary Board' (the supreme policy-making body of the Bank of Korea), was in charge of the supervision and regular examination of banking institutions. (Arts. 39 and 40 of the old Bank of Korea Act). However, the government, indirectly, could exercise the bank supervision function through the Monetary Board, because the Minister of Finance and Economy ('MOFE') held the chairmanship of the Monetary Board, and five out of the seven non ex-officio members of the Board were appointed on the recommendation of the Government Ministers. Also, the Governor of the BOK was appointed by the President on the recommendation of the Minister. Moreover, the Minister could request the Board to reconsider any resolution it had adopted and also had the right to appoint the Auditor for the BOK and to make bank examinations of the BOK. (*See* Research Department of the Bank of Korea, *The Main Points of Reshaping the Central Banking and Financial Supervision System in Korea* 1–2 (Jan. 1998)).

[148] The government's intervention over the bank management was exercised, indirectly, through the appointment of bank officers including the president or directors. Even though bank officers could be appointed at the shareholders' meeting under the general Banking Act and the Commercial Code, sometimes, unofficially and influenced by the government or politicians before the shareholders' meeting, these decisions had already been decided on before the

hazard.[149] To develop Korea's economy after the Korean War, government controls over financial and corporate sectors were considered necessary for Korea's economic development; and, in many ways, such policies succeeded in developing the economy for over four decades. However, continued government controls over the financial sectors after deregulation, liberalisation and internationalisation of the financial system worked against developing an efficient and prudential financial sector. As time passed, the Korean government slowly gave the Korean banking system more autonomy. Nonetheless, the Korean government continued to control parts of the financial system through government legislation and government practices throughout the 1990s. This control or intervention left an inefficient banking sector, which in turn led to a highly leveraged corporate sector that lacked effective market discipline, and finally became one of active causes of the recent financial crisis.

Under these circumstances, the Korean banks initially underestimated the severity of the recent financial crisis. The large share of the responsibility for the financial instability should fall on the long tradition of government intervention in loan approvals and the bail-outs, but this does not excuse the banks for substandard management practices. In fact, the banking sector should have shown its willingness to create responsible management structures, but obviously, this did not occur.[150] Considering the past and current Korean economic situations, government controls over banking and financial institutions cannot be eliminated entirely. However, such controls should be limited to the 'safety and soundness' of financial institutions and used only out of necessity and on a strictly legal basis. The new Bank of Korea Act and the new General Banking Act have been changed to reflect this viewpoint.

In conclusion, the recent financial reforms should not be the end but

meeting. Because of this government intervention, the bank officers or presidents who had significant power over lending decisions tended to follow the government's decisions and directions.

149 The government's past bail-out practice also created a special situation of moral hazard which the banks could carry on lending to inefficient or failing businesses in the belief that they would eventually be bailed out because whenever banks had carried large non-performing loans, the government and the central bank had consistently bailed them out. Practically speaking, banks have relied on an implicit guarantee by the government which had involved itself heavily in resource allocation, picking target sectors for support. Under these circumstances, banks tended not to develop credit-analysis skills but to lend funds chiefly against real-estate collateral. (*See* Shee Yul Ryoo, *Principal Measures to Secure Financial Stability in Korea*, 2nd G-10 Working Party Meeting Paper (20 Dec. 1996), at 2–3) This special relationship between banks and the government in supporting the financial sector reflected a special bank management culture, but it had an inherent problem that has been one of main causes of the recent bank bankruptcies in Korea because the government could not guarantee any bail-outs for troubled banks any more during the country's financial crisis.

150 'Government Intervention in Banking' (editorial), *Chosun Ilbo* (daily newspaper), 3 Mar. 1998.

rather the beginning of a thorough and a long process of financial reform in Korea. The introduction of a 'bank holding company', appropriate loan documentation in lending, the government's international policies in such matters as the newly established EC bank, and the introduction of refinance technology that enables a refinancing institution to invest foreign capital directly into domestic companies and businesses should be complemented with further financial reform in Korea.

Chapter 20

The Japanese Banking Crisis: Historical and Regulatory Perspectives

*Yoshihisa Hayakawa**

'Japanese financial institutions are building rapidly on their successes in a few chosen fields in the US, to turn themselves into powerful full-line firms that will pose a growing competitive threat to their American counterparts.'

Financial Times, 16 February 1987

'As Japan's economy boomed during the heady years of the 1980s 'bubble' its banks made aggressive forays overseas, triggering fears of Japanese 'take-over' of Wall Street. Ten years later, in a bitter irony, Japan's financial sector is once again triggering alarm—but this time because of its weakness, rather than strength.'

Financial Times, 2 October 1998

I. INTRODUCTION

A. *Change in Reputation of the Japanese Banking System*

Both of the above two quotes are on the reputation of the Japanese banking system. The former was made in 1980s and the latter was made in 1990s. What makes these comments so different?

The 1980s are called the 'Bubble Era' in Japan. During this decade, the booming stock and real estate markets made banks and other financial institutions extend their business, domestically and internationally, to various areas.

However, from the end of the 1980s, banks and other financial institutions have been struggling with large amounts of non-performing loans. Most of them had to restructure their business including withdrawal from foreign countries. In spite of their restructuring efforts, many banks and other financial institutions failed in the 1990s.

Is the burst of the bubble economy, however, the only reason for the too long struggle of banks and other financial institutions?

* The author wishes to express special thanks to Professor Joseph J. Norton. The author is indebted to Ms Mamiko Yokoi for the linguistic revision of this chapter.

B. Traditional Japanese Regulatory System of Financial Institutions

Since the end of the Second World War, the first priority of Japan has been to catch up with Western economies. For this purpose, the financial industry, especially the banking industry, has been treated as the most important industry in order to provide enough capital to other industries. The Japanese government protected banks and other financial institutions from competition, like many developing countries, to keep their business steady. In fact, until recently, it was difficult, not only for a foreign competitor but also for a domestic new comer, to enter the Japanese financial industry.[1]

Under the protective regulatory system, the regulatory agency, the Ministry of Finance (MOF), had huge power over the Japanese financial industry. As the MOF also had powers to prepare the national budget as a fiscal authority and to deal with the tax matters, the MOF had large discretion, legally and practically, on every matter of any financial institution.[2]

Some point out that the recent struggle of the banks and other financial institutions were caused by this protective regulatory system. This system had spoiled the banks and other financial institutions for a long period until the change of the governmental policy. In the 1980s the government opened its protective barrier and the banks and financial institutions suddenly faced competition. But, fortunately or unfortunately, this decade was the Bubble Era. The impact of opening the market was not so serious during this decade. In the 1990s, however, the burst of the bubble economy multiplied the impact against the banks and other financial institutions.

Others add that the system was filled with too much discretion, which was more serious. They point out that this type of system does not work any more, especially to make the banks and other financial institutions revive and competitive again.

Since the end of the 1990s, Japan has begun to change its systems in many areas of finance. The common keyword in these changes is 'transparency'. This new phenomenon is deeply influenced by the above mentioned critical views against the traditional Japanese system.

Especially in the area of reorganisation of failed banks, we can clearly find this new phenomenon. This chapter will describe the recent drastic changes in the way that failed banks are reorganised in Japan. It symbolises drastic changes not only in the financial industry but also in the whole of Japan.

1 Masao Kyuno, *Kin'yu Fuan* [Fear of the Financial System] 51–5 (1998).

2 *See* Curtis J. Milhaupt, 'Managing the Market: The Ministry of Finance and Securities Regulation in Japan', 30 *Stan J Int'l L* 423 (Summer 1994).

II. BANKING CRISIS

A. *Japanese System of Banking Institutions*

Japan has two types of banking institutions. One is called '*Shinkin*' or '*Shinkumi*'. These banking institutions are relatively small and equivalent to savings and loan institutions ('S&L') in the US.[3] The other type is relatively big and called '*Ginko*', which means bank in Japanese.

The banks in Japan are divided into four groups according to their historical backgrounds or roles. They are '*Toshigin* and *Choshingin*', first-tier '*Chiho Ginko*', second-tier '*Chiho Ginko*' and '*Shintaku Ginko*'[4].

At the end of 1980s, there were sixteen banks belonging to the '*Toshi Ginko* and *Choshingin*' group.[5] It is a group for major banks located in the large cities of Japan (this chapter refers to them as 'major banks').

Regional banks, located in the suburban or countryside areas of Japan, are divided into two groups by their historical backgrounds, ie first-tier '*Chiho Ginko*' and second-tier '*Chiho Ginko*' (this chapter refers to '*Chiho Ginko*' as 'regional banks').

The other, called '*Shintaku Ginko*', is the group of banks mainly engaged in trust business (this chapter refers to them as 'trust banks').

B. *Banking Crisis*

In the first four years of 1990s, four S&Ls failed.[6] Although one bank (*Toho Sogo Ginko*) also failed in 1992, this bank was a small one classified as a second-tier regional bank.[7]

However, the crisis suddenly accelerated (the second stage).

In 1994, after the failure of three S&Ls[8] and one trust bank (*Nippon Shintaku Ginko*),[9] two S&Ls (*Tokyo Kyowa Shinkumi* and *Anzen Shinkumi*) announced their failures with large losses.[10]

3 '*Shinkin*' is a shortened form of '*Shin'yo Kinko*' and '*Shinkumi*' is a shortened form of '*Shin'yo Kyodo Kumiai*'.

4 '*Toshigin*' is a shortened form of '*Toshi Ginko*' and '*Choshingin*' is a shortened form of '*Choki Shin'yo Ginko*'.

5 They were *Daiichi Kangyo Ginko*, *Daiwa Ginko*, *Fuji Ginko*, *Hokkaido Takushoku Ginko*, *Kyowa Ginko*, *Mitsubishi Ginko*, *Mitsui Ginko*, *Saitama Ginko*, *Sanwa Ginko*, *Sumitomo Ginko*, *Taiyo Kobe Ginko*, *Tokai Ginko*, *Tokyo Ginko*, *Nihon Kogyo Ginko*, *Nihon Choki Shin'yo Ginko*, and *Nihon Saiken Shin'yo Ginko*.

6 They were *Sanwa Shinkin*, *Toyo Shinkin*, *Kamaishi Shinkin*, and *Osaka Fumin Shinkumi*. *Financial Times*, 31 Mar. 1991; ibid. 29 Apr. 1992; ibid. 25 May 1993; ibid. 2 Aug. 1993.

7 Ibid. 25 July 1991.

8 The failed three S&L were *Matsuura Shinkumi*, *Tokyo Daiwa Shinkumi*, and *Shinkumi Gifu Shogin*. *New York Times*, 18 Oct. 1994; *Nikkei Weekly*, 31 Oct. 1994; ibid. 28 Nov. 1994.

9 *Financial Times*, 13 Oct. 1994; ibid. 17 Oct. 1994.

10 Ibid. 10 Dec. 1994; ibid. 16 Dec. 1994.

In 1995, in addition to the failure of three S&Ls,[11] two other S&Ls (*Cosmo Shinkumi* and *Kizu Shinkumi*) and one second-tier regional bank (*Hyogo Ginko*) failed with huge losses.[12]

In 1996, in addition to the failure of six S&Ls,[13] two second-tier regional banks (*Taiheiyo Ginko* and *Hanwa Ginko*) failed with huge losses.[14]

Japanese remember 1997 as the year of the failures of big financial institutions (the third stage).

Besides the failure of banking institutions, five stock brokerage companies and one life insurance company failed.[15] It was shocking that two of the failed stock brokerage companies were prestigious ones. One had approximately 450 thousand personal customers at the time of its failure (*San'yo Shoken*).[16] The other was one of the biggest four stock brokerage companies in Japan with more than 10 thousand employees (*Yamaichi Shoken*).[17]

Moreover, in addition to the failure of seven S&Ls,[18] three banks failed. Two of them were second-tier regional banks (*Kyoto Kyoei Ginko* and *Tokuyo City Ginko*),[19] but the other was a major bank whose assets were nearly US$100 billion (*Hokkaido Takushoku Ginko*).[20] Japanese were shocked by the news that even one of the major banks had failed.

In 1998 the failure of S&Ls continued and various rumours about the next failing bank began to spread (the fourth stage). The rumours about two mammoth major banks seemed especially credible.

In August the stock price of one major bank dropped to nearly 30 cents (*Nihon Choki Shin'yo Ginko*).[21] This bank is known in English as the 'Long-term Credit Bank of Japan' or LTCB. (This chapter refers to it as

[11] They were *Yuai Shinkumi*, *Fukuiken Daiichi Shinkumi*, and *Osaka Shinkumi*. *Nikkei Weekly*, 6 Feb. 1995; *Financial Times*, 8 Dec. 1995; *Japan Weekly Monitor*, 26 Aug. 1996.

[12] *Financial Times*, 31 July 1995; *Daily Yomiuri*, 31 Aug. 1995; *Financial Times*, 10 Apr. 1995; ibid. 17 Apr. 1995.

[13] They were *Yukuhashi Shinkin*, *San'yo Shinkumi*, *Kenmin Daiwa Shinkumi*, *Noshiro Shinkin*, *Musashino Shinkin*, and *Sampuku Shinkumi*. *Daily Yomiuri*, 7 June 1992; *Jiji Press Ticker Service*, 18 Mar. 1996; *Wall Street Journal*, 15 Apr. 1996; *Nikkei Weekly*, 22 Apr. 1996; *Financial Times*, 13 Sept. 1996; *Daily Yomiuri*, 9 Nov. 1996.

[14] *Financial Times*, 30 Mar. 1996; ibid. 1 Apr. 1996; ibid. 29 May 1996; ibid. 22 Nov. 1996; *New York Times*, 26 Nov. 1996.

[15] Except for the two prestigious stock brokerage companies, the failed stock brokerage or life insurance companies were *Ogawa Shoken*, *Echigo Shoken*, and *Nissan Seimei*. *New York Times*, 24 May 1997; *Japan Weekly Monitor*, 13 Oct. 1997; *Financial Times*, 26 Apr. 1997.

[16] Ibid. 4 Nov. 1997; ibid. 5 Nov. 1997; ibid. 10 Nov. 1997.

[17] Ibid. 24 Nov. 1997; ibid. 25 Nov. 1997; ibid. 27 Nov. 1997.

[18] They were *Hanshin Rodo Shinkumi*, *Toki Shinkumi*, *Tokai Shinkumi*, *Kitakyushu Shinkumi*, *Kanagawaken Shinkumi*, *Tanabe Shinkumi*, and *Chogin Osaka Shinkumi*. *Japan Weekly Monitor*, 7 Apr. 1997; *Daily Yomiuri*, 15 May 1997; *Nikkei Weekly*, 19 May 1997; *Japan Weekly Monitor*, 27 Oct. 1997;

[19] *Financial Times*, 15 Oct. 1997; *Daily Yomiuri*, 27 Nov. 1997.

[20] *Financial Times*, 17 Nov. 1997; ibid. 18 Nov. 1997.

[21] On 11 Aug. 1998, the stock price of LTCB dropped to 38 yen. *Financial Times*, 12 Aug. 1998.

'LTCB'). The stock price of the other major bank also continued to decrease (*Nihon Saiken Shin'yo Ginko*). This bank is also known by its English name as Nippon Credit Bank or NCB. (This chapter refers to it as 'NCB').[22]

The situation became worse stage by stage. Until this stage, what were the Japanese governmental regulatory bodies or politicians doing for this banking crisis? Or, if their attempts to settle this crisis did not work sufficiently (this chapter refers to it as 'old approach'), what was the reason?

III. OLD APPROACH

A. *Old Approach*

Traditionally, the Japanese regulatory agency, the MOF, used its power to rescue the failed banking institutions as follows.

First, asserting strong pressure, the MOF requests a banking institution, which has a close relationship with the failing banking institution, to merge it, make it a subsidiary, or purchase its whole business including all branches and employees.[23] As the MOF had large discretion on every matter of any banking institution, the institution could not refuse its proposal. Further, if the banking institution accepted the proposal, some privileges were sometimes given to the relevant institution by the MOF.[24] As a result, failing banking institutions were always rescued and most of the banking failures did not surface.[25]

For instance, in 1986, at the time of the Bubble Era, one second-tier regional bank failed with big losses (*Heiwa Sogo Ginko*). At first, although the MOF asked some banks to merge with this failed bank, all of them hesitated and no bank accepted the MOF's proposal. The MOF strengthened pressure on these banks, especially after the news that one foreign bank had a strong interest in merging with the failed bank. Finally, one of the major banks (*Sumitomo Ginko*) merged with the failed bank with all of its branches and employees.[26]

This technique was also used to rescue the failed S&Ls. In 1984, one S&L based in Osaka failed (*Jitsugyo Shinkumi*). After some tough negotiations, finally, one S&L merged with the failed one.[27]

Secondly, in order to assist the rescue plan accepted by the closest banking institution, the MOF frequently asked other banking institutions to provide capital for the rescue plan.[28] Usually the MOF asked the banking institutions which have some relations with the failed bank to contribute.

22 *See* <http://www.ncb.co.jp/Ir/English/1998/index.html>.

23 *See* above n 1, at 56–60.

24 Ibid.

25 Ibid.

26 *Financial Times*, 27 Dec. 1985; ibid. 13 Feb. 1986; ibid. 18 Feb. 1986.

27 Jiji Press Ticker Service, 7 Dec. 1995.

28 *See* above n 23.

But sometimes the MOF asked other banking institutions that have no relation with it. On such occasions, some united associations of banks and administrative organisations of S&Ls were useful.[29]

In 1979, for instance, one second-tier regional bank completely failed (*Taiko Sogo Bank*). However, owing to the money and guarantee that a number of related banks reluctantly provided, this bank has continued to operate until now.[30]

In the *Jitsugyo Shinkumi* case in 1984, at first, the S&L industry organisation (*Zenshinren*) rejected to provide money to this failed S&L. However, finally, this organisation had to cooperate in a rescue merger plan with other institutions.[31]

It is noteworthy that public funds were not used in the scheme of the old approach. It was a long-time taboo in Japan.

It is not easily accepted by taxpayers to use their money only for one or more private entities in a specific industry. Besides, in Japan, the regulatory agency was the MOF, which was also the fiscal authority. Moreover, at the beginning of the recent banking crisis, another incident occurred.

In the first half of the 1990s, at the first and second stage of the banking crisis, there was another financial crisis in Japan. There were a number of non-banks, called '*Jusen*', established mainly by major banks to provide housing loans to individuals.[32] However, in the Bubble Era, their main business shifted to investments to real estate developers. After the burst of the bubble economy, these non-banks failed with huge amounts of non-performing loans, totalling approximately US$60 billion at the time of June 1995. The main lenders to these non-banks were agricultural financial institutions. The agricultural financial institutions and agricultural pressure groups made strong objections against the liquidation of these non-banks under the Bankruptcy Law. Although the people engaged in the agricultural industry are not the majority of the population nowadays, the agricultural pressure groups are very strong in the Japanese political process. Finally, in 1996, more than US$6.5 billion of public funds were provided exclusively for the rescue of the *Jusen*.[33] As a result, strong resistances against the use

[29] There are a number of united associations of banks and administrative organisations of S&Ls in Japan. *See* <http://www.zenginkyo.or.jp/en/index.htm; http://www.chiginkyo.or.jp/>; <http://www.dainichiginkyo.or.jp/>; <http://www.shintaku-kyokai.or.jp/images/e-1.htm>; <http://www.shinkin.co.jp/scb/e/1999/cont.htm>; <http://www5.mediagalaxy.c o.jp/zshinkumi/>.

[30] *Nikkei Weekly*, 28 Sept. 1991.

[31] *See* above n 27.

[32] There were eight non-banks called '*Jusen*'. Seven of them were established by banks to provide housing loans to individuals.

[33] *See* Curtis J Milhaupt and Geoffrey P Miller, 'Cooperation, Conflict and Convergence in Japanese Finance: Evidence from the "Jusen" Problem', 29 *L & Pol'y Int'l Bus* 35 (Fall 1997). *See also* Howard M Felson, 'Closing the Book on Jusen: an Account of the Bad Loan Crisis and a New Chapter for Securitization in Japan', 47 *Duke LJ* 567 (1997); Edward L Rubin, 'Communing with Disaster: What We can Learn From the Jusen and the Savings and Loan Crises', 29 *Law & Pol'y Int'l Bus* 79 (Fall 1997).

of public funds for financial institutions spread among the Japanese taxpayers.

The old approach had prepared a scheme for providing sufficient money for a banking failure. It is the establishment of the Deposit Insurance Corporation of Japan (DIC). Although this corporation was established by a special act in 1971,[34] it is independent from the Japanese government (the capital of this corporation was raised by the Japanese government, the Bank of Japan (BOJ) and private banking institutions).[35] Thus, strictly speaking, the money provided by the DIC is not that of taxpayers.

Besides this system, the special loans provided by the BOJ were regarded as a strong measure against the failure of financial institutions.[36] In 1961, a big stock brokerage company revived from its first insolvency owing to BOJ loans (however, as noted above, this company faced its second failure and was closed in 1997).[37]

It is also noteworthy that, although the insurance repayment of the Japanese deposit insurance system is legally limited to within 10 million yen, less than US$100 thousand per depositor (so-called 'pay-off'), the pay-off has been never executed since its establishment in 1971.[38]

In the *Jitsugyo Shinkumi* case in 1984, after the administrative organisation of S&Ls rejected the proposed rescue plan, once informed that the other alternative was pay-off, the organisation suddenly accepted the rescue plan.[39]

Pay-off has been another taboo in Japan.

B. Deadlock of the Old Approach

In the recent banking crisis, the old approach barely worked in the first stage.

Three of the failed S&Ls and one failed bank were merged into related banking institutions including major banks (*Tokai Ginko* and *Sanwa Ginko*).[40] The business of the other failed S&L was purchased by several banking institutions with all the branches and employees.[41]

In four of these cases, many banking institutions, one industry organisation of S&Ls, and the DIC were asked to provide capital for the rescue plans. And they did.[42]

34 *Yokin Hoken Ho* [Deposit Insurance Law], Law No 34 of 1971.

35 *See* <http://www.dic.go.jp/info/info2.html>.

36 *See* <http://www.boj.or.jp/en/about/about_f.htm>.

37 *See Daily Yomiuri*, 1 Sept. 1995.

38 *See* Art. 54 of *Yokin Hoken Ho*.

39 *See* above n 27.

40 *Sanwa Shinkin* was merged into *Tokai Ginko* and *Toyo Shinkin* was merged into *Sanwa Ginko*. *Osaka Fumin Shinkumi* was merged into *Shinkumi Osaka Koyo* and Toho Sogo Ginko was merged into *IyoGinko*, a first-tier regional bank. *See* above n 6 and 7.

41 *See* above n 6.

42 *See* above nn 6 and 7.

Although the DIC provided more than US$700 million, the use of public funds was still a taboo as well as the pay-off.

In the second stage, the old approach faced so many difficulties that the techniques of the approach had to be modified in a number of cases.

Five of the failed S&Ls were merged with related S&Ls.[43] The failed trust bank (*Nihon Shintaku Ginko*) fortunately became a subsidiary of one major bank (*Mitsubishi Ginko* before the merger into *Tokyo-Mitsubishi Ginko*).[44] The business of the six failed S&Ls was purchased by a number of banking institutions, including one major bank (*Tokai Ginko*), with their branches and employees.[45]

However, since the number of banks which could rescue failed banks decreased as the banking crisis progressed, the traditional techniqus of the old approach did not work as it had before. In the *Taiheiyo Ginko* case, a new bank had to be established (*Wakashio Ginko*) by one major bank (*Sakura Ginko*) with the support of three major banks (*Fuji Ginko*, *Tokai Ginko*, and *Sanwa Ginko*) to purchase the business of the failed bank.[46] In the *Tokyo Kyowa Shinkumi* and *Anzen Shinkumi* case, it was necessary to establish a new bank (*Tokyo Kyodo Ginko*) by the BOJ and many other banking institutions.[47] In the *Hyogo Ginko* case, a new bank (*Midori Ginko*) was also needed with investments from many banks and companies.[48]

But the newly established *Tokyo Kyodo Ginko* became quickly insolvent. In September 1996, the DIC invested large sums in this failed bank and changed it into a body only for purchasing business of failed banking institutions and collecting non-performing loans (newly named as *Seiri Kaishu Ginko*, Resolution and Collection Bank or ROB. This paper refers to it as 'ROB').[49]

On the other hand, for the other failed banking institutions (*Hanwa Ginko*, *Cosmo Shinkumi*, *Kizu Shinkumi* and one more S&L), there was no other way but to terminate them. In the *Hanwa Ginko* case, a new financial institution (*Kii Yokin Kanri Ginko*) was established only for the liquidation of this failed bank.[50] In other cases, the newly established ROB (or its former body) worked to liquidate them.[51]

Besides the deadlock of one technique of the old approach, the other technique also faced some problems. First, it became more difficult to collect money from other banking institutions for the rescue plans due to

[43] *Tokyo Daiwa Shinkumi* was merged into *Shonan Shinkin* and *Shinkumi Gifu Shogin* was merged into *Shinkumi Kansai Kogin*. *Yuai Shinkumi* was merged into *Kanagawaken Rodokinko*. *Noshiro Shinkin* was merged into *Omagari Shinkin* and *Musashino Shinkumi* was merged into *Oji Shinkin*. *See* above n 8, 11, and 13.

[44] *See* above n 9.

[45] *See* above nn 8, 11, and 13. *Tokai Ginko* merged into *Osaka Shinkumi*.

[46] *See* above n 14.

[47] *See* above n 10.

[48] *See* above n 12.

[49] *Financial Times*, 13 Sept. 1996.

[50] *See* above n 14.

[51] *See* above nn 12, 14, and 13.

the progress of the banking crisis. They were operating, but not healthy. Second, some of them hesitated to cooperate with the rescue plans proposed by the regulatory bodies. Especially, it is symbolic that the new Governor of the Tokyo Metropolis clearly rejected to cooperate with the plan proposed by the MOF and BOJ in the *Tokyo Kyowa Shinkumi* and *Anzen Shinkumi* case.[52]

In a deadlock of the old approach, the DIC had to provide more money to assist many rescue plans. Nearly US$20 billion were provided by DIC for the rescue of the banking institutions that failed in the second stage.[53] In addition to such huge money, DIC used nearly US$3 billion to purchase the loans and assets of the failed banking institutions with the ROB.[54]

In this stage, as already noted, the taboo of public funds was strengthened due to the *Jusen* problem. Regarding the other taboo, a special provision was added to the Deposit Insurance Law that any deposit would be fully insured until the end of March 2001.[55] This taboo was legally authorised at this stage.

In the third stage, the year 1997, fortunately the business of all failed S&Ls was purchased by a number of banking institutions.[56] As a condition, the DIC had to provide nearly US$5 billion to assist the rescue plans and the ROB's purchase of non-performing loans and assets.

However, all of the proposed plans could not rescue the failed banks.

In the *Hokkaido Takushoku Ginko* case, at first, a merger plan with one of the second-tier regional banks (*Hokkaido Ginko*) was arranged in April 1997.[57] But *Hokkaido Ginko* gradually became suspicious of the true contents of the balance sheet of *Hokkaido Takushoku*. In September, they announced the extension of their merger date.[58] Finally, in November, *Hokkaido Takushoku* failed.[59] Although a part of the business was purchased by one of the second-tier regional banks and another by one trust bank, the majority of operations terminated.[60]

In the *Tokuyo City Ginko* case, a merger plan with three second-tier regional banks had been proposed since 1994.[61] However, since it was clear that the purpose of the merger plan was only for the rescue of *Tokuyo City*, the other banks finally rejected this plan.[62] As a result, *Tokuyo City* failed and its business was purchased by several banking institutions.[63]

52 *Daily Yomiuri*, 2 Sept. 1995.

53 Annual Report 1998 Deposit Insurance Corporation of Japan 64 (1999). A PDF file of this annual report is available on the web site: <http://www.dic.go.jp/annual/h10/h10-e.pdf>.

54 Ibid.

55 *See* Art. 54 and Additional Art. 17 of *Yokin Hoken Ho*.

56 *See* above n 18.

57 *New York Times*, 1 Apr. 1997; *Washington Post*, 2 Apr. 1997.

58 *Financial Times*, 15 Sept. 1997; *New York Times*, 13 Sept. 1997.

59 *See* above n 20.

60 *New York Times*, 18 Feb. 1998; ibid. 11 June 1998.

61 *Financial Times*, 21 Apr. 1994.

62 Ibid. 3 June 1994; ibid. 20 June 1994.

63 *See* above n 19.

The *Kyoto Kyoei Ginko* case is more serious. First, a merger plan with four second-tier regional banks (*Kyoto Kyoei Ginko*, *Kofuku Ginko*, *Fukutoku Ginko* and *Naniwa Ginko*) was proposed.[64] But *Kyoto Kyoei* and *Kofuku* rejected this merger plan.[65] It finally caused the failure of *Kyoto Kyoei*.[66] *Kofuku* had to acquire the business of *Kyoto Kyoei*.[67] The other two banks in the merger plan above, *Fukutoku* and *Naniwa*, merged into one bank, *Namihaya Ginko*, according to the newly modified merger plan.[68] In 1999, however, the *Kofuku* and the *Namihaya* failed.[69] After all, these four banks could not avoid disasters, whether they had accepted the proposed rescue plan or not.

Of course, the DIC had to provide large amounts of money for these failed banks, as well as BOJ loans, because of the taboos of the public fund and pay-off.[70]

The first priority of the regulatory bodies in the forth stage, from January to September in 1998, was to prevent disasters occurring from the failure of the two mammoth major banks, LTCB and NCB. At the critical point of the banking crisis, the political-side actively cooperated. However, the techniques used by them were still those of the old approach.

In June, the rescue plan of LTCB, a merger plan with one of the trust banks (*Sumitomo Shintaku Ginko*) was announced with the support of the regulatory agency and the BOJ.[71] But *Sumitomo Shintaku* became gradually suspicious about the real state of the balance sheet of LTCB. In August, surprisingly, the Japanese Prime Minister invited the president of *Sumitomo Shintaku* to his office and requested him, with the Minister of Finance and the Chief Cabinet Secretary, to proceed with the merger plan.[72] The president of the trust bank, however, did not give them clear consent to do so. Finally the agreement for merger was cancelled.[73]

Regarding NCB, many financial institutions had been forced to purchase its newly issued shares since 1997.[74] However, this major bank did not recover from the serious sickness.

In a deadlock of the old approach, in order to prolong the lives of the banks, huge money was lent, directly or via the DIC, by the BOJ.[75] However, these two banks were too large to be rescued. At last, the political-side decided to break away from the taboo of public funds and to use the taxpayers' money for the two banks. But it would be difficult to gain

[64] *Daily Yomiuri*, 10 Oct. 1997.
[65] Ibid.
[66] *See* above n 19.
[67] *See* above n 64.
[68] *Japan Times*, 19 Aug. 1998; *Daily Yomiuri*, 1 Oct. 1998; *Japan Times*, 2 Oct. 1998.
[69] *Financial Times*, 14 Apr. 1999; ibid. 12 May 1999; ibid. 24 May 1999; *Daily Yomiuri*, 8 Aug. 1999; *Financial Times*, 9 Aug. 1999.
[70] *See* above n 53, at 65.
[71] *Financial Times*, 27 June 1998; ibid. 29 June 1998.
[72] *Daily Yomiuri*, 21 Aug. 1998.
[73] *Nikkei Weekly*, 12 Oct. 1998.
[74] *New York Times*, 6 June 1997.
[75] *See* above n 53, at 65.

the approval of the taxpayers to use their money only for these two private entities. Thus, the political-side made special laws under the pretext of stabilising the entire banking system and prepared nearly US$300 billion in order to purchase newly issued stock of these banks.[76] All of the major banks (except the closed *Hokkaido Takushoku Ginko*) and trust banks and some regional banks were asked if they wanted their stock purchased.[77] All of them responded to this proposal and applied to the scheme.[78] Finally, the vast amount of public funds was pumped into these two seriously distressed banks as well as the other viable (but not healthy) banks. After the failures of LTCB and NBC in the next stage, the investments into the two banks turned out to be a total loss of money.

C. *Reasons for the Deadlock*

Why did the old approach not work in the recent banking crisis?

Obviously, one reason is the burst of the bubble economy. The long-lasting serious recession after the burst of the bubble had caused many failed companies and non-performing loans. Besides, banking institutions themselves had been conducting various risky businesses, eg investments to real estate developers, and losing great amounts of money.

The huge losses made many Japanese banking institutions unsound. It is difficult for one which is ill to look after another which is ill. Thus, some of them began to reject the proposed merger plans. And some of them failed after merging with failed banks.

Several of the environmental changes are more important for the failure of many banking institutions. The burst of the bubble is regarded to be a trigger that multiplied the impact of such structural changes.

Since the end of the Second World War, the Japanese economy had continually grown without stopping until the burst of the bubble. Some attributed this high growth rate to the superiority of the Japanese social and economic system, especially in the Bubble Era. Recently, however, many have pointed out that it was a phenomenon mainly caused by several environmental factors. After their disappearance through liberalisation, Japan has become an ordinary developed country with a low growth rate.[79]

Regarding the Japanese financial industry, the biggest cause for its growth was, as noted above, the protective regulatory system. Since the 1980s, various protective measures were gradually removed. Especially the

76 *Kin'yu Kino no Anteika no tameno Kinkyu Sochi ni kansuru Horitsu* [Law concerning Emergency Measures for the Stabilisation of the Function of the Financial System], Law No 5 of 1998.

77 *International Herald Tribune*, 6 Mar. 1998.

78 *Financial Times*, 14 Mar. 1998.

79 See <http://www.epa.go.jp/2000/g/qe001/nen.gif>.

recent dismantling of the restrictions on the financial industry, called 'Big-Bang in Japan', was drastic.[80] These changes stimulated competition. Competition will make the Japanese financial industry more robust. On the other hand, many banking institutions were defeated not only by Japanese competitors but also by foreign ones.

A structural change also appeared on the side of the regulatory bodies. The MOF was powerful because it had great discretion through the protective measures. As the restrictions disappeared, the MOF gradually lost the tools for asserting pressure or giving privileges. Moreover, it also lost the support of public opinion because of some scandals in the 1990s.[81] In the third stage and the fourth stage, at least, the MOF was not so powerful as it used to be.

Instead of obeying the MOF's instructions, in the 1990s, Japanese banking institutions had to follow various global rules for banking stability, eg the Basel capital adequacy standard, the use of rating agencies for credit risk, the requirements of disclosure, and the application of international accounting rules.

Further, the amendment of the provisions on litigation fees in 1992 made the stockholders' representative action much easier.[82] After this amendment, directors of the banking institutions could no longer ignore corporate governance by the stockholders.

It became more difficult for banks to provide money to help other failing banks.

C. *Disaster under 'No Approach'*

The deadlock of the old approach caused the sudden death of the *Hokkaido Takushoku Ginko*. The death of the huge major bank resulted in lack of liquidity in the *Hokkaido* Area where this failed bank was based. Many private companies in this area also terminated business as a result of this problem.[83]

A similar situation happened after the termination of the *Hanwa Ginko*, around the area where this bank was based.[84]

'No approach' resulted in the termination of banking institutions and lack of liquidity. An additional measure of a 'new approach' to reorganising the banking institutions was seriously needed.

In the fourth stage, however, the MOF lost many members of staff due to the scandals noted above. This governmental authority was not suitable

80 *See* <http://www.fsa.go.jp/p_mof/english/big-bang/big-bang.htm>.

81 *Mainichi Daily News*, 11 Mar. 1998; ibid. 28 Apr. 1998; ibid. 27 May 1998.

82 *See Sho Ho* [Commcercial Code], Law 48 of 1899. The relevant provision was added in Art. 267 in 1992.

83 *See Daily Yomiuri*, 2 June 1998.

84 *See* above n 14.

to form a new regulatory direction without discretion, which was the source of its power in the past.

Older generations in politics, especially influential members of the Liberal Democratic Party (LDP), a long-time governing party in Japan, were not suitable either. They were too accustomed to only cooperating with the MOF.

In the crisis, however, urgency changed the Japanese traditional political process and made it possible to take such a new direction. Surprisingly, new bills were jointly drafted by the younger politicians of the LDP and those of the opposition parties.[85]

What was the 'New Approach' proposed by these bills? And how did it work?

IV. NEW APPROACH

A. *Financial Reorganisation Law*

Various bills were approved in the Japanese Diet in October 1998. One of them was the Law concerning Emergency Measures for the Reconstruction of the Function of the Financial System (so-called 'Financial Reorganisation Law').[86]

It provided the temporary framework for the reorganisation of the banking institutions until the end of March 2001. There are two schemes, one for ordinary banks and a special one for large banks whose failures might lead to a series of other failures and have an impact on international financial markets.

In the former scheme, financial administrators will be appointed for managing the failed banking institution. In the event that a private party comes forward to take over the failed one, the business of the failed one will be transferred to that banking institution. If such a successor does not emerge, the business will be assumed by a newly established bridge bank. The bridge bank will continue to make loans to sound borrowers in good faith, on a temporary base, until the business is taken over by a private party.[87]

In the latter scheme, it will be mandatory for the DIC to acquire all of the shares of the failed bank. In other words, the failed bank will be temporarily nationalised. When it is rehabilitated in accordance with the

85 *See* Motohisa Ikeda, *Kin'yu Saisei Kanren Ho* [Laws concerning Financial Reorganisation] (1), 529 Hogaku Seminar 114 (1999); Nobuteru Ishihara, *Kin'yu Saisei Kanren Ho* (2), 530 Hogaku Seminar 116 (1999).

86 *See Kin'yu Kino no Saisei no tameno Kinkyu Sochi ni kansuru Horitsu* [Law concerning Emergency Measures for the Reconstruction of the Function of the Financial System (Financial Reorganisation Law)], Law No 132 of 1998.

87 *See* Part 3 of Financial Reorganisation Law.

plan to restore soundness of the management, its business is then transferred to another private banking institution, or its shares are transferred or disposed of, the special public management will be terminated. It is noteworthy that this scheme will be used not only for failed banks but also for banks in danger of failure.[88]

The Financial Reorganisation Law was accompanied by some new laws and amendments to the present law. One of them is the Law for the Establishment of the Financial Reorganisation Commission.[89]

The Financial Reorganisation Commission (FRC) is a temporary commission, until the end of 2000, as an external bureau of the Prime Minister's Office.[90] This completely new authority, of course independent from the MOF, assumes full responsibility for dealing with failed banking institutions.[91]

The Deposit Insurance Law was also amended to establish a new legal entity. This is the Resolution and Collection Corporation (ROC).[92] It is the successor to a corporation established for the *Jusen* problem and the ROB. The ROC purchases and collects non-performing loans of failed banks. Under the new special reorganisation scheme, LTCB and NCB were temporarily nationalised in 1999 (in the fifth stage).

The publicly managed LTCB found its private successor and reached a basic agreement with it in December 1999.[93] The DIC, as the holder of all the shares, LTCB and the successor made a final agreement in February 2000.[94] Since March 2000, it has become a newly born bank named '*Shinsei Ginko*'.[95]

The successor to the publicly managed NCB was decided in February 2000.[96] The successor and NCB made a final agreement with the DIC and are waiting for the day of renewed opening.[97]

The process of choosing LTCB's and NCB's successors was open to the public. As a result, the successor to LTCB was a foreign financial group and NCB a group organised by an IT company.[98] It is symbolic.

[88] *See* Part 2 of Financial Reorganisation Law.

[89] *Kin'yu Saisei Iinkai Secchi Ho* [Law for the Establishment of the Financial Reorganisation Commission], Law No 130 of 1998.

[90] *See* Part 2 of Law for the Establishment of the Financial Reorganisation Commission. *See* <http://www.fsa.go.jp/frc/indexe.html>.

[91] *See* ibid.

[92] *See* <http://www.kaisyukikou.co.jp/>.

[93] *See* <http://www.fsa.go.jp/frc/newse/ne014a.html>.

[94] *See* <http://www.fsa.go.jp/frc/news/n082a.html>.

[95] *See* <http://www.fsa.go.jp/frc/news/n089.html>; <http://www.shinseibank.co.jp/indexe.htm>.

[96] *See* <http://www.fsa.go.jp/frc/newse/ne016.html>.

[97] *See* <http://www.fsa.go.jp/frc/news/n131.html>.

[98] The successor to LTCB was a financial group organised by Ripplewood Holdings LLC and the successor to NCB was a financial group consisted with Softbank, Orix, and Tokyo Marine and Fire Insurance.

Before this stage, the process of making and implementing the rescue plans had been strictly closed. After the rescue, retired bureaucrats of the MOF usually took over the presidency of the failed banking institutions.[99] However, now, the new president of *Shinsei Ginko* was formerly a president of a Japanese subsidiary of a foreign bank.[100] There are no retired bureaucrats among the new directors of the new bank.[101]

According to the ordinary reorganisation scheme, five second-tier regional banks accepted financial administrators under the reorganisation scheme. They were *Kokumin Ginko*, *Kofuku Ginko*, *Tokyo Sowa Ginko*, *Namihaya Ginko* and *Niigata Chuo Ginko*.[102]

Among them, *Kokumin* has already been taken over by *Yachiyo Ginko*, a second-tier regional bank.[103] The successors to the *Kofuku* and *Namihaya* were decided in May 2000.[104] The former was a foreign financial group and the latter was a group organised by a major bank.[105] And the successor to the *Tokyo Sowa* was decided in June 2000.[106] It too was a foreign financial group.[107]

B. Change of Regulatory System

The regulatory system itself has been also drastically changed. The removal of the financial regulatory functions from the MOF, also a fiscal authority, had been debated in the political arena. Finally, in June 1998, the Financial Supervisory Agency (FSA) was established and the regulatory functions were removed from the MOF, except planning the financial system framework and the resolution of systemic failure.[108]

Moreover, since the fifth stage, the FRC has been responsible, jointly with the MOF, for planning the resolution of systemic failure.[109]

The status of the FSA has also changed due to the establishment of the

99 *Mainichi Daily News*, 6 Feb. 1998. *See also* ibid. 29 Mar. 1998.

100 *See* above n 95.

101 *See* ibid.

102 *See* <http://www.fsa.go.jp/frc/newse/ne003.html>; <http://www.fsa.go.jp/frc/newse/ne005.html> <http://www.fsa.go.jp/frc/newse/ne008.html>; <http://www.fsa.go.jp/frc/newse/ne011.html>; <http://www.fsa.go.jp/frc/newse/ne013.html>. *See* also above n 69.

103 *See* <http://www.fsa.go.jp/frc/news/n091.html>; <http://www.fsa.go.jp/frc/news/n098.html>.

104 *See* <http://www.fsa.go.jp/frc/news/n110.html>; <http://www.fsa.go.jp/frc/news/n118.html>.

105 The former one was a financial group organised by Asia Recovery Fund and the latter one was a group organised by *Daiwa Ginko*.

106 *See* <http://www.fsa.go.jp/frc/news/n128.html>.

107 It was a financial group organised by Asian Recovery Fund.

108 *Kin'yu Kantoku Cho Secchi Ho* [Law for the Establishment of the Financial Supervisory Authority], Law No 101 of 1997.

109 *See* Arts. 3 and 4 of Law for the Establishment of the Financial Reorganisation Commission.

FRC. At first, the FSA was established as an external bureau of the Prime Minister's Office.[110] However, after the establishment of the FRC, it was placed under the FRC.[111] This means that the FRC is an authority for the inspection and supervision of banking institutions as well and delegates its authority to the FSA with few exceptions.

Under the new system, there is less room for discretion than previously. Also, the Japanese general public has become more critical of inspection and supervision. When the second chairman of the FRC made a speech in front of his electoral district, he used some expressions implying he could influence the inspection of the FSA. The outroar of public opinion caused the Prime Minister to quickly sack him without hesitation.[112]

C. *Public Funds for Reorganisation of the Banking System*

As noted above, the taboo of the public fund was broken in the fourth stage. But the purpose was only to prolong the lives of LTCB and NCB.

In the Financial Reorganisation Law, governmental guarantees were prepared, of nearly US$180 billion, for the operation of the reorganisation, such as the establishment of bridge banks, special public management and purchase of banking institutions' assets.[113]

At the same time, separate from the Financial Reorganisation Law, nearly US$600 billion were prepared for the Financial Function Early Strengthening Law operation.[114] The fund was to acquire undercapitalised banks' shares, provided that they submitted to the ROC the plans for restoring the soundness of management and obtained the approval of the ROC.[115]

It is interesting that, although most major banks applied to this scheme, one major bank (*Tokyo-Mitsubishi Ginko*) did not apply indicating conviction of its soundness.[116]

Several of the applying banks had to make drastic restructuring plans to get the approval of the ROC.[117] Public funds were used for this purpose, too.

[110] *See* Art. 2 of Law for the Establishment of the Financial Supervisory Authority.
[111] *See* Arts. 16, 17 and 18 of Law for the Establishment of the Financial Reorganisation Commission.
[112] *Daily Yomiuri*, 25 Feb. 2000; ibid. 26 Feb. 2000; *Nikkei Weekly*, 28 Feb. 2000. *See also Financial Times*, 5 Oct. 1999
[113] *See* above n 53, at 12 and 16–17.
[114] *Kin'yu Kino no Soki Kenzenka no tameno Kin'kyu Sochi ni kansuru Horitsu* [Law concerning Emergency Measures for the Early Strengthening of the Function of the Financial System (Financial Function Early Strengthening Law)], Law No 143 of 1998.
[115] *See* above n 53, at 12–13 and 17.
[116] *Daily Yomiuri*, 12 Mar. 1999.
[117] *Financial Times*, 21 June 1999.

This type of public fund injection to the banks ended by the end of March 2001.[118]

D. *New Scheme from 2001 and Pay-Off from 2002*

As noted above, the FRC was a temporary entity until the end of 2000 and the reorganisation scheme under the Financial Reorganisation Law was also temporary until the end of March 2001.

However, it has already been decided that the basic procedure of the temporary reorganisation schemes will be kept. In May 2000, the Deposit Insurance Law was amended to incorporate permanent reorganisation schemes, similar to the temporary ones.[119]

The differences are as follows. First, the Financial Services Agency will replace the FRC.[120] It was established in July 2000 as a successor to the FSA. However, it is also responsible for planning the financial system framework, instead of the MOF. At first, it was placed under the FRC. But, after the termination of the FRC, it will become the only permanent governmental authority for the financial industry. It will be responsible for inspecting and supervising the banking institutions, dealing with the failures of banking institutions, and planning the financial system framework and the resolution of systematic failure (however, the resolution of systematic failure will be planned jointly with the MOF).[121]

Secondly, the new reorganisation schemes will be used, not only for failed banking institutions or institutions in danger of failure, but also for insolvent banking institutions.[122]

Thirdly, the transfer of the failed bank's business to the purchasing bank will be more speedy.[123]

Fourthly, the special scheme will be exceptional for financial crisis, ie systemic risk.[124]

Finally, the special commission for the financial crisis will be prepared for exceptional measures of emergency.[125]

Most of these differences are improving the new schemes.

Moreover, the most drastic change will be added to the new approach from April 2002. It is to break away from the taboo of pay-off.[126] Each depositor will be insured only to 10 million yen, less than US$100 thousand.

118 *See* Art. 4 of Financial Function Early Strengthening Law.

119 *Yokin Hoken Ho To no Ichibu wo Kaisei suru Horitsu* [Law for the amendment of the Deposit Insurance Law], Law No 93 of 2000.

120 *See* <http://www.fsa.go.jp/indexe.html>.

121 *See* ibid.

122 *See* Art. 74 of Deposit Insurance Law.

123 *See* Art. 90 of Deposit Insurance Law.

124 *See* Art. 102 of Deposit Insurance Law.

125 Ibid.

126 *See* <http://www.dic.go.jp/qa/qa05.html>.

Each depositor has to be responsible for his or her selection of banking institution without expecting paternalistic protection.

V. CONCLUSION

A. *Financial Regulatory System and Reorganisation Scheme in the 21st Century*

After the banking crisis, Japan learned some lessons from the many failures. They are not novel, but very important.

First, a regulatory system or reorganisation scheme with too much discretion will not work any more, especially in the twenty-first century. It is most important to establish transparent rules without discretion. Japanese began to esteem this idea not only for the financial industry but also for the whole system of Japan. Although, unfortunately, the burst of the bubble economy seriously damaged the Japanese economy, fortunately, it gave us a valuable chance to improve our whole system.

At the end of the 1980s, as mentioned above, there were sixteen major banks in Japan. By the end of the 1990s, six of them had disappeared because of their failure or merger.[127] Now, under the new system, the rest of them have begun to find their merger partner or partners. According to the recent announcements of merger plans, the number of competitive major banks will become only four in one or two years.[128] This phenomenon is completely different from the mergers in the days of the old approach. The banks voluntarily made their merger plans to survive in the coming competitive environment. And the merger partners were not failing banks, but successful ones.

Secondly, there was a ridiculous proverb, 'Too big to fail', in the financial industry. In order to prolong the lives of some large banks, a large amount of money was wasted in Japan. It only caused moral hazard in the failing banks.

If the bank is too big, it is sufficient to prepare a reorganisation scheme for such a size.

If the impact of the failure is too big, it is sufficient to prepare a countermeasure for such an impact.

[127] *Mitsui Ginko* and *Taiyo Kobe Ginko* merged into *Sakura Ginko* in 1990. *Kyowa Ginko* and *Saitama Ginko* merged into *Asahi Ginko* in 1991. *Mitsubishi Ginko* and *Tokyo Ginko* merged into *Tokyo–Mitsubishi Ginko* in 1996. *Hokkaido Takushoku Ginko* disappeared in 1997. LTCB and NCB were temporarily nationalised in 1998.

[128] *Daiichi Kangyo Ginko*, *Fuji Ginko*, and *Nihon Kogyo Ginko* will form one financial group '*Mizuho*'. *Sakura Ginko*, and *Sumitomo Ginko* will merge into *Mitsui Sumitomo Ginko*. *Sanwa Ginko* and *Tokai Ginko* will merge into one bank with a trust bank, *Toyo Shintaku Ginko*. These three and *Tokyo–Mitsubishi Ginko* will be 'Big Four' in Japan.

Thirdly, if necessary, we should not hesitate to use pubic funds in a banking crisis. Public funds were used at the later stage of the crisis in Japan. However, it was said that the amount of the public fund would have been much smaller if it had been used at an earlier stage.

Finally, we have to be responsible for our selections of banking institutions. Pay-oOff will sometimes cause confusion. But we cannot avoid it any more.

B. One More Lesson

In the recent banking crisis, many rumours spread in Japan. One of them was, as noted above, 'Too big to fail'. Even before the recent banking crisis, such special treatment was strictly criticised.

However, in the recent crisis, the need for special treatment was emphasised from a different viewpoint. It was said that, in the interdependent world economy, especially international financial markets, the failure of large banks would have serious impacts all over the world, and the large banks had to be maintained as they were from this viewpoint.[129]

The present world lacks systems or structures for cross-border bankruptcy, especially for banking institutions. No one can estimate the transnational impact of a major cross-border banking failure. This fact resulted in the continuation of the old approach until the later stage of the banking crisis in Japan.

Under the new system, we still cannot estimate the transnational impact of banking failure. We have to continue to examine the problems in cross-border bankruptcy.[130]

[129] Shin'ichiro Suda, *Chogin Hatan* [The Crash of the Long-Term Credit Bank of Japan] 78–9 (1998).

[130] *See* Yoshihisa Hayakawa, 'International Bankruptcy from the viewpoint of Private International Law and International Civil Procedure' in *Legal Aspects of Globalisation* 165 (J. Basedow and T. Kono (eds), 2000). *See also* Takashi Hamano, 'Japan' in *International Bank Insolvencies* 117 (M. Giovanoli and G. Heinrich (eds), 1999).

Chapter 21

Conclusion: Lessons for the 21st Century

Douglas Arner, Mamiko Yokoi-Arai, and Zhongfei Zhou

Over the past fifty years, the international financial system has dramatically changed from an essentially fixed relationship between isolated national financial systems, to an increasingly global, integrated and volatile financial system. A number of underlying trends are indicative of this change. First, there has been a liberalisation of capital flows and financial systems from the original closed and fixed structure established under the Bretton Woods system. Secondly, financial markets both internationally and domestically have undergone a process of disintermediation, as financial flows have moved from traditional banks to capital markets. Thirdly, technological innovation has increased the speed with which information is transferred around the world. Fourthly, financial innovations have developed to meet the challenges of changing financial markets and their participants. Fifthly, there has been a reduction in the role of centralised economic decision-making, evidenced by the spread of privatisation around the world since the early 1980s.

By the beginning of the 1990s, these trends had fundamentally altered the financial landscape around the world. As the decade progressed, a clear feature of international financial markets in the last decade of the twentieth century has been the occurrence of a series of financial crises, often with international or global implications, of a sort not seen since the late ninetheenth century—exactly the sort of crises that the Bretton Woods system was designed to prevent. In many ways, financial crises have been a defining feature of the last decade of the twentieth century. As these crises have occurred, there has been an increasing focus on their causes, resolution and possible future prevention—often under the rubric of the 'new international financial architecture' (NIFA), ie a reassessment of the Bretton Woods system, its constituents and the issues with which it was designed to address.

This volume has not looked at the NIFA, but rather has sought to integrate a series of analyses of some of the individual crises which have occurred during the 1990s and to draw some lessons from those experiences, not only for the countries concerned and for those similarly situated, but also for the international institutions and actors and to inform the debate on the NIFA.

As a starting point, in chapter 1, Mamiko Yokoi-Arai presented an introduction to financial crises and early warning systems and institutional mechanisms in the UK, US, and Japan. She concluded that such early warning systems are essential, but that no single system provides complete assurance against crises and that each country must carefully analyse its own circumstances to develop an appropriate and effective system. This background laid the framework for the individual studies which comprise the majority of this volume.

PART I: PRELUDE: 1990–5

In Part I, the authors discuss financial crises during the first half of the 1990s in the United States (a domestic crisis in a developed country), Mexico (an international crisis in a developing country), Venezuela (a domestic crisis in a developing country), and Bulgaria (a domestic crisis in a transition country). These crises foreshadowed the sorts of crises that occurred in the second half of the 1990s in developed, developing, and transitioning economies. Further, these crises hold important lessons for the crises that occurred around the world in the second half of the 1990s and seem to be continuing into the twenty-first century, with recent examples in Argentina and Turkey.

In Chapter 2, Gerald Olson discussed the American debt crisis of the late 1980s and early 1990s. Olson suggests that the crisis was one of 'capital inadequacy' and draws lessons and recommends approaches from the US experiences for other countries around the world experiencing similar situations, which unfortunately have occurred with some frequency during the 1990s and are likely to continue into the twenty-first century.

In Chapter 3, Douglas Arner and Thomas Slover analysed the Mexican currency crisis of 1995. They conclude that while Mexico has largely been successful in resolving that crisis, continuing structural reform of the financial system is required in order to reduce the likelihood of similar crises in the future.

In Chapter 4, Ruth de Krivoy discussed the Venezuelan Banking Crisis of 1994–5. De Krivoy suggests that Venezuela's experiences were similar to those in other countries during the 1990s, suggesting the strong importance of non-political prudential regulation and supervision of financial institutions, but that the key factor remains the expertise of bankers themselves.

In Chapter 5, Georgi Spasov analysed regulatory issues resulting from the banking crisis in Bulgaria. Spasov concludes that the crisis in Bulgaria was the result of the transition process, exacerbated by conflicting goals and inappropriate advice from the international community. In future, Bulgaria (and others) need to carefully analyse the domestic situation in order to develop appropriate and workable systems—especially in the context of transition.

In many ways, the experiences of the US in liberalising its financial system in the 1970s and 1980s as a reaction to the internationalisation of financial markets are similar to the crises experienced in other countries throughout the 1990s, not only in developing and transitioning countries, but also in the developed countries of Europe and Japan. The crises in Mexico and Venezuela were largely similar to those which occurred in East Asia, beginning in Thailand in 1997. The crisis in Bulgaria was very similar to that which occurred in Russia in 1998. Crises in Brazil, Argentina, and Turkey follow similar patterns. In other words, the writing was on the wall, but no one outside of the immediately effected countries was reading it.

PART II: THE EAST ASIAN FINANCIAL CRISIS: 1997–8

In Part II, the authors analyse the financial crises in East Asia. The East Asian financial crisis began in Thailand in the summer of 1997 and spread to Malaysia, Indonesia, the Philippines, South Korea and Hong Kong. Fundamentally, these were all international crises in developing countries that in many ways were foreshadowed by the crises discussed in Part I, the lessons of which were unfortunately largely ignored both at the domestic level and at the international level, with direct and significant consequences for hundreds of millions of people in East Asia.

In Chapter 6, Tull Traisorat discussed the Thai financial and economic crisis of 1997–8, which served as the trigger event for the East Asian financial crisis of 1997–8. He concludes that the crisis in many ways was the result of structures developed in a domestic context being exposed to international financial markets without adequate *ex ante* reform. He suggests that while the effects have been very severe, the crisis may serve as an opportunity to re-address financial system fundamentals in order to secure financial stability and economic growth in the future.

In Chapter 7, Joseph Norton and Mamiko Yokoi-Arai discussed Indonesia's financial crisis beginning in 1997 and its attempts at reform after the crisis. They conclude that the crisis in many ways resulted from structural problems that had developed as a result of its domestic political system that were exposed to the international financial community as a result of the reassessment of risks following the Thai financial crisis. Norton and Yokoi-Arai suggest that it is necessary for Indonesia to fundamentally restructure its financial system in order to succeed in the international financial system.

In Chapter 8, Sungchul Shin analysed Korea's search for a viable social safety net through pension and financial market reform. Shin concludes that Korea must develop an effective social safety net based on an appropriately designed pension system in order to ensure social and therefore economic stability in the future.

In Chapter 9, Berry Hsu discussed Hong Kong's experiences during the East Asian financial crisis, suggesting that in fact the crisis brought to the surface important deficiencies necessitating reform and transparency. Hsu concludes that significant legislative reforms are necessary in order to secure Hong Kong's place as an international financial centre in the twenty-first century.

As with the crises in the first half of the 1990s, the East Asian financial crises occurred in individual countries as a result of the exposure of idiosyncratic domestic systems to the international financial markets. In all cases, reform should have preceded liberalisation but did not. This must be seen as a key lesson from the crises. Further, the experiences of each of the countries discussed (Thailand, Indonesia, South Korea, and Hong Kong) demonstrate the inadequacies of the framework applied by the IMF in the various East Asian countries and the need for analysis and action with respect to the NIFA.

PART III: INTERNATIONAL CONTAGION: 1995 AND 1998–9

Part three presents studies of the effects of international contagion in 1995 (following the Mexican crisis) and in 1998–99 (following the East Asian financial crises). While in each case, contagion may have been the triggering cause of a crisis (or near crisis, in the case of Brazil), the authors suggest that underlying domestic weaknesses in effect provided the trigger for the contagion. In other words, domestic weaknesses were exposed by international reactions to problems in another country viewed to have similar circumstances.

In Chapter 10, Manuela Tortora discussed crisis and contagion in Latin America and the implications for the management of the international financial system. Tortora suggests that the experiences of Latin America indicate a clear lack of knowledge and leadership internationally in respect to solving problems of the new financial crises that have occurred with frequency during the 1990s and highlight a clear need for further analysis of the larger picture in order to devise appropriate solutions.

In Chapter 11, Jorge Guira presented a case study of the experiences of Brazil in preventing and containing international financial crisis and contagion throughout the 1990s and its own crisis in 1999. Guira suggests that the international responses are an important first step, but that continuing efforts, both at the international and domestic levels are required. Importantly, however, he concludes that in Brazil's case in 1999, the preventative measures developed at the international level prevented a financial crisis, but that these preventative measures would not have been effective without prior and continuing domestic restructuring.

In Chapter 12, Marcelo Tavarone discussed the Argentina's experiences with contagion in 1995 and 1997. Tavarone suggests that Argentina was largely successful in weathering the contagion in both periods, but that significant structural weaknesses remain, which must be addressed to ensure future stability. In fact, Argentina's current on-going crisis may be seen to some extent to be the result of these continuing structural problems.

In Chapter 13, Christine Lang and Shlomo Weber analysed the financial crisis of 1998 as the result of 10 years of economic reforms in Russia. While they conclude that the events of 1998 were caused by internal problems primarily, they also conclude that the experience may be a vital event on the path from a centrally planned political and economic system to a functioning democratic and market system.

In Chapter 14, Kai Chen discussed the failure of GITIC in the PRC. He concludes that the failure of GITIC highlights the importance of strengthening regulatory and supervisory power over financial institutions in the PRC and the need to move to a more law-based financial system prior to further liberalisation in order to underpin future economic growth and financial stability. Further, he suggests that while GITIC's failure may be more properly attributable to domestic problems, it is not dissimilar to the situation faced in other countries in East Asia, in that GITIC was in the business of intermediating foreign capital flows into the PRC.

In Chapter 15, Maria Patiño discussed the financial crisis in Ecuador in 1999. She concludes that the crisis was in many ways the result of Ecuador's integration into the global financial system and the consequent exposure of existing structural weaknesses to external forces which the financial system was (and is) unequipped to cope.

In this section, the authors both confirm the vital causative role of domestic weaknesses and the triggering effect of contagion from external events. The experiences also suggest that the interaction between external contagion through the international financial system and problematic domestic structural conditions can at least to some extent be seen as a result of policies encouraged by the international community and especially the US, through the so-called 'Washington Consensus'. At present, the key result of the experiences of the contagion-affected economies may be a new focus on the importance of domestic restructuring through development of appropriate legal infrastructure in order to better equip economies to weather the risks of contagion apparently inherent in participation in the international financial system.

PART IV: FINANCIAL REFORM FOLLOWING THE EAST ASIAN CRISES

In this final section, the authors look at the continuing efforts of countries to restructure their financial systems in order to successfully integrate into the international financial system (Taiwan and Mainland China) or to recover from a crisis resulting from earlier integration (Korea and Japan).

In Chapter 16, Chuanjie Li discussed China's financial reforms and their implications. He concludes that further domestic structural reform is necessary prior to further liberalisation and that such reform must be law-based in order to protect against exposures of internal structural problems to international forces.

In Chapter 17, Zhongfei Zhou evaluated China's banking reforms following the East Asian financial crisis. Zhou concludes that the financial crisis was a wake-up call to the PRC and that structural problems are being addressed, but that more remains to be done. He suggests that future efforts should focus on developing a common value system to underlie the financial system and that that system must be implemented through a law-based structure.

In Chapter 18, Chunghsing Chou presented the experiences of Taiwan during and after the East Asian crisis and the lessons for other countries. Chou concludes that the experiences of Taiwan in weathering financial contagion during the 1990s have important lessons for countries seeking democratisation, liberalisation, and internationalisation, most especially the need for careful sequencing in any process of reform. While Taiwan is still resolving a number of significant domestic issues with respect to financial restructuring and liberalisation, from its experiences to date, one can conclude that in many ways its path to development and participation in the international financial system has been relatively more successful than that of many of its neighbours in East Asia.

In Chapter 19, Byung-Tae Kim analysed Korea's recent financial reforms resulting from the 1997 financial crisis. He concludes that the crisis has in fact given Korea the impetus to reform its financial system in order to be more successful in the future. Past problems resulted from the politicised nature of the system; to be successful, the new system must be law-based and transparent. In many ways, the reforms Kim discusses must be seen as domestic restructuring brought on by Korea's increasing participation in the international financial system and their structure is clearly indicative of the typical path presently being pursued in similarly situated economies around the world.

In Chapter 20, Yoshihisa Hayakawa discussed the historical and regulatory aspects of the on-going Japanese banking crisis. He concludes that the key lessons from Japan's experience is the need for a transparent, rule-based system operating outside of political influence. Further, in order to reduce the political constraints of the doctrine of 'too big to fail', effort needs to be focused on the development of a workable system for dealing with international financial insolvencies.

The key conclusion of all the authors in this section is the need for financial sector restructuring as an imperative of participation in the international financial system. In each case, such restructuring needs to be carefully structured as a rule-based system which addresses the current underlying system presently in existence in the individual country *vis-à-vis* the needs and requirements of participation in the international financial system.

CONCLUSION: LESSONS FOR THE TWENTY-FIRST CENTURY

In reading through the case studies which make up this volume, one cannot avoid a number of lessons. First, in order to become full participants in the international financial system while at the same time maintaining both domestic and international financial stability requires careful domestic restructuring as part of any process of liberalisation. Throughout the studies, liberalisation without appropriate restructuring has been followed by crisis, and those crises have often had international or even global impact. Secondly, the policies and systems advocated by the Bretton Woods and other international financial organisations during the 1990s did not adequately take into account the risks inherent in financial sector liberalisation and likewise provided insufficient guidance on the requirements necessary to implement domestically in the context of restructuring. Thirdly, developments in one country are no longer restricted to its own borders in today's increasingly globalised financial markets and therefore there is an imperative need to readdress the Bretton Woods system and to design an appropriate 'new international financial architecture' in much the same way that was done originally at Bretton Woods. Fourth, all of these systems, whether domestic or international, need to be based upon transparent, rule-based structures, ie upon the 'rule of law'. The lesson of this volume then is that if these key lessons are not addressed, financial crises similar to those common in the past decade (and in fact in likewise in the nineteenth century) will continue to be commonplace in the twenty-first century.

Sir Joseph Gold Memorial Series — Vol. 4

International Financial & Economic Law

FINANCIAL CRISES IN THE 1990s

Edited by Douglas Arner, Mamiko Yokoi-Arai, and Zhongfei Zhou

The success of the incipient 'new international financial architecture' needs to be based in large part upon the lessons learned from the series of financial crises in the 1990s. This volume provides the historical perspectives and context to assist scholars and policymakers in their analysis.

Financial Crises in the 1990s analyses financial crises in over sixteen divergent jurisdictions during a span from the end of the 1980s to the end of the 1990s. Through comprehensive discussion, this book unfolds similar causes rooted in financial crises, whether in developing and transitional countries or in developed countries. It further indicates that these lessons unfortunately were largely ignored both at the domestic and international levels, with the result that a similar tragedy occurred in East Asia.

Based on studies of the effects of international contagion following financial crises, the book presents to readers the interaction process between external contagion and problematic domestic structural conditions. Moreover, the book introduces the necessity of a rule-based system in restructuring the financial system in crises-hit countries.

Douglas Arner is Assistant Professor and Deputy Director, Asian Institute of International Financial Law at the University of Hong Kong and Visiting Fellow at the Centre for Commercial Law Studies, University of London.

Mamiko Yokoi-Arai is Sir John Lubbock Research Fellow i
International Fi
for Commercial

Zhongfei Zhou i
Law at Shangha
Economics, Pe